nickelodeon

降击神通

AVATAR

THE LAST AIRBENDER

THE PROMISE

Created by
BRYAN KONIETZKO
MICHAEL DANTE DIMARTINO

script
GENE LUEN YANG

art and cover
GURIHIRU

lettering
MICHAEL HEISLER

DARK HORSE BOOKS

publisher
MIKE RICHARDSON

editor
RACHEL ROBERTS

assistant editor
JENNY BLENK

designer
DAVID NESTELLE

digital art technician
SAMANTHA HUMMER

Special thanks to Linda Lee, James Salerno,
and Joan Hilty at Nickelodeon, and to Bryan Konietzko
and Michael Dante DiMartino.

This book collects *Avatar: The Last Airbender—The Promise* parts one through three.

Published by
Dark Horse Books
A division of
Dark Horse Comics LLC
10956 SE Main Street
Milwaukie, OR 97222

DarkHorse.com
Nick.com

To find a comics shop in your area,
visit ComicShopLocator.com

First edition: June 2020
ISBN 978-1-50671-784-5

5 7 9 10 8 6
Printed in China

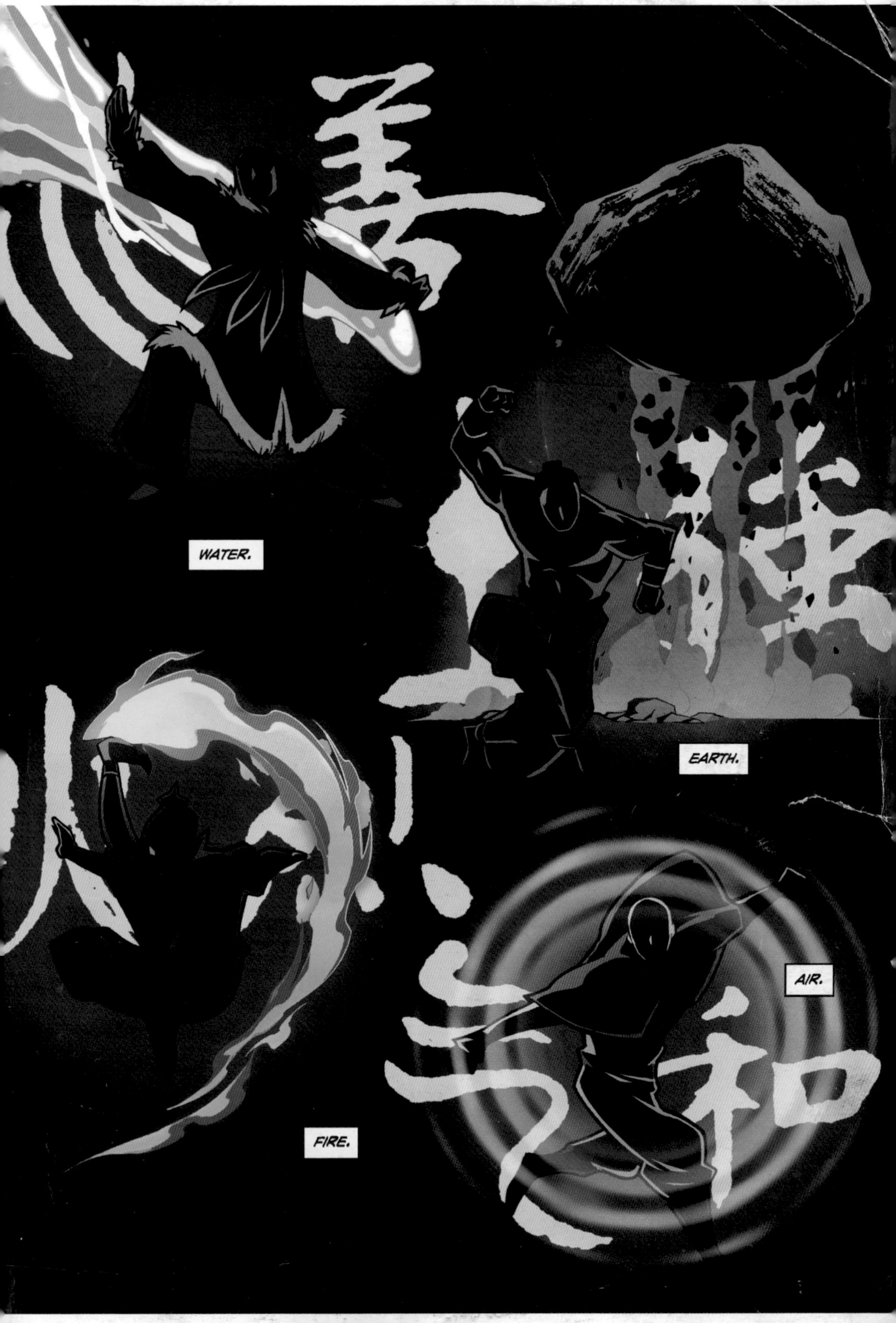
WATER.
EARTH.
FIRE.
AIR.

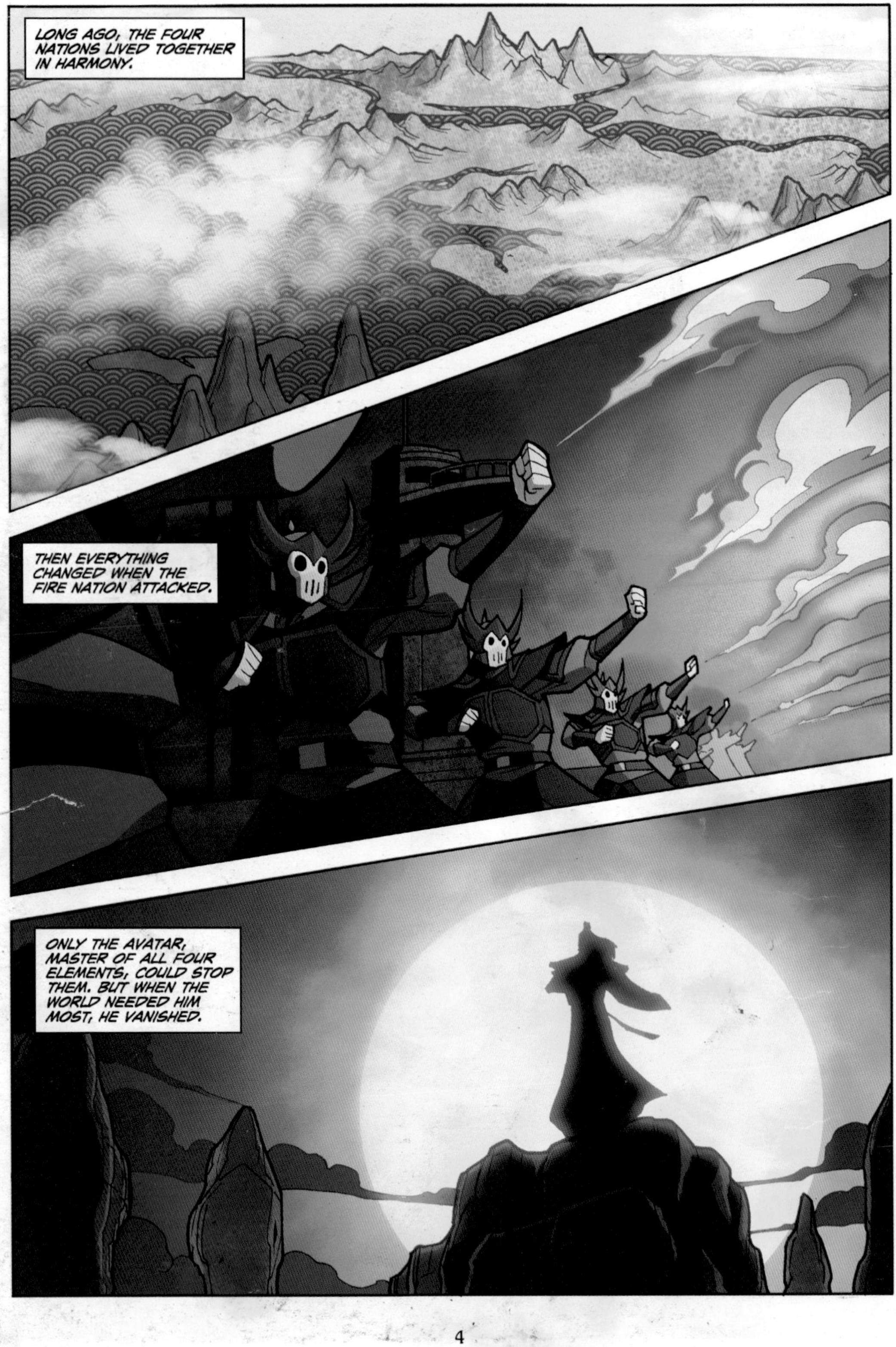
LONG AGO, THE FOUR NATIONS LIVED TOGETHER IN HARMONY.
THEN EVERYTHING CHANGED WHEN THE FIRE NATION ATTACKED.
ONLY THE AVATAR, MASTER OF ALL FOUR ELEMENTS, COULD STOP THEM. BUT WHEN THE WORLD NEEDED HIM MOST, HE VANISHED.

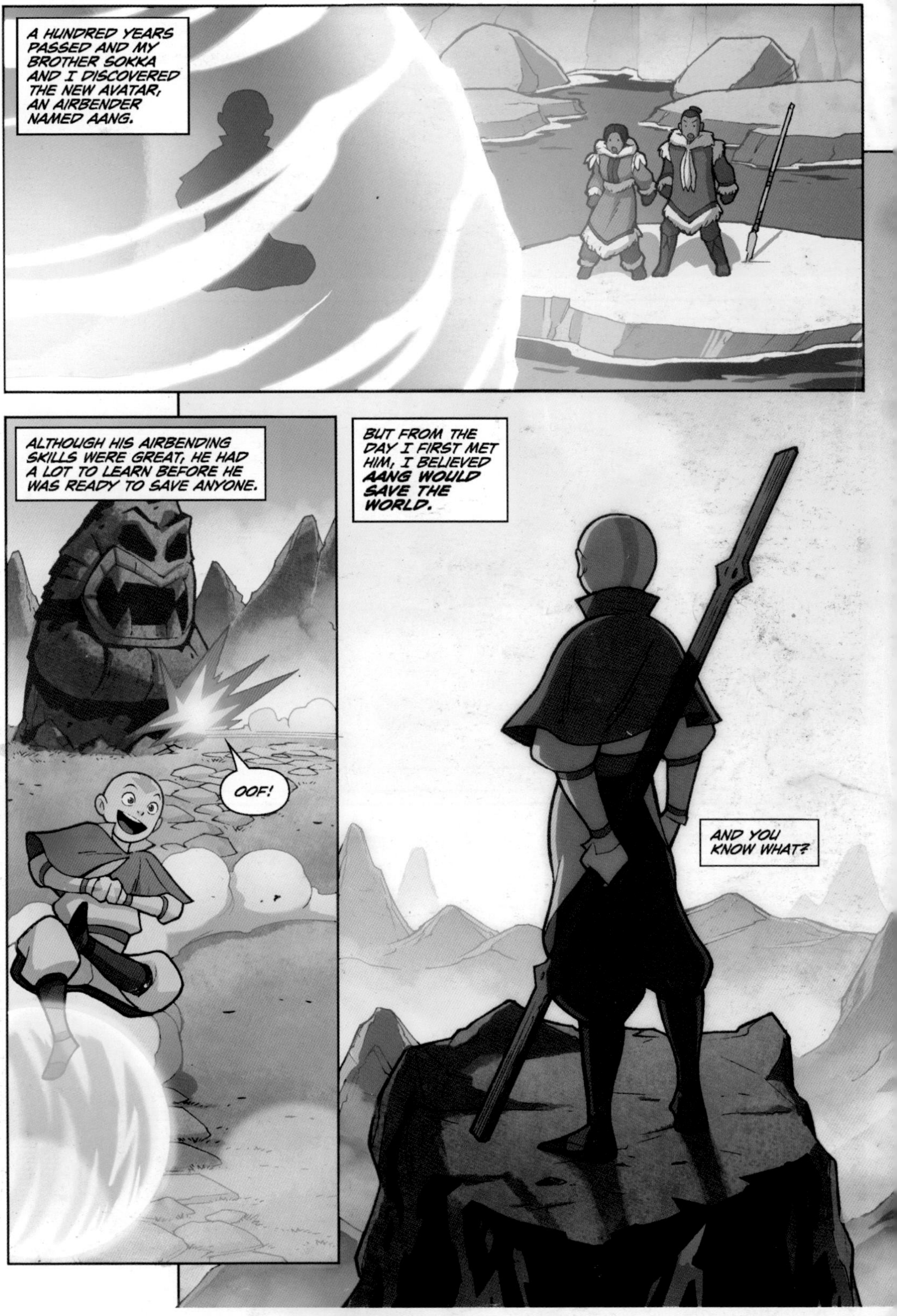
A HUNDRED YEARS PASSED AND MY BROTHER SOKKA AND I DISCOVERED THE NEW AVATAR, AN AIRBENDER NAMED AANG.
ALTHOUGH HIS AIRBENDING SKILLS WERE GREAT, HE HAD A LOT TO LEARN BEFORE HE WAS READY TO SAVE ANYONE.
OOF!
BUT FROM THE DAY I FIRST MET HIM, I BELIEVED AANG WOULD SAVE THE WORLD.
AND YOU KNOW WHAT?

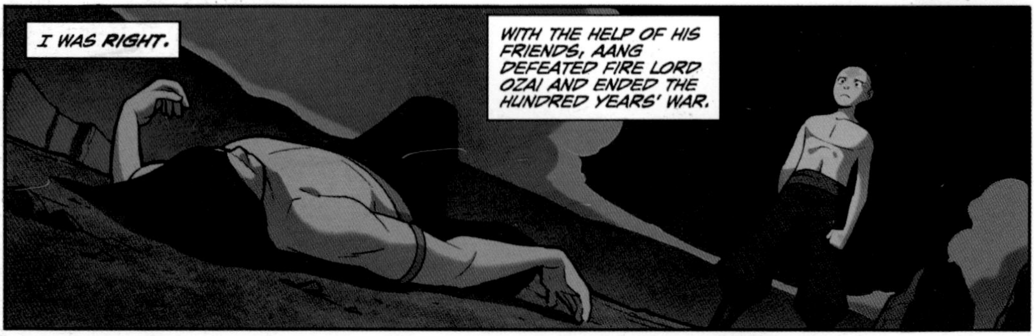
I WAS RIGHT.
WITH THE HELP OF HIS FRIENDS, AANG DEFEATED FIRE LORD OZAI AND ENDED THE HUNDRED YEARS' WAR.

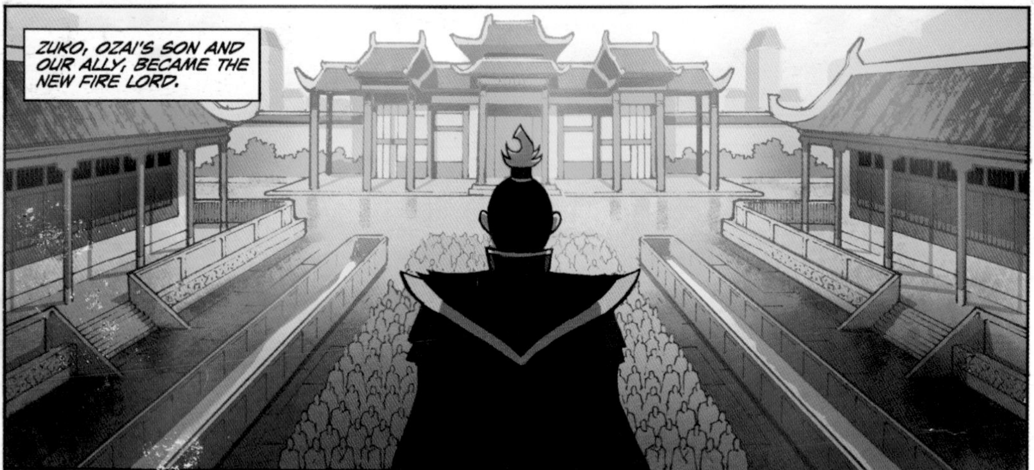
ZUKO, OZAI'S SON AND OUR ALLY, BECAME THE NEW FIRE LORD.

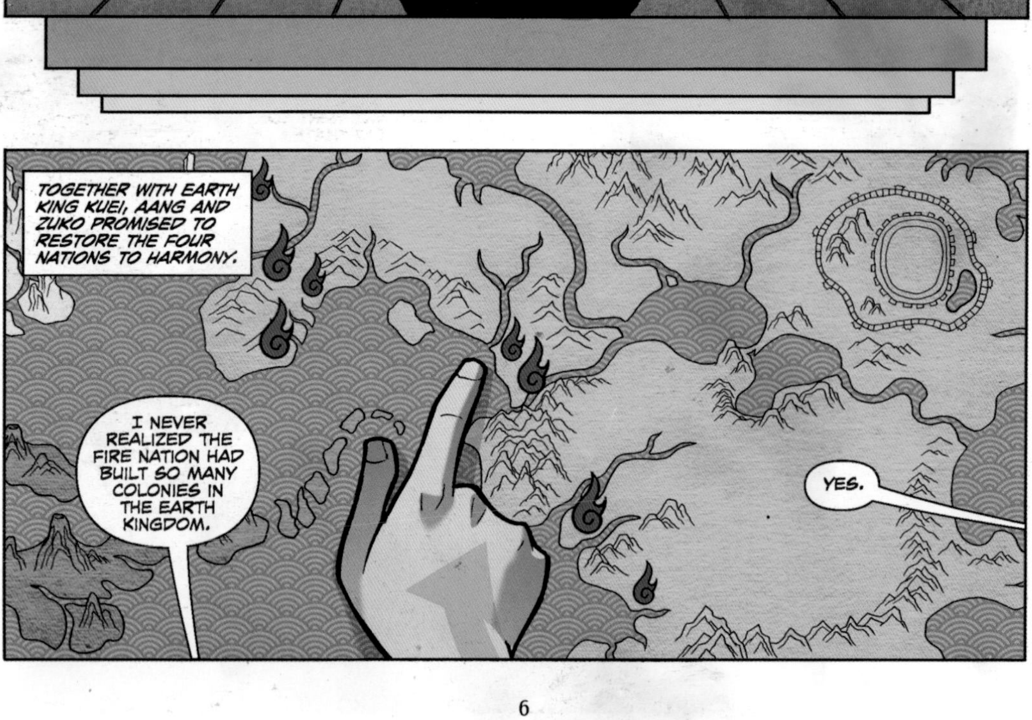
TOGETHER WITH EARTH KING KUEI, AANG AND ZUKO PROMISED TO RESTORE THE FOUR NATIONS TO HARMONY.
I NEVER REALIZED THE FIRE NATION HAD BUILT SO MANY COLONIES IN THE EARTH KINGDOM.
YES.

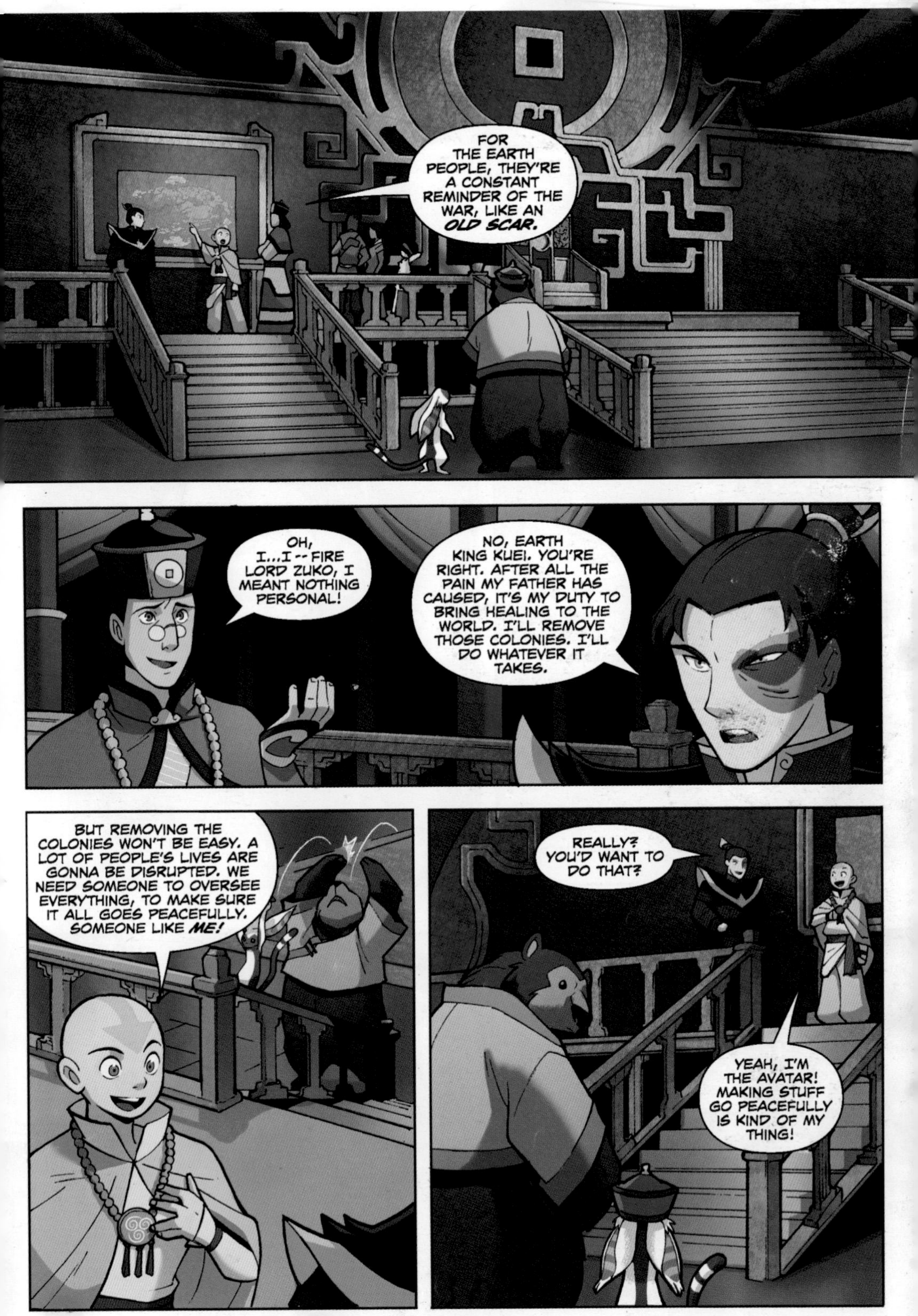
FOR THE EARTH PEOPLE, THEY'RE A CONSTANT REMINDER OF THE WAR, LIKE AN OLD SCAR.
OH, I...I -- FIRE LORD ZUKO, I MEANT NOTHING PERSONAL!
NO, EARTH KING KUEI. YOU'RE RIGHT. AFTER ALL THE PAIN MY FATHER HAS CAUSED, IT'S MY DUTY TO BRING HEALING TO THE WORLD. I'LL REMOVE THOSE COLONIES. I'LL DO WHATEVER IT TAKES.
BUT REMOVING THE COLONIES WON'T BE EASY. A LOT OF PEOPLE'S LIVES ARE GONNA BE DISRUPTED. WE NEED SOMEONE TO OVERSEE EVERYTHING, TO MAKE SURE IT ALL GOES PEACEFULLY. SOMEONE LIKE ME!
REALLY? YOU'D WANT TO DO THAT?
YEAH, I'M THE AVATAR! MAKING STUFF GO PEACEFULLY IS KIND OF MY THING!

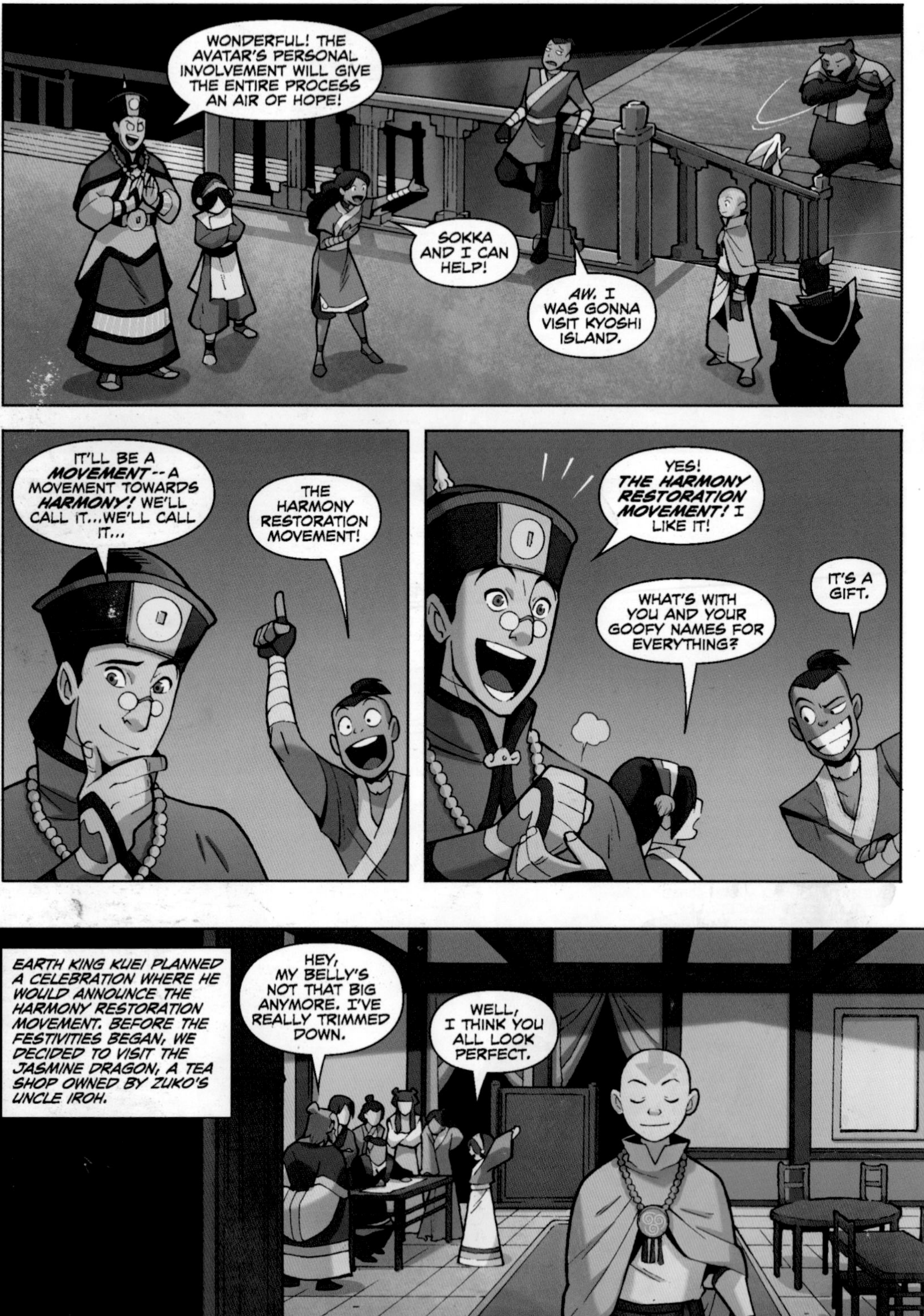
WONDERFUL! THE AVATAR'S PERSONAL INVOLVEMENT WILL GIVE THE ENTIRE PROCESS AN AIR OF HOPE!
SOKKA AND I CAN HELP!
AW. I WAS GONNA VISIT KYOSHI ISLAND.
IT'LL BE A MOVEMENT-- A MOVEMENT TOWARDS HARMONY! WE'LL CALL IT...WE'LL CALL IT...
THE HARMONY RESTORATION MOVEMENT!
YES! THE HARMONY RESTORATION MOVEMENT! I LIKE IT!
WHAT'S WITH YOU AND YOUR GOOFY NAMES FOR EVERYTHING?
IT'S A GIFT.
EARTH KING KUEI PLANNED A CELEBRATION WHERE HE WOULD ANNOUNCE THE HARMONY RESTORATION MOVEMENT. BEFORE THE FESTIVITIES BEGAN, WE DECIDED TO VISIT THE JASMINE DRAGON, A TEA SHOP OWNED BY ZUKO'S UNCLE IROH.
HEY, MY BELLY'S NOT THAT BIG ANYMORE. I'VE REALLY TRIMMED DOWN.
WELL, I THINK YOU ALL LOOK PERFECT.

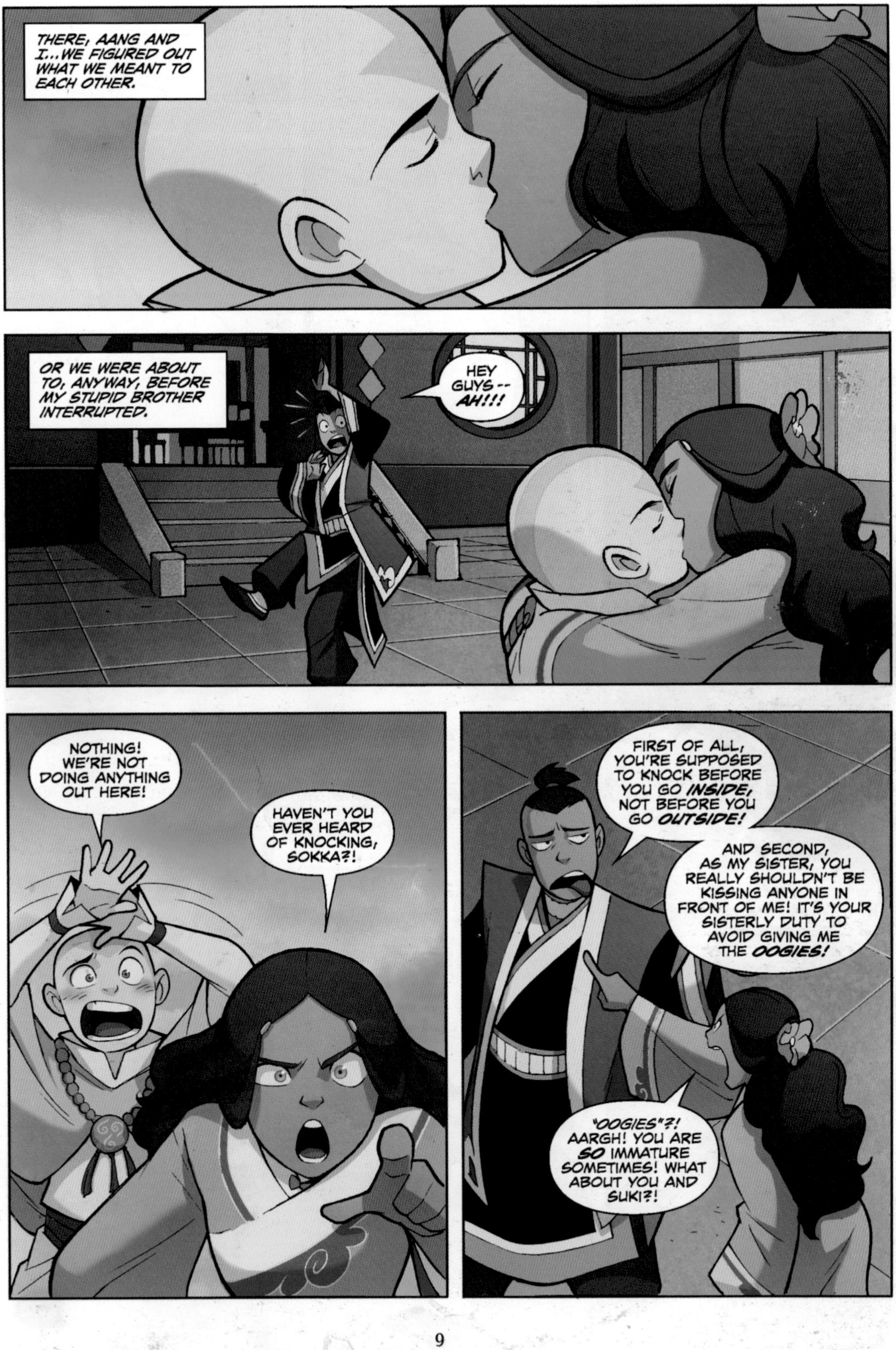
THERE, AANG AND I...WE FIGURED OUT WHAT WE MEANT TO EACH OTHER.
OR WE WERE ABOUT TO, ANYWAY, BEFORE MY STUPID BROTHER INTERRUPTED.
HEY GUYS-- AH!!!
NOTHING! WE'RE NOT DOING ANYTHING OUT HERE!
HAVEN'T YOU EVER HEARD OF KNOCKING, SOKKA?!
FIRST OF ALL, YOU'RE SUPPOSED TO KNOCK BEFORE YOU GO INSIDE, NOT BEFORE YOU GO OUTSIDE!
AND SECOND, AS MY SISTER, YOU REALLY SHOULDN'T BE KISSING ANYONE IN FRONT OF ME! IT'S YOUR SISTERLY DUTY TO AVOID GIVING ME THE OOGIES!
"OOGIES"?! AARGH! YOU ARE SO IMMATURE SOMETIMES! WHAT ABOUT YOU AND SUKI?!

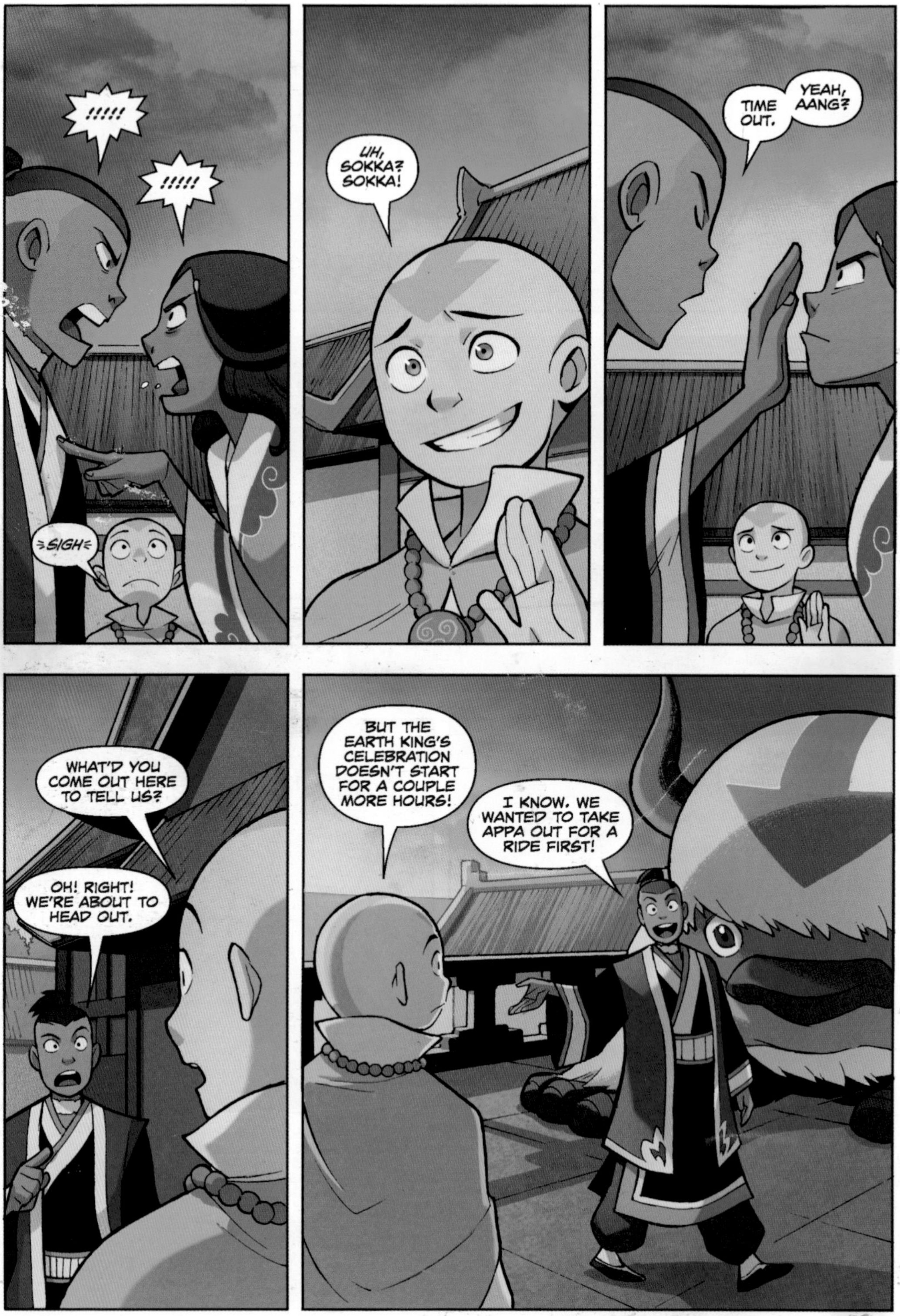
!!!!!
!!!!!
SIGH
UH, SOKKA? SOKKA!
TIME OUT.
YEAH, AANG?
WHAT'D YOU COME OUT HERE TO TELL US?
OH! RIGHT! WE'RE ABOUT TO HEAD OUT.
BUT THE EARTH KING'S CELEBRATION DOESN'T START FOR A COUPLE MORE HOURS!
I KNOW. WE WANTED TO TAKE APPA OUT FOR A RIDE FIRST!

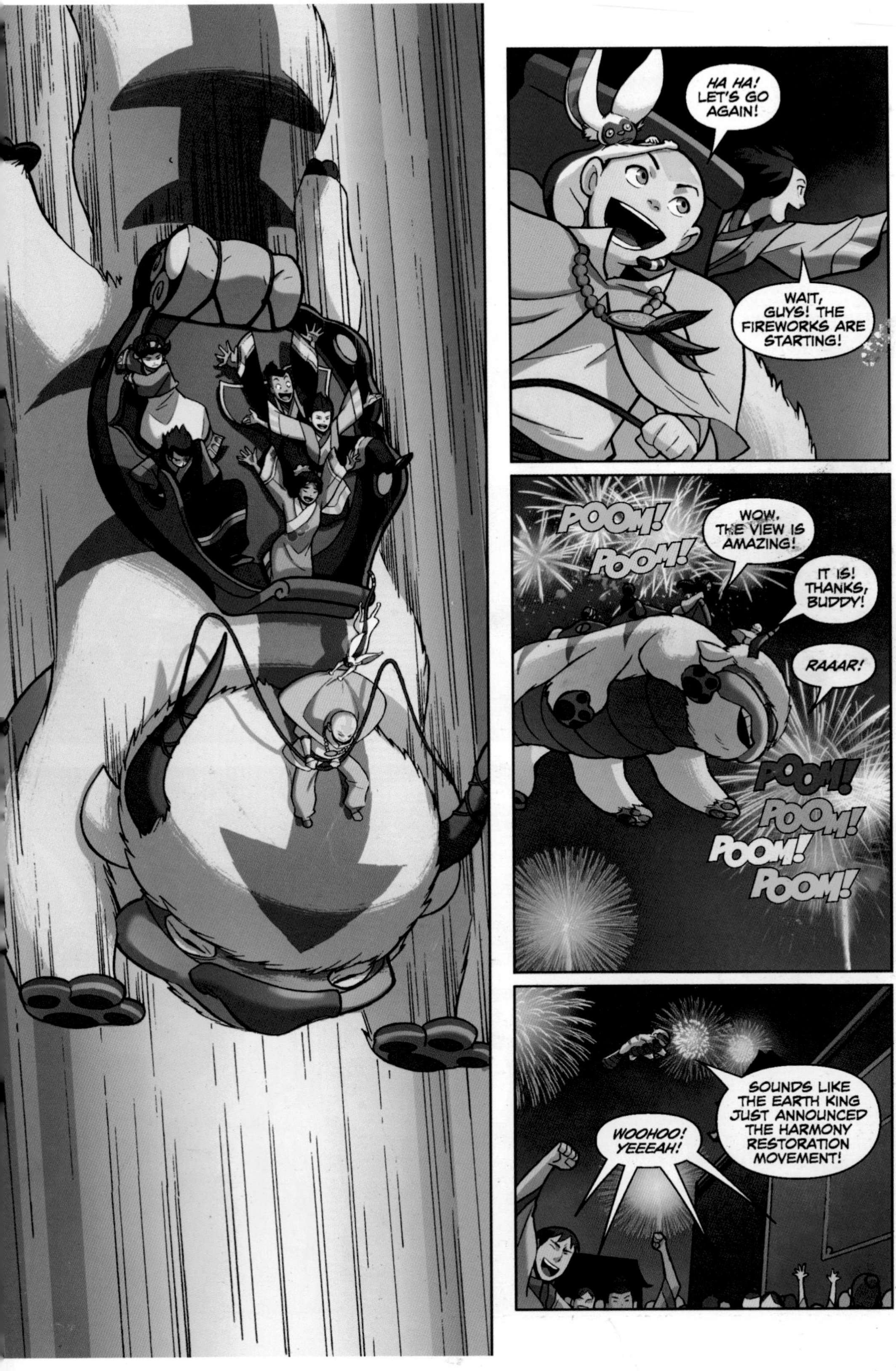
HA HA! LET'S GO AGAIN!
WAIT, GUYS! THE FIREWORKS ARE STARTING!
POOM!
POOM!
WOW, THE VIEW IS AMAZING!
IT IS! THANKS, BUDDY!
RAAAR!
POOM!
POOM!
POOM!
POOM!
SOUNDS LIKE THE EARTH KING JUST ANNOUNCED THE HARMONY RESTORATION MOVEMENT!
WOOHOO! YEEEAH!

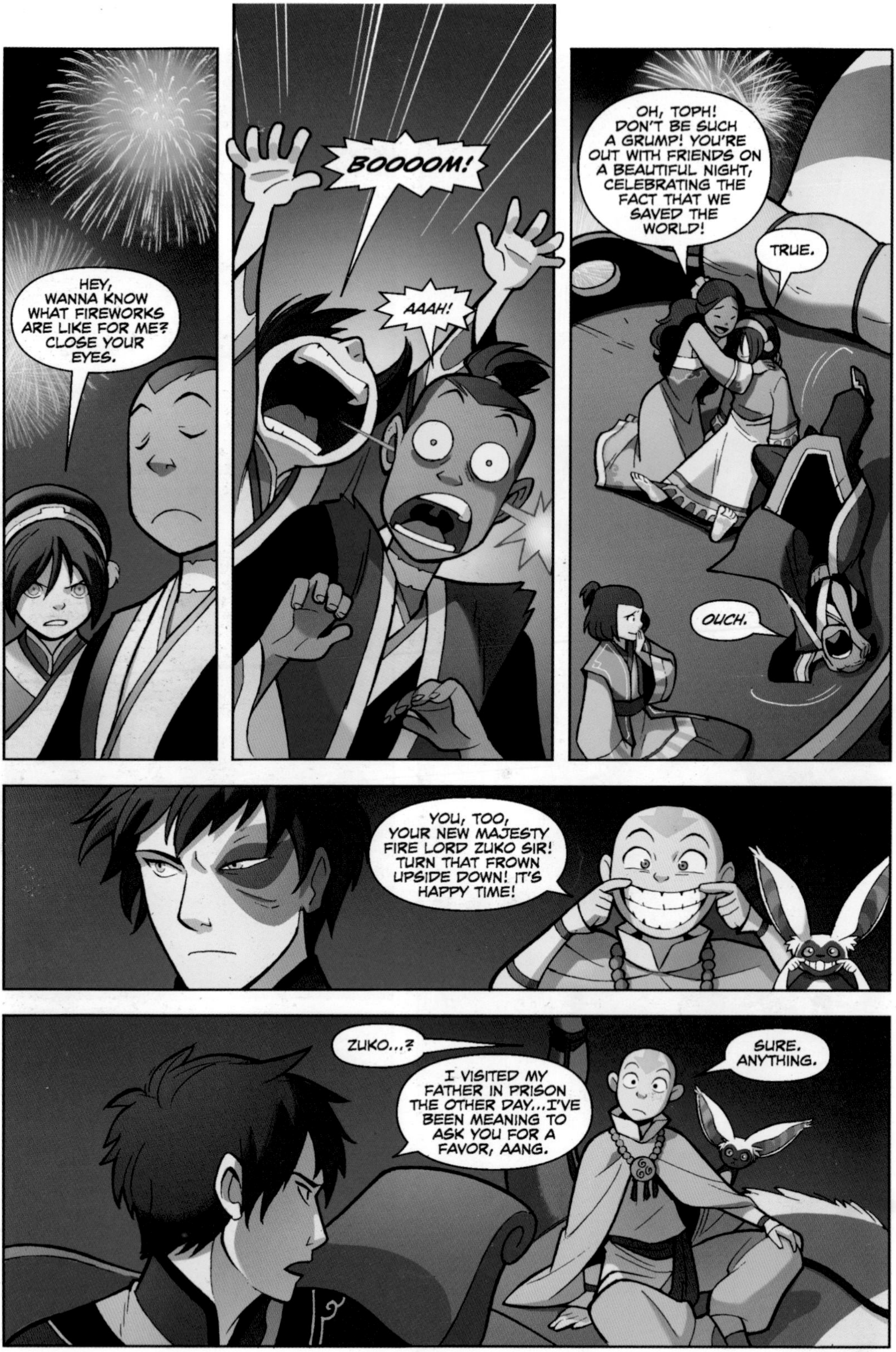
HEY, WANNA KNOW WHAT FIREWORKS ARE LIKE FOR ME? CLOSE YOUR EYES.
BOOOOM!
AAAH!
OH, TOPH! DON'T BE SUCH A GRUMP! YOU'RE OUT WITH FRIENDS ON A BEAUTIFUL NIGHT, CELEBRATING THE FACT THAT WE SAVED THE WORLD!
TRUE.
OUCH.
YOU, TOO, YOUR NEW MAJESTY FIRE LORD ZUKO SIR! TURN THAT FROWN UPSIDE DOWN! IT'S HAPPY TIME!
ZUKO...?
SURE. ANYTHING.
I VISITED MY FATHER IN PRISON THE OTHER DAY...I'VE BEEN MEANING TO ASK YOU FOR A FAVOR, AANG.

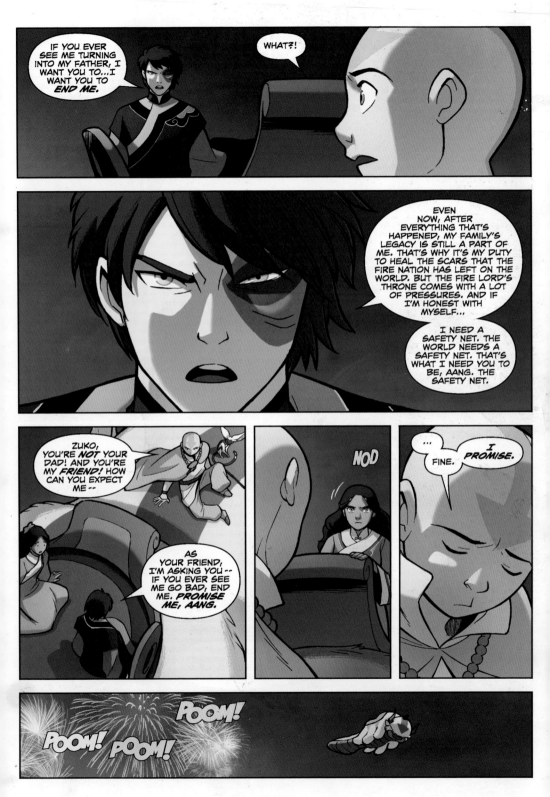

IF YOU EVER SEE ME TURNING INTO MY FATHER, I WANT YOU TO...I WANT YOU TO *END ME.*

WHAT?!

EVEN NOW, AFTER EVERYTHING THAT'S HAPPENED, MY FAMILY'S LEGACY IS STILL A PART OF ME. THAT'S WHY IT'S MY DUTY TO HEAL THE SCARS THAT THE FIRE NATION HAS LEFT ON THE WORLD. BUT THE FIRE LORD'S THRONE COMES WITH A LOT OF PRESSURES. AND IF I'M HONEST WITH MYSELF...

I NEED A SAFETY NET. THE WORLD NEEDS A SAFETY NET. THAT'S WHAT I NEED YOU TO BE, AANG. THE SAFETY NET.

ZUKO, YOU'RE *NOT* YOUR DAD! AND YOU'RE MY *FRIEND!* HOW CAN YOU EXPECT ME --

AS YOUR FRIEND, I'M ASKING YOU -- IF YOU EVER SEE ME GO BAD, END ME. *PROMISE ME, AANG.*

NOD

... FINE.

I *PROMISE.*

POOM!

POOM! POOM!

13

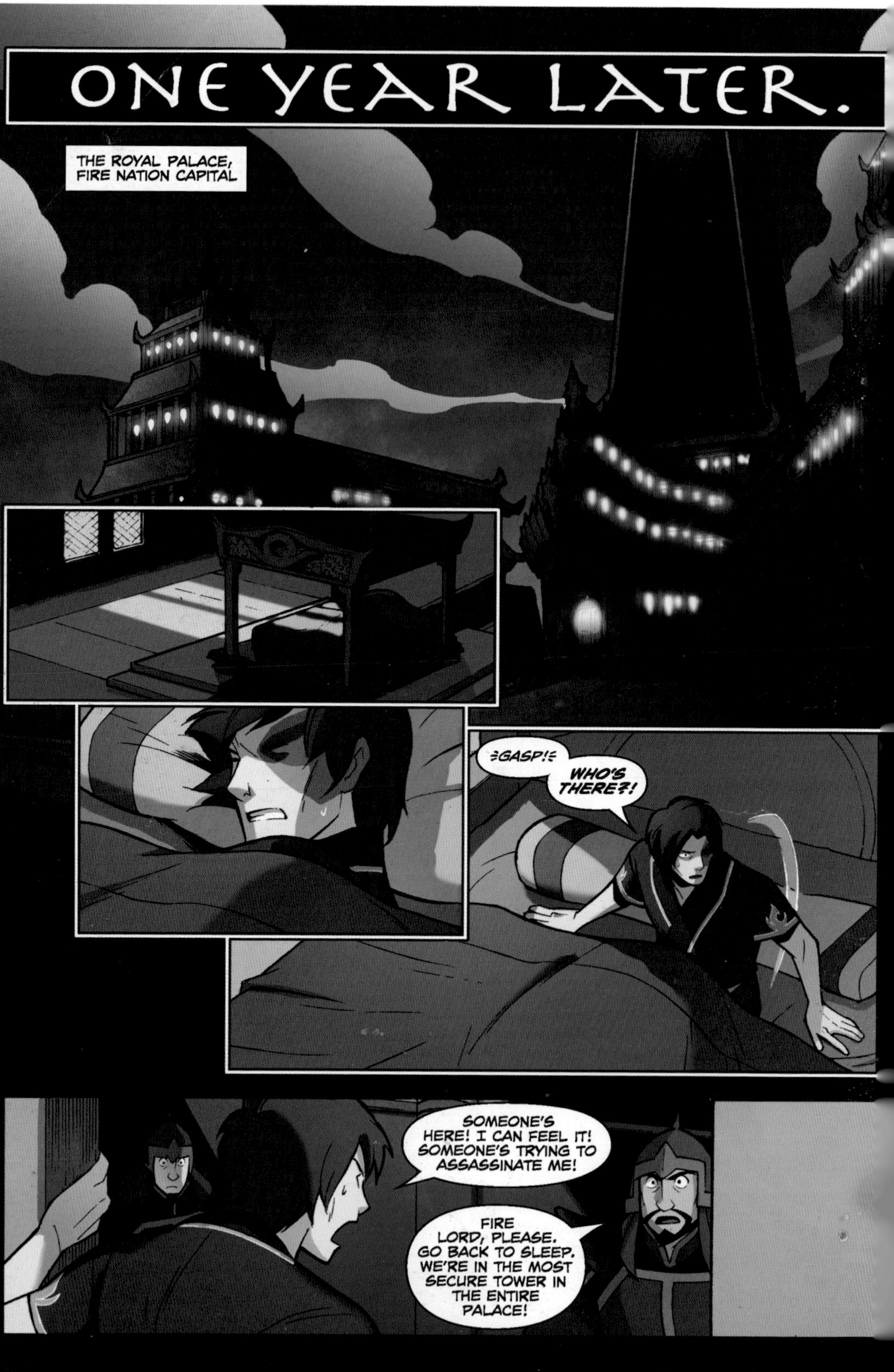
ONE YEAR LATER.
THE ROYAL PALACE, FIRE NATION CAPITAL
GASP!
WHO'S THERE?!
SOMEONE'S HERE! I CAN FEEL IT! SOMEONE'S TRYING TO ASSASSINATE ME!
FIRE LORD, PLEASE. GO BACK TO SLEEP. WE'RE IN THE MOST SECURE TOWER IN THE ENTIRE PALACE!

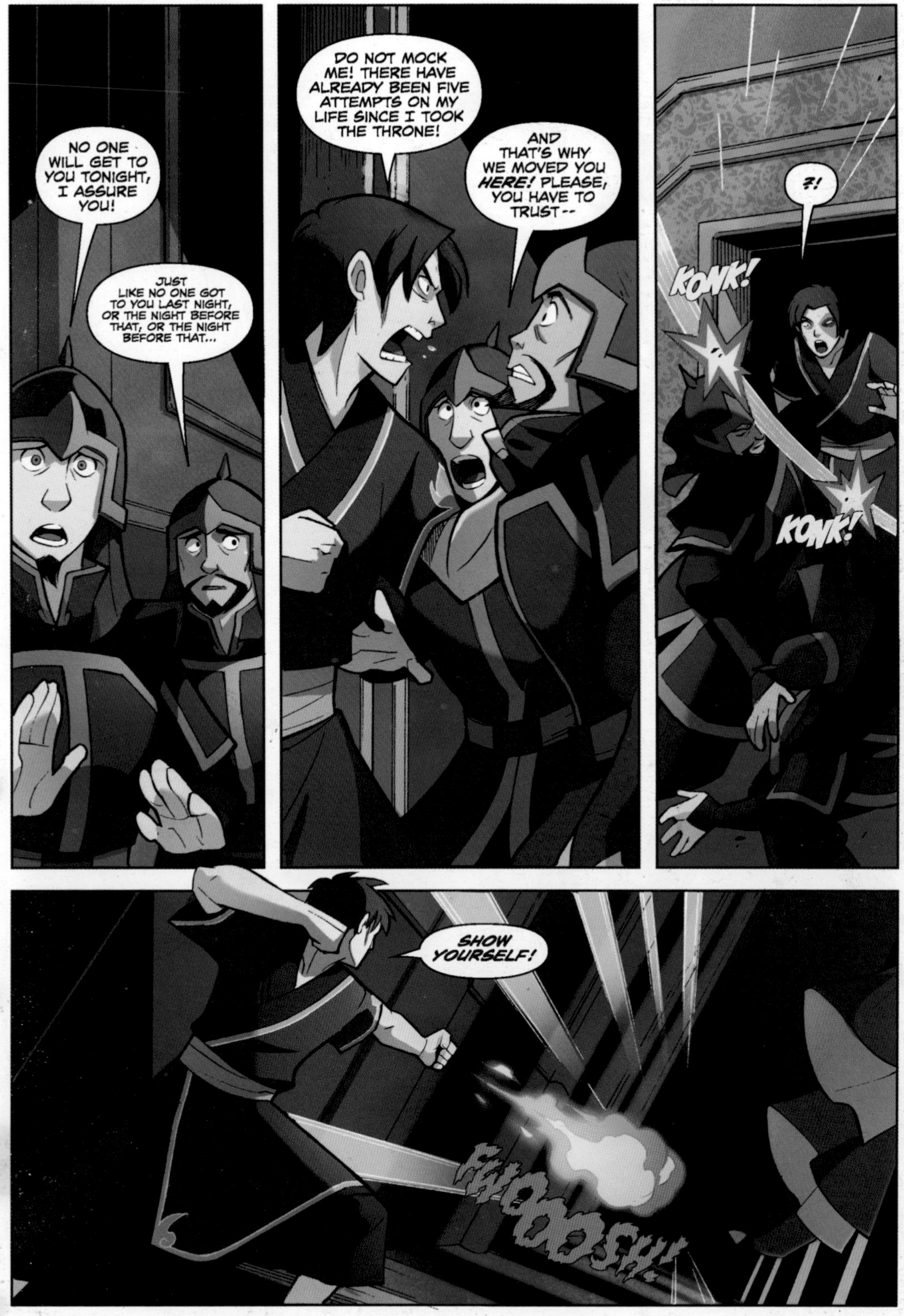
NO ONE WILL GET TO YOU TONIGHT, I ASSURE YOU!
JUST LIKE NO ONE GOT TO YOU LAST NIGHT, OR THE NIGHT BEFORE THAT, OR THE NIGHT BEFORE THAT...
DO NOT MOCK ME! THERE HAVE ALREADY BEEN FIVE ATTEMPTS ON MY LIFE SINCE I TOOK THE THRONE!
AND THAT'S WHY WE MOVED YOU HERE! PLEASE, YOU HAVE TO TRUST--
?!
KONK!
KONK!
SHOW YOURSELF!
FWOOOSH!

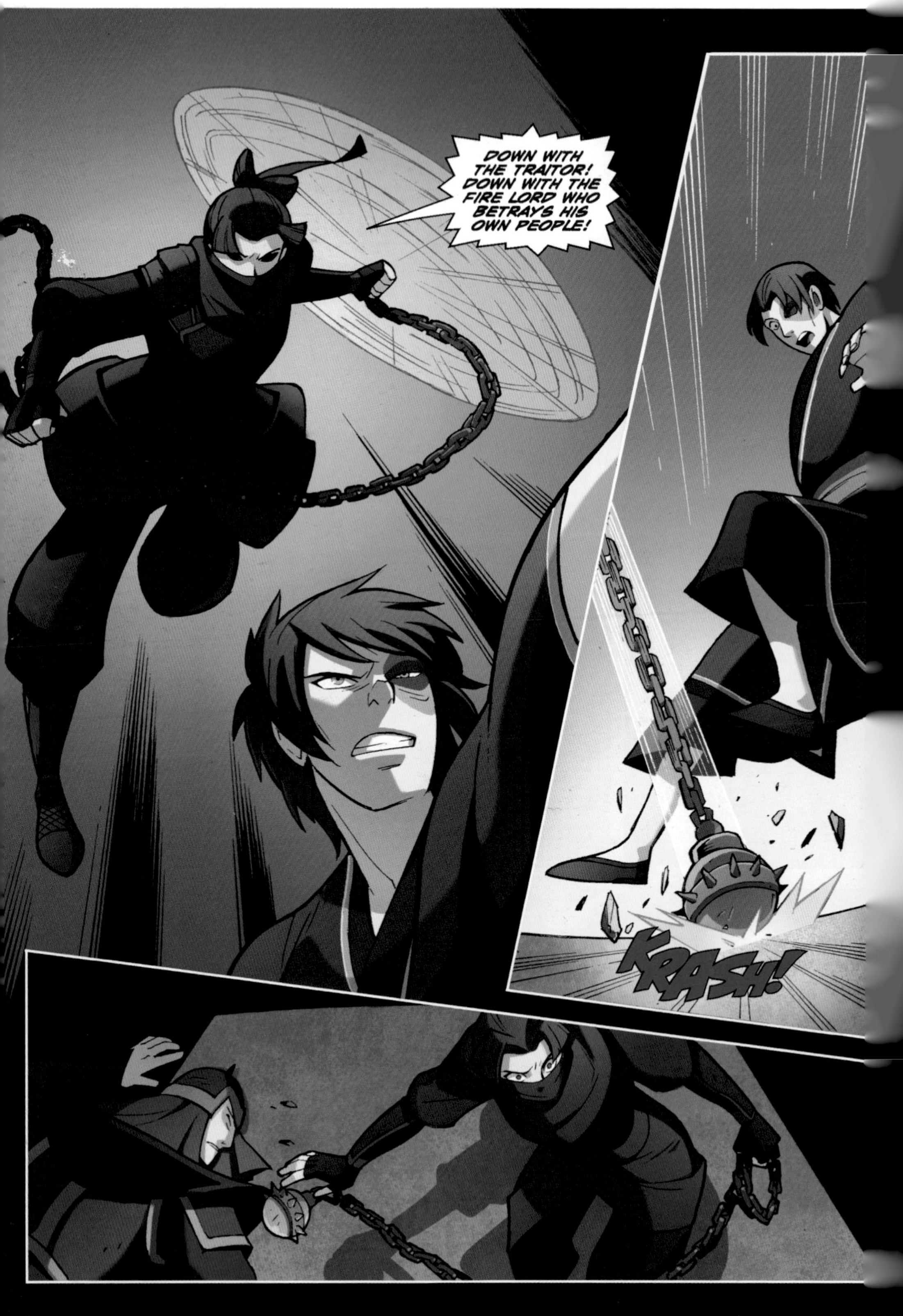
DOWN WITH THE TRAITOR! DOWN WITH THE FIRE LORD WHO BETRAYS HIS OWN PEOPLE!
KRASH!

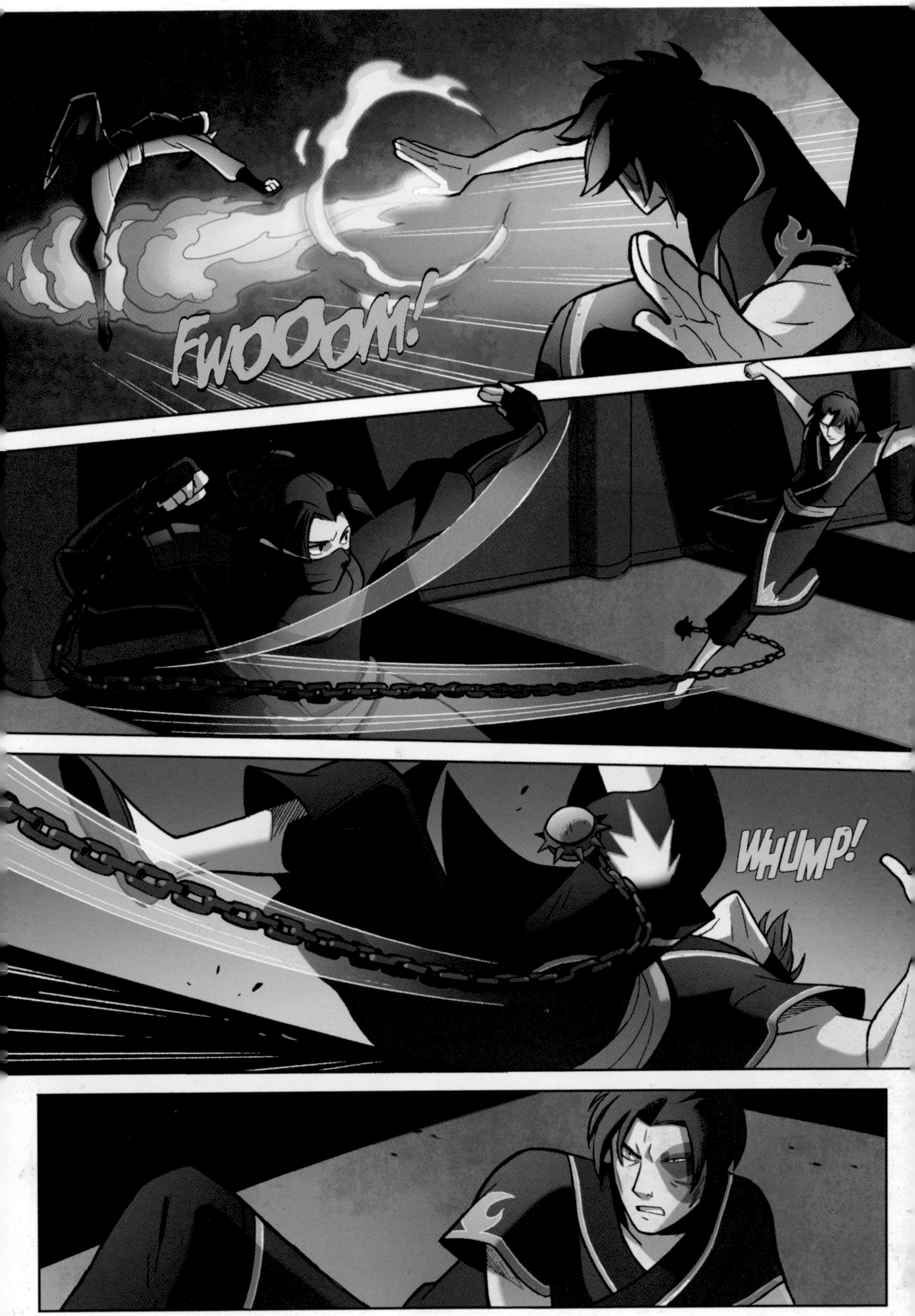
FWOOOM!
WHUMP!

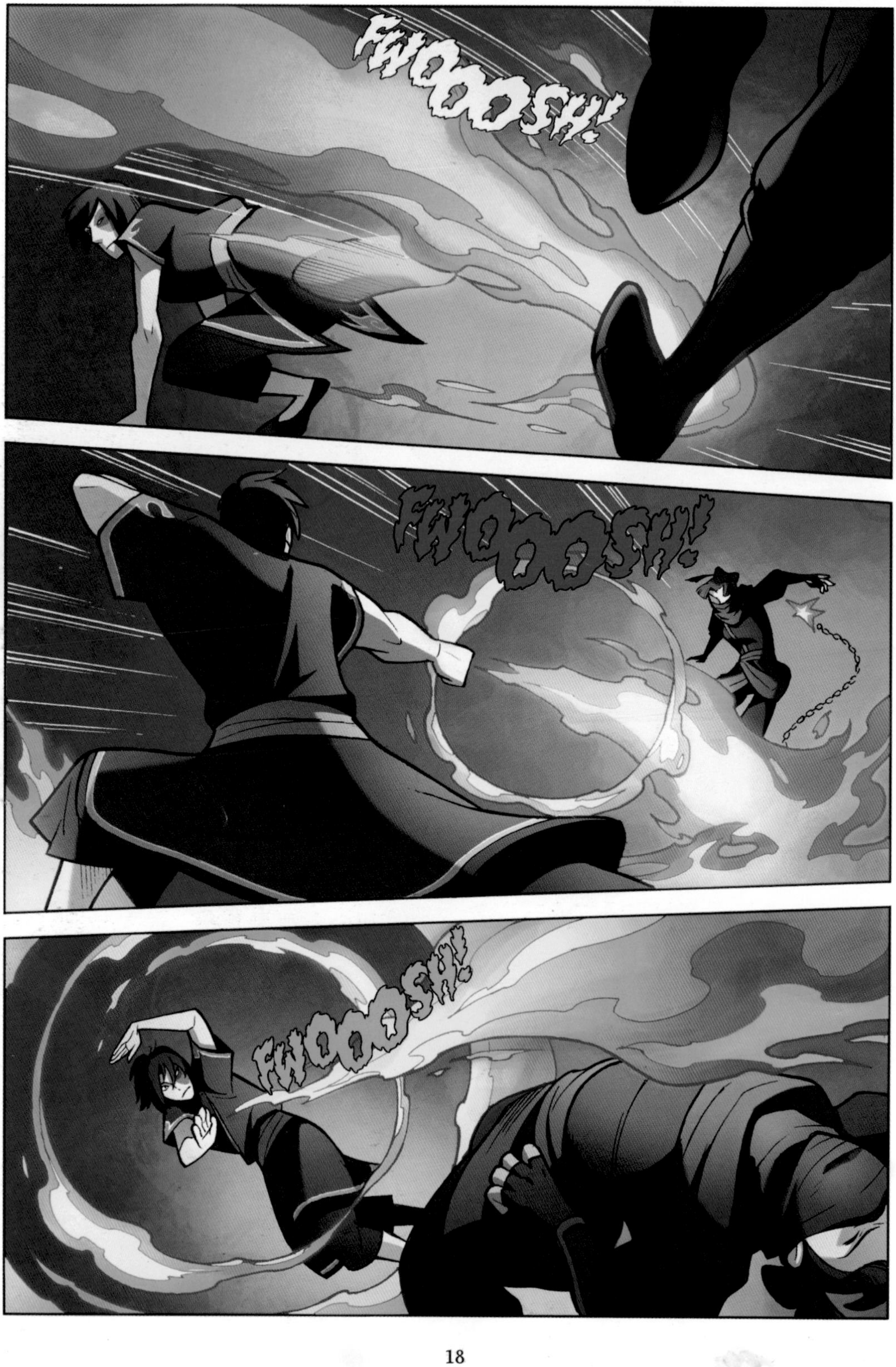
FWOOOSH!
FWOOOSH!
FWOOOSH!

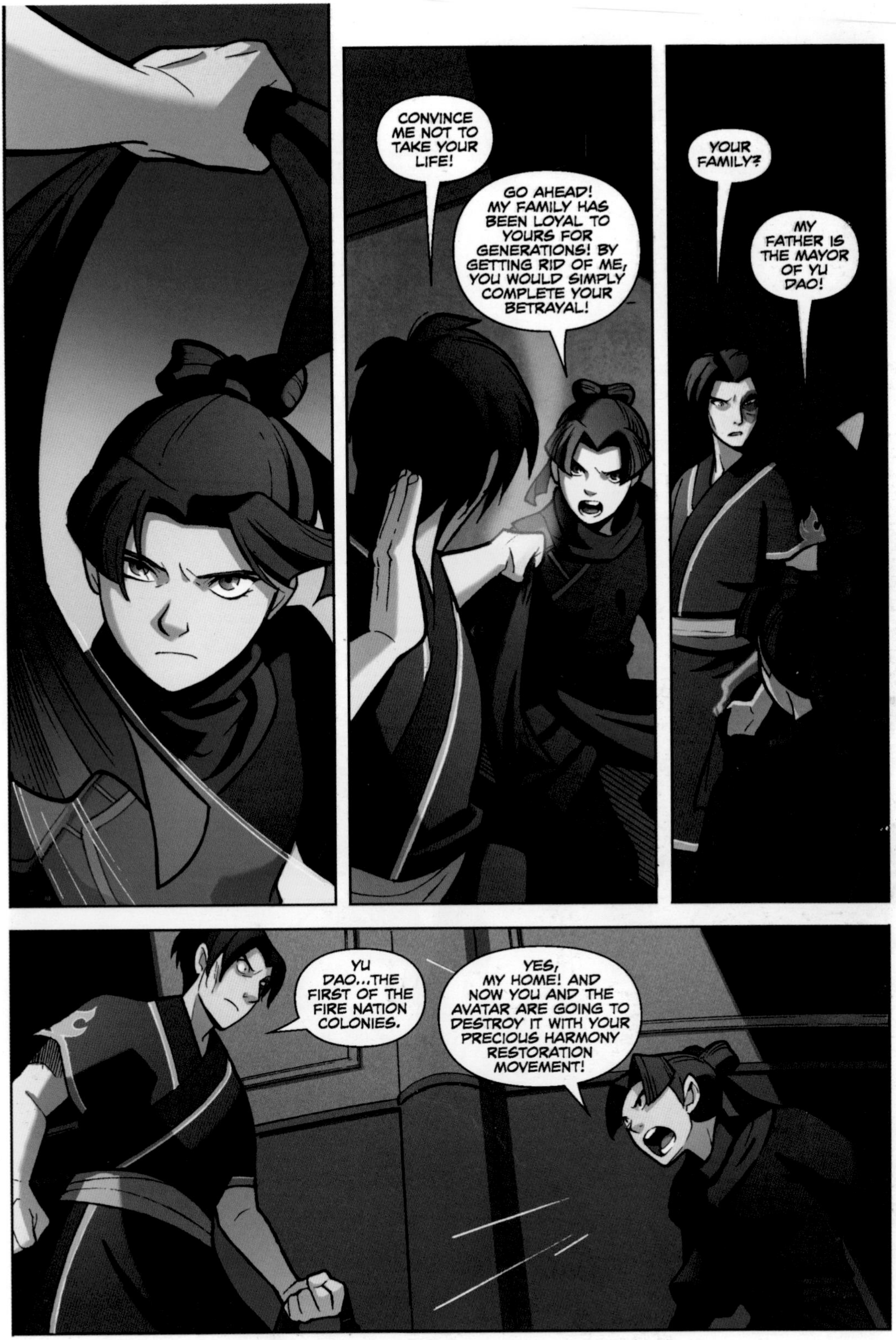
CONVINCE ME NOT TO TAKE YOUR LIFE!
GO AHEAD! MY FAMILY HAS BEEN LOYAL TO YOURS FOR GENERATIONS! BY GETTING RID OF ME, YOU WOULD SIMPLY COMPLETE YOUR BETRAYAL!
YOUR FAMILY?
MY FATHER IS THE MAYOR OF YU DAO!
YU DAO...THE FIRST OF THE FIRE NATION COLONIES.
YES, MY HOME! AND NOW YOU AND THE AVATAR ARE GOING TO DESTROY IT WITH YOUR PRECIOUS HARMONY RESTORATION MOVEMENT!

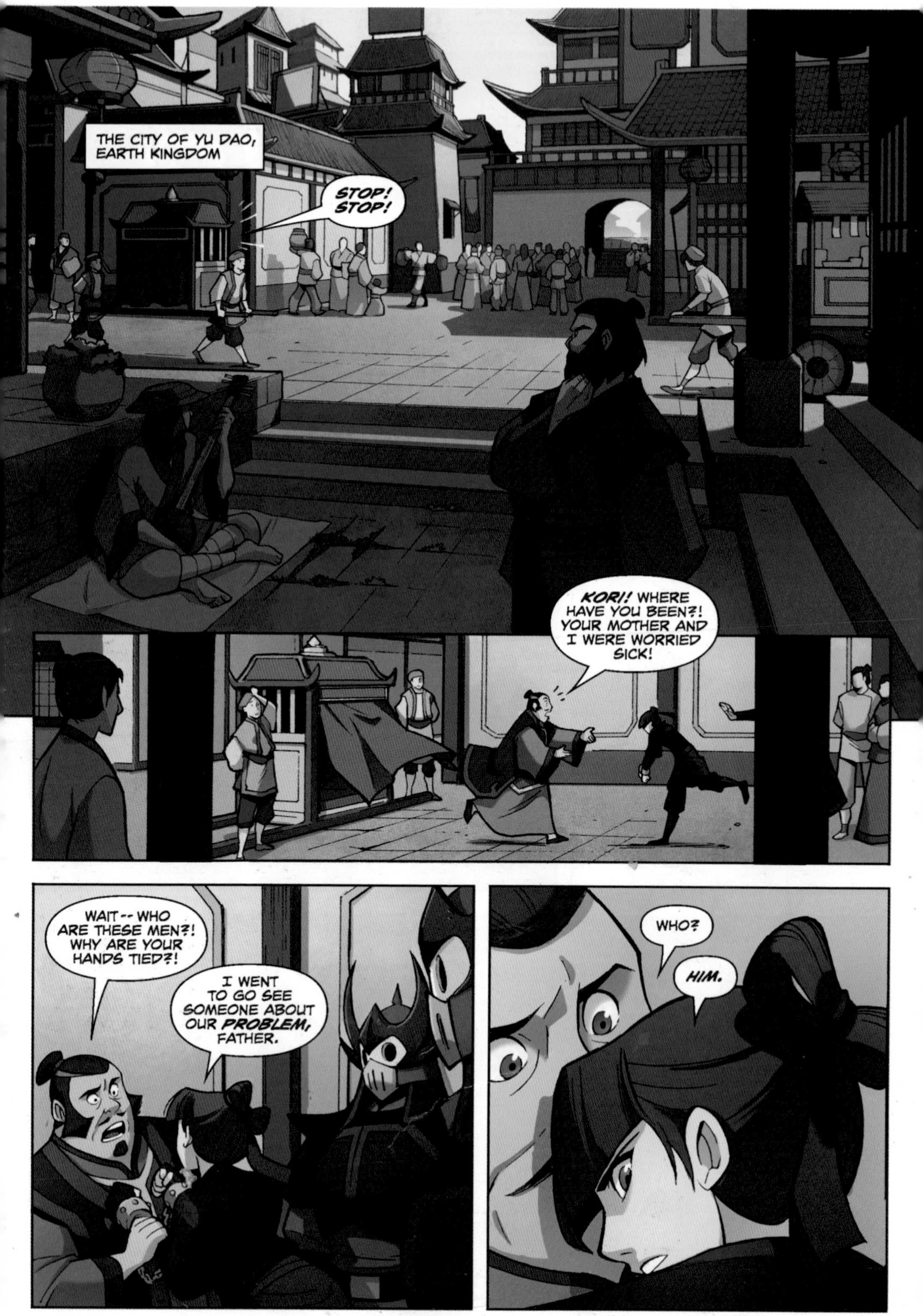
THE CITY OF YU DAO, EARTH KINGDOM
STOP! STOP!
KORI! WHERE HAVE YOU BEEN?! YOUR MOTHER AND I WERE WORRIED SICK!
WAIT-- WHO ARE THESE MEN?! WHY ARE YOUR HANDS TIED?!
I WENT TO GO SEE SOMEONE ABOUT OUR PROBLEM, FATHER.
WHO?
HIM.

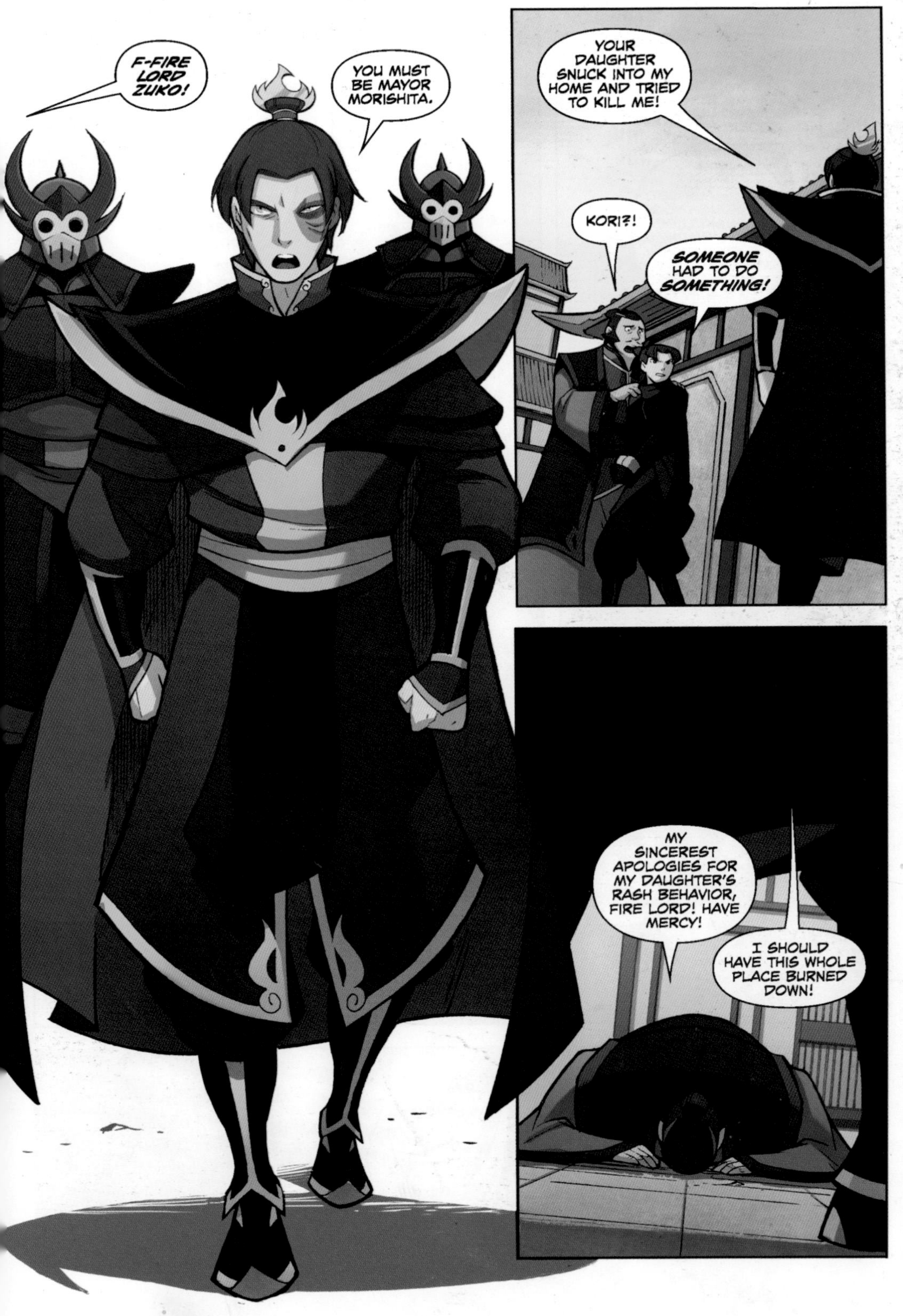
F-FIRE LORD ZUKO!
YOU MUST BE MAYOR MORISHITA.
YOUR DAUGHTER SNUCK INTO MY HOME AND TRIED TO KILL ME!
KORI?!
SOMEONE HAD TO DO SOMETHING!
MY SINCEREST APOLOGIES FOR MY DAUGHTER'S RASH BEHAVIOR, FIRE LORD! HAVE MERCY!
I SHOULD HAVE THIS WHOLE PLACE BURNED DOWN!

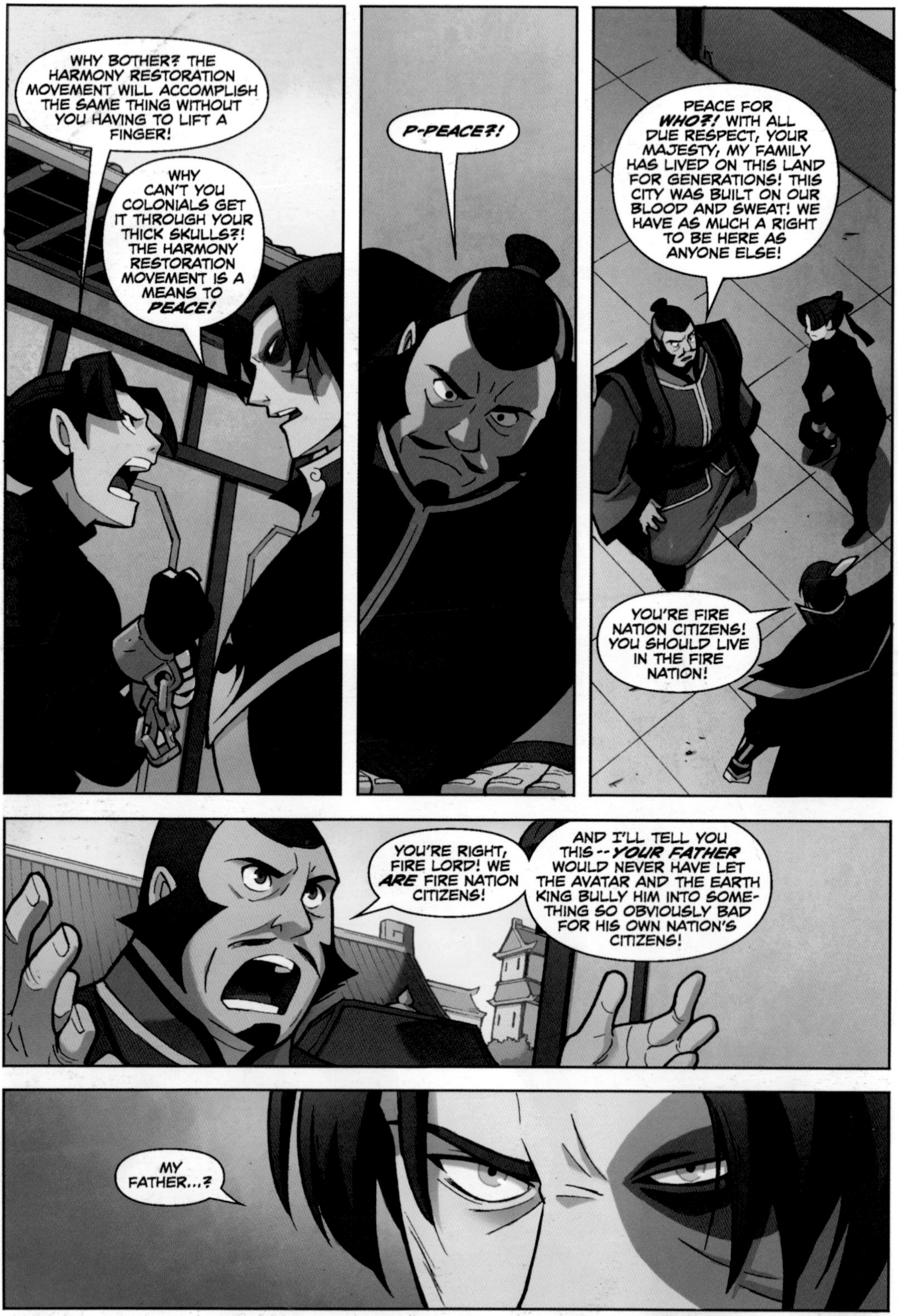
WHY BOTHER? THE HARMONY RESTORATION MOVEMENT WILL ACCOMPLISH THE SAME THING WITHOUT YOU HAVING TO LIFT A FINGER!
WHY CAN'T YOU COLONIALS GET IT THROUGH YOUR THICK SKULLS?! THE HARMONY RESTORATION MOVEMENT IS A MEANS TO PEACE!
P-PEACE?!
PEACE FOR WHO?! WITH ALL DUE RESPECT, YOUR MAJESTY, MY FAMILY HAS LIVED ON THIS LAND FOR GENERATIONS! THIS CITY WAS BUILT ON OUR BLOOD AND SWEAT! WE HAVE AS MUCH A RIGHT TO BE HERE AS ANYONE ELSE!
YOU'RE FIRE NATION CITIZENS! YOU SHOULD LIVE IN THE FIRE NATION!
YOU'RE RIGHT, FIRE LORD! WE ARE FIRE NATION CITIZENS!
AND I'LL TELL YOU THIS--YOUR FATHER WOULD NEVER HAVE LET THE AVATAR AND THE EARTH KING BULLY HIM INTO SOMETHING SO OBVIOUSLY BAD FOR HIS OWN NATION'S CITIZENS!
MY FATHER...?

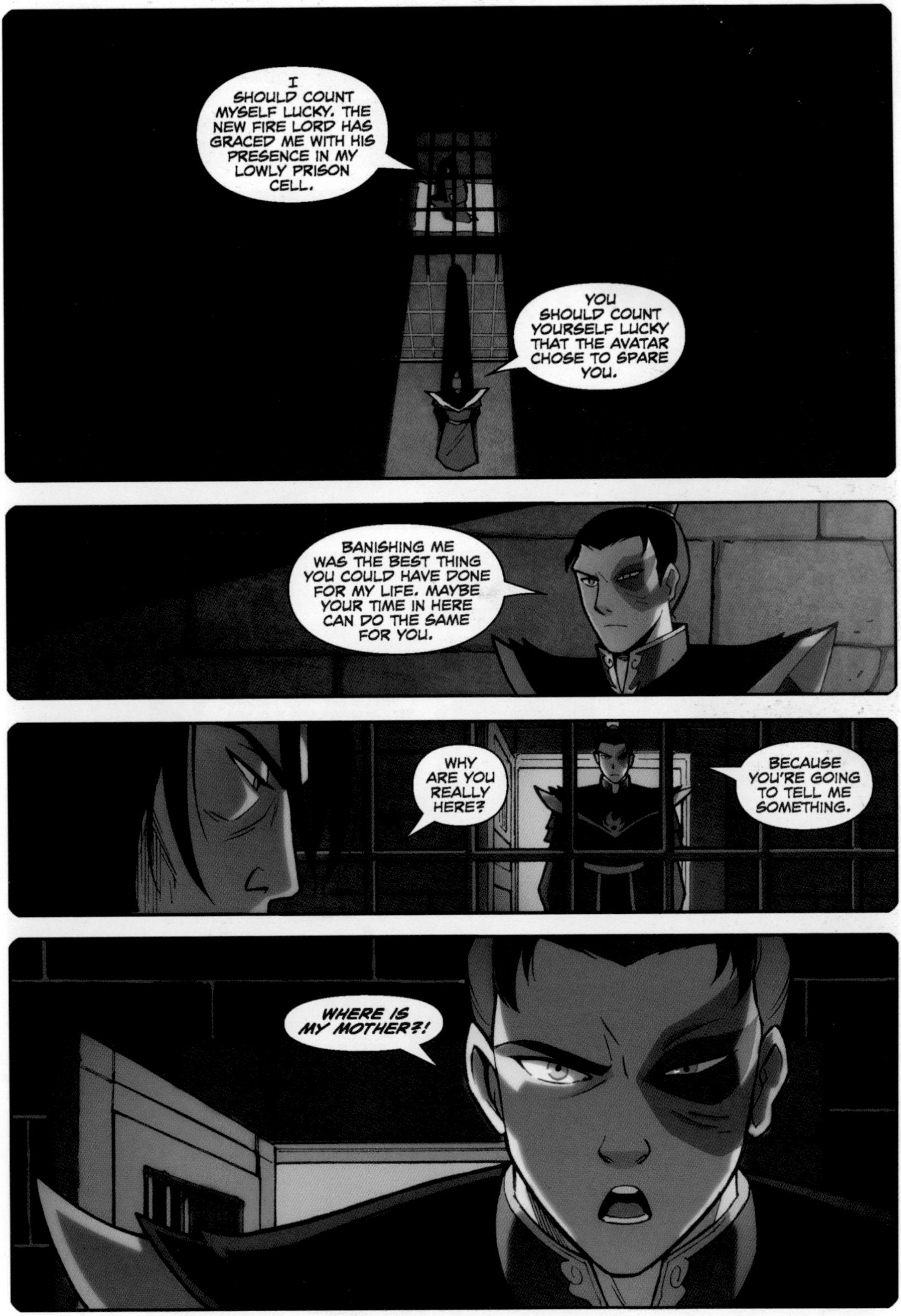
I SHOULD COUNT MYSELF LUCKY. THE NEW FIRE LORD HAS GRACED ME WITH HIS PRESENCE IN MY LOWLY PRISON CELL.
YOU SHOULD COUNT YOURSELF LUCKY THAT THE AVATAR CHOSE TO SPARE YOU.
BANISHING ME WAS THE BEST THING YOU COULD HAVE DONE FOR MY LIFE. MAYBE YOUR TIME IN HERE CAN DO THE SAME FOR YOU.
WHY ARE YOU REALLY HERE?
BECAUSE YOU'RE GOING TO TELL ME SOMETHING.
WHERE IS MY MOTHER?!

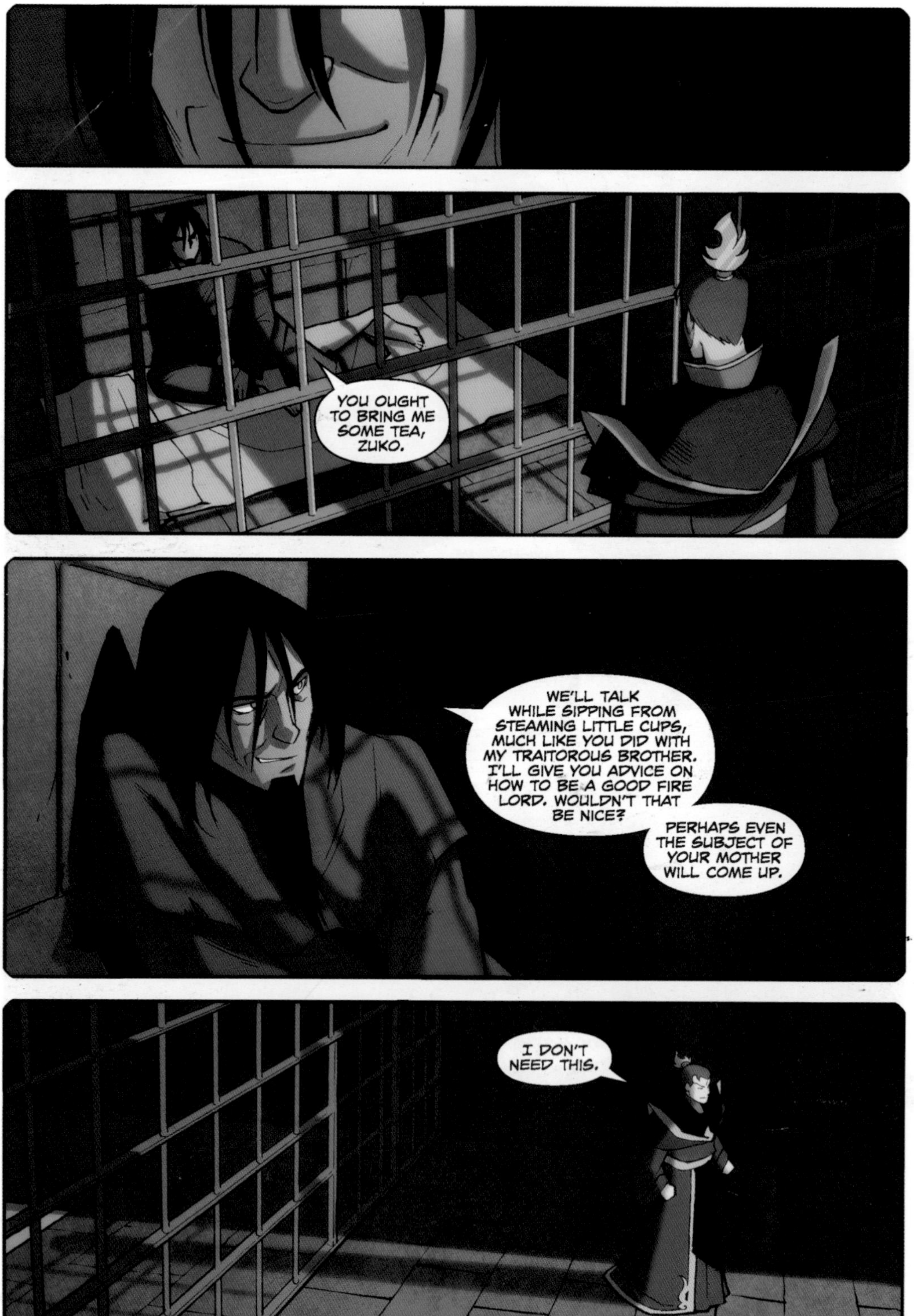
YOU OUGHT TO BRING ME SOME TEA, ZUKO.
WE'LL TALK WHILE SIPPING FROM STEAMING LITTLE CUPS, MUCH LIKE YOU DID WITH MY TRAITOROUS BROTHER. I'LL GIVE YOU ADVICE ON HOW TO BE A GOOD FIRE LORD. WOULDN'T THAT BE NICE?
PERHAPS EVEN THE SUBJECT OF YOUR MOTHER WILL COME UP.
I DON'T NEED THIS.

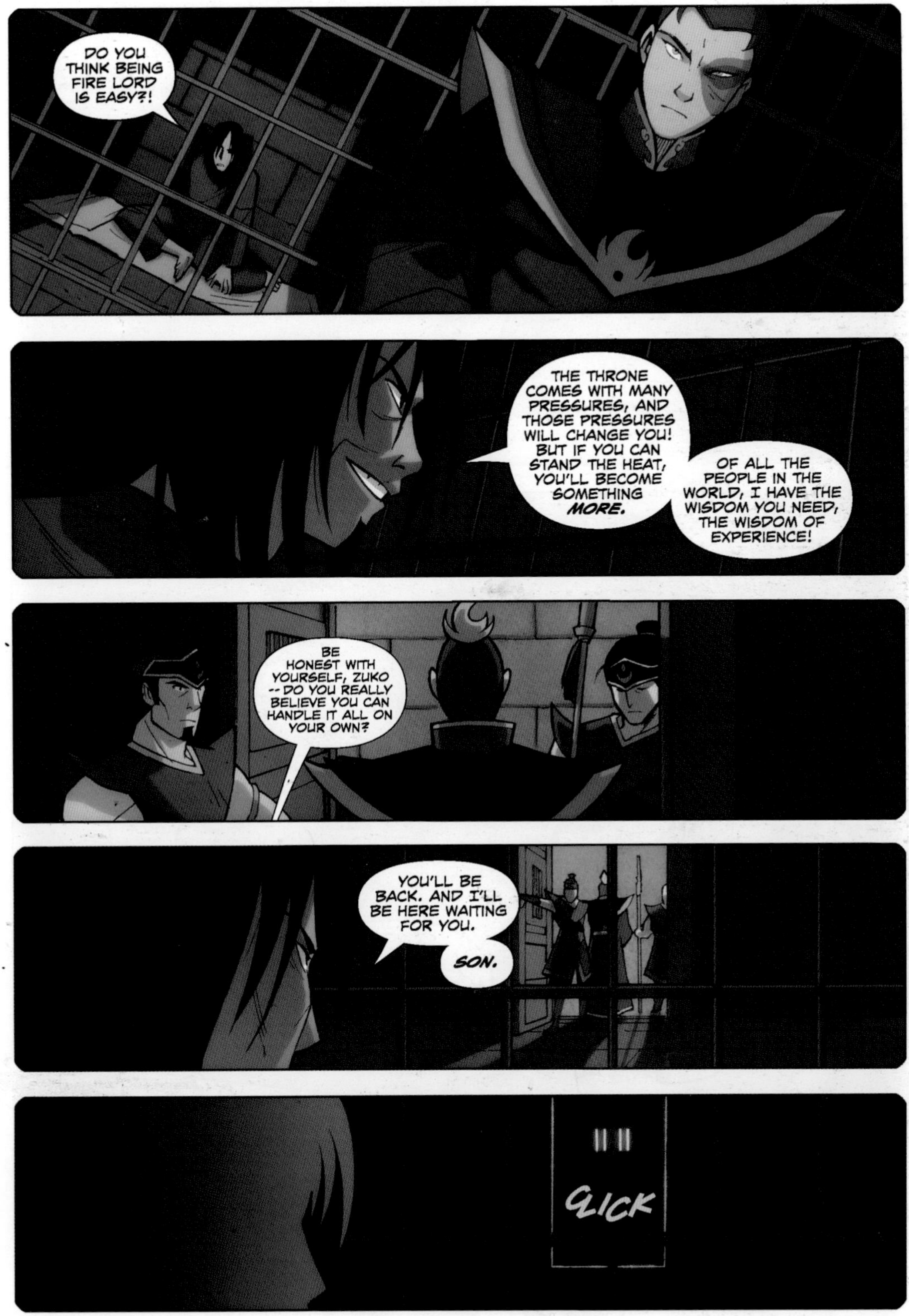
DO YOU THINK BEING FIRE LORD IS EASY?!
THE THRONE COMES WITH MANY PRESSURES, AND THOSE PRESSURES WILL CHANGE YOU! BUT IF YOU CAN STAND THE HEAT, YOU'LL BECOME SOMETHING *MORE.*
OF ALL THE PEOPLE IN THE WORLD, I HAVE THE WISDOM YOU NEED, THE WISDOM OF EXPERIENCE!
BE HONEST WITH YOURSELF, ZUKO -- DO YOU REALLY BELIEVE YOU CAN HANDLE IT ALL ON YOUR OWN?
YOU'LL BE BACK. AND I'LL BE HERE WAITING FOR YOU.
SON.
CLICK

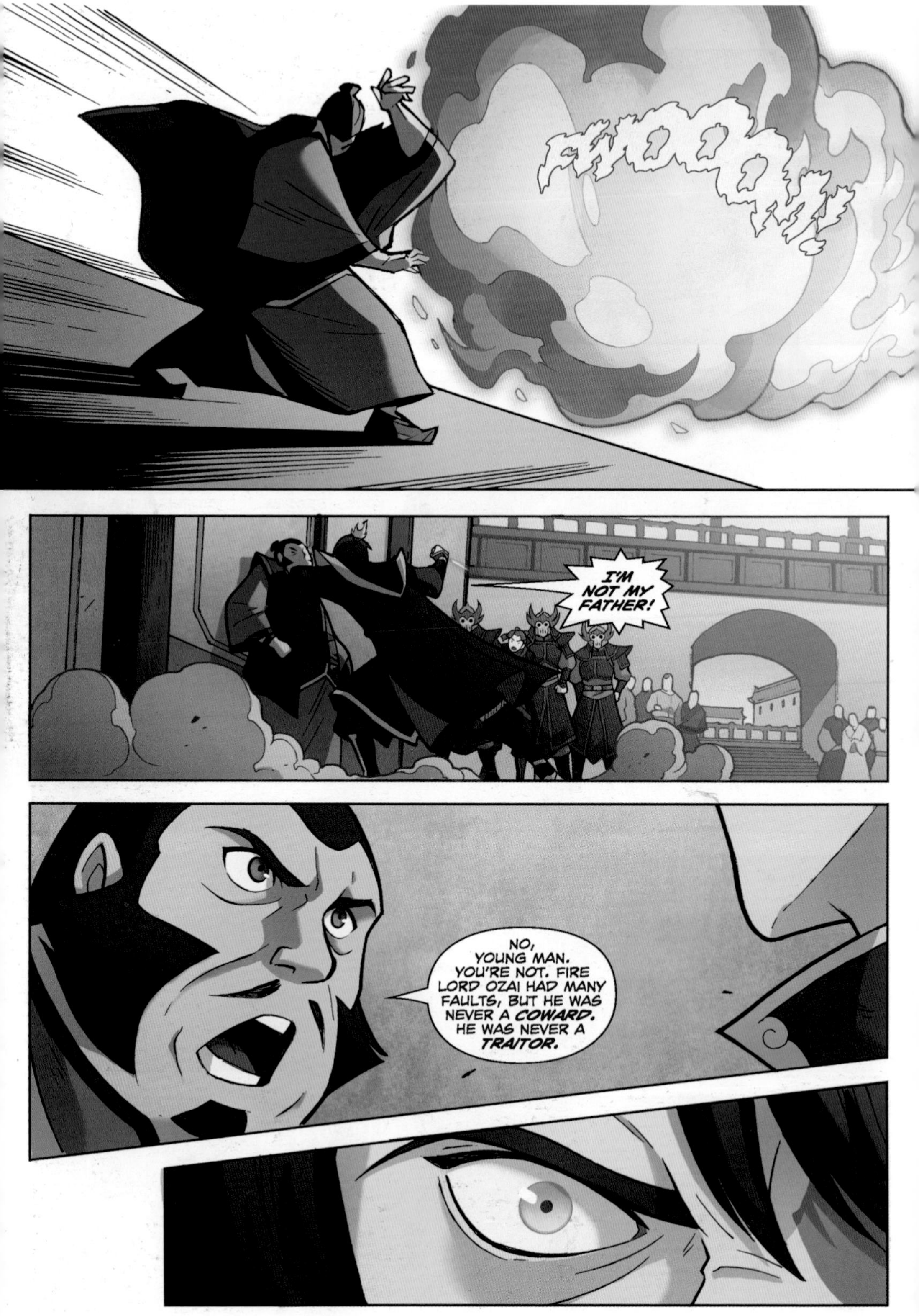
FWOOOM!
I'M NOT MY FATHER!
NO, YOUNG MAN. YOU'RE NOT. FIRE LORD OZAI HAD MANY FAULTS, BUT HE WAS NEVER A *COWARD*. HE WAS NEVER A *TRAITOR*.

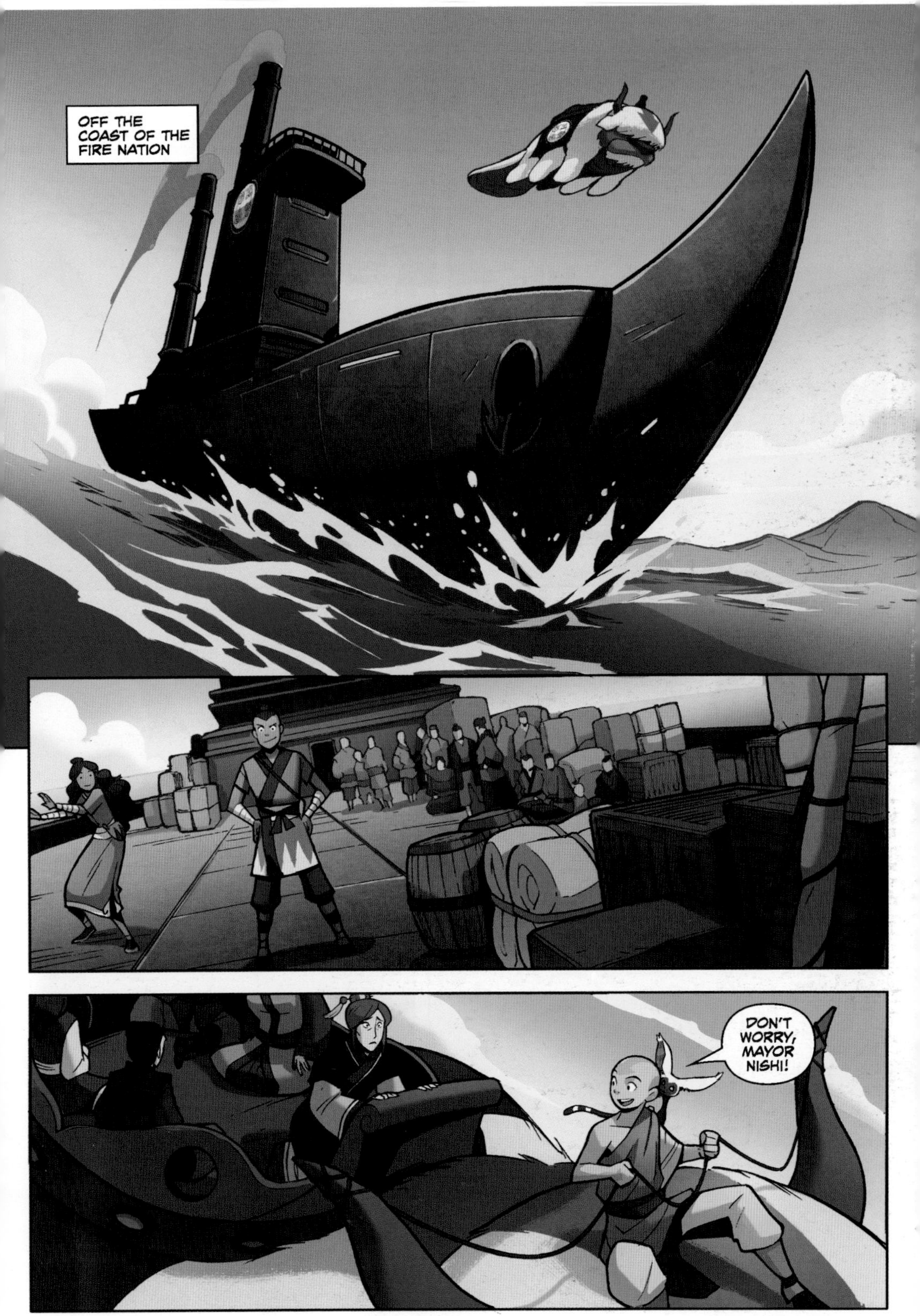
OFF THE COAST OF THE FIRE NATION
DON'T WORRY, MAYOR NISHI!

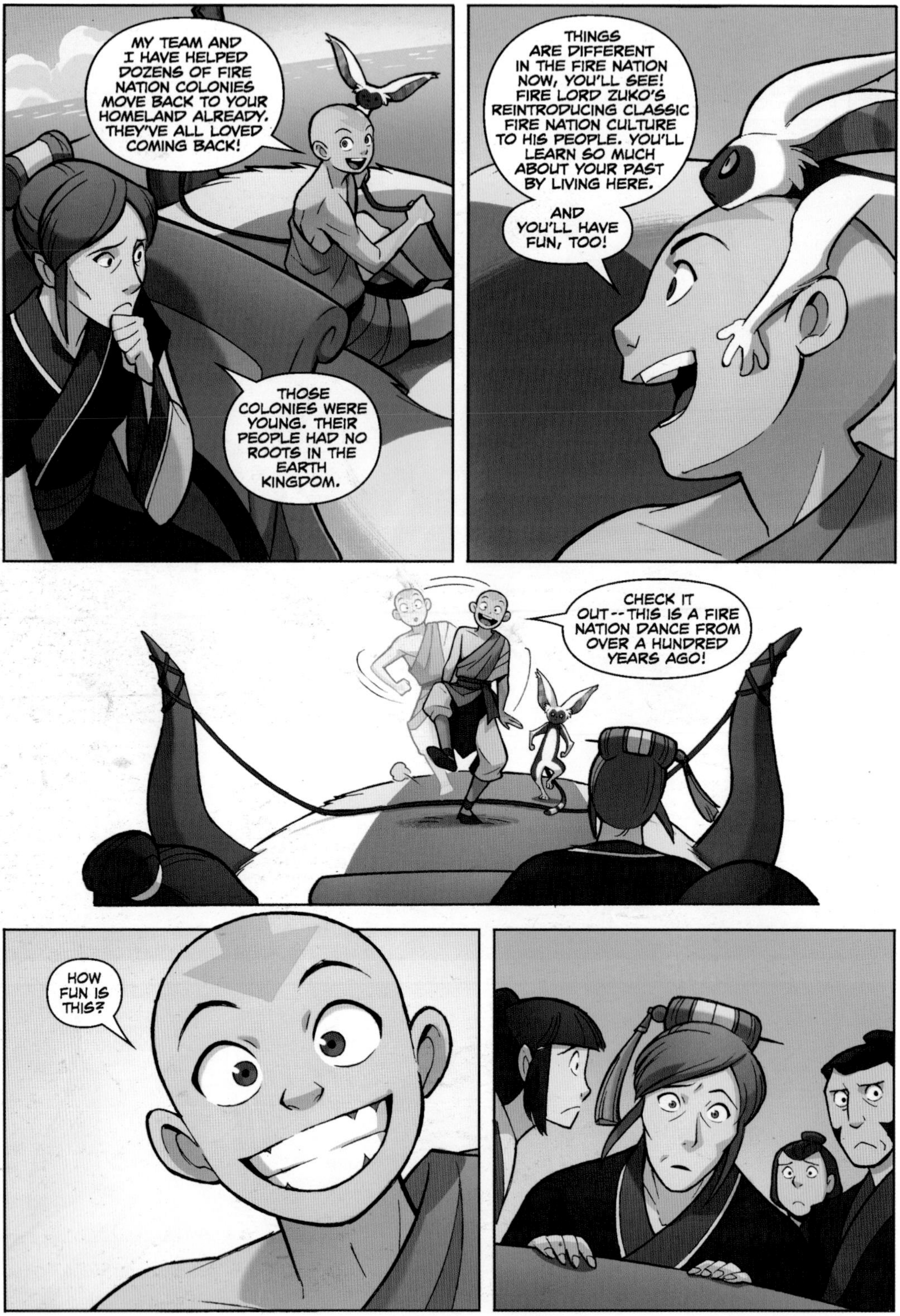
MY TEAM AND I HAVE HELPED DOZENS OF FIRE NATION COLONIES MOVE BACK TO YOUR HOMELAND ALREADY. THEY'VE ALL LOVED COMING BACK!
THOSE COLONIES WERE YOUNG. THEIR PEOPLE HAD NO ROOTS IN THE EARTH KINGDOM.
THINGS ARE DIFFERENT IN THE FIRE NATION NOW, YOU'LL SEE! FIRE LORD ZUKO'S REINTRODUCING CLASSIC FIRE NATION CULTURE TO HIS PEOPLE. YOU'LL LEARN SO MUCH ABOUT YOUR PAST BY LIVING HERE.
AND YOU'LL HAVE FUN, TOO!
CHECK IT OUT--THIS IS A FIRE NATION DANCE FROM OVER A HUNDRED YEARS AGO!
HOW FUN IS THIS?

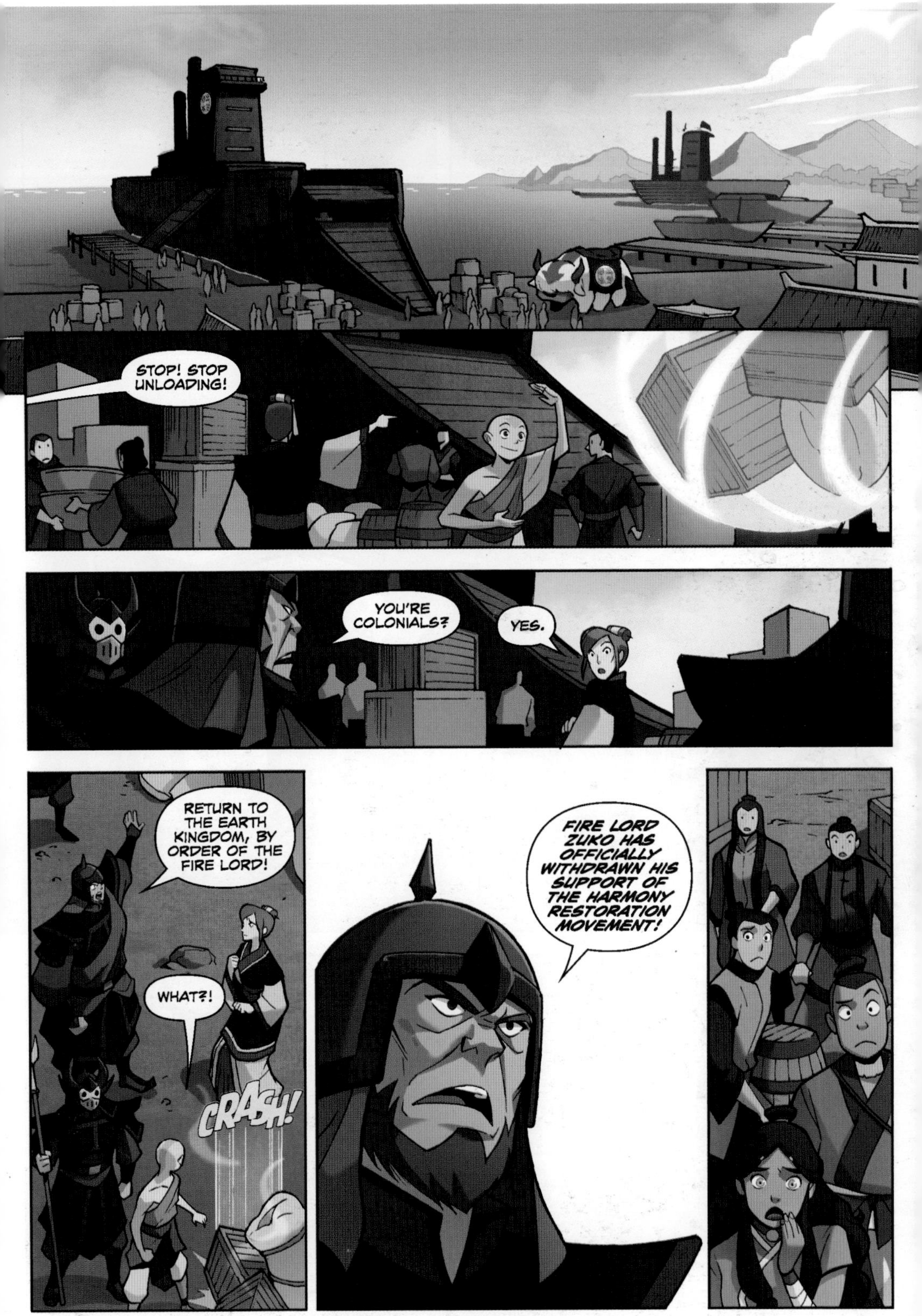
STOP! STOP UNLOADING!
YOU'RE COLONIALS?
YES.
RETURN TO THE EARTH KINGDOM, BY ORDER OF THE FIRE LORD!
WHAT?!
CRASH!
FIRE LORD ZUKO HAS OFFICIALLY WITHDRAWN HIS SUPPORT OF THE HARMONY RESTORATION MOVEMENT!

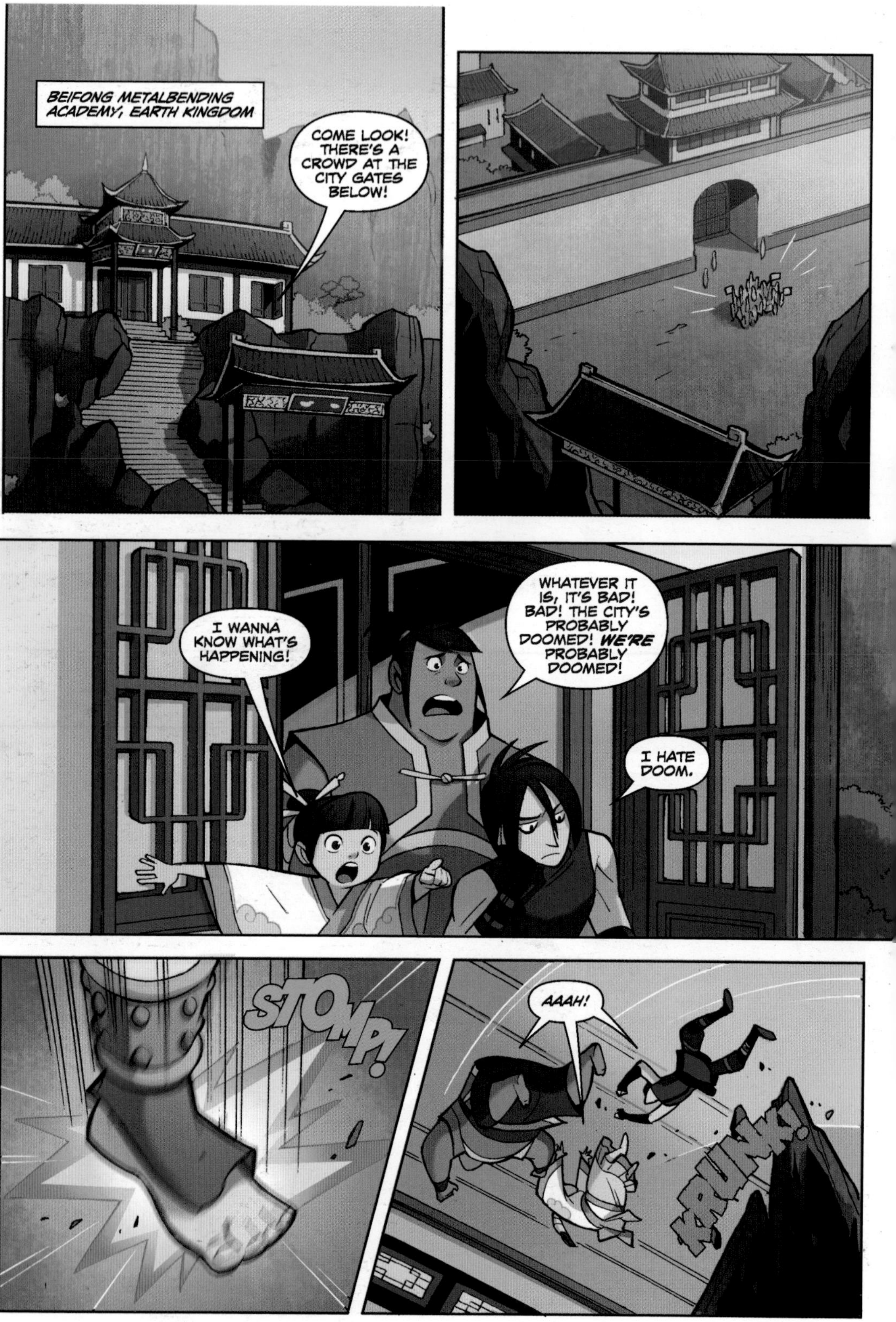
BEIFONG METALBENDING ACADEMY, EARTH KINGDOM
COME LOOK! THERE'S A CROWD AT THE CITY GATES BELOW!
I WANNA KNOW WHAT'S HAPPENING!
WHATEVER IT IS, IT'S BAD! BAD! THE CITY'S PROBABLY DOOMED! WE'RE PROBABLY DOOMED!
I HATE DOOM.
STOMP!
AAAH!
KRUNK!

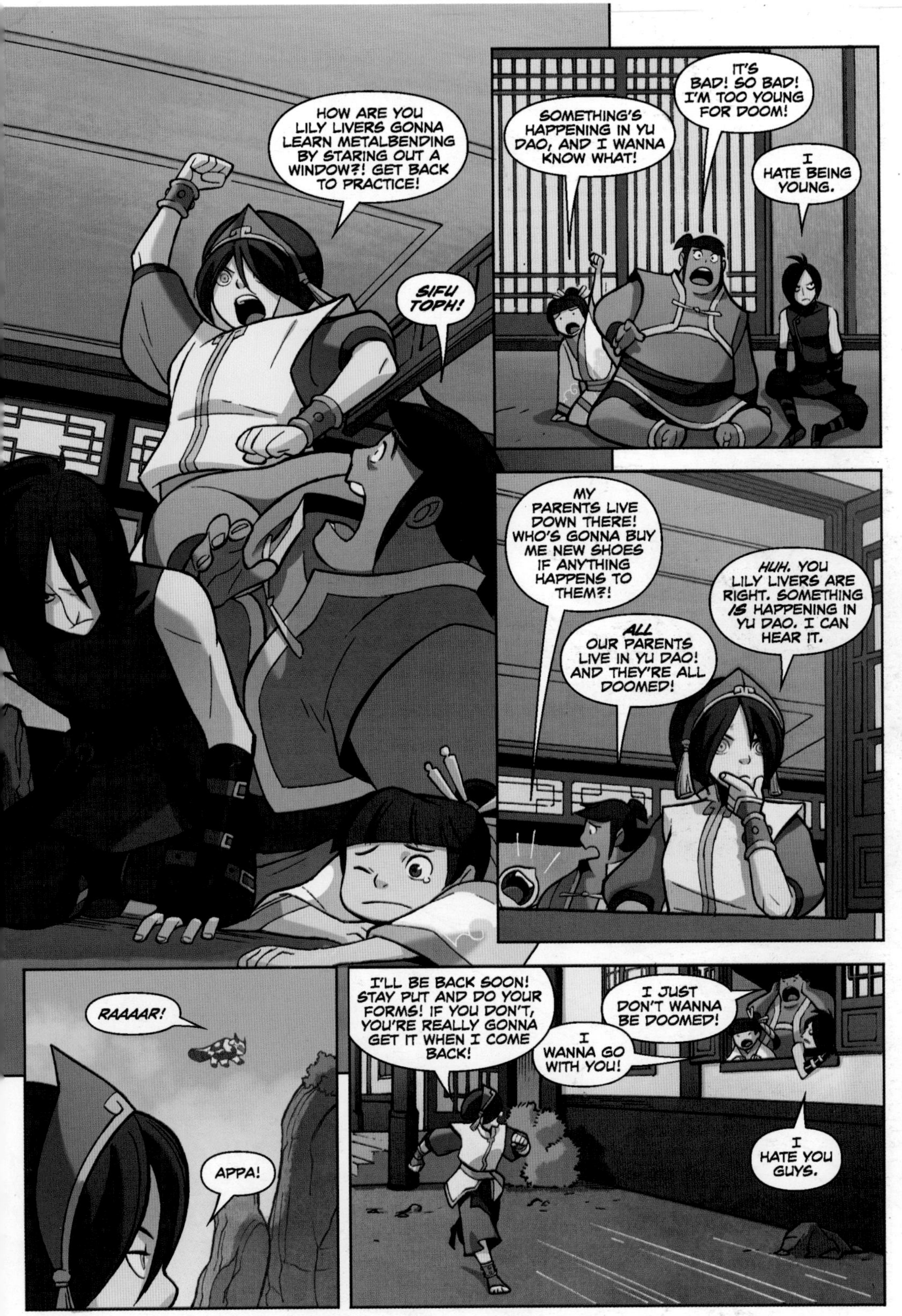
HOW ARE YOU LILY LIVERS GONNA LEARN METALBENDING BY STARING OUT A WINDOW?! GET BACK TO PRACTICE!
SIFU TOPH!
SOMETHING'S HAPPENING IN YU DAO, AND I WANNA KNOW WHAT!
IT'S BAD! SO BAD! I'M TOO YOUNG FOR DOOM!
I HATE BEING YOUNG.
MY PARENTS LIVE DOWN THERE! WHO'S GONNA BUY ME NEW SHOES IF ANYTHING HAPPENS TO THEM?!
ALL OUR PARENTS LIVE IN YU DAO! AND THEY'RE ALL DOOMED!
HUH. YOU LILY LIVERS ARE RIGHT. SOMETHING IS HAPPENING IN YU DAO. I CAN HEAR IT.
RAAAAR!
APPA!
I'LL BE BACK SOON! STAY PUT AND DO YOUR FORMS! IF YOU DON'T, YOU'RE REALLY GONNA GET IT WHEN I COME BACK!
I JUST DON'T WANNA BE DOOMED!
I WANNA GO WITH YOU!
I HATE YOU GUYS.

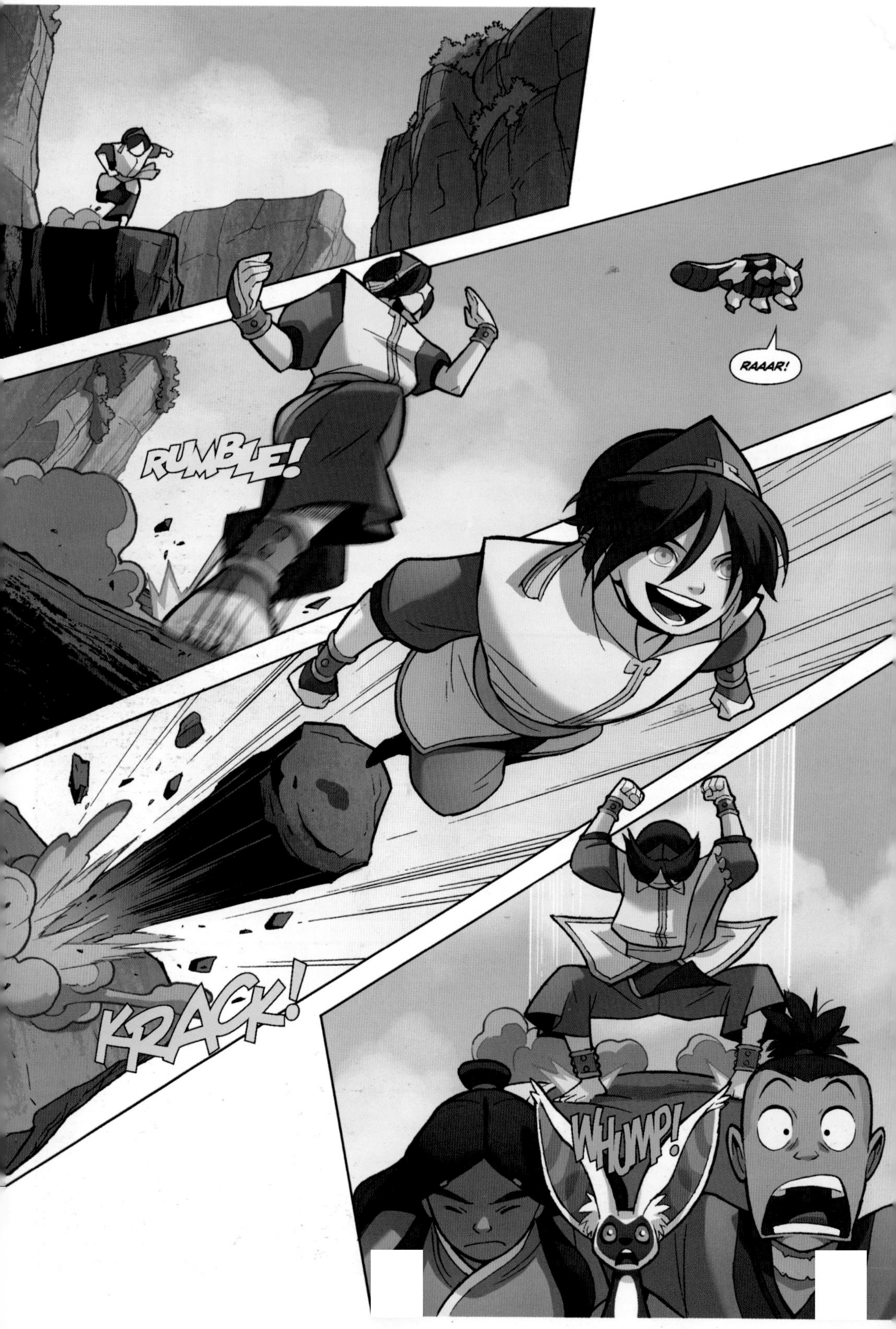
RAAAR!
RUMBLE!
KRACK!
WHUMP!

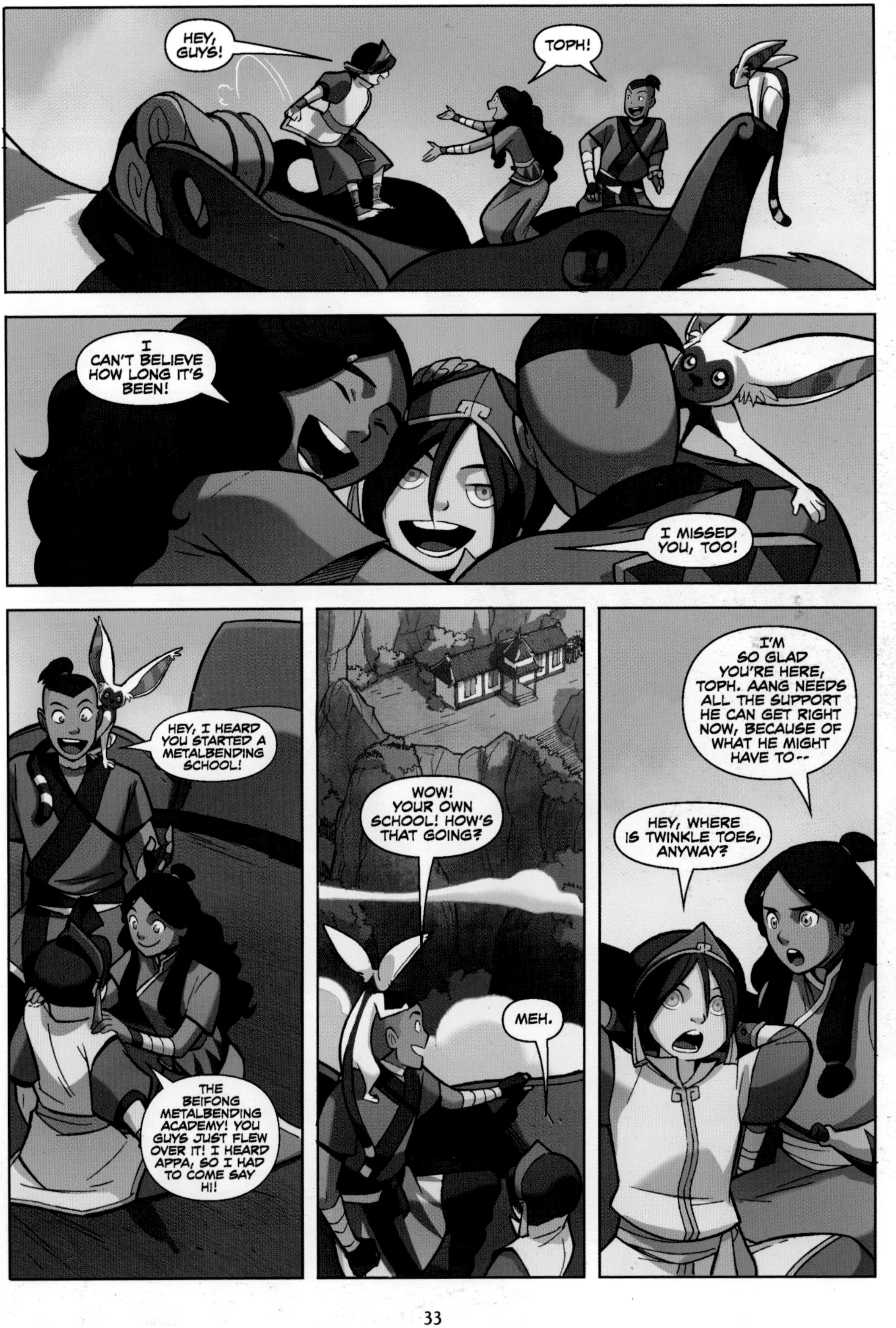
HEY, GUYS!
TOPH!
I CAN'T BELIEVE HOW LONG IT'S BEEN!
I MISSED YOU, TOO!
HEY, I HEARD YOU STARTED A METALBENDING SCHOOL!
THE BEIFONG METALBENDING ACADEMY! YOU GUYS JUST FLEW OVER IT! I HEARD APPA, SO I HAD TO COME SAY HI!
WOW! YOUR OWN SCHOOL! HOW'S THAT GOING?
MEH.
I'M SO GLAD YOU'RE HERE, TOPH. AANG NEEDS ALL THE SUPPORT HE CAN GET RIGHT NOW, BECAUSE OF WHAT HE MIGHT HAVE TO--
HEY, WHERE IS TWINKLE TOES, ANYWAY?

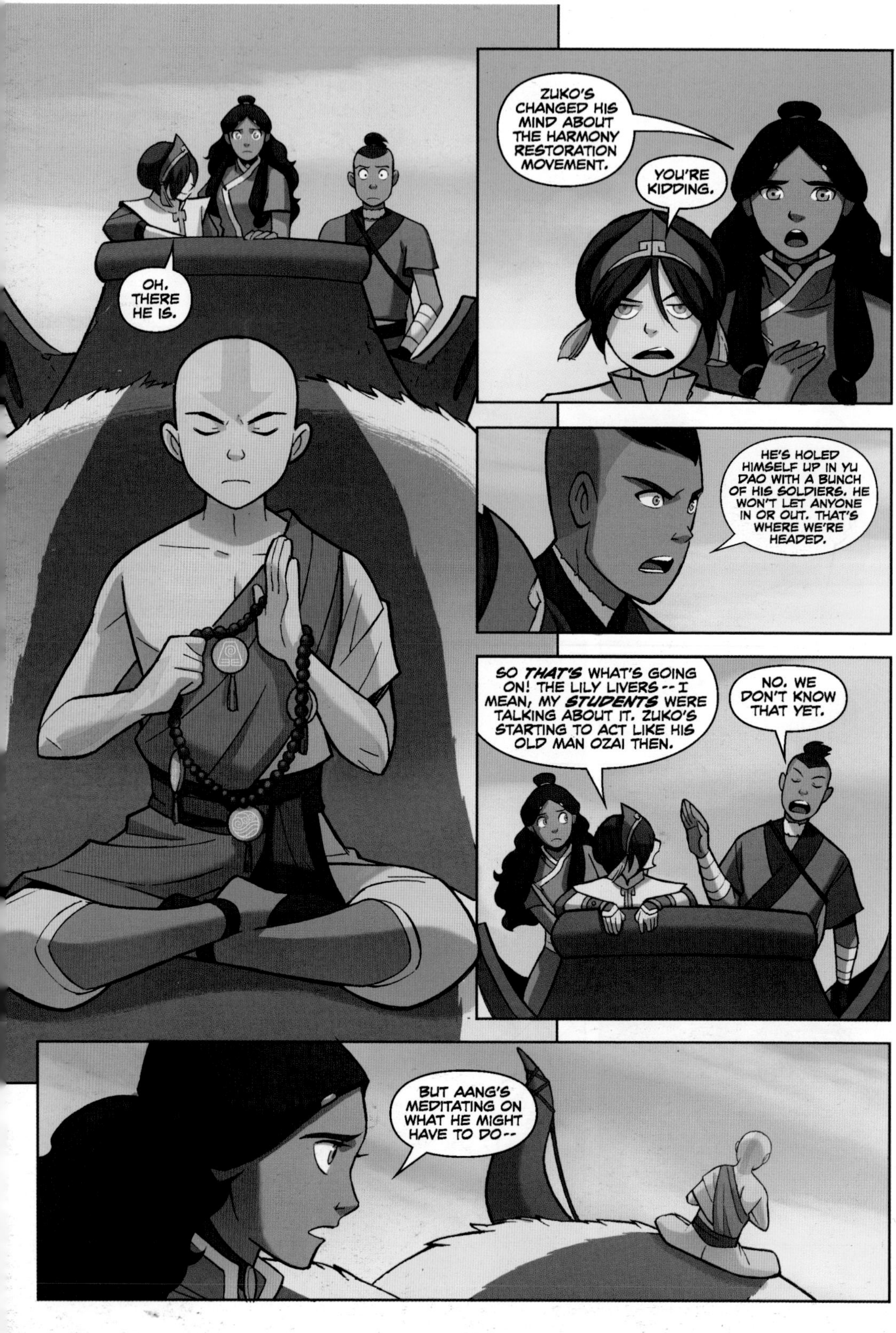
OH. THERE HE IS.
ZUKO'S CHANGED HIS MIND ABOUT THE HARMONY RESTORATION MOVEMENT.
YOU'RE KIDDING.
HE'S HOLED HIMSELF UP IN YU DAO WITH A BUNCH OF HIS SOLDIERS. HE WON'T LET ANYONE IN OR OUT. THAT'S WHERE WE'RE HEADED.
SO *THAT'S* WHAT'S GOING ON! THE LILY LIVERS -- I MEAN, MY *STUDENTS* WERE TALKING ABOUT IT. ZUKO'S STARTING TO ACT LIKE HIS OLD MAN OZAI THEN.
NO. WE DON'T KNOW THAT YET.
BUT AANG'S MEDITATING ON WHAT HE MIGHT HAVE TO DO--

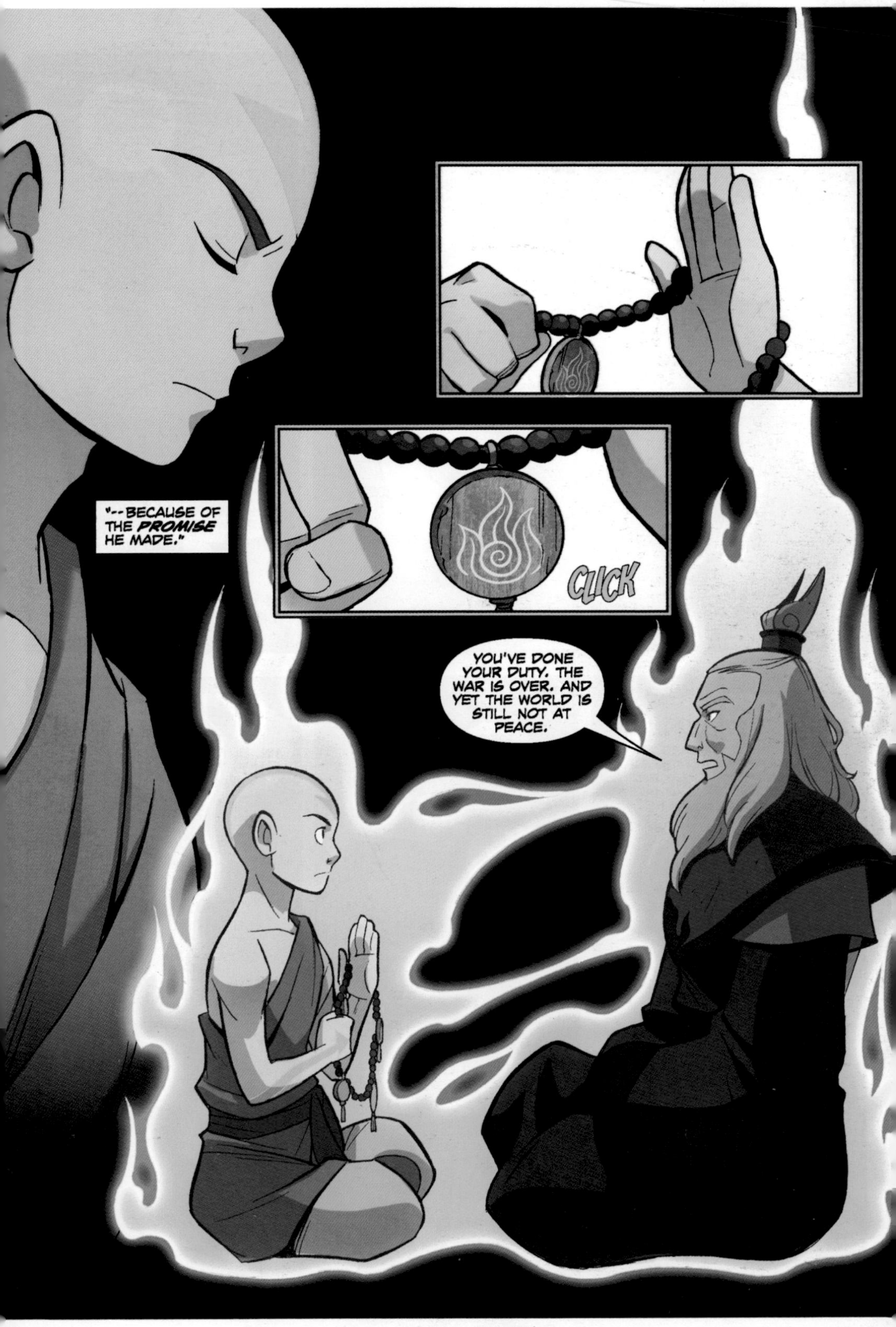
"--BECAUSE OF THE PROMISE HE MADE."
CLICK
YOU'VE DONE YOUR DUTY. THE WAR IS OVER. AND YET THE WORLD IS STILL NOT AT PEACE.

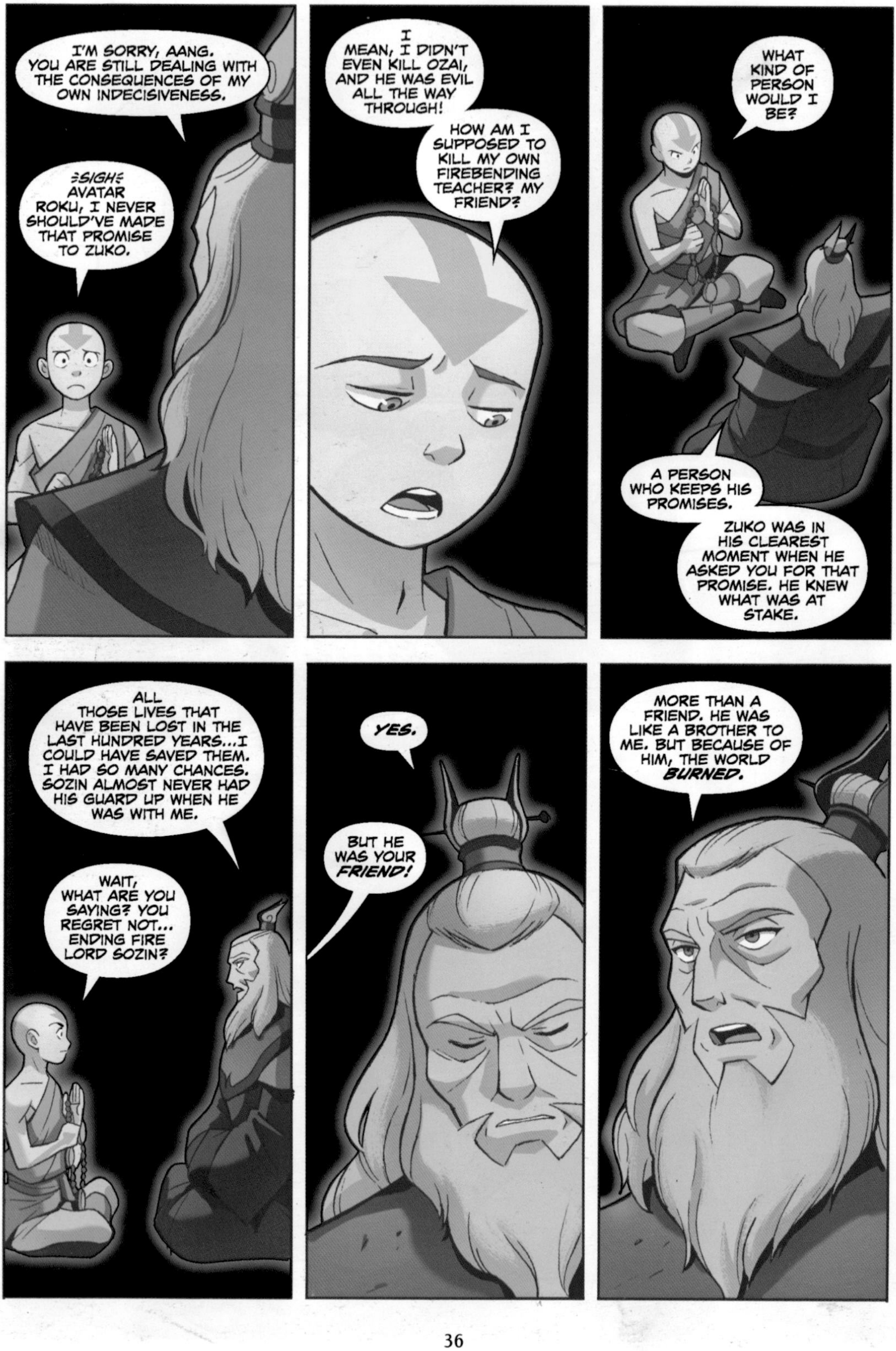
I'M SORRY, AANG. YOU ARE STILL DEALING WITH THE CONSEQUENCES OF MY OWN INDECISIVENESS.
SIGH AVATAR ROKU, I NEVER SHOULD'VE MADE THAT PROMISE TO ZUKO.
I MEAN, I DIDN'T EVEN KILL OZAI, AND HE WAS EVIL ALL THE WAY THROUGH!
HOW AM I SUPPOSED TO KILL MY OWN FIREBENDING TEACHER? MY FRIEND?
WHAT KIND OF PERSON WOULD I BE?
A PERSON WHO KEEPS HIS PROMISES.
ZUKO WAS IN HIS CLEAREST MOMENT WHEN HE ASKED YOU FOR THAT PROMISE. HE KNEW WHAT WAS AT STAKE.
ALL THOSE LIVES THAT HAVE BEEN LOST IN THE LAST HUNDRED YEARS...I COULD HAVE SAVED THEM. I HAD SO MANY CHANCES. SOZIN ALMOST NEVER HAD HIS GUARD UP WHEN HE WAS WITH ME.
WAIT, WHAT ARE YOU SAYING? YOU REGRET NOT... ENDING FIRE LORD SOZIN?
YES.
BUT HE WAS YOUR FRIEND!
MORE THAN A FRIEND. HE WAS LIKE A BROTHER TO ME. BUT BECAUSE OF HIM, THE WORLD BURNED.

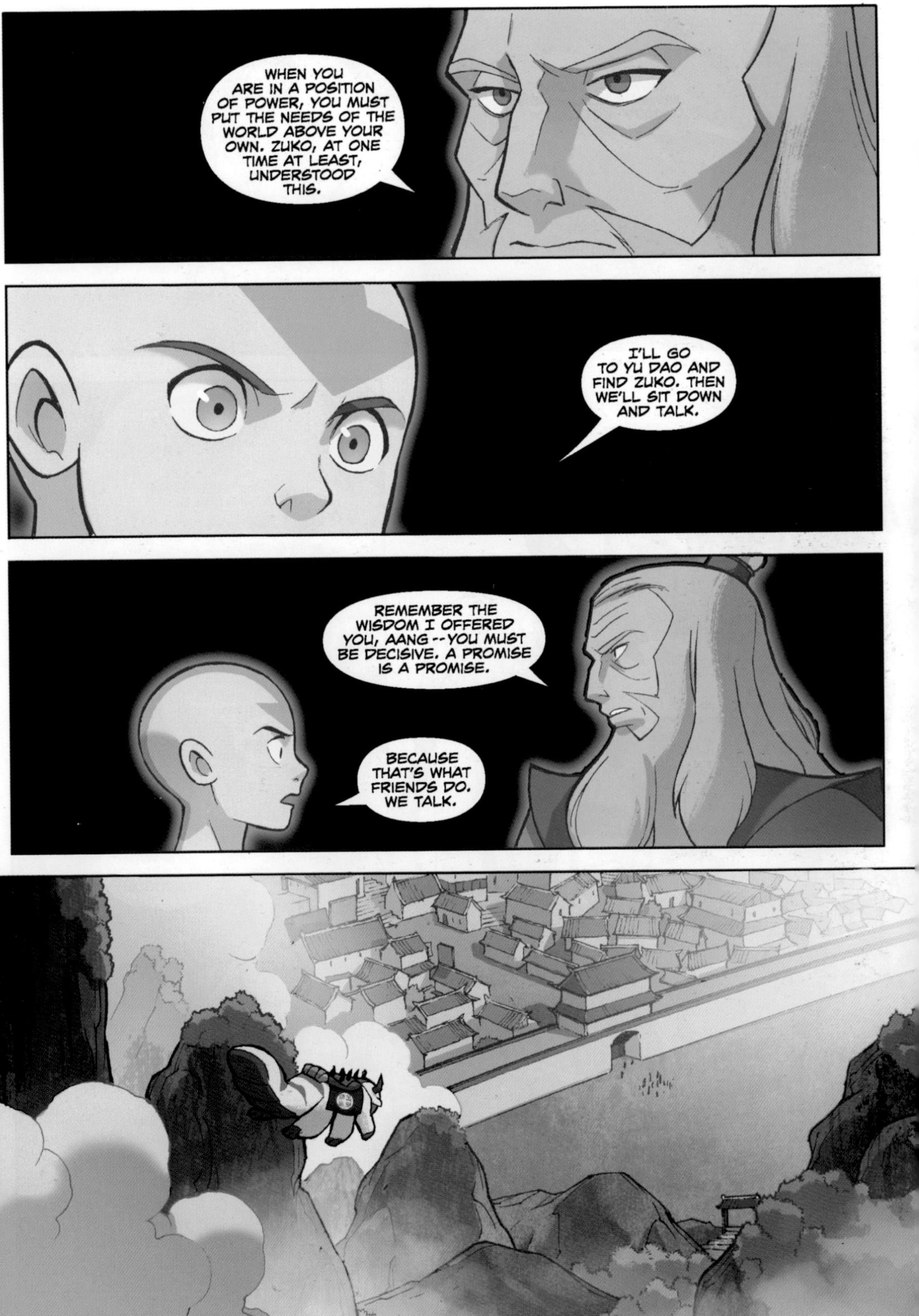
WHEN YOU ARE IN A POSITION OF POWER, YOU MUST PUT THE NEEDS OF THE WORLD ABOVE YOUR OWN. ZUKO, AT ONE TIME AT LEAST, UNDERSTOOD THIS.
I'LL GO TO YU DAO AND FIND ZUKO. THEN WE'LL SIT DOWN AND TALK.
REMEMBER THE WISDOM I OFFERED YOU, AANG--YOU MUST BE DECISIVE. A PROMISE IS A PROMISE.
BECAUSE THAT'S WHAT FRIENDS DO. WE TALK.

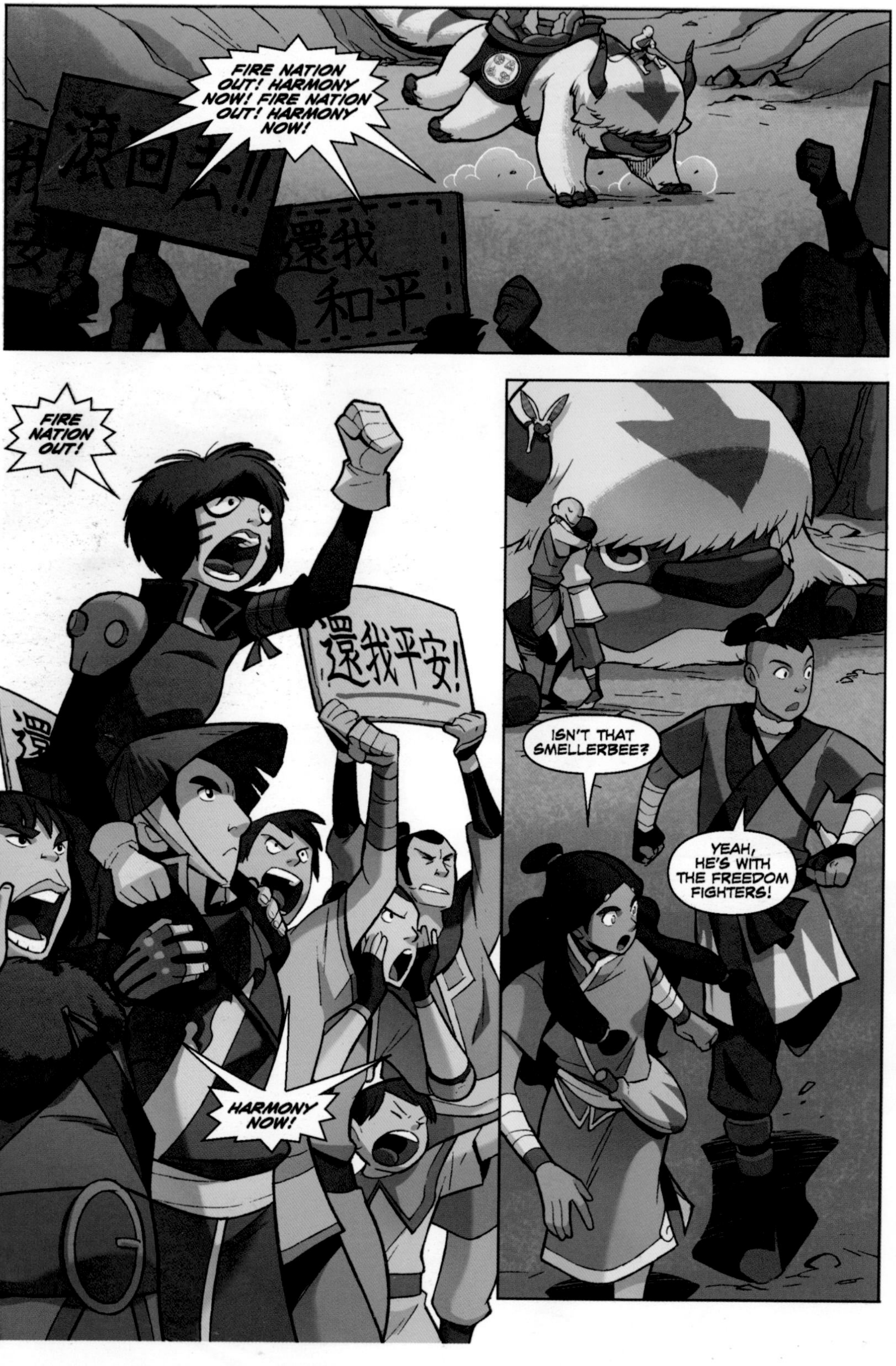
FIRE NATION OUT! HARMONY NOW! FIRE NATION OUT! HARMONY NOW!
滚回去!!
還我和平
FIRE NATION OUT!
還我平安!
HARMONY NOW!
ISN'T THAT SMELLERBEE?
YEAH, HE'S WITH THE FREEDOM FIGHTERS!

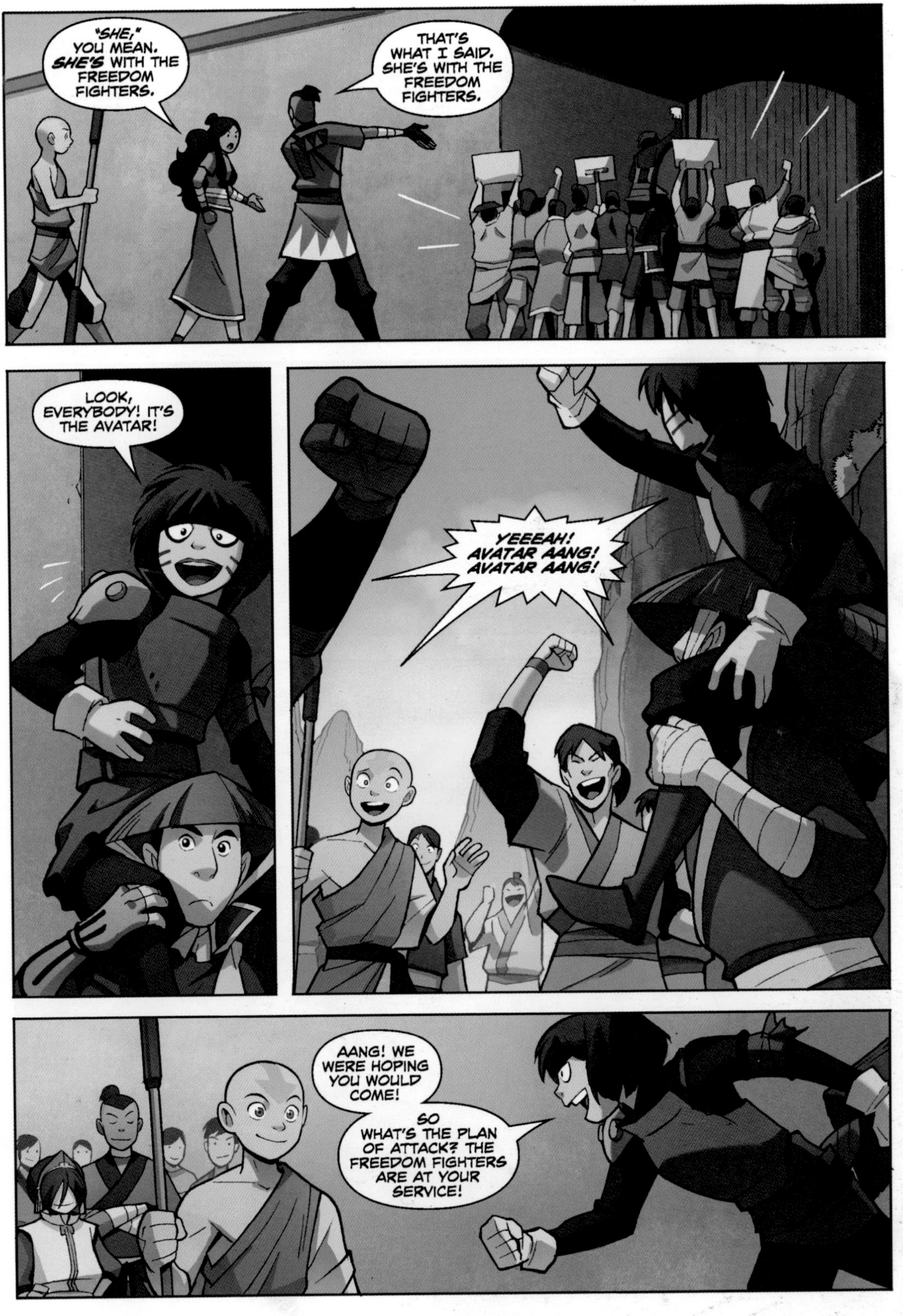
"SHE," YOU MEAN. SHE'S WITH THE FREEDOM FIGHTERS.
THAT'S WHAT I SAID. SHE'S WITH THE FREEDOM FIGHTERS.
LOOK, EVERYBODY! IT'S THE AVATAR!
YEEEAH! AVATAR AANG! AVATAR AANG!
AANG! WE WERE HOPING YOU WOULD COME!
SO WHAT'S THE PLAN OF ATTACK? THE FREEDOM FIGHTERS ARE AT YOUR SERVICE!

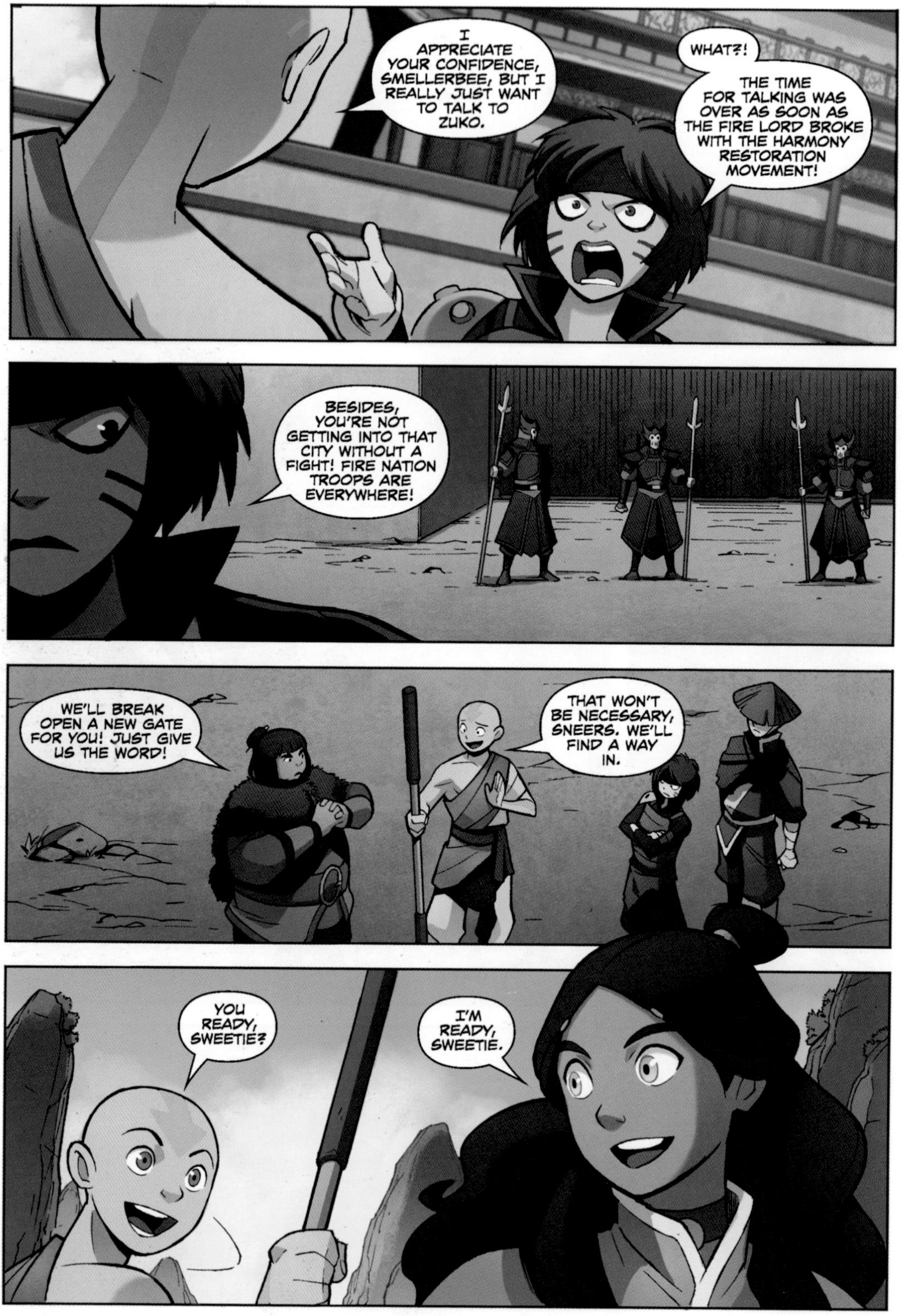
I APPRECIATE YOUR CONFIDENCE, SMELLERBEE, BUT I REALLY JUST WANT TO TALK TO ZUKO.
WHAT?!
THE TIME FOR TALKING WAS OVER AS SOON AS THE FIRE LORD BROKE WITH THE HARMONY RESTORATION MOVEMENT!
BESIDES, YOU'RE NOT GETTING INTO THAT CITY WITHOUT A FIGHT! FIRE NATION TROOPS ARE EVERYWHERE!
WE'LL BREAK OPEN A NEW GATE FOR YOU! JUST GIVE US THE WORD!
THAT WON'T BE NECESSARY, SNEERS. WE'LL FIND A WAY IN.
YOU READY, SWEETIE?
I'M READY, SWEETIE.

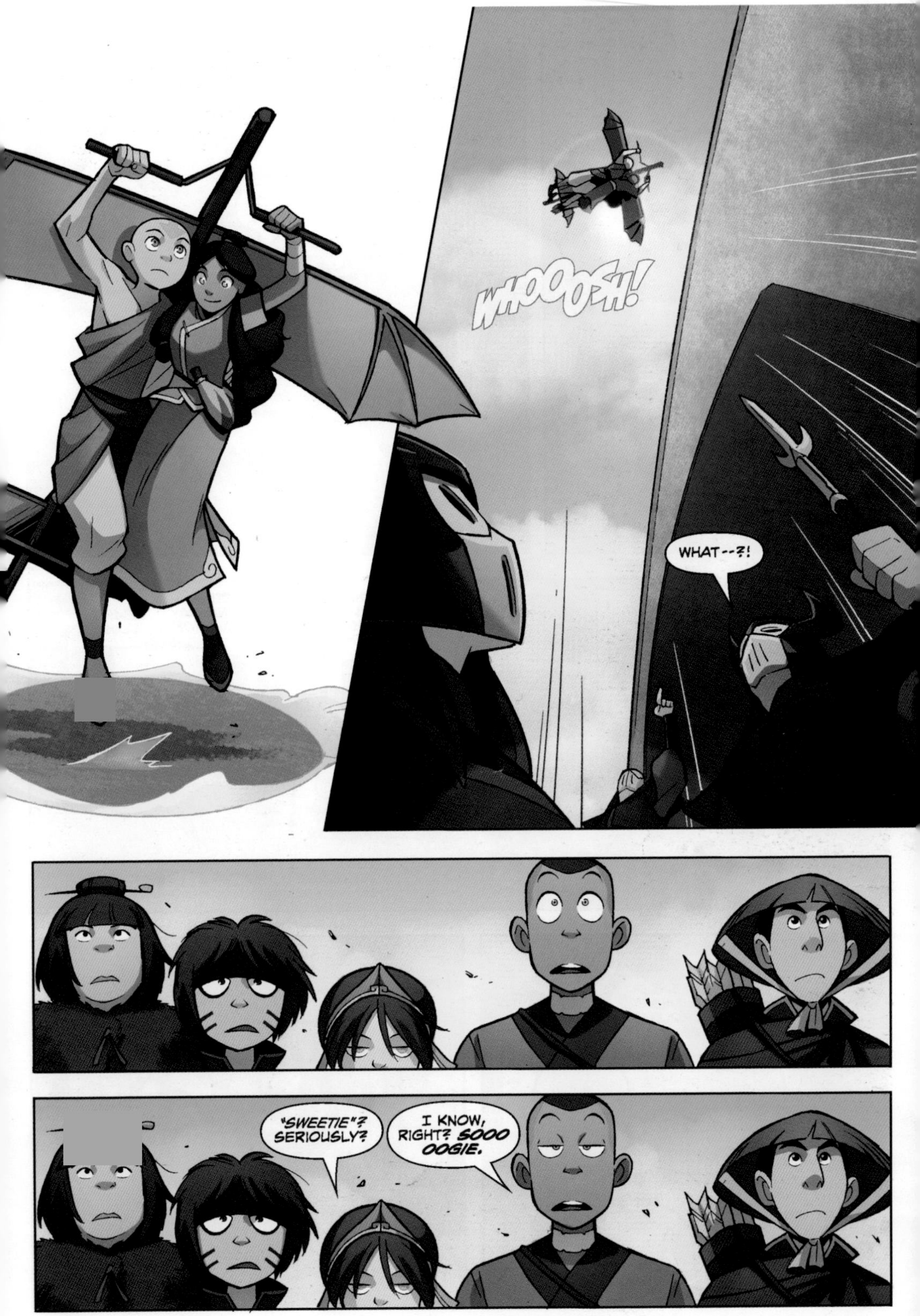
WHOOOSH!
WHAT--?!
"SWEETIE"? SERIOUSLY?
I KNOW, RIGHT? SOOO OOGIE.

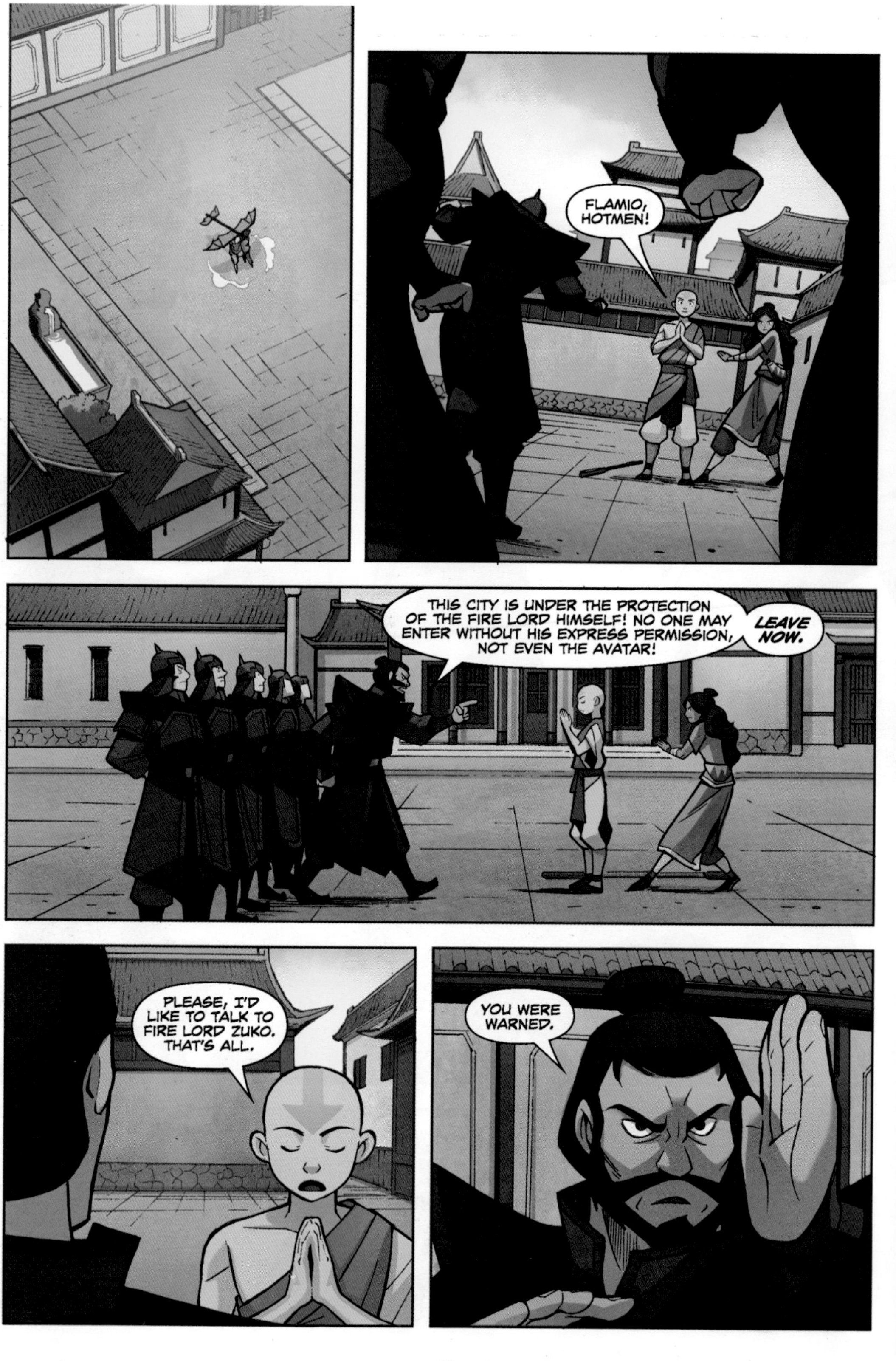
FLAMIO, HOTMEN!
THIS CITY IS UNDER THE PROTECTION OF THE FIRE LORD HIMSELF! NO ONE MAY ENTER WITHOUT HIS EXPRESS PERMISSION, NOT EVEN THE AVATAR!
LEAVE NOW.
PLEASE, I'D LIKE TO TALK TO FIRE LORD ZUKO. THAT'S ALL.
YOU WERE WARNED.

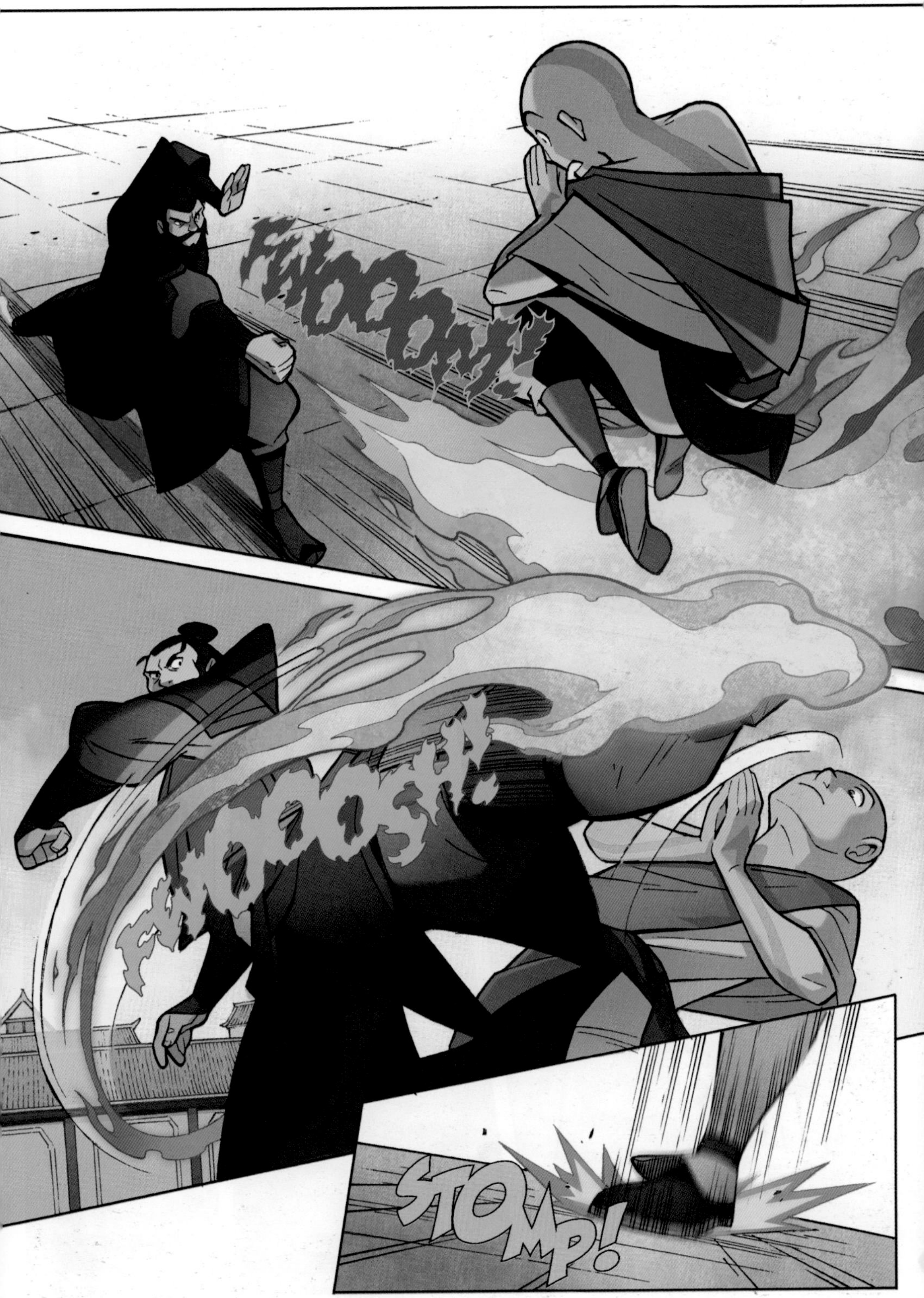
FWOOOM!
WHOOOSH!
STOMP!

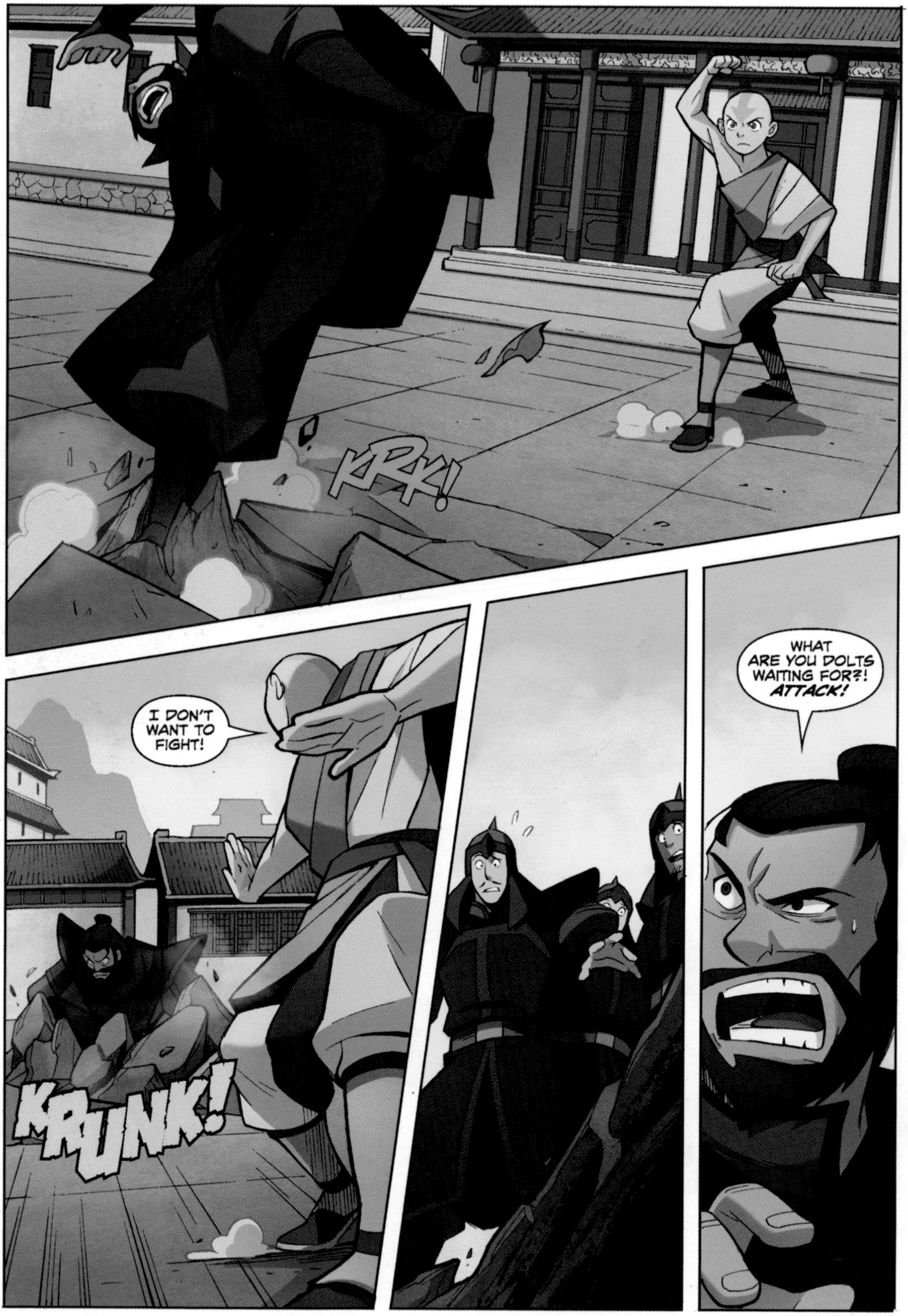
KRK!
I DON'T WANT TO FIGHT!
KRUNK!
WHAT ARE YOU DOLTS WAITING FOR?! ATTACK!

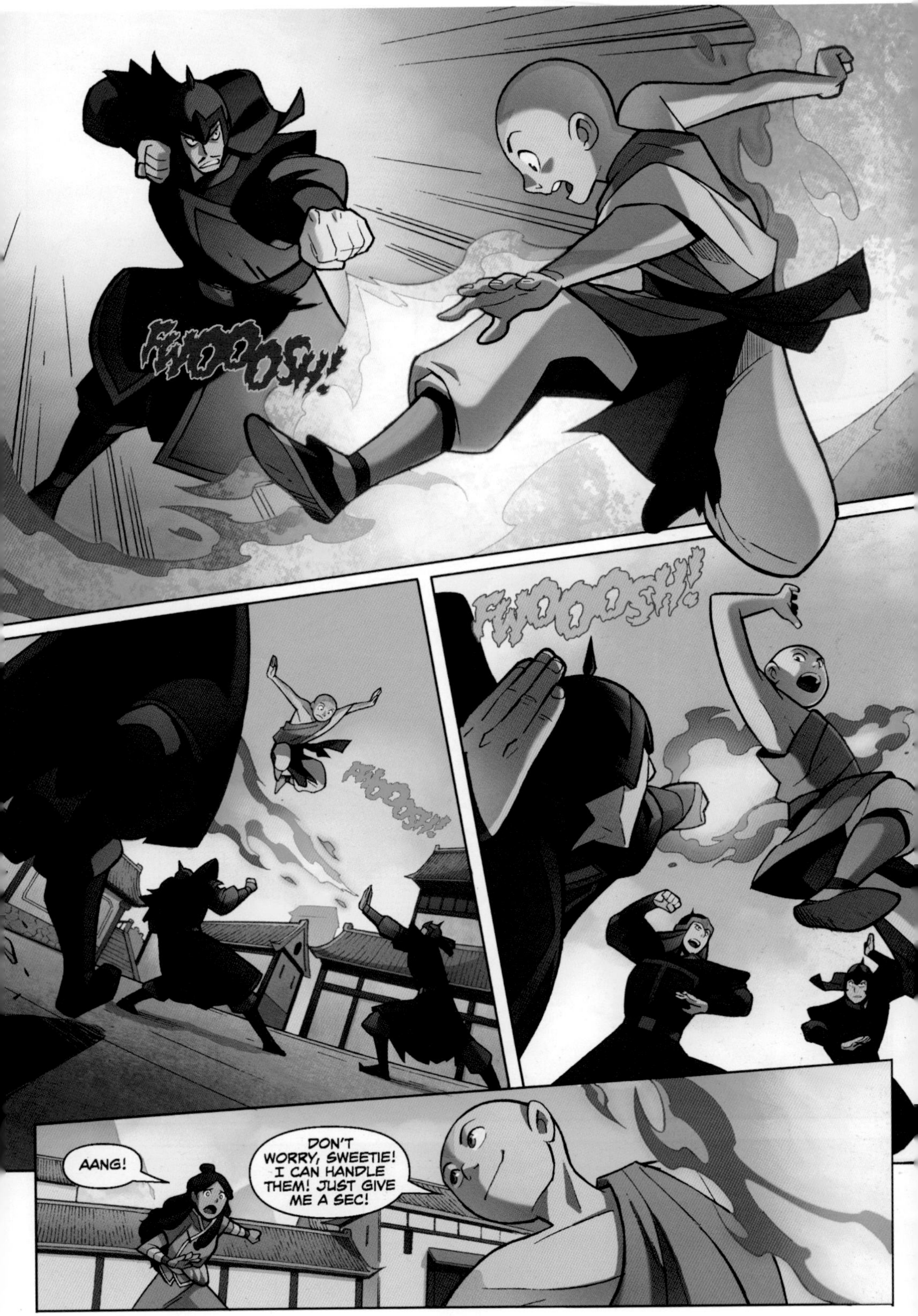
FWOOOSH!
FWOOOSH!
FWOOOSH!
AANG!
DON'T WORRY, SWEETIE! I CAN HANDLE THEM! JUST GIVE ME A SEC!

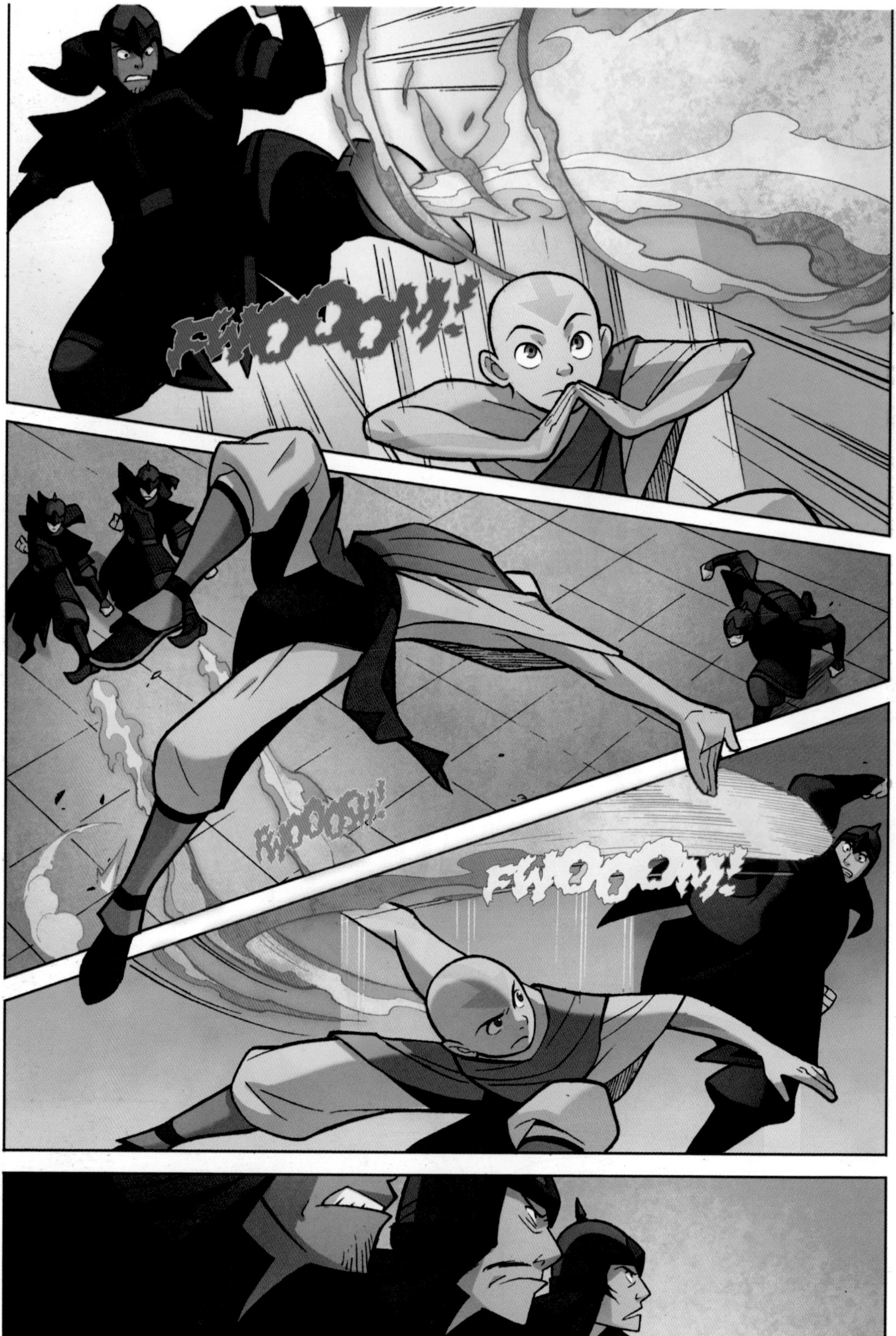
FWOOOM!
FWOOOSH!
FWOOOM!

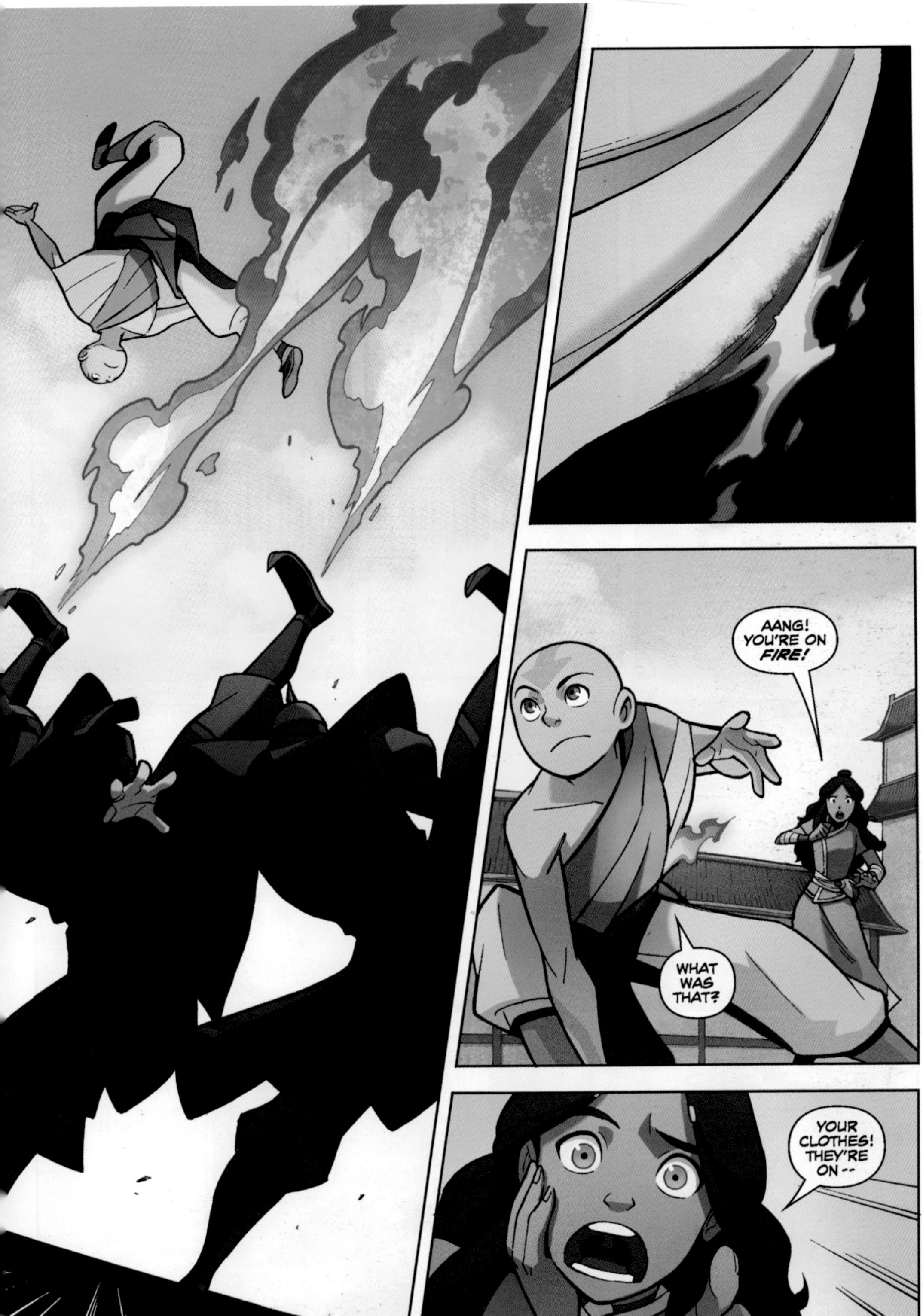
AANG! YOU'RE ON FIRE!
WHAT WAS THAT?
YOUR CLOTHES! THEY'RE ON --

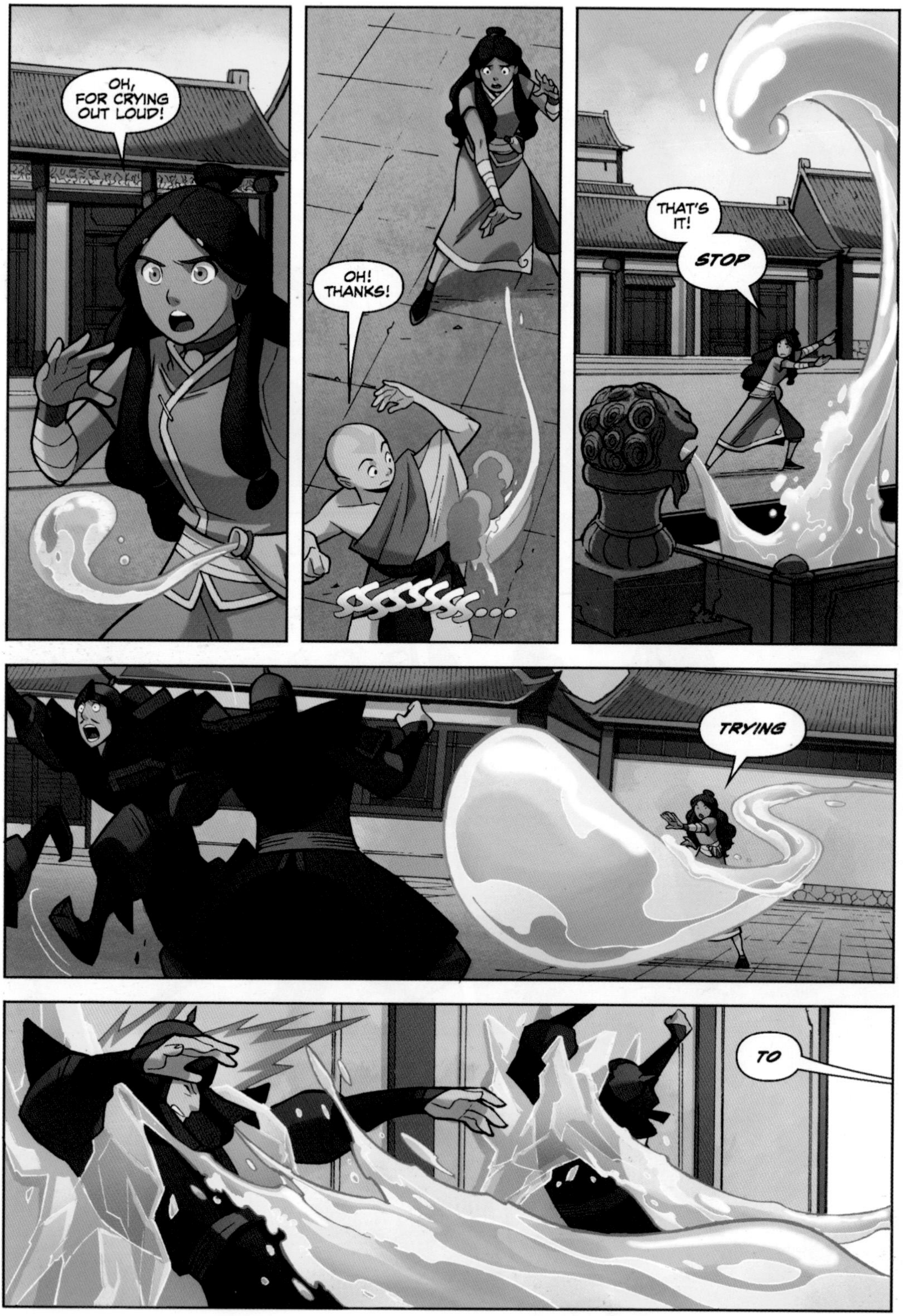
OH, FOR CRYING OUT LOUD!
OH! THANKS!
SSSSSSS...
THAT'S IT!
STOP
TRYING
TO

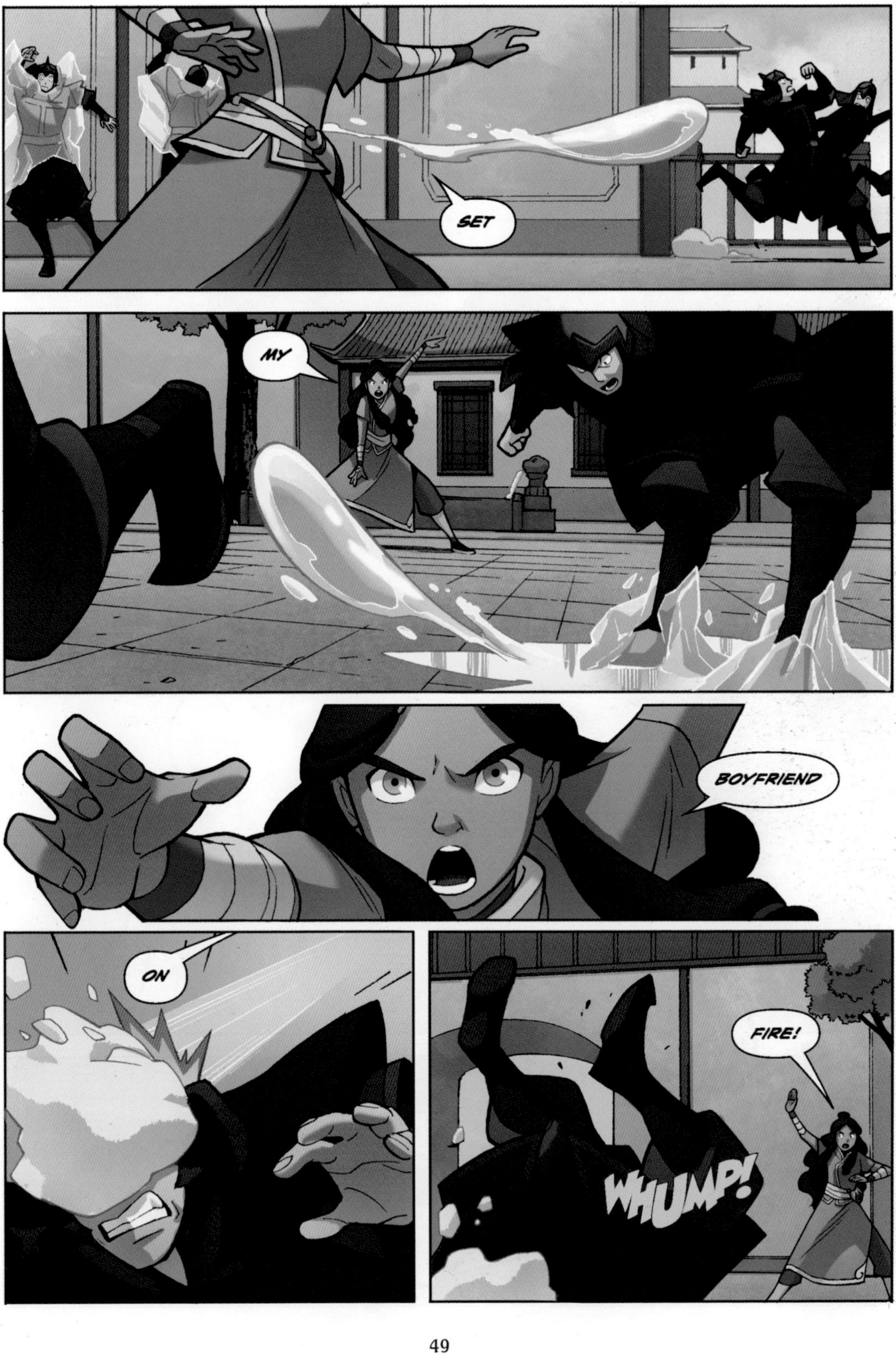
SET
MY
BOYFRIEND
ON
WHUMP!
FIRE!

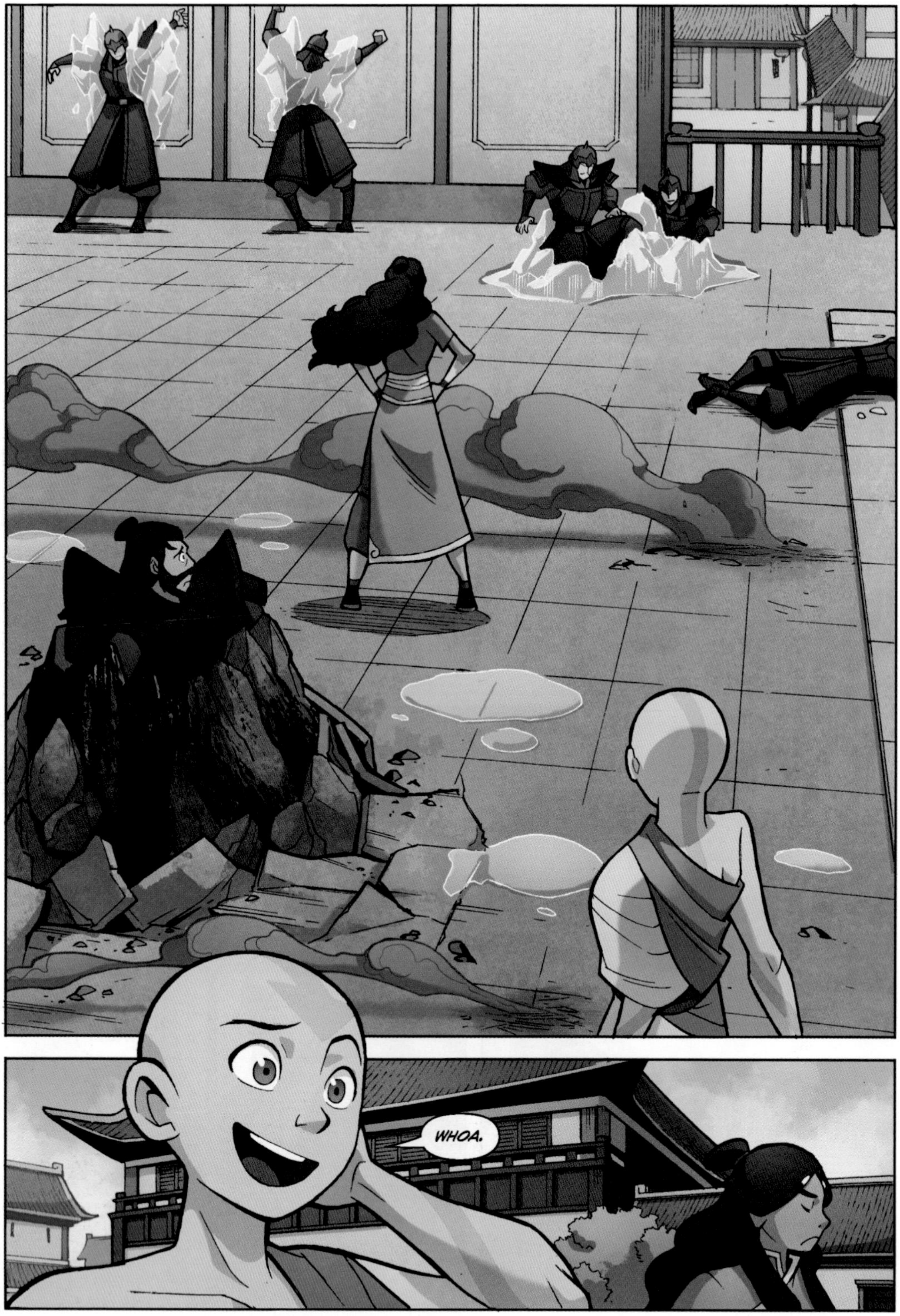
WHOA.

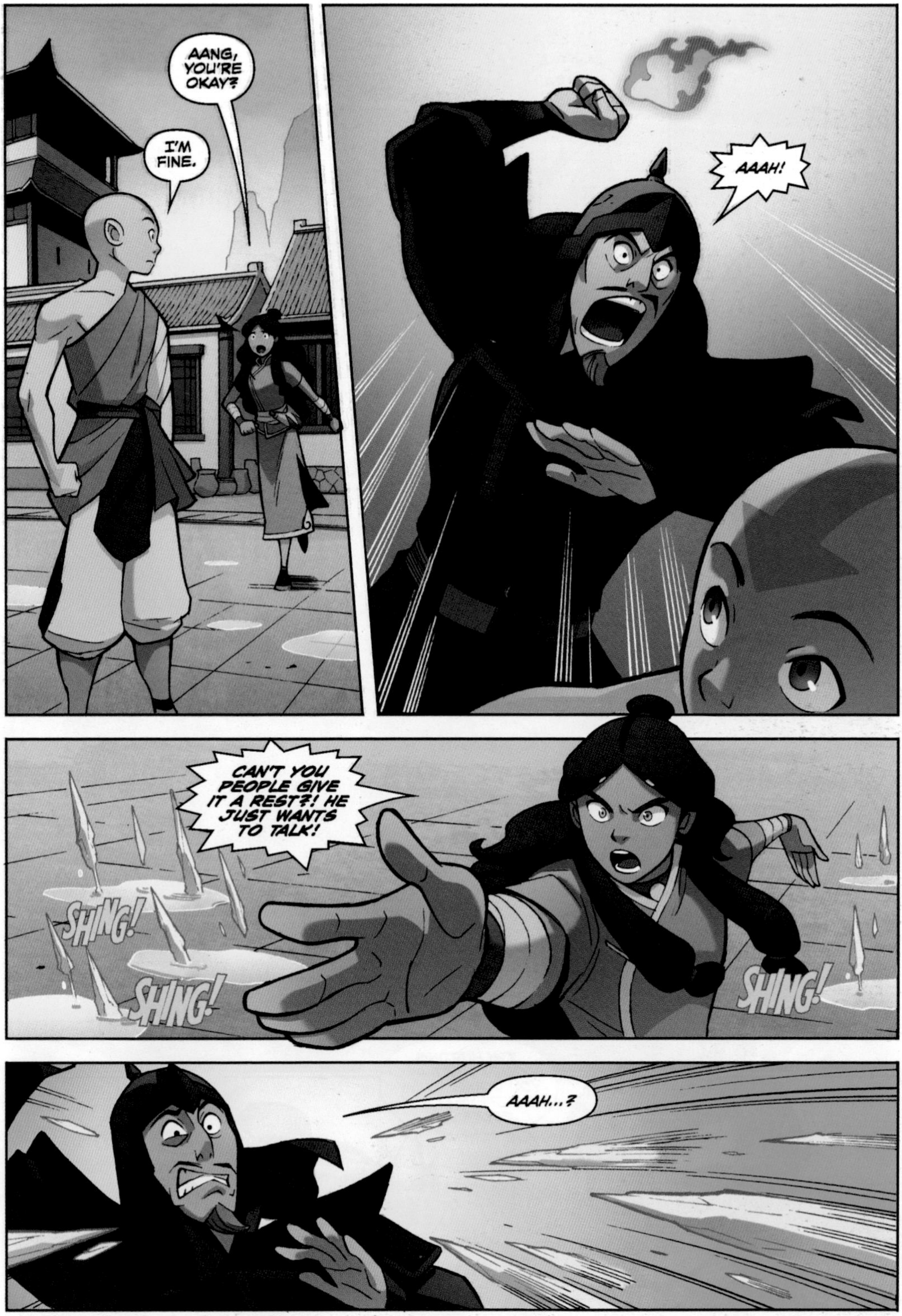
AANG, YOU'RE OKAY?
I'M FINE.
AAAH!
CAN'T YOU PEOPLE GIVE IT A REST?! HE JUST WANTS TO TALK!
SHING!
SHING!
SHING!
AAAH...?

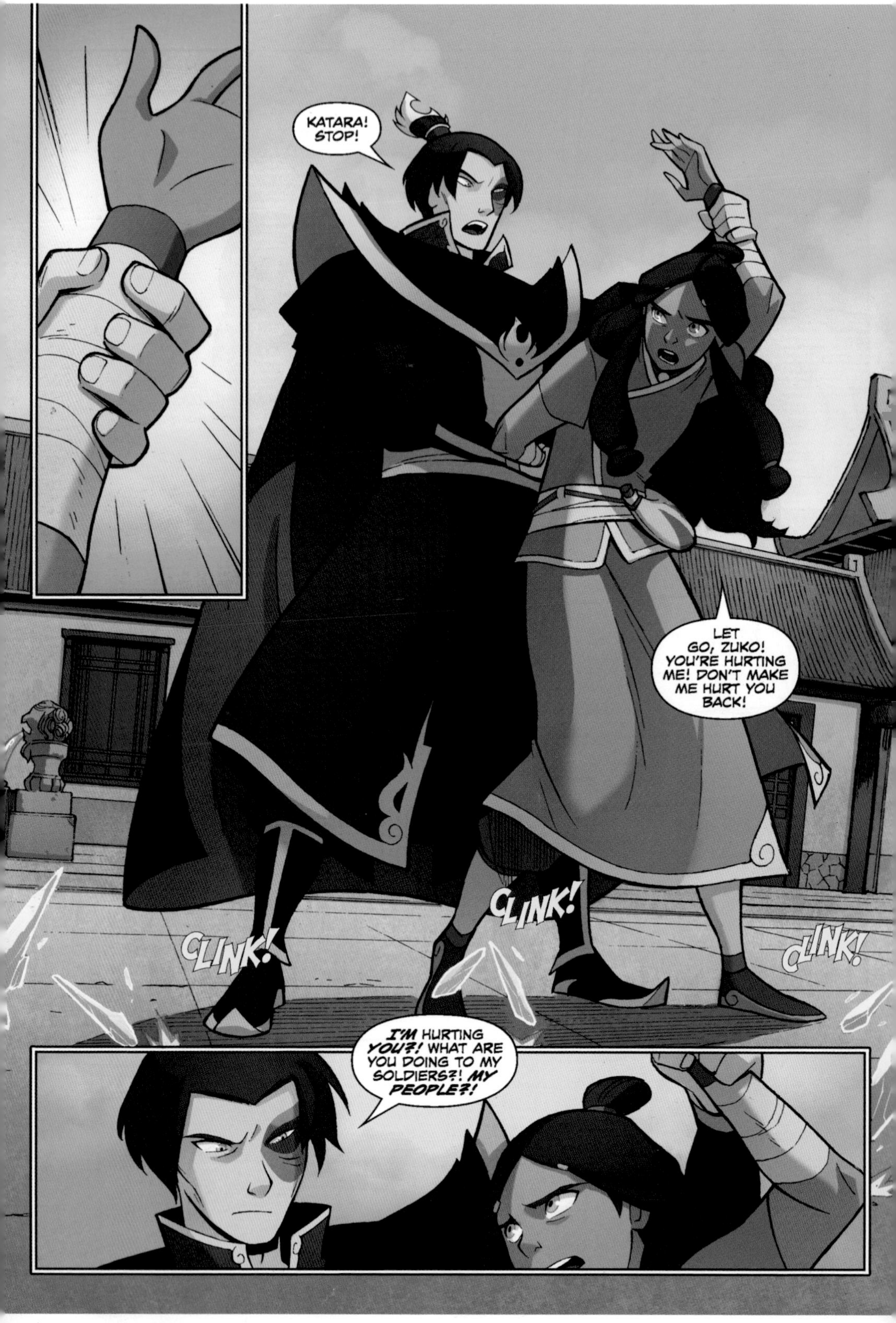
KATARA! STOP!
LET GO, ZUKO! YOU'RE HURTING ME! DON'T MAKE ME HURT YOU BACK!
CLINK!
CLINK!
CLINK!
I'M HURTING YOU?! WHAT ARE YOU DOING TO MY SOLDIERS?! MY PEOPLE?!

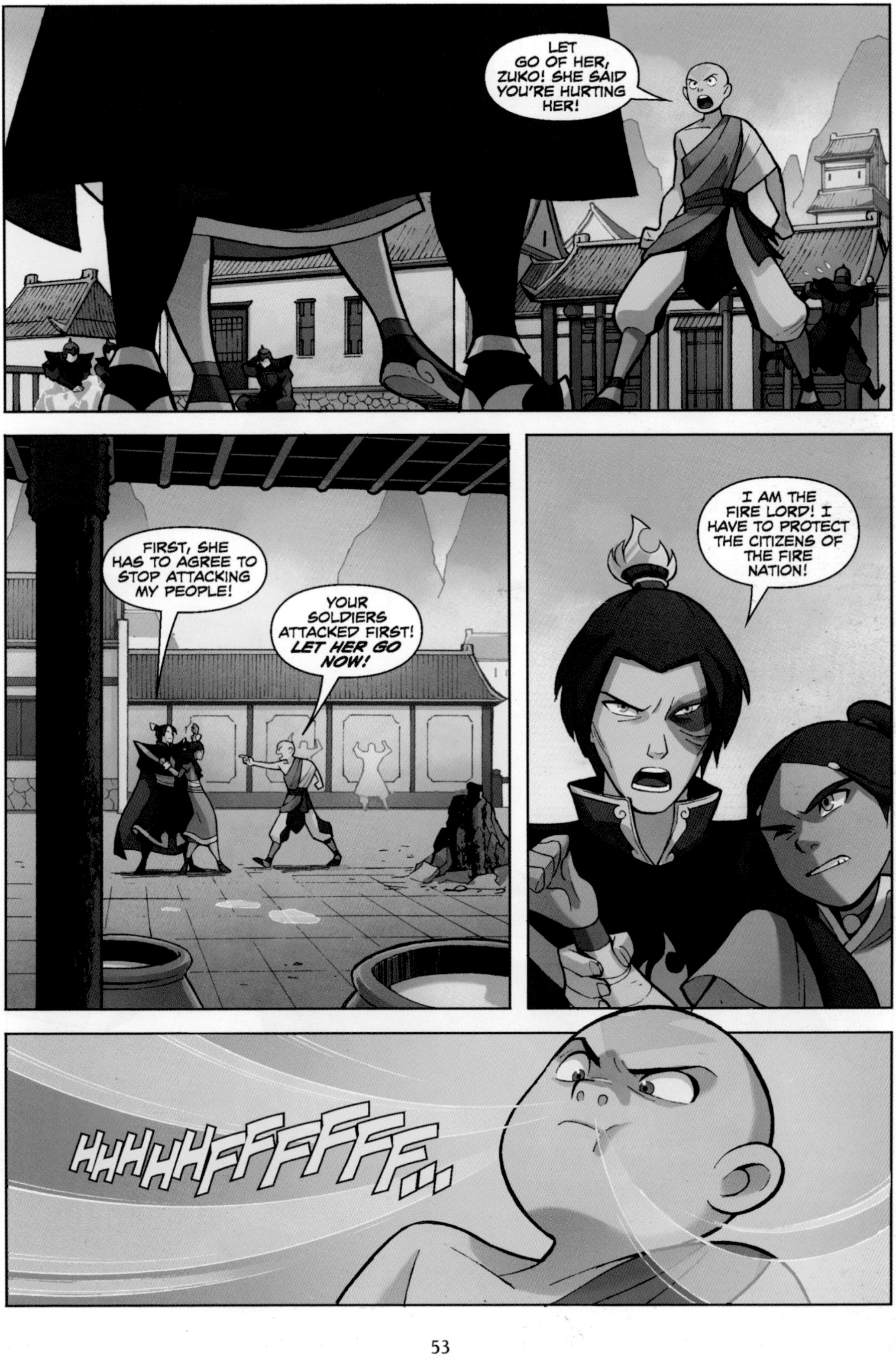
LET GO OF HER, ZUKO! SHE SAID YOU'RE HURTING HER!
FIRST, SHE HAS TO AGREE TO STOP ATTACKING MY PEOPLE!
YOUR SOLDIERS ATTACKED FIRST! ***LET HER GO NOW!***
I AM THE FIRE LORD! I HAVE TO PROTECT THE CITIZENS OF THE FIRE NATION!
HHHHHFFFFFFF...

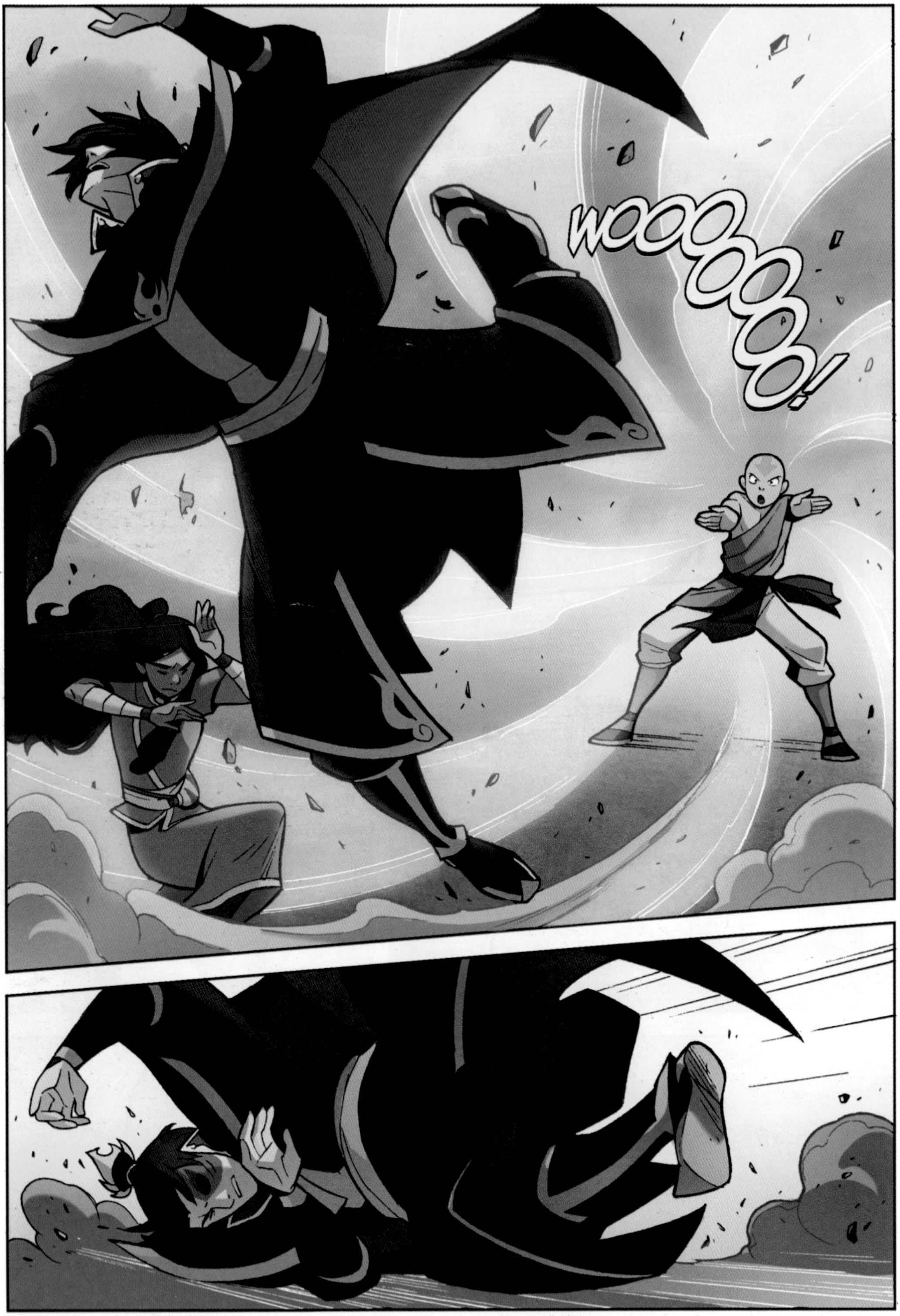
WOOOOOOOO!

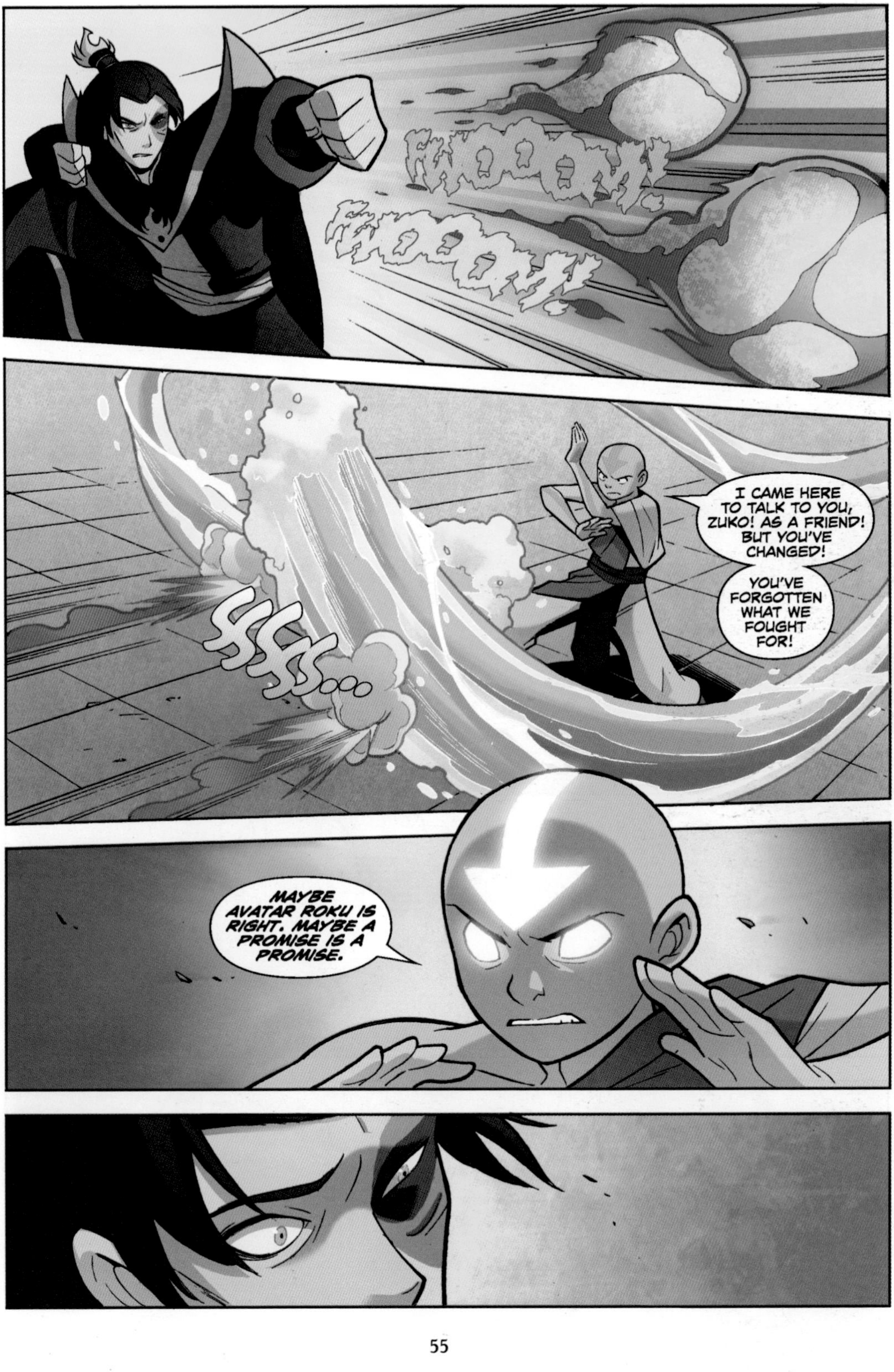
FWOOOM!
FWOOOM!
SSSS...
I CAME HERE TO TALK TO YOU, ZUKO! AS A FRIEND! BUT YOU'VE CHANGED!
YOU'VE FORGOTTEN WHAT WE FOUGHT FOR!
MAYBE AVATAR ROKU IS RIGHT. MAYBE A PROMISE IS A PROMISE.

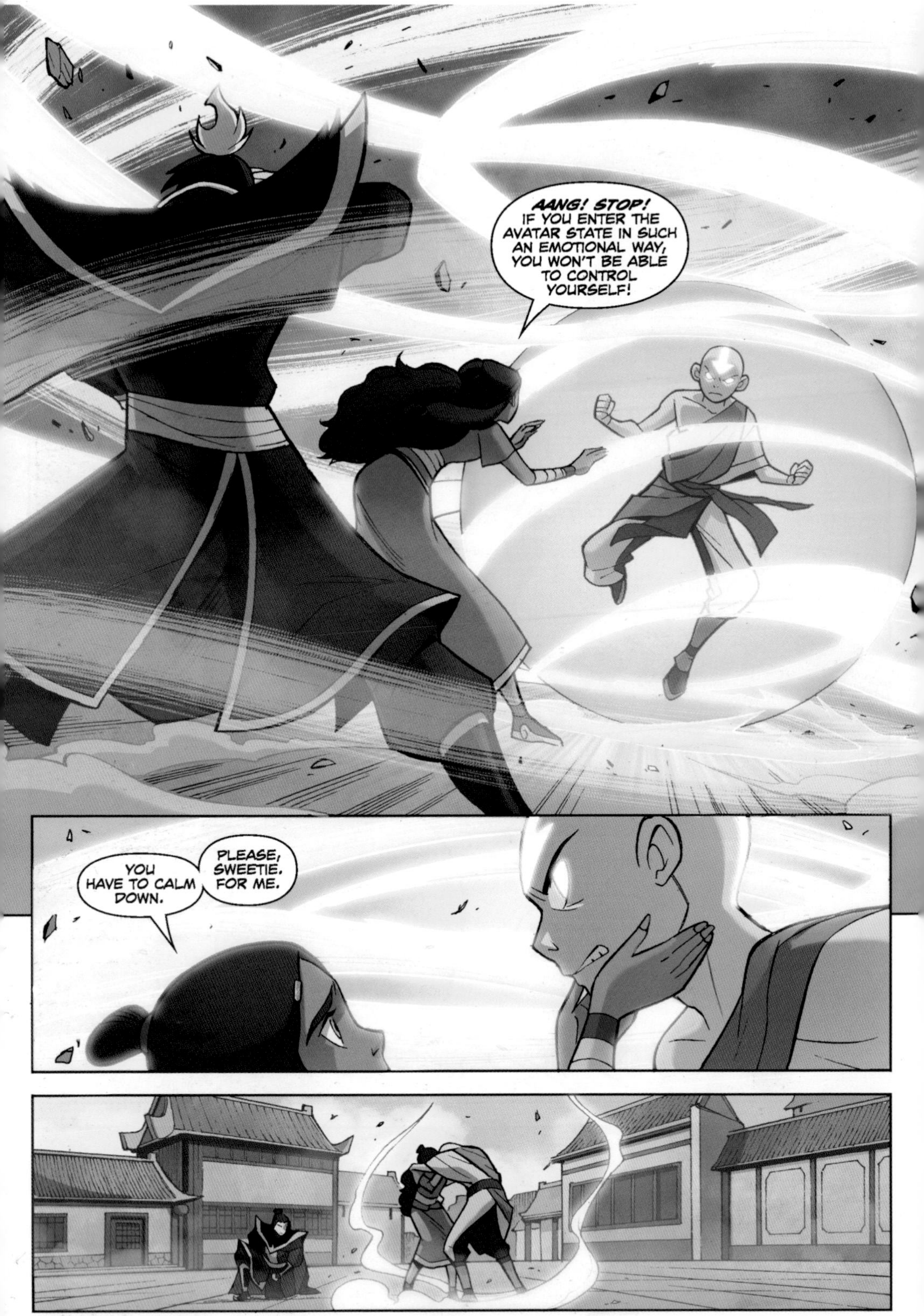
AANG! STOP! IF YOU ENTER THE AVATAR STATE IN SUCH AN EMOTIONAL WAY, YOU WON'T BE ABLE TO CONTROL YOURSELF!
YOU HAVE TO CALM DOWN.
PLEASE, SWEETIE. FOR ME.

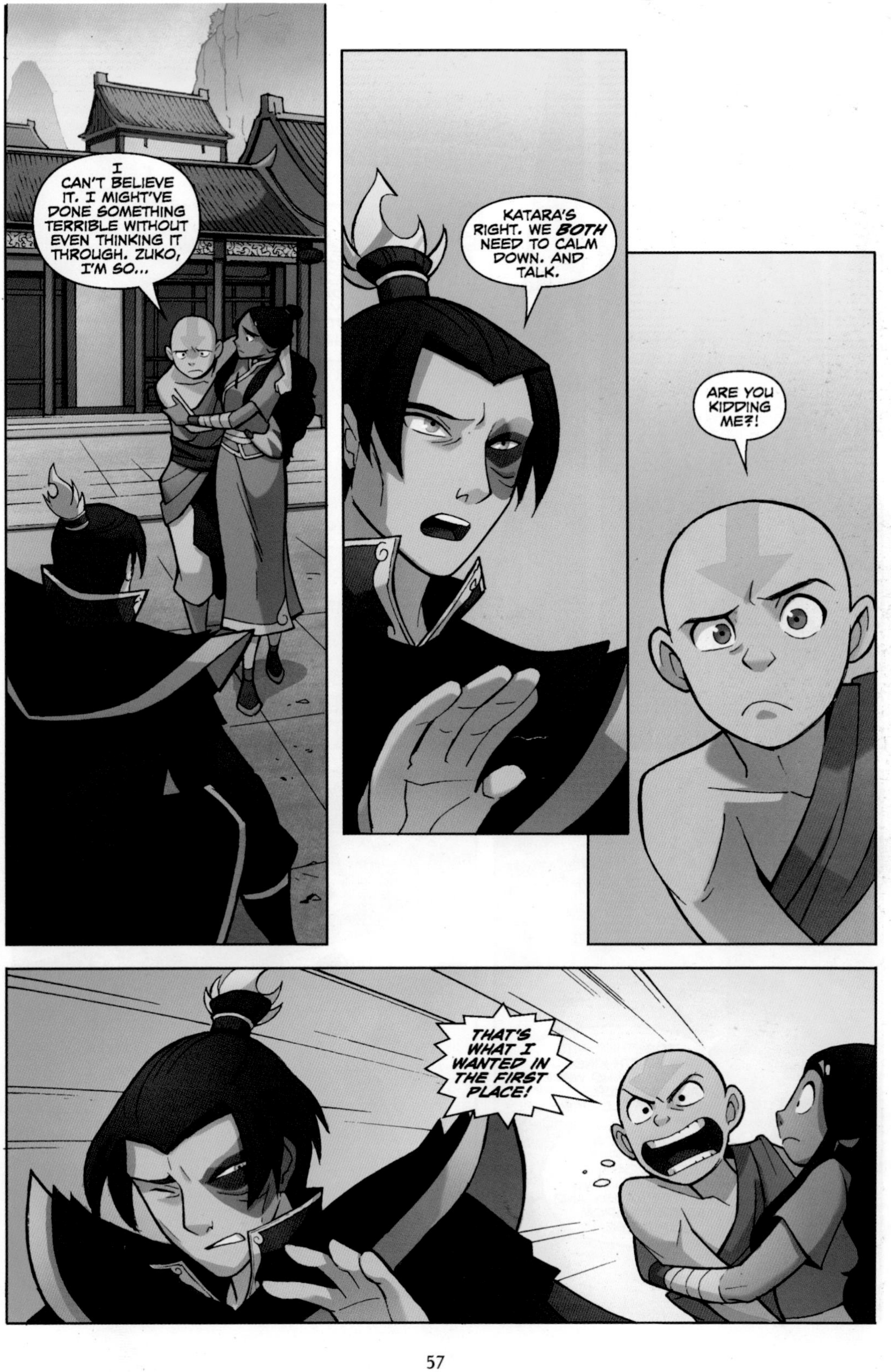
I CAN'T BELIEVE IT. I MIGHT'VE DONE SOMETHING TERRIBLE WITHOUT EVEN THINKING IT THROUGH. ZUKO, I'M SO...
KATARA'S RIGHT. WE *BOTH* NEED TO CALM DOWN. AND TALK.
ARE YOU KIDDING ME?!
THAT'S WHAT I WANTED IN THE FIRST PLACE!

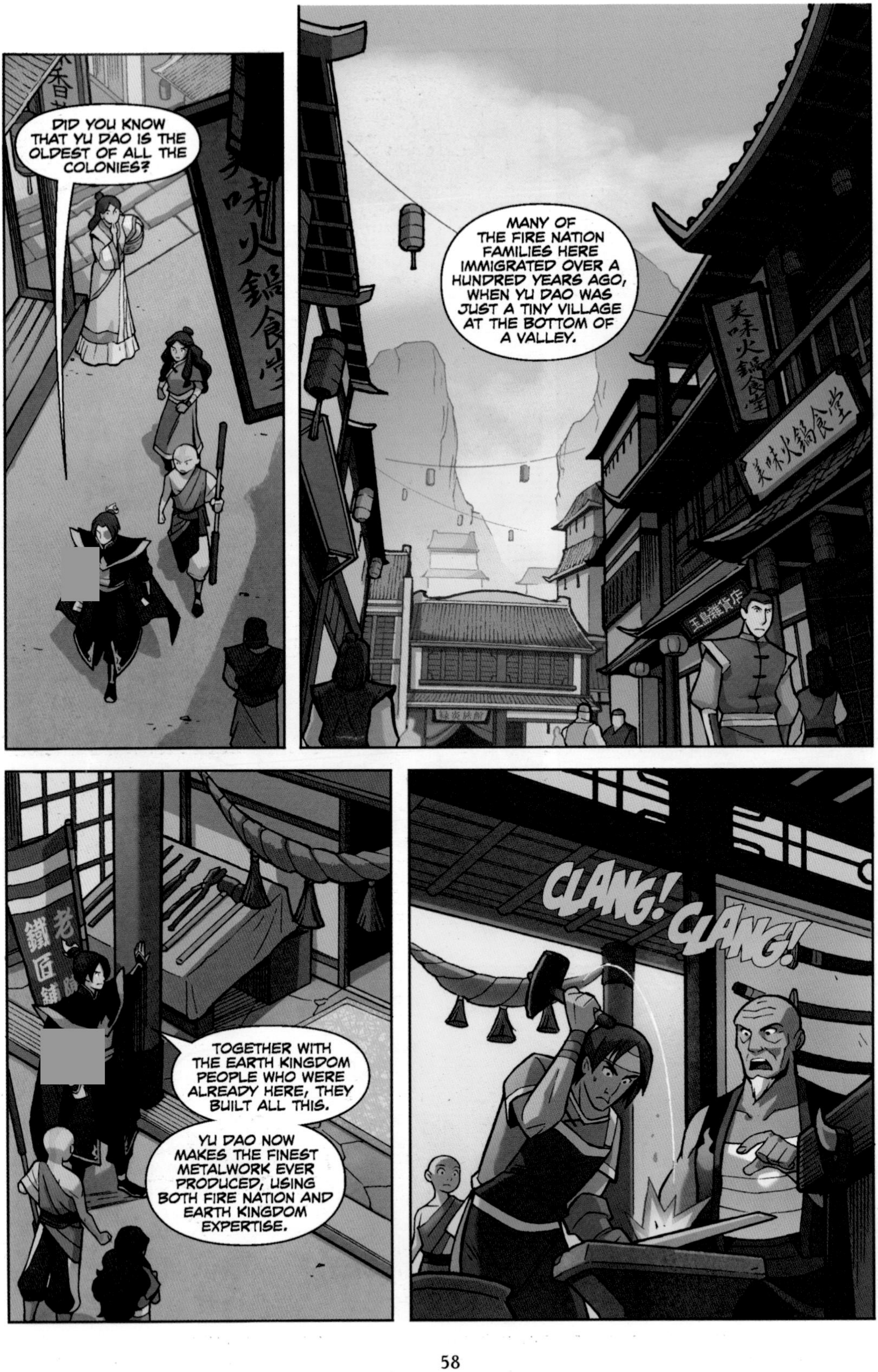
DID YOU KNOW THAT YU DAO IS THE OLDEST OF ALL THE COLONIES?
MANY OF THE FIRE NATION FAMILIES HERE IMMIGRATED OVER A HUNDRED YEARS AGO, WHEN YU DAO WAS JUST A TINY VILLAGE AT THE BOTTOM OF A VALLEY.
TOGETHER WITH THE EARTH KINGDOM PEOPLE WHO WERE ALREADY HERE, THEY BUILT ALL THIS.
YU DAO NOW MAKES THE FINEST METALWORK EVER PRODUCED, USING BOTH FIRE NATION AND EARTH KINGDOM EXPERTISE.
CLANG! CLANG!

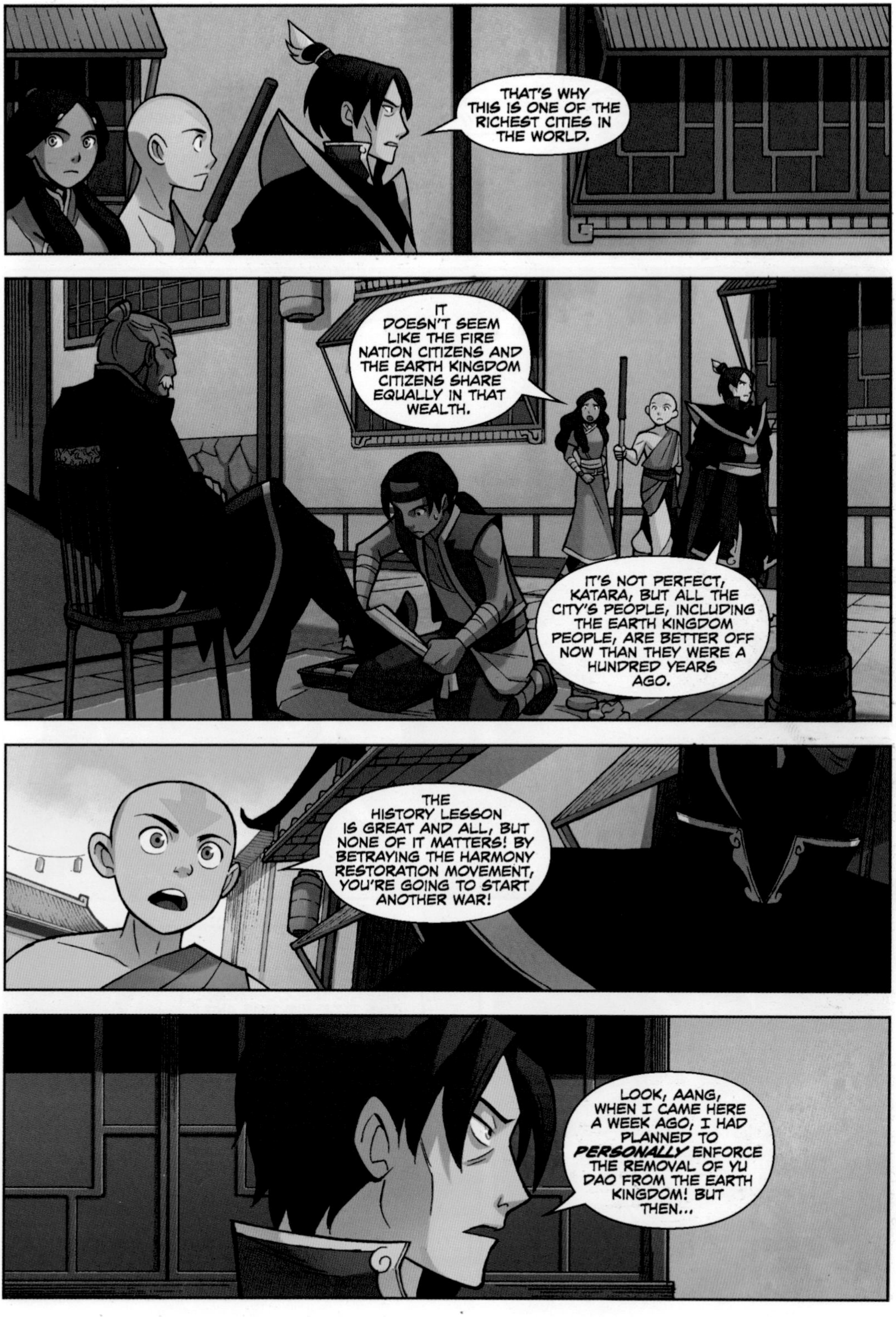
THAT'S WHY THIS IS ONE OF THE RICHEST CITIES IN THE WORLD.
IT DOESN'T SEEM LIKE THE FIRE NATION CITIZENS AND THE EARTH KINGDOM CITIZENS SHARE EQUALLY IN THAT WEALTH.
IT'S NOT PERFECT, KATARA, BUT ALL THE CITY'S PEOPLE, INCLUDING THE EARTH KINGDOM PEOPLE, ARE BETTER OFF NOW THAN THEY WERE A HUNDRED YEARS AGO.
THE HISTORY LESSON IS GREAT AND ALL, BUT NONE OF IT MATTERS! BY BETRAYING THE HARMONY RESTORATION MOVEMENT, YOU'RE GOING TO START ANOTHER WAR!
LOOK, AANG, WHEN I CAME HERE A WEEK AGO, I HAD PLANNED TO *PERSONALLY* ENFORCE THE REMOVAL OF YU DAO FROM THE EARTH KINGDOM! BUT THEN...

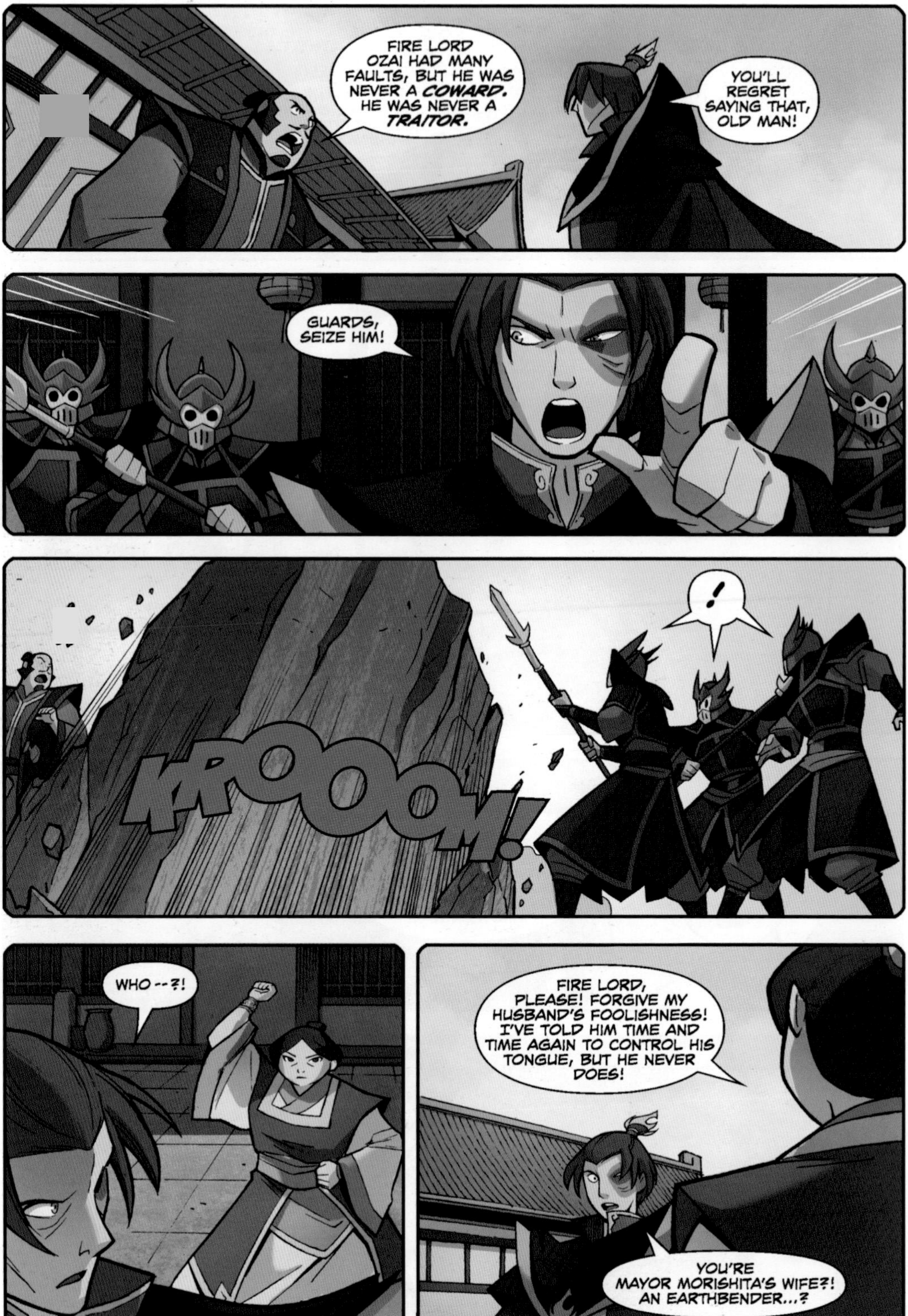
FIRE LORD OZAI HAD MANY FAULTS, BUT HE WAS NEVER A COWARD. HE WAS NEVER A TRAITOR.
YOU'LL REGRET SAYING THAT, OLD MAN!
GUARDS, SEIZE HIM!
!
KROOOOM!
WHO--?!
FIRE LORD, PLEASE! FORGIVE MY HUSBAND'S FOOLISHNESS! I'VE TOLD HIM TIME AND TIME AGAIN TO CONTROL HIS TONGUE, BUT HE NEVER DOES!
YOU'RE MAYOR MORISHITA'S WIFE?! AN EARTHBENDER...?

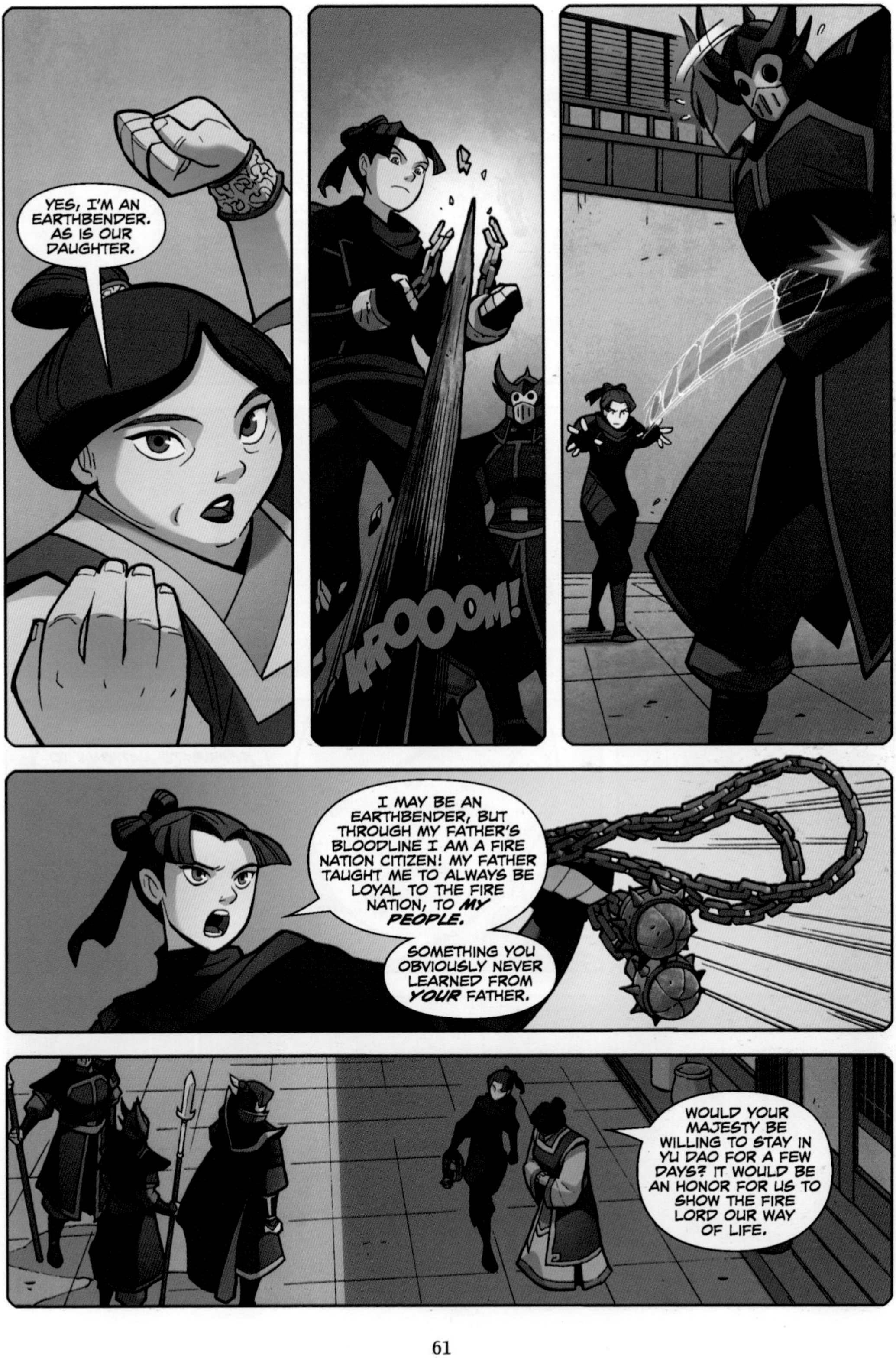
YES, I'M AN EARTHBENDER. AS IS OUR DAUGHTER.
KRROOOM!
I MAY BE AN EARTHBENDER, BUT THROUGH MY FATHER'S BLOODLINE I AM A FIRE NATION CITIZEN! MY FATHER TAUGHT ME TO ALWAYS BE LOYAL TO THE FIRE NATION, TO MY PEOPLE.
SOMETHING YOU OBVIOUSLY NEVER LEARNED FROM YOUR FATHER.
WOULD YOUR MAJESTY BE WILLING TO STAY IN YU DAO FOR A FEW DAYS? IT WOULD BE AN HONOR FOR US TO SHOW THE FIRE LORD OUR WAY OF LIFE.

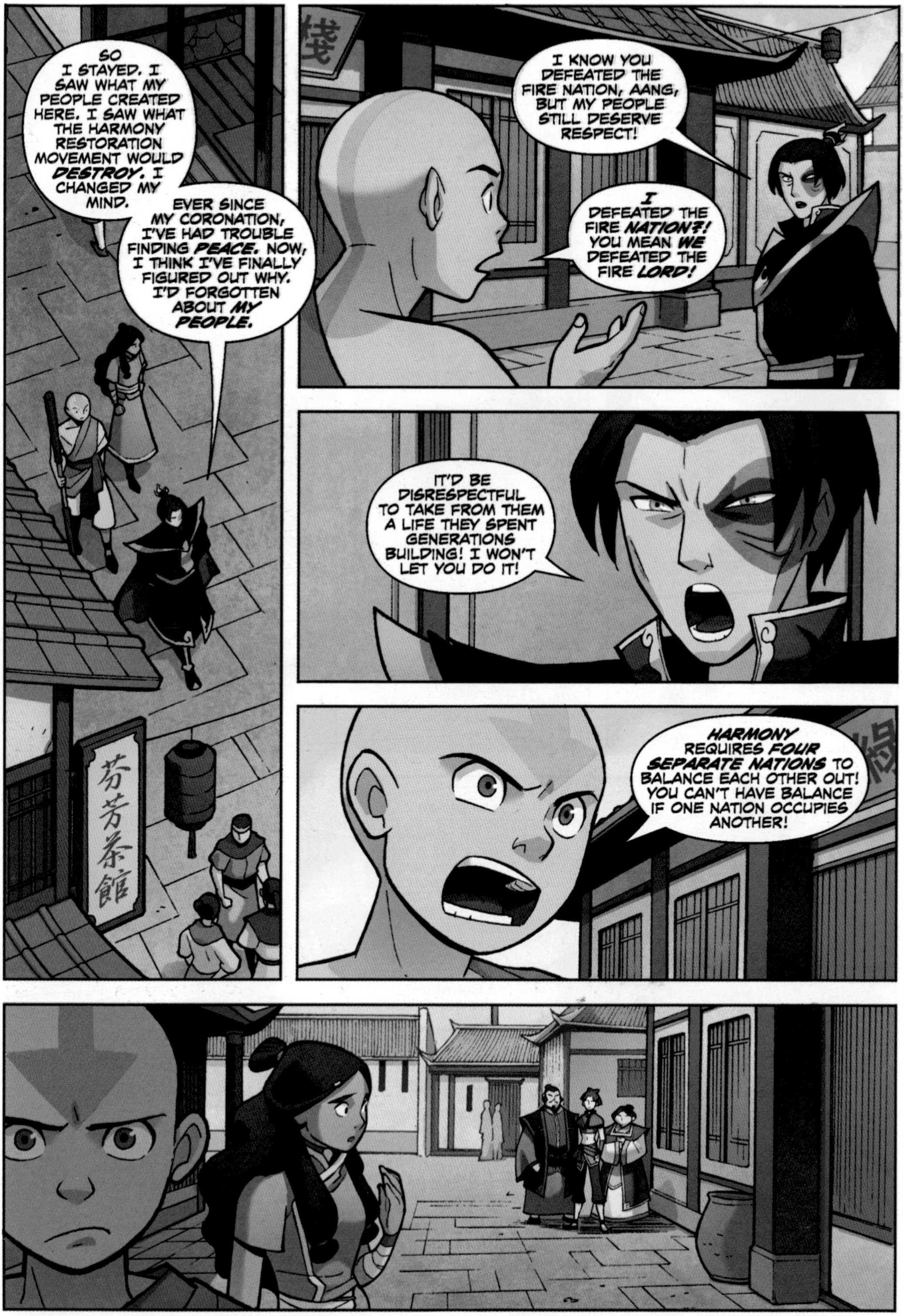
SO I STAYED. I SAW WHAT MY PEOPLE CREATED HERE. I SAW WHAT THE HARMONY RESTORATION MOVEMENT WOULD DESTROY. I CHANGED MY MIND.
EVER SINCE MY CORONATION, I'VE HAD TROUBLE FINDING PEACE. NOW, I THINK I'VE FINALLY FIGURED OUT WHY. I'D FORGOTTEN ABOUT MY PEOPLE.
I KNOW YOU DEFEATED THE FIRE NATION, AANG, BUT MY PEOPLE STILL DESERVE RESPECT!
I DEFEATED THE FIRE NATION?! YOU MEAN WE DEFEATED THE FIRE LORD!
IT'D BE DISRESPECTFUL TO TAKE FROM THEM A LIFE THEY SPENT GENERATIONS BUILDING! I WON'T LET YOU DO IT!
HARMONY REQUIRES FOUR SEPARATE NATIONS TO BALANCE EACH OTHER OUT! YOU CAN'T HAVE BALANCE IF ONE NATION OCCUPIES ANOTHER!

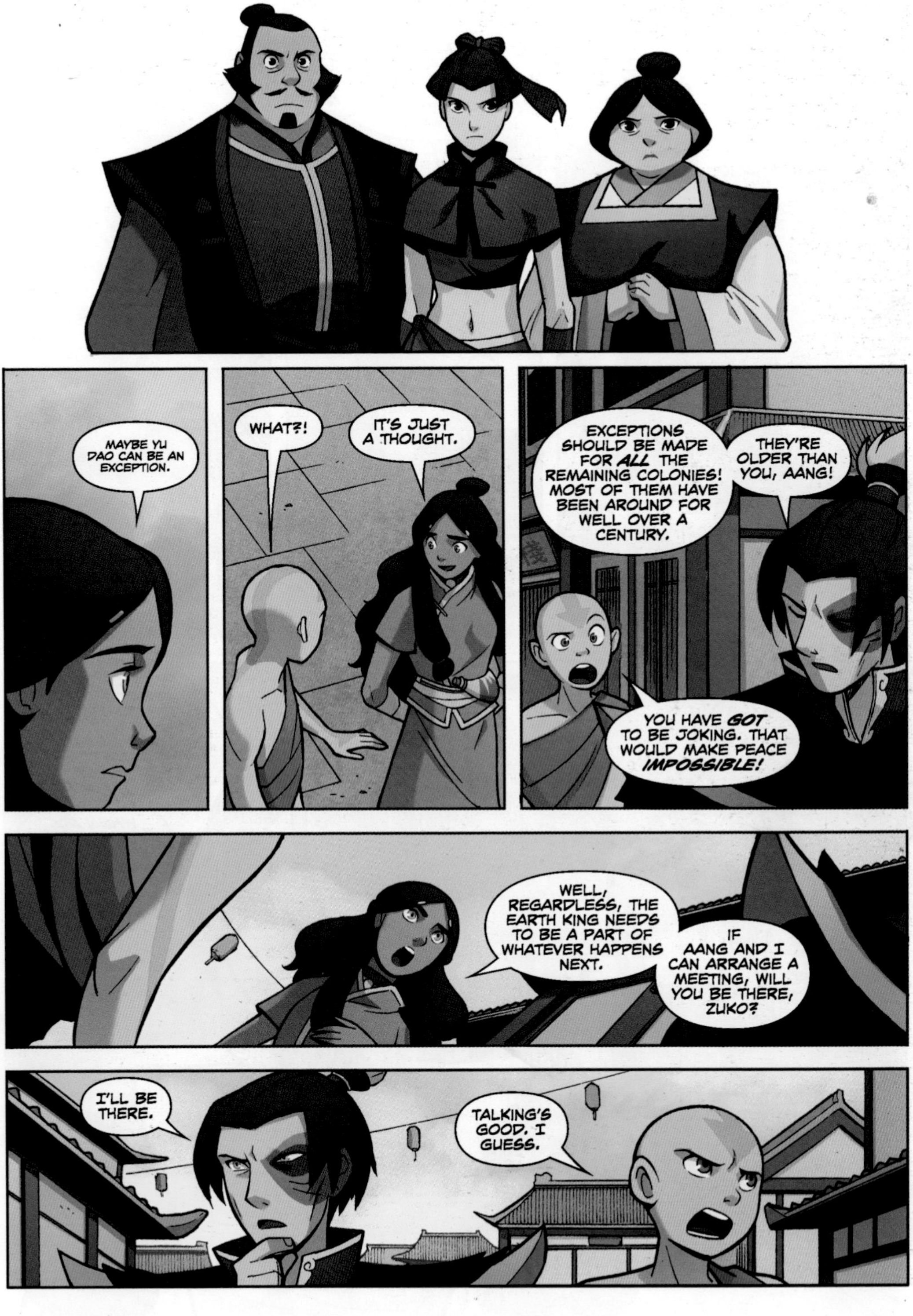
MAYBE YU DAO CAN BE AN EXCEPTION.
WHAT?!
IT'S JUST A THOUGHT.
EXCEPTIONS SHOULD BE MADE FOR ALL THE REMAINING COLONIES! MOST OF THEM HAVE BEEN AROUND FOR WELL OVER A CENTURY.
THEY'RE OLDER THAN YOU, AANG!
YOU HAVE GOT TO BE JOKING. THAT WOULD MAKE PEACE IMPOSSIBLE!
WELL, REGARDLESS, THE EARTH KING NEEDS TO BE A PART OF WHATEVER HAPPENS NEXT.
IF AANG AND I CAN ARRANGE A MEETING, WILL YOU BE THERE, ZUKO?
I'LL BE THERE.
TALKING'S GOOD, I GUESS.

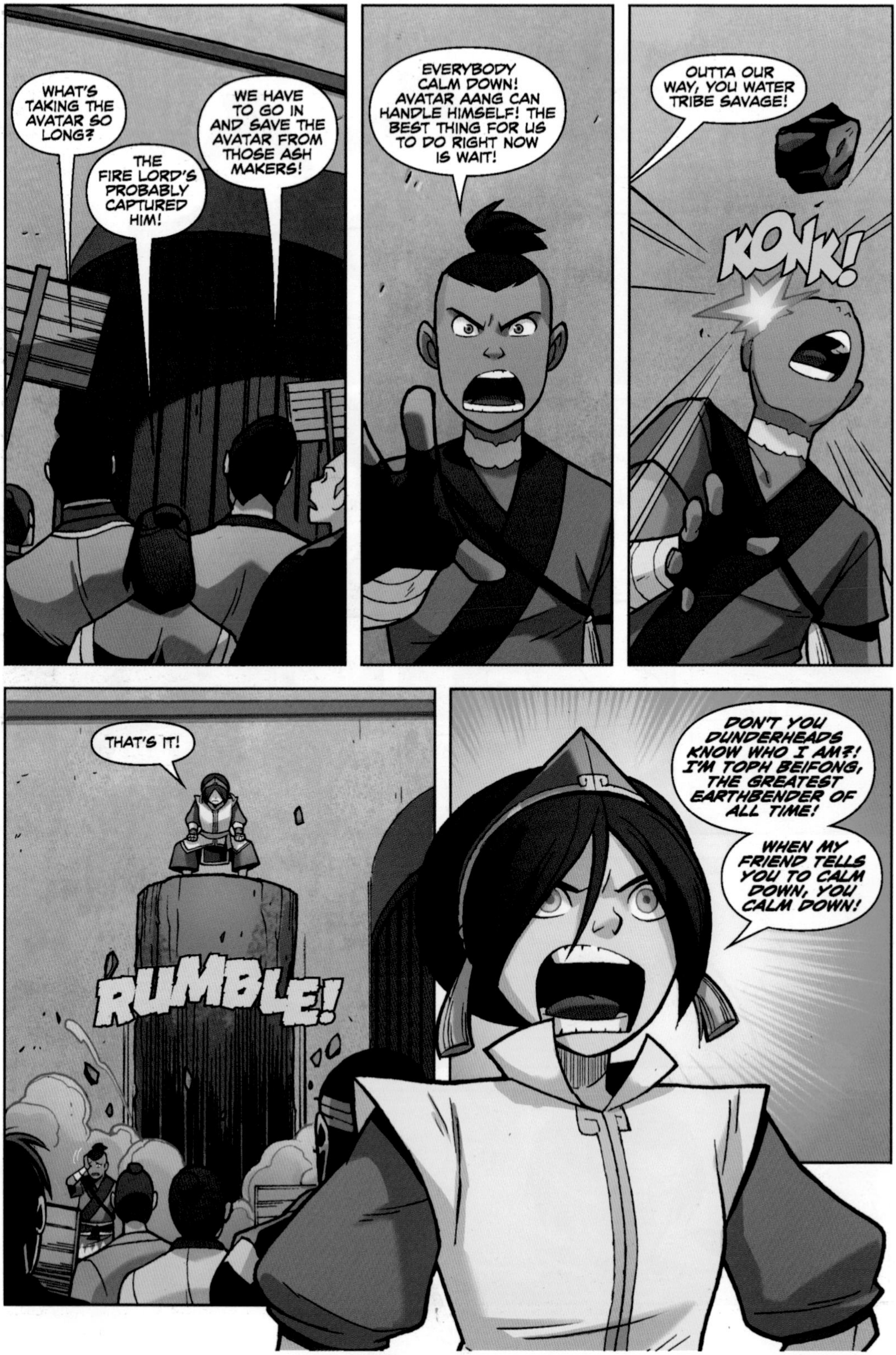
WHAT'S TAKING THE AVATAR SO LONG?
THE FIRE LORD'S PROBABLY CAPTURED HIM!
WE HAVE TO GO IN AND SAVE THE AVATAR FROM THOSE ASH MAKERS!
EVERYBODY CALM DOWN! AVATAR AANG CAN HANDLE HIMSELF! THE BEST THING FOR US TO DO RIGHT NOW IS WAIT!
OUTTA OUR WAY, YOU WATER TRIBE SAVAGE!
KONK!
THAT'S IT!
RUMBLE!
DON'T YOU DUNDERHEADS KNOW WHO I AM?! I'M TOPH BEIFONG, THE GREATEST EARTHBENDER OF ALL TIME!
WHEN MY FRIEND TELLS YOU TO CALM DOWN, YOU CALM DOWN!

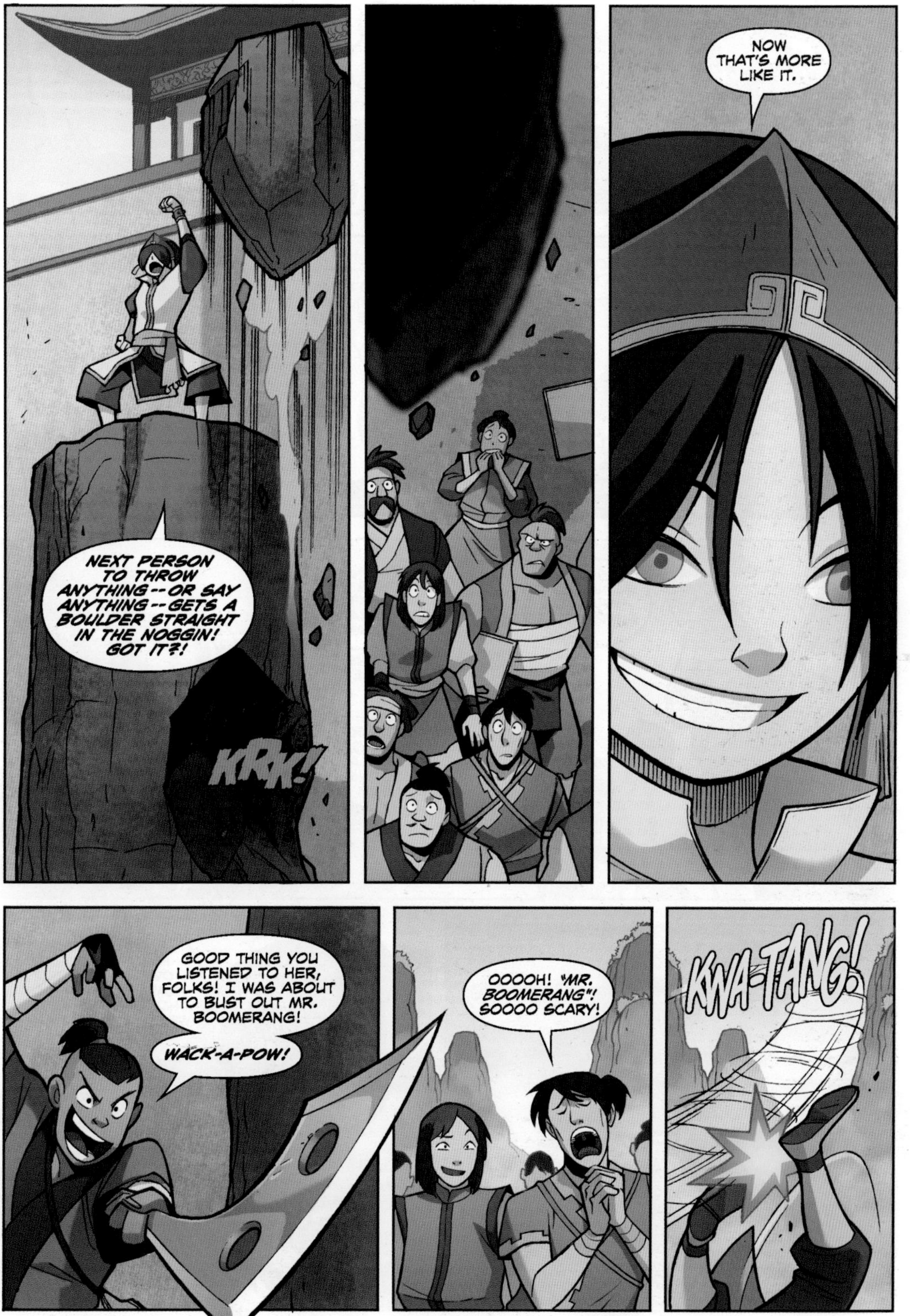

NEXT PERSON TO THROW ANYTHING--OR SAY ANYTHING--GETS A BOULDER STRAIGHT IN THE NOGGIN! GOT IT?!
KRK!
NOW THAT'S MORE LIKE IT.
GOOD THING YOU LISTENED TO HER, FOLKS! I WAS ABOUT TO BUST OUT MR. BOOMERANG!
WACK-A-POW!
OOOOH! "MR. BOOMERANG"! SOOOO SCARY!
KWA-TANG!

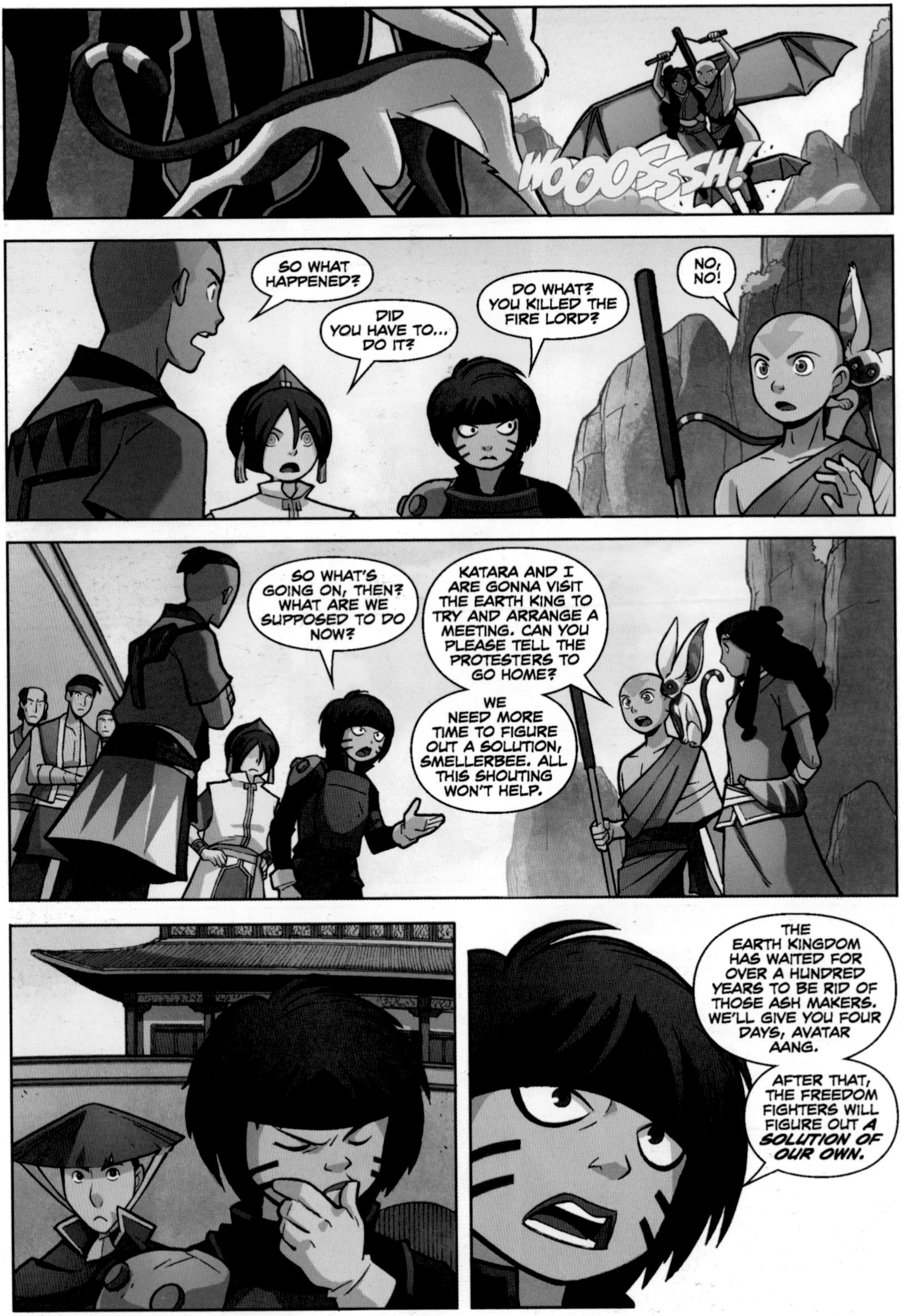
WOOOSSSH!
SO WHAT HAPPENED?
DID YOU HAVE TO... DO IT?
DO WHAT? YOU KILLED THE FIRE LORD?
NO, NO!
SO WHAT'S GOING ON, THEN? WHAT ARE WE SUPPOSED TO DO NOW?
KATARA AND I ARE GONNA VISIT THE EARTH KING TO TRY AND ARRANGE A MEETING. CAN YOU PLEASE TELL THE PROTESTERS TO GO HOME?
WE NEED MORE TIME TO FIGURE OUT A SOLUTION, SMELLERBEE. ALL THIS SHOUTING WON'T HELP.
THE EARTH KINGDOM HAS WAITED FOR OVER A HUNDRED YEARS TO BE RID OF THOSE ASH MAKERS. WE'LL GIVE YOU FOUR DAYS, AVATAR AANG.
AFTER THAT, THE FREEDOM FIGHTERS WILL FIGURE OUT *A SOLUTION OF OUR OWN.*

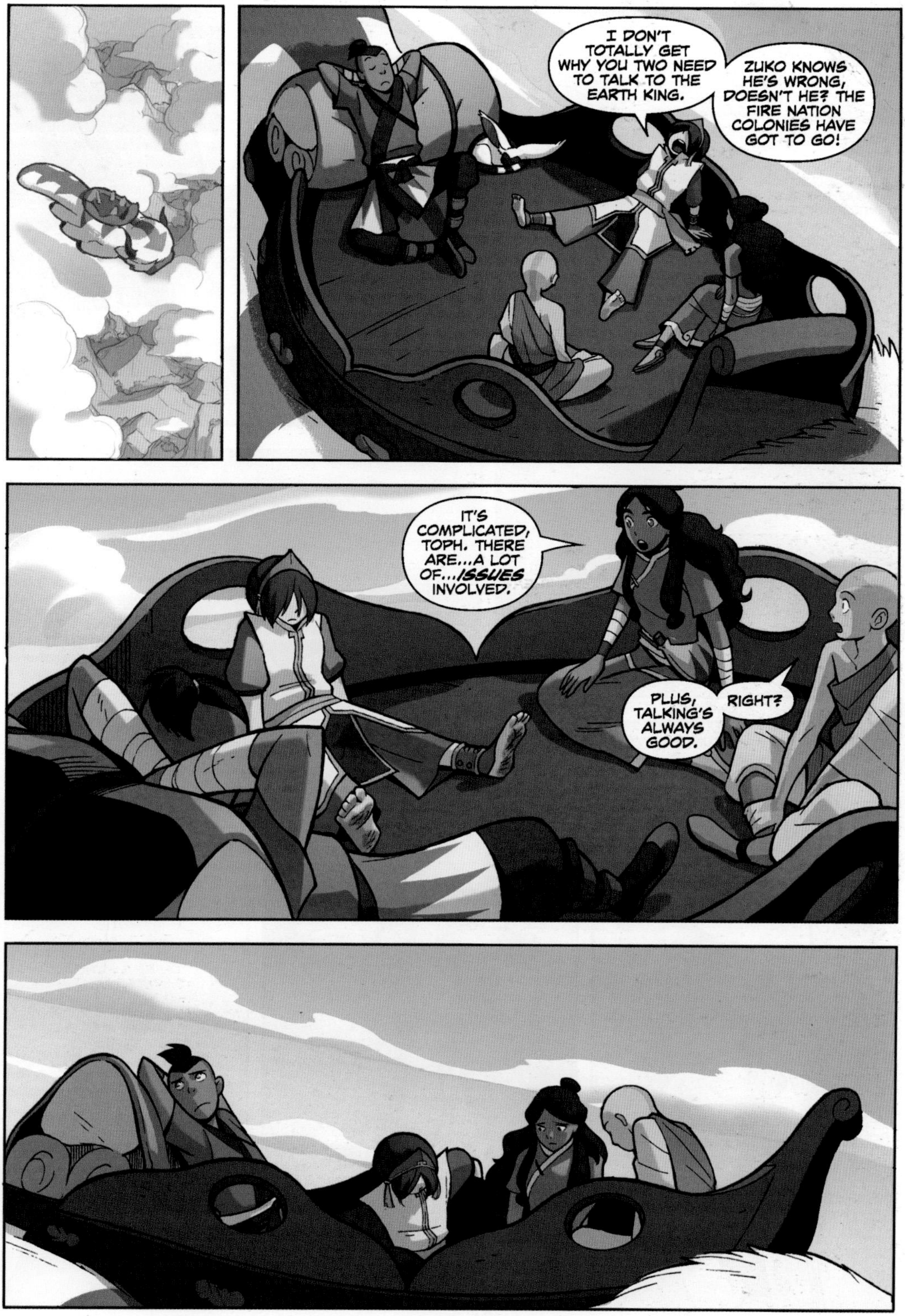
I DON'T TOTALLY GET WHY YOU TWO NEED TO TALK TO THE EARTH KING.
ZUKO KNOWS HE'S WRONG, DOESN'T HE? THE FIRE NATION COLONIES HAVE GOT TO GO!
IT'S COMPLICATED, TOPH. THERE ARE...A LOT OF...ISSUES INVOLVED.
PLUS, TALKING'S ALWAYS GOOD.
RIGHT?

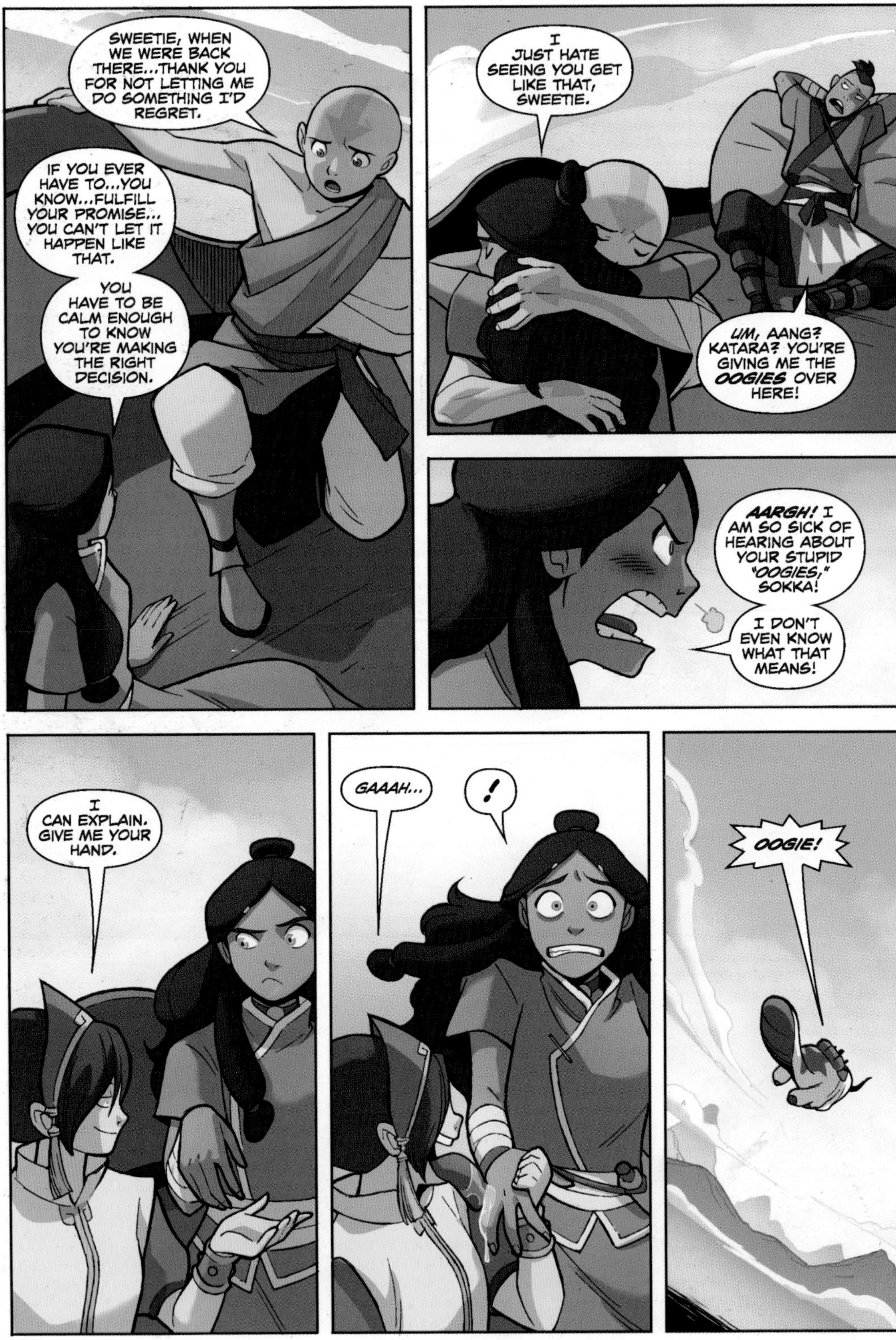
SWEETIE, WHEN WE WERE BACK THERE...THANK YOU FOR NOT LETTING ME DO SOMETHING I'D REGRET.
IF YOU EVER HAVE TO...YOU KNOW...FULFILL YOUR PROMISE... YOU CAN'T LET IT HAPPEN LIKE THAT.
YOU HAVE TO BE CALM ENOUGH TO KNOW YOU'RE MAKING THE RIGHT DECISION.
I JUST HATE SEEING YOU GET LIKE THAT, SWEETIE.
UM, AANG? KATARA? YOU'RE GIVING ME THE OOGIES OVER HERE!
AARGH! I AM SO SICK OF HEARING ABOUT YOUR STUPID "OOGIES," SOKKA!
I DON'T EVEN KNOW WHAT THAT MEANS!
I CAN EXPLAIN. GIVE ME YOUR HAND.
GAAAH...
!
OOGIE!

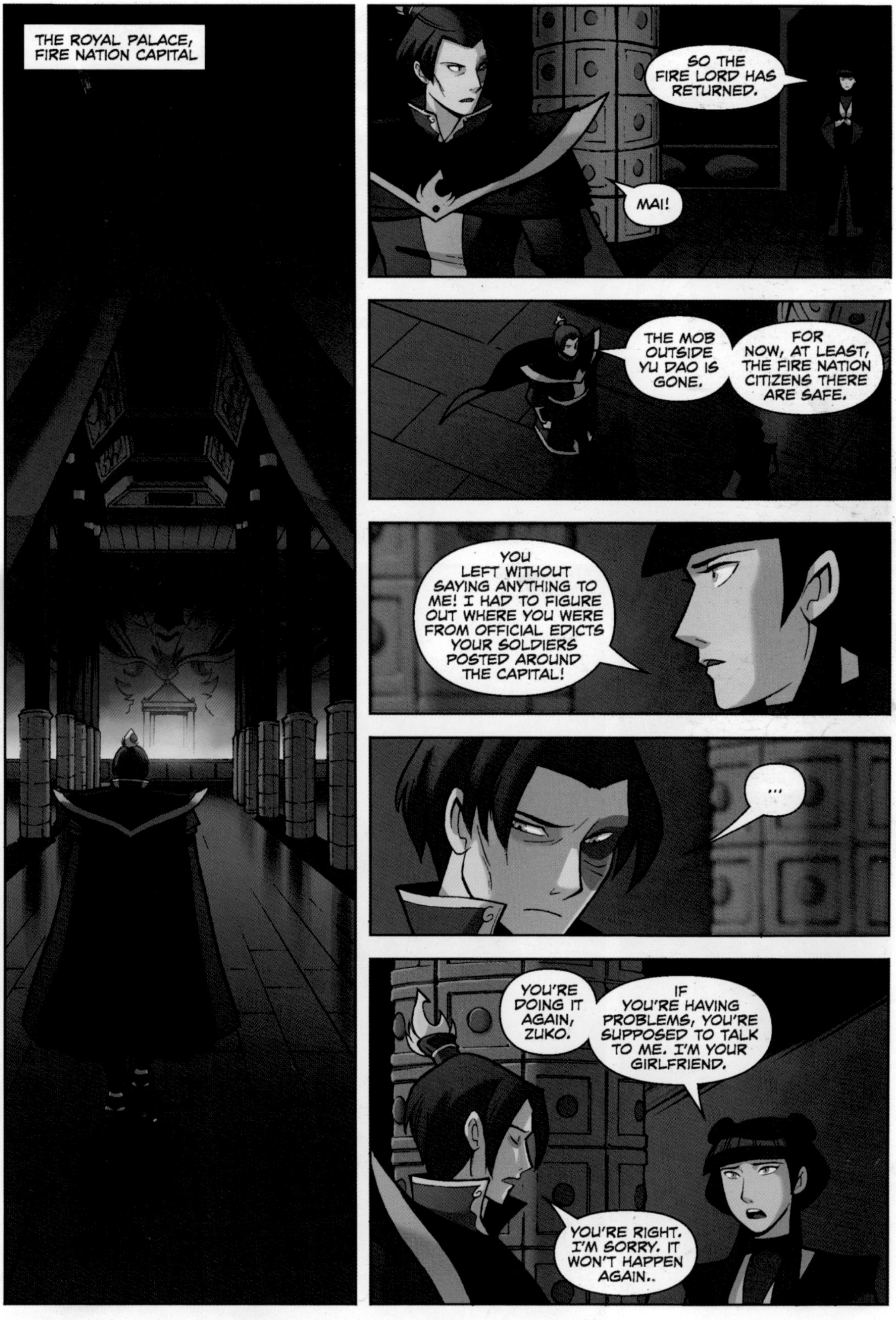
THE ROYAL PALACE, FIRE NATION CAPITAL
SO THE FIRE LORD HAS RETURNED.
MAI!
THE MOB OUTSIDE YU DAO IS GONE.
FOR NOW, AT LEAST, THE FIRE NATION CITIZENS THERE ARE SAFE.
YOU LEFT WITHOUT SAYING ANYTHING TO ME! I HAD TO FIGURE OUT WHERE YOU WERE FROM OFFICIAL EDICTS YOUR SOLDIERS POSTED AROUND THE CAPITAL!
...
YOU'RE DOING IT AGAIN, ZUKO.
IF YOU'RE HAVING PROBLEMS, YOU'RE SUPPOSED TO TALK TO ME. I'M YOUR GIRLFRIEND.
YOU'RE RIGHT. I'M SORRY. IT WON'T HAPPEN AGAIN..

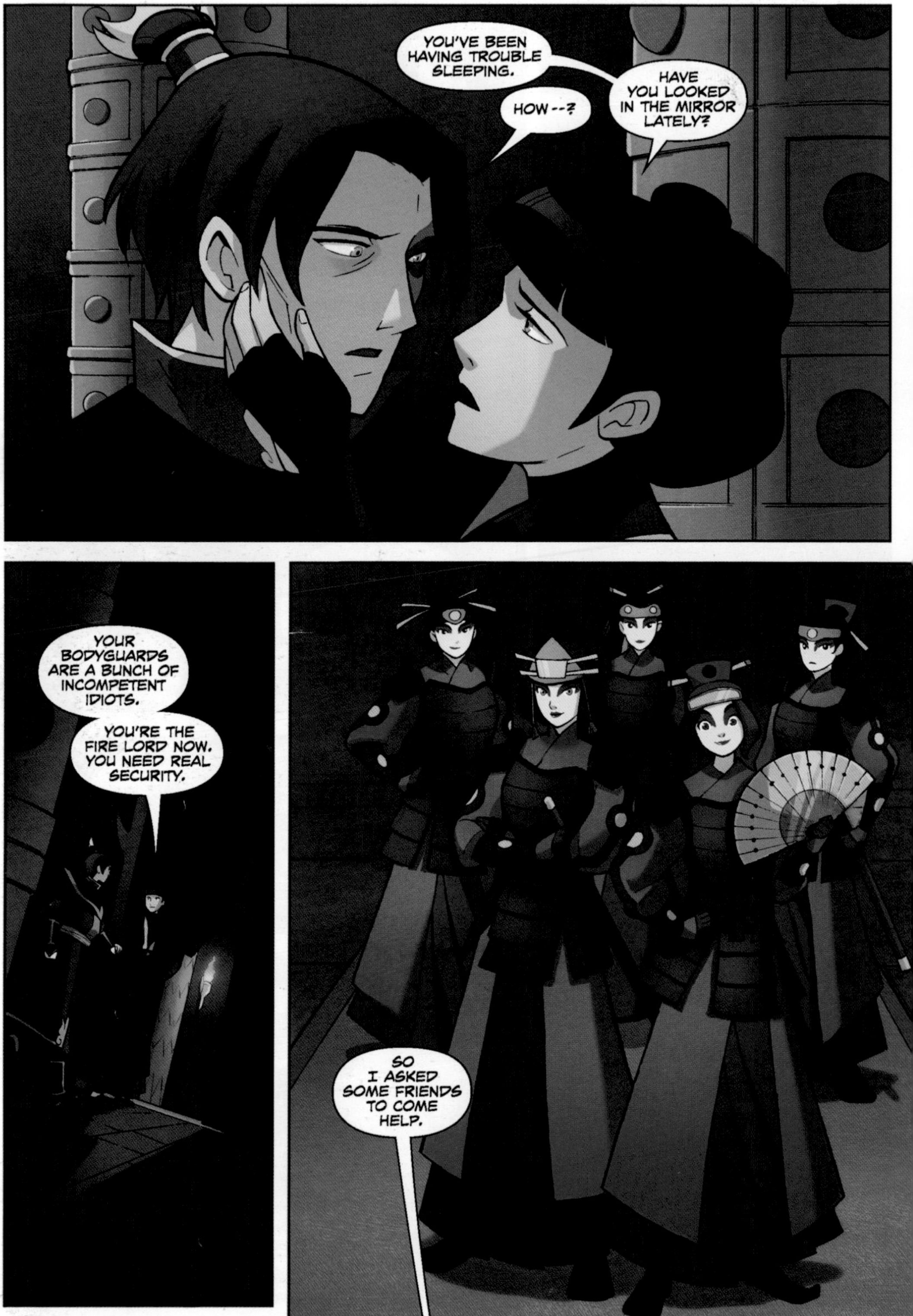
YOU'VE BEEN HAVING TROUBLE SLEEPING.
HOW--?
HAVE YOU LOOKED IN THE MIRROR LATELY?
YOUR BODYGUARDS ARE A BUNCH OF INCOMPETENT IDIOTS.
YOU'RE THE FIRE LORD NOW. YOU NEED REAL SECURITY.
SO I ASKED SOME FRIENDS TO COME HELP.

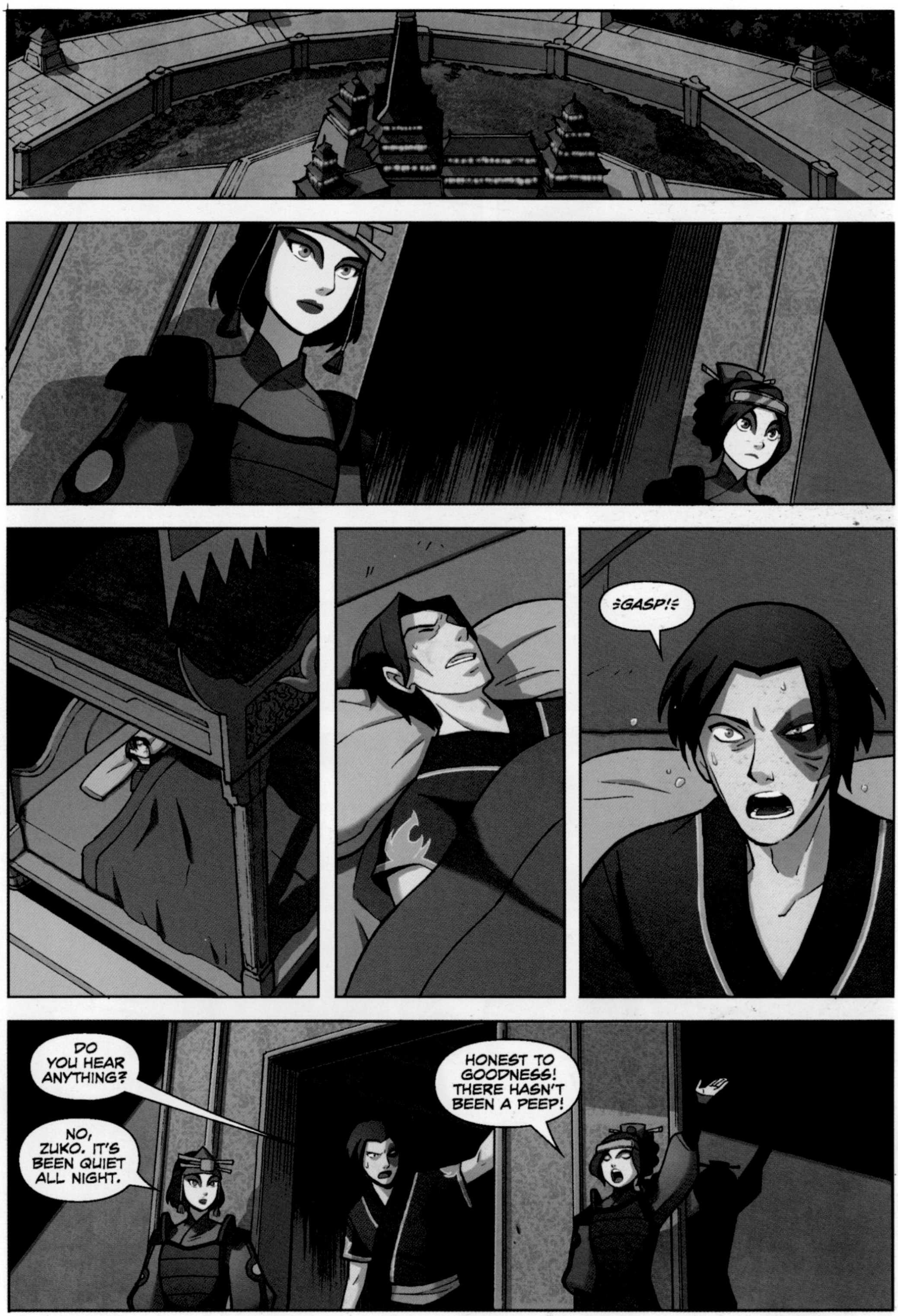

GASP!
DO YOU HEAR ANYTHING?
NO, ZUKO. IT'S BEEN QUIET ALL NIGHT.
HONEST TO GOODNESS! THERE HASN'T BEEN A PEEP!

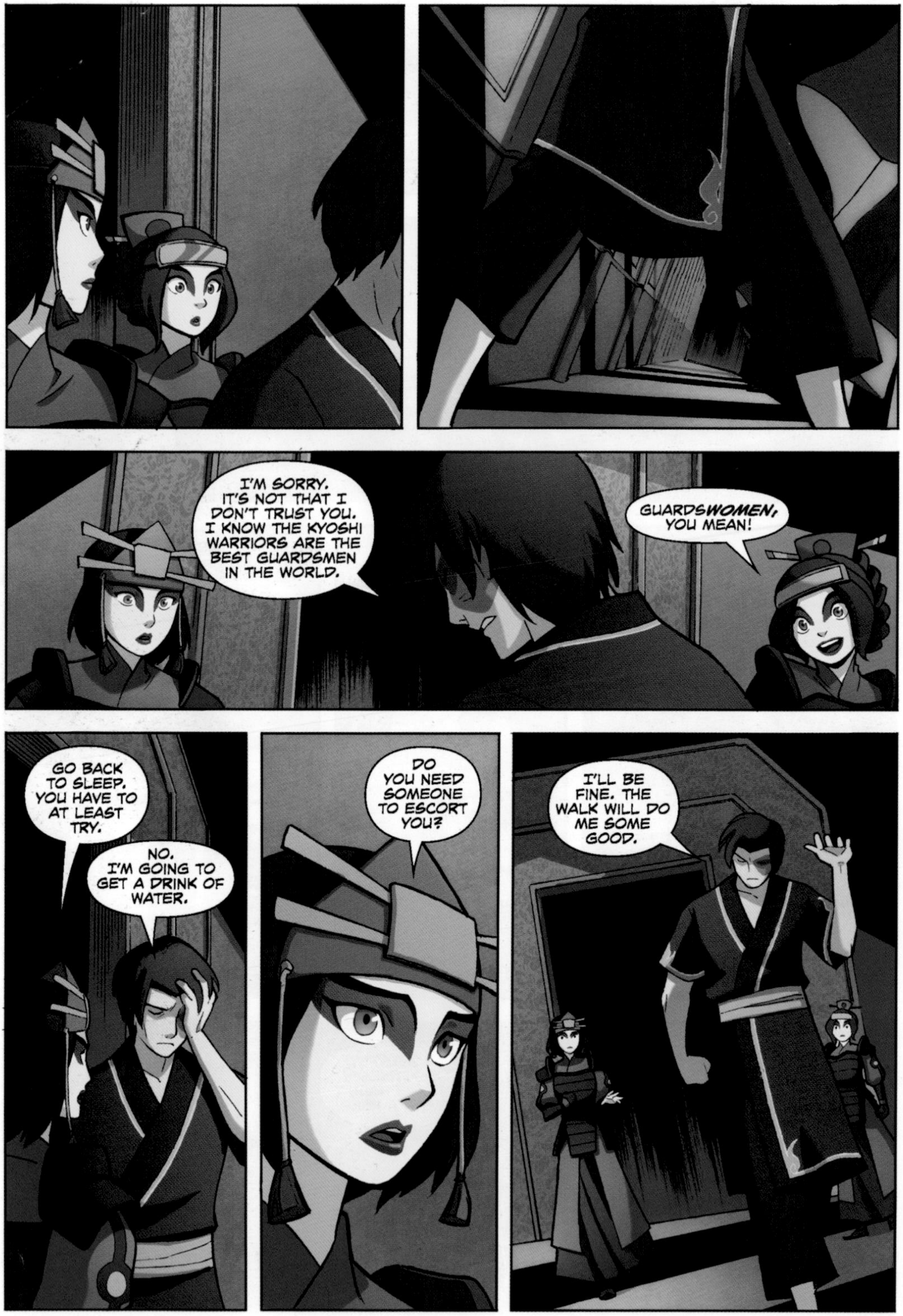
I'M SORRY. IT'S NOT THAT I DON'T TRUST YOU. I KNOW THE KYOSHI WARRIORS ARE THE BEST GUARDSMEN IN THE WORLD.
GUARDSWOMEN, YOU MEAN!
GO BACK TO SLEEP. YOU HAVE TO AT LEAST TRY.
NO. I'M GOING TO GET A DRINK OF WATER.
DO YOU NEED SOMEONE TO ESCORT YOU?
I'LL BE FINE. THE WALK WILL DO ME SOME GOOD.

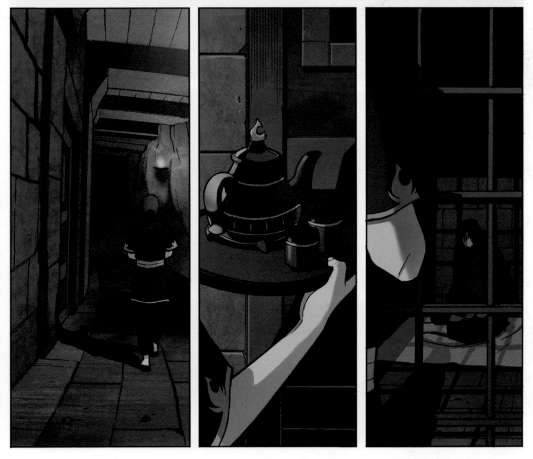

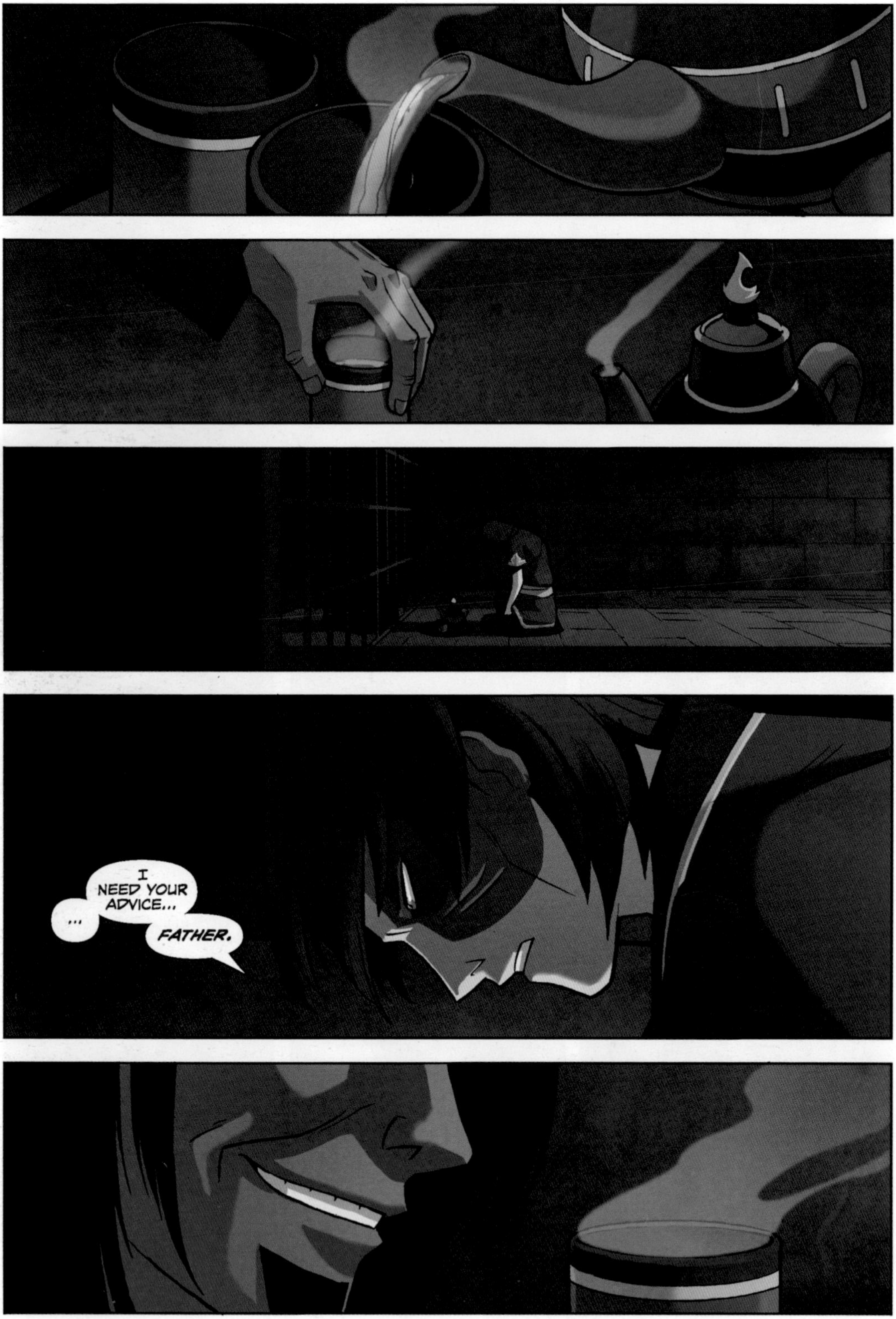
I NEED YOUR ADVICE...
...
FATHER.

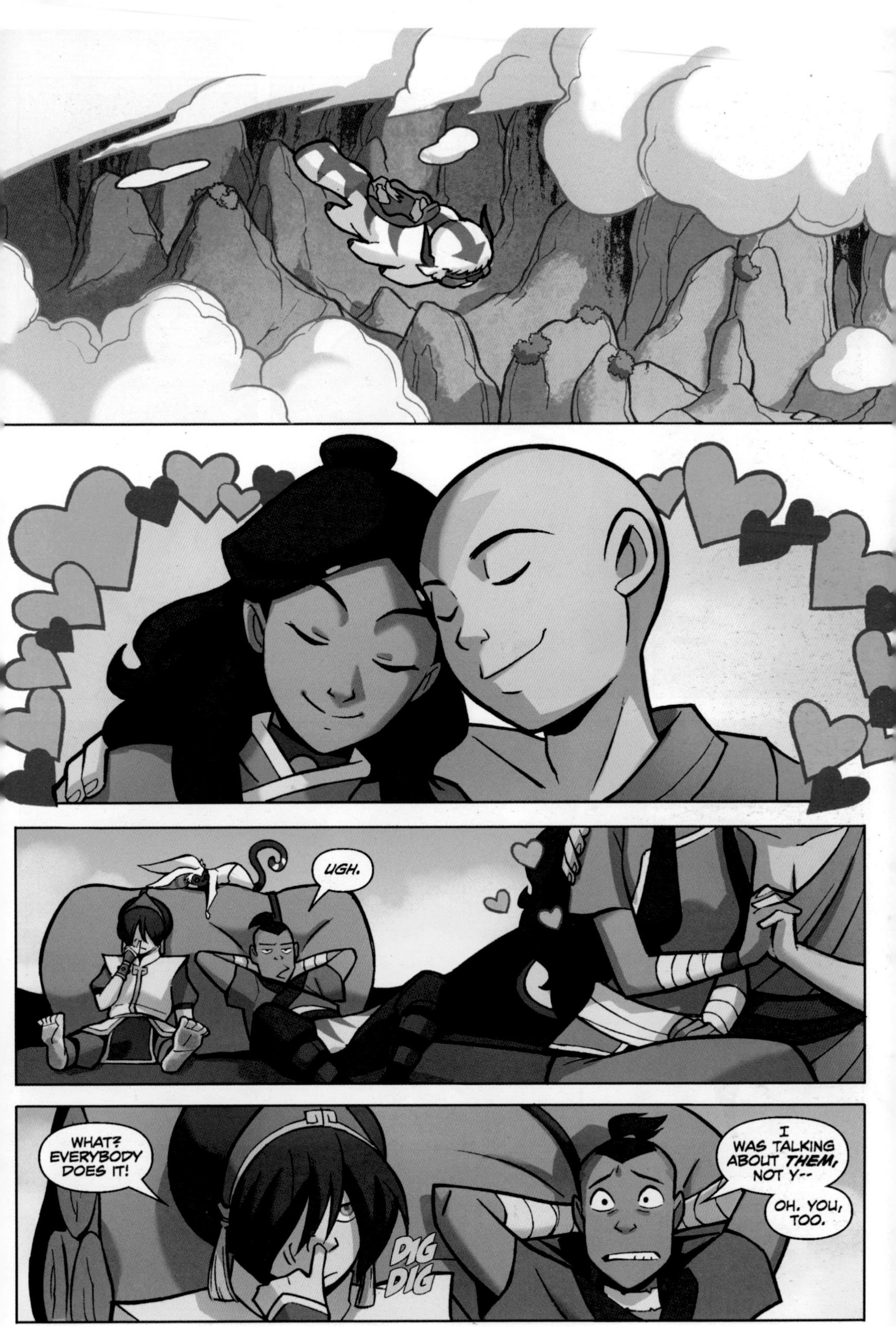
UGH.
WHAT? EVERYBODY DOES IT!
DIG DIG
I WAS TALKING ABOUT *THEM,* NOT Y--
OH. YOU, TOO.

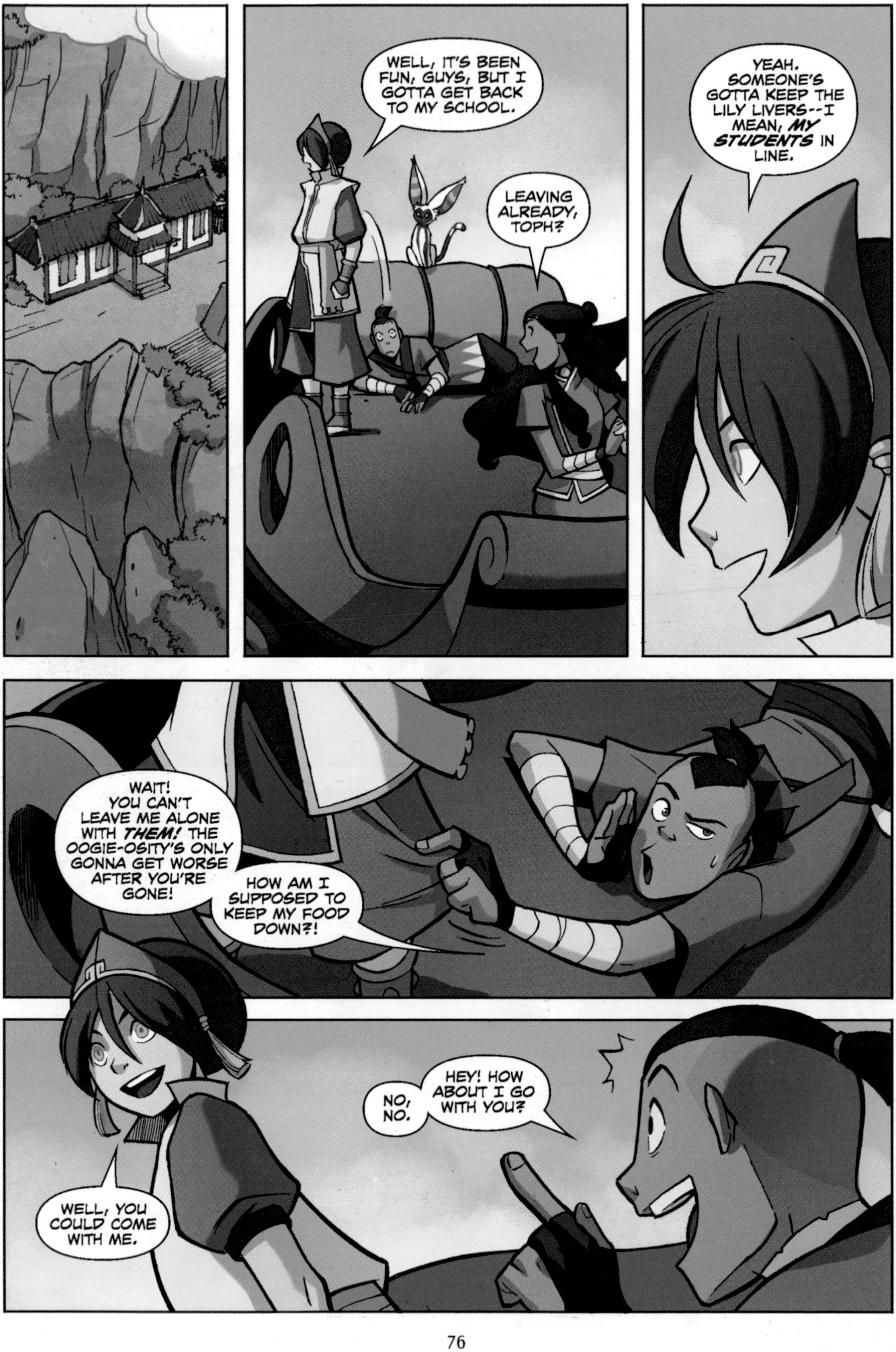
WELL, IT'S BEEN FUN, GUYS, BUT I GOTTA GET BACK TO MY SCHOOL.
LEAVING ALREADY, TOPH?
YEAH. SOMEONE'S GOTTA KEEP THE LILY LIVERS--I MEAN, *MY STUDENTS* IN LINE.
WAIT! YOU CAN'T LEAVE ME ALONE WITH *THEM!* THE OOGIE-OSITY'S ONLY GONNA GET WORSE AFTER YOU'RE GONE!
HOW AM I SUPPOSED TO KEEP MY FOOD DOWN?!
WELL, YOU COULD COME WITH ME.
HEY! HOW ABOUT I GO WITH YOU?
NO, NO.

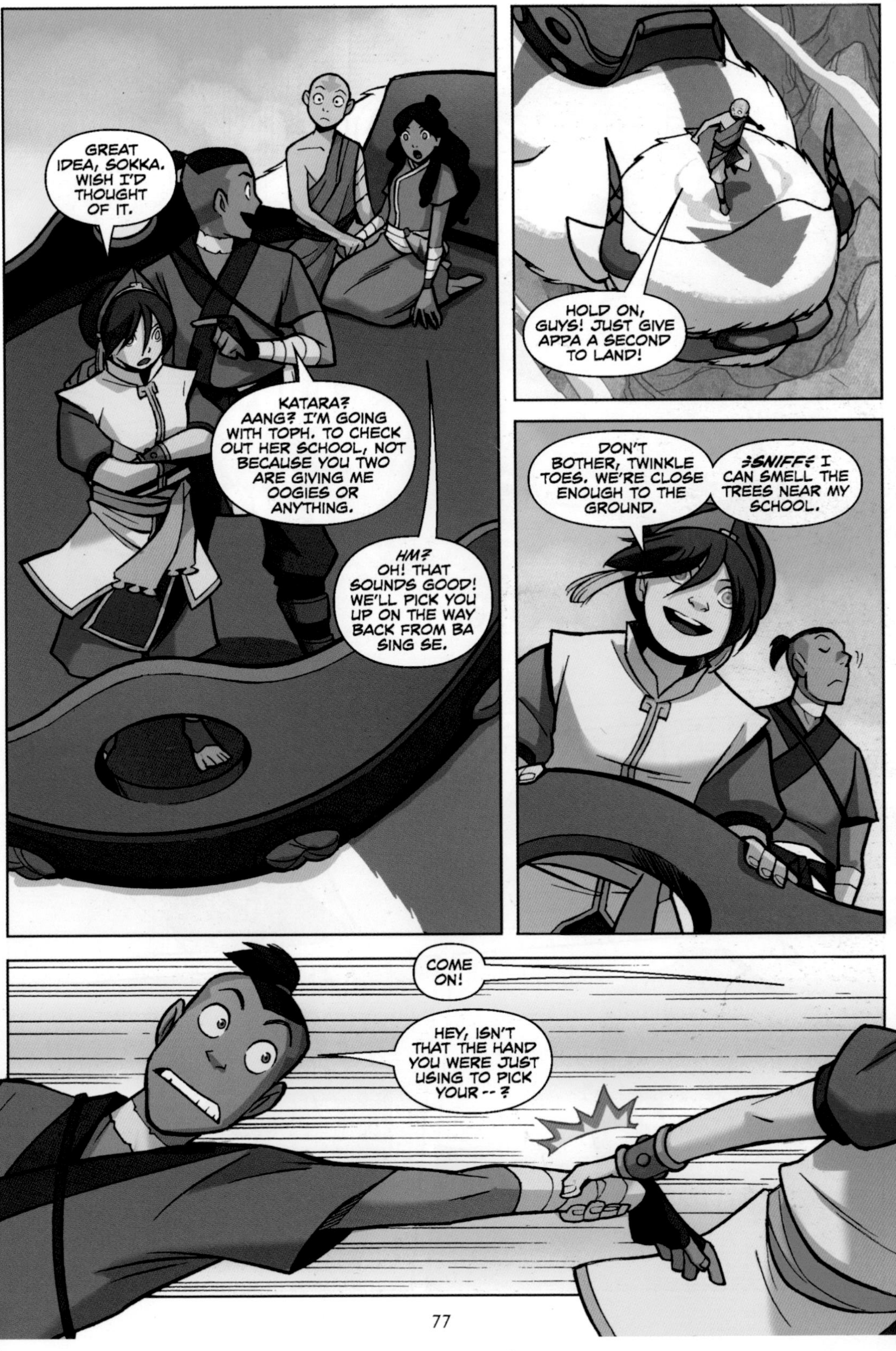
GREAT IDEA, SOKKA. WISH I'D THOUGHT OF IT.
KATARA? AANG? I'M GOING WITH TOPH. TO CHECK OUT HER SCHOOL, NOT BECAUSE YOU TWO ARE GIVING ME OOGIES OR ANYTHING.
HM? OH! THAT SOUNDS GOOD! WE'LL PICK YOU UP ON THE WAY BACK FROM BA SING SE.
HOLD ON, GUYS! JUST GIVE APPA A SECOND TO LAND!
DON'T BOTHER, TWINKLE TOES. WE'RE CLOSE ENOUGH TO THE GROUND.
SNIFF I CAN SMELL THE TREES NEAR MY SCHOOL.
COME ON!
HEY, ISN'T THAT THE HAND YOU WERE JUST USING TO PICK YOUR--?

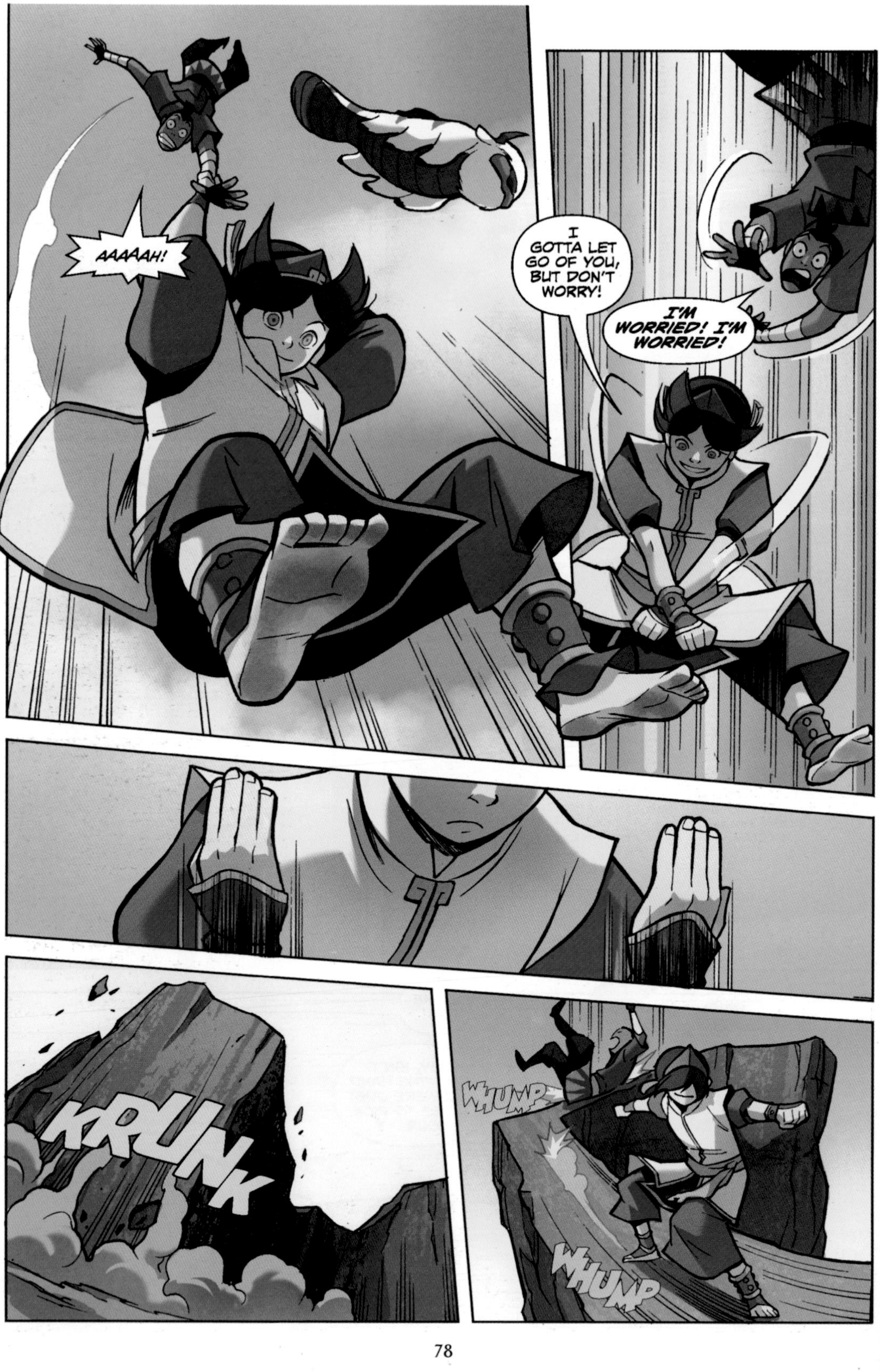
AAAAAH!
I GOTTA LET GO OF YOU, BUT DON'T WORRY!
I'M WORRIED! I'M WORRIED!
KRUNK
WHUMP
WHUMP

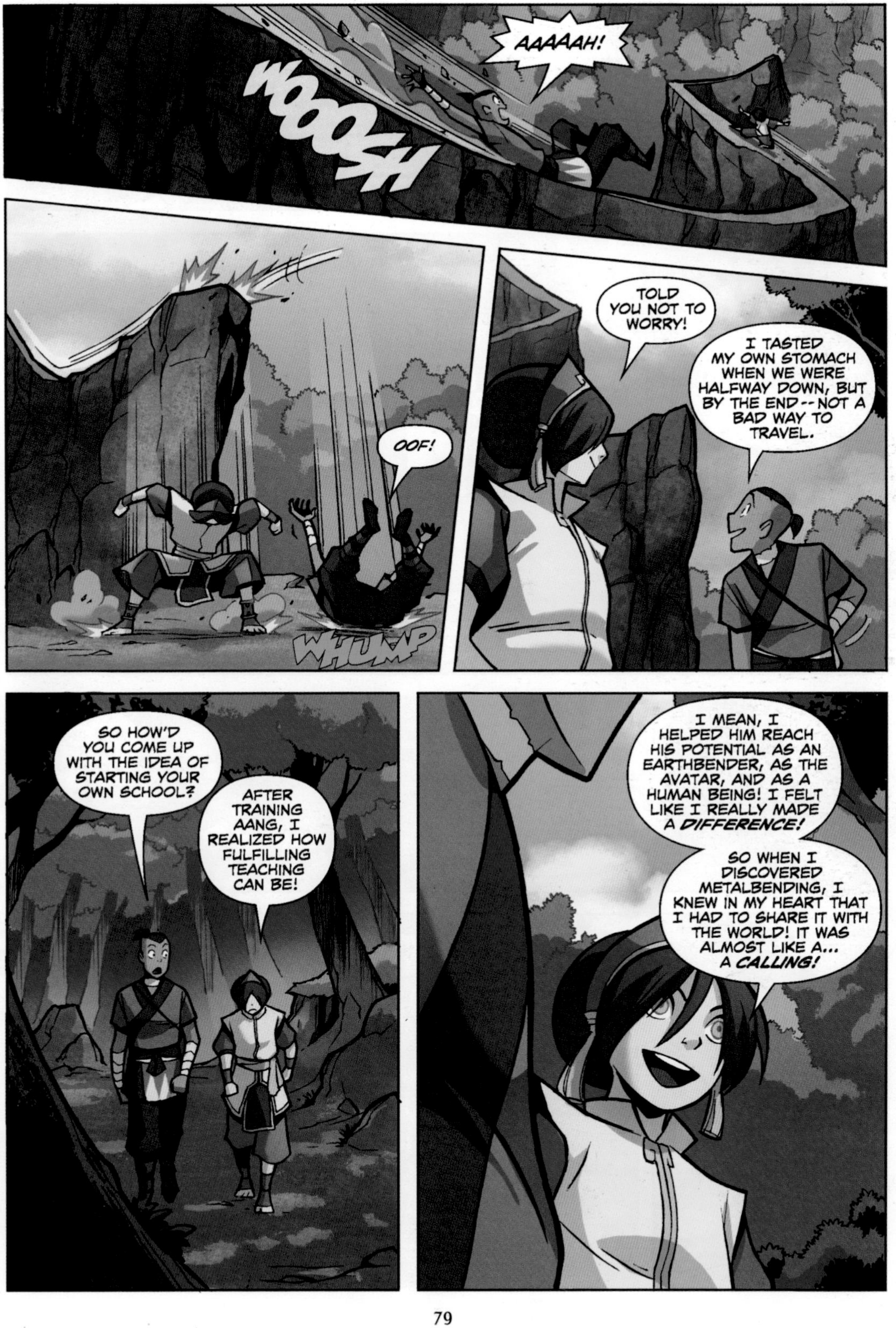

AAAAAH!
WOOOSH
OOF!
WHUMP
TOLD YOU NOT TO WORRY!
I TASTED MY OWN STOMACH WHEN WE WERE HALFWAY DOWN, BUT BY THE END--NOT A BAD WAY TO TRAVEL.
SO HOW'D YOU COME UP WITH THE IDEA OF STARTING YOUR OWN SCHOOL?
AFTER TRAINING AANG, I REALIZED HOW FULFILLING TEACHING CAN BE!
I MEAN, I HELPED HIM REACH HIS POTENTIAL AS AN EARTHBENDER, AS THE AVATAR, AND AS A HUMAN BEING! I FELT LIKE I REALLY MADE A *DIFFERENCE!*
SO WHEN I DISCOVERED METALBENDING, I KNEW IN MY HEART THAT I HAD TO SHARE IT WITH THE WORLD! IT WAS ALMOST LIKE A... A *CALLING!*

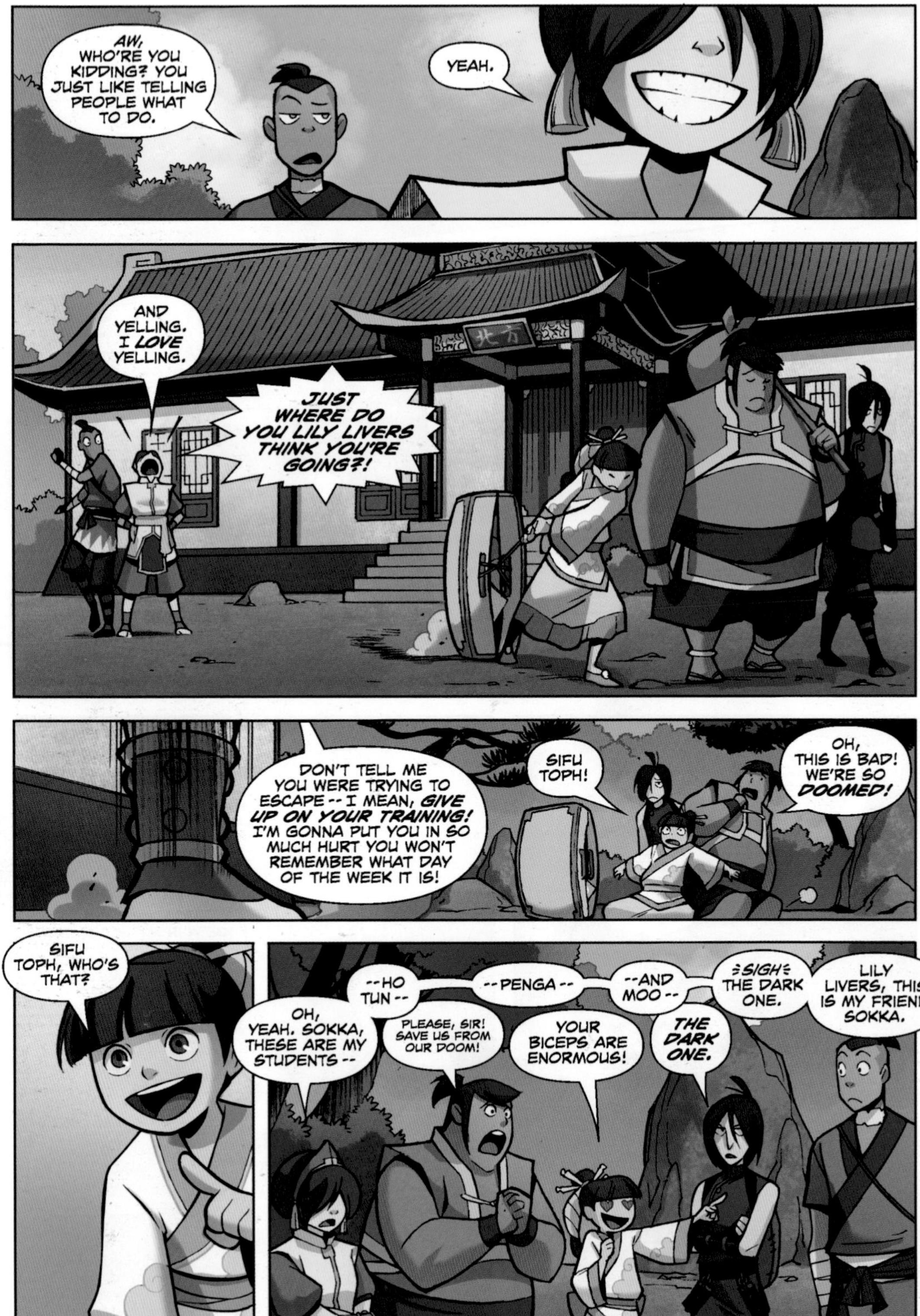

AW, WHO'RE YOU KIDDING? YOU JUST LIKE TELLING PEOPLE WHAT TO DO.
YEAH.
AND YELLING. I *LOVE* YELLING.
JUST WHERE DO YOU LILY LIVERS THINK YOU'RE GOING?!
DON'T TELL ME YOU WERE TRYING TO ESCAPE -- I MEAN, *GIVE UP ON YOUR TRAINING!* I'M GONNA PUT YOU IN SO MUCH HURT YOU WON'T REMEMBER WHAT DAY OF THE WEEK IT IS!
SIFU TOPH!
OH, THIS IS BAD! WE'RE SO *DOOMED!*
SIFU TOPH, WHO'S THAT?
OH, YEAH. SOKKA, THESE ARE MY STUDENTS --
--HO TUN --
PLEASE, SIR! SAVE US FROM OUR DOOM!
-- PENGA --
YOUR BICEPS ARE ENORMOUS!
--AND MOO --
THE DARK ONE.
SIGH THE DARK ONE.
LILY LIVERS, THIS IS MY FRIEND SOKKA.

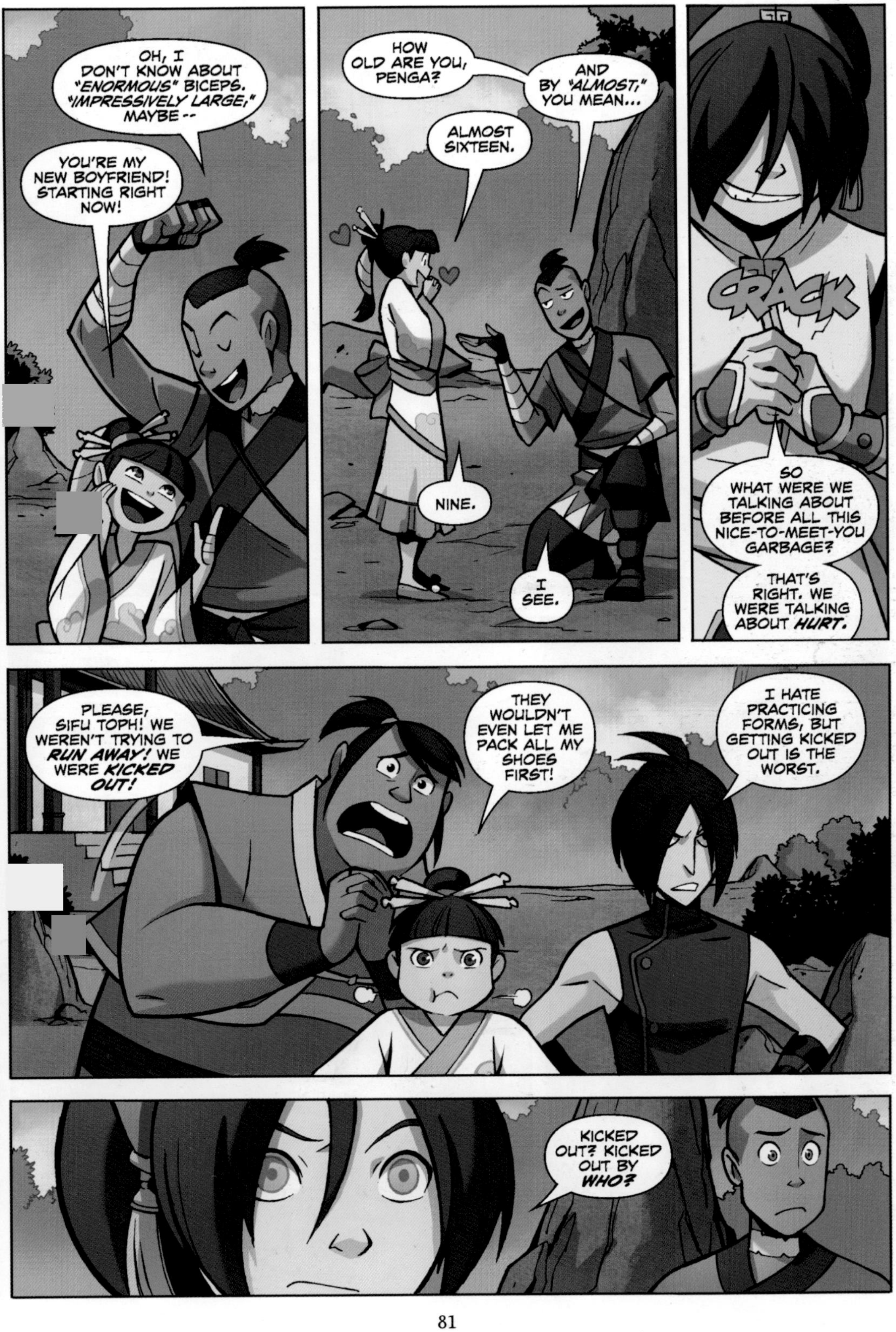
OH, I DON'T KNOW ABOUT *"ENORMOUS"* BICEPS. *"IMPRESSIVELY LARGE,"* MAYBE --
YOU'RE MY NEW BOYFRIEND! STARTING RIGHT NOW!
HOW OLD ARE YOU, PENGA?
ALMOST SIXTEEN.
AND BY *"ALMOST,"* YOU MEAN...
NINE.
I SEE.
CRACK
SO WHAT WERE WE TALKING ABOUT BEFORE ALL THIS NICE-TO-MEET-YOU GARBAGE?
THAT'S RIGHT. WE WERE TALKING ABOUT ***HURT.***
PLEASE, SIFU TOPH! WE WEREN'T TRYING TO ***RUN AWAY!*** WE WERE ***KICKED OUT!***
THEY WOULDN'T EVEN LET ME PACK ALL MY SHOES FIRST!
I HATE PRACTICING FORMS, BUT GETTING KICKED OUT IS THE WORST.
KICKED OUT? KICKED OUT BY ***WHO?***

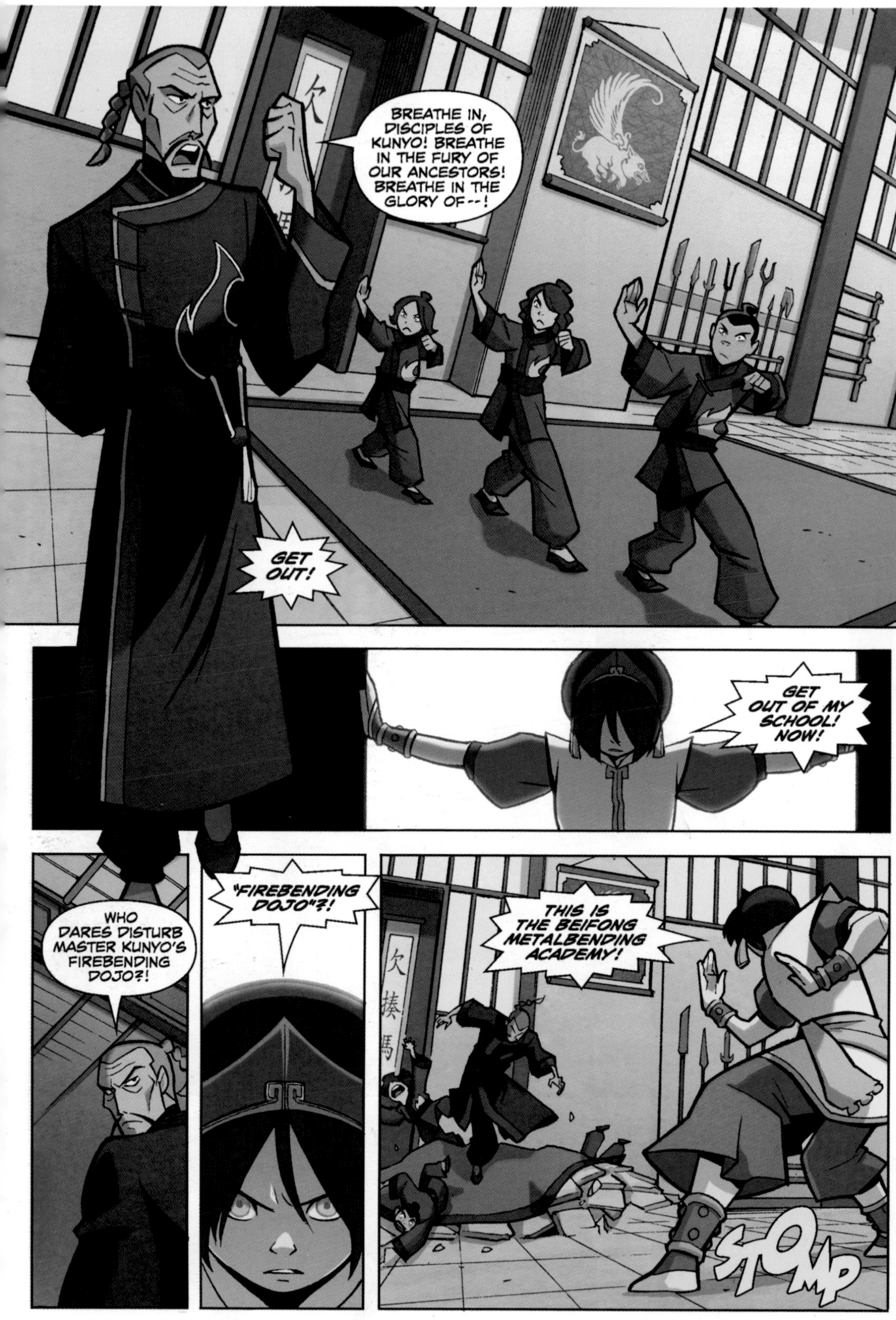
BREATHE IN, DISCIPLES OF KUNYO! BREATHE IN THE FURY OF OUR ANCESTORS! BREATHE IN THE GLORY OF--!
GET OUT!
GET OUT OF MY SCHOOL! NOW!
WHO DARES DISTURB MASTER KUNYO'S FIREBENDING DOJO?!
"FIREBENDING DOJO"?!
THIS IS THE BEIFONG METALBENDING ACADEMY!
STOMP

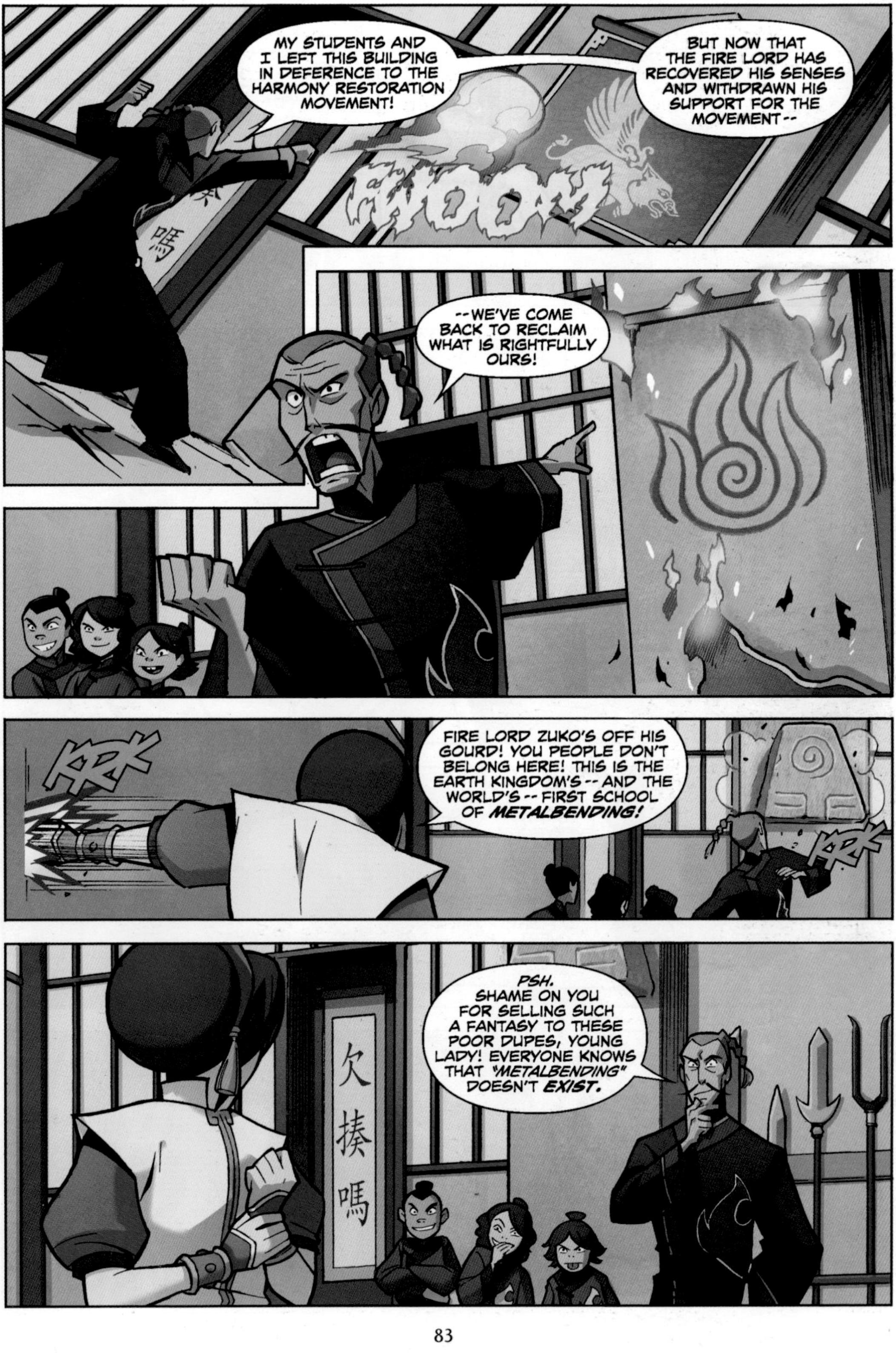
MY STUDENTS AND I LEFT THIS BUILDING IN DEFERENCE TO THE HARMONY RESTORATION MOVEMENT!
BUT NOW THAT THE FIRE LORD HAS RECOVERED HIS SENSES AND WITHDRAWN HIS SUPPORT FOR THE MOVEMENT--
FWOOM
--WE'VE COME BACK TO RECLAIM WHAT IS RIGHTFULLY OURS!
KRK
FIRE LORD ZUKO'S OFF HIS GOURD! YOU PEOPLE DON'T BELONG HERE! THIS IS THE EARTH KINGDOM'S-- AND THE WORLD'S-- FIRST SCHOOL OF *METALBENDING!*
KRK
PSH. SHAME ON YOU FOR SELLING SUCH A FANTASY TO THESE POOR DUPES, YOUNG LADY! EVERYONE KNOWS THAT *"METALBENDING"* DOESN'T *EXIST.*
欠揍嗎

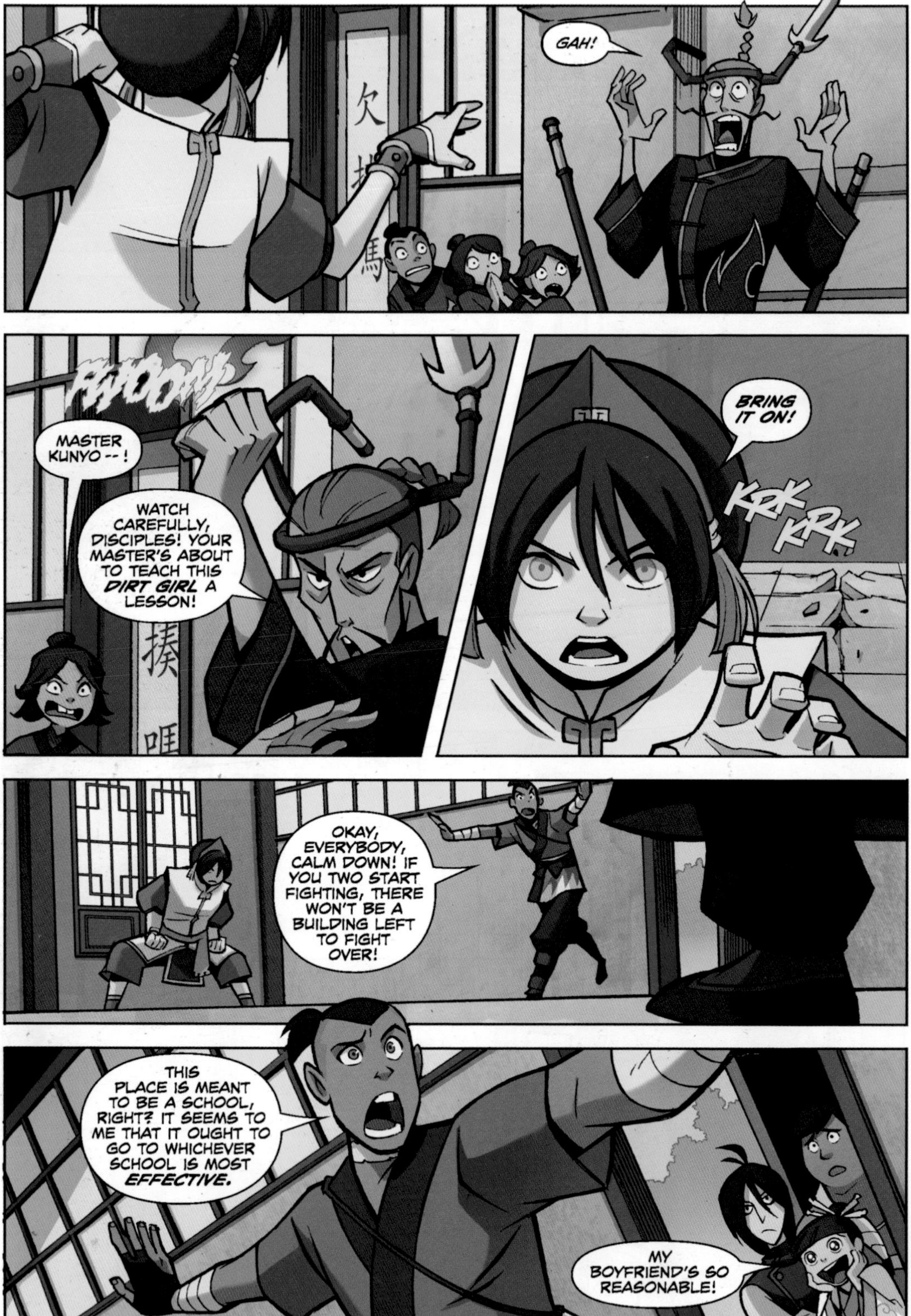
GAH!
FWOOM
MASTER KUNYO -- !
WATCH CAREFULLY, DISCIPLES! YOUR MASTER'S ABOUT TO TEACH THIS DIRT GIRL A LESSON!
BRING IT ON!
KRK KRK
OKAY, EVERYBODY, CALM DOWN! IF YOU TWO START FIGHTING, THERE WON'T BE A BUILDING LEFT TO FIGHT OVER!
THIS PLACE IS MEANT TO BE A SCHOOL, RIGHT? IT SEEMS TO ME THAT IT OUGHT TO GO TO WHICHEVER SCHOOL IS MOST EFFECTIVE.
MY BOYFRIEND'S SO REASONABLE!

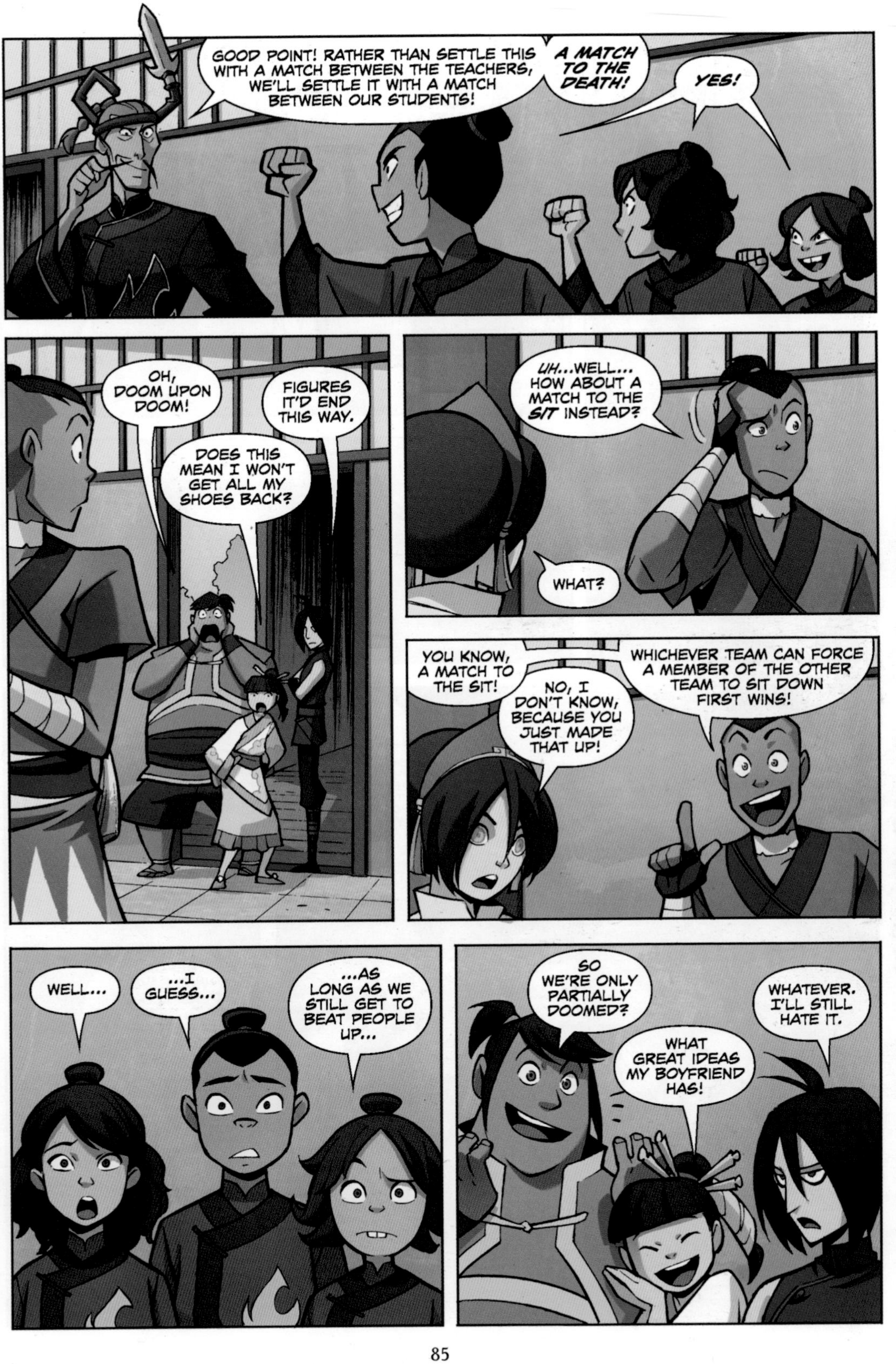
GOOD POINT! RATHER THAN SETTLE THIS WITH A MATCH BETWEEN THE TEACHERS, WE'LL SETTLE IT WITH A MATCH BETWEEN OUR STUDENTS!
A MATCH TO THE DEATH!
YES!
OH, DOOM UPON DOOM!
FIGURES IT'D END THIS WAY.
DOES THIS MEAN I WON'T GET ALL MY SHOES BACK?
UH...WELL... HOW ABOUT A MATCH TO THE SIT INSTEAD?
WHAT?
YOU KNOW, A MATCH TO THE SIT!
NO, I DON'T KNOW, BECAUSE YOU JUST MADE THAT UP!
WHICHEVER TEAM CAN FORCE A MEMBER OF THE OTHER TEAM TO SIT DOWN FIRST WINS!
WELL...
...I GUESS...
...AS LONG AS WE STILL GET TO BEAT PEOPLE UP...
SO WE'RE ONLY PARTIALLY DOOMED?
WHAT GREAT IDEAS MY BOYFRIEND HAS!
WHATEVER. I'LL STILL HATE IT.

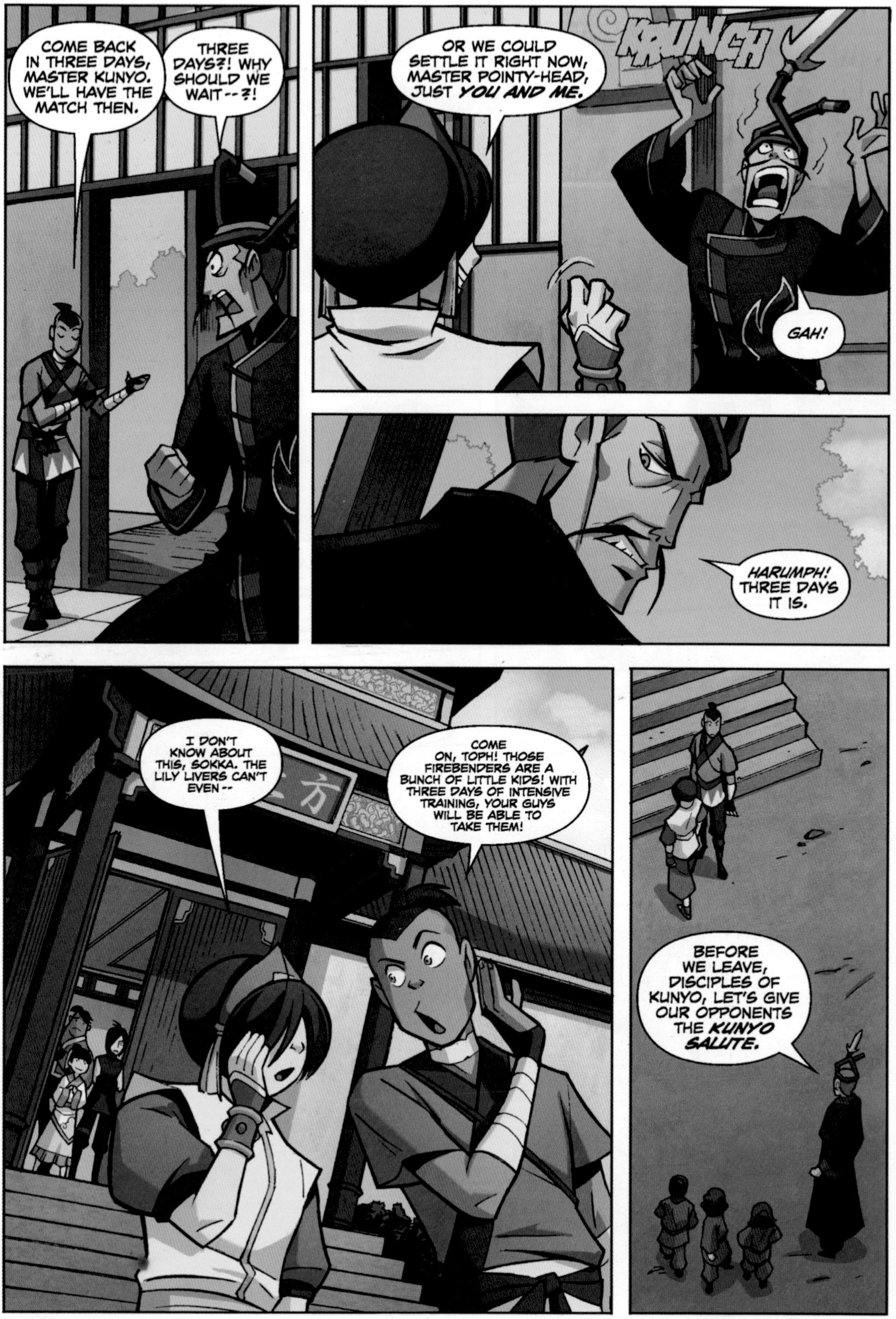
COME BACK IN THREE DAYS, MASTER KUNYO. WE'LL HAVE THE MATCH THEN.
THREE DAYS?! WHY SHOULD WE WAIT--?!
OR WE COULD SETTLE IT RIGHT NOW, MASTER POINTY-HEAD, JUST YOU AND ME.
KRUNCH
GAH!
HARUMPH! THREE DAYS IT IS.
I DON'T KNOW ABOUT THIS, SOKKA. THE LILY LIVERS CAN'T EVEN--
COME ON, TOPH! THOSE FIREBENDERS ARE A BUNCH OF LITTLE KIDS! WITH THREE DAYS OF INTENSIVE TRAINING, YOUR GUYS WILL BE ABLE TO TAKE THEM!
BEFORE WE LEAVE, DISCIPLES OF KUNYO, LET'S GIVE OUR OPPONENTS THE KUNYO SALUTE.

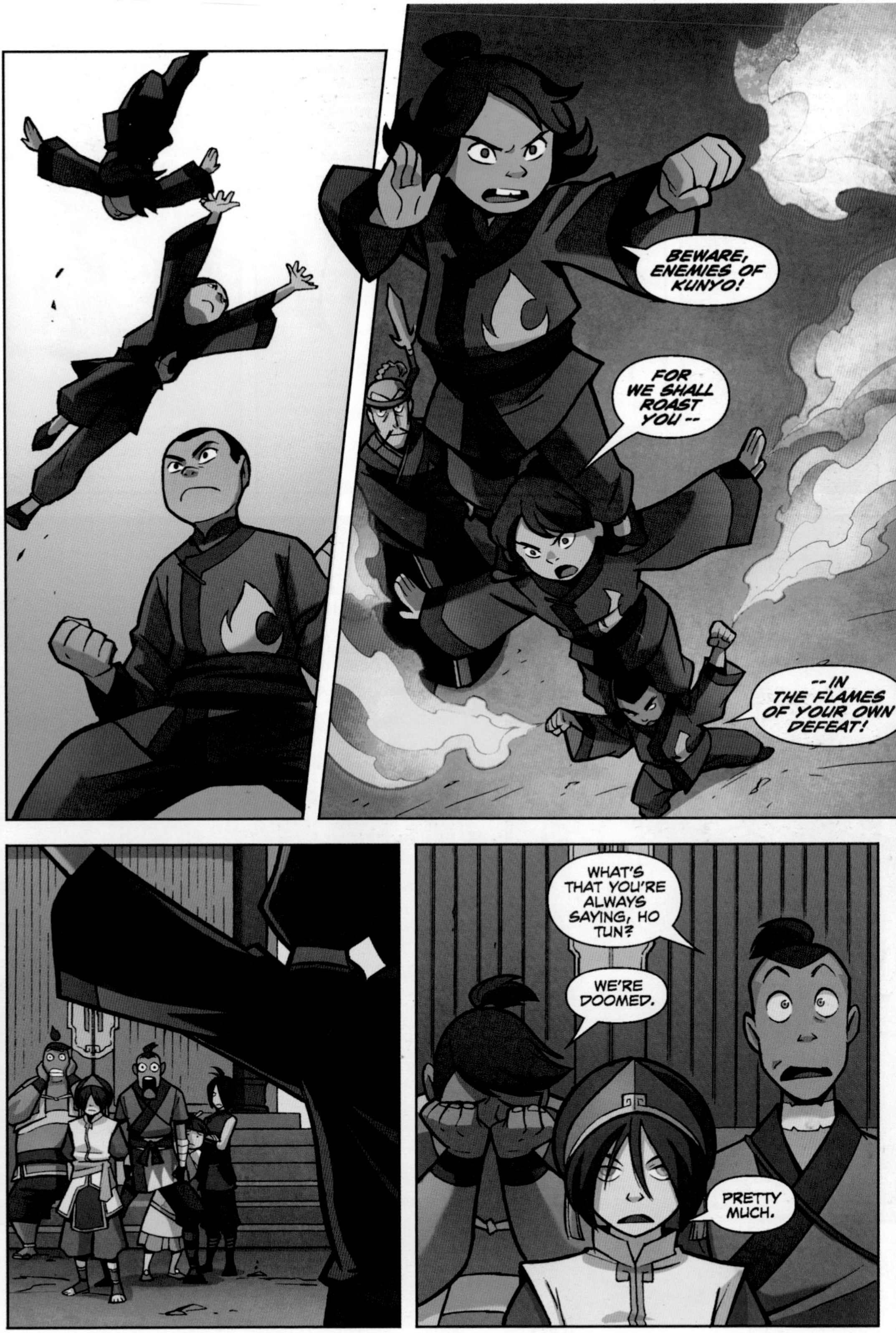
BEWARE, ENEMIES OF KUNYO!
FOR WE SHALL ROAST YOU --
-- IN THE FLAMES OF YOUR OWN DEFEAT!
WHAT'S THAT YOU'RE ALWAYS SAYING, HO TUN?
WE'RE DOOMED.
PRETTY MUCH.

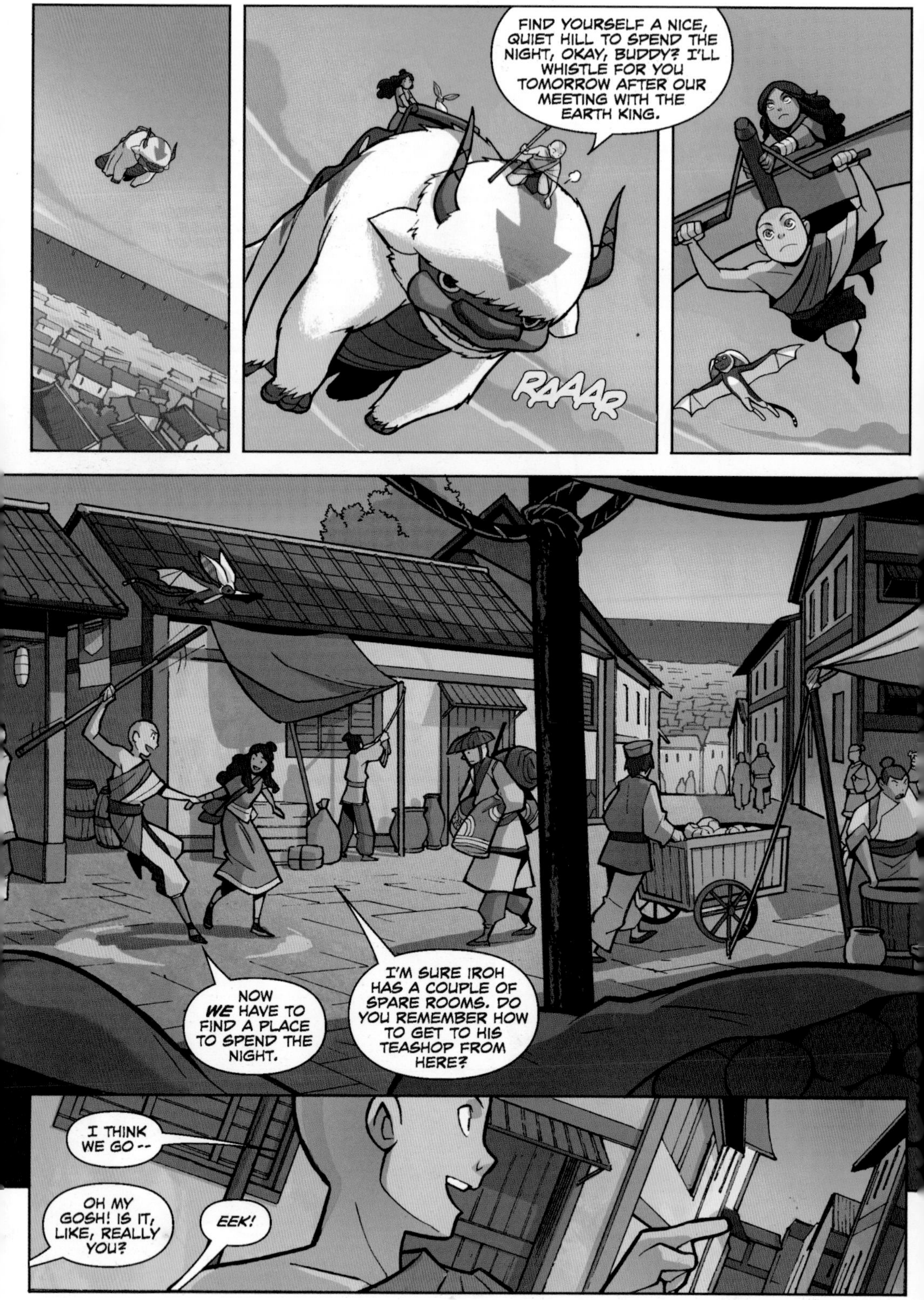
FIND YOURSELF A NICE, QUIET HILL TO SPEND THE NIGHT, OKAY, BUDDY? I'LL WHISTLE FOR YOU TOMORROW AFTER OUR MEETING WITH THE EARTH KING.
RAAAR
NOW *WE* HAVE TO FIND A PLACE TO SPEND THE NIGHT.
I'M SURE IROH HAS A COUPLE OF SPARE ROOMS. DO YOU REMEMBER HOW TO GET TO HIS TEASHOP FROM HERE?
I THINK WE GO --
OH MY GOSH! IS IT, LIKE, REALLY YOU?
EEK!

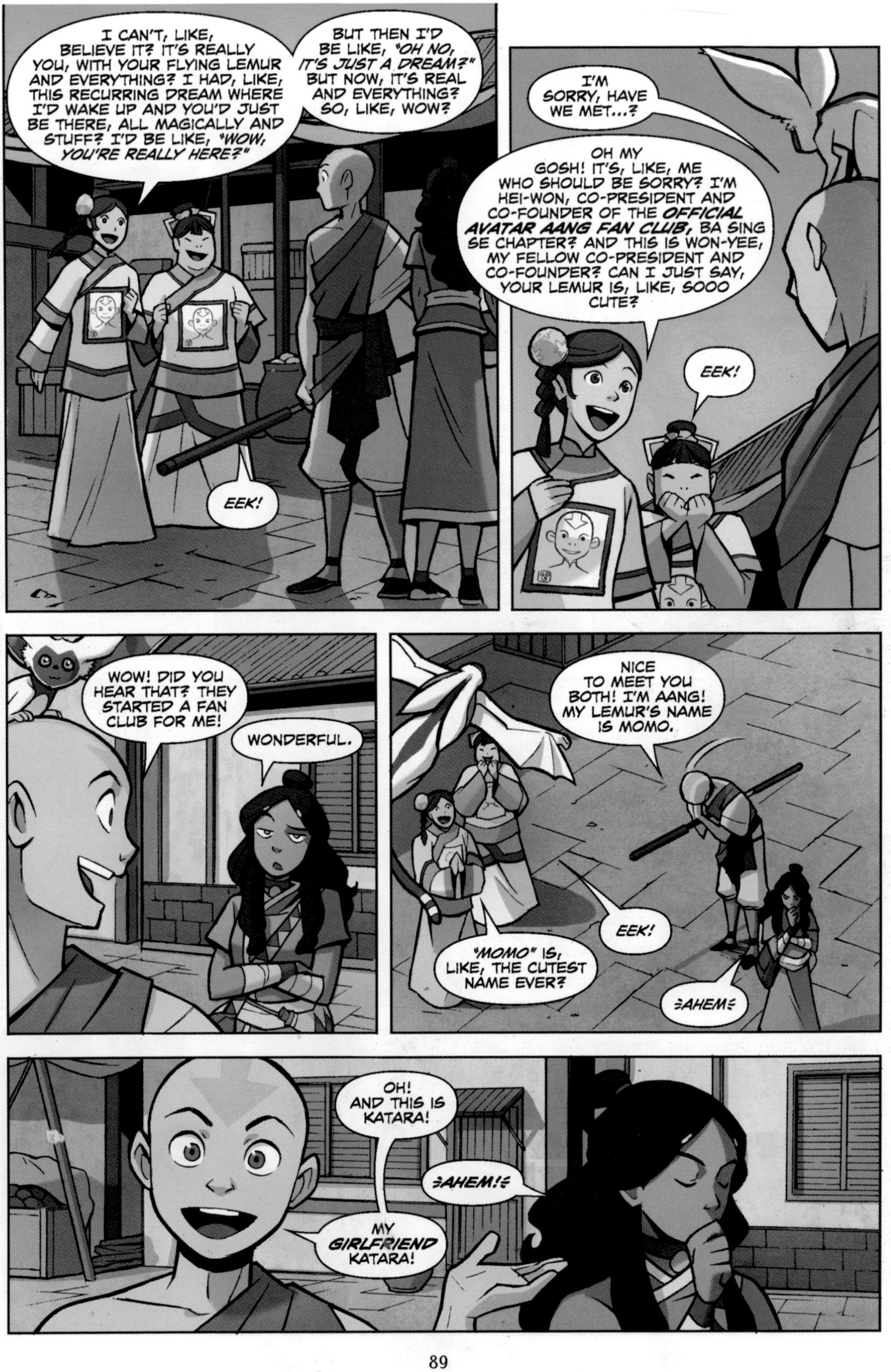
I CAN'T, LIKE, BELIEVE IT? IT'S REALLY YOU, WITH YOUR FLYING LEMUR AND EVERYTHING? I HAD, LIKE, THIS RECURRING DREAM WHERE I'D WAKE UP AND YOU'D JUST BE THERE, ALL MAGICALLY AND STUFF? I'D BE LIKE, "WOW, YOU'RE REALLY HERE?"
BUT THEN I'D BE LIKE, "OH NO, IT'S JUST A DREAM?" BUT NOW, IT'S REAL AND EVERYTHING? SO, LIKE, WOW?
EEK!
I'M SORRY, HAVE WE MET...?
OH MY GOSH! IT'S, LIKE, ME WHO SHOULD BE SORRY? I'M HEI-WON, CO-PRESIDENT AND CO-FOUNDER OF THE OFFICIAL AVATAR AANG FAN CLUB, BA SING SE CHAPTER? AND THIS IS WON-YEE, MY FELLOW CO-PRESIDENT AND CO-FOUNDER? CAN I JUST SAY, YOUR LEMUR IS, LIKE, SOOO CUTE?
EEK!
WOW! DID YOU HEAR THAT? THEY STARTED A FAN CLUB FOR ME!
WONDERFUL.
NICE TO MEET YOU BOTH! I'M AANG! MY LEMUR'S NAME IS MOMO.
EEK!
"MOMO" IS, LIKE, THE CUTEST NAME EVER?
AHEM
OH! AND THIS IS KATARA!
AHEM!
MY GIRLFRIEND KATARA!

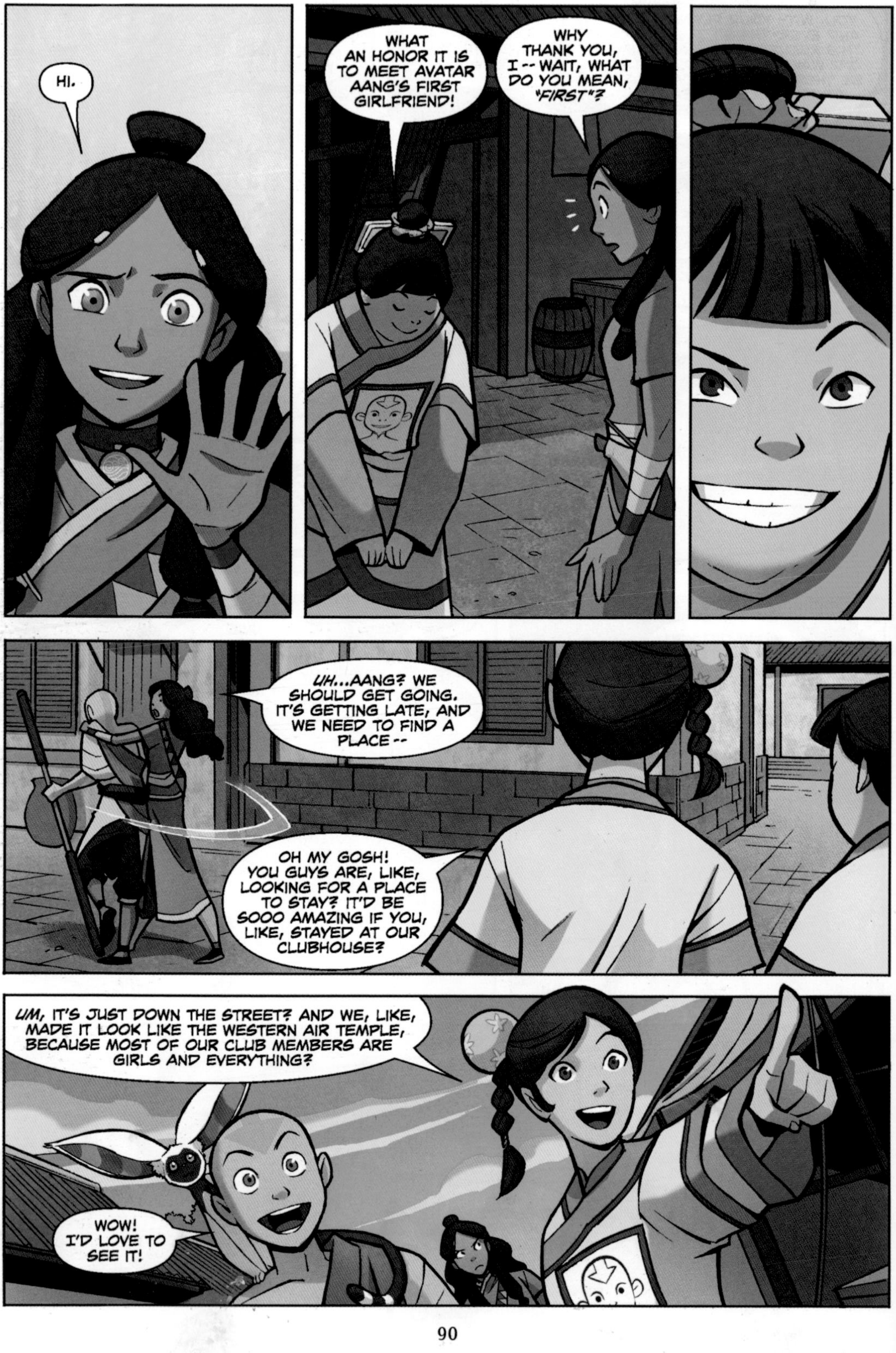
HI.
WHAT AN HONOR IT IS TO MEET AVATAR AANG'S FIRST GIRLFRIEND!
WHY THANK YOU, I -- WAIT, WHAT DO YOU MEAN, "FIRST"?
UH...AANG? WE SHOULD GET GOING. IT'S GETTING LATE, AND WE NEED TO FIND A PLACE --
OH MY GOSH! YOU GUYS ARE, LIKE, LOOKING FOR A PLACE TO STAY? IT'D BE SOOO AMAZING IF YOU, LIKE, STAYED AT OUR CLUBHOUSE?
UM, IT'S JUST DOWN THE STREET? AND WE, LIKE, MADE IT LOOK LIKE THE WESTERN AIR TEMPLE, BECAUSE MOST OF OUR CLUB MEMBERS ARE GIRLS AND EVERYTHING?
WOW! I'D LOVE TO SEE IT!

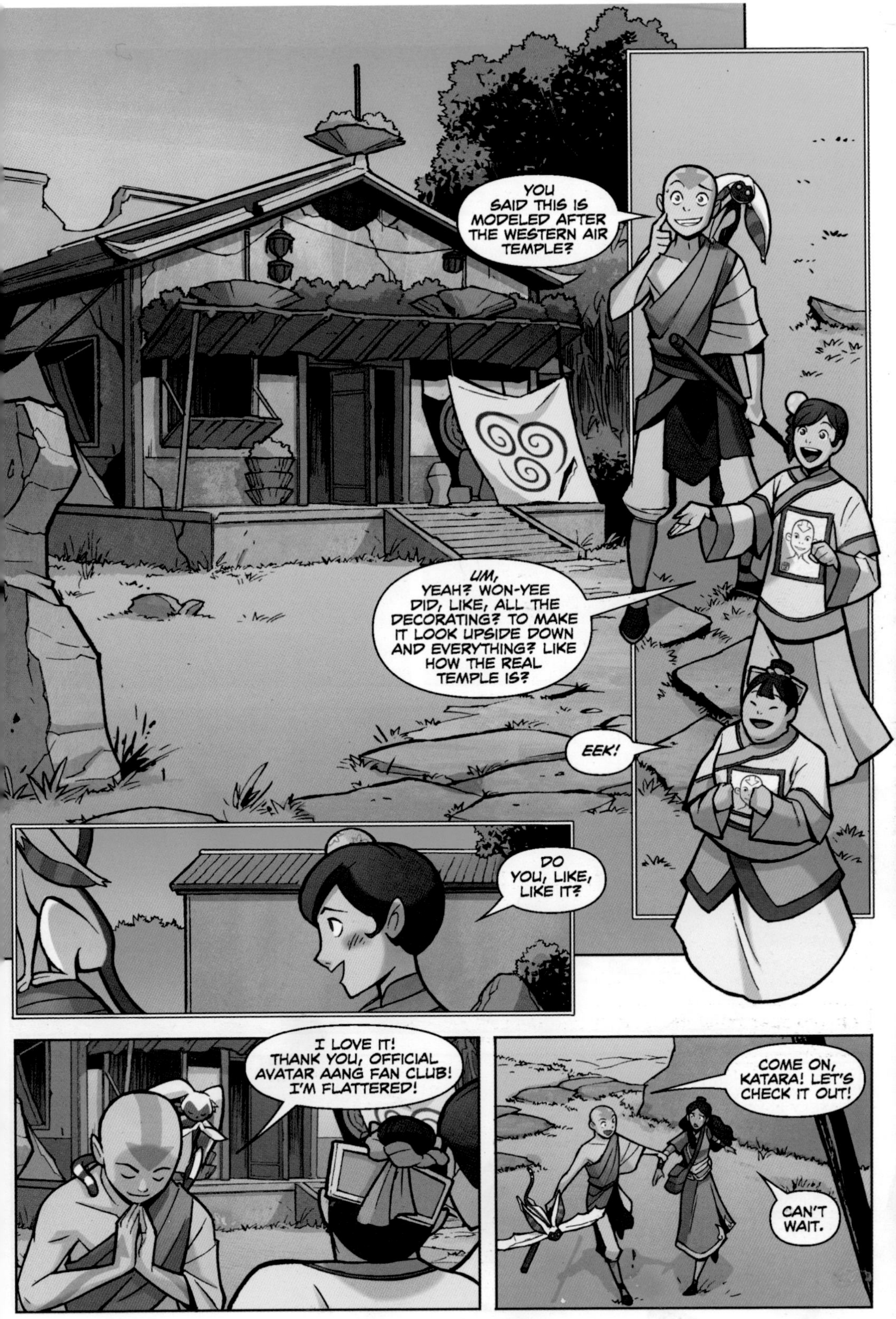
YOU SAID THIS IS MODELED AFTER THE WESTERN AIR TEMPLE?
UM, YEAH? WON-YEE DID, LIKE, ALL THE DECORATING? TO MAKE IT LOOK UPSIDE DOWN AND EVERYTHING? LIKE HOW THE REAL TEMPLE IS?
EEK!
DO YOU, LIKE, LIKE IT?
I LOVE IT! THANK YOU, OFFICIAL AVATAR AANG FAN CLUB! I'M FLATTERED!
COME ON, KATARA! LET'S CHECK IT OUT!
CAN'T WAIT.

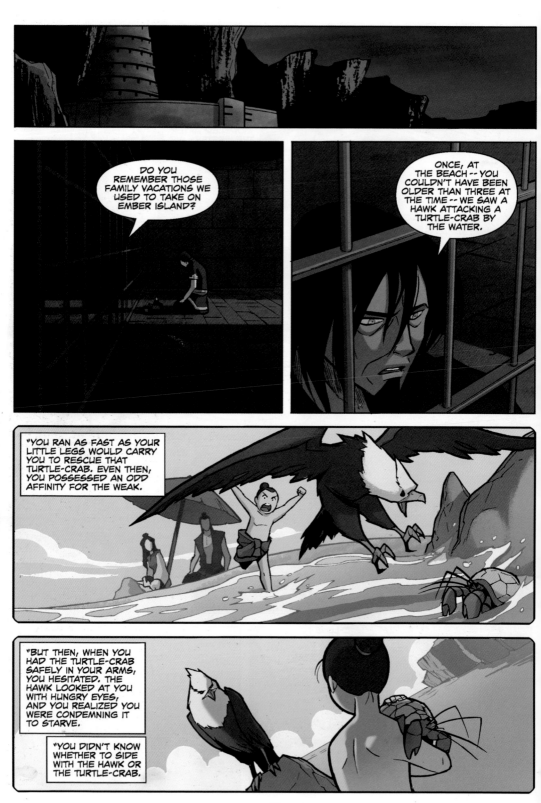

DO YOU REMEMBER THOSE FAMILY VACATIONS WE USED TO TAKE ON EMBER ISLAND?

ONCE, AT THE BEACH -- YOU COULDN'T HAVE BEEN OLDER THAN THREE AT THE TIME -- WE SAW A HAWK ATTACKING A TURTLE-CRAB BY THE WATER.

"YOU RAN AS FAST AS YOUR LITTLE LEGS WOULD CARRY YOU TO RESCUE THAT TURTLE-CRAB. EVEN THEN, YOU POSSESSED AN ODD AFFINITY FOR THE WEAK.

"BUT THEN, WHEN YOU HAD THE TURTLE-CRAB SAFELY IN YOUR ARMS, YOU HESITATED. THE HAWK LOOKED AT YOU WITH HUNGRY EYES, AND YOU REALIZED YOU WERE CONDEMNING IT TO STARVE.

"YOU DIDN'T KNOW WHETHER TO SIDE WITH THE HAWK OR THE TURTLE-CRAB.

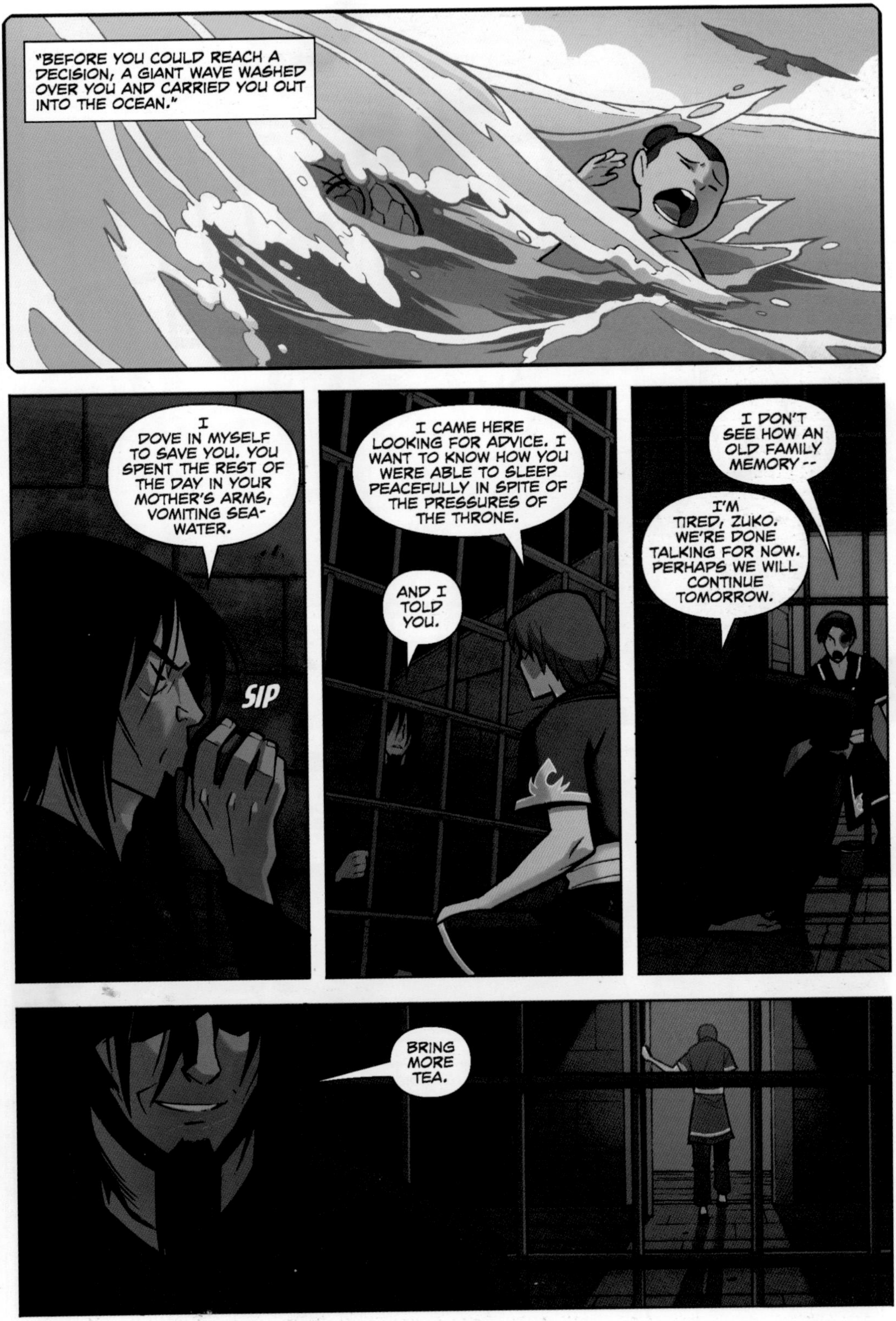
"BEFORE YOU COULD REACH A DECISION, A GIANT WAVE WASHED OVER YOU AND CARRIED YOU OUT INTO THE OCEAN."
I DOVE IN MYSELF TO SAVE YOU. YOU SPENT THE REST OF THE DAY IN YOUR MOTHER'S ARMS, VOMITING SEA-WATER.
SIP
I CAME HERE LOOKING FOR ADVICE. I WANT TO KNOW HOW YOU WERE ABLE TO SLEEP PEACEFULLY IN SPITE OF THE PRESSURES OF THE THRONE.
AND I TOLD YOU.
I DON'T SEE HOW AN OLD FAMILY MEMORY --
I'M TIRED, ZUKO. WE'RE DONE TALKING FOR NOW. PERHAPS WE WILL CONTINUE TOMORROW.
BRING MORE TEA.

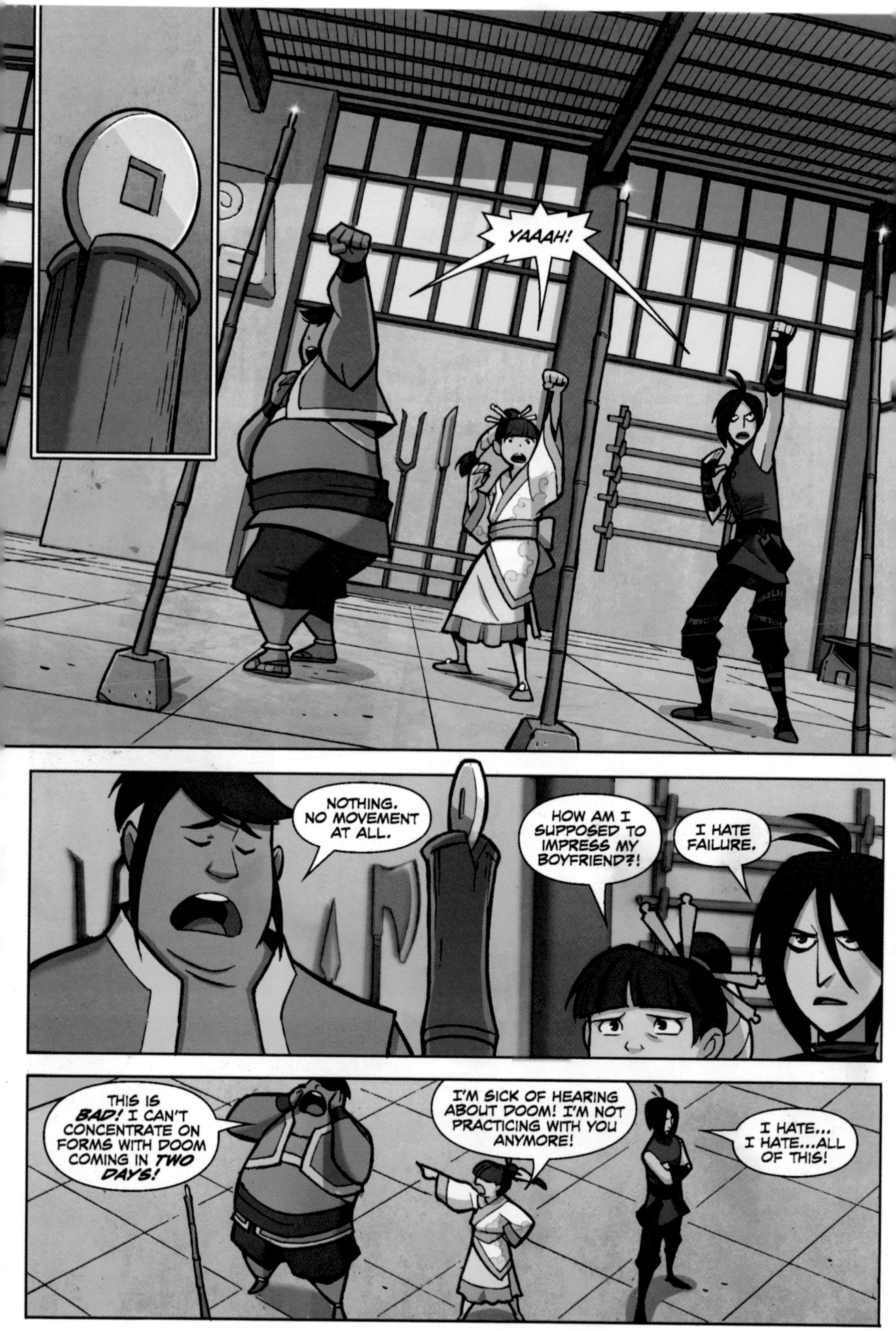
YAAAH!
NOTHING. NO MOVEMENT AT ALL.
HOW AM I SUPPOSED TO IMPRESS MY BOYFRIEND?!
I HATE FAILURE.
THIS IS *BAD!* I CAN'T CONCENTRATE ON FORMS WITH DOOM COMING IN *TWO DAYS!*
I'M SICK OF HEARING ABOUT DOOM! I'M NOT PRACTICING WITH YOU ANYMORE!
I HATE... I HATE...ALL OF THIS!

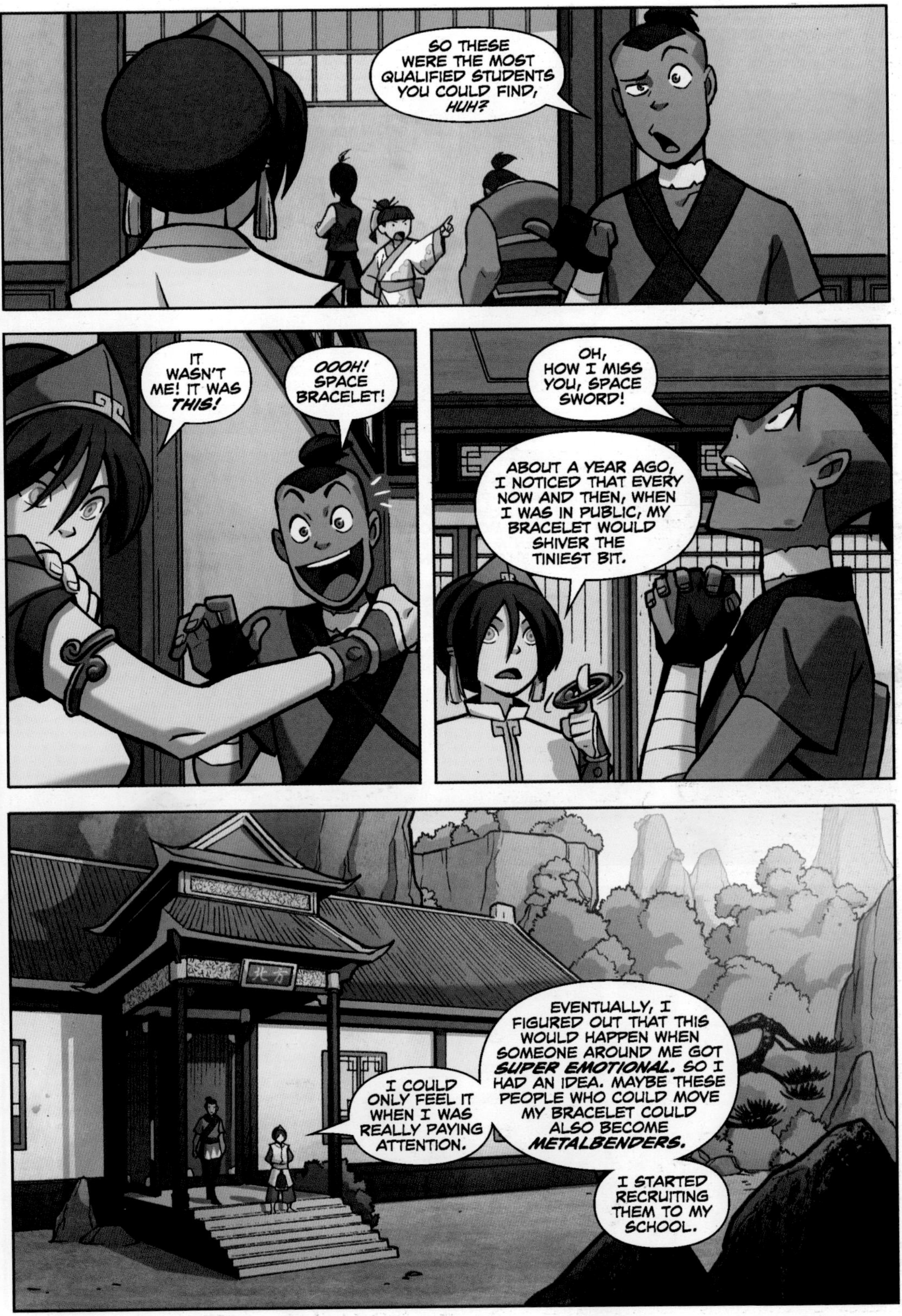
SO THESE WERE THE MOST QUALIFIED STUDENTS YOU COULD FIND, HUH?
IT WASN'T ME! IT WAS THIS!
OOOH! SPACE BRACELET!
OH, HOW I MISS YOU, SPACE SWORD!
ABOUT A YEAR AGO, I NOTICED THAT EVERY NOW AND THEN, WHEN I WAS IN PUBLIC, MY BRACELET WOULD SHIVER THE TINIEST BIT.
I COULD ONLY FEEL IT WHEN I WAS REALLY PAYING ATTENTION.
EVENTUALLY, I FIGURED OUT THAT THIS WOULD HAPPEN WHEN SOMEONE AROUND ME GOT SUPER EMOTIONAL. SO I HAD AN IDEA. MAYBE THESE PEOPLE WHO COULD MOVE MY BRACELET COULD ALSO BECOME METALBENDERS.
I STARTED RECRUITING THEM TO MY SCHOOL.

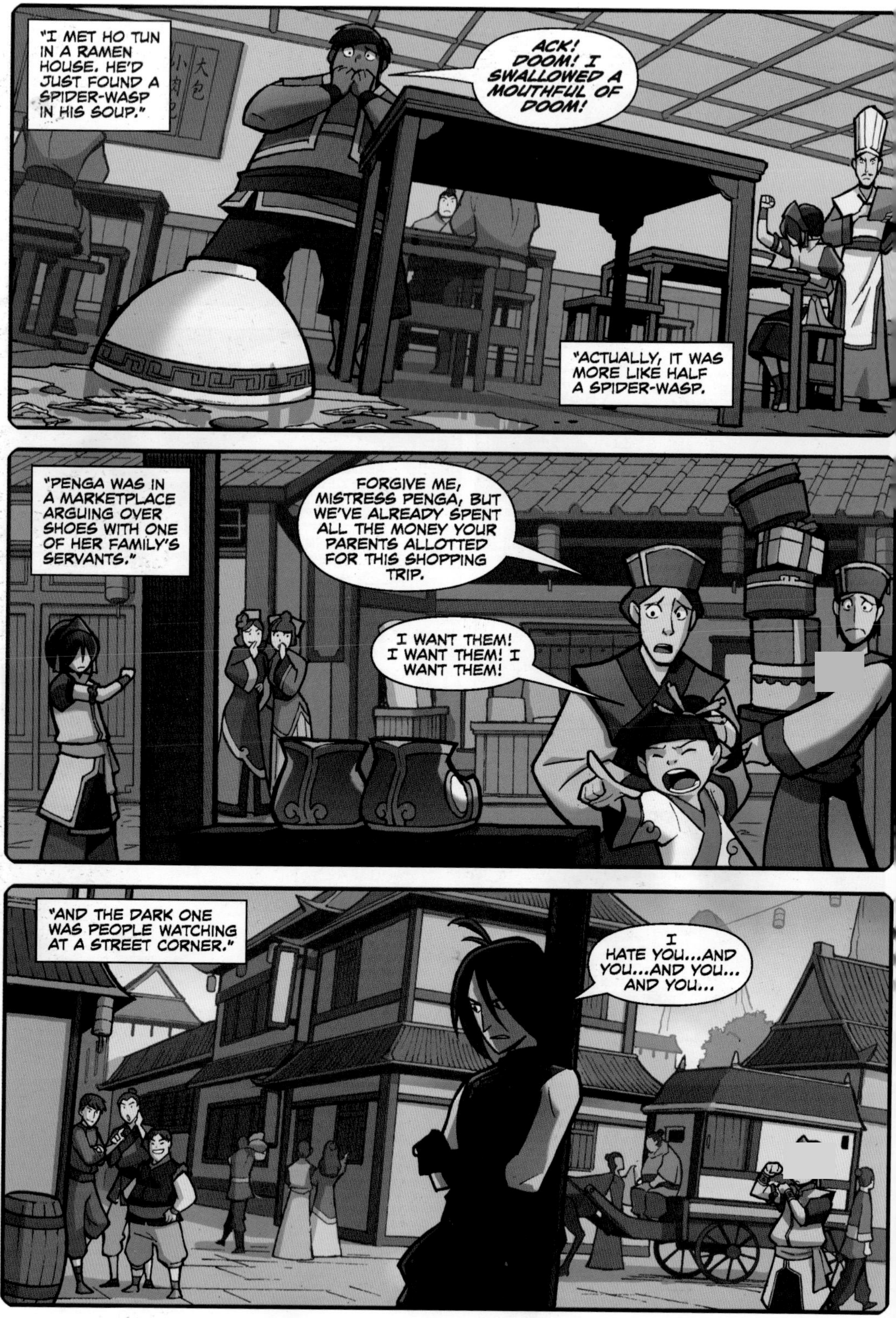
"I MET HO TUN IN A RAMEN HOUSE. HE'D JUST FOUND A SPIDER-WASP IN HIS SOUP."
ACK! DOOM! I SWALLOWED A MOUTHFUL OF DOOM!
"ACTUALLY, IT WAS MORE LIKE HALF A SPIDER-WASP.
"PENGA WAS IN A MARKETPLACE ARGUING OVER SHOES WITH ONE OF HER FAMILY'S SERVANTS."
FORGIVE ME, MISTRESS PENGA, BUT WE'VE ALREADY SPENT ALL THE MONEY YOUR PARENTS ALLOTTED FOR THIS SHOPPING TRIP.
I WANT THEM! I WANT THEM! I WANT THEM!
"AND THE DARK ONE WAS PEOPLE WATCHING AT A STREET CORNER."
I HATE YOU...AND YOU...AND YOU... AND YOU...

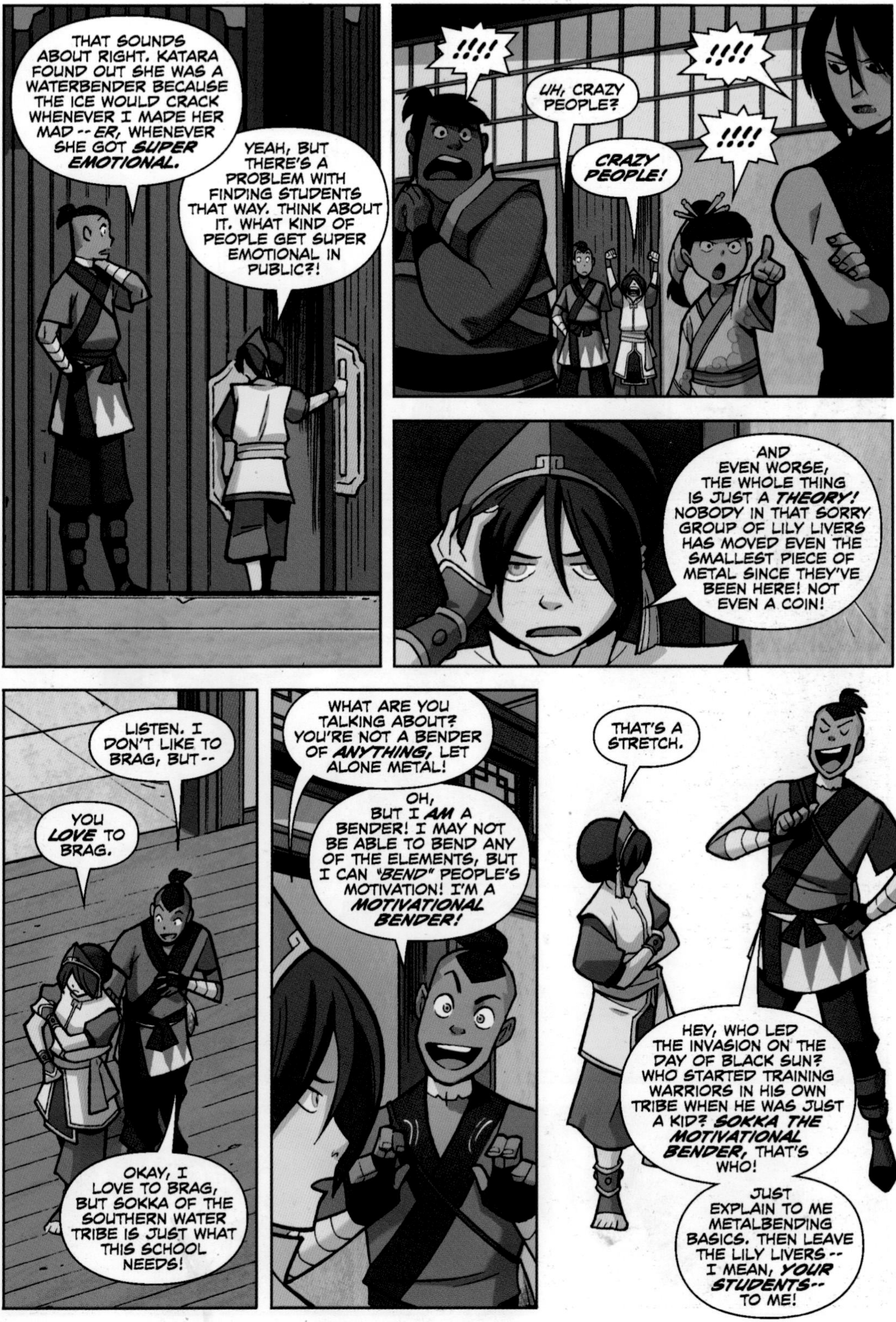
THAT SOUNDS ABOUT RIGHT. KATARA FOUND OUT SHE WAS A WATERBENDER BECAUSE THE ICE WOULD CRACK WHENEVER I MADE HER MAD -- *ER,* WHENEVER SHE GOT ***SUPER EMOTIONAL.***
YEAH, BUT THERE'S A PROBLEM WITH FINDING STUDENTS THAT WAY. THINK ABOUT IT. WHAT KIND OF PEOPLE GET SUPER EMOTIONAL IN PUBLIC?!
!!!!
UH, CRAZY PEOPLE?
!!!!
!!!!
CRAZY PEOPLE!
AND EVEN WORSE, THE WHOLE THING IS JUST A ***THEORY!*** NOBODY IN THAT SORRY GROUP OF LILY LIVERS HAS MOVED EVEN THE SMALLEST PIECE OF METAL SINCE THEY'VE BEEN HERE! NOT EVEN A COIN!
LISTEN. I DON'T LIKE TO BRAG, BUT--
YOU ***LOVE*** TO BRAG.
OKAY, I LOVE TO BRAG, BUT SOKKA OF THE SOUTHERN WATER TRIBE IS JUST WHAT THIS SCHOOL NEEDS!
WHAT ARE YOU TALKING ABOUT? YOU'RE NOT A BENDER OF ***ANYTHING,*** LET ALONE METAL!
OH, BUT I ***AM*** A BENDER! I MAY NOT BE ABLE TO BEND ANY OF THE ELEMENTS, BUT I CAN *"BEND"* PEOPLE'S MOTIVATION! I'M A ***MOTIVATIONAL BENDER!***
THAT'S A STRETCH.
HEY, WHO LED THE INVASION ON THE DAY OF BLACK SUN? WHO STARTED TRAINING WARRIORS IN HIS OWN TRIBE WHEN HE WAS JUST A KID? ***SOKKA THE MOTIVATIONAL BENDER,*** THAT'S WHO!
JUST EXPLAIN TO ME METALBENDING BASICS. THEN LEAVE THE LILY LIVERS -- I MEAN, ***YOUR STUDENTS***-- TO ME!

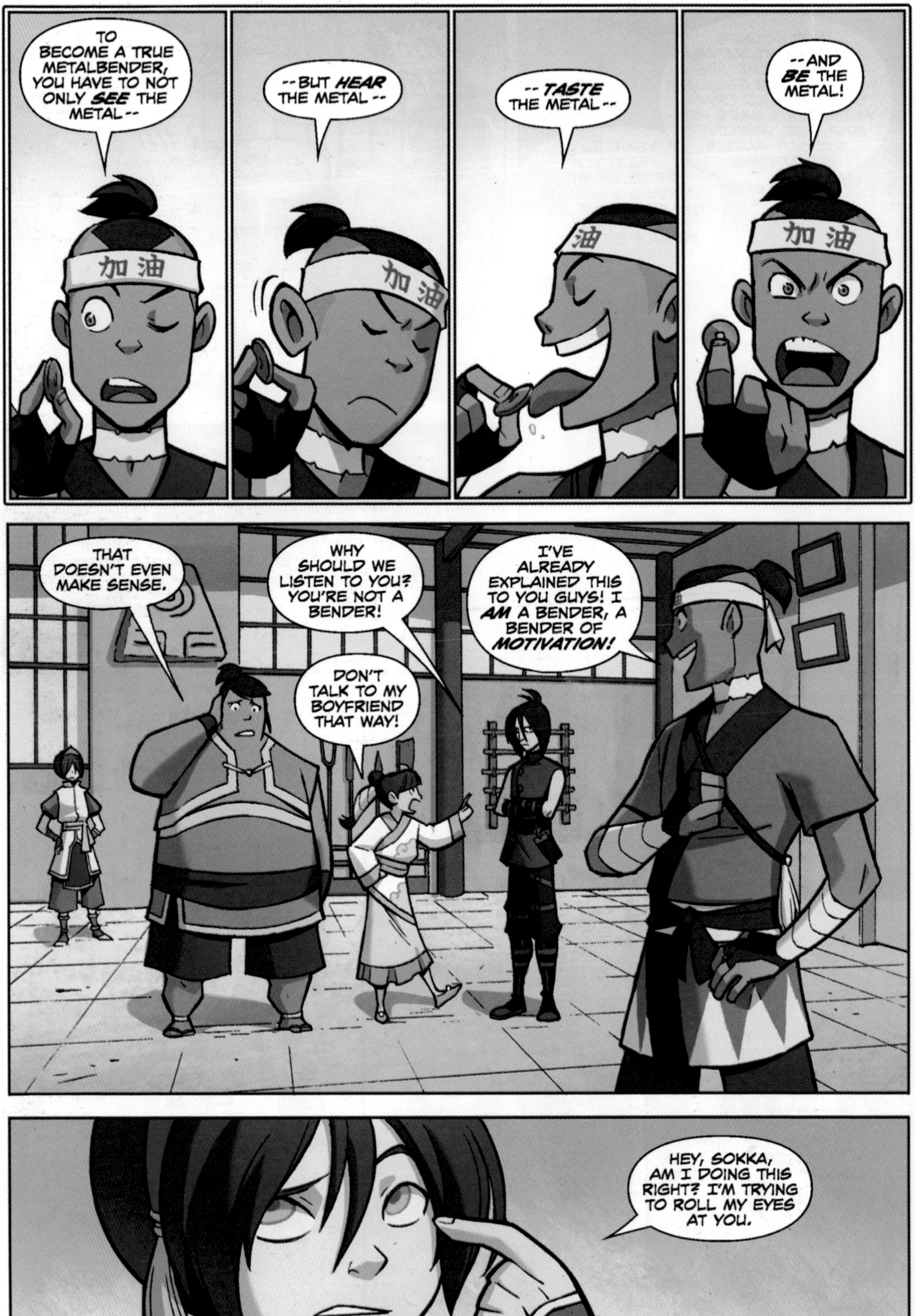
TO BECOME A TRUE METALBENDER, YOU HAVE TO NOT ONLY SEE THE METAL--
加油
--BUT HEAR THE METAL--
加油
--TASTE THE METAL--
油
--AND BE THE METAL!
加油
THAT DOESN'T EVEN MAKE SENSE.
WHY SHOULD WE LISTEN TO YOU? YOU'RE NOT A BENDER!
DON'T TALK TO MY BOYFRIEND THAT WAY!
I'VE ALREADY EXPLAINED THIS TO YOU GUYS! I AM A BENDER, A BENDER OF MOTIVATION!
HEY, SOKKA, AM I DOING THIS RIGHT? I'M TRYING TO ROLL MY EYES AT YOU.

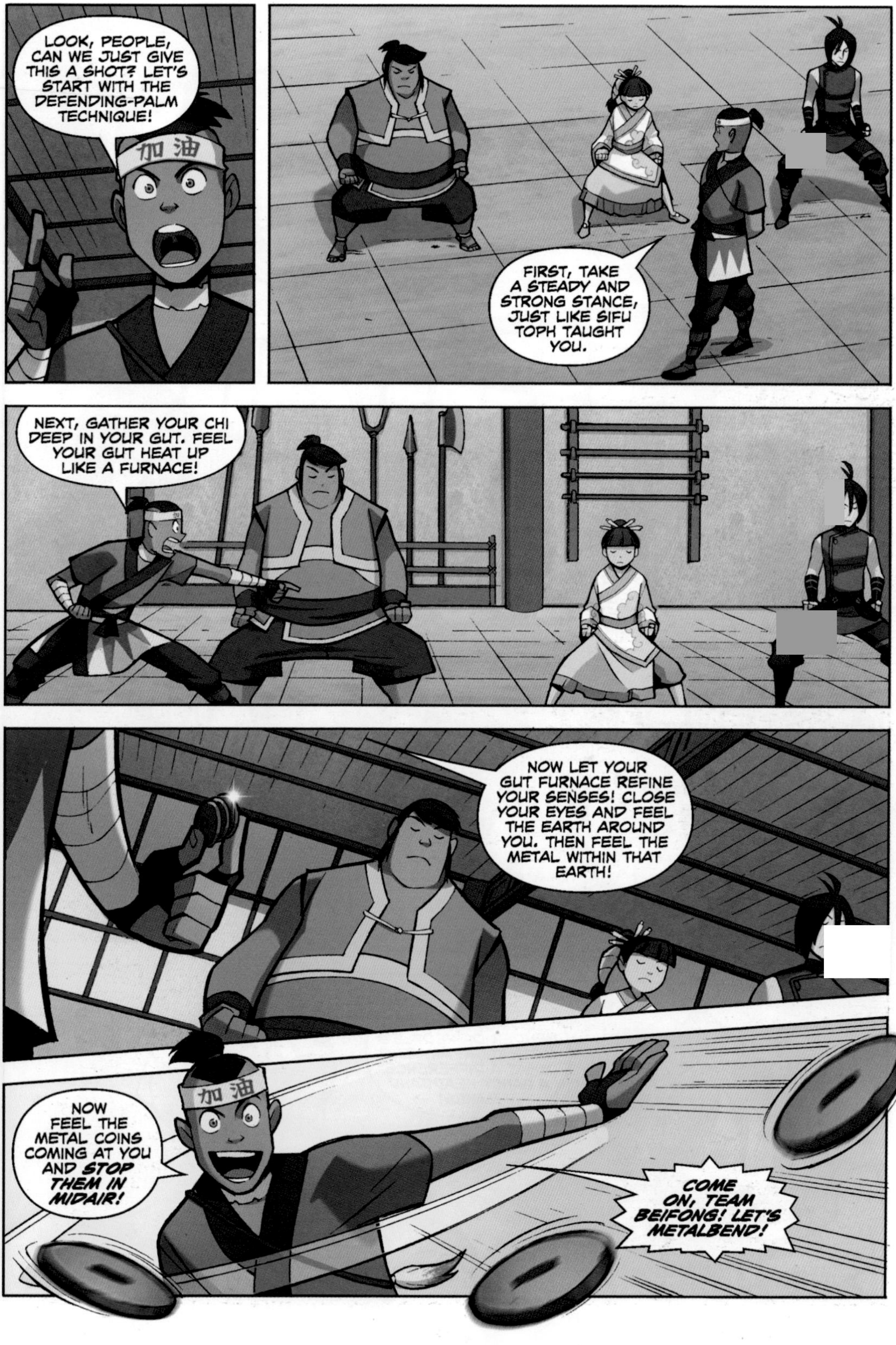

LOOK, PEOPLE, CAN WE JUST GIVE THIS A SHOT? LET'S START WITH THE DEFENDING-PALM TECHNIQUE!
加油
FIRST, TAKE A STEADY AND STRONG STANCE, JUST LIKE SIFU TOPH TAUGHT YOU.
NEXT, GATHER YOUR CHI DEEP IN YOUR GUT. FEEL YOUR GUT HEAT UP LIKE A FURNACE!
NOW LET YOUR GUT FURNACE REFINE YOUR SENSES! CLOSE YOUR EYES AND FEEL THE EARTH AROUND YOU. THEN FEEL THE METAL WITHIN THAT EARTH!
加油
NOW FEEL THE METAL COINS COMING AT YOU AND *STOP THEM IN MIDAIR!*
COME ON, TEAM BEIFONG! LET'S METALBEND!

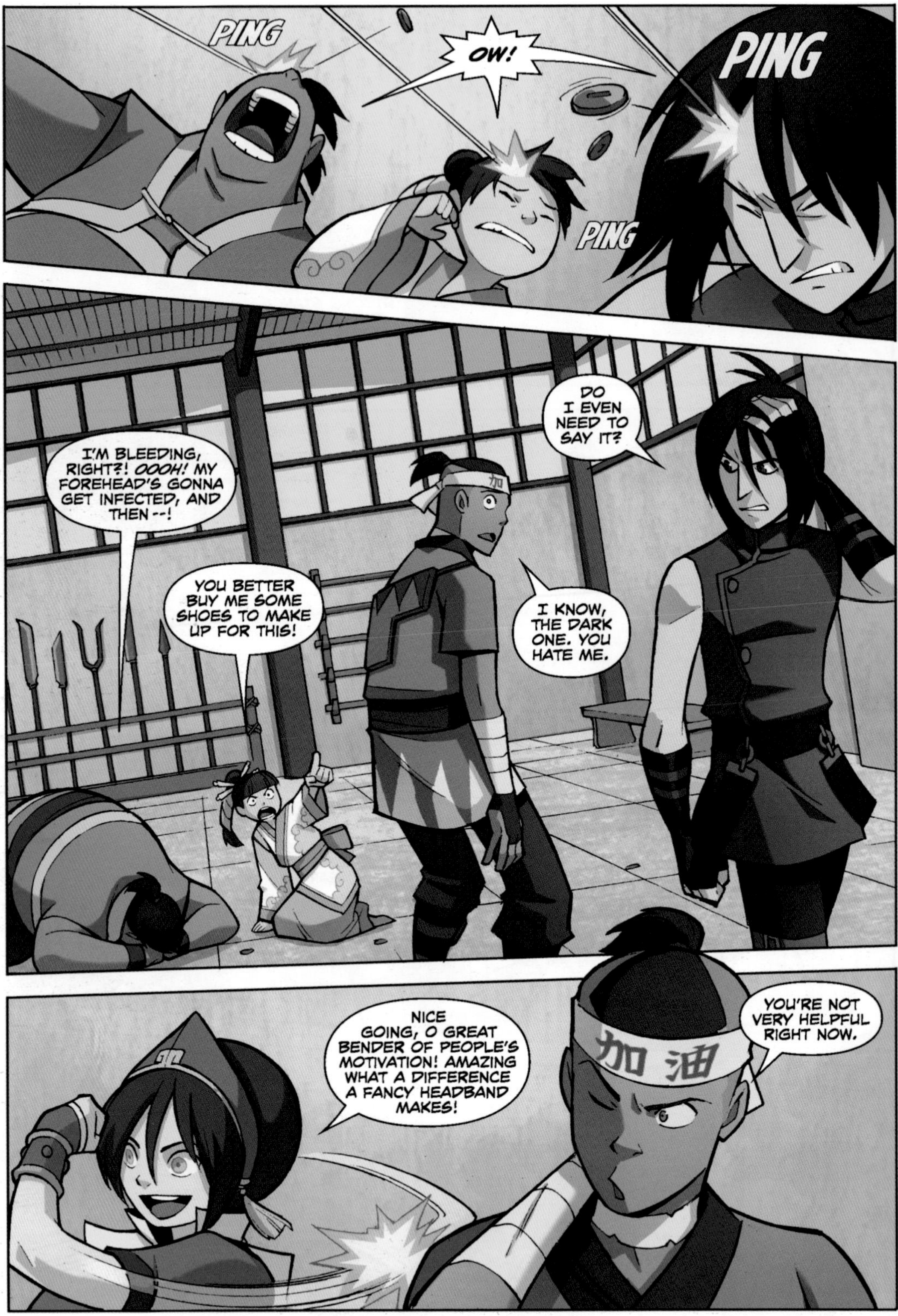
PING
OW!
PING
PING
I'M BLEEDING, RIGHT?! OOOH! MY FOREHEAD'S GONNA GET INFECTED, AND THEN --!
YOU BETTER BUY ME SOME SHOES TO MAKE UP FOR THIS!
DO I EVEN NEED TO SAY IT?
I KNOW, THE DARK ONE. YOU HATE ME.
NICE GOING, O GREAT BENDER OF PEOPLE'S MOTIVATION! AMAZING WHAT A DIFFERENCE A FANCY HEADBAND MAKES!
YOU'RE NOT VERY HELPFUL RIGHT NOW.
加油

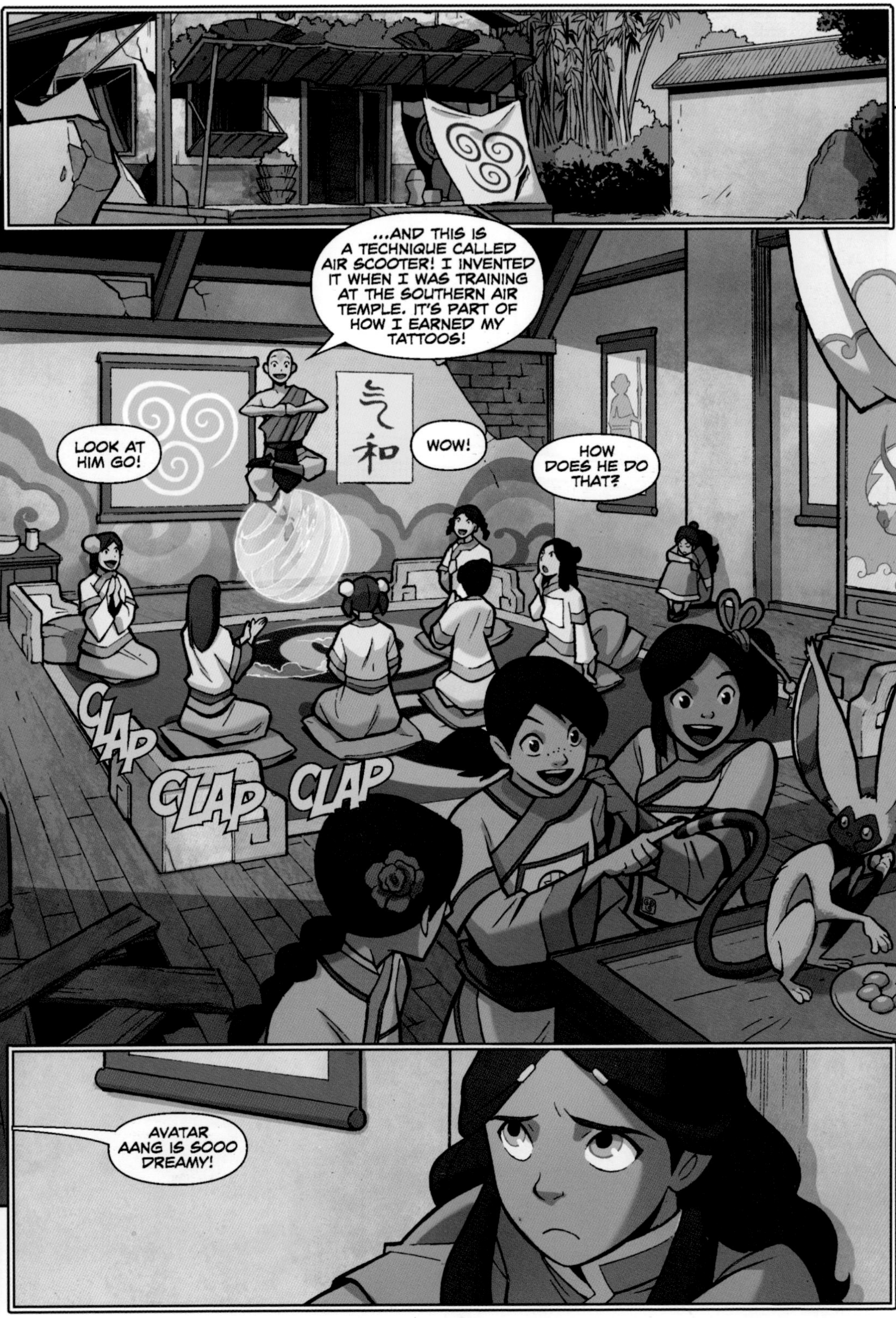
...AND THIS IS A TECHNIQUE CALLED AIR SCOOTER! I INVENTED IT WHEN I WAS TRAINING AT THE SOUTHERN AIR TEMPLE. IT'S PART OF HOW I EARNED MY TATTOOS!
LOOK AT HIM GO!
WOW!
HOW DOES HE DO THAT?
CLAP
CLAP
CLAP
AVATAR AANG IS SOOO DREAMY!

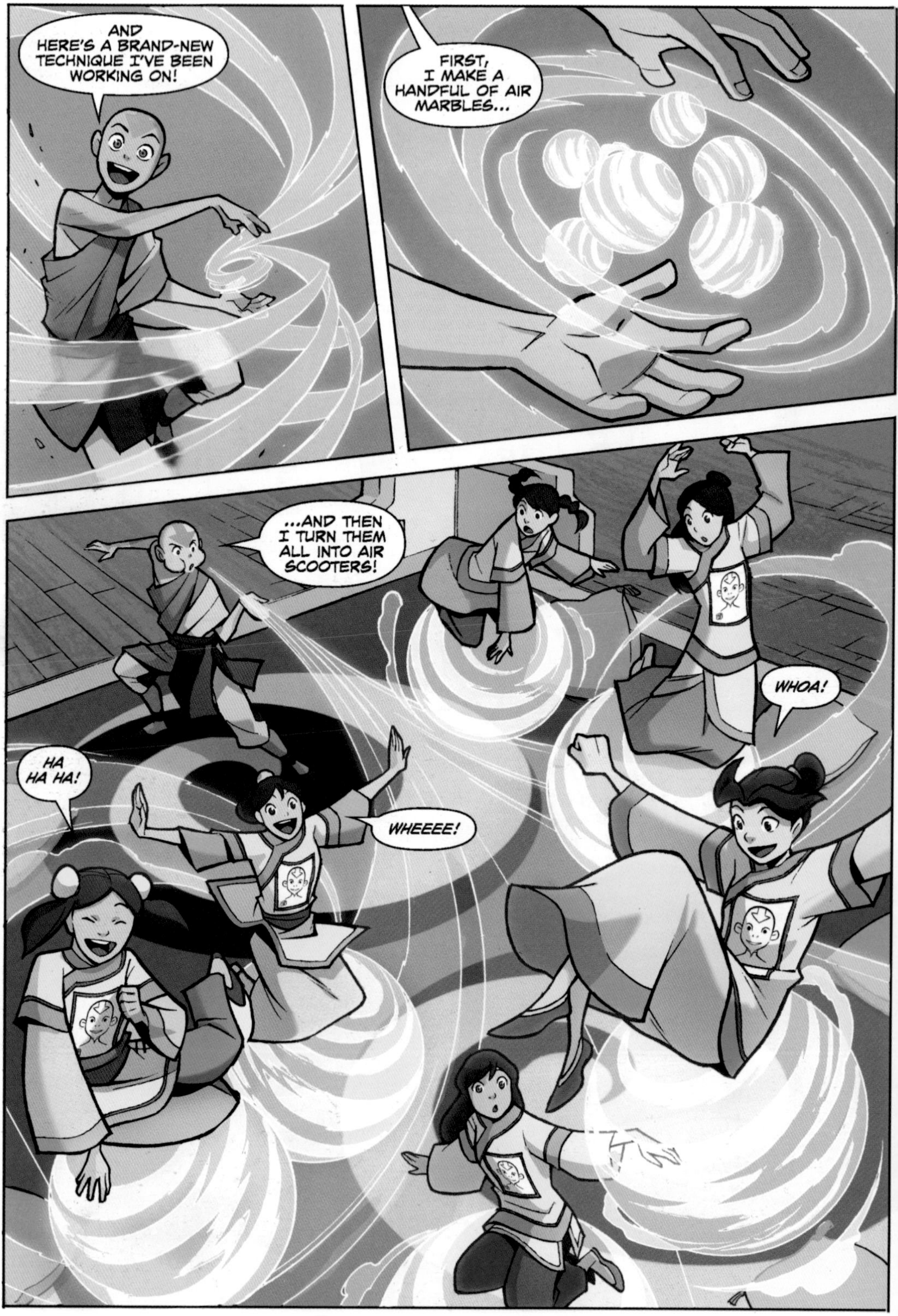
AND HERE'S A BRAND-NEW TECHNIQUE I'VE BEEN WORKING ON!
FIRST, I MAKE A HANDFUL OF AIR MARBLES...
...AND THEN I TURN THEM ALL INTO AIR SCOOTERS!
WHOA!
HA HA HA!
WHEEEE!

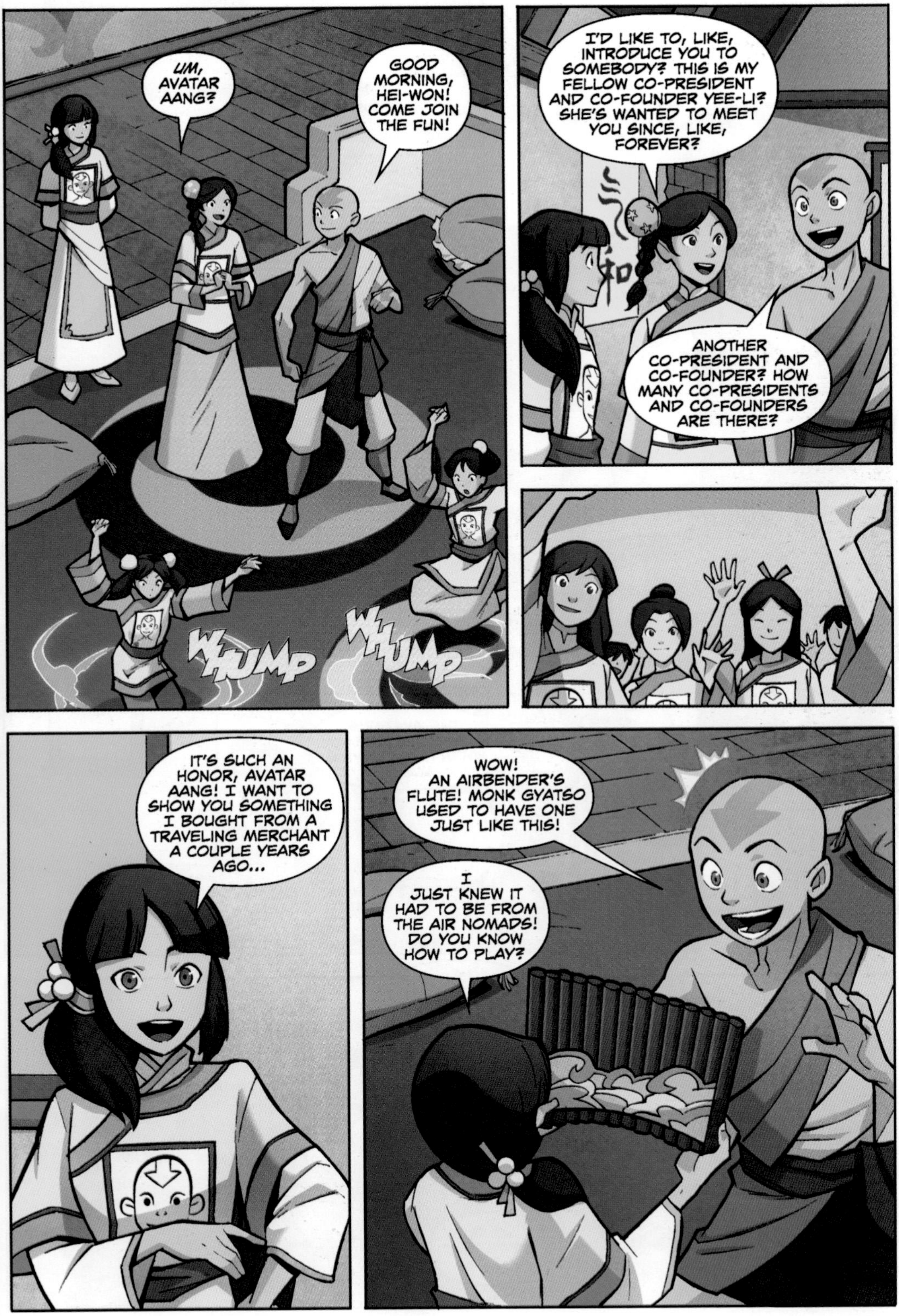
UM, AVATAR AANG?
GOOD MORNING, HEI-WON! COME JOIN THE FUN!
WHUMP
WHUMP
I'D LIKE TO, LIKE, INTRODUCE YOU TO SOMEBODY? THIS IS MY FELLOW CO-PRESIDENT AND CO-FOUNDER YEE-LI? SHE'S WANTED TO MEET YOU SINCE, LIKE, FOREVER?
ANOTHER CO-PRESIDENT AND CO-FOUNDER? HOW MANY CO-PRESIDENTS AND CO-FOUNDERS ARE THERE?
IT'S SUCH AN HONOR, AVATAR AANG! I WANT TO SHOW YOU SOMETHING I BOUGHT FROM A TRAVELING MERCHANT A COUPLE YEARS AGO...
WOW! AN AIRBENDER'S FLUTE! MONK GYATSO USED TO HAVE ONE JUST LIKE THIS!
I JUST KNEW IT HAD TO BE FROM THE AIR NOMADS! DO YOU KNOW HOW TO PLAY?

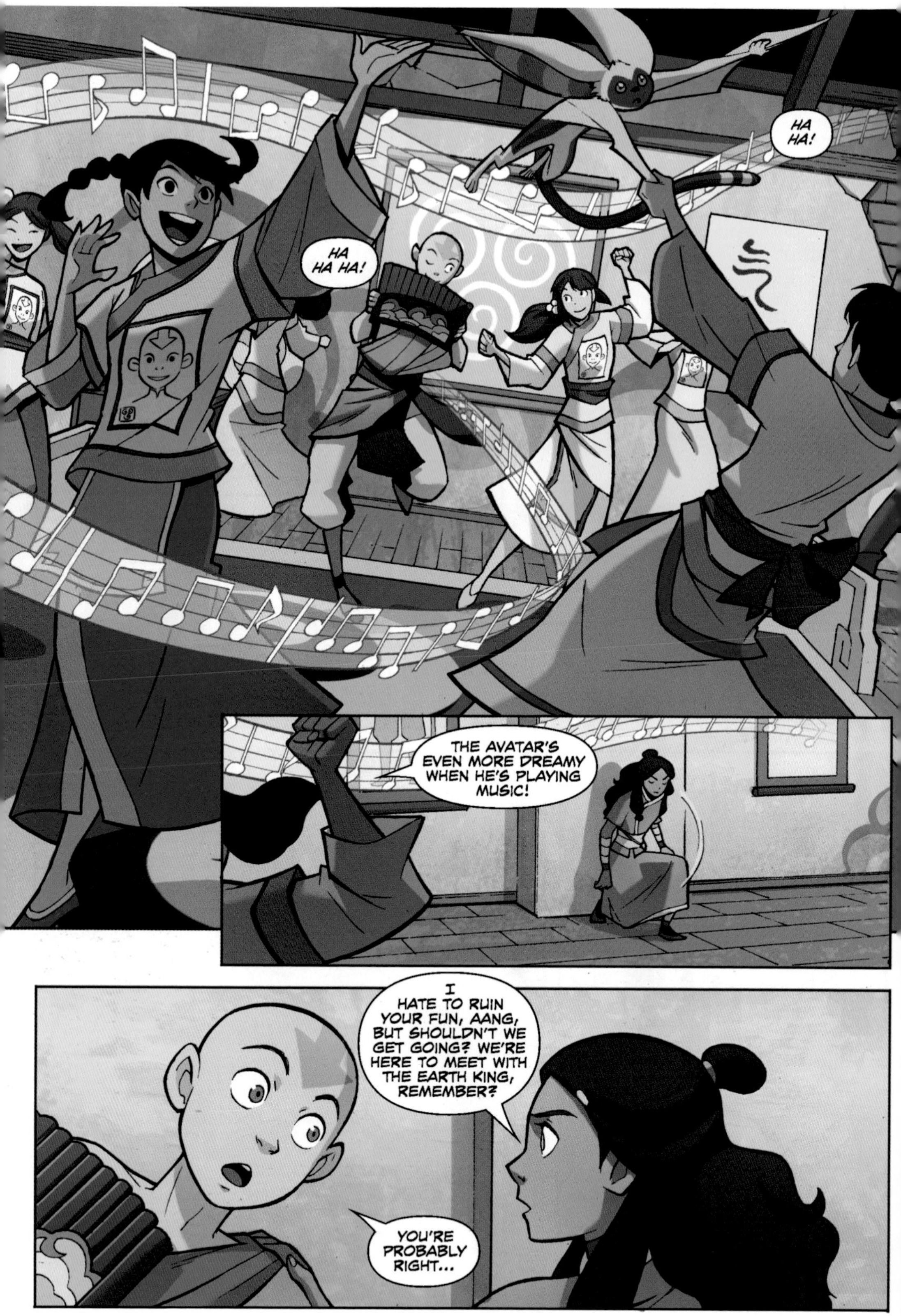
HA HA!
HA HA HA!
THE AVATAR'S EVEN MORE DREAMY WHEN HE'S PLAYING MUSIC!
I HATE TO RUIN YOUR FUN, AANG, BUT SHOULDN'T WE GET GOING? WE'RE HERE TO MEET WITH THE EARTH KING, REMEMBER?
YOU'RE PROBABLY RIGHT...

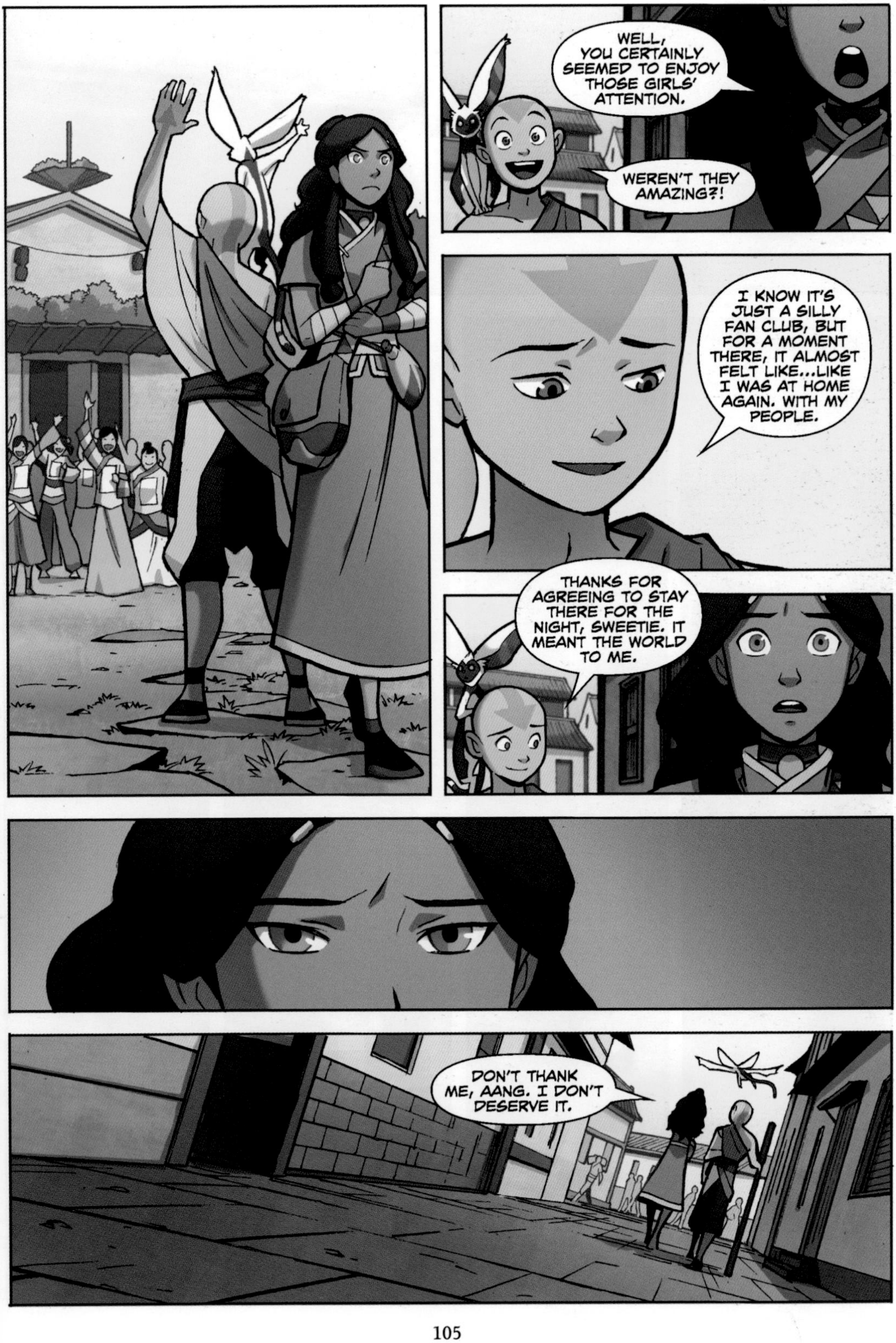
WELL, YOU CERTAINLY SEEMED TO ENJOY THOSE GIRLS' ATTENTION.
WEREN'T THEY AMAZING?!
I KNOW IT'S JUST A SILLY FAN CLUB, BUT FOR A MOMENT THERE, IT ALMOST FELT LIKE...LIKE I WAS AT HOME AGAIN. WITH MY PEOPLE.
THANKS FOR AGREEING TO STAY THERE FOR THE NIGHT, SWEETIE. IT MEANT THE WORLD TO ME.
DON'T THANK ME, AANG. I DON'T DESERVE IT.

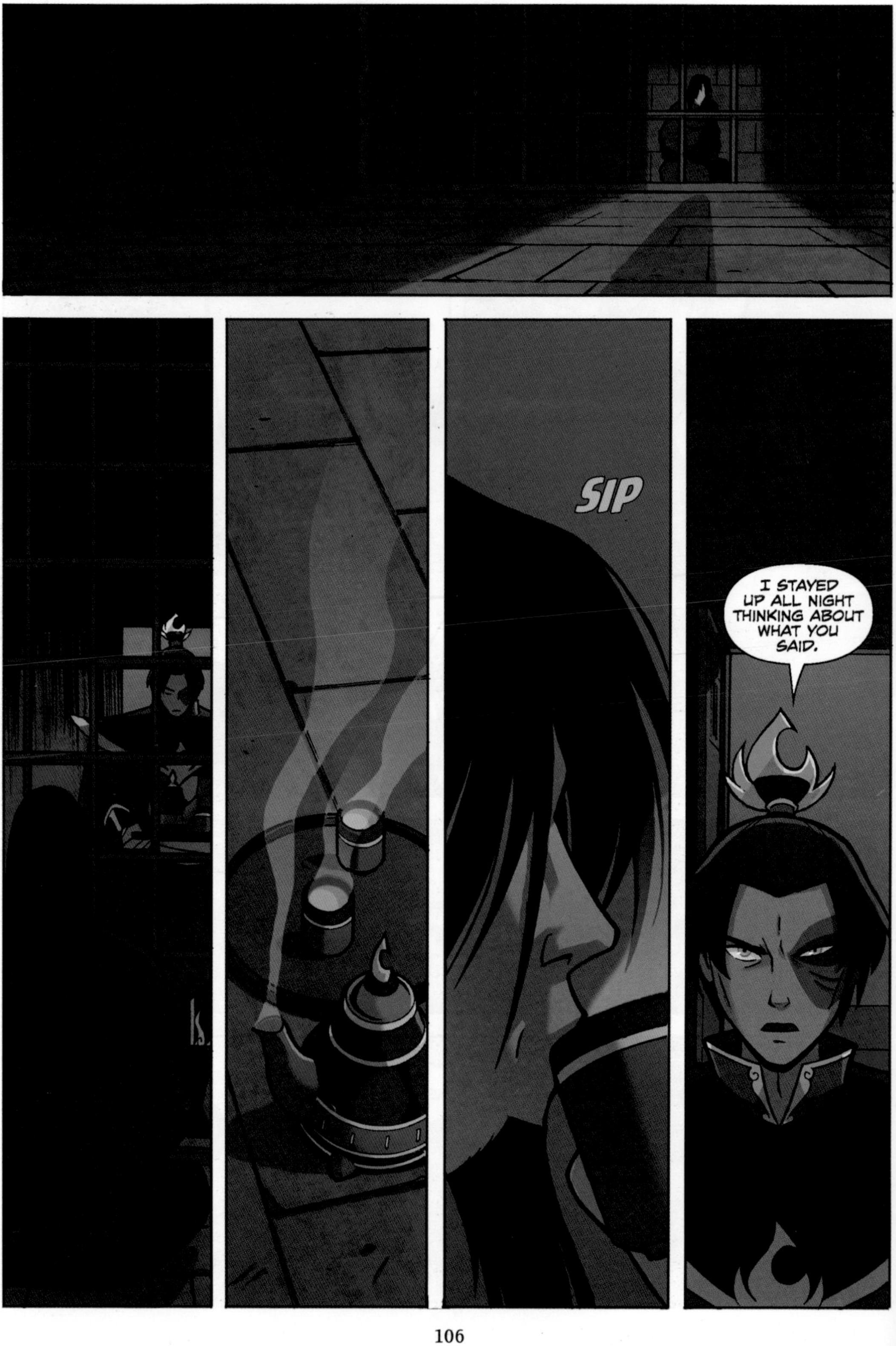
SIP
I STAYED UP ALL NIGHT THINKING ABOUT WHAT YOU SAID.

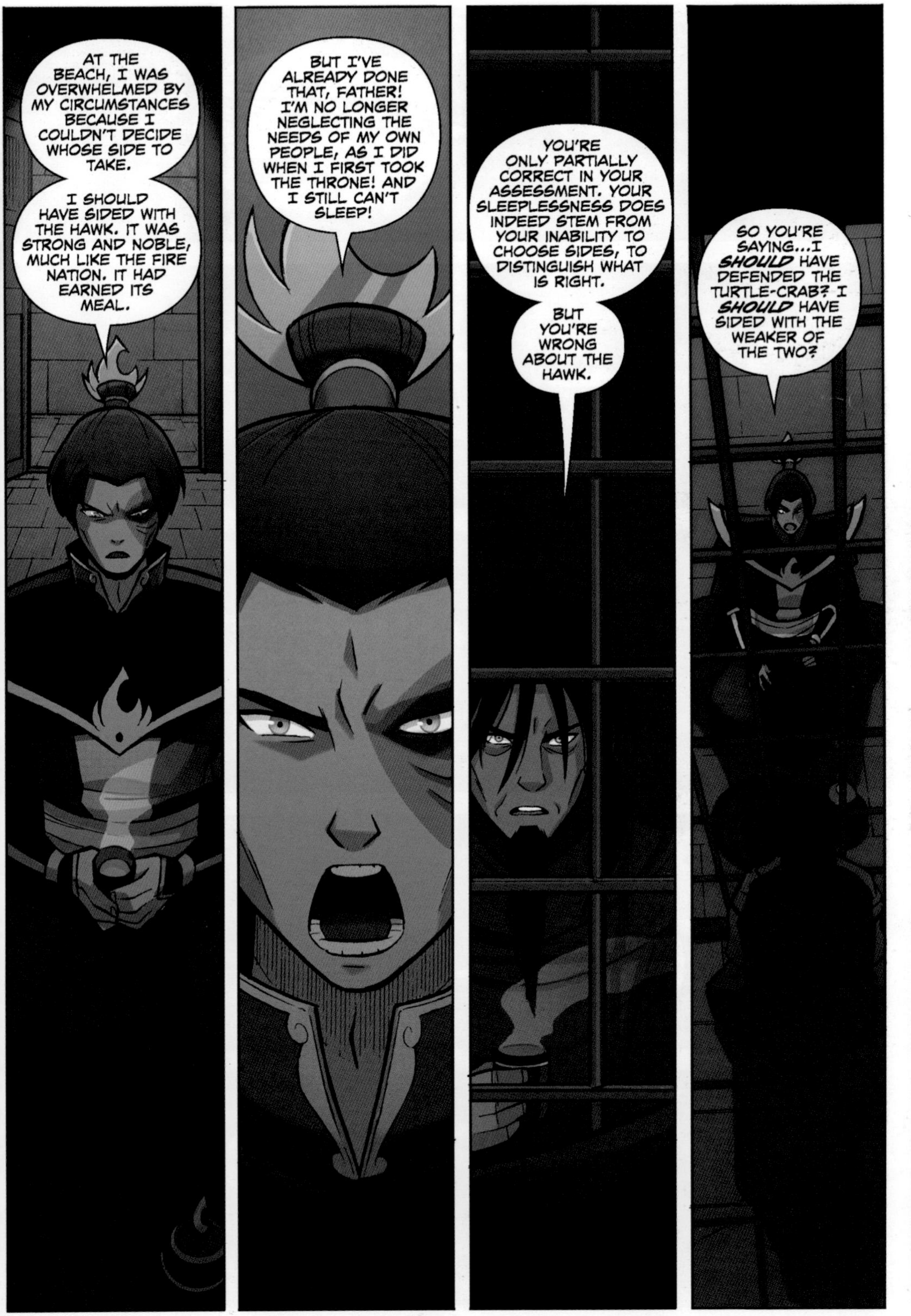

AT THE BEACH, I WAS OVERWHELMED BY MY CIRCUMSTANCES BECAUSE I COULDN'T DECIDE WHOSE SIDE TO TAKE.
I SHOULD HAVE SIDED WITH THE HAWK. IT WAS STRONG AND NOBLE, MUCH LIKE THE FIRE NATION. IT HAD EARNED ITS MEAL.
BUT I'VE ALREADY DONE THAT, FATHER! I'M NO LONGER NEGLECTING THE NEEDS OF MY OWN PEOPLE, AS I DID WHEN I FIRST TOOK THE THRONE! AND I STILL CAN'T SLEEP!
YOU'RE ONLY PARTIALLY CORRECT IN YOUR ASSESSMENT. YOUR SLEEPLESSNESS DOES INDEED STEM FROM YOUR INABILITY TO CHOOSE SIDES, TO DISTINGUISH WHAT IS RIGHT.
BUT YOU'RE WRONG ABOUT THE HAWK.
SO YOU'RE SAYING...I SHOULD HAVE DEFENDED THE TURTLE-CRAB? I SHOULD HAVE SIDED WITH THE WEAKER OF THE TWO?

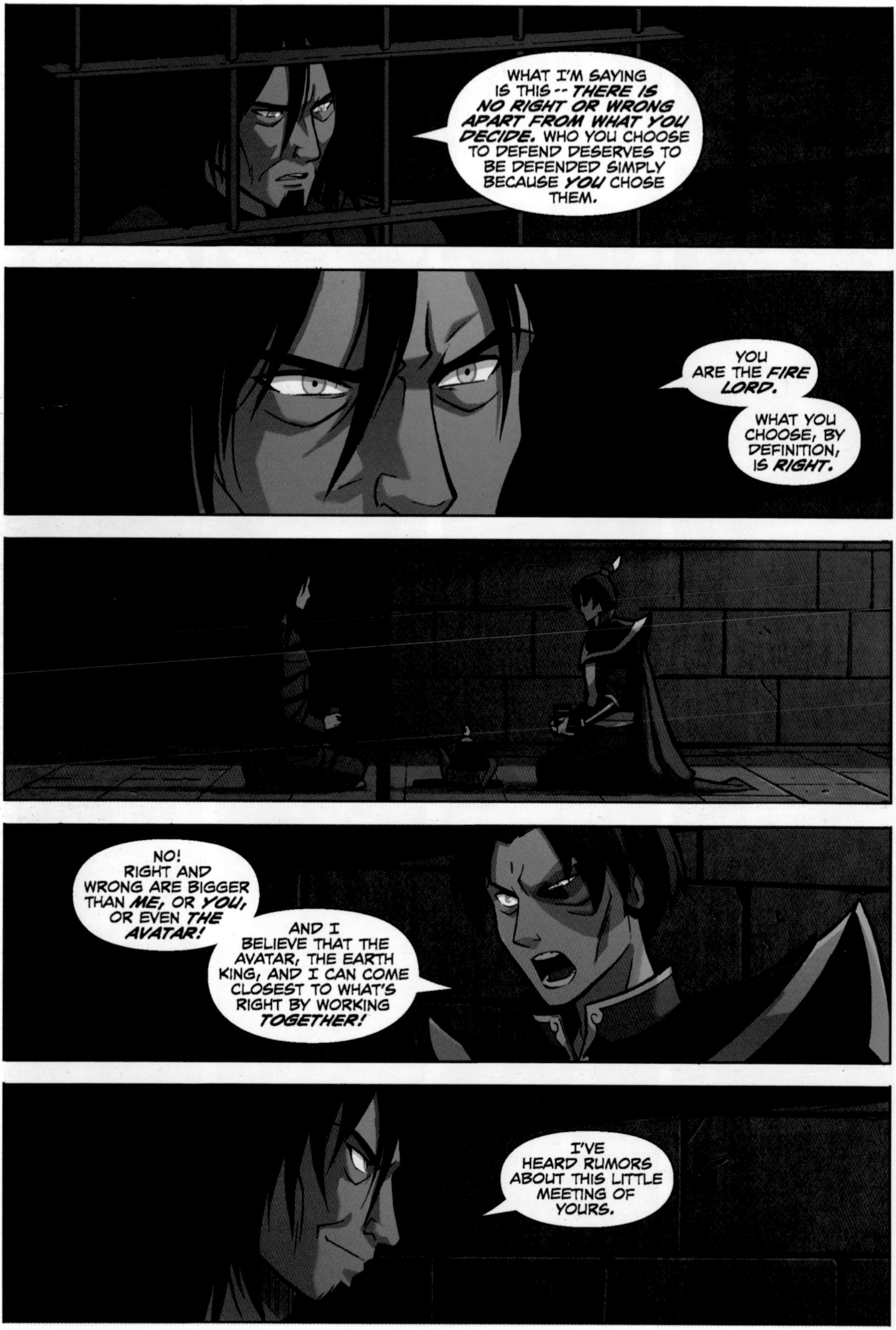
WHAT I'M SAYING IS THIS -- THERE IS NO RIGHT OR WRONG APART FROM WHAT YOU DECIDE. WHO YOU CHOOSE TO DEFEND DESERVES TO BE DEFENDED SIMPLY BECAUSE YOU CHOSE THEM.
YOU ARE THE FIRE LORD.
WHAT YOU CHOOSE, BY DEFINITION, IS RIGHT.
NO! RIGHT AND WRONG ARE BIGGER THAN ME, OR YOU, OR EVEN THE AVATAR!
AND I BELIEVE THAT THE AVATAR, THE EARTH KING, AND I CAN COME CLOSEST TO WHAT'S RIGHT BY WORKING TOGETHER!
I'VE HEARD RUMORS ABOUT THIS LITTLE MEETING OF YOURS.

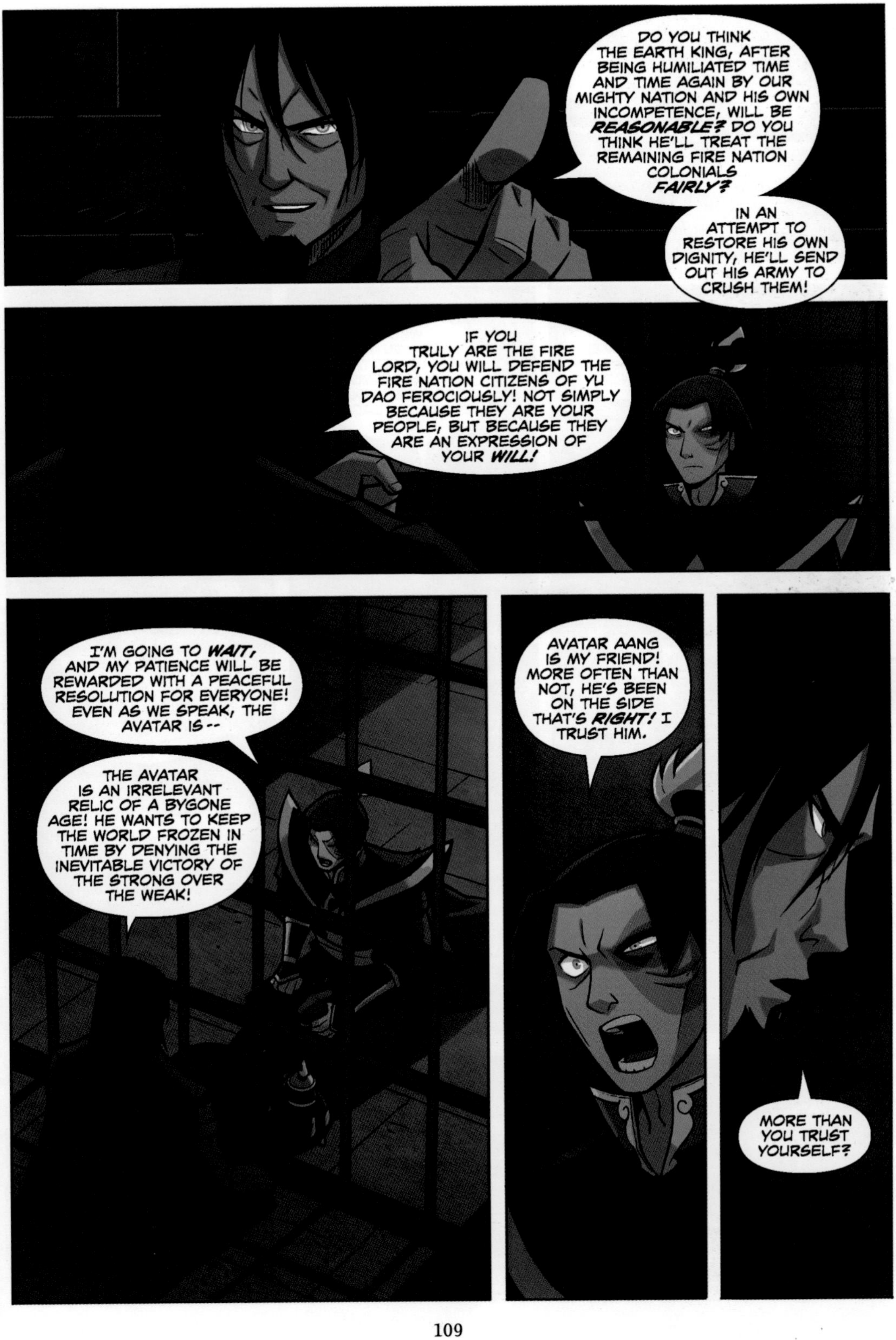
DO YOU THINK THE EARTH KING, AFTER BEING HUMILIATED TIME AND TIME AGAIN BY OUR MIGHTY NATION AND HIS OWN INCOMPETENCE, WILL BE REASONABLE? DO YOU THINK HE'LL TREAT THE REMAINING FIRE NATION COLONIALS FAIRLY?
IN AN ATTEMPT TO RESTORE HIS OWN DIGNITY, HE'LL SEND OUT HIS ARMY TO CRUSH THEM!
IF YOU TRULY ARE THE FIRE LORD, YOU WILL DEFEND THE FIRE NATION CITIZENS OF YU DAO FEROCIOUSLY! NOT SIMPLY BECAUSE THEY ARE YOUR PEOPLE, BUT BECAUSE THEY ARE AN EXPRESSION OF YOUR WILL!
I'M GOING TO WAIT, AND MY PATIENCE WILL BE REWARDED WITH A PEACEFUL RESOLUTION FOR EVERYONE! EVEN AS WE SPEAK, THE AVATAR IS --
THE AVATAR IS AN IRRELEVANT RELIC OF A BYGONE AGE! HE WANTS TO KEEP THE WORLD FROZEN IN TIME BY DENYING THE INEVITABLE VICTORY OF THE STRONG OVER THE WEAK!
AVATAR AANG IS MY FRIEND! MORE OFTEN THAN NOT, HE'S BEEN ON THE SIDE THAT'S RIGHT! I TRUST HIM.
MORE THAN YOU TRUST YOURSELF?

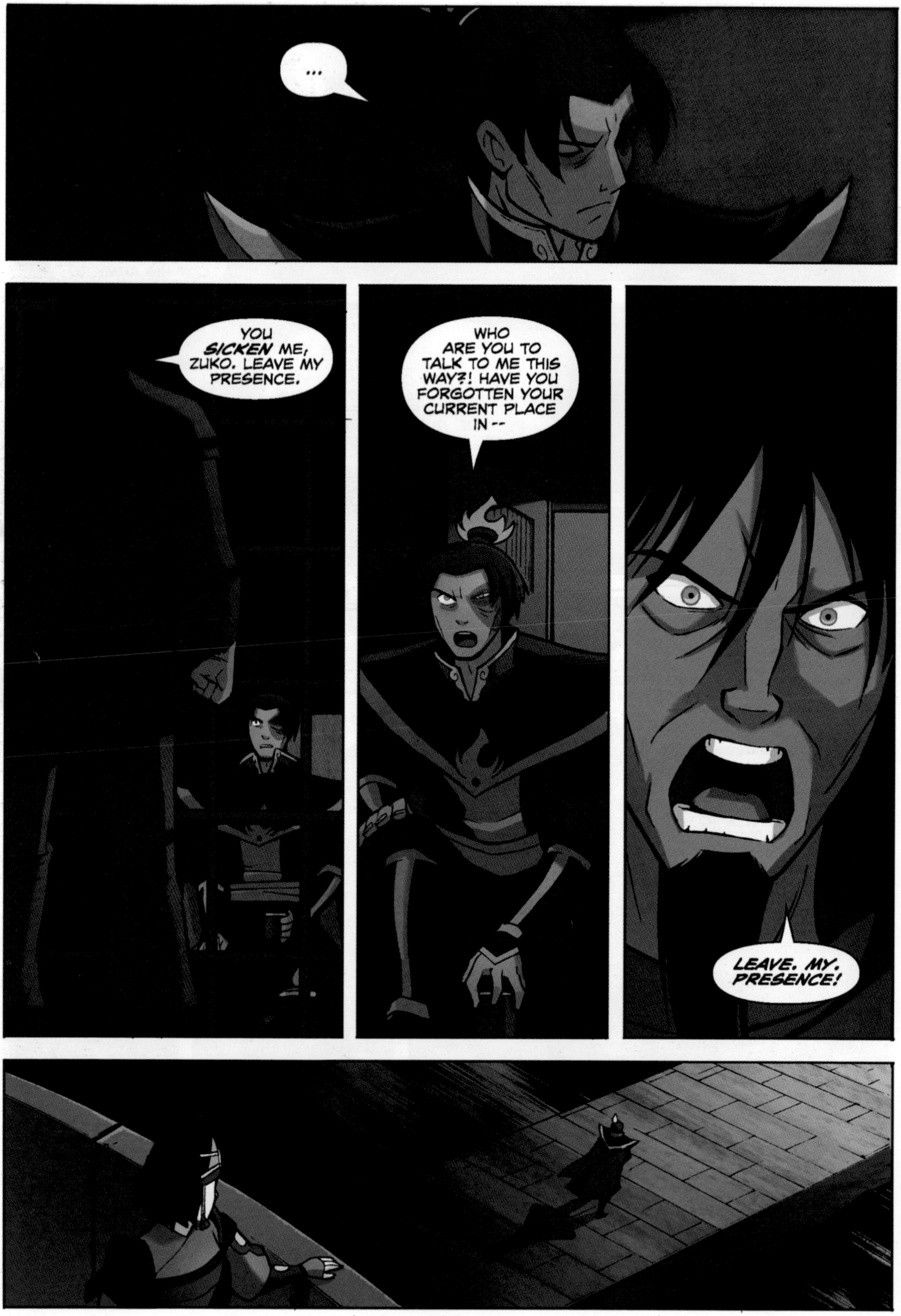
...
YOU SICKEN ME, ZUKO. LEAVE MY PRESENCE.
WHO ARE YOU TO TALK TO ME THIS WAY?! HAVE YOU FORGOTTEN YOUR CURRENT PLACE IN --
LEAVE. MY. PRESENCE!

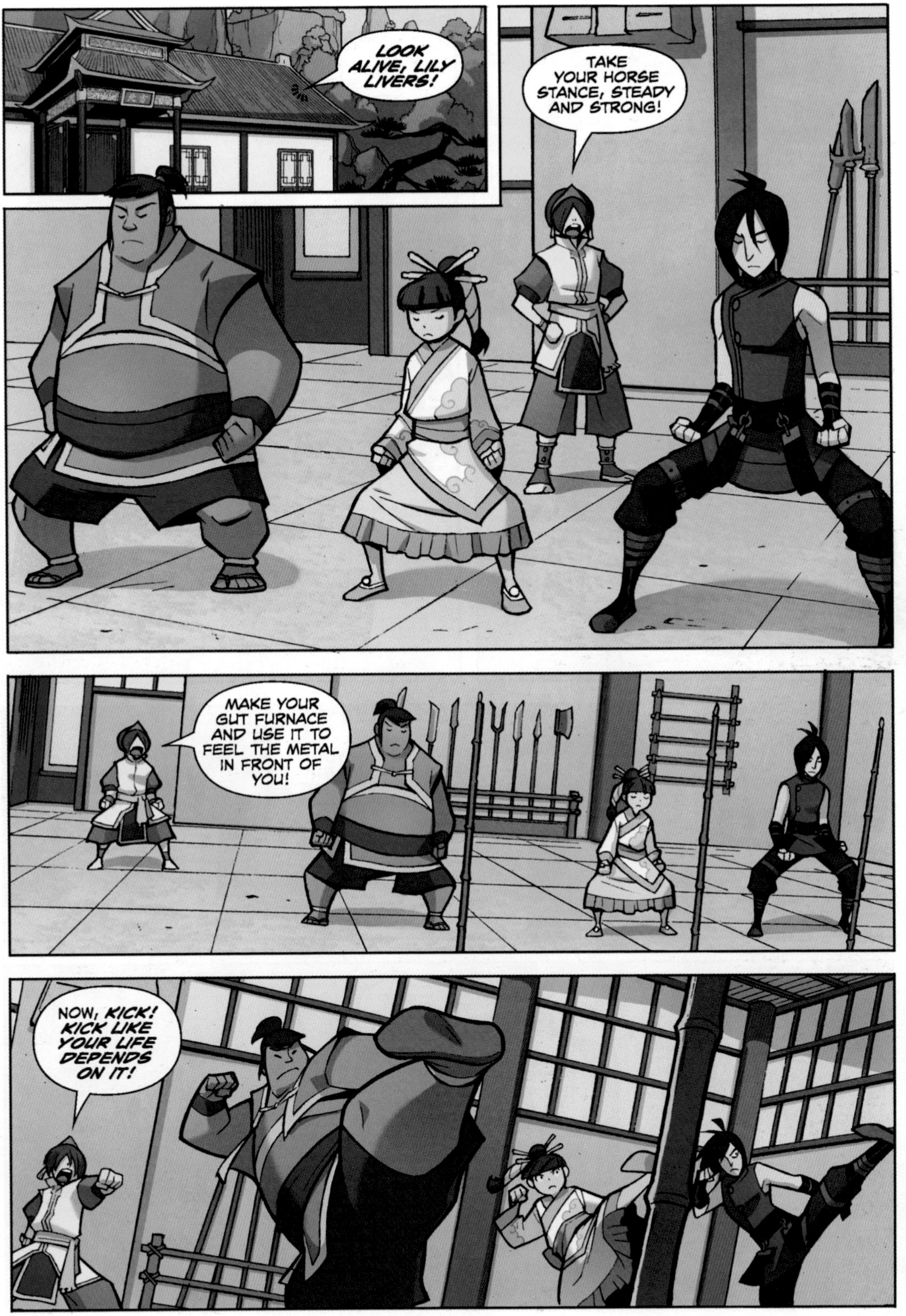
LOOK ALIVE, LILY LIVERS!
TAKE YOUR HORSE STANCE, STEADY AND STRONG!
MAKE YOUR GUT FURNACE AND USE IT TO FEEL THE METAL IN FRONT OF YOU!
NOW, KICK! KICK LIKE YOUR LIFE DEPENDS ON IT!

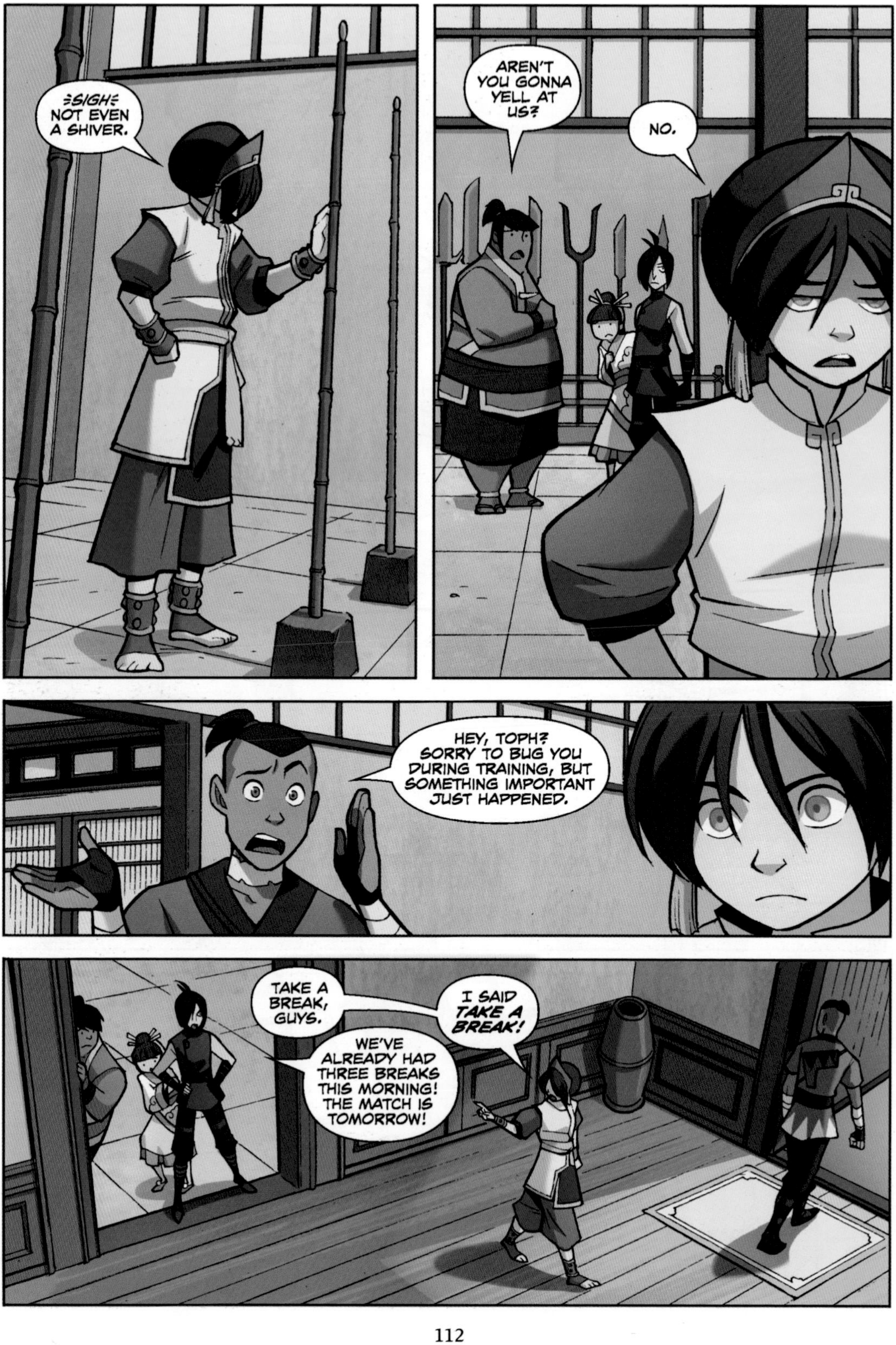

≈SIGH≈ NOT EVEN A SHIVER.
AREN'T YOU GONNA YELL AT US?
NO.
HEY, TOPH? SORRY TO BUG YOU DURING TRAINING, BUT SOMETHING IMPORTANT JUST HAPPENED.
TAKE A BREAK, GUYS.
WE'VE ALREADY HAD THREE BREAKS THIS MORNING! THE MATCH IS TOMORROW!
I SAID *TAKE A BREAK!*

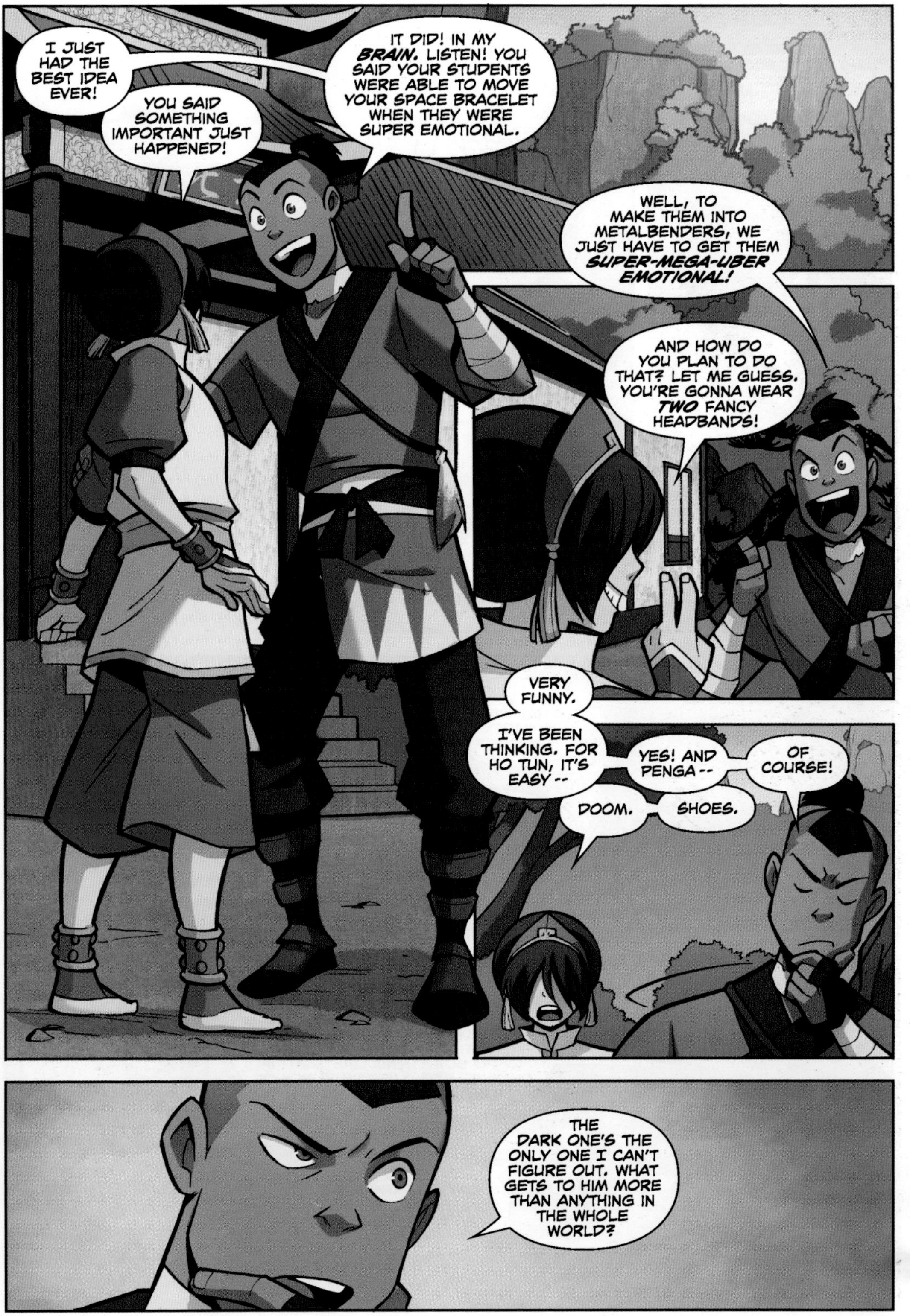
I JUST HAD THE BEST IDEA EVER!
YOU SAID SOMETHING IMPORTANT JUST HAPPENED!
IT DID! IN MY **BRAIN.** LISTEN! YOU SAID YOUR STUDENTS WERE ABLE TO MOVE YOUR SPACE BRACELET WHEN THEY WERE SUPER EMOTIONAL.
WELL, TO MAKE THEM INTO METALBENDERS, WE JUST HAVE TO GET THEM ***SUPER-MEGA-UBER EMOTIONAL!***
AND HOW DO YOU PLAN TO DO THAT? LET ME GUESS. YOU'RE GONNA WEAR ***TWO*** FANCY HEADBANDS!
VERY FUNNY.
I'VE BEEN THINKING. FOR HO TUN, IT'S EASY --
DOOM.
YES! AND PENGA --
SHOES.
OF COURSE!
THE DARK ONE'S THE ONLY ONE I CAN'T FIGURE OUT. WHAT GETS TO HIM MORE THAN ANYTHING IN THE WHOLE WORLD?

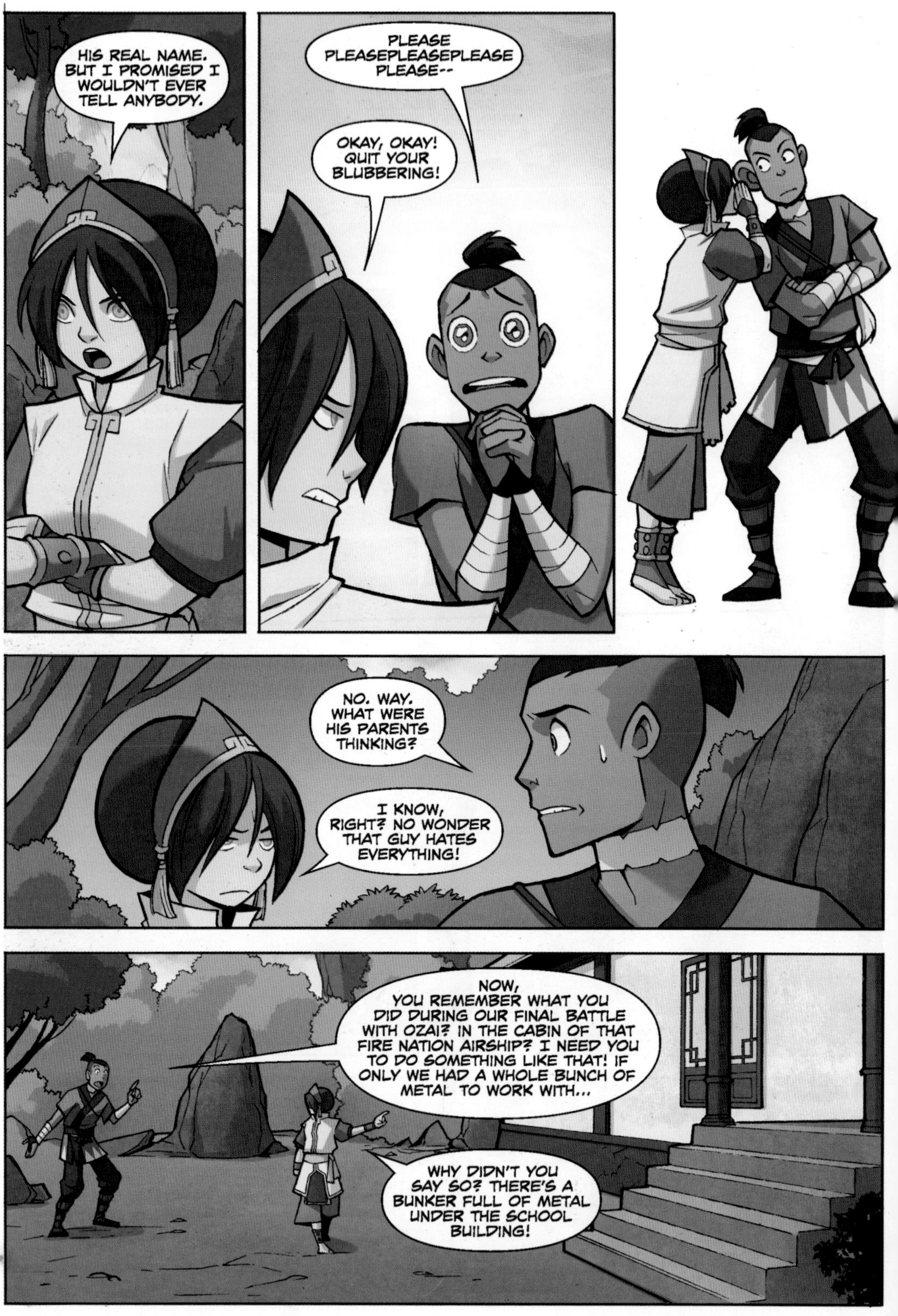
HIS REAL NAME. BUT I PROMISED I WOULDN'T EVER TELL ANYBODY.
PLEASE PLEASEPLEASEPLEASE PLEASE--
OKAY, OKAY! QUIT YOUR BLUBBERING!
NO. WAY. WHAT WERE HIS PARENTS THINKING?
I KNOW, RIGHT? NO WONDER THAT GUY HATES EVERYTHING!
NOW, YOU REMEMBER WHAT YOU DID DURING OUR FINAL BATTLE WITH OZAI? IN THE CABIN OF THAT FIRE NATION AIRSHIP? I NEED YOU TO DO SOMETHING LIKE THAT! IF ONLY WE HAD A WHOLE BUNCH OF METAL TO WORK WITH...
WHY DIDN'T YOU SAY SO? THERE'S A BUNKER FULL OF METAL UNDER THE SCHOOL BUILDING!

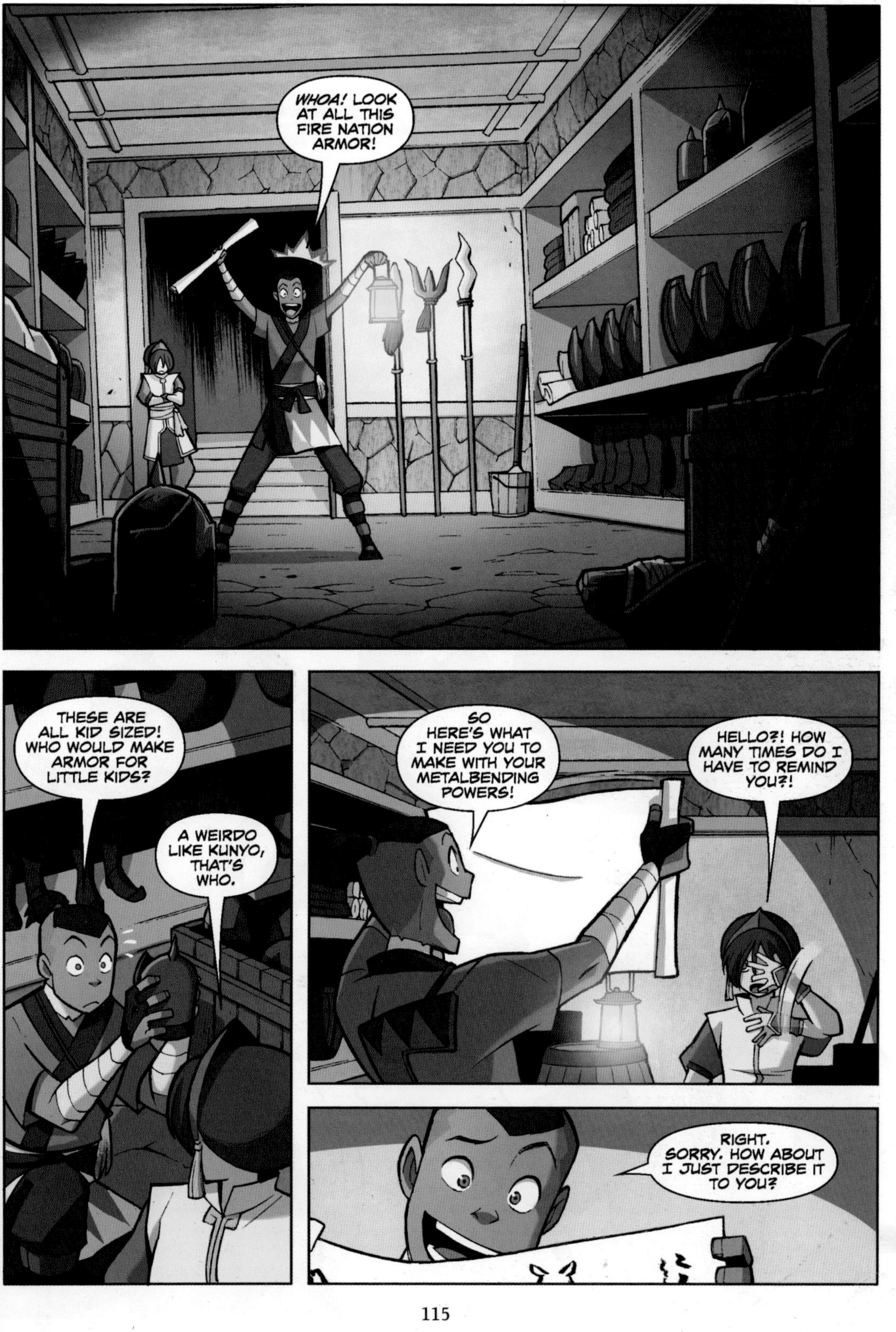
WHOA! LOOK AT ALL THIS FIRE NATION ARMOR!
THESE ARE ALL KID SIZED! WHO WOULD MAKE ARMOR FOR LITTLE KIDS?
A WEIRDO LIKE KUNYO, THAT'S WHO.
SO HERE'S WHAT I NEED YOU TO MAKE WITH YOUR METALBENDING POWERS!
HELLO?! HOW MANY TIMES DO I HAVE TO REMIND YOU?!
RIGHT. SORRY. HOW ABOUT I JUST DESCRIBE IT TO YOU?

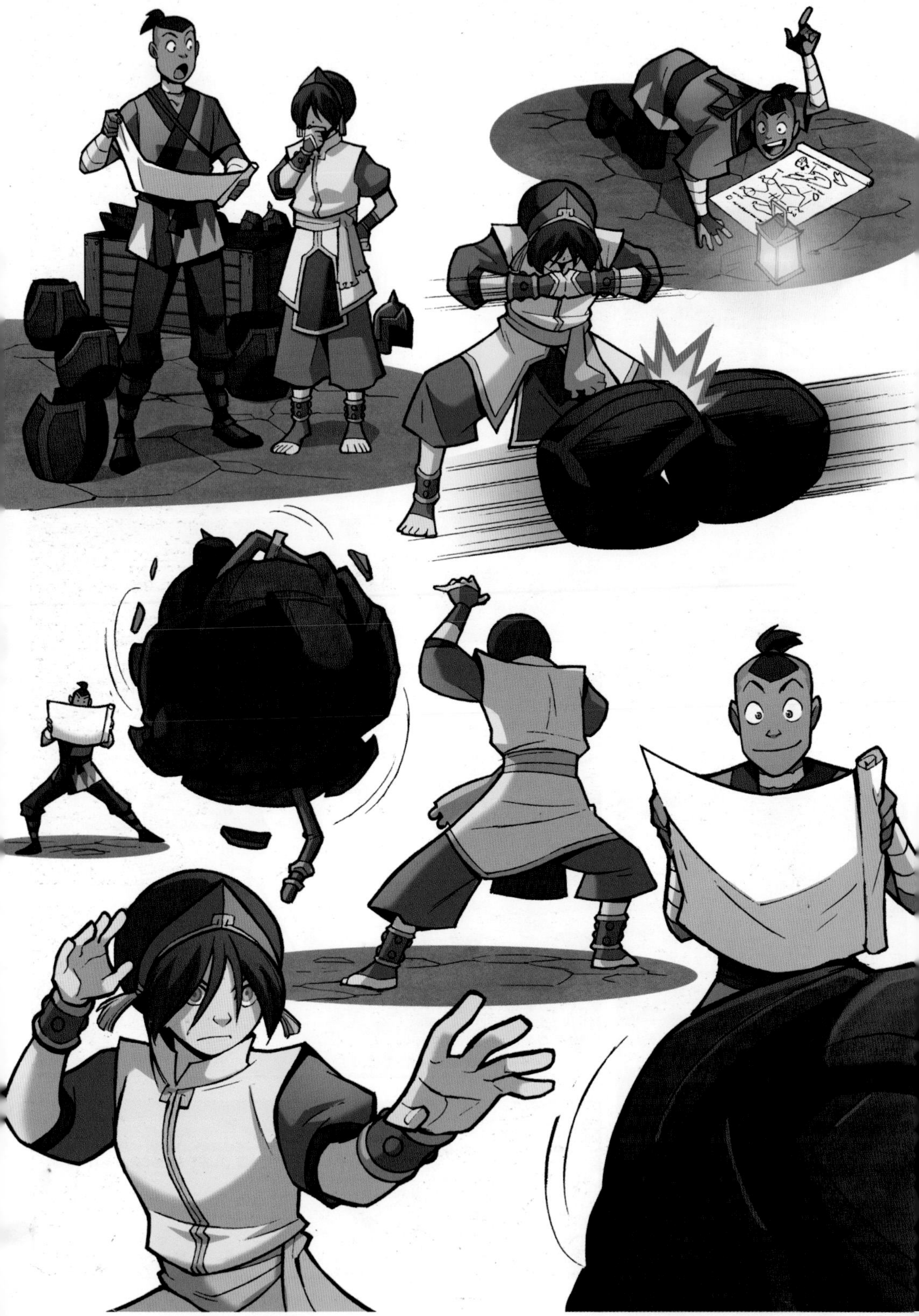

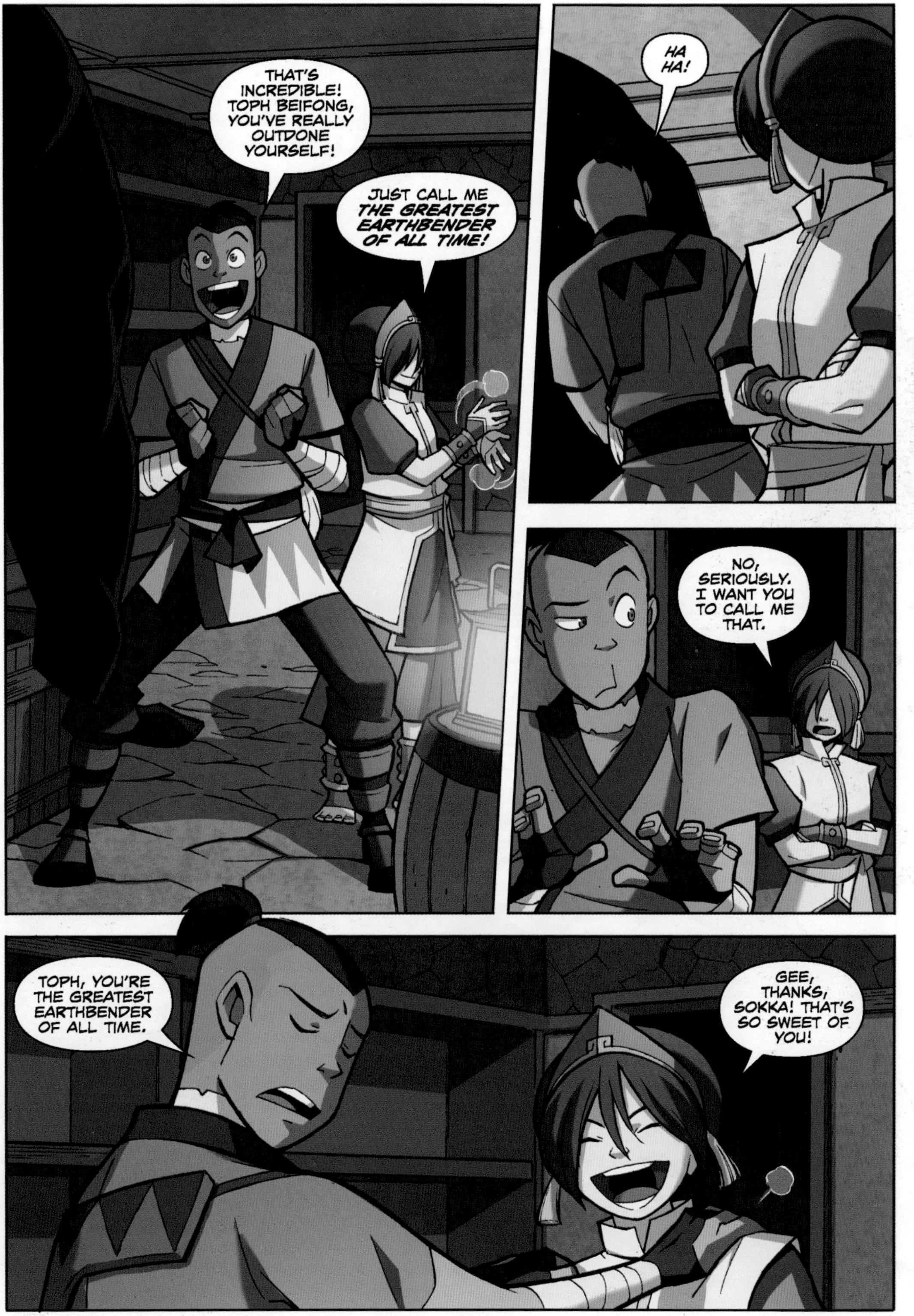
THAT'S INCREDIBLE! TOPH BEIFONG, YOU'VE REALLY OUTDONE YOURSELF!
JUST CALL ME *THE GREATEST EARTHBENDER OF ALL TIME!*
HA HA!
NO, SERIOUSLY. I WANT YOU TO CALL ME THAT.
TOPH, YOU'RE THE GREATEST EARTHBENDER OF ALL TIME.
GEE, THANKS, SOKKA! THAT'S SO SWEET OF YOU!

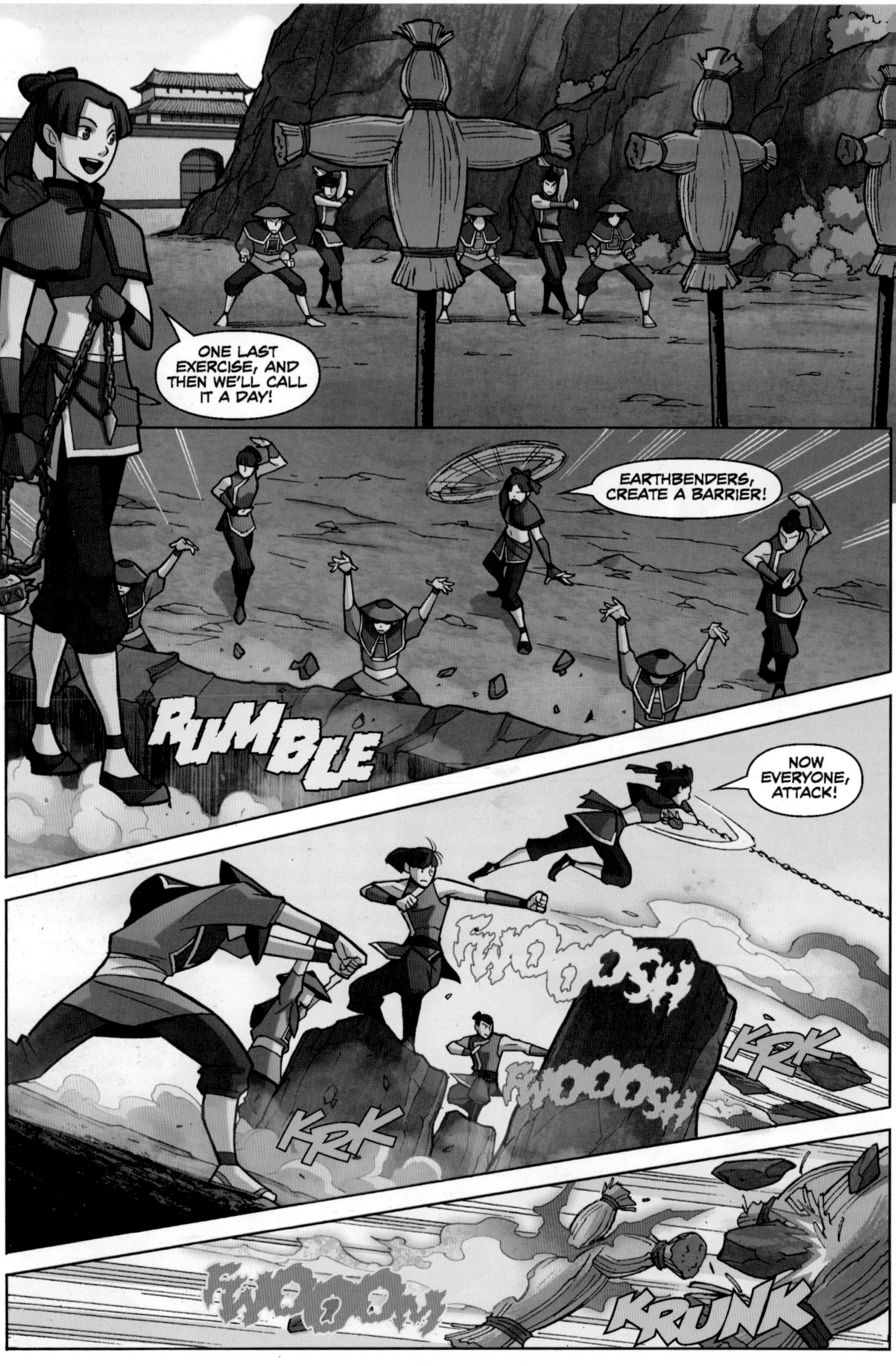
ONE LAST EXERCISE, AND THEN WE'LL CALL IT A DAY!
EARTHBENDERS, CREATE A BARRIER!
RUMBLE
NOW EVERYONE, ATTACK!
FWOOOSH
KRK
FWOOOSH
KRK
FWOOOM
KRUNK

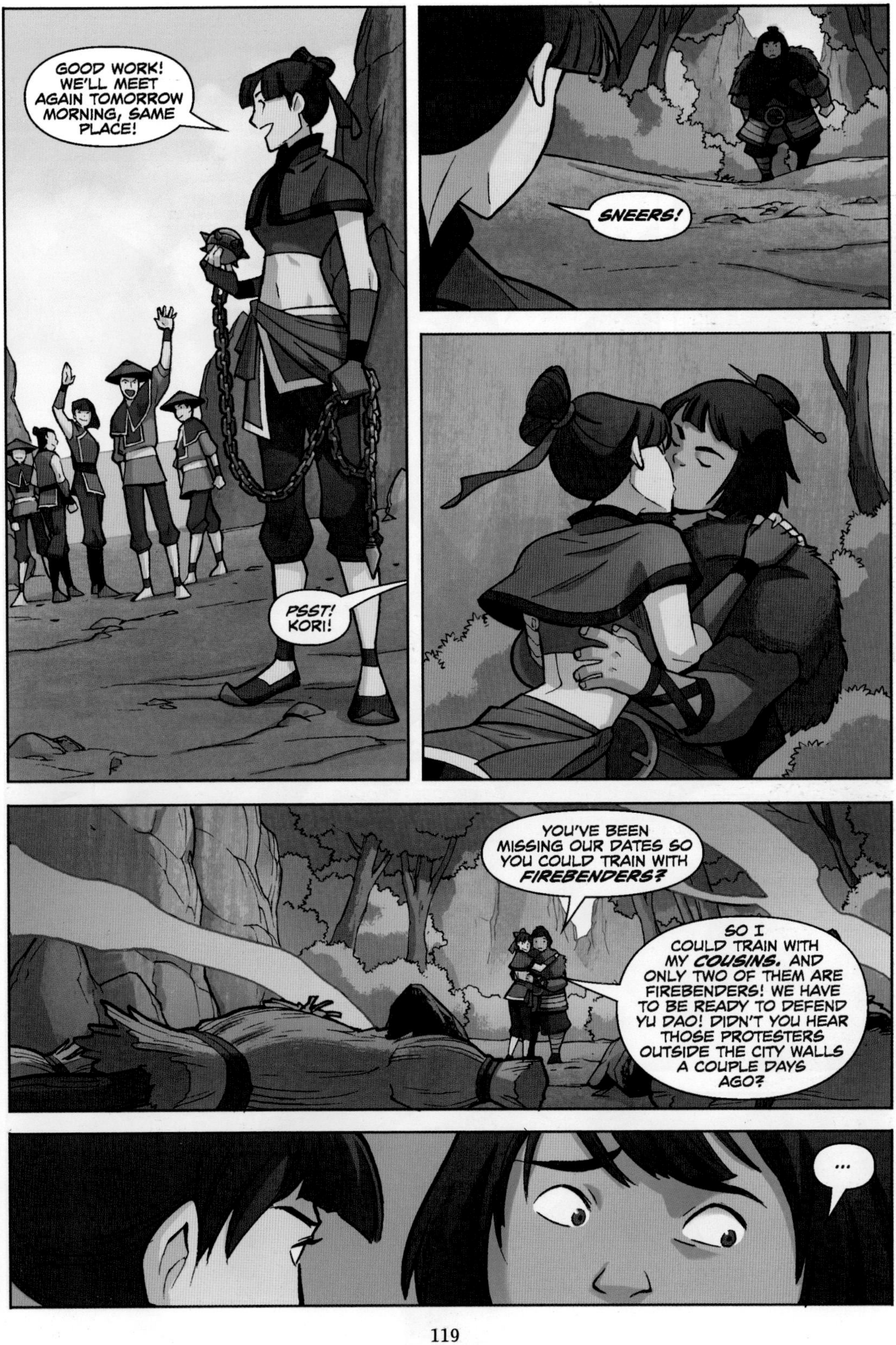
GOOD WORK! WE'LL MEET AGAIN TOMORROW MORNING, SAME PLACE!
PSST! KORI!
SNEERS!
YOU'VE BEEN MISSING OUR DATES SO YOU COULD TRAIN WITH FIREBENDERS?
SO I COULD TRAIN WITH MY COUSINS. AND ONLY TWO OF THEM ARE FIREBENDERS! WE HAVE TO BE READY TO DEFEND YU DAO! DIDN'T YOU HEAR THOSE PROTESTERS OUTSIDE THE CITY WALLS A COUPLE DAYS AGO?
...

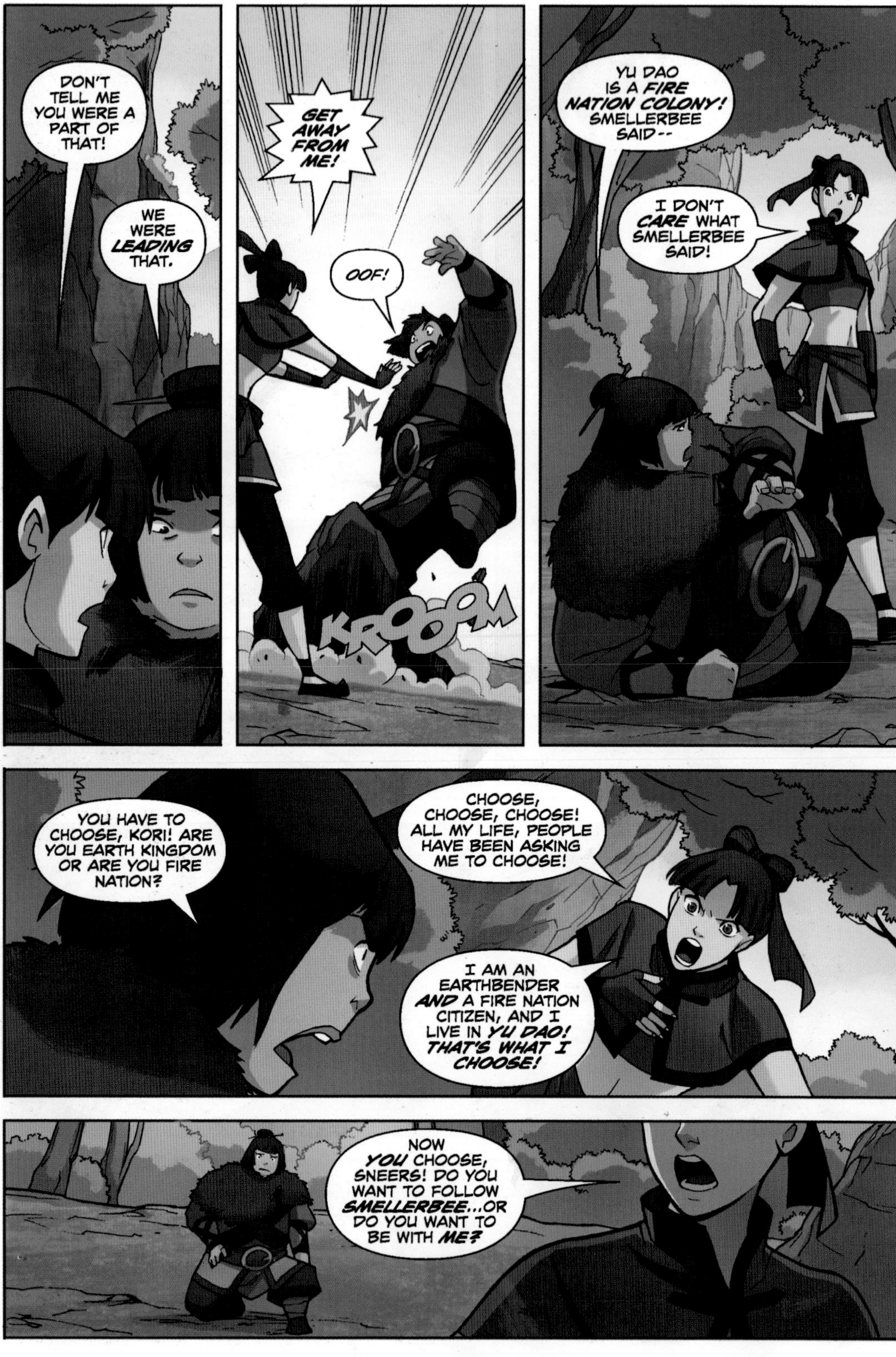
DON'T TELL ME YOU WERE A PART OF THAT!
WE WERE LEADING THAT.
GET AWAY FROM ME!
OOF!
KROOOM
YU DAO IS A FIRE NATION COLONY! SMELLERBEE SAID--
I DON'T CARE WHAT SMELLERBEE SAID!
YOU HAVE TO CHOOSE, KORI! ARE YOU EARTH KINGDOM OR ARE YOU FIRE NATION?
CHOOSE, CHOOSE, CHOOSE! ALL MY LIFE, PEOPLE HAVE BEEN ASKING ME TO CHOOSE!
I AM AN EARTHBENDER AND A FIRE NATION CITIZEN, AND I LIVE IN YU DAO! THAT'S WHAT I CHOOSE!
NOW YOU CHOOSE, SNEERS! DO YOU WANT TO FOLLOW SMELLERBEE...OR DO YOU WANT TO BE WITH ME?

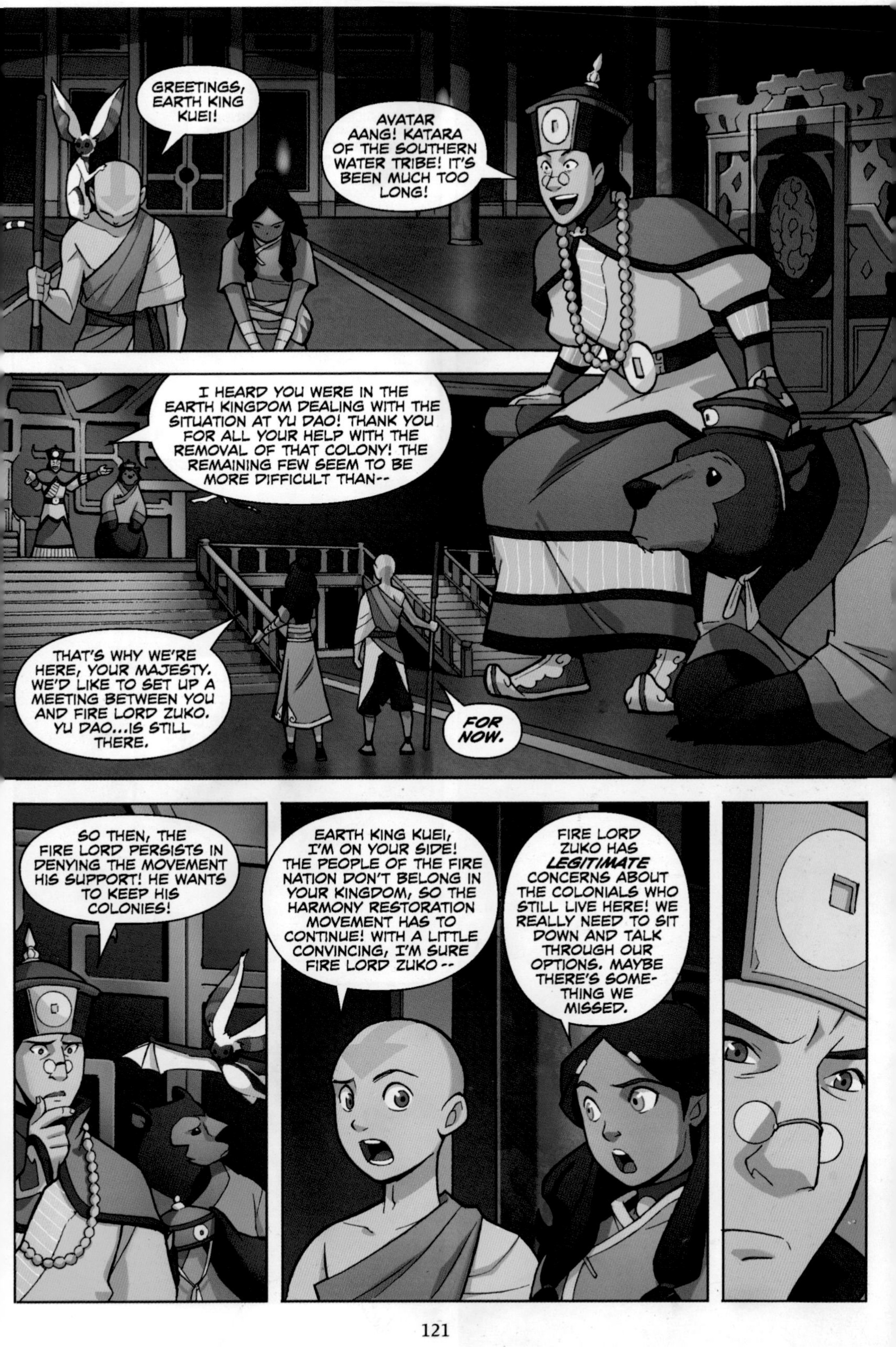
GREETINGS, EARTH KING KUEI!
AVATAR AANG! KATARA OF THE SOUTHERN WATER TRIBE! IT'S BEEN MUCH TOO LONG!
I HEARD YOU WERE IN THE EARTH KINGDOM DEALING WITH THE SITUATION AT YU DAO! THANK YOU FOR ALL YOUR HELP WITH THE REMOVAL OF THAT COLONY! THE REMAINING FEW SEEM TO BE MORE DIFFICULT THAN--
THAT'S WHY WE'RE HERE, YOUR MAJESTY. WE'D LIKE TO SET UP A MEETING BETWEEN YOU AND FIRE LORD ZUKO. YU DAO...IS STILL THERE.
FOR NOW.
SO THEN, THE FIRE LORD PERSISTS IN DENYING THE MOVEMENT HIS SUPPORT! HE WANTS TO KEEP HIS COLONIES!
EARTH KING KUEI, I'M ON YOUR SIDE! THE PEOPLE OF THE FIRE NATION DON'T BELONG IN YOUR KINGDOM, SO THE HARMONY RESTORATION MOVEMENT HAS TO CONTINUE! WITH A LITTLE CONVINCING, I'M SURE FIRE LORD ZUKO--
FIRE LORD ZUKO HAS LEGITIMATE CONCERNS ABOUT THE COLONIALS WHO STILL LIVE HERE! WE REALLY NEED TO SIT DOWN AND TALK THROUGH OUR OPTIONS. MAYBE THERE'S SOME-THING WE MISSED.

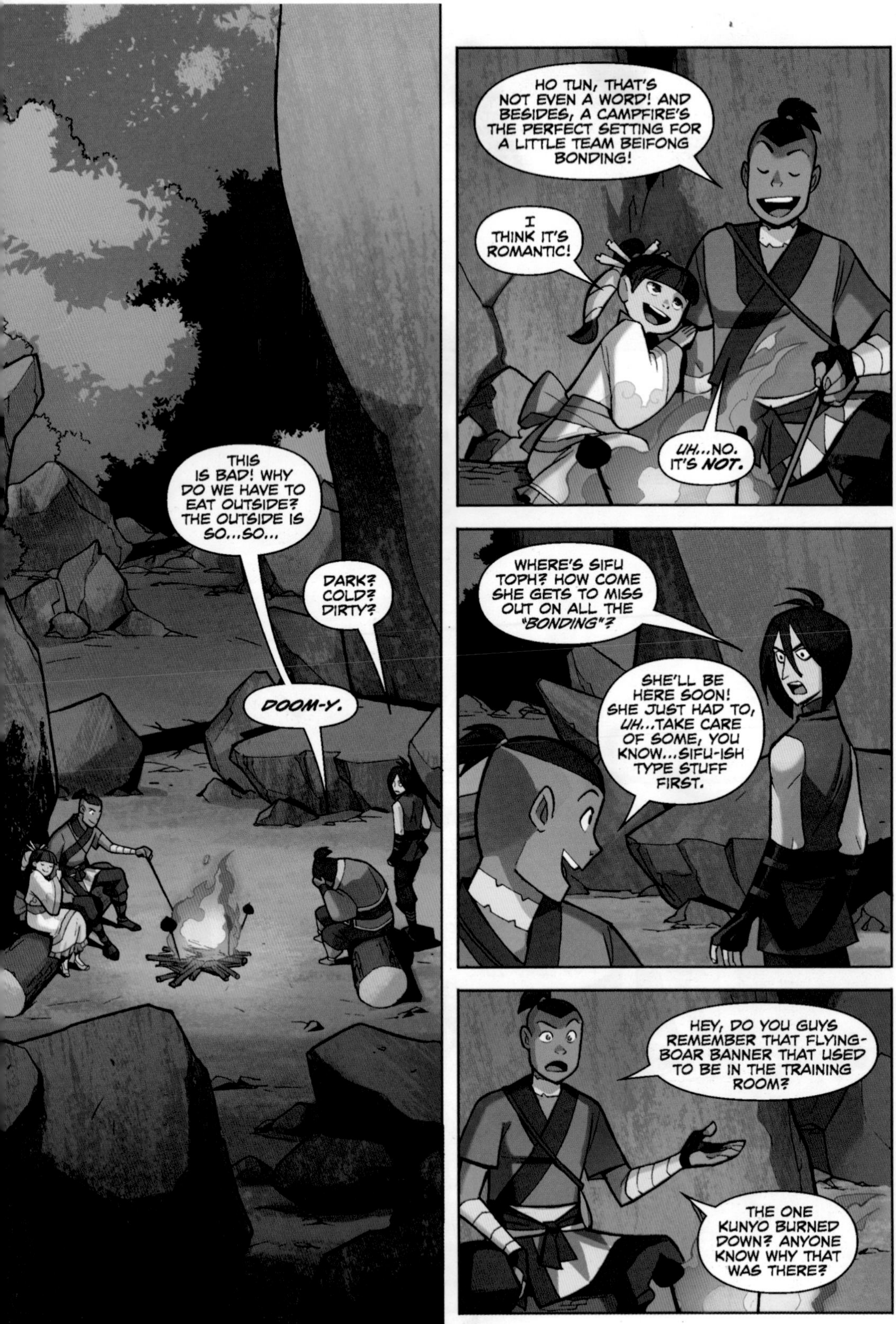
THIS IS BAD! WHY DO WE HAVE TO EAT OUTSIDE? THE OUTSIDE IS SO...SO...
DARK? COLD? DIRTY?
DOOM-Y.
HO TUN, THAT'S NOT EVEN A WORD! AND BESIDES, A CAMPFIRE'S THE PERFECT SETTING FOR A LITTLE TEAM BEIFONG BONDING!
I THINK IT'S ROMANTIC!
UH...NO. IT'S NOT.
WHERE'S SIFU TOPH? HOW COME SHE GETS TO MISS OUT ON ALL THE "BONDING"?
SHE'LL BE HERE SOON! SHE JUST HAD TO, UH...TAKE CARE OF SOME, YOU KNOW...SIFU-ISH TYPE STUFF FIRST.
HEY, DO YOU GUYS REMEMBER THAT FLYING-BOAR BANNER THAT USED TO BE IN THE TRAINING ROOM?
THE ONE KUNYO BURNED DOWN? ANYONE KNOW WHY THAT WAS THERE?

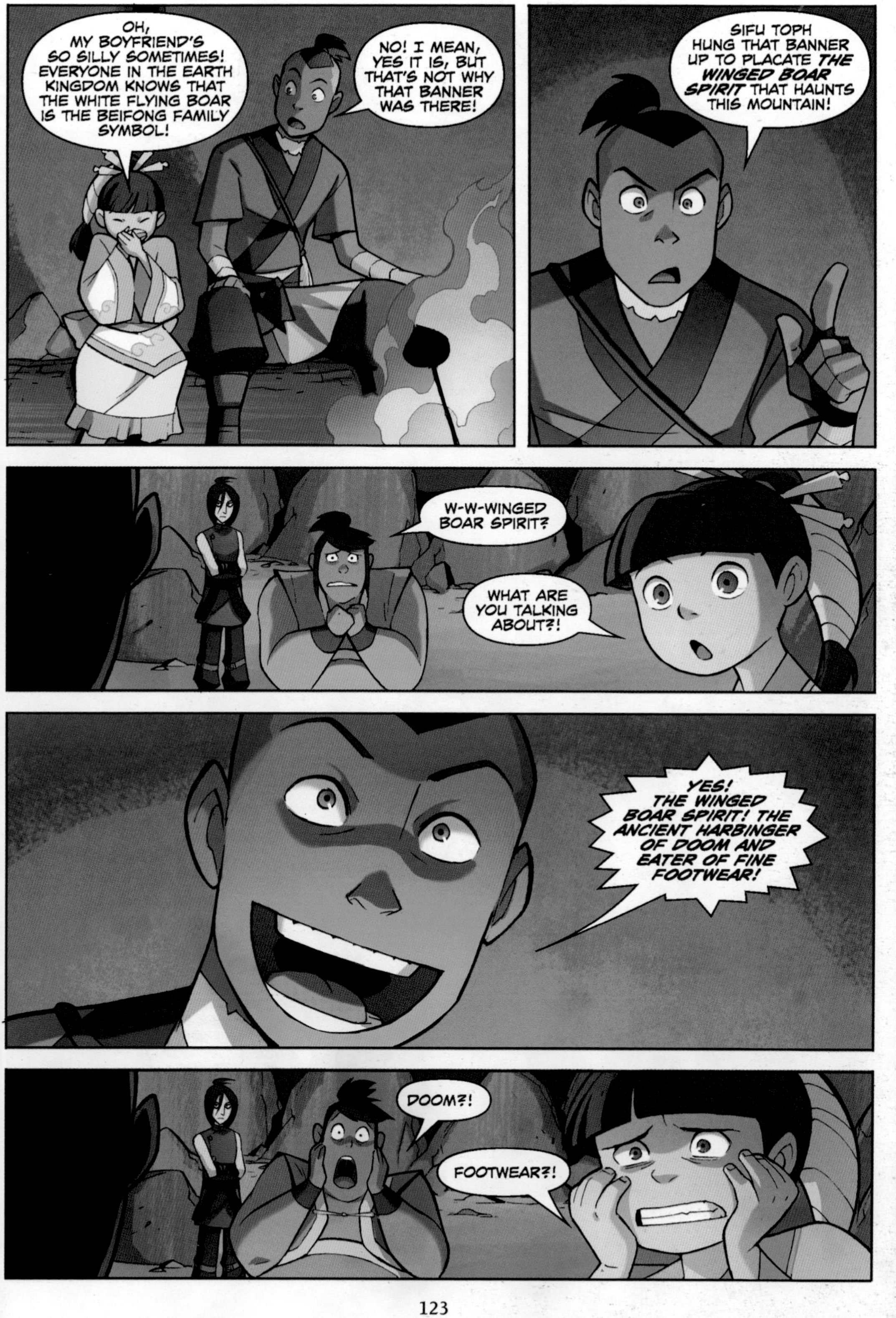
OH, MY BOYFRIEND'S SO SILLY SOMETIMES! EVERYONE IN THE EARTH KINGDOM KNOWS THAT THE WHITE FLYING BOAR IS THE BEIFONG FAMILY SYMBOL!
NO! I MEAN, YES IT IS, BUT THAT'S NOT WHY THAT BANNER WAS THERE!
SIFU TOPH HUNG THAT BANNER UP TO PLACATE ***THE WINGED BOAR SPIRIT*** THAT HAUNTS THIS MOUNTAIN!
W-W-WINGED BOAR SPIRIT?
WHAT ARE YOU TALKING ABOUT?!
YES! THE WINGED BOAR SPIRIT! THE ANCIENT HARBINGER OF DOOM AND EATER OF FINE FOOTWEAR!
DOOM?!
FOOTWEAR?!

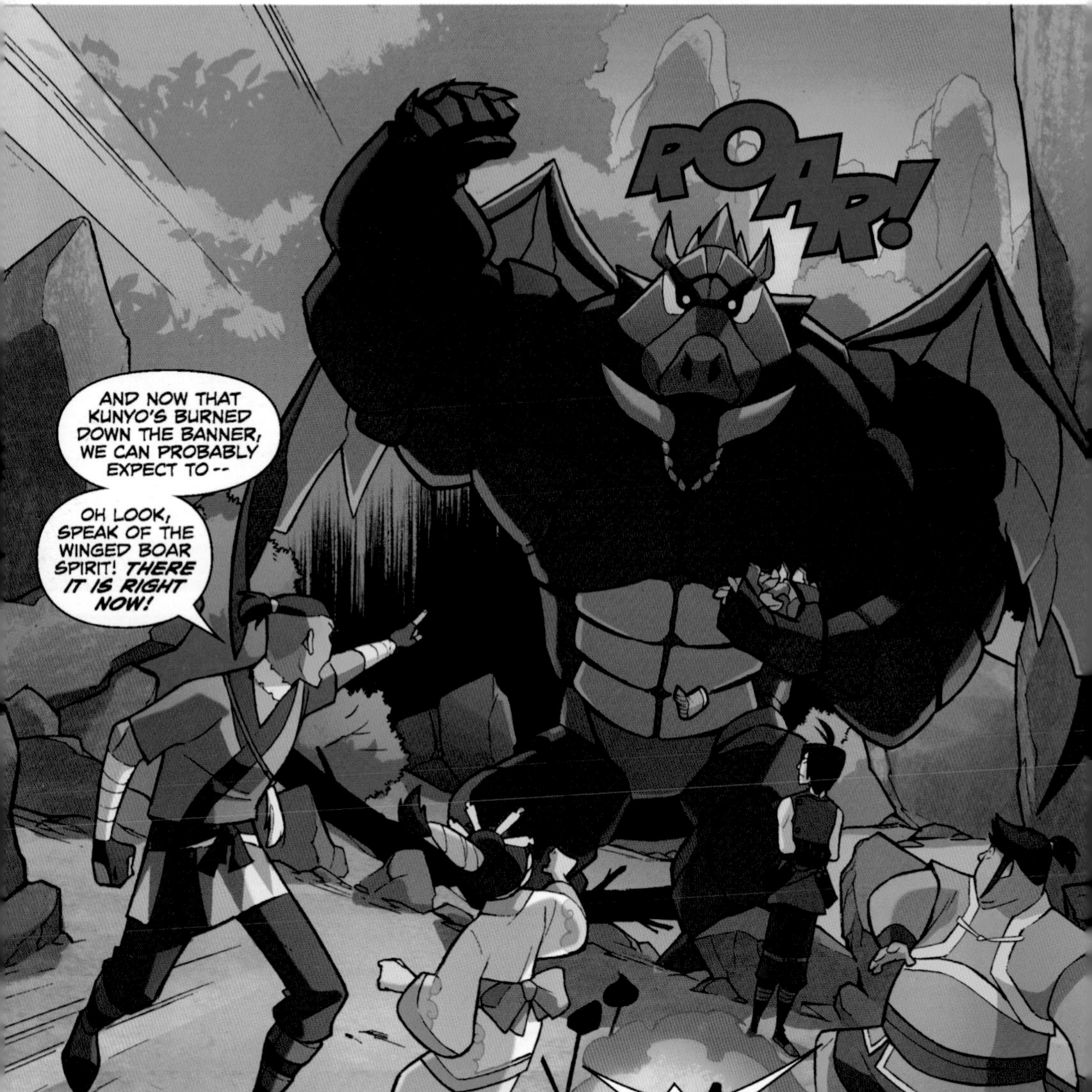
ROAR!
AND NOW THAT KUNYO'S BURNED DOWN THE BANNER, WE CAN PROBABLY EXPECT TO --
OH LOOK, SPEAK OF THE WINGED BOAR SPIRIT! THERE IT IS RIGHT NOW!
AAAH!

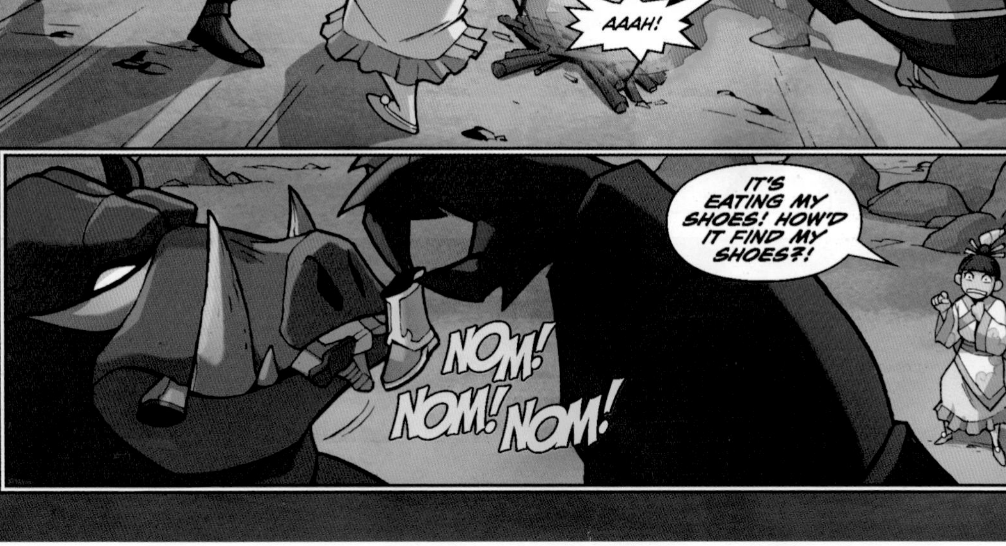
IT'S EATING MY SHOES! HOW'D IT FIND MY SHOES?!
NOM! NOM! NOM!

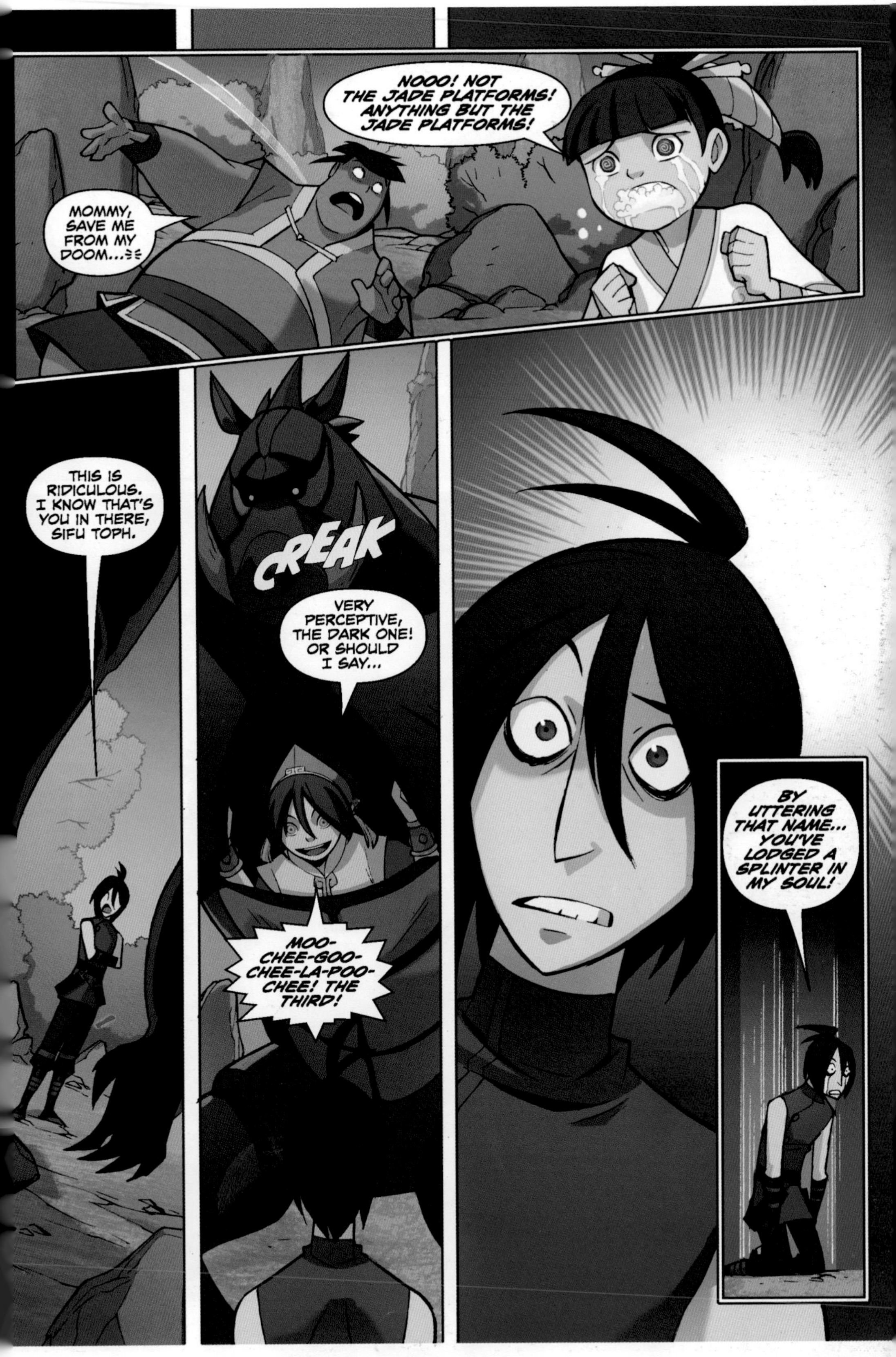
MOMMY, SAVE ME FROM MY DOOM...
NOOO! NOT THE JADE PLATFORMS! ANYTHING BUT THE JADE PLATFORMS!
THIS IS RIDICULOUS. I KNOW THAT'S YOU IN THERE, SIFU TOPH.
CREAK
VERY PERCEPTIVE, THE DARK ONE! OR SHOULD I SAY...
MOO-CHEE-GOO-CHEE-LA-POO-CHEE! THE THIRD!
BY UTTERING THAT NAME... YOU'VE LODGED A SPLINTER IN MY SOUL!

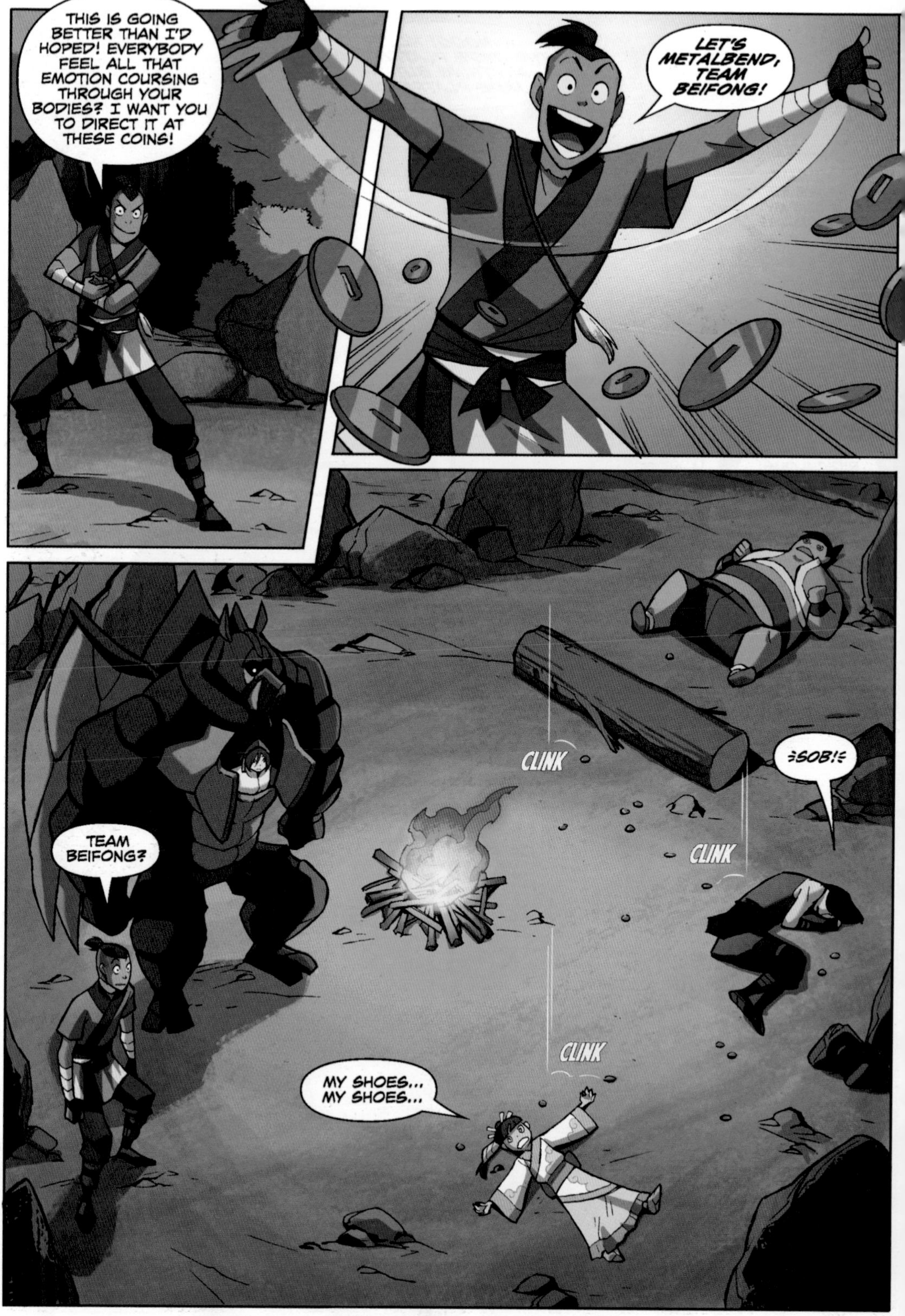
THIS IS GOING BETTER THAN I'D HOPED! EVERYBODY FEEL ALL THAT EMOTION COURSING THROUGH YOUR BODIES? I WANT YOU TO DIRECT IT AT THESE COINS!
LET'S METALBEND, TEAM BEIFONG!
CLINK
SOB!
CLINK
TEAM BEIFONG?
CLINK
MY SHOES... MY SHOES...

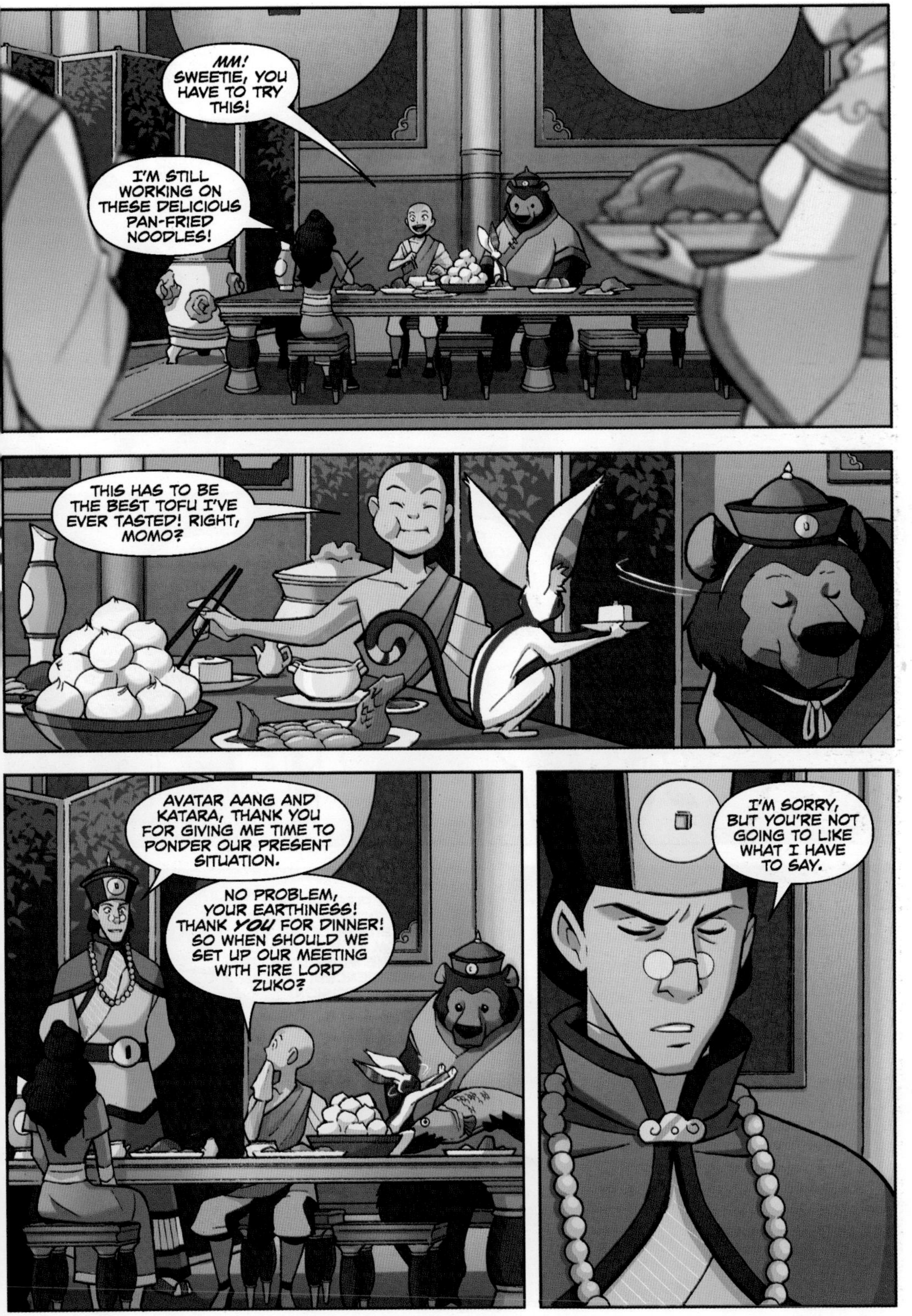
MM! SWEETIE, YOU HAVE TO TRY THIS!
I'M STILL WORKING ON THESE DELICIOUS PAN-FRIED NOODLES!
THIS HAS TO BE THE BEST TOFU I'VE EVER TASTED! RIGHT, MOMO?
AVATAR AANG AND KATARA, THANK YOU FOR GIVING ME TIME TO PONDER OUR PRESENT SITUATION.
NO PROBLEM, YOUR EARTHINESS! THANK YOU FOR DINNER! SO WHEN SHOULD WE SET UP OUR MEETING WITH FIRE LORD ZUKO?
I'M SORRY, BUT YOU'RE NOT GOING TO LIKE WHAT I HAVE TO SAY.

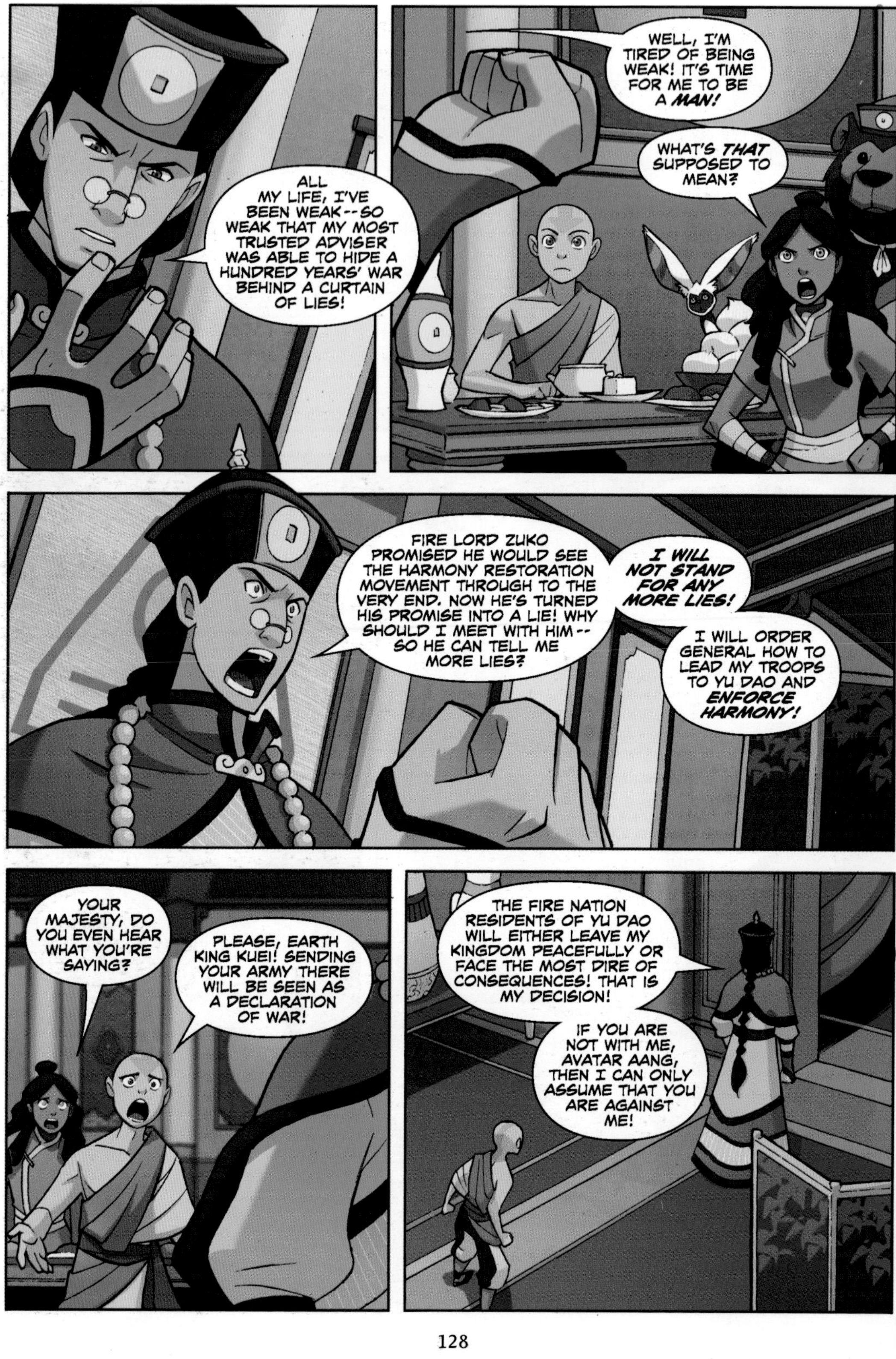
ALL MY LIFE, I'VE BEEN WEAK--SO WEAK THAT MY MOST TRUSTED ADVISER WAS ABLE TO HIDE A HUNDRED YEARS' WAR BEHIND A CURTAIN OF LIES!
WELL, I'M TIRED OF BEING WEAK! IT'S TIME FOR ME TO BE A *MAN!*
WHAT'S *THAT* SUPPOSED TO MEAN?
FIRE LORD ZUKO PROMISED HE WOULD SEE THE HARMONY RESTORATION MOVEMENT THROUGH TO THE VERY END. NOW HE'S TURNED HIS PROMISE INTO A LIE! WHY SHOULD I MEET WITH HIM--SO HE CAN TELL ME MORE LIES?
I WILL NOT STAND FOR ANY MORE LIES!
I WILL ORDER GENERAL HOW TO LEAD MY TROOPS TO YU DAO AND *ENFORCE HARMONY!*
YOUR MAJESTY, DO YOU EVEN HEAR WHAT YOU'RE SAYING?
PLEASE, EARTH KING KUEI! SENDING YOUR ARMY THERE WILL BE SEEN AS A DECLARATION OF WAR!
THE FIRE NATION RESIDENTS OF YU DAO WILL EITHER LEAVE MY KINGDOM PEACEFULLY OR FACE THE MOST DIRE OF CONSEQUENCES! THAT IS MY DECISION!
IF YOU ARE NOT WITH ME, AVATAR AANG, THEN I CAN ONLY ASSUME THAT YOU ARE AGAINST ME!

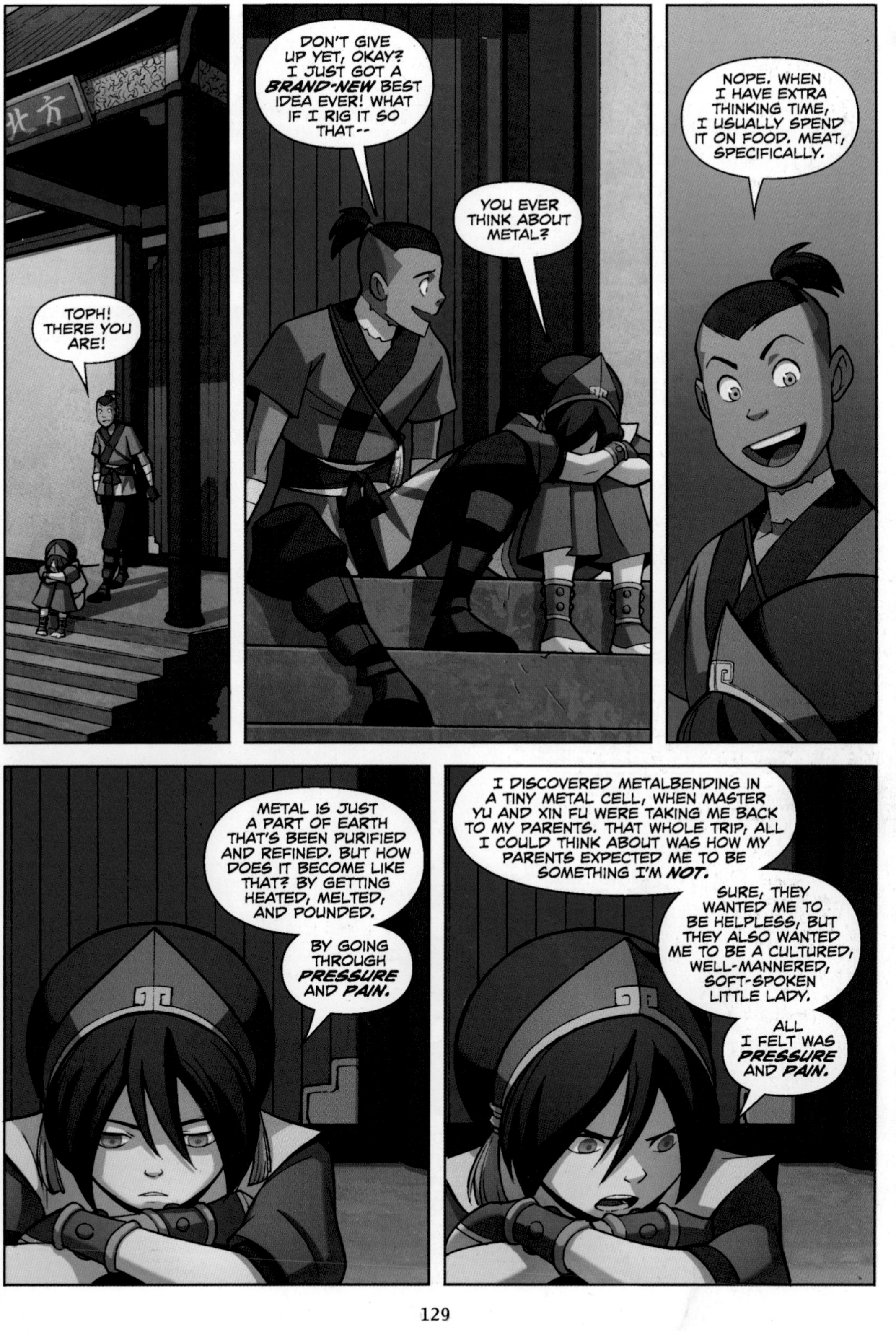

TOPH! THERE YOU ARE!
DON'T GIVE UP YET, OKAY? I JUST GOT A BRAND-NEW BEST IDEA EVER! WHAT IF I RIG IT SO THAT--
YOU EVER THINK ABOUT METAL?
NOPE. WHEN I HAVE EXTRA THINKING TIME, I USUALLY SPEND IT ON FOOD. MEAT, SPECIFICALLY.
METAL IS JUST A PART OF EARTH THAT'S BEEN PURIFIED AND REFINED. BUT HOW DOES IT BECOME LIKE THAT? BY GETTING HEATED, MELTED, AND POUNDED.
BY GOING THROUGH PRESSURE AND PAIN.
I DISCOVERED METALBENDING IN A TINY METAL CELL, WHEN MASTER YU AND XIN FU WERE TAKING ME BACK TO MY PARENTS. THAT WHOLE TRIP, ALL I COULD THINK ABOUT WAS HOW MY PARENTS EXPECTED ME TO BE SOMETHING I'M NOT.
SURE, THEY WANTED ME TO BE HELPLESS, BUT THEY ALSO WANTED ME TO BE A CULTURED, WELL-MANNERED, SOFT-SPOKEN LITTLE LADY.
ALL I FELT WAS PRESSURE AND PAIN.

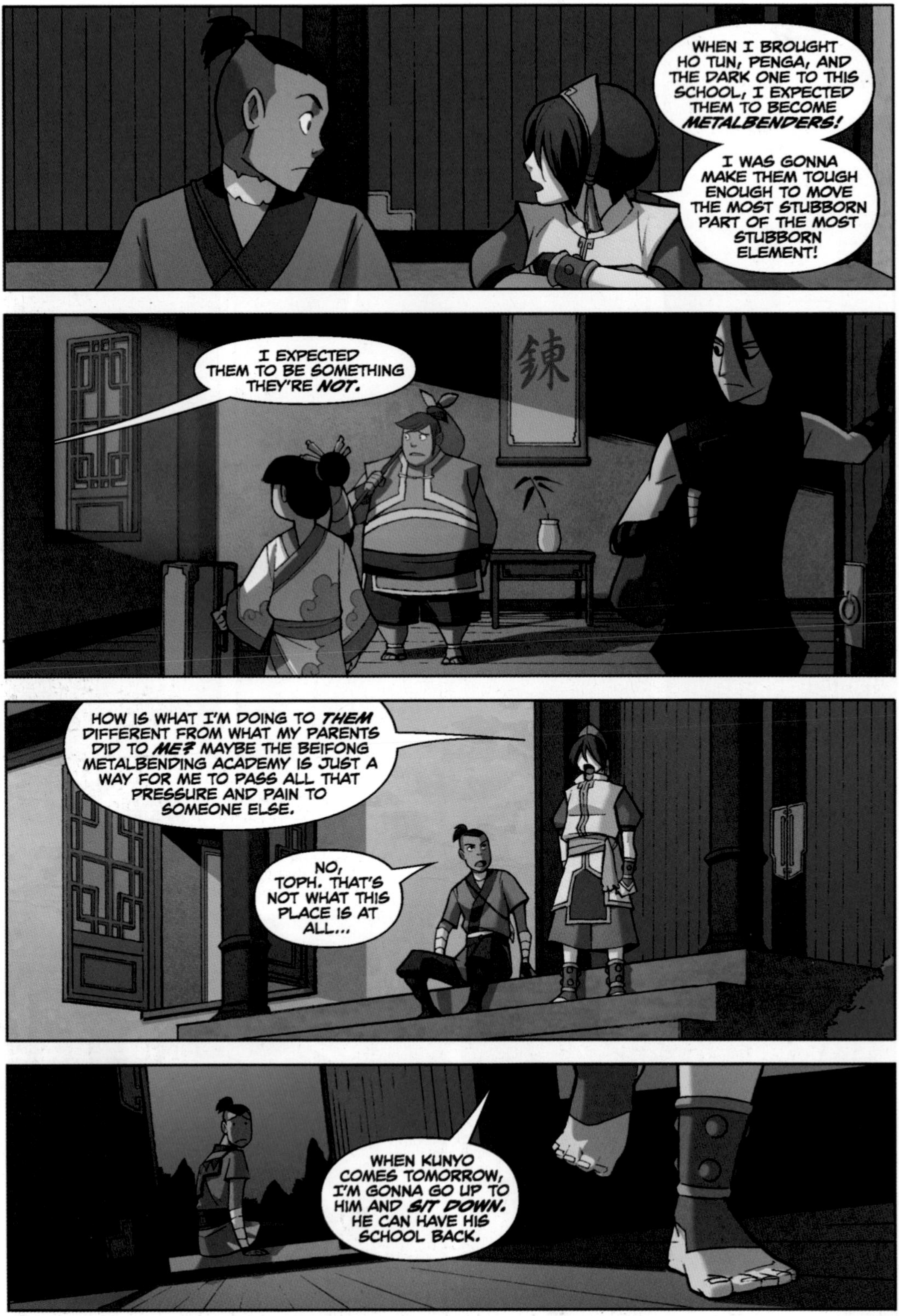
WHEN I BROUGHT HO TUN, PENGA, AND THE DARK ONE TO THIS SCHOOL, I EXPECTED THEM TO BECOME METALBENDERS!
I WAS GONNA MAKE THEM TOUGH ENOUGH TO MOVE THE MOST STUBBORN PART OF THE MOST STUBBORN ELEMENT!
I EXPECTED THEM TO BE SOMETHING THEY'RE NOT.
HOW IS WHAT I'M DOING TO THEM DIFFERENT FROM WHAT MY PARENTS DID TO ME? MAYBE THE BEIFONG METALBENDING ACADEMY IS JUST A WAY FOR ME TO PASS ALL THAT PRESSURE AND PAIN TO SOMEONE ELSE.
NO, TOPH. THAT'S NOT WHAT THIS PLACE IS AT ALL...
WHEN KUNYO COMES TOMORROW, I'M GONNA GO UP TO HIM AND SIT DOWN. HE CAN HAVE HIS SCHOOL BACK.

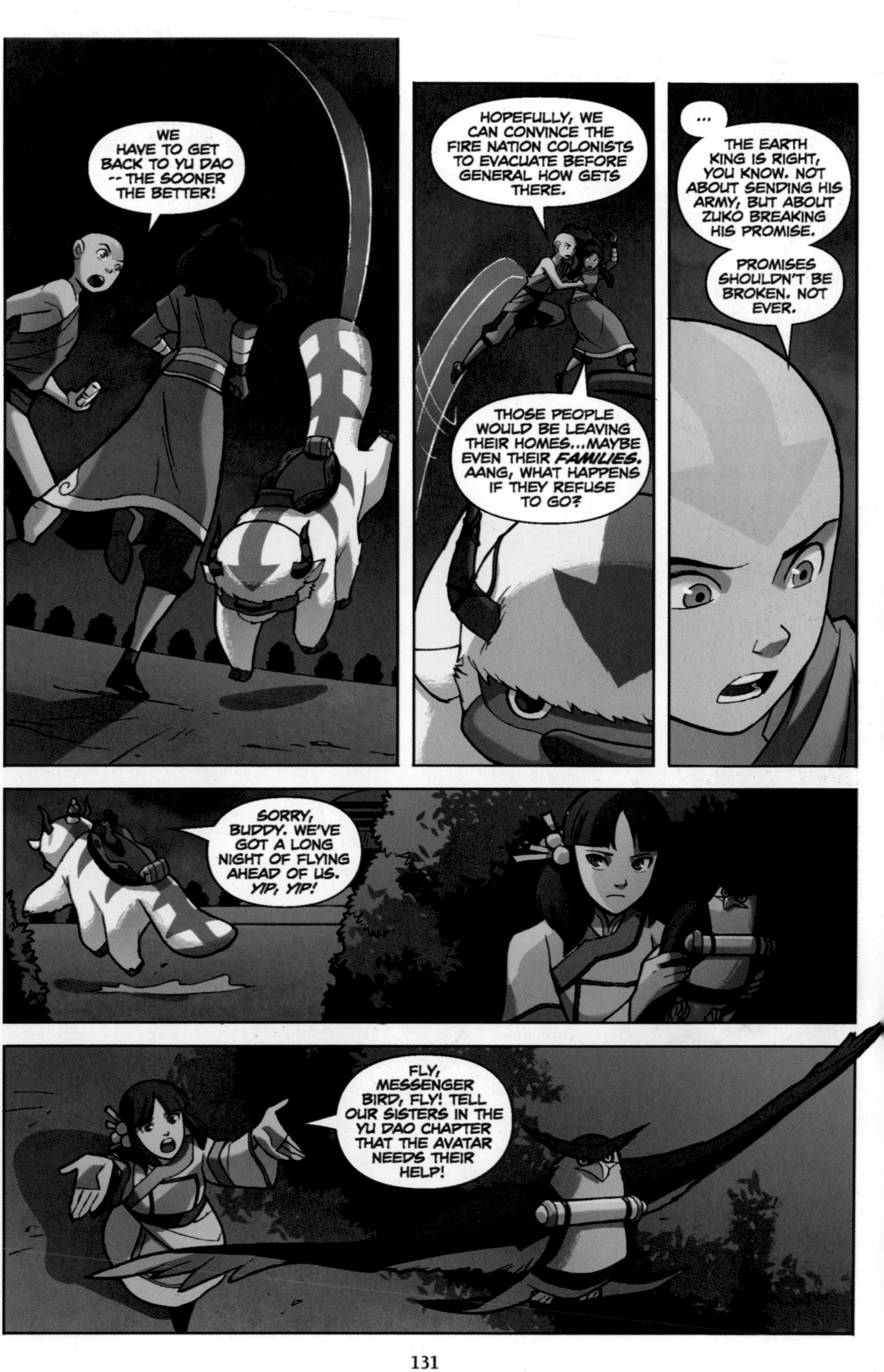
WE HAVE TO GET BACK TO YU DAO -- THE SOONER THE BETTER!
HOPEFULLY, WE CAN CONVINCE THE FIRE NATION COLONISTS TO EVACUATE BEFORE GENERAL HOW GETS THERE.
THOSE PEOPLE WOULD BE LEAVING THEIR HOMES...MAYBE EVEN THEIR *FAMILIES.* AANG, WHAT HAPPENS IF THEY REFUSE TO GO?
...
THE EARTH KING IS RIGHT, YOU KNOW. NOT ABOUT SENDING HIS ARMY, BUT ABOUT ZUKO BREAKING HIS PROMISE.
PROMISES SHOULDN'T BE BROKEN. NOT EVER.
SORRY, BUDDY. WE'VE GOT A LONG NIGHT OF FLYING AHEAD OF US. *YIP, YIP!*
FLY, MESSENGER BIRD, FLY! TELL OUR SISTERS IN THE YU DAO CHAPTER THAT THE AVATAR NEEDS THEIR HELP!

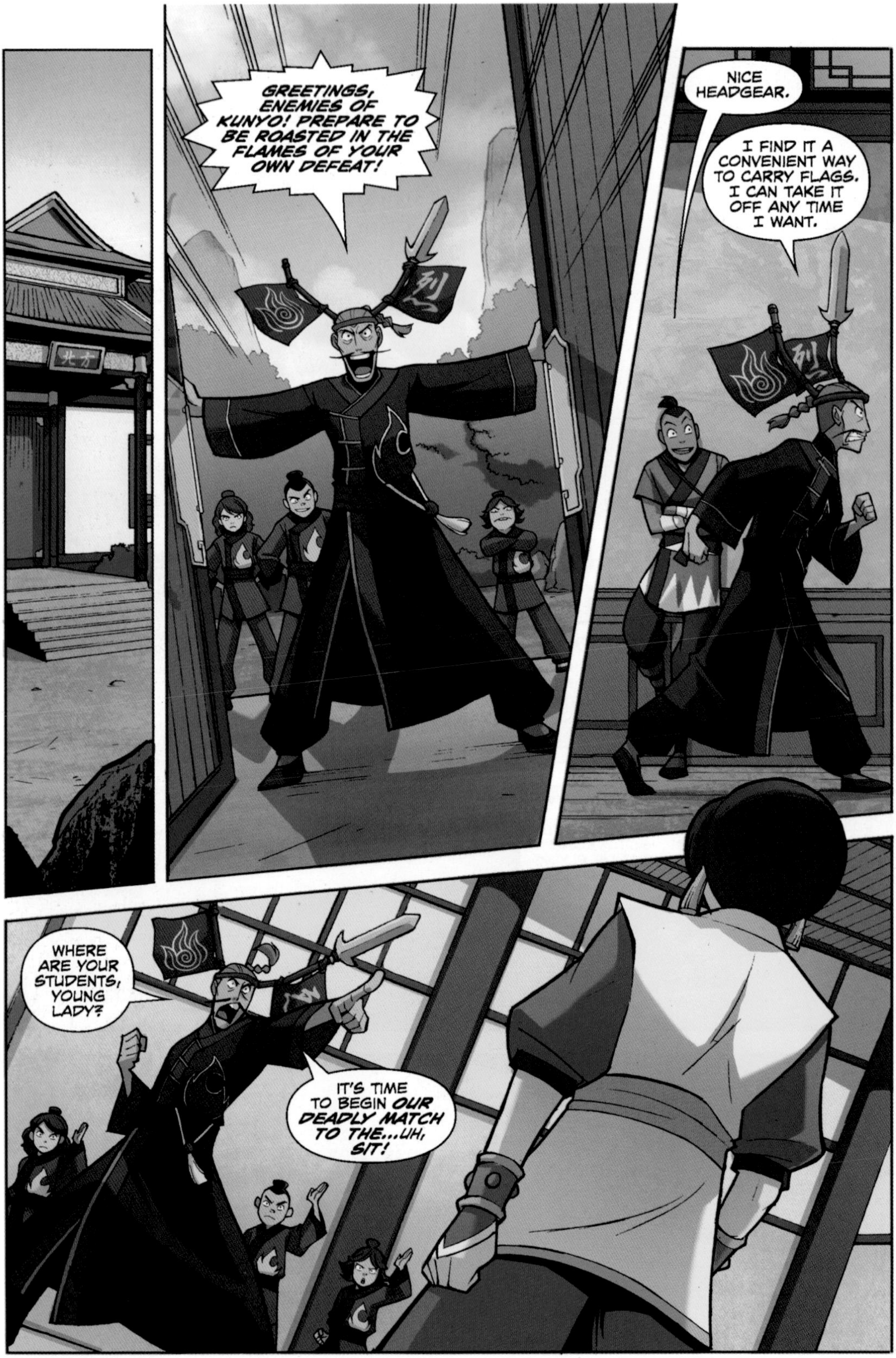

GREETINGS, ENEMIES OF KUNYO! PREPARE TO BE ROASTED IN THE FLAMES OF YOUR OWN DEFEAT!
NICE HEADGEAR.
I FIND IT A CONVENIENT WAY TO CARRY FLAGS. I CAN TAKE IT OFF ANY TIME I WANT.
WHERE ARE YOUR STUDENTS, YOUNG LADY?
IT'S TIME TO BEGIN OUR DEADLY MATCH TO THE...UH, SIT!

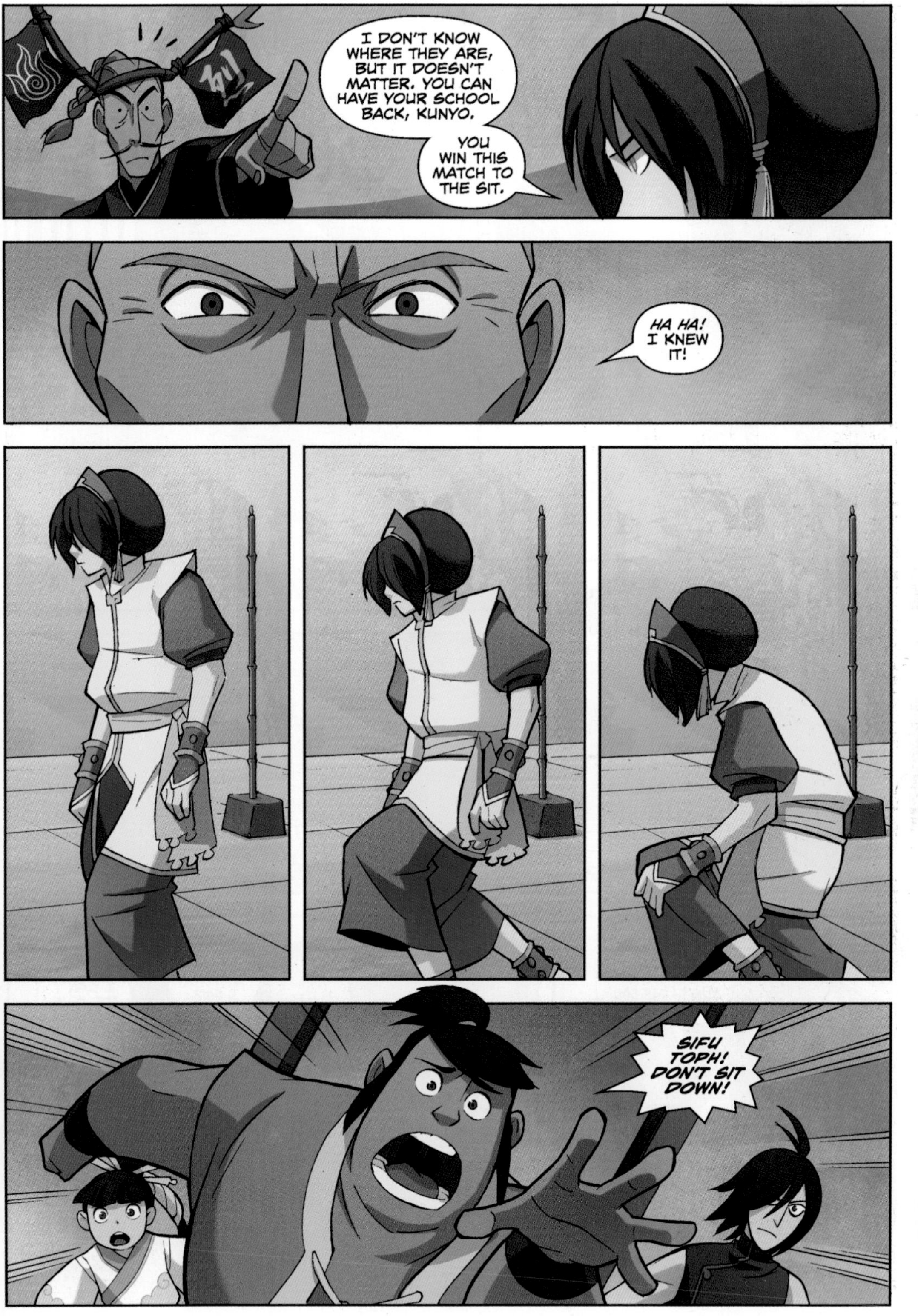
I DON'T KNOW WHERE THEY ARE, BUT IT DOESN'T MATTER. YOU CAN HAVE YOUR SCHOOL BACK, KUNYO.
YOU WIN THIS MATCH TO THE SIT.
HA HA! I KNEW IT!
SIFU TOPH! DON'T SIT DOWN!

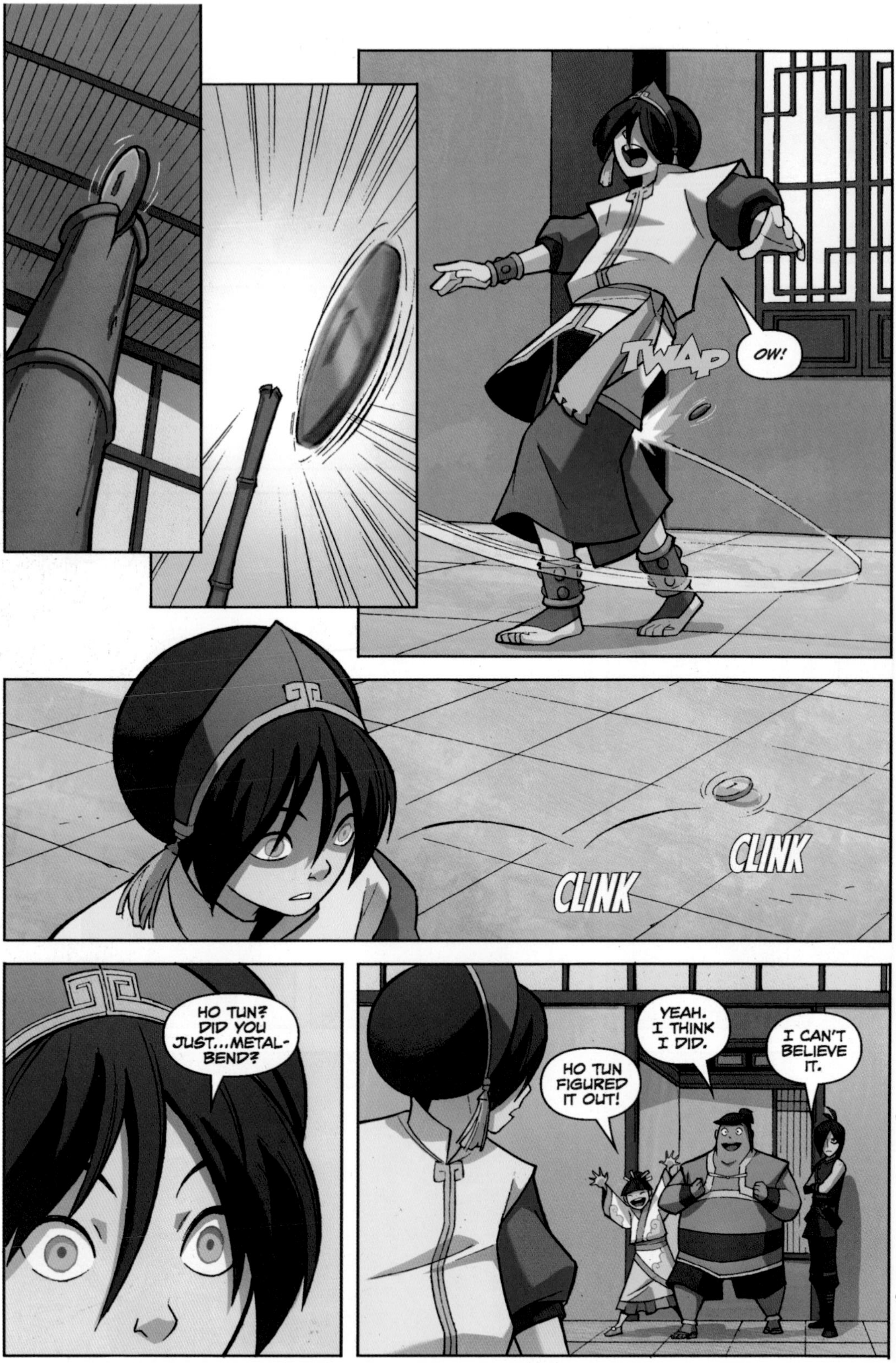

TWAP
OW!
CLINK
CLINK
HO TUN? DID YOU JUST...METAL-BEND?
HO TUN FIGURED IT OUT!
YEAH. I THINK I DID.
I CAN'T BELIEVE IT.

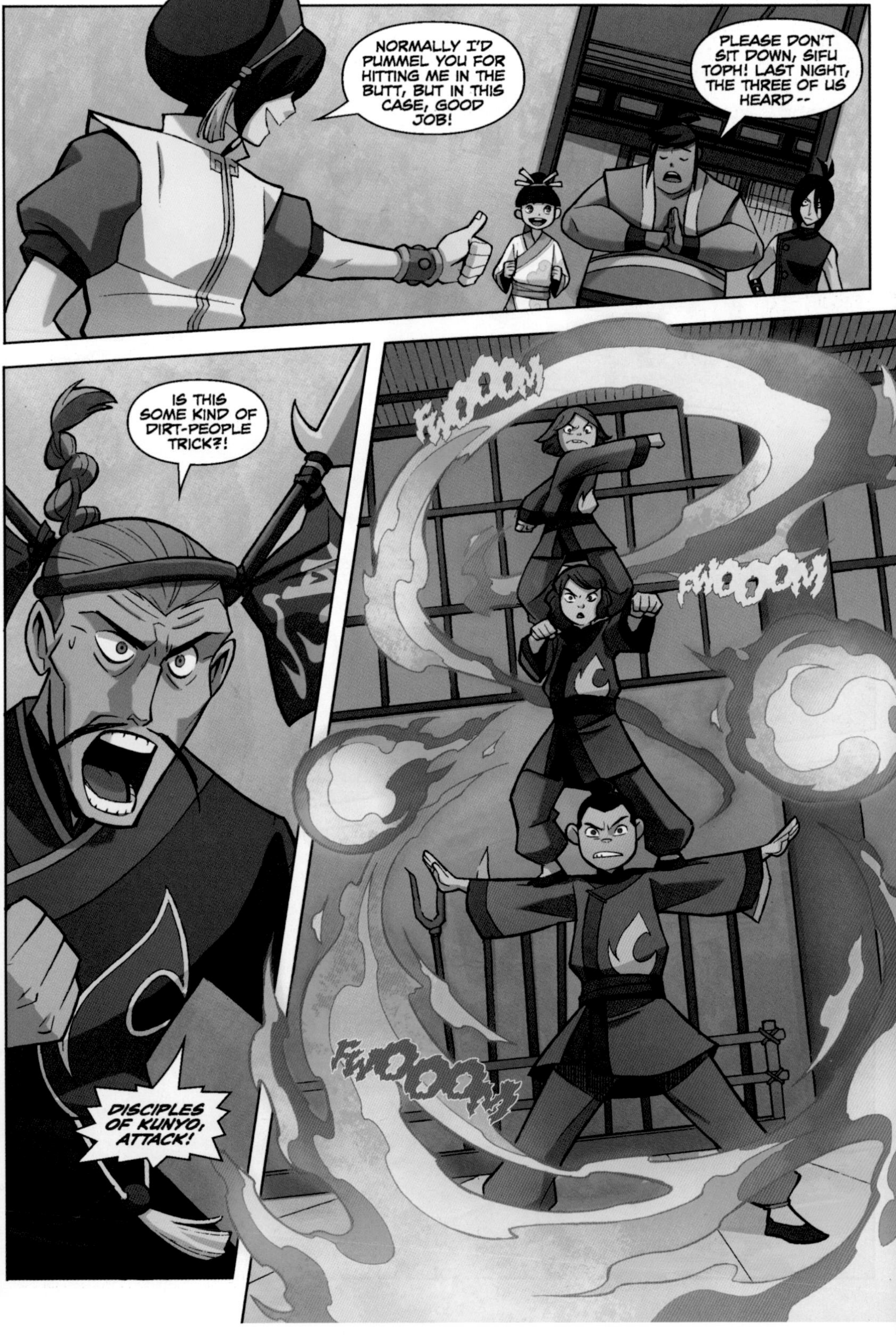
NORMALLY I'D PUMMEL YOU FOR HITTING ME IN THE BUTT, BUT IN THIS CASE, GOOD JOB!
PLEASE DON'T SIT DOWN, SIFU TOPH! LAST NIGHT, THE THREE OF US HEARD --
IS THIS SOME KIND OF DIRT-PEOPLE TRICK?!
DISCIPLES OF KUNYO, ATTACK!
FWOOOM
FWOOOM
FWOOOM

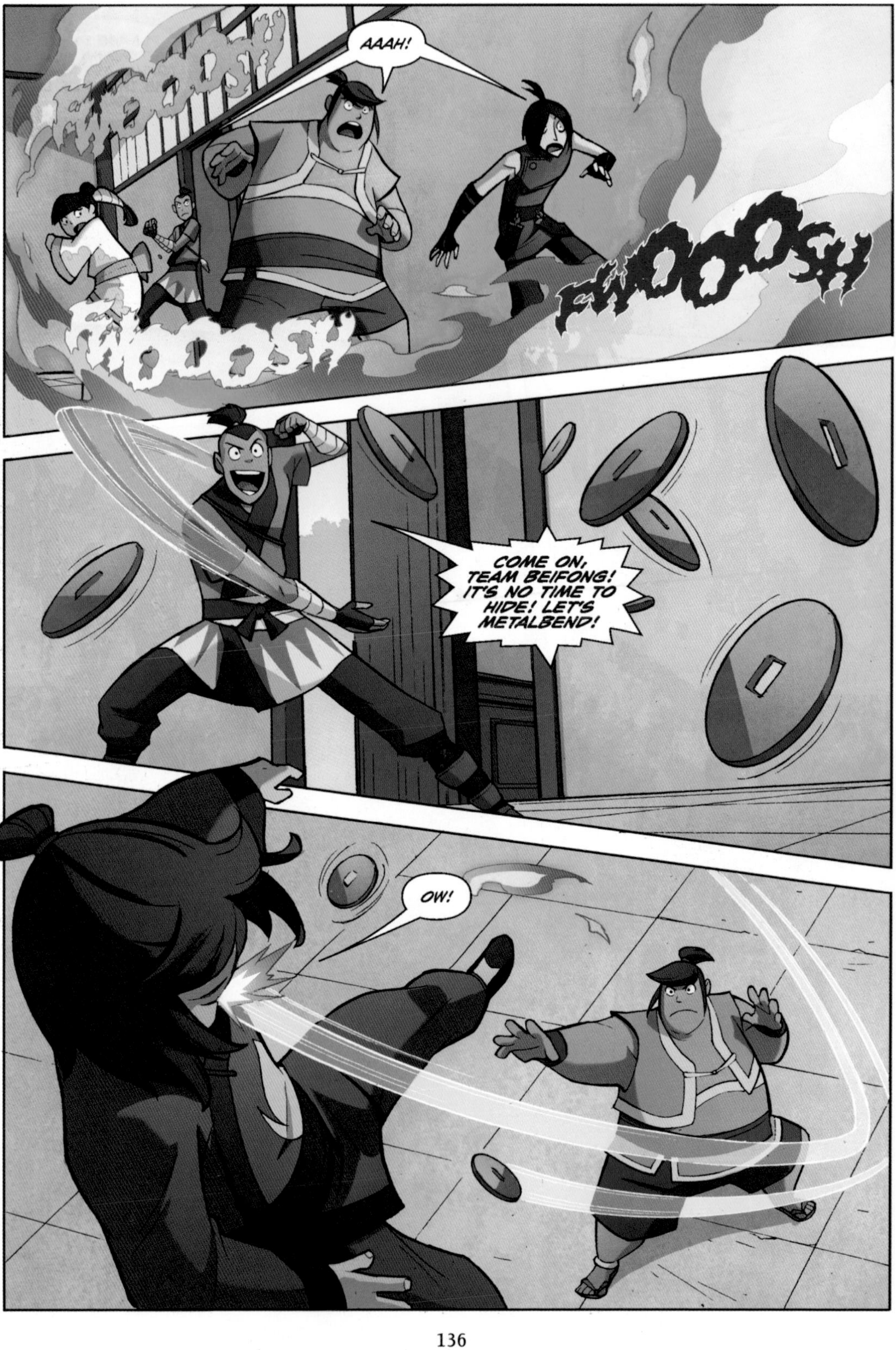
FWOOOSH
AAAH!
FWOOOSH
FWOOOSH
COME ON, TEAM BEIFONG! IT'S NO TIME TO HIDE! LET'S METALBEND!
OW!

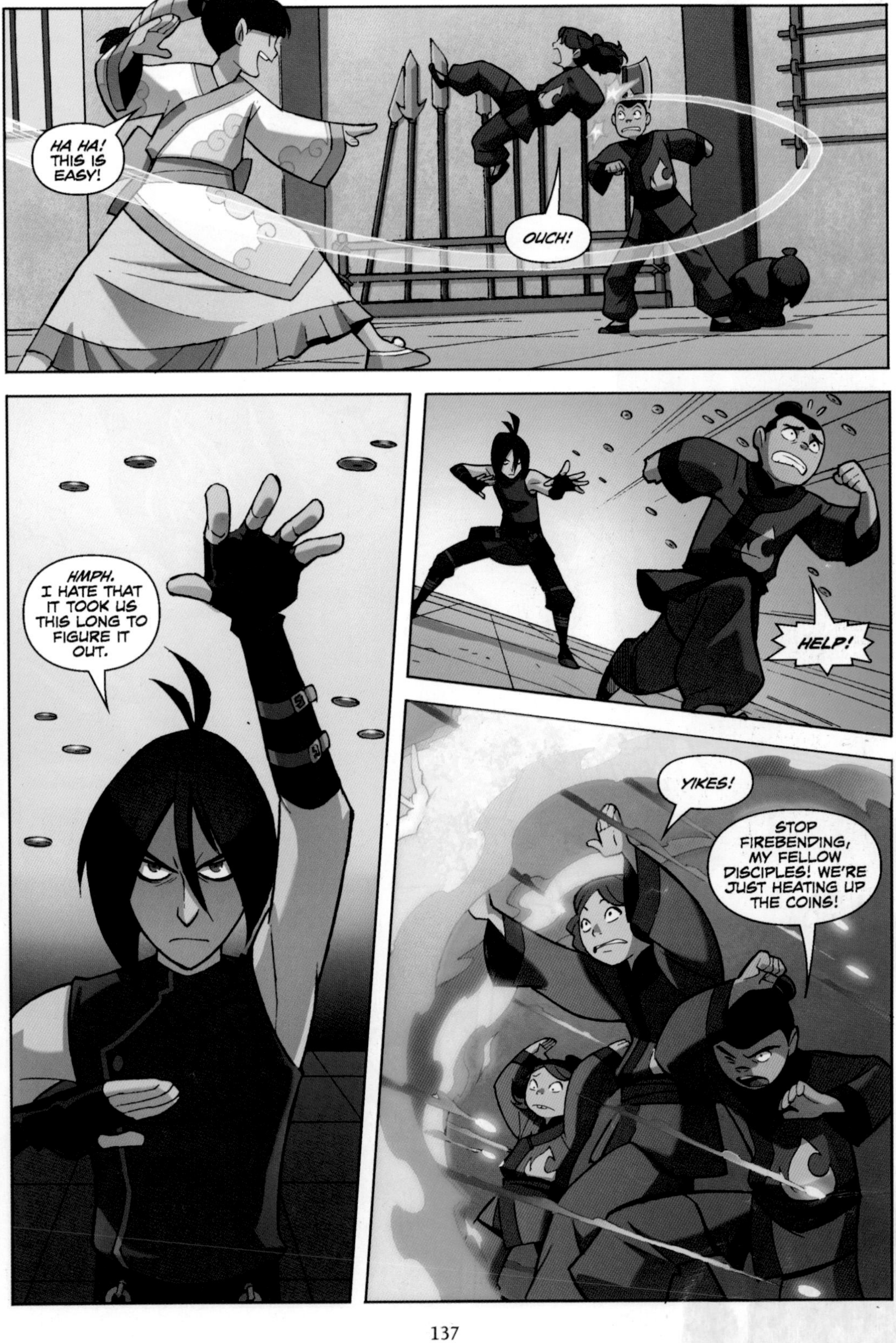
HA HA! THIS IS EASY!
OUCH!
HMPH. I HATE THAT IT TOOK US THIS LONG TO FIGURE IT OUT.
HELP!
YIKES!
STOP FIREBENDING, MY FELLOW DISCIPLES! WE'RE JUST HEATING UP THE COINS!

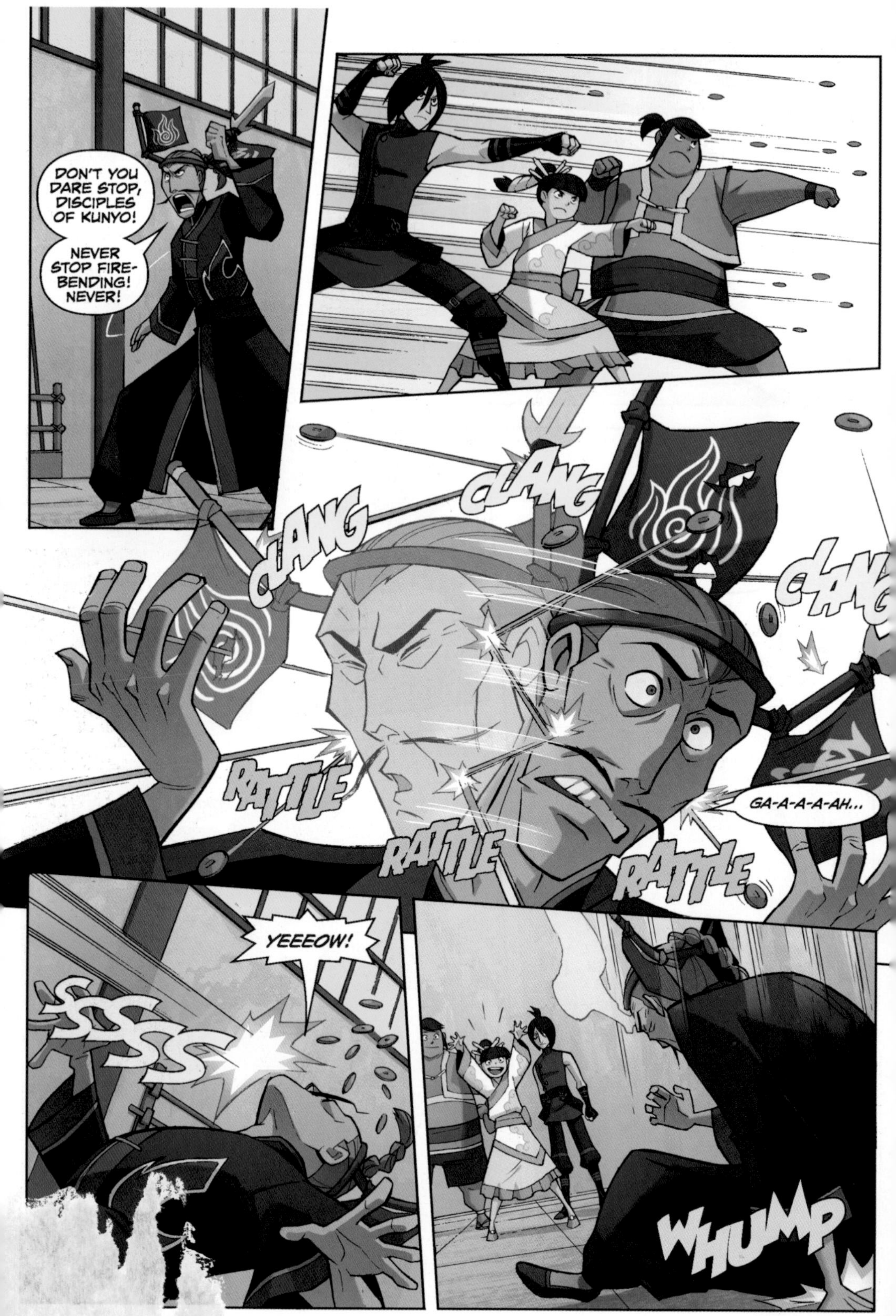
DON'T YOU DARE STOP, DISCIPLES OF KUNYO!
NEVER STOP FIRE-BENDING! NEVER!
CLANG
CLANG
CLANG
RATTLE
RATTLE
RATTLE
GA-A-A-A-AH...
YEEEOW!
SSSSS
WHUMP

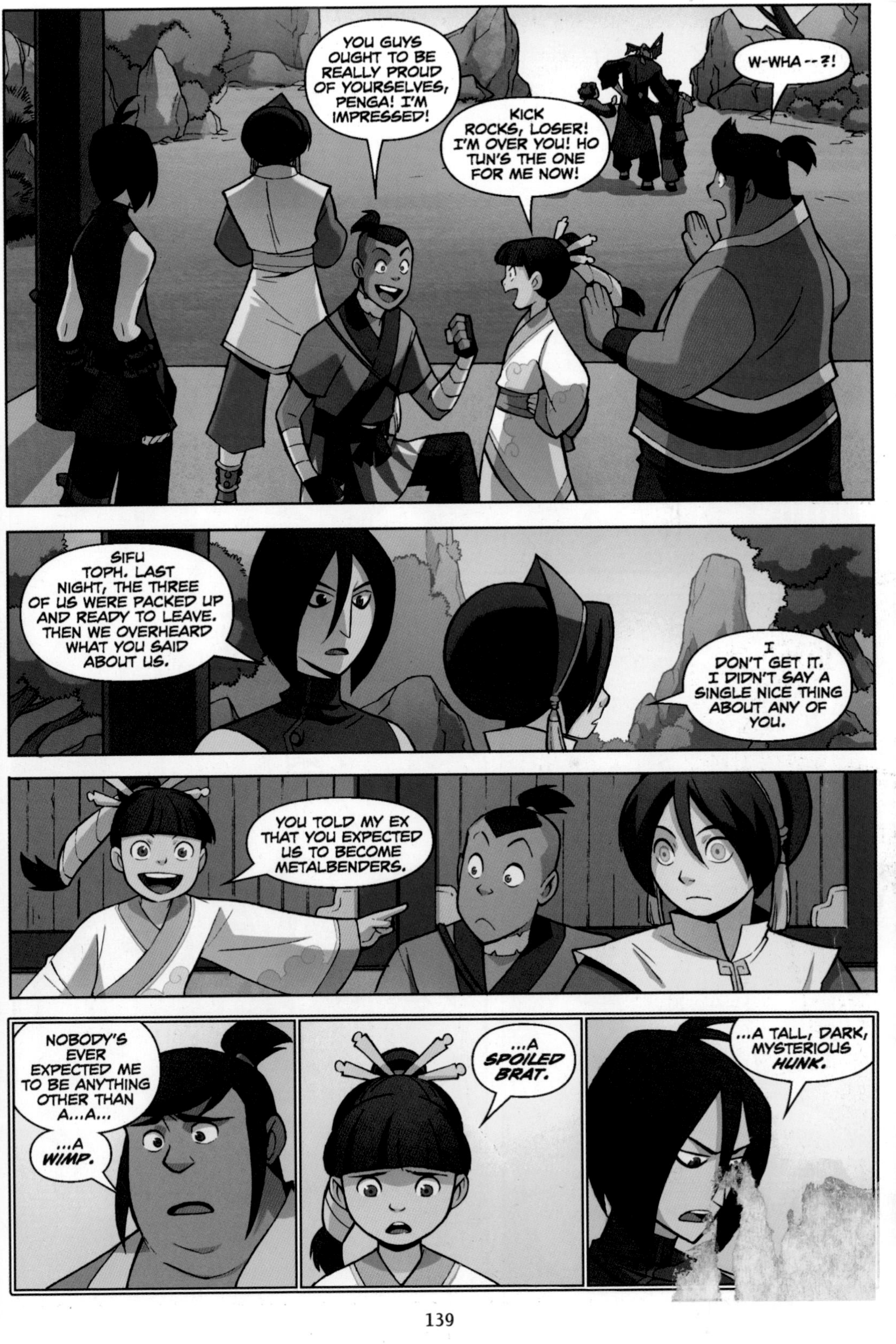
YOU GUYS OUGHT TO BE REALLY PROUD OF YOURSELVES, PENGA! I'M IMPRESSED!
KICK ROCKS, LOSER! I'M OVER YOU! HO TUN'S THE ONE FOR ME NOW!
W-WHA--?!
SIFU TOPH. LAST NIGHT, THE THREE OF US WERE PACKED UP AND READY TO LEAVE. THEN WE OVERHEARD WHAT YOU SAID ABOUT US.
I DON'T GET IT. I DIDN'T SAY A SINGLE NICE THING ABOUT ANY OF YOU.
YOU TOLD MY EX THAT YOU EXPECTED US TO BECOME METALBENDERS.
NOBODY'S EVER EXPECTED ME TO BE ANYTHING OTHER THAN A...A...
...A WIMP.
...A SPOILED BRAT.
...A TALL, DARK, MYSTERIOUS HUNK.

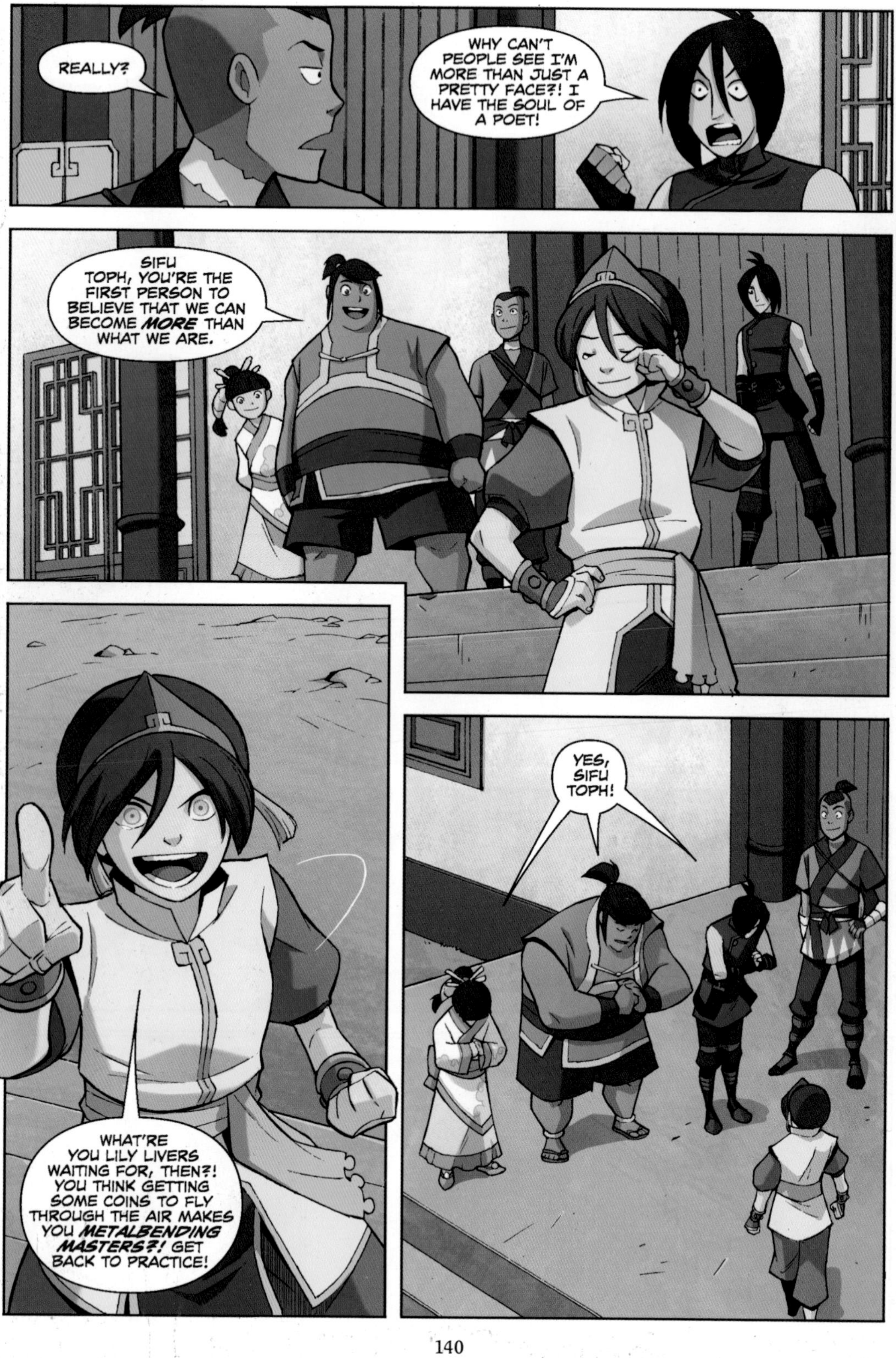
REALLY?
WHY CAN'T PEOPLE SEE I'M MORE THAN JUST A PRETTY FACE?! I HAVE THE SOUL OF A POET!
SIFU TOPH, YOU'RE THE FIRST PERSON TO BELIEVE THAT WE CAN BECOME MORE THAN WHAT WE ARE.
WHAT'RE YOU LILY LIVERS WAITING FOR, THEN?! YOU THINK GETTING SOME COINS TO FLY THROUGH THE AIR MAKES YOU METALBENDING MASTERS?! GET BACK TO PRACTICE!
YES, SIFU TOPH!

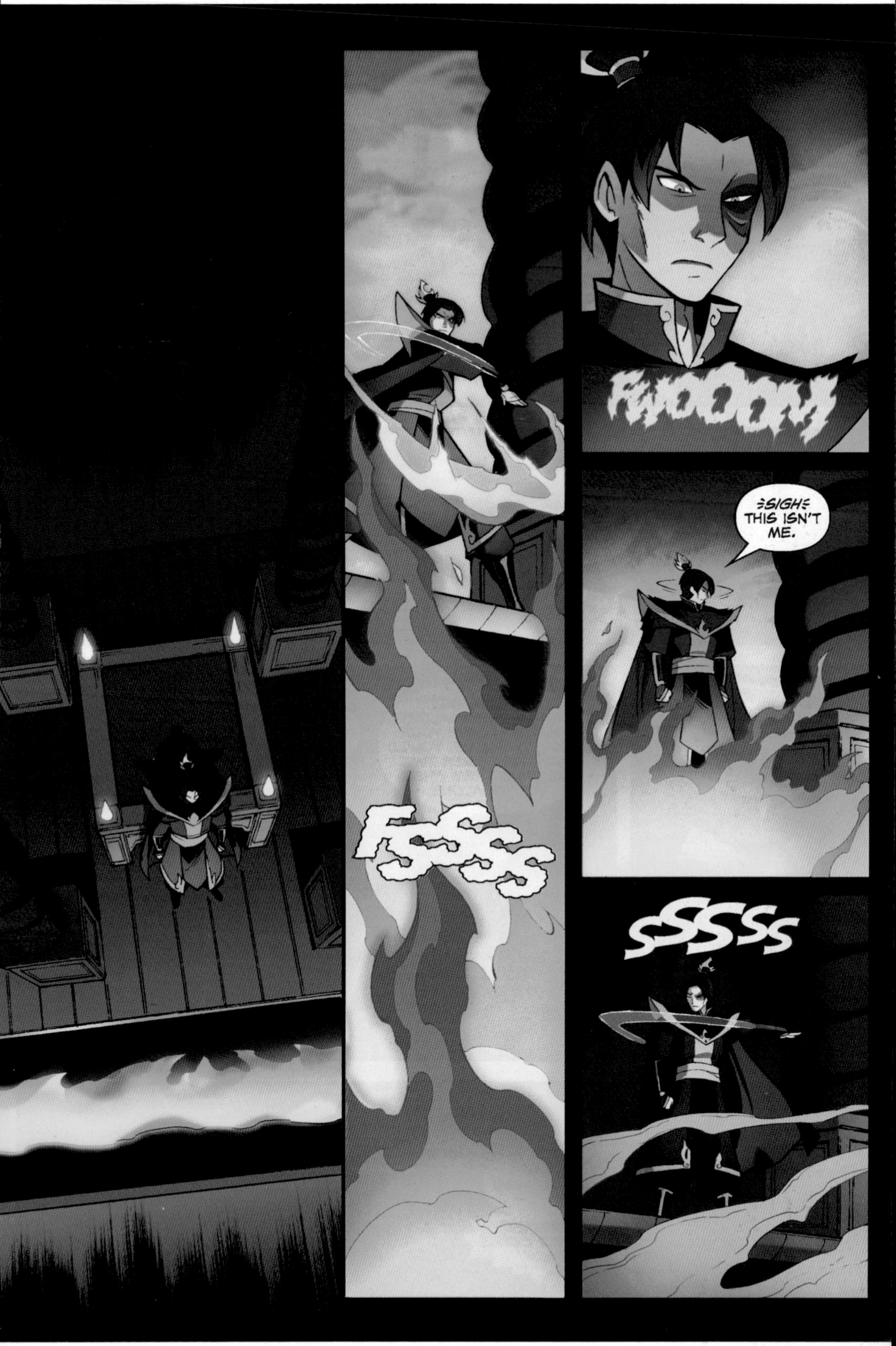
FWOOOM
FSSSS
≈SIGH≈
THIS ISN'T
ME.
SSSSS

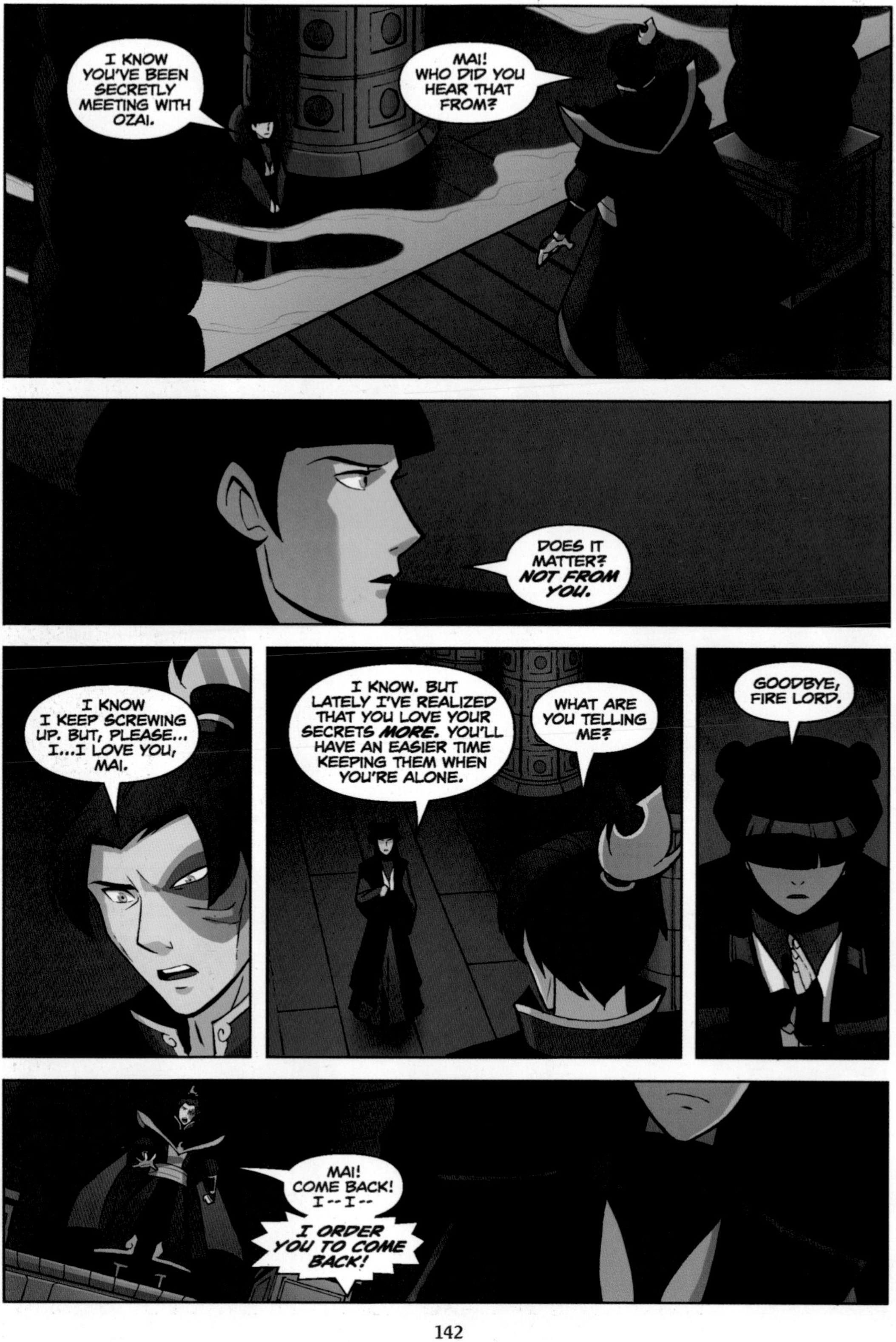
I KNOW YOU'VE BEEN SECRETLY MEETING WITH OZAI.
MAI! WHO DID YOU HEAR THAT FROM?
DOES IT MATTER? NOT FROM YOU.
I KNOW I KEEP SCREWING UP. BUT, PLEASE... I...I LOVE YOU, MAI.
I KNOW. BUT LATELY I'VE REALIZED THAT YOU LOVE YOUR SECRETS MORE. YOU'LL HAVE AN EASIER TIME KEEPING THEM WHEN YOU'RE ALONE.
WHAT ARE YOU TELLING ME?
GOODBYE, FIRE LORD.
MAI! COME BACK! I -- I --
I ORDER YOU TO COME BACK!

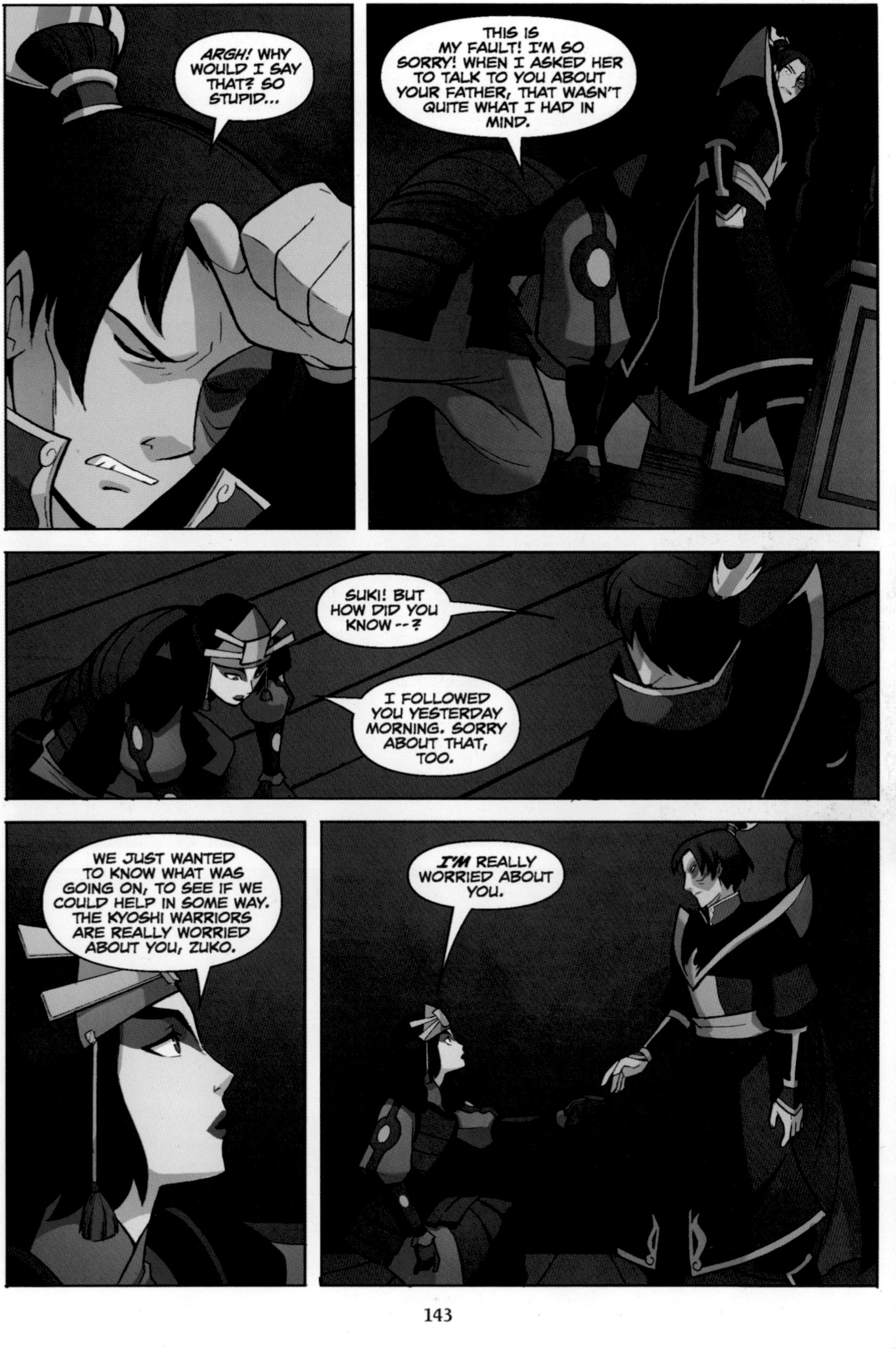
ARGH! WHY WOULD I SAY THAT? SO STUPID...
THIS IS MY FAULT! I'M SO SORRY! WHEN I ASKED HER TO TALK TO YOU ABOUT YOUR FATHER, THAT WASN'T QUITE WHAT I HAD IN MIND.
SUKI! BUT HOW DID YOU KNOW --?
I FOLLOWED YOU YESTERDAY MORNING. SORRY ABOUT THAT, TOO.
WE JUST WANTED TO KNOW WHAT WAS GOING ON, TO SEE IF WE COULD HELP IN SOME WAY. THE KYOSHI WARRIORS ARE REALLY WORRIED ABOUT YOU, ZUKO.
I'M REALLY WORRIED ABOUT YOU.

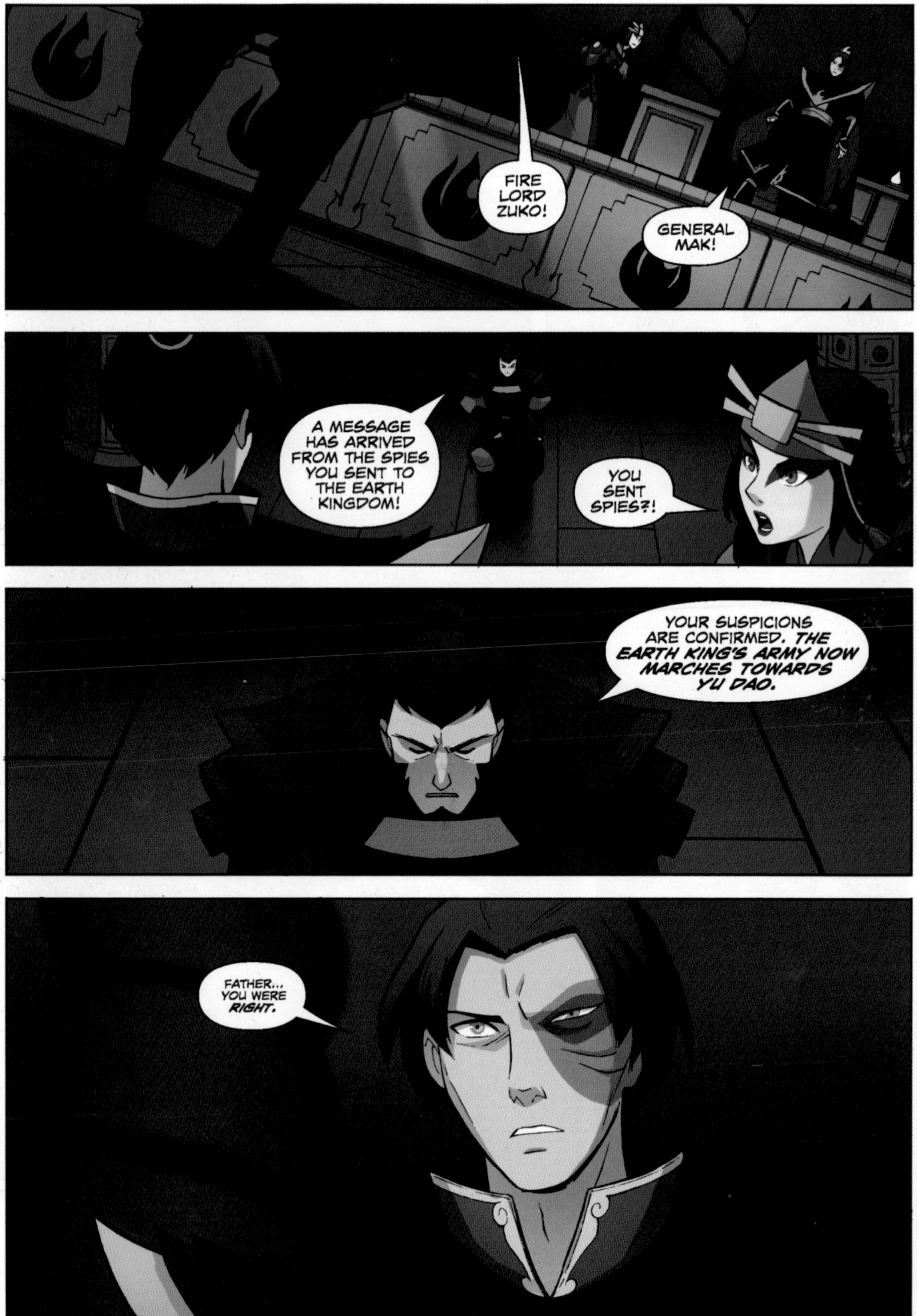
FIRE LORD ZUKO!
GENERAL MAK!
A MESSAGE HAS ARRIVED FROM THE SPIES YOU SENT TO THE EARTH KINGDOM!
YOU SENT SPIES?!
YOUR SUSPICIONS ARE CONFIRMED. THE EARTH KING'S ARMY NOW MARCHES TOWARDS YU DAO.
FATHER... YOU WERE RIGHT.

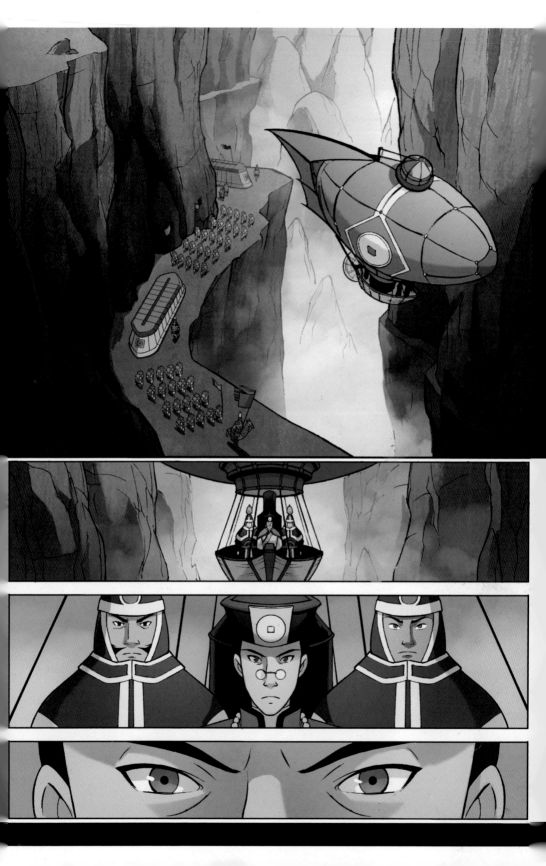

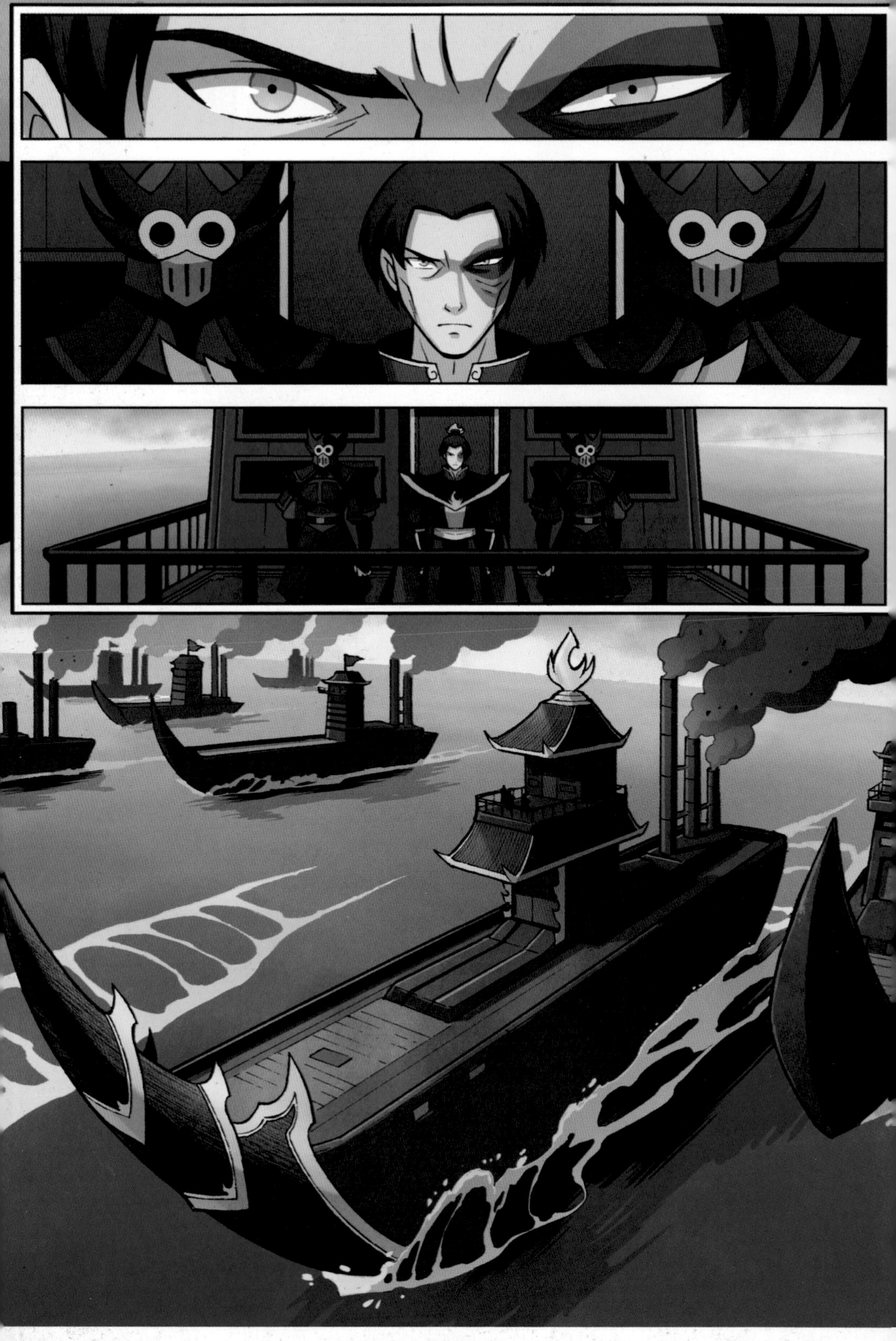

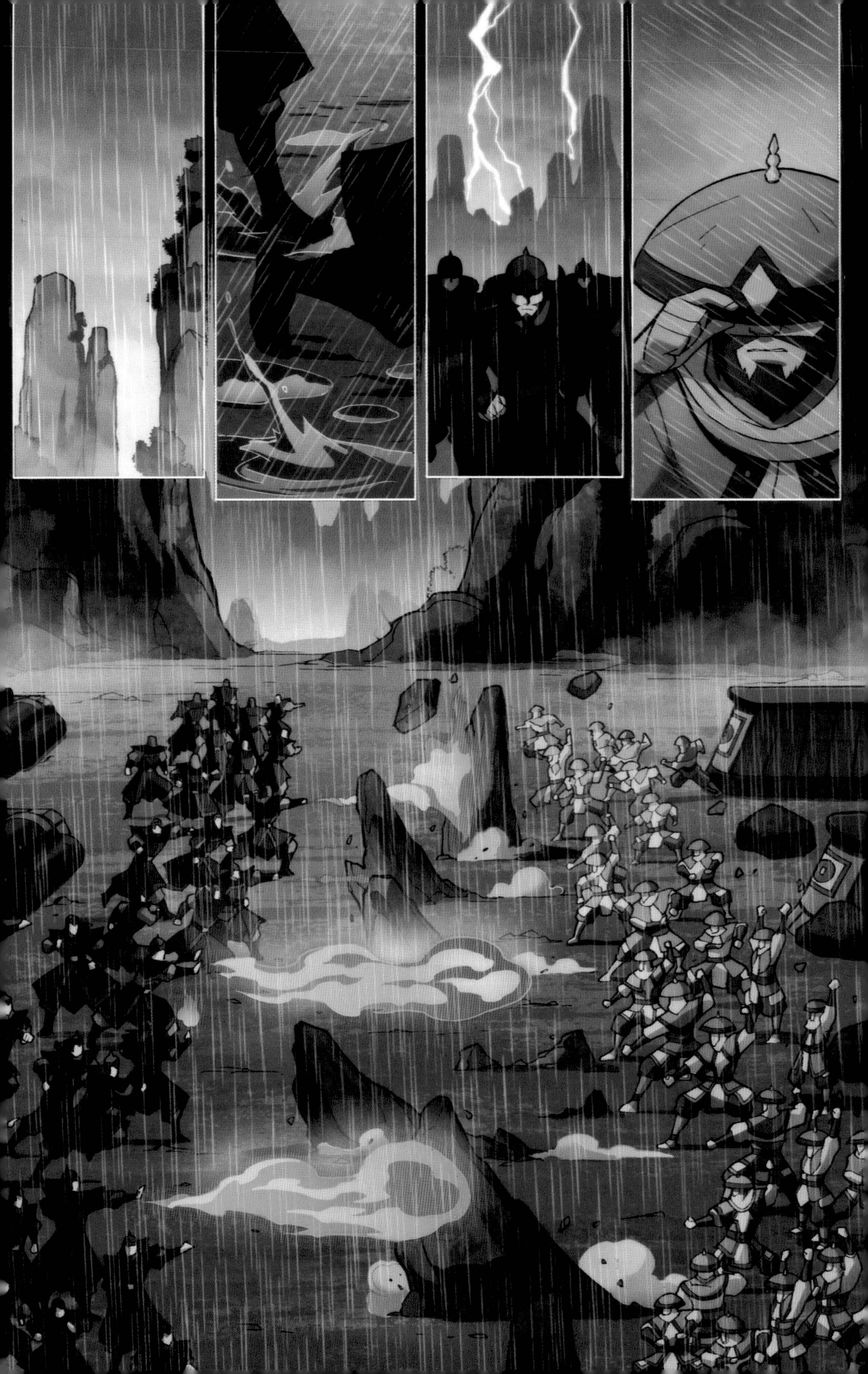

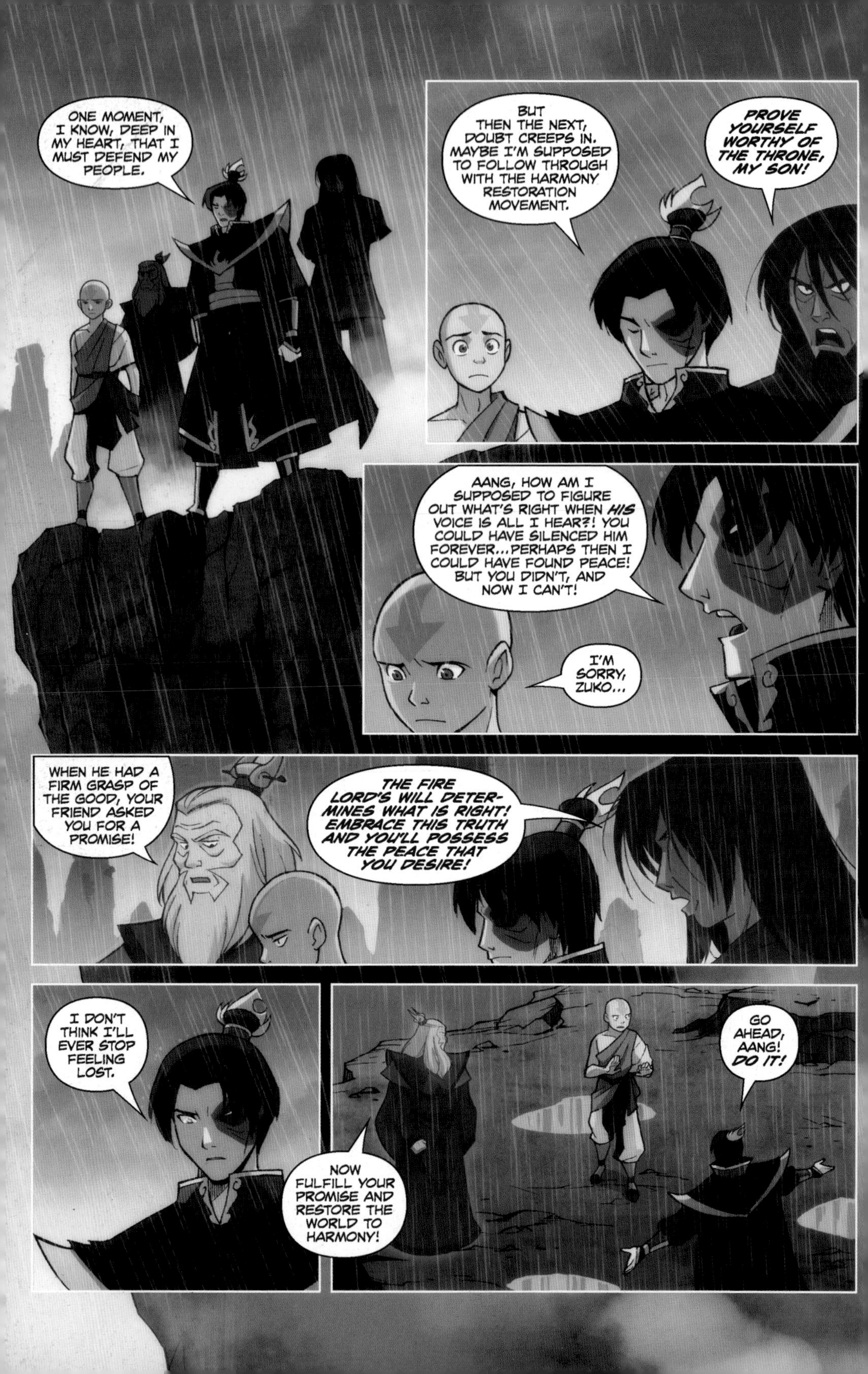
ONE MOMENT, I KNOW, DEEP IN MY HEART, THAT I MUST DEFEND MY PEOPLE.
BUT THEN THE NEXT, DOUBT CREEPS IN. MAYBE I'M SUPPOSED TO FOLLOW THROUGH WITH THE HARMONY RESTORATION MOVEMENT.
PROVE YOURSELF WORTHY OF THE THRONE, MY SON!
AANG, HOW AM I SUPPOSED TO FIGURE OUT WHAT'S RIGHT WHEN HIS VOICE IS ALL I HEAR?! YOU COULD HAVE SILENCED HIM FOREVER...PERHAPS THEN I COULD HAVE FOUND PEACE! BUT YOU DIDN'T, AND NOW I CAN'T!
I'M SORRY, ZUKO...
WHEN HE HAD A FIRM GRASP OF THE GOOD, YOUR FRIEND ASKED YOU FOR A PROMISE!
THE FIRE LORD'S WILL DETERMINES WHAT IS RIGHT! EMBRACE THIS TRUTH AND YOU'LL POSSESS THE PEACE THAT YOU DESIRE!
I DON'T THINK I'LL EVER STOP FEELING LOST.
NOW FULFILL YOUR PROMISE AND RESTORE THE WORLD TO HARMONY!
GO AHEAD, AANG! DO IT!

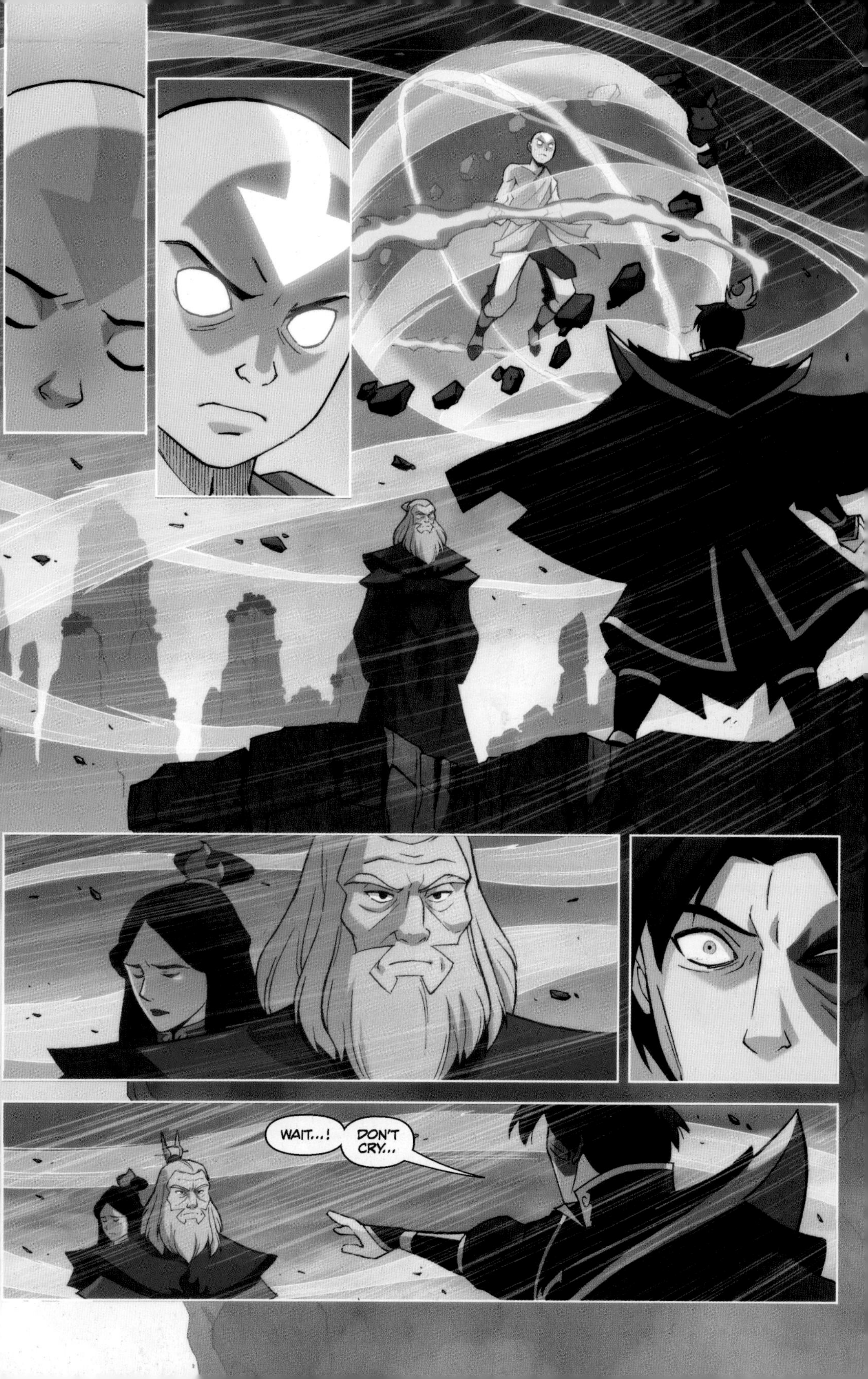
WAIT...!
DON'T CRY...

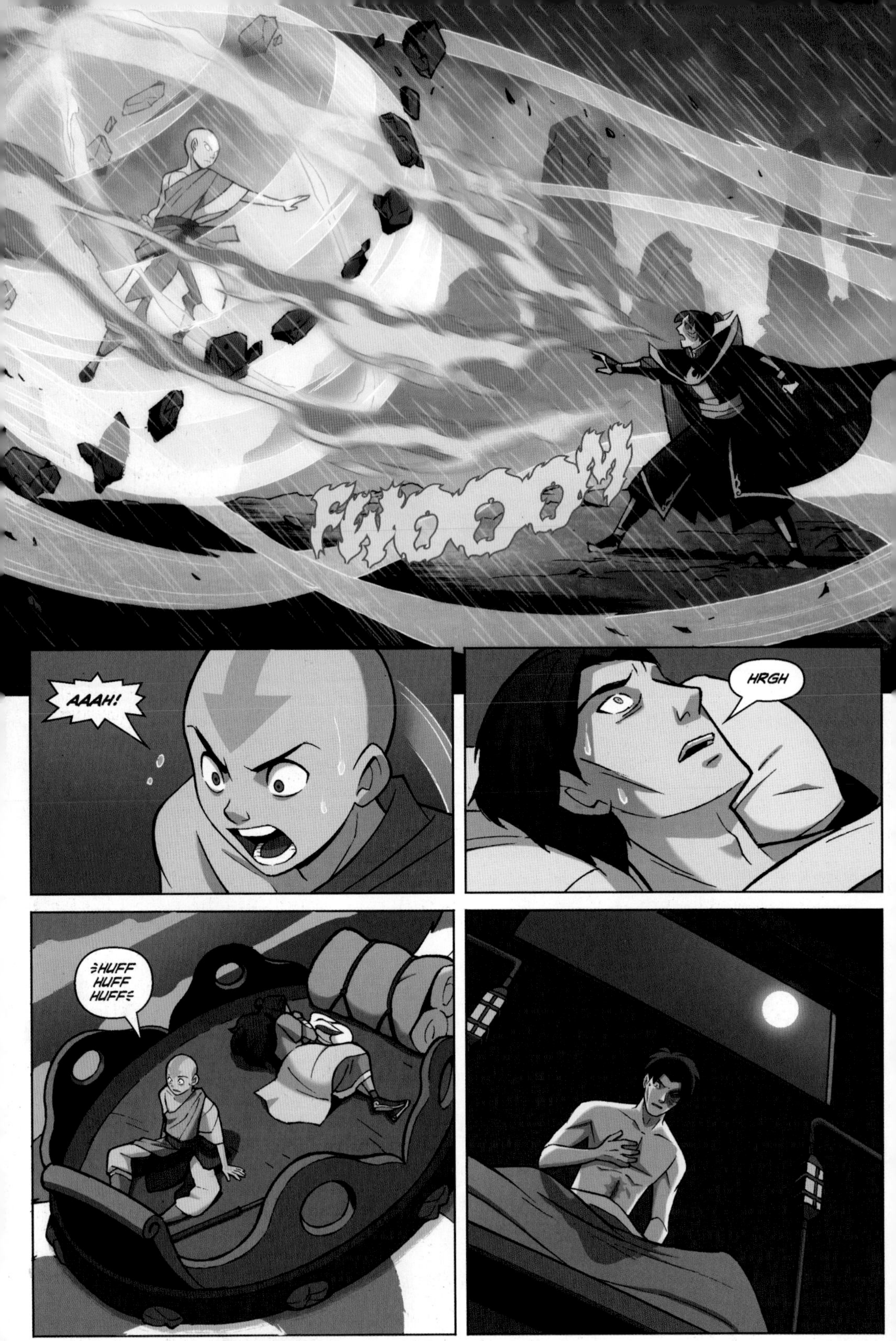
FWOOOOM
AAAH!
HRGH
HUFF HUFF HUFF

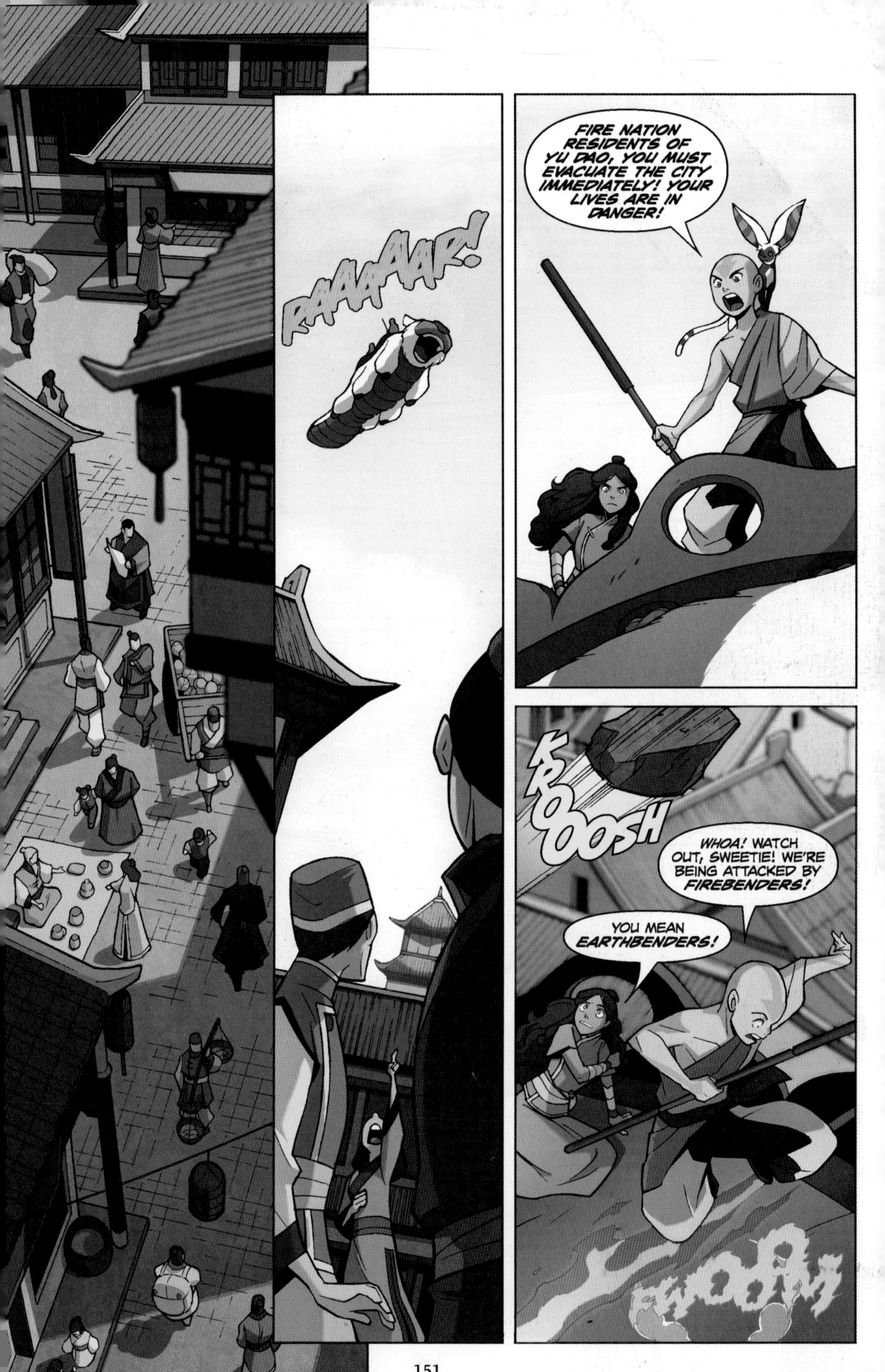
RAAAAAR!
FIRE NATION RESIDENTS OF YU DAO, YOU MUST EVACUATE THE CITY IMMEDIATELY! YOUR LIVES ARE IN DANGER!
KROOOOSH
WHOA! WATCH OUT, SWEETIE! WE'RE BEING ATTACKED BY FIREBENDERS!
YOU MEAN EARTHBENDERS!
FWOOM

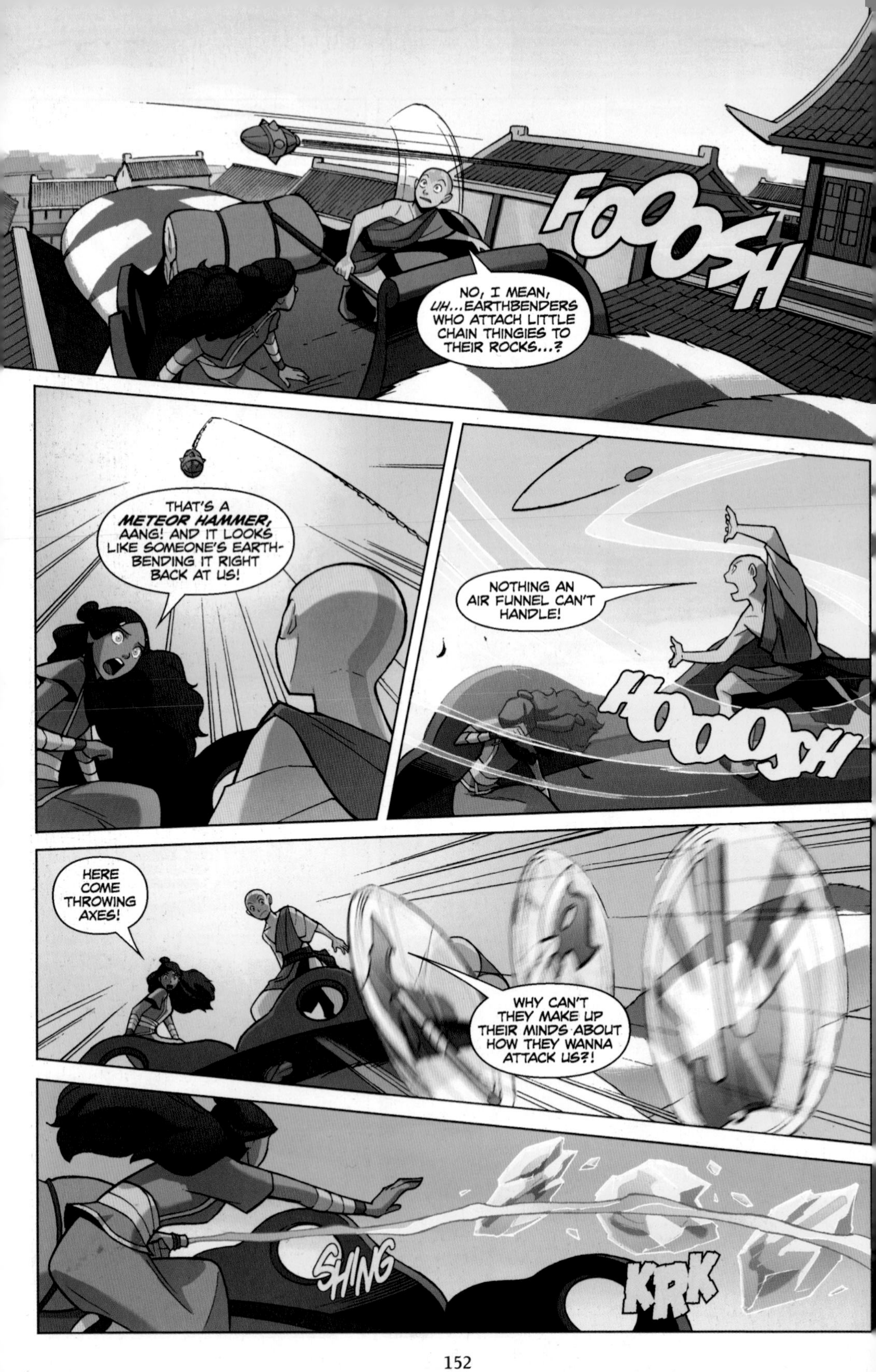
FOOOSH
NO, I MEAN, UH... EARTHBENDERS WHO ATTACH LITTLE CHAIN THINGIES TO THEIR ROCKS...?
THAT'S A METEOR HAMMER, AANG! AND IT LOOKS LIKE SOMEONE'S EARTH-BENDING IT RIGHT BACK AT US!
NOTHING AN AIR FUNNEL CAN'T HANDLE!
HOOOSH
HERE COME THROWING AXES!
WHY CAN'T THEY MAKE UP THEIR MINDS ABOUT HOW THEY WANNA ATTACK US?!
SHING
KRK

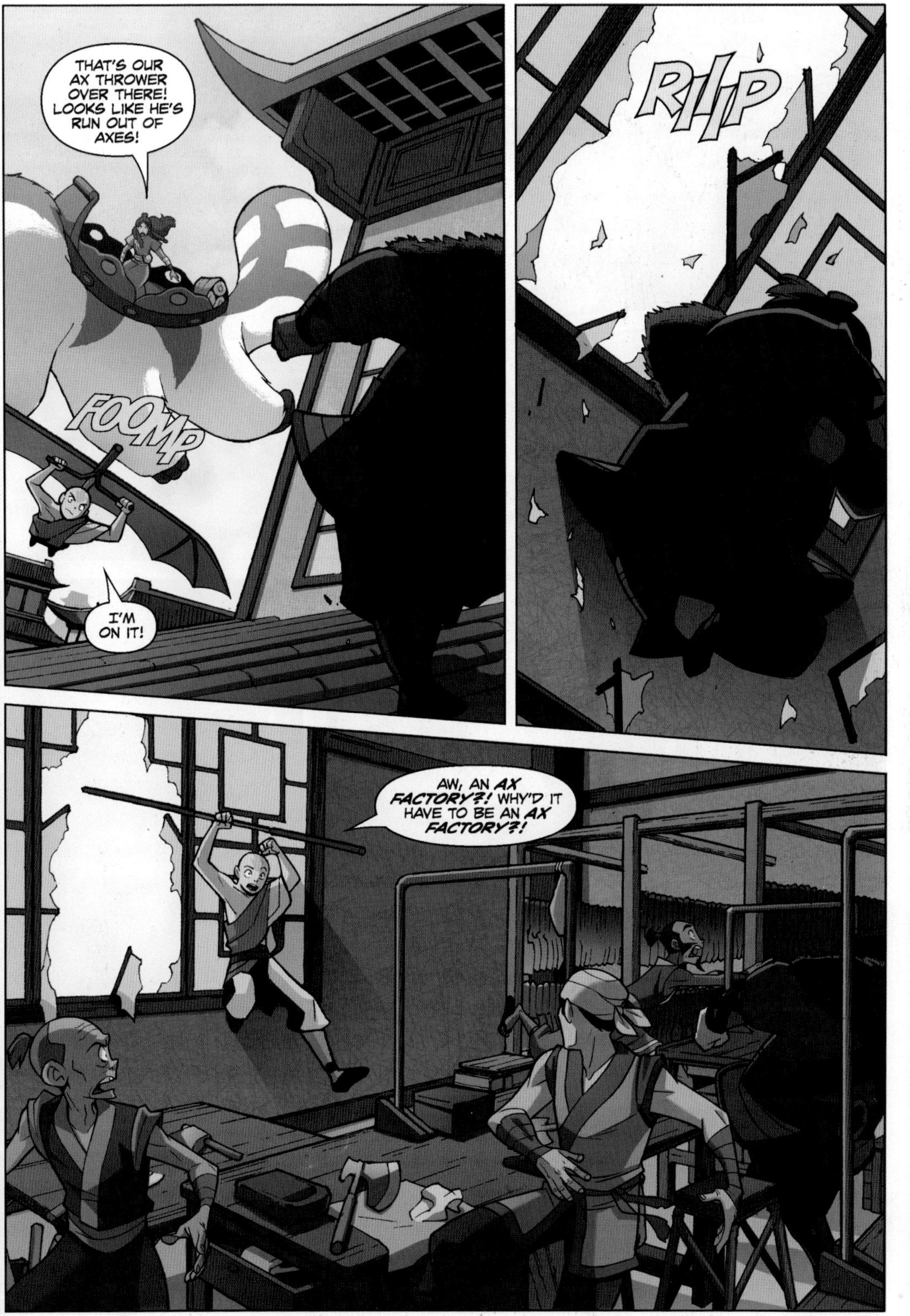
THAT'S OUR AX THROWER OVER THERE! LOOKS LIKE HE'S RUN OUT OF AXES!
FOOMP
I'M ON IT!
RIIP
AW, AN AX FACTORY?! WHY'D IT HAVE TO BE AN AX FACTORY?!

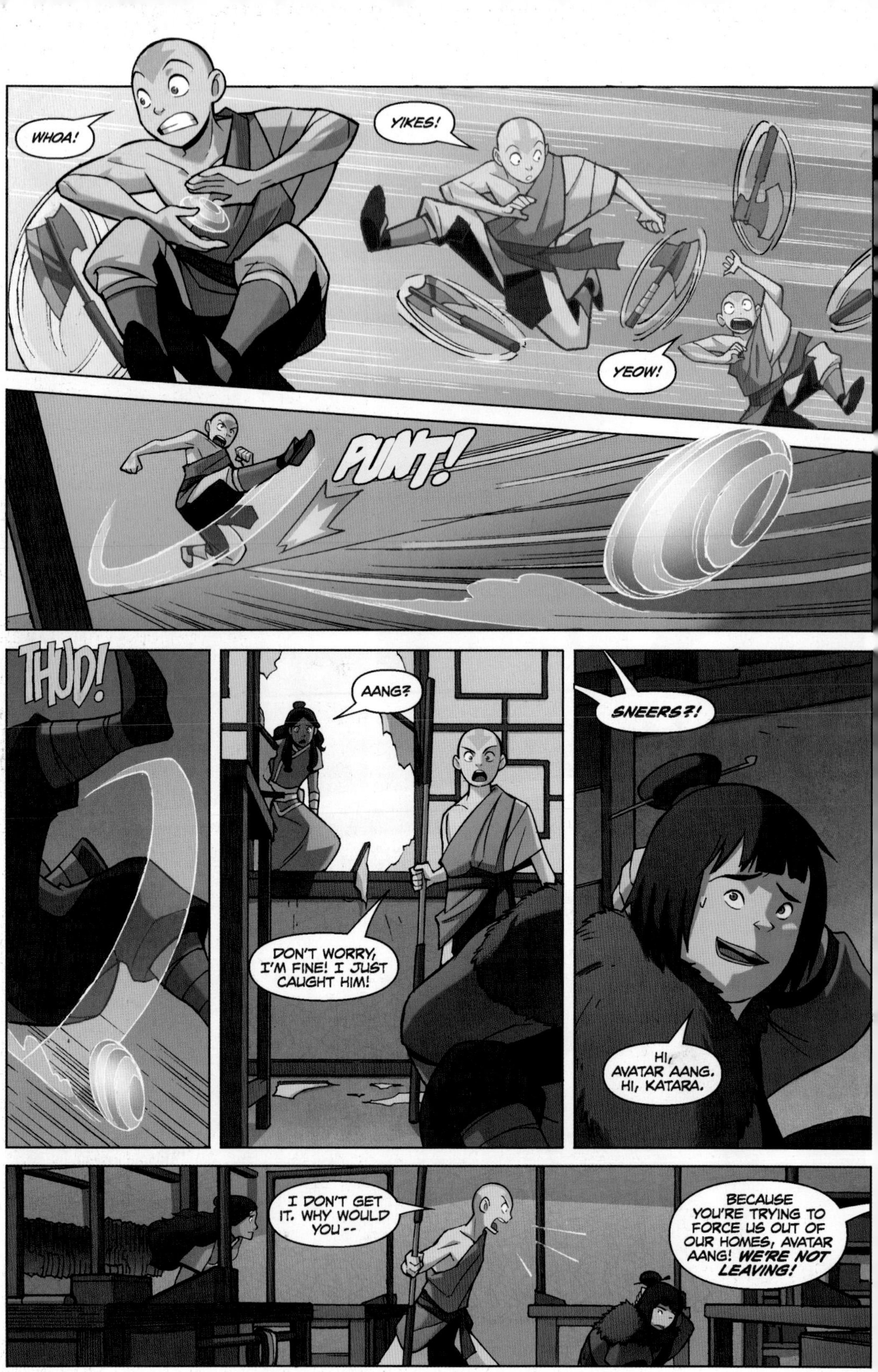
WHOA!
YIKES!
YEOW!
PUNT!
THUD!
AANG?
DON'T WORRY, I'M FINE! I JUST CAUGHT HIM!
SNEERS?!
HI, AVATAR AANG. HI, KATARA.
I DON'T GET IT. WHY WOULD YOU --
BECAUSE YOU'RE TRYING TO FORCE US OUT OF OUR HOMES, AVATAR AANG! WE'RE NOT LEAVING!

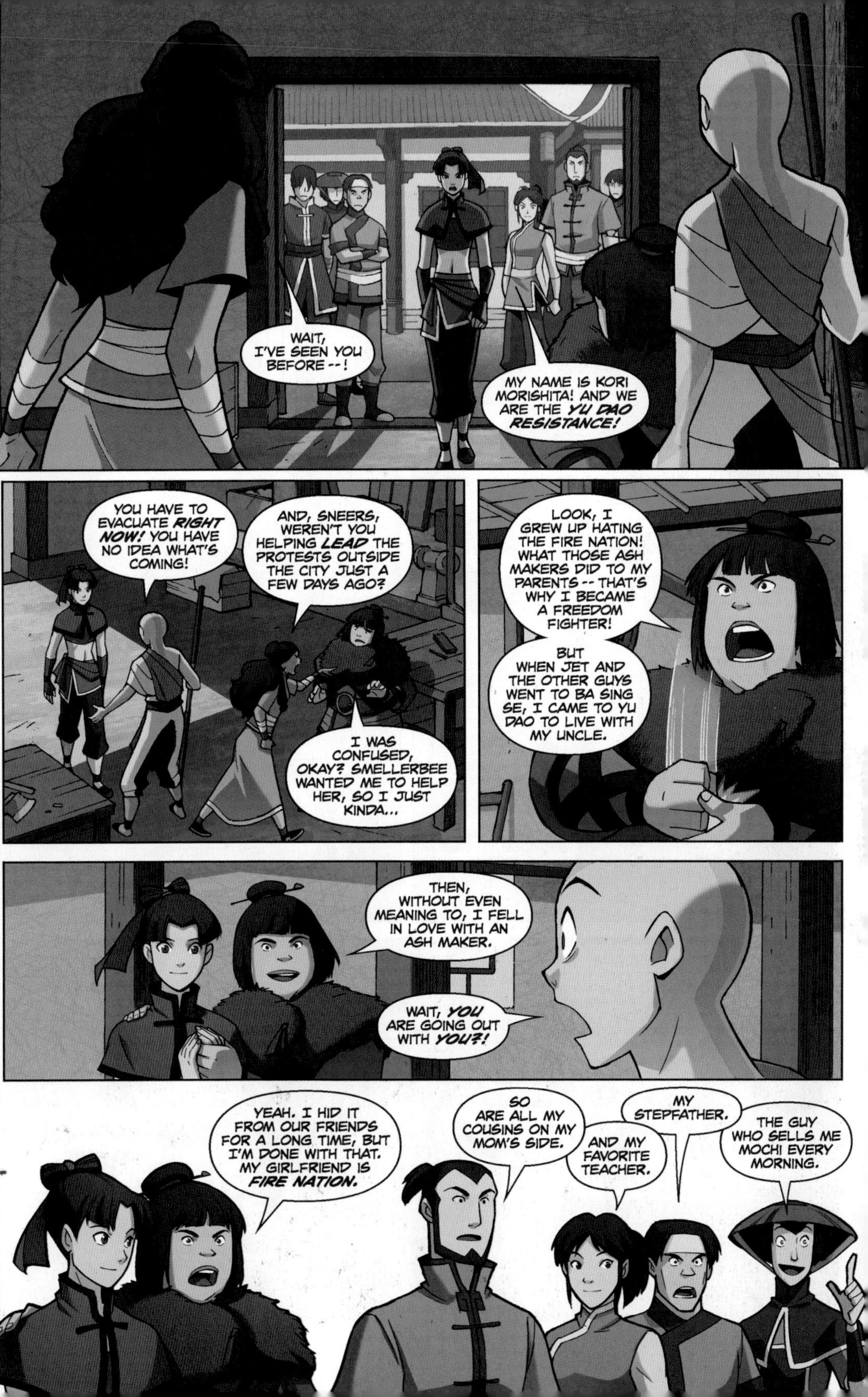
WAIT, I'VE SEEN YOU BEFORE--!
MY NAME IS KORI MORISHITA! AND WE ARE THE YU DAO RESISTANCE!
YOU HAVE TO EVACUATE RIGHT NOW! YOU HAVE NO IDEA WHAT'S COMING!
AND, SNEERS, WEREN'T YOU HELPING LEAD THE PROTESTS OUTSIDE THE CITY JUST A FEW DAYS AGO?
I WAS CONFUSED, OKAY? SMELLERBEE WANTED ME TO HELP HER, SO I JUST KINDA...
LOOK, I GREW UP HATING THE FIRE NATION! WHAT THOSE ASH MAKERS DID TO MY PARENTS -- THAT'S WHY I BECAME A FREEDOM FIGHTER!
BUT WHEN JET AND THE OTHER GUYS WENT TO BA SING SE, I CAME TO YU DAO TO LIVE WITH MY UNCLE.
THEN, WITHOUT EVEN MEANING TO, I FELL IN LOVE WITH AN ASH MAKER.
WAIT, YOU ARE GOING OUT WITH YOU?!
YEAH. I HID IT FROM OUR FRIENDS FOR A LONG TIME, BUT I'M DONE WITH THAT. MY GIRLFRIEND IS FIRE NATION.
SO ARE ALL MY COUSINS ON MY MOM'S SIDE.
AND MY FAVORITE TEACHER.
MY STEPFATHER.
THE GUY WHO SELLS ME MOCHI EVERY MORNING.

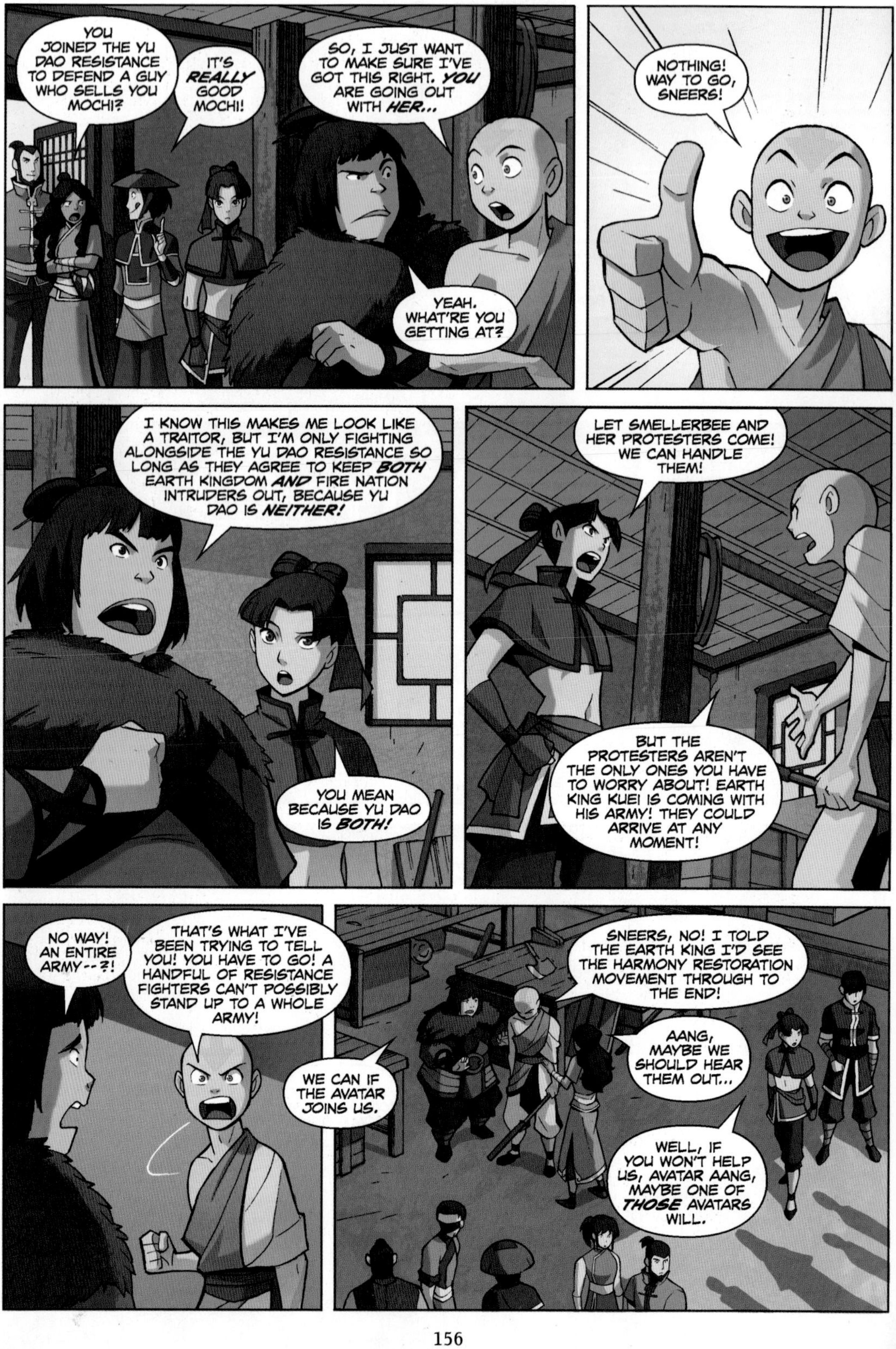

YOU JOINED THE YU DAO RESISTANCE TO DEFEND A GUY WHO SELLS YOU MOCHI?
IT'S REALLY GOOD MOCHI!
SO, I JUST WANT TO MAKE SURE I'VE GOT THIS RIGHT. YOU ARE GOING OUT WITH HER...
YEAH. WHAT'RE YOU GETTING AT?
NOTHING! WAY TO GO, SNEERS!
I KNOW THIS MAKES ME LOOK LIKE A TRAITOR, BUT I'M ONLY FIGHTING ALONGSIDE THE YU DAO RESISTANCE SO LONG AS THEY AGREE TO KEEP BOTH EARTH KINGDOM AND FIRE NATION INTRUDERS OUT, BECAUSE YU DAO IS NEITHER!
YOU MEAN BECAUSE YU DAO IS BOTH!
LET SMELLERBEE AND HER PROTESTERS COME! WE CAN HANDLE THEM!
BUT THE PROTESTERS AREN'T THE ONLY ONES YOU HAVE TO WORRY ABOUT! EARTH KING KUEI IS COMING WITH HIS ARMY! THEY COULD ARRIVE AT ANY MOMENT!
NO WAY! AN ENTIRE ARMY--?!
THAT'S WHAT I'VE BEEN TRYING TO TELL YOU! YOU HAVE TO GO! A HANDFUL OF RESISTANCE FIGHTERS CAN'T POSSIBLY STAND UP TO A WHOLE ARMY!
WE CAN IF THE AVATAR JOINS US.
SNEERS, NO! I TOLD THE EARTH KING I'D SEE THE HARMONY RESTORATION MOVEMENT THROUGH TO THE END!
AANG, MAYBE WE SHOULD HEAR THEM OUT...
WELL, IF YOU WON'T HELP US, AVATAR AANG, MAYBE ONE OF THOSE AVATARS WILL.

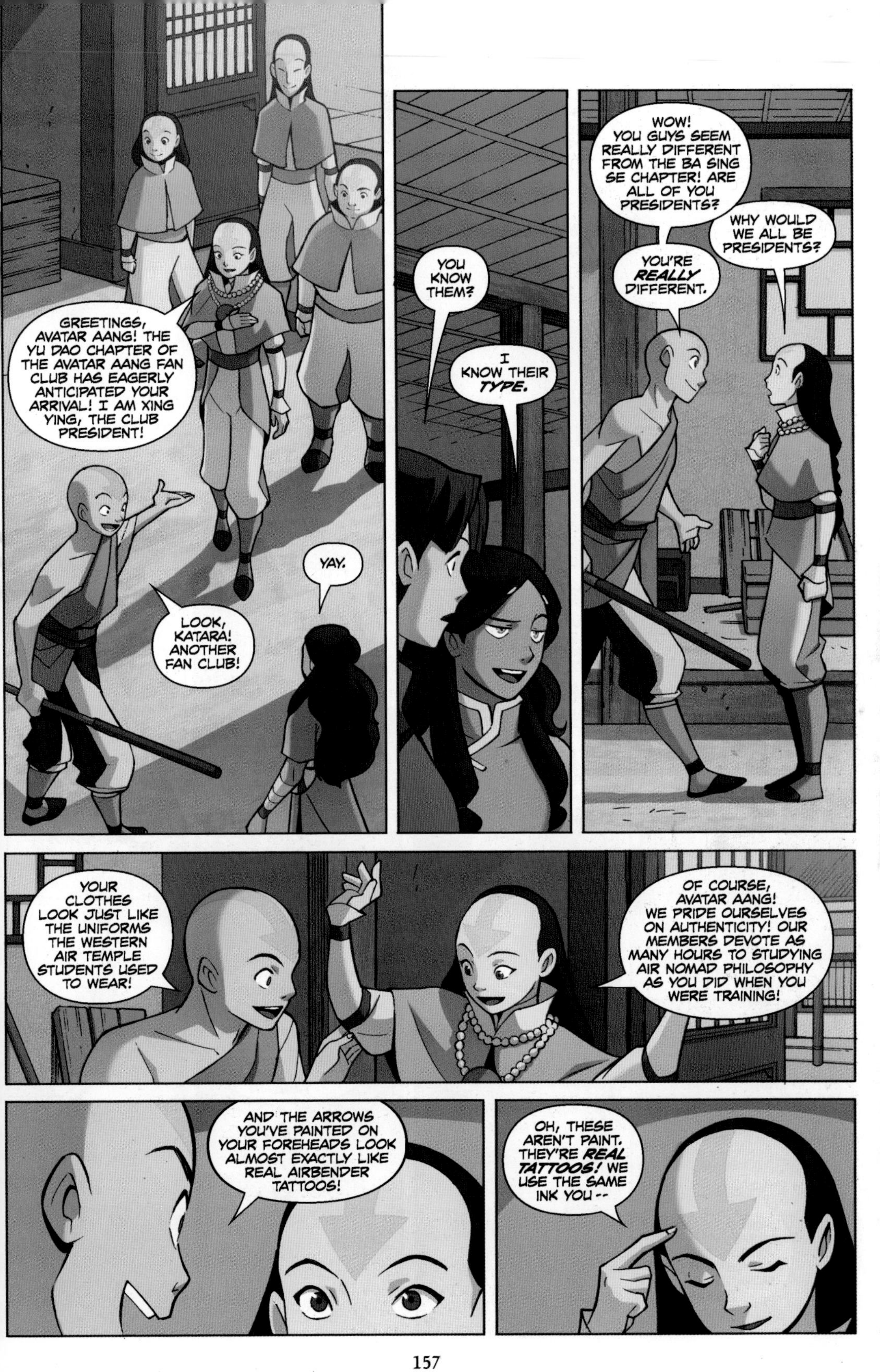
GREETINGS, AVATAR AANG! THE YU DAO CHAPTER OF THE AVATAR AANG FAN CLUB HAS EAGERLY ANTICIPATED YOUR ARRIVAL! I AM XING YING, THE CLUB PRESIDENT!
LOOK, KATARA! ANOTHER FAN CLUB!
YAY.
YOU KNOW THEM?
I KNOW THEIR *TYPE.*
WOW! YOU GUYS SEEM REALLY DIFFERENT FROM THE BA SING SE CHAPTER! ARE ALL OF YOU PRESIDENTS?
YOU'RE *REALLY* DIFFERENT.
WHY WOULD WE ALL BE PRESIDENTS?
YOUR CLOTHES LOOK JUST LIKE THE UNIFORMS THE WESTERN AIR TEMPLE STUDENTS USED TO WEAR!
OF COURSE, AVATAR AANG! WE PRIDE OURSELVES ON AUTHENTICITY! OUR MEMBERS DEVOTE AS MANY HOURS TO STUDYING AIR NOMAD PHILOSOPHY AS YOU DID WHEN YOU WERE TRAINING!
AND THE ARROWS YOU'VE PAINTED ON YOUR FOREHEADS LOOK ALMOST EXACTLY LIKE REAL AIRBENDER TATTOOS!
OH, THESE AREN'T PAINT. THEY'RE *REAL TATTOOS!* WE USE THE SAME INK YOU --

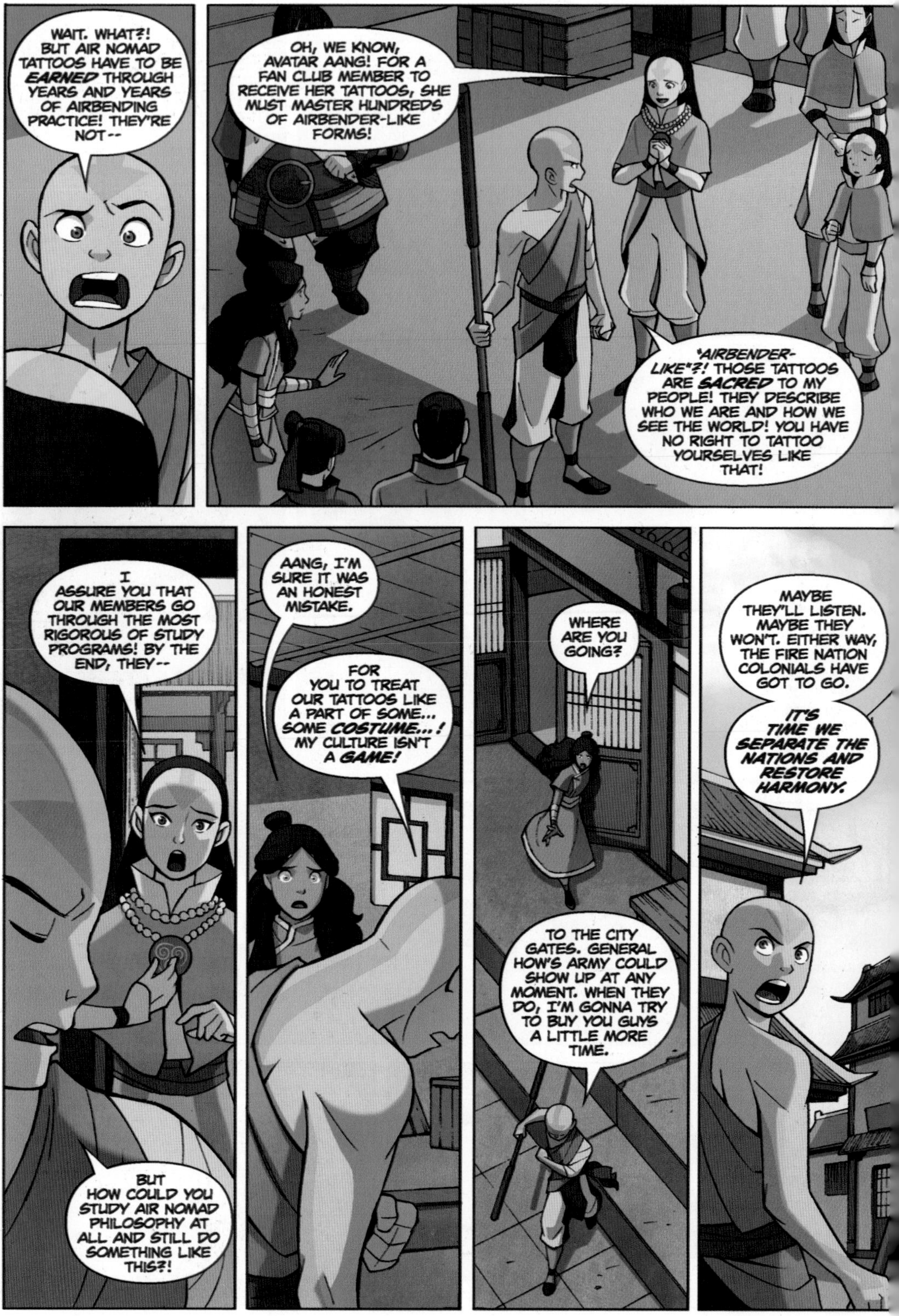
WAIT. WHAT?! BUT AIR NOMAD TATTOOS HAVE TO BE EARNED THROUGH YEARS AND YEARS OF AIRBENDING PRACTICE! THEY'RE NOT --
OH, WE KNOW, AVATAR AANG! FOR A FAN CLUB MEMBER TO RECEIVE HER TATTOOS, SHE MUST MASTER HUNDREDS OF AIRBENDER-LIKE FORMS!
"AIRBENDER-LIKE"?! THOSE TATTOOS ARE SACRED TO MY PEOPLE! THEY DESCRIBE WHO WE ARE AND HOW WE SEE THE WORLD! YOU HAVE NO RIGHT TO TATTOO YOURSELVES LIKE THAT!
I ASSURE YOU THAT OUR MEMBERS GO THROUGH THE MOST RIGOROUS OF STUDY PROGRAMS! BY THE END, THEY--
BUT HOW COULD YOU STUDY AIR NOMAD PHILOSOPHY AT ALL AND STILL DO SOMETHING LIKE THIS?!
AANG, I'M SURE IT WAS AN HONEST MISTAKE.
FOR YOU TO TREAT OUR TATTOOS LIKE A PART OF SOME... SOME COSTUME...! MY CULTURE ISN'T A GAME!
WHERE ARE YOU GOING?
TO THE CITY GATES. GENERAL HOW'S ARMY COULD SHOW UP AT ANY MOMENT. WHEN THEY DO, I'M GONNA TRY TO BUY YOU GUYS A LITTLE MORE TIME.
MAYBE THEY'LL LISTEN. MAYBE THEY WON'T. EITHER WAY, THE FIRE NATION COLONIALS HAVE GOT TO GO.
IT'S TIME WE SEPARATE THE NATIONS AND RESTORE HARMONY.

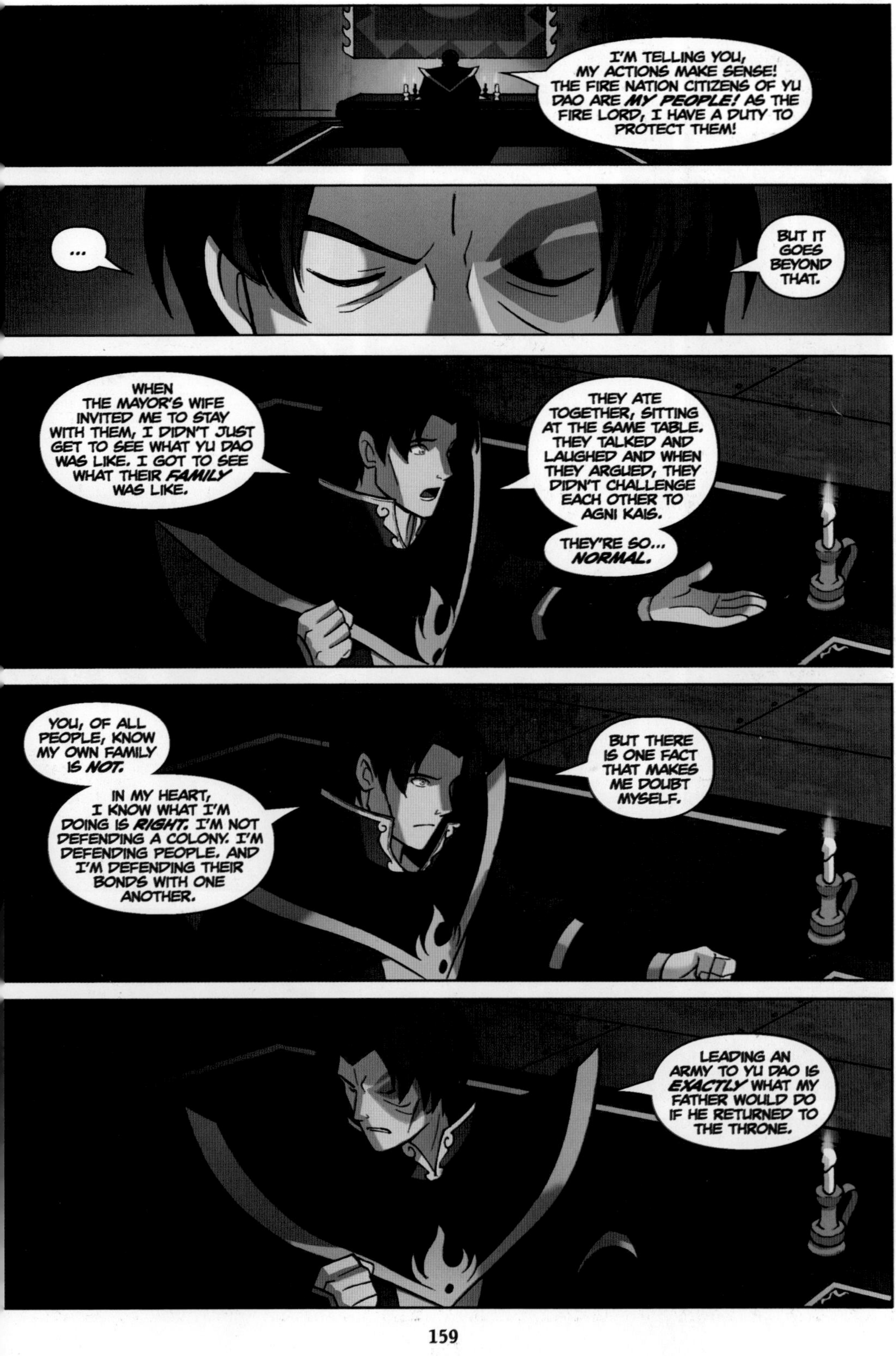
I'M TELLING YOU, MY ACTIONS MAKE SENSE! THE FIRE NATION CITIZENS OF YU DAO ARE MY PEOPLE! AS THE FIRE LORD, I HAVE A DUTY TO PROTECT THEM!
...
BUT IT GOES BEYOND THAT.
WHEN THE MAYOR'S WIFE INVITED ME TO STAY WITH THEM, I DIDN'T JUST GET TO SEE WHAT YU DAO WAS LIKE. I GOT TO SEE WHAT THEIR FAMILY WAS LIKE.
THEY ATE TOGETHER, SITTING AT THE SAME TABLE. THEY TALKED AND LAUGHED AND WHEN THEY ARGUED, THEY DIDN'T CHALLENGE EACH OTHER TO AGNI KAIS.
THEY'RE SO... NORMAL.
YOU, OF ALL PEOPLE, KNOW MY OWN FAMILY IS NOT.
IN MY HEART, I KNOW WHAT I'M DOING IS RIGHT. I'M NOT DEFENDING A COLONY. I'M DEFENDING PEOPLE. AND I'M DEFENDING THEIR BONDS WITH ONE ANOTHER.
BUT THERE IS ONE FACT THAT MAKES ME DOUBT MYSELF.
LEADING AN ARMY TO YU DAO IS EXACTLY WHAT MY FATHER WOULD DO IF HE RETURNED TO THE THRONE.

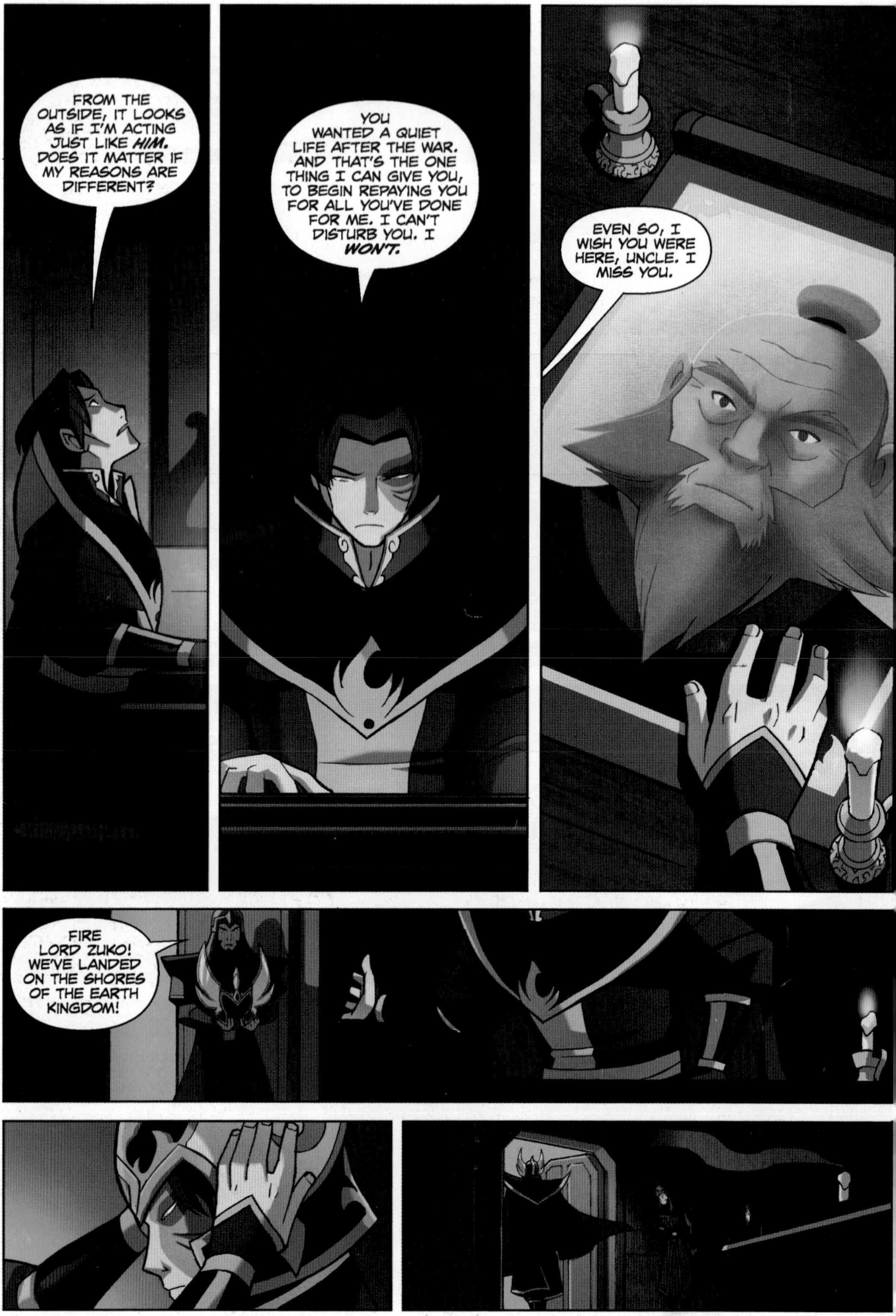
FROM THE OUTSIDE, IT LOOKS AS IF I'M ACTING JUST LIKE *HIM*. DOES IT MATTER IF MY REASONS ARE DIFFERENT?
YOU WANTED A QUIET LIFE AFTER THE WAR. AND THAT'S THE ONE THING I CAN GIVE YOU, TO BEGIN REPAYING YOU FOR ALL YOU'VE DONE FOR ME. I CAN'T DISTURB YOU. I *WON'T*.
EVEN SO, I WISH YOU WERE HERE, UNCLE. I MISS YOU.
FIRE LORD ZUKO! WE'VE LANDED ON THE SHORES OF THE EARTH KINGDOM!

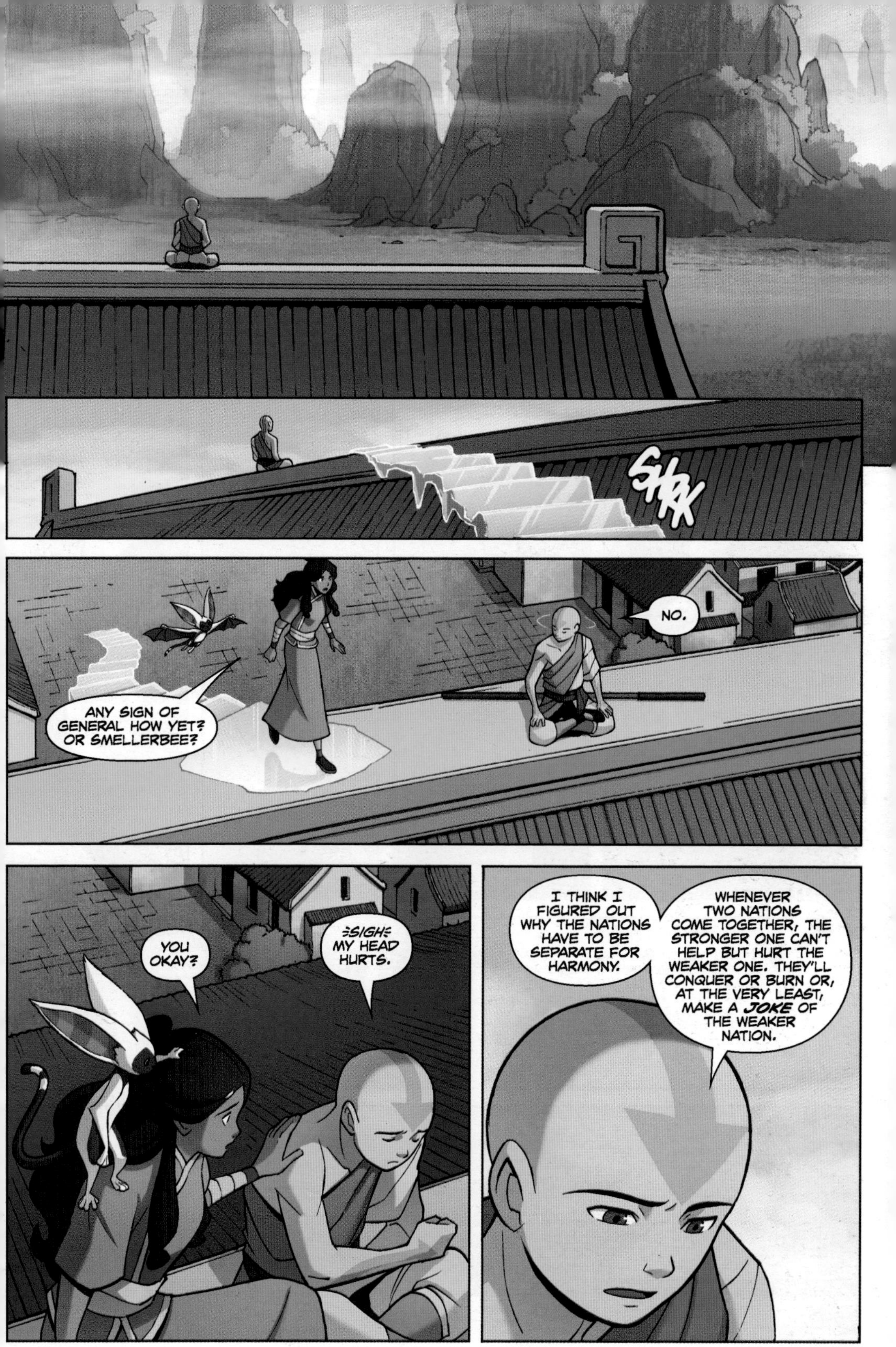
SHKK
ANY SIGN OF GENERAL HOW YET? OR SMELLERBEE?
NO.
YOU OKAY?
SIGH MY HEAD HURTS.
I THINK I FIGURED OUT WHY THE NATIONS HAVE TO BE SEPARATE FOR HARMONY.
WHENEVER TWO NATIONS COME TOGETHER, THE STRONGER ONE CAN'T HELP BUT HURT THE WEAKER ONE. THEY'LL CONQUER OR BURN OR, AT THE VERY LEAST, MAKE A JOKE OF THE WEAKER NATION.

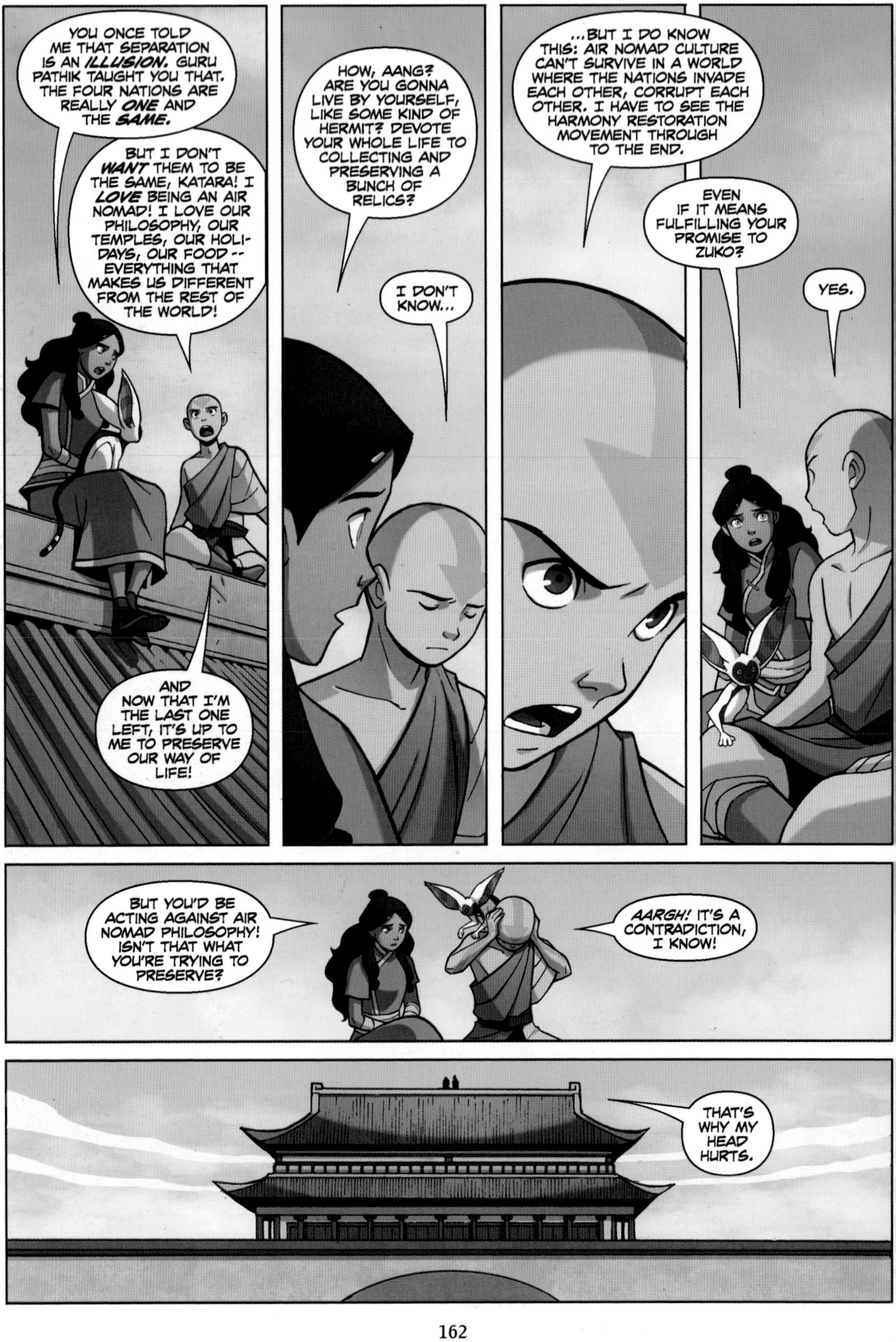
YOU ONCE TOLD ME THAT SEPARATION IS AN *ILLUSION.* GURU PATHIK TAUGHT YOU THAT. THE FOUR NATIONS ARE REALLY *ONE* AND THE *SAME.*
BUT I DON'T *WANT* THEM TO BE THE SAME, KATARA! I *LOVE* BEING AN AIR NOMAD! I LOVE OUR PHILOSOPHY, OUR TEMPLES, OUR HOLI-DAYS, OUR FOOD-- EVERYTHING THAT MAKES US DIFFERENT FROM THE REST OF THE WORLD!
AND NOW THAT I'M THE LAST ONE LEFT, IT'S UP TO ME TO PRESERVE OUR WAY OF LIFE!
HOW, AANG? ARE YOU GONNA LIVE BY YOURSELF, LIKE SOME KIND OF HERMIT? DEVOTE YOUR WHOLE LIFE TO COLLECTING AND PRESERVING A BUNCH OF RELICS?
I DON'T KNOW...
...BUT I DO KNOW THIS: AIR NOMAD CULTURE CAN'T SURVIVE IN A WORLD WHERE THE NATIONS INVADE EACH OTHER, CORRUPT EACH OTHER. I HAVE TO SEE THE HARMONY RESTORATION MOVEMENT THROUGH TO THE END.
EVEN IF IT MEANS FULFILLING YOUR PROMISE TO ZUKO?
YES.
BUT YOU'D BE ACTING AGAINST AIR NOMAD PHILOSOPHY! ISN'T THAT WHAT YOU'RE TRYING TO PRESERVE?
AARGH! IT'S A CONTRADICTION, I KNOW!
THAT'S WHY MY HEAD HURTS.

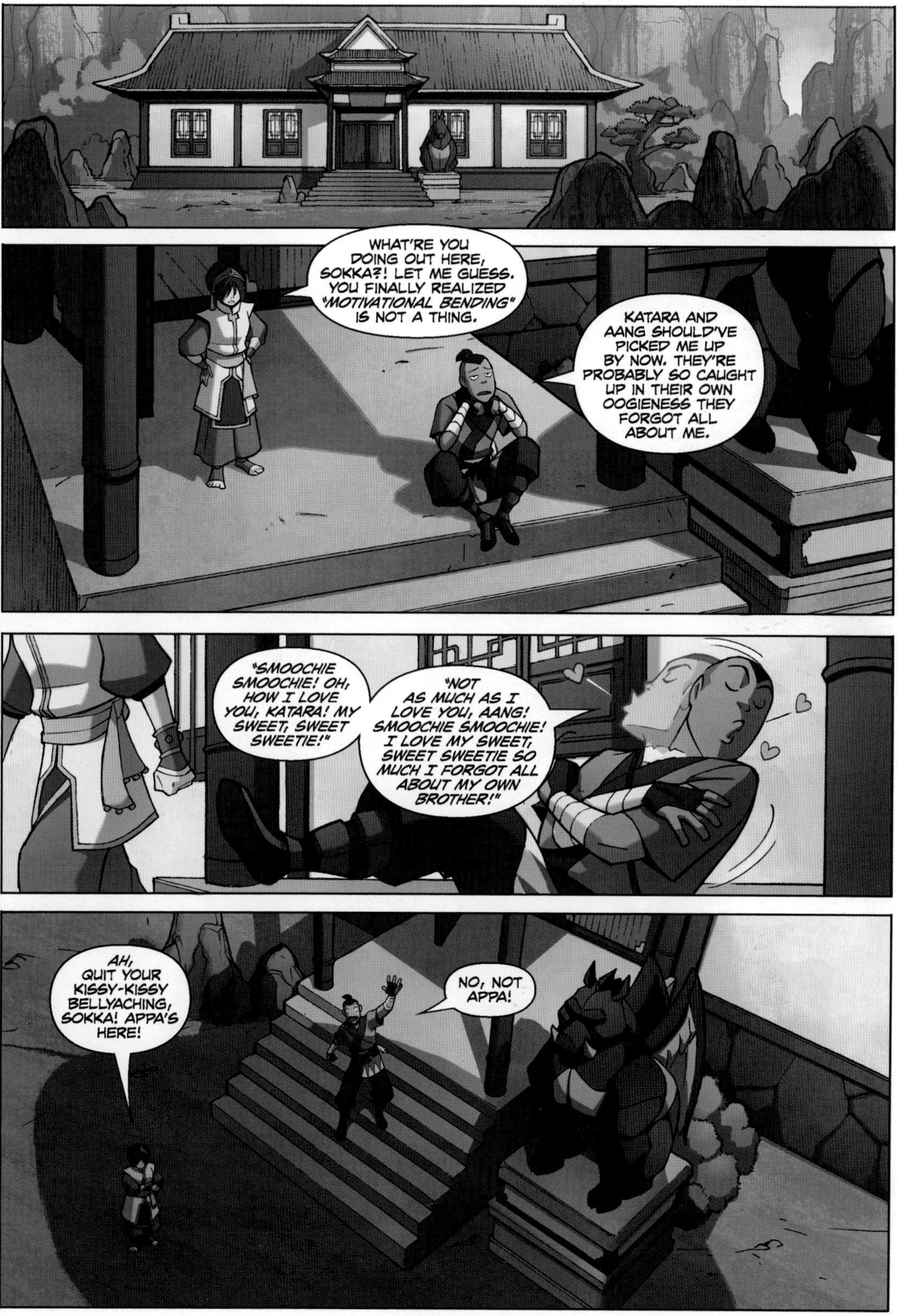
WHAT'RE YOU DOING OUT HERE, SOKKA?! LET ME GUESS. YOU FINALLY REALIZED "MOTIVATIONAL BENDING" IS NOT A THING.
KATARA AND AANG SHOULD'VE PICKED ME UP BY NOW. THEY'RE PROBABLY SO CAUGHT UP IN THEIR OWN OOGIENESS THEY FORGOT ALL ABOUT ME.
"SMOOCHIE SMOOCHIE! OH, HOW I LOVE YOU, KATARA! MY SWEET, SWEET SWEETIE!"
"NOT AS MUCH AS I LOVE YOU, AANG! SMOOCHIE SMOOCHIE! I LOVE MY SWEET, SWEET SWEETIE SO MUCH I FORGOT ALL ABOUT MY OWN BROTHER!"
AH, QUIT YOUR KISSY-KISSY BELLYACHING, SOKKA! APPA'S HERE!
NO, NOT APPA!

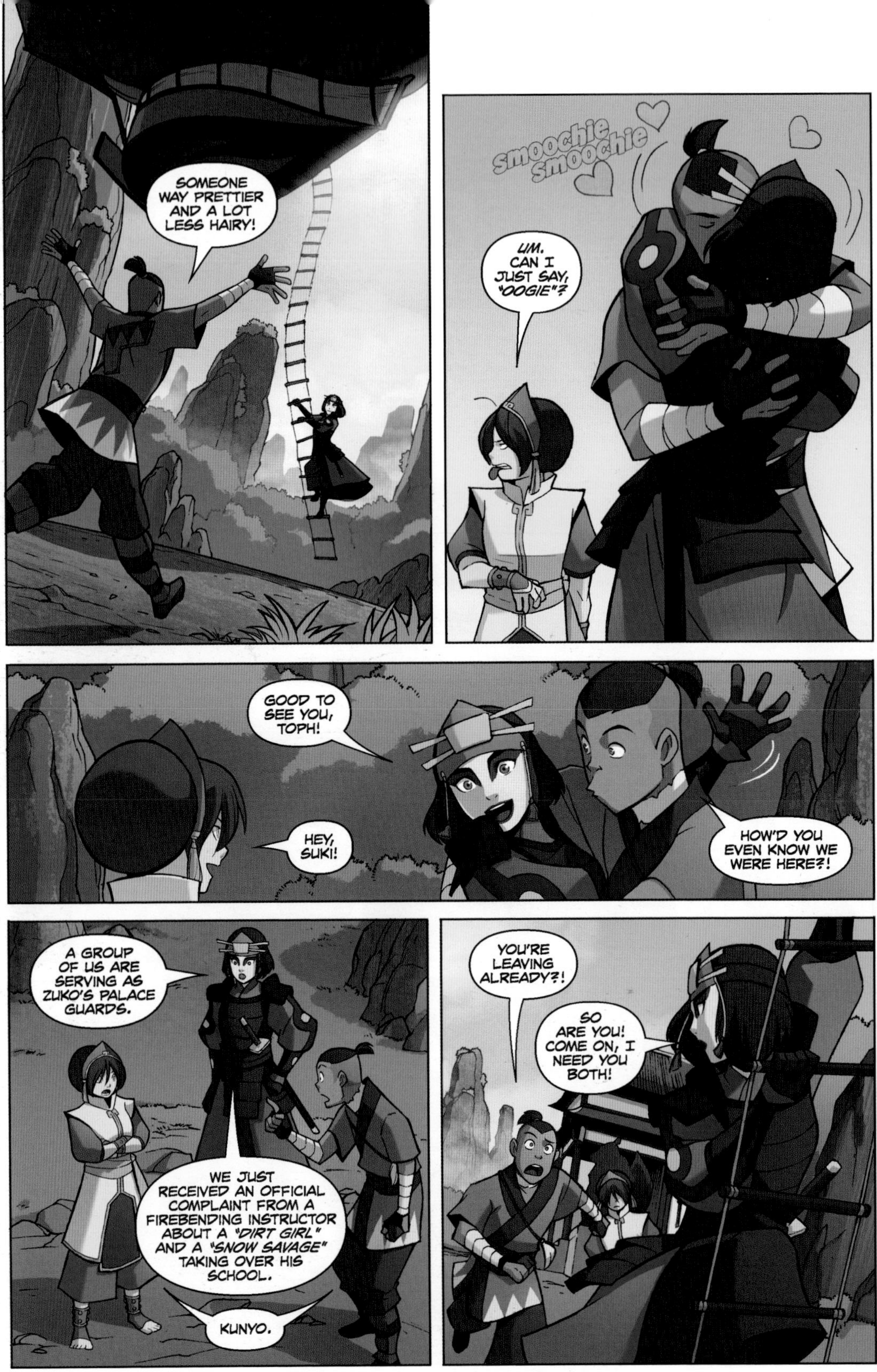
SOMEONE WAY PRETTIER AND A LOT LESS HAIRY!
SMOOCHIE SMOOCHIE
UM. CAN I JUST SAY, "OOGIE"?
GOOD TO SEE YOU, TOPH!
HEY, SUKI!
HOW'D YOU EVEN KNOW WE WERE HERE?!
A GROUP OF US ARE SERVING AS ZUKO'S PALACE GUARDS.
WE JUST RECEIVED AN OFFICIAL COMPLAINT FROM A FIREBENDING INSTRUCTOR ABOUT A "DIRT GIRL" AND A "SNOW SAVAGE" TAKING OVER HIS SCHOOL.
KUNYO.
YOU'RE LEAVING ALREADY?!
SO ARE YOU! COME ON, I NEED YOU BOTH!

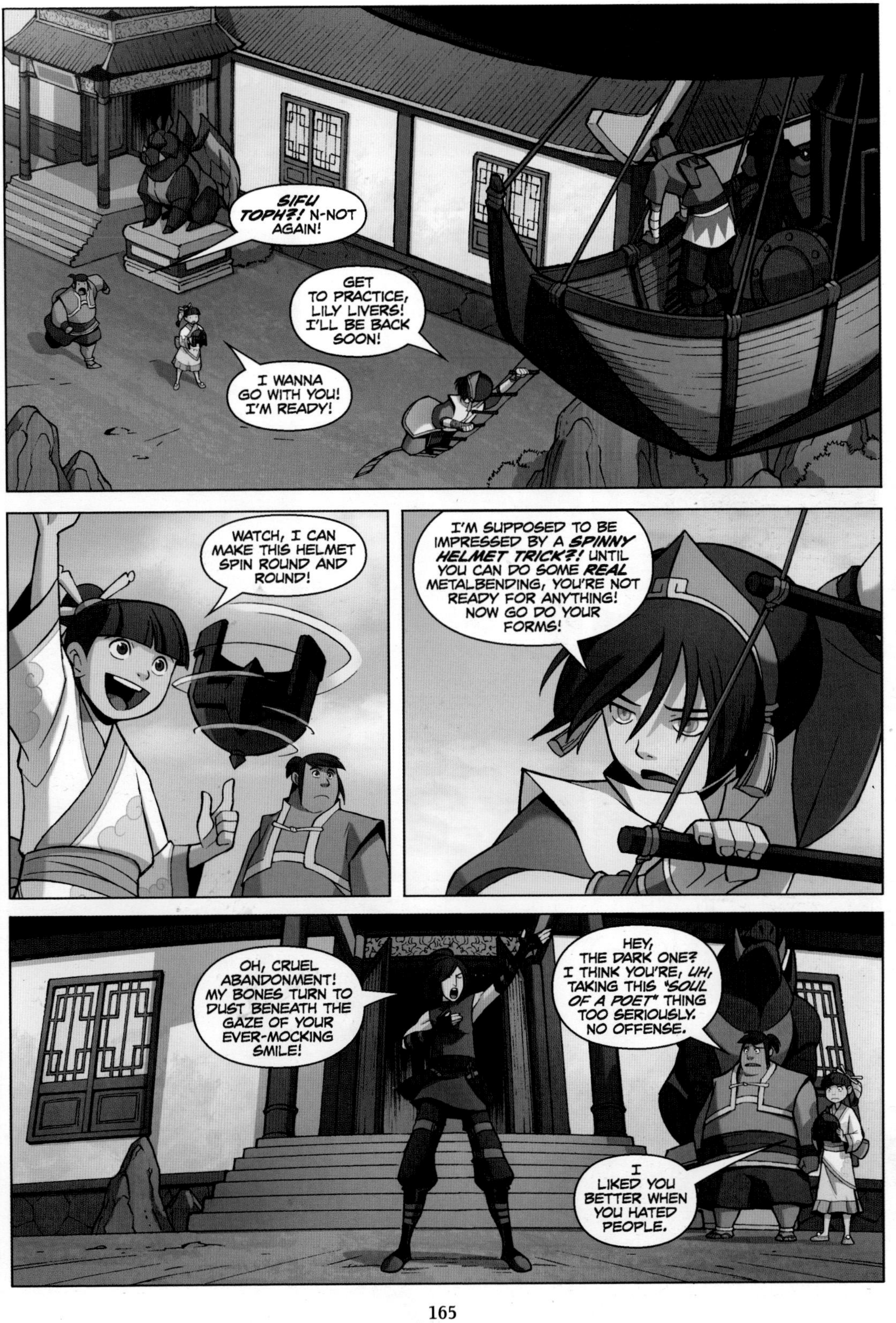
SIFU TOPH?! N-NOT AGAIN!
GET TO PRACTICE, LILY LIVERS! I'LL BE BACK SOON!
I WANNA GO WITH YOU! I'M READY!
WATCH, I CAN MAKE THIS HELMET SPIN ROUND AND ROUND!
I'M SUPPOSED TO BE IMPRESSED BY A SPINNY HELMET TRICK?! UNTIL YOU CAN DO SOME REAL METALBENDING, YOU'RE NOT READY FOR ANYTHING! NOW GO DO YOUR FORMS!
OH, CRUEL ABANDONMENT! MY BONES TURN TO DUST BENEATH THE GAZE OF YOUR EVER-MOCKING SMILE!
HEY, THE DARK ONE? I THINK YOU'RE, UH, TAKING THIS "SOUL OF A POET" THING TOO SERIOUSLY. NO OFFENSE.
I LIKED YOU BETTER WHEN YOU HATED PEOPLE.

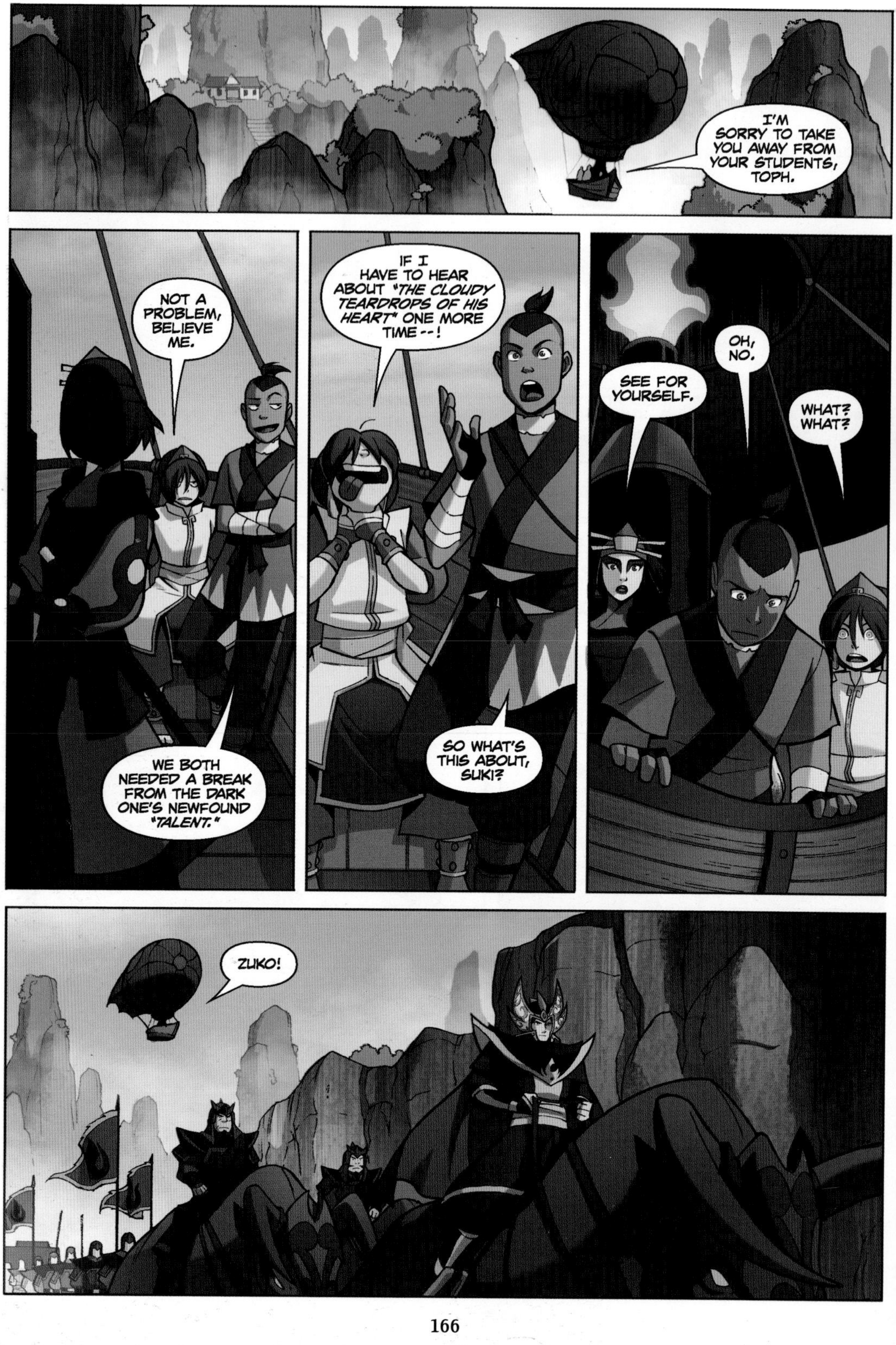
I'M SORRY TO TAKE YOU AWAY FROM YOUR STUDENTS, TOPH.
NOT A PROBLEM, BELIEVE ME.
WE BOTH NEEDED A BREAK FROM THE DARK ONE'S NEWFOUND "TALENT."
IF I HAVE TO HEAR ABOUT "THE CLOUDY TEARDROPS OF HIS HEART" ONE MORE TIME --!
SO WHAT'S THIS ABOUT, SUKI?
SEE FOR YOURSELF.
OH, NO.
WHAT? WHAT?
ZUKO!

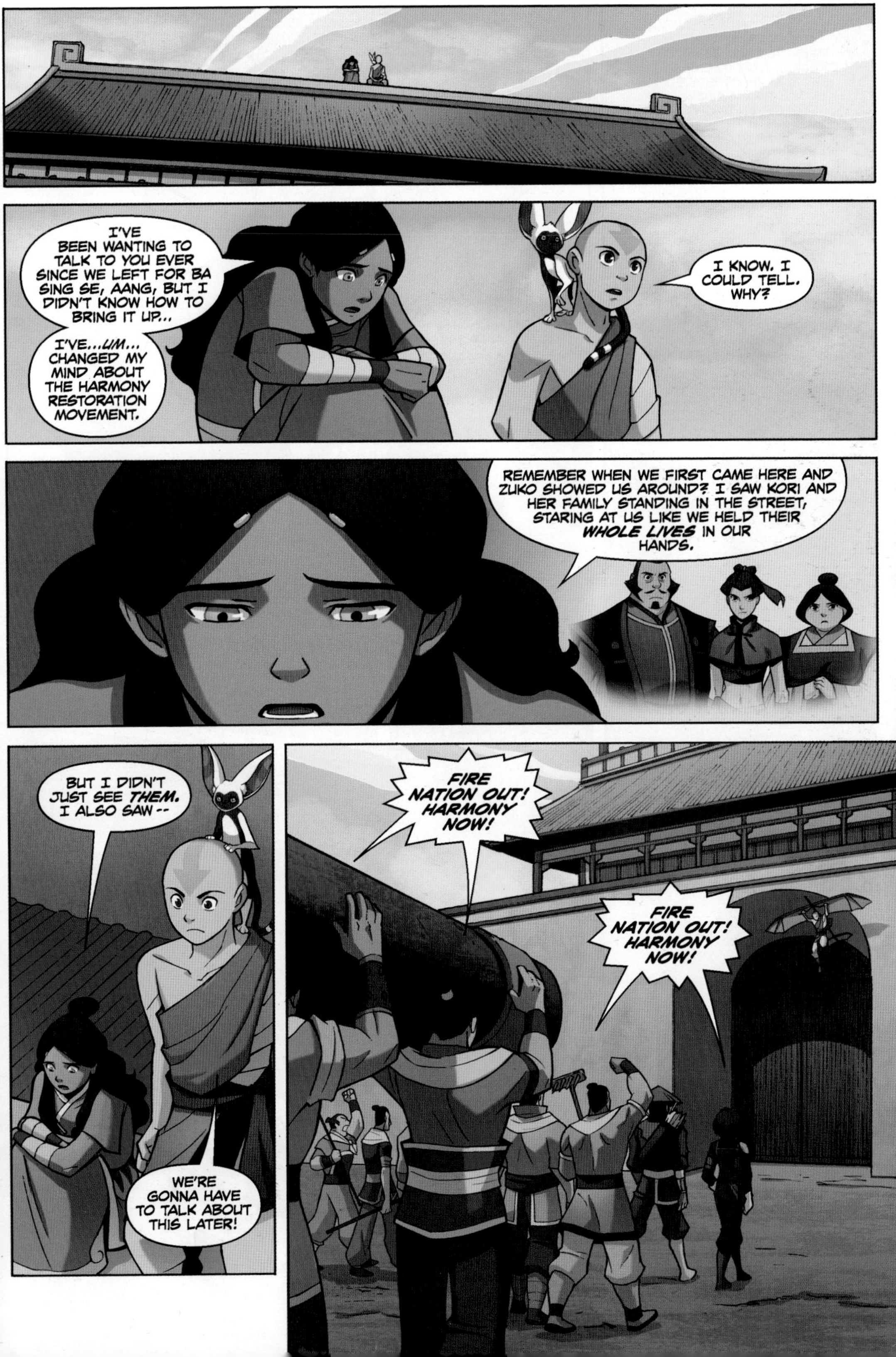
I'VE BEEN WANTING TO TALK TO YOU EVER SINCE WE LEFT FOR BA SING SE, AANG, BUT I DIDN'T KNOW HOW TO BRING IT UP...
I'VE...UM... CHANGED MY MIND ABOUT THE HARMONY RESTORATION MOVEMENT.
I KNOW. I COULD TELL. WHY?
REMEMBER WHEN WE FIRST CAME HERE AND ZUKO SHOWED US AROUND? I SAW KORI AND HER FAMILY STANDING IN THE STREET, STARING AT US LIKE WE HELD THEIR WHOLE LIVES IN OUR HANDS.
BUT I DIDN'T JUST SEE THEM. I ALSO SAW --
WE'RE GONNA HAVE TO TALK ABOUT THIS LATER!
FIRE NATION OUT! HARMONY NOW!
FIRE NATION OUT! HARMONY NOW!

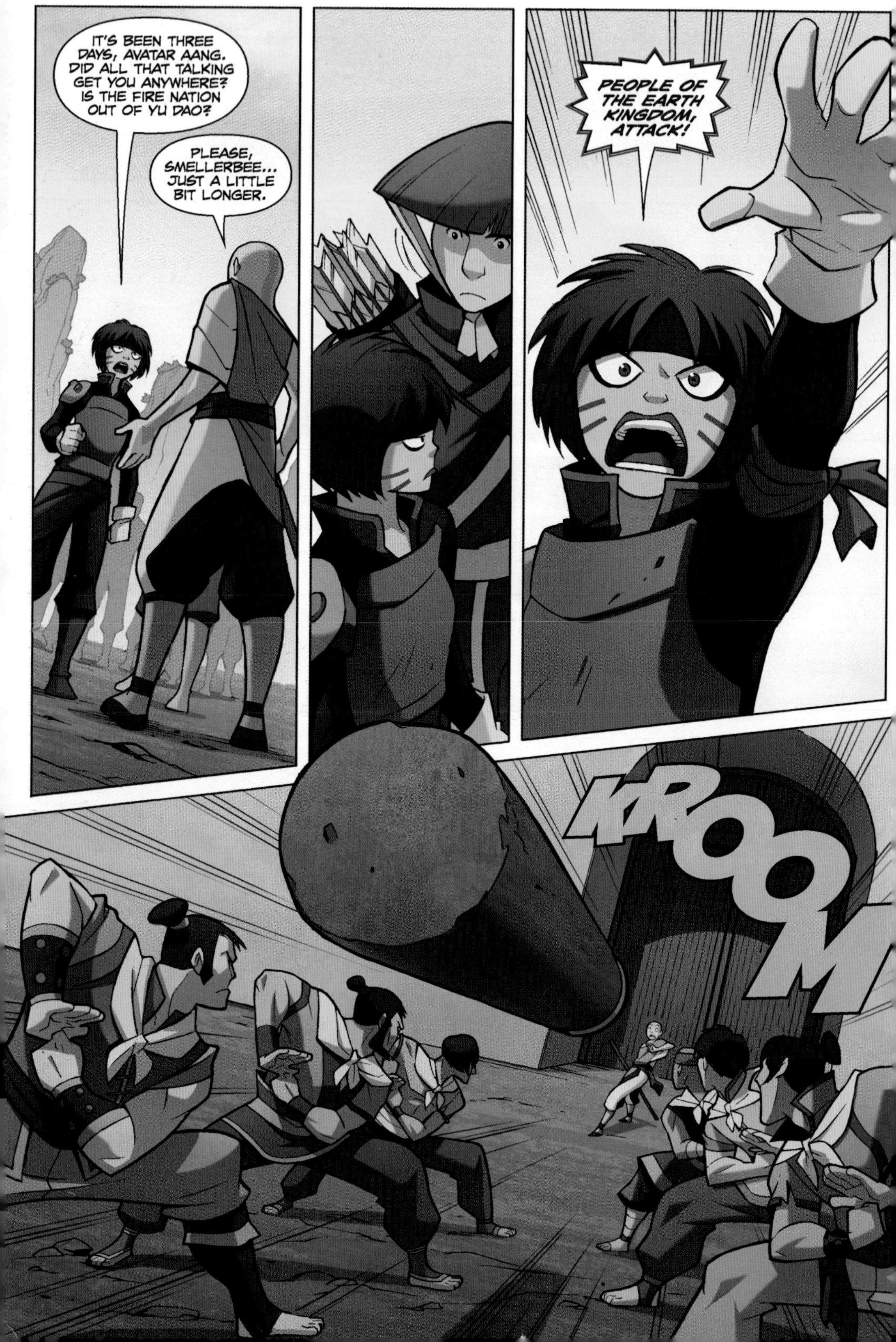

IT'S BEEN THREE DAYS, AVATAR AANG. DID ALL THAT TALKING GET YOU ANYWHERE? IS THE FIRE NATION OUT OF YU DAO?
PLEASE, SMELLERBEE... JUST A LITTLE BIT LONGER.
PEOPLE OF THE EARTH KINGDOM, ATTACK!
KROOM

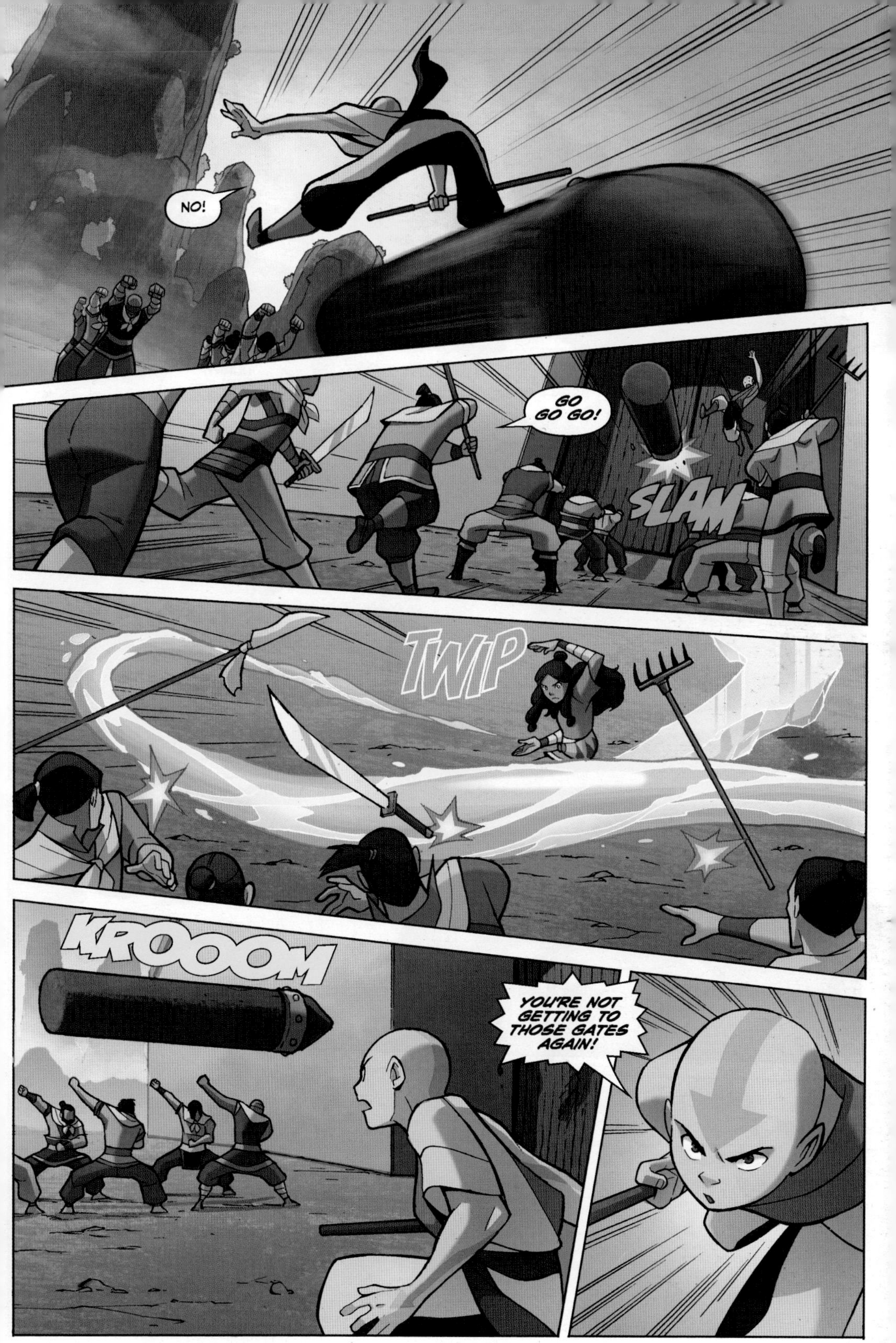
NO!
GO GO GO!
SLAM
TWIP
KROOOM
YOU'RE NOT GETTING TO THOSE GATES AGAIN!

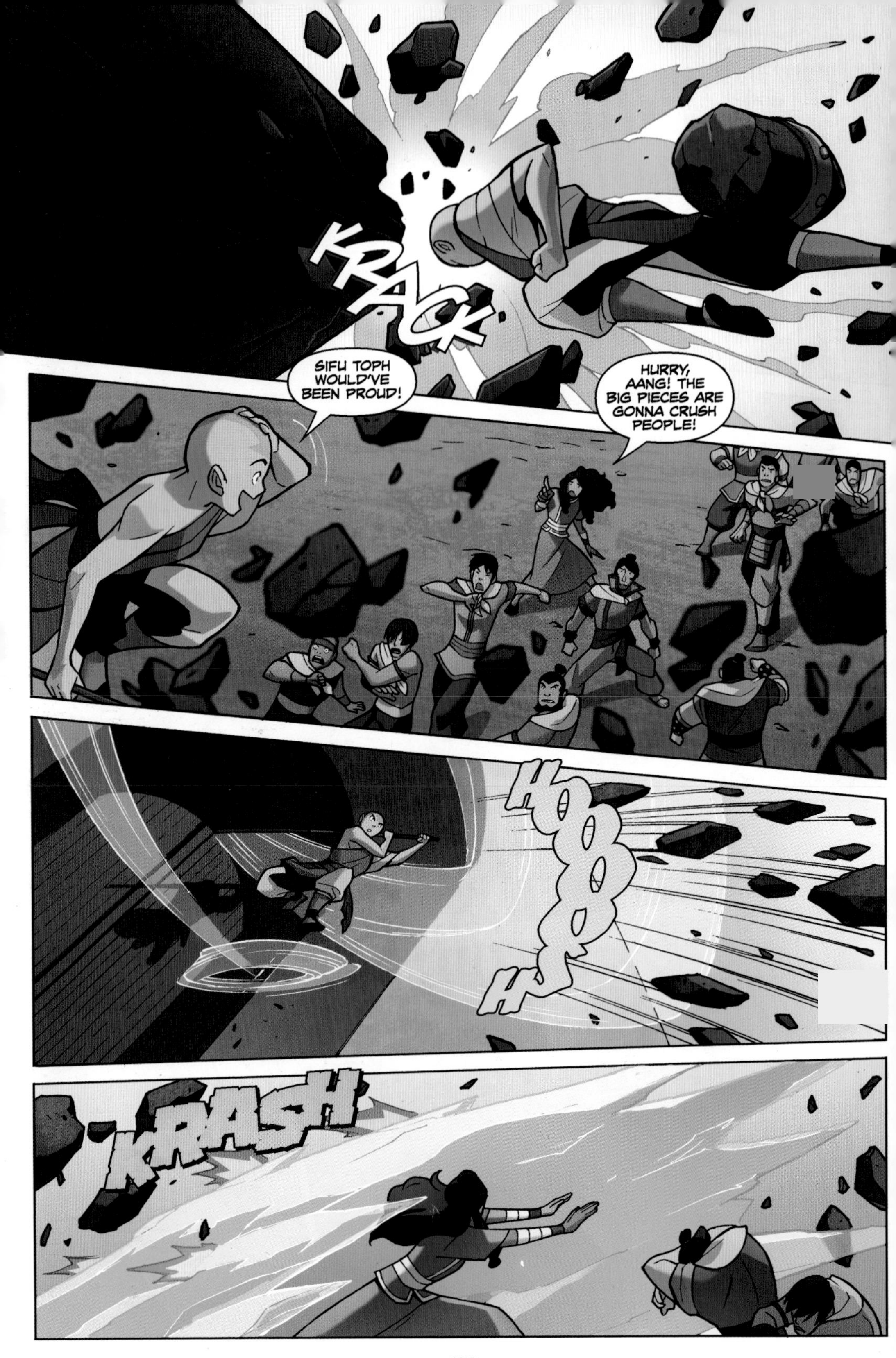
KRACK
SIFU TOPH WOULD'VE BEEN PROUD!
HURRY, AANG! THE BIG PIECES ARE GONNA CRUSH PEOPLE!
HOOOSH
KRASH

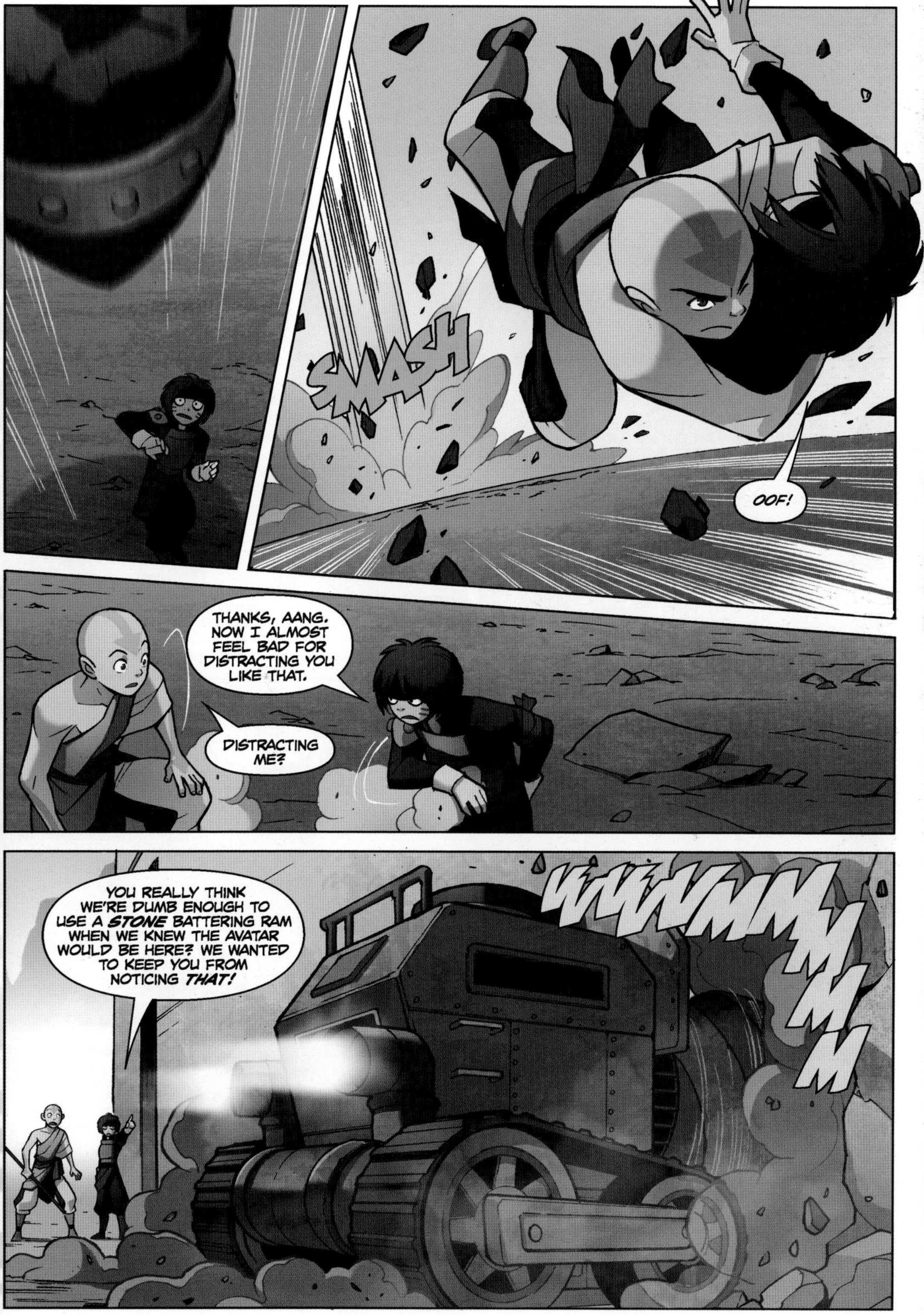
SMASH
OOF!
THANKS, AANG. NOW I ALMOST FEEL BAD FOR DISTRACTING YOU LIKE THAT.
DISTRACTING ME?
YOU REALLY THINK WE'RE DUMB ENOUGH TO USE A STONE BATTERING RAM WHEN WE KNEW THE AVATAR WOULD BE HERE? WE WANTED TO KEEP YOU FROM NOTICING THAT!
VVVVVMMMMMMM

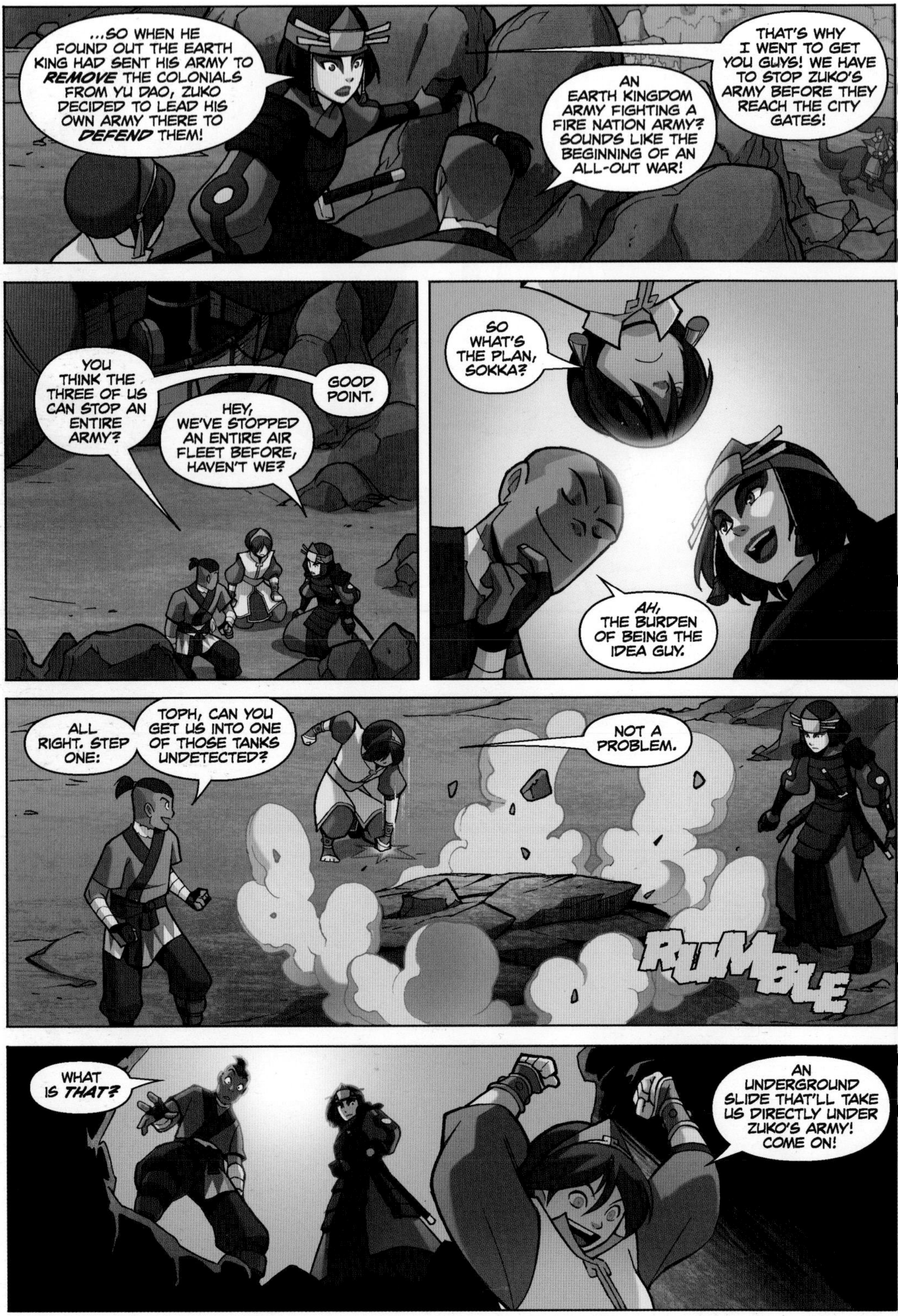
...SO WHEN HE FOUND OUT THE EARTH KING HAD SENT HIS ARMY TO *REMOVE* THE COLONIALS FROM YU DAO, ZUKO DECIDED TO LEAD HIS OWN ARMY THERE TO *DEFEND* THEM!
AN EARTH KINGDOM ARMY FIGHTING A FIRE NATION ARMY? SOUNDS LIKE THE BEGINNING OF AN ALL-OUT WAR!
THAT'S WHY I WENT TO GET YOU GUYS! WE HAVE TO STOP ZUKO'S ARMY BEFORE THEY REACH THE CITY GATES!
YOU THINK THE THREE OF US CAN STOP AN ENTIRE ARMY?
HEY, WE'VE STOPPED AN ENTIRE AIR FLEET BEFORE, HAVEN'T WE?
GOOD POINT.
SO WHAT'S THE PLAN, SOKKA?
AH, THE BURDEN OF BEING THE IDEA GUY.
ALL RIGHT. STEP ONE:
TOPH, CAN YOU GET US INTO ONE OF THOSE TANKS UNDETECTED?
NOT A PROBLEM.
RUMBLE
WHAT IS *THAT?*
AN UNDERGROUND SLIDE THAT'LL TAKE US DIRECTLY UNDER ZUKO'S ARMY! COME ON!

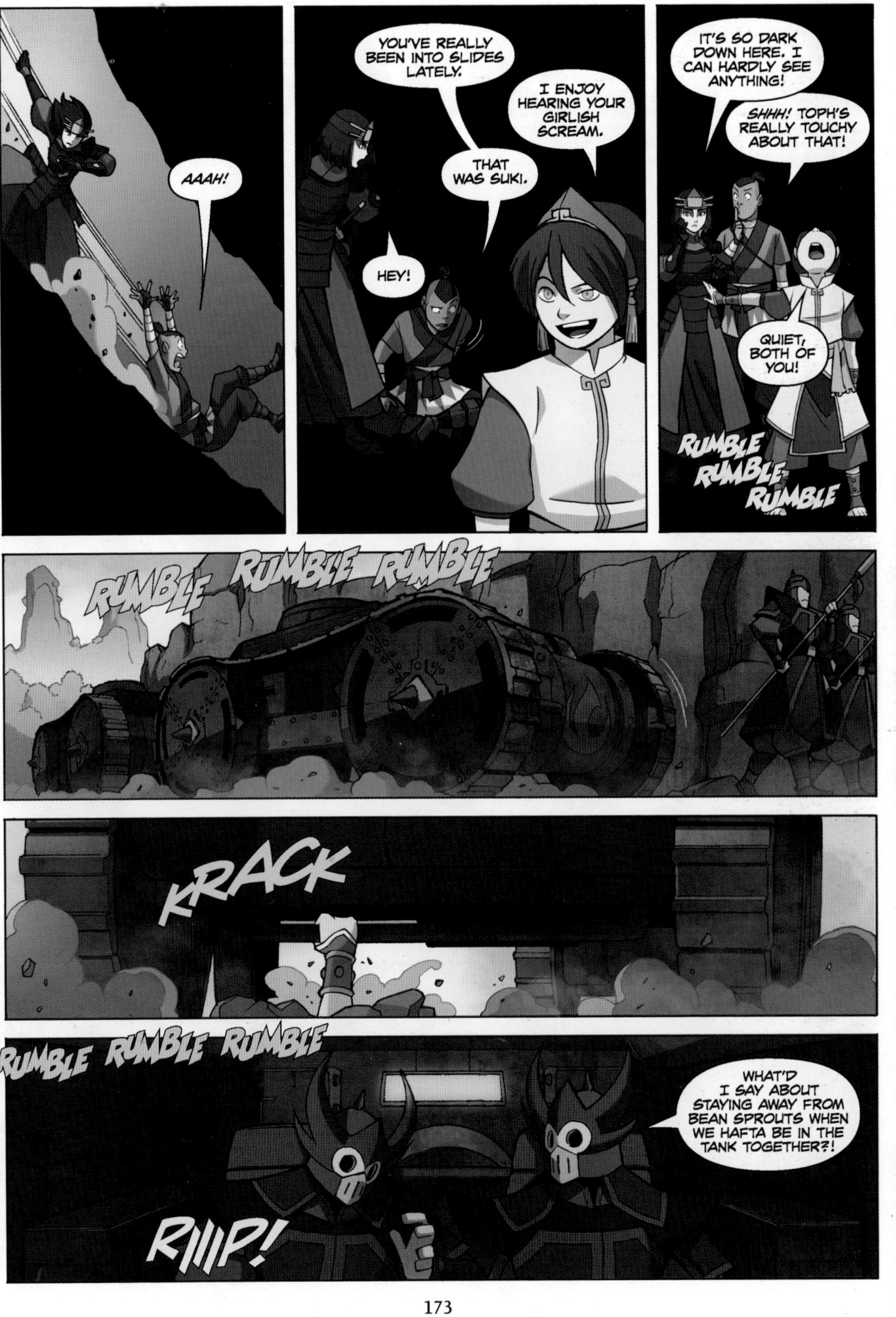
AAAH!
YOU'VE REALLY BEEN INTO SLIDES LATELY.
I ENJOY HEARING YOUR GIRLISH SCREAM.
THAT WAS SUKI.
HEY!
IT'S SO DARK DOWN HERE. I CAN HARDLY SEE ANYTHING!
SHHH! TOPH'S REALLY TOUCHY ABOUT THAT!
QUIET, BOTH OF YOU!
RUMBLE RUMBLE RUMBLE
RUMBLE RUMBLE RUMBLE
KRACK
RUMBLE RUMBLE RUMBLE
WHAT'D I SAY ABOUT STAYING AWAY FROM BEAN SPROUTS WHEN WE HAFTA BE IN THE TANK TOGETHER?!
RIIIP!

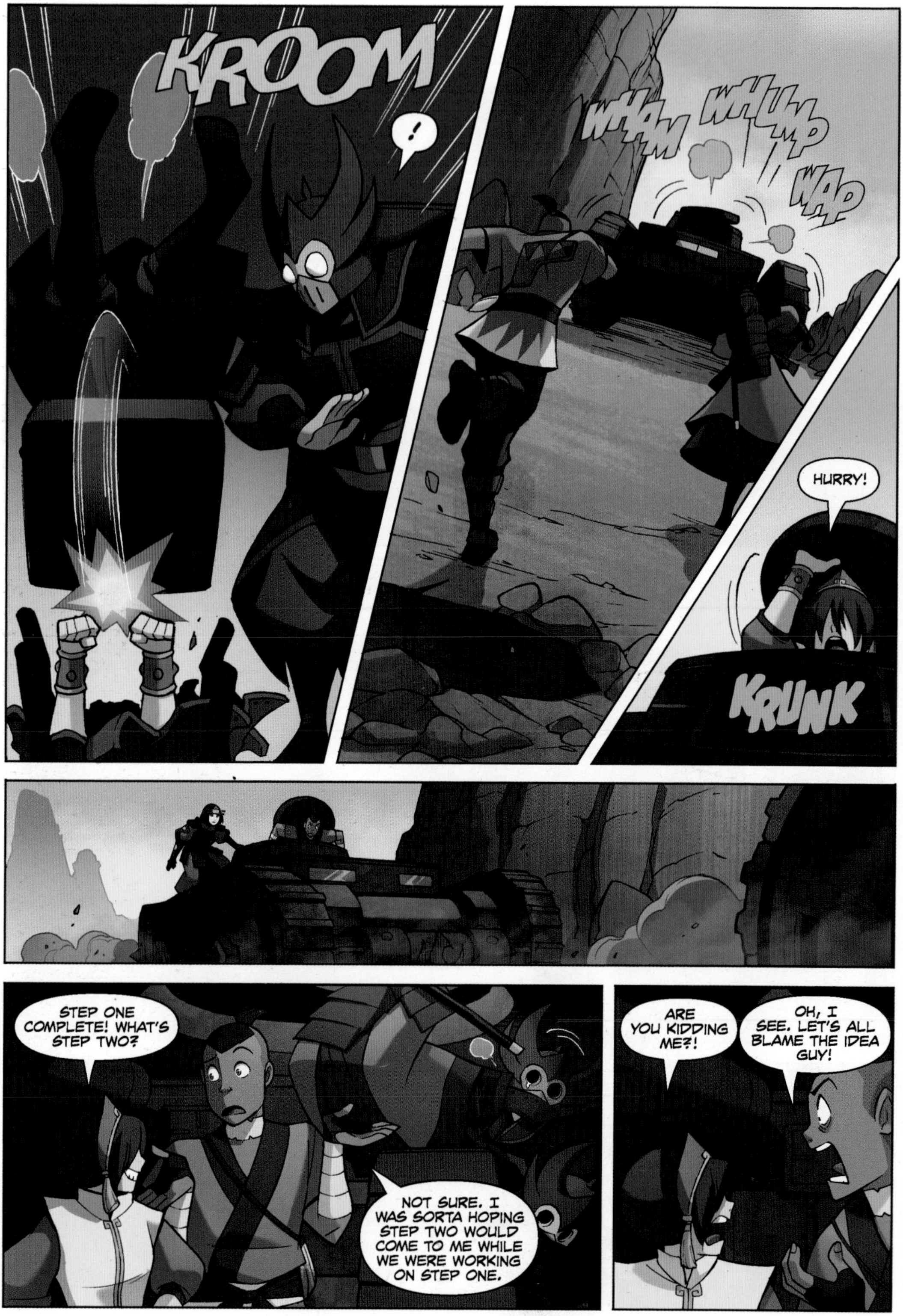
KROOM
!
WHAM
WHUMP
WAP
HURRY!
KRUNK
STEP ONE COMPLETE! WHAT'S STEP TWO?
NOT SURE. I WAS SORTA HOPING STEP TWO WOULD COME TO ME WHILE WE WERE WORKING ON STEP ONE.
ARE YOU KIDDING ME?!
OH, I SEE. LET'S ALL BLAME THE IDEA GUY!

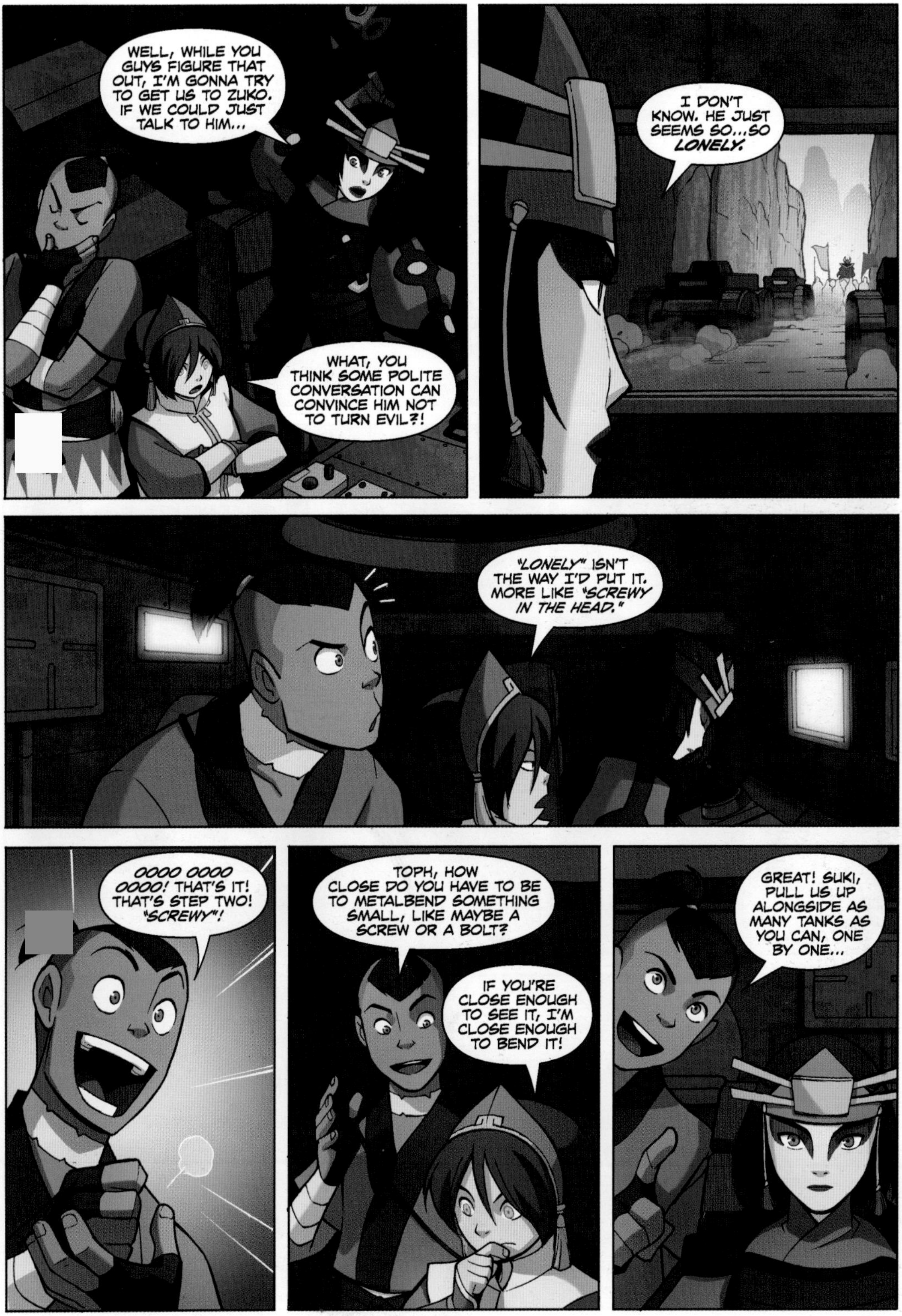
WELL, WHILE YOU GUYS FIGURE THAT OUT, I'M GONNA TRY TO GET US TO ZUKO. IF WE COULD JUST TALK TO HIM...
WHAT, YOU THINK SOME POLITE CONVERSATION CAN CONVINCE HIM NOT TO TURN EVIL?!
I DON'T KNOW. HE JUST SEEMS SO...SO *LONELY.*
"LONELY" ISN'T THE WAY I'D PUT IT. MORE LIKE *"SCREWY IN THE HEAD."*
OOOO OOOO OOOO! THAT'S IT! THAT'S STEP TWO! *"SCREWY"*!
TOPH, HOW CLOSE DO YOU HAVE TO BE TO METALBEND SOMETHING SMALL, LIKE MAYBE A SCREW OR A BOLT?
IF YOU'RE CLOSE ENOUGH TO SEE IT, I'M CLOSE ENOUGH TO BEND IT!
GREAT! SUKI, PULL US UP ALONGSIDE AS MANY TANKS AS YOU CAN, ONE BY ONE...

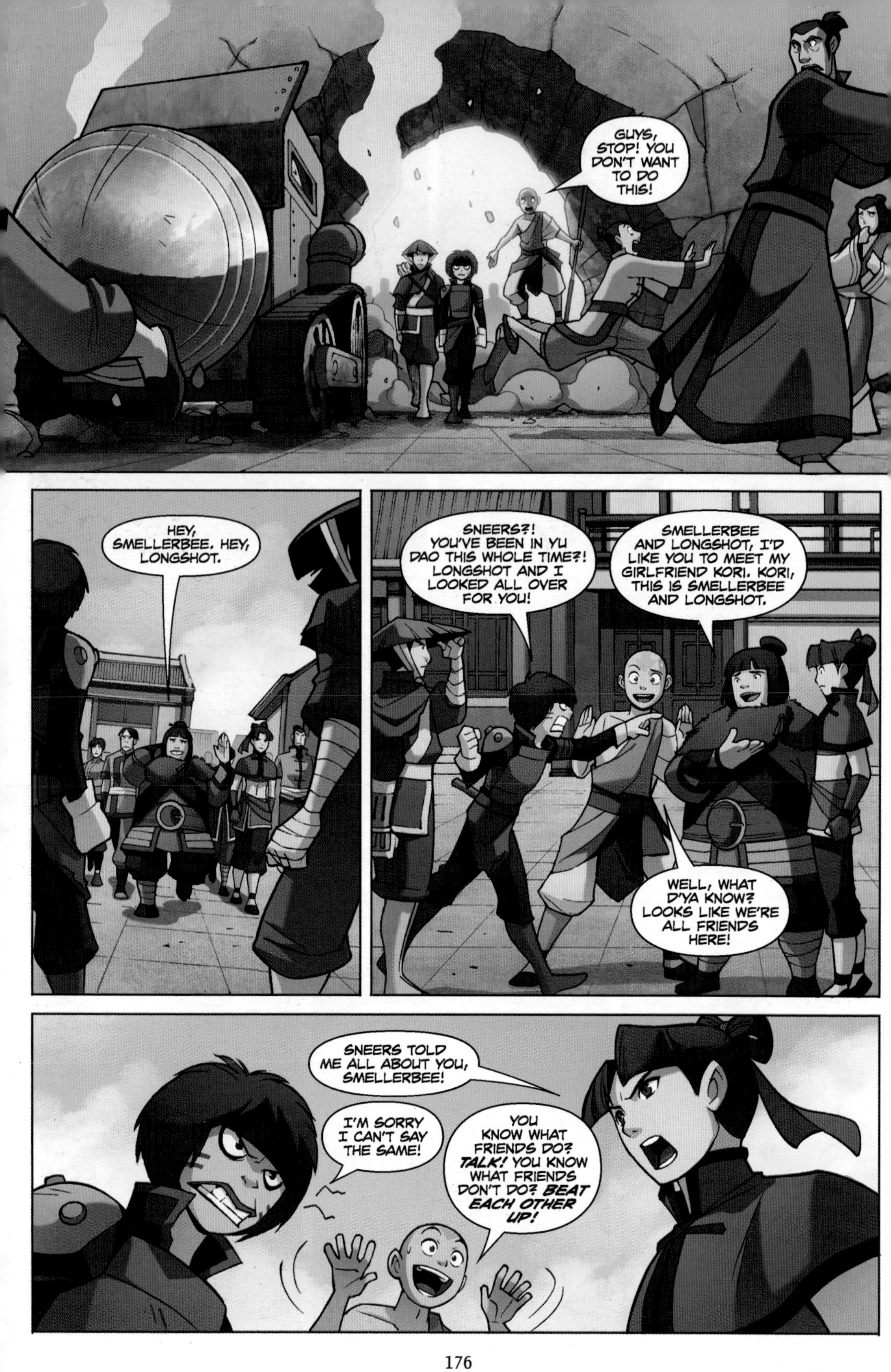
GUYS, STOP! YOU DON'T WANT TO DO THIS!
HEY, SMELLERBEE. HEY, LONGSHOT.
SNEERS?! YOU'VE BEEN IN YU DAO THIS WHOLE TIME?! LONGSHOT AND I LOOKED ALL OVER FOR YOU!
SMELLERBEE AND LONGSHOT, I'D LIKE YOU TO MEET MY GIRLFRIEND KORI. KORI, THIS IS SMELLERBEE AND LONGSHOT.
WELL, WHAT D'YA KNOW? LOOKS LIKE WE'RE ALL FRIENDS HERE!
SNEERS TOLD ME ALL ABOUT YOU, SMELLERBEE!
I'M SORRY I CAN'T SAY THE SAME!
YOU KNOW WHAT FRIENDS DO? TALK! YOU KNOW WHAT FRIENDS DON'T DO? BEAT EACH OTHER UP!

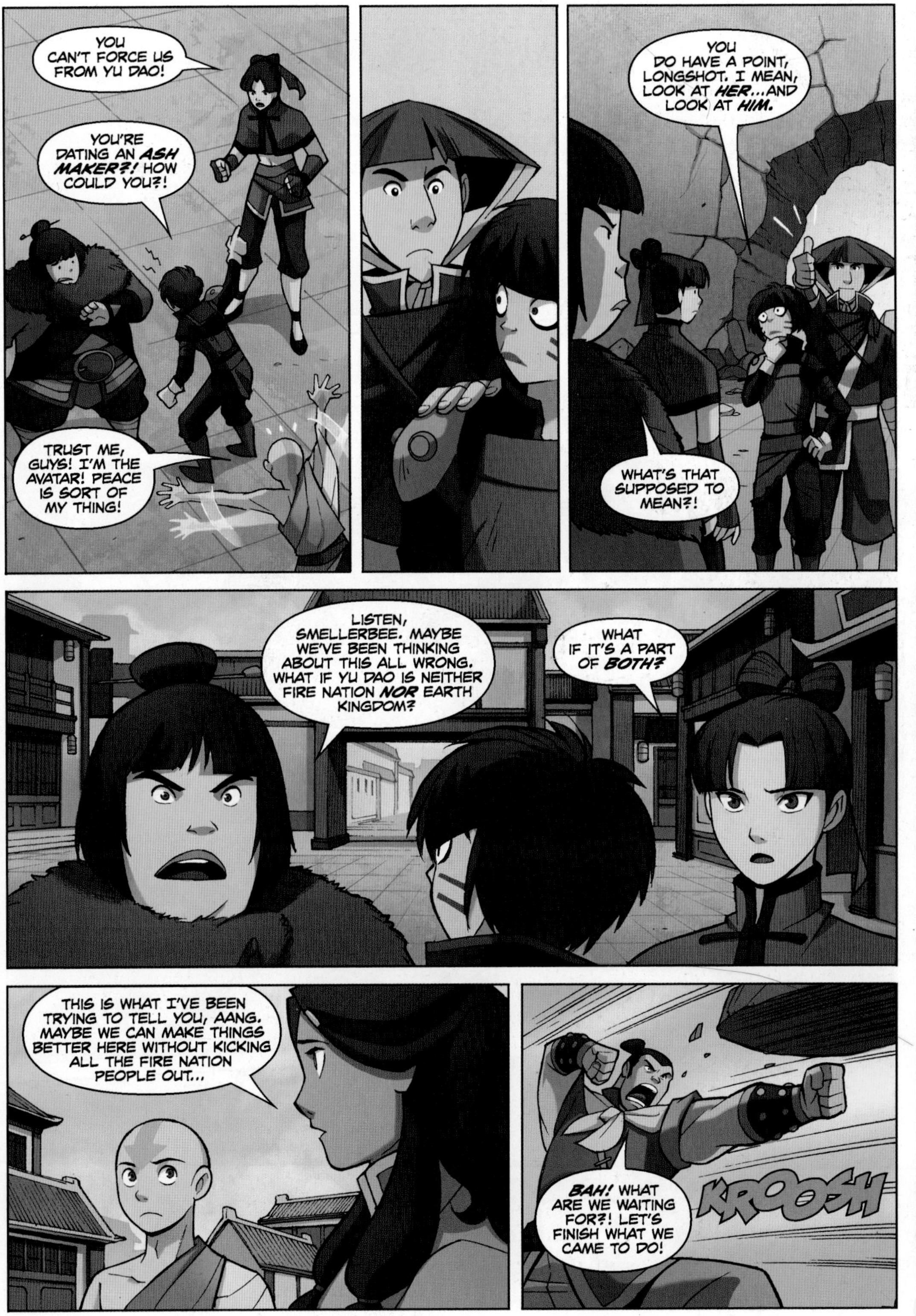
YOU CAN'T FORCE US FROM YU DAO!
YOU'RE DATING AN ASH MAKER?! HOW COULD YOU?!
TRUST ME, GUYS! I'M THE AVATAR! PEACE IS SORT OF MY THING!
YOU DO HAVE A POINT, LONGSHOT. I MEAN, LOOK AT HER...AND LOOK AT HIM.
WHAT'S THAT SUPPOSED TO MEAN?!
LISTEN, SMELLERBEE. MAYBE WE'VE BEEN THINKING ABOUT THIS ALL WRONG. WHAT IF YU DAO IS NEITHER FIRE NATION NOR EARTH KINGDOM?
WHAT IF IT'S A PART OF BOTH?
THIS IS WHAT I'VE BEEN TRYING TO TELL YOU, AANG. MAYBE WE CAN MAKE THINGS BETTER HERE WITHOUT KICKING ALL THE FIRE NATION PEOPLE OUT...
BAH! WHAT ARE WE WAITING FOR?! LET'S FINISH WHAT WE CAME TO DO!
KROOSH

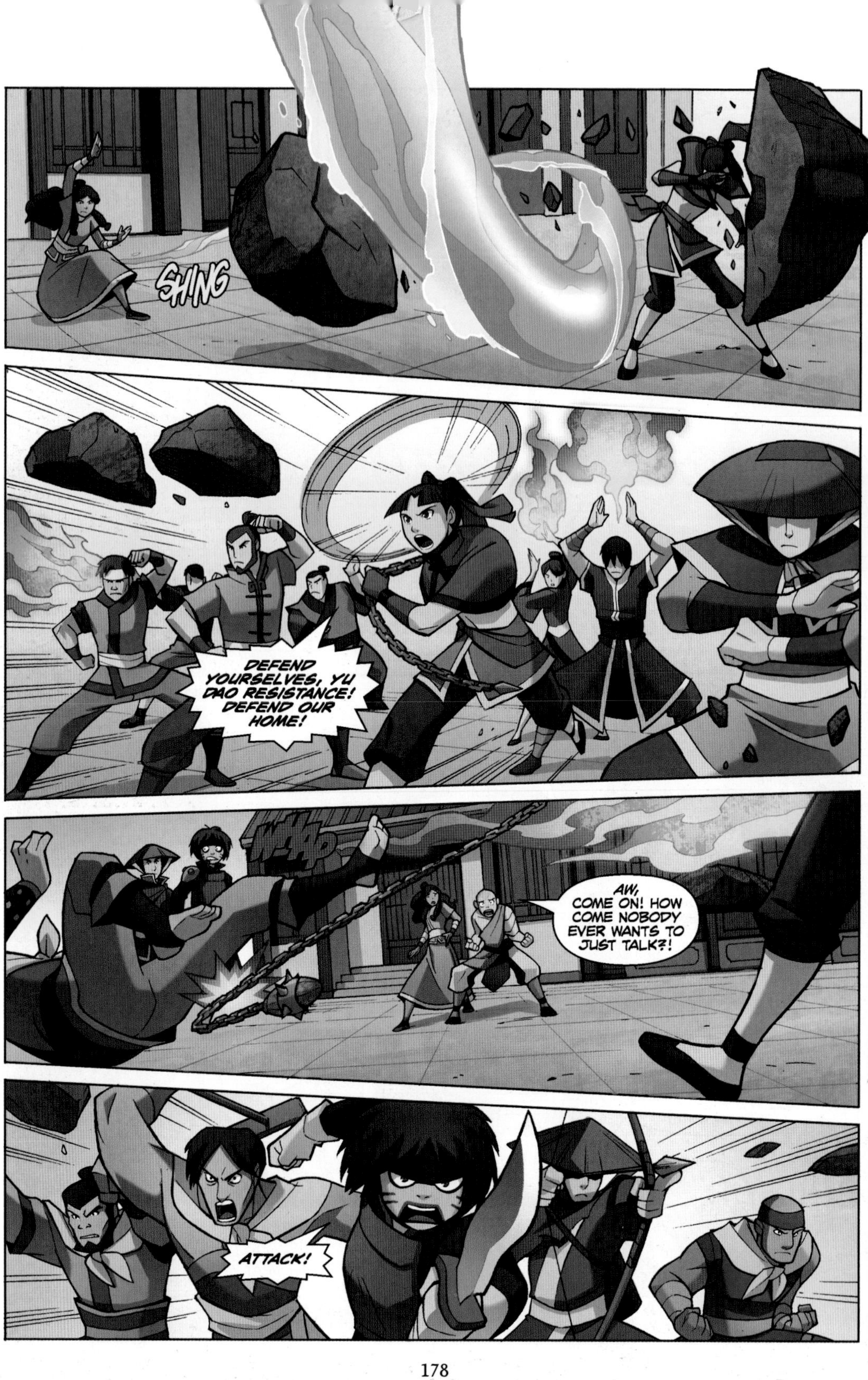
SHING
DEFEND YOURSELVES, YU DAO RESISTANCE! DEFEND OUR HOME!
AW, COME ON! HOW COME NOBODY EVER WANTS TO JUST TALK?!
ATTACK!

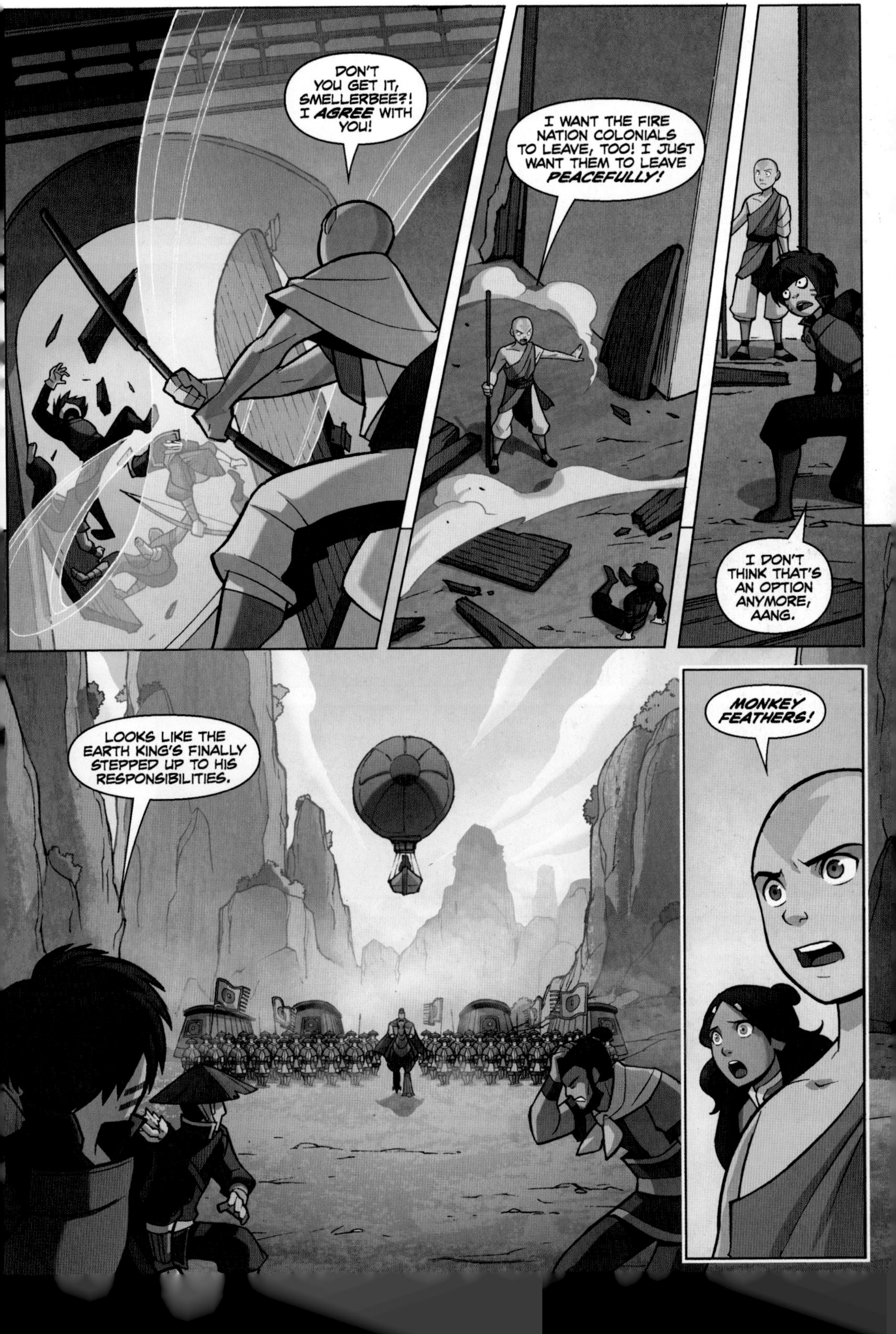
DON'T YOU GET IT, SMELLERBEE?! I AGREE WITH YOU!
I WANT THE FIRE NATION COLONIALS TO LEAVE, TOO! I JUST WANT THEM TO LEAVE PEACEFULLY!
I DON'T THINK THAT'S AN OPTION ANYMORE, AANG.
LOOKS LIKE THE EARTH KING'S FINALLY STEPPED UP TO HIS RESPONSIBILITIES.
MONKEY FEATHERS!

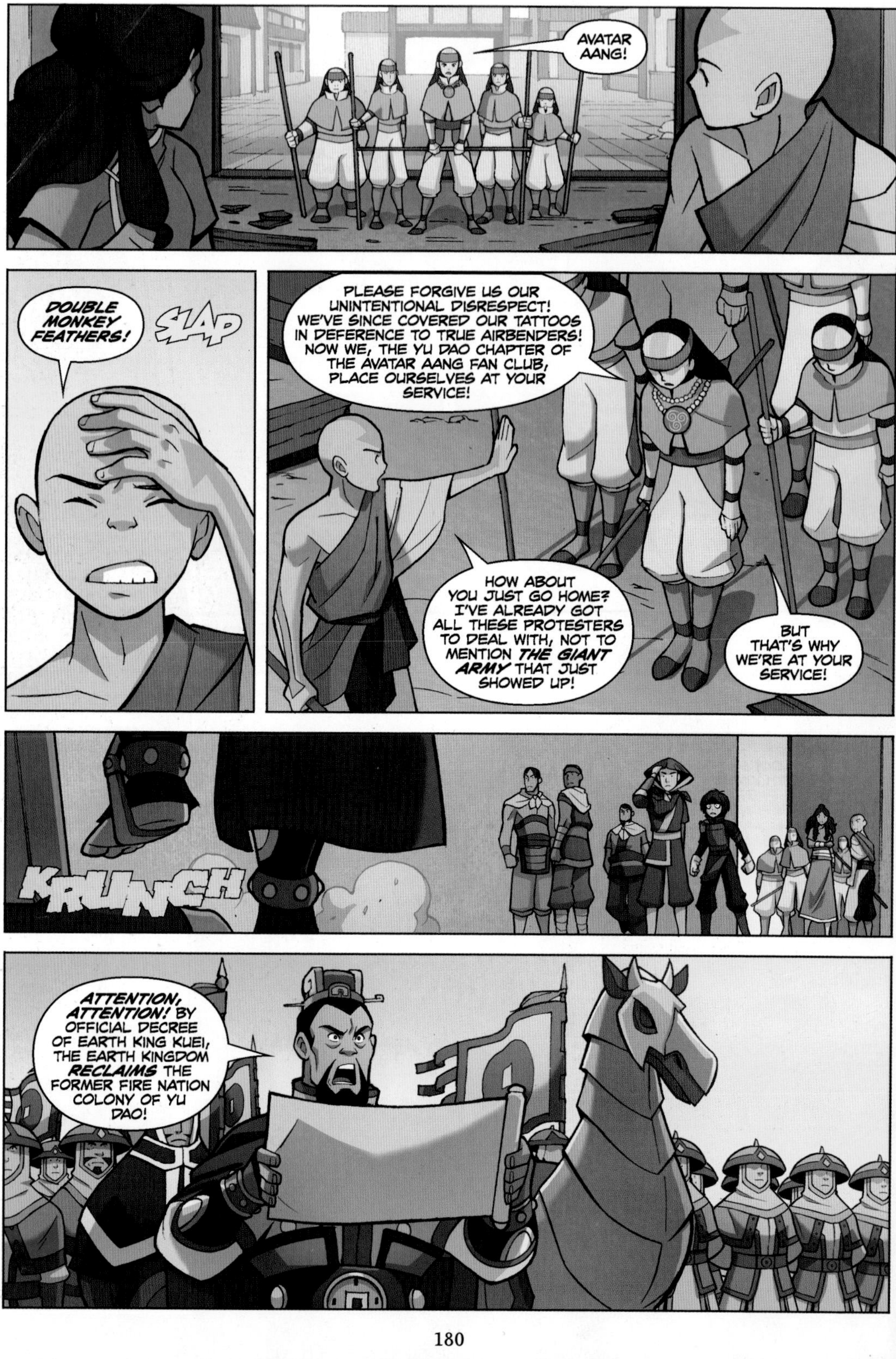
AVATAR AANG!
DOUBLE MONKEY FEATHERS!
SLAP
PLEASE FORGIVE US OUR UNINTENTIONAL DISRESPECT! WE'VE SINCE COVERED OUR TATTOOS IN DEFERENCE TO TRUE AIRBENDERS! NOW WE, THE YU DAO CHAPTER OF THE AVATAR AANG FAN CLUB, PLACE OURSELVES AT YOUR SERVICE!
HOW ABOUT YOU JUST GO HOME? I'VE ALREADY GOT ALL THESE PROTESTERS TO DEAL WITH, NOT TO MENTION THE GIANT ARMY THAT JUST SHOWED UP!
BUT THAT'S WHY WE'RE AT YOUR SERVICE!
KRUNCH
ATTENTION, ATTENTION! BY OFFICIAL DECREE OF EARTH KING KUEI, THE EARTH KINGDOM RECLAIMS THE FORMER FIRE NATION COLONY OF YU DAO!

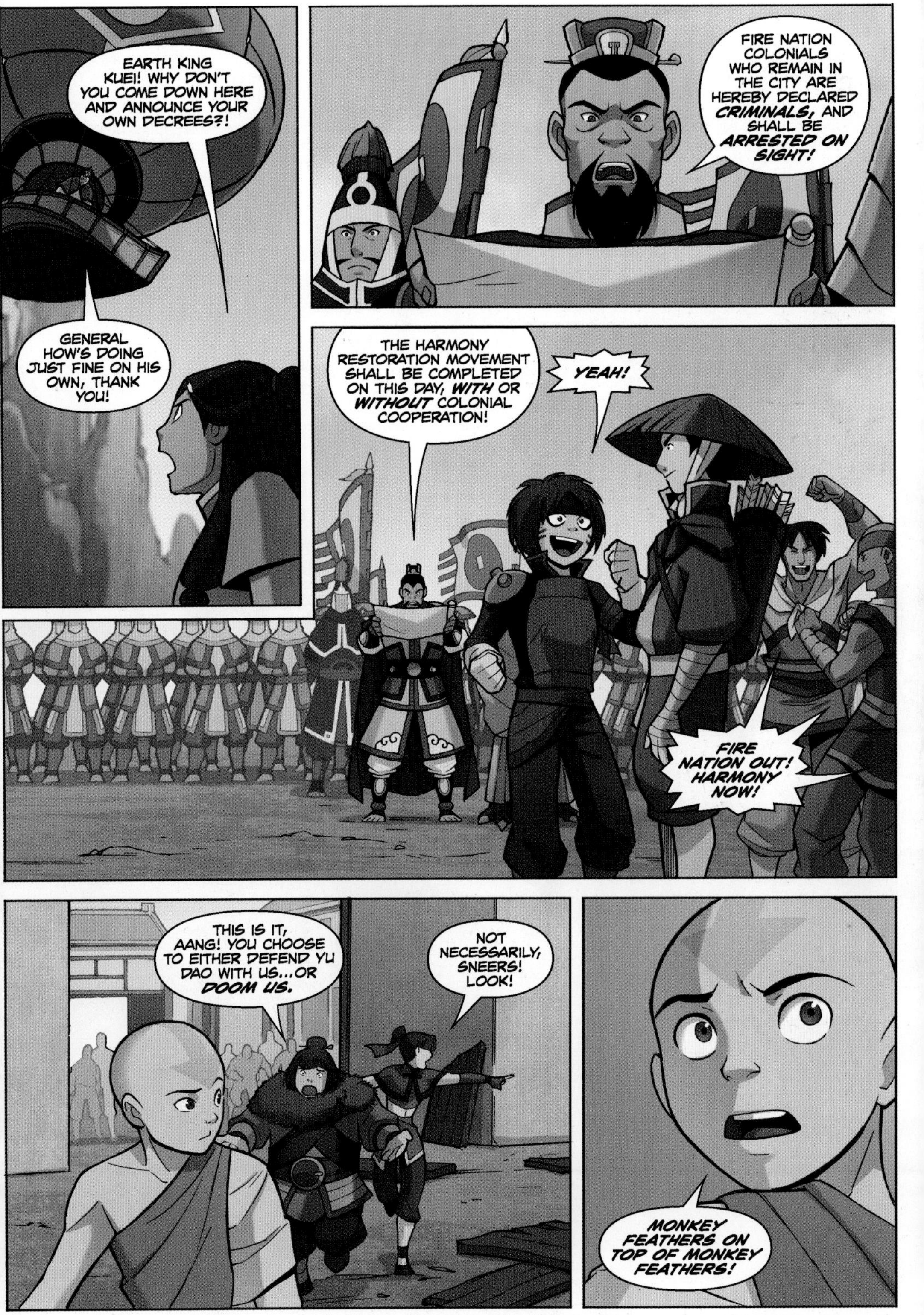
EARTH KING KUEI! WHY DON'T YOU COME DOWN HERE AND ANNOUNCE YOUR OWN DECREES?!
GENERAL HOW'S DOING JUST FINE ON HIS OWN, THANK YOU!
FIRE NATION COLONIALS WHO REMAIN IN THE CITY ARE HEREBY DECLARED CRIMINALS, AND SHALL BE ARRESTED ON SIGHT!
THE HARMONY RESTORATION MOVEMENT SHALL BE COMPLETED ON THIS DAY, WITH OR WITHOUT COLONIAL COOPERATION!
YEAH!
FIRE NATION OUT! HARMONY NOW!
THIS IS IT, AANG! YOU CHOOSE TO EITHER DEFEND YU DAO WITH US...OR DOOM US.
NOT NECESSARILY, SNEERS! LOOK!
MONKEY FEATHERS ON TOP OF MONKEY FEATHERS!

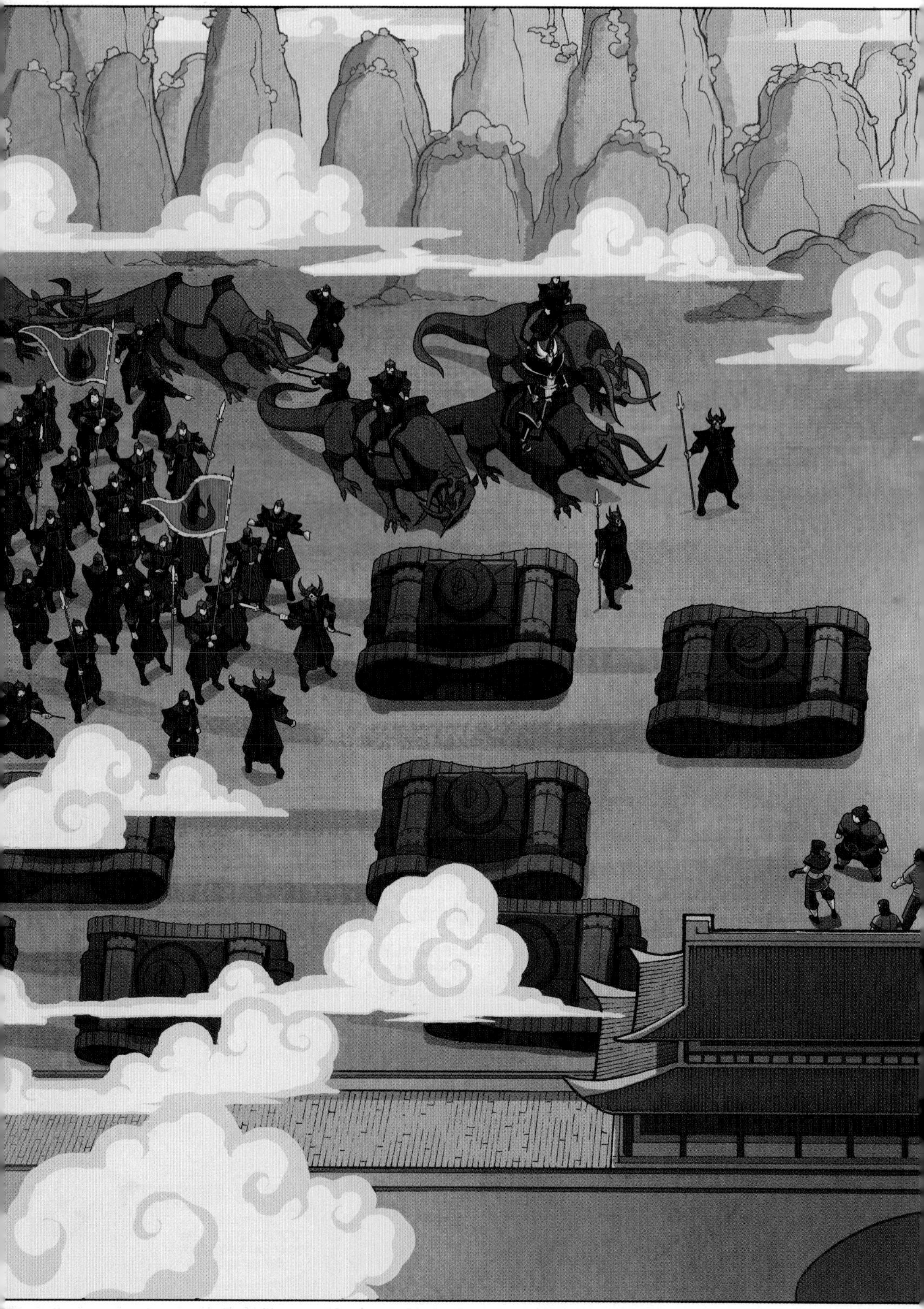

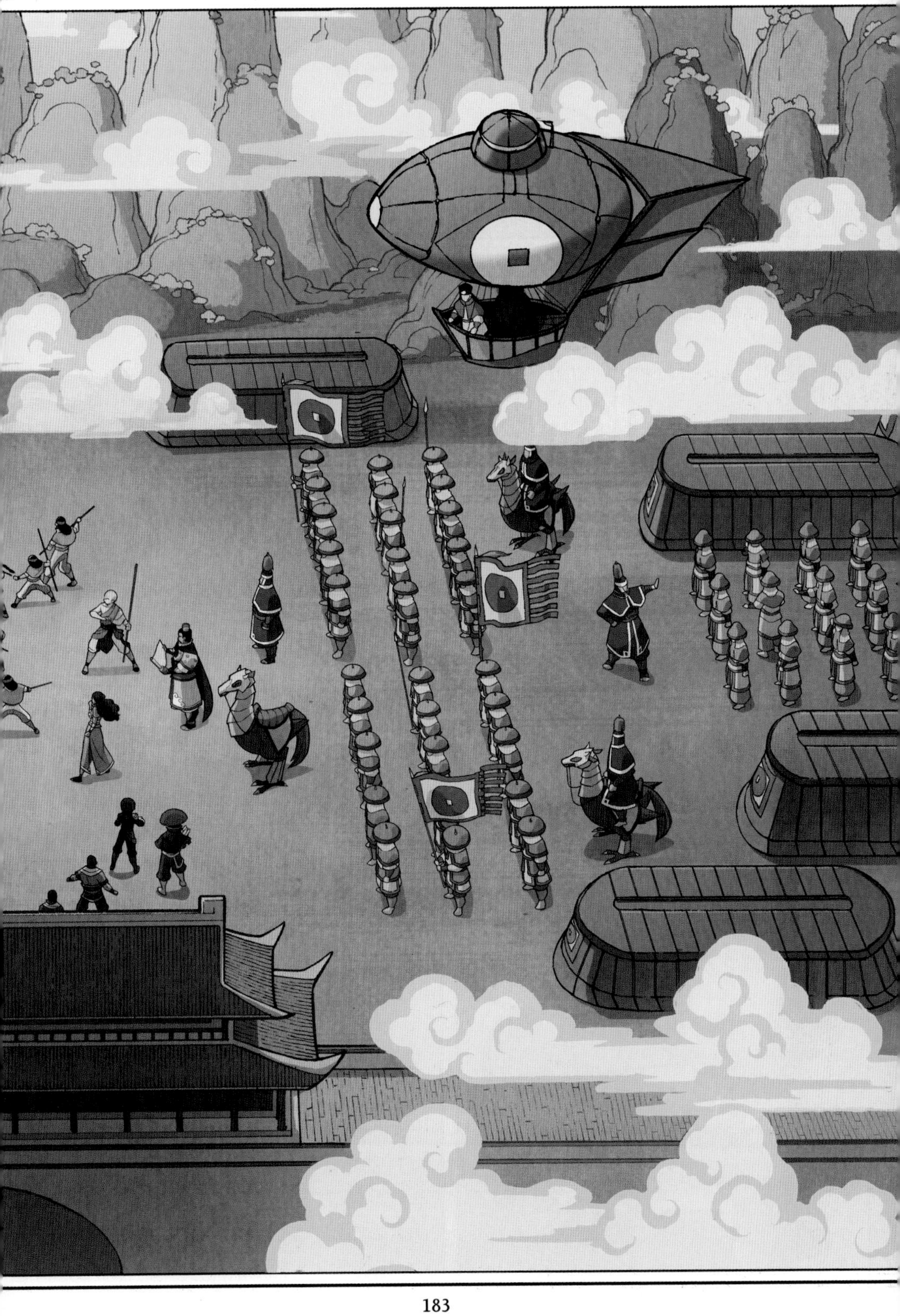

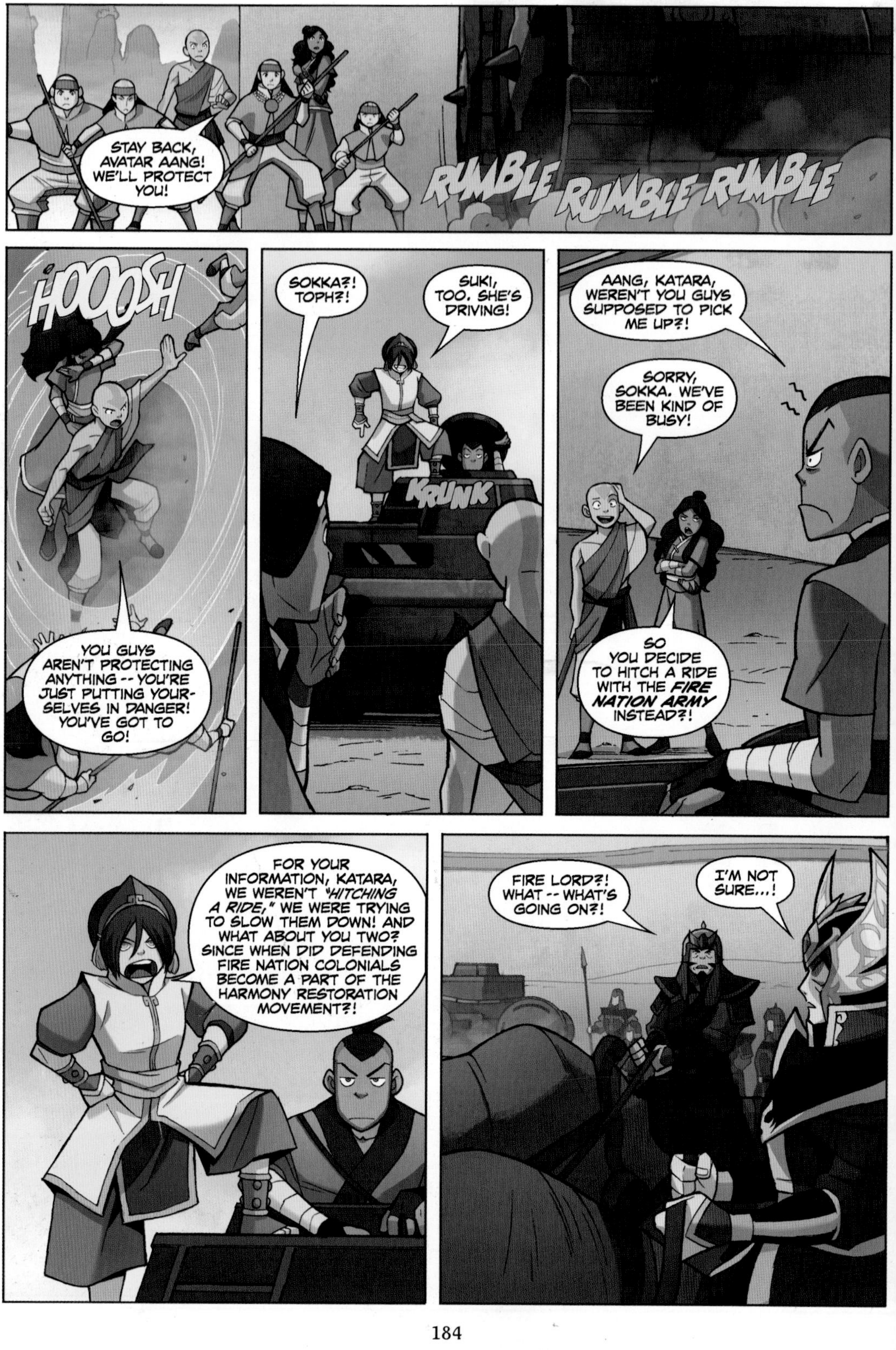
STAY BACK, AVATAR AANG! WE'LL PROTECT YOU!
RUMBLE RUMBLE RUMBLE
HOOOSH
YOU GUYS AREN'T PROTECTING ANYTHING -- YOU'RE JUST PUTTING YOURSELVES IN DANGER! YOU'VE GOT TO GO!
SOKKA?! TOPH?!
SUKI, TOO. SHE'S DRIVING!
KRUNK
AANG, KATARA, WEREN'T YOU GUYS SUPPOSED TO PICK ME UP?!
SORRY, SOKKA. WE'VE BEEN KIND OF BUSY!
SO YOU DECIDE TO HITCH A RIDE WITH THE *FIRE NATION ARMY* INSTEAD?!
FOR YOUR INFORMATION, KATARA, WE WEREN'T *"HITCHING A RIDE,"* WE WERE TRYING TO SLOW THEM DOWN! AND WHAT ABOUT YOU TWO? SINCE WHEN DID DEFENDING FIRE NATION COLONIALS BECOME A PART OF THE HARMONY RESTORATION MOVEMENT?!
FIRE LORD?! WHAT -- WHAT'S GOING ON?!
I'M NOT SURE...!

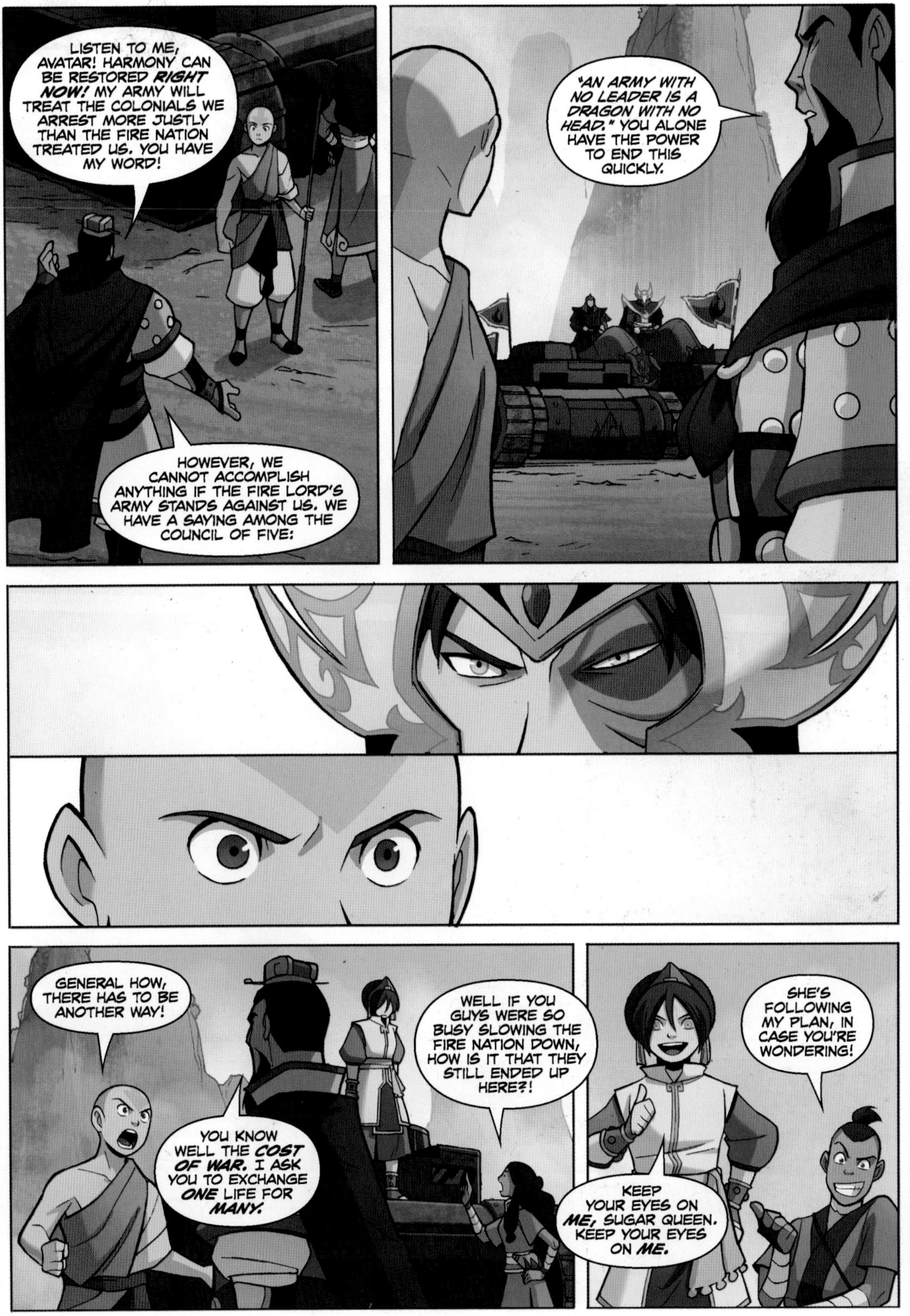
LISTEN TO ME, AVATAR! HARMONY CAN BE RESTORED *RIGHT NOW!* MY ARMY WILL TREAT THE COLONIALS WE ARREST MORE JUSTLY THAN THE FIRE NATION TREATED US. YOU HAVE MY WORD!
HOWEVER, WE CANNOT ACCOMPLISH ANYTHING IF THE FIRE LORD'S ARMY STANDS AGAINST US. WE HAVE A SAYING AMONG THE COUNCIL OF FIVE:
"AN ARMY WITH NO LEADER IS A DRAGON WITH NO HEAD." YOU ALONE HAVE THE POWER TO END THIS QUICKLY.
GENERAL HOW, THERE HAS TO BE ANOTHER WAY!
YOU KNOW WELL THE *COST OF WAR.* I ASK YOU TO EXCHANGE *ONE* LIFE FOR *MANY.*
WELL IF YOU GUYS WERE SO BUSY SLOWING THE FIRE NATION DOWN, HOW IS IT THAT THEY STILL ENDED UP HERE?!
SHE'S FOLLOWING MY PLAN, IN CASE YOU'RE WONDERING!
KEEP YOUR EYES ON *ME,* SUGAR QUEEN. KEEP YOUR EYES ON *ME.*

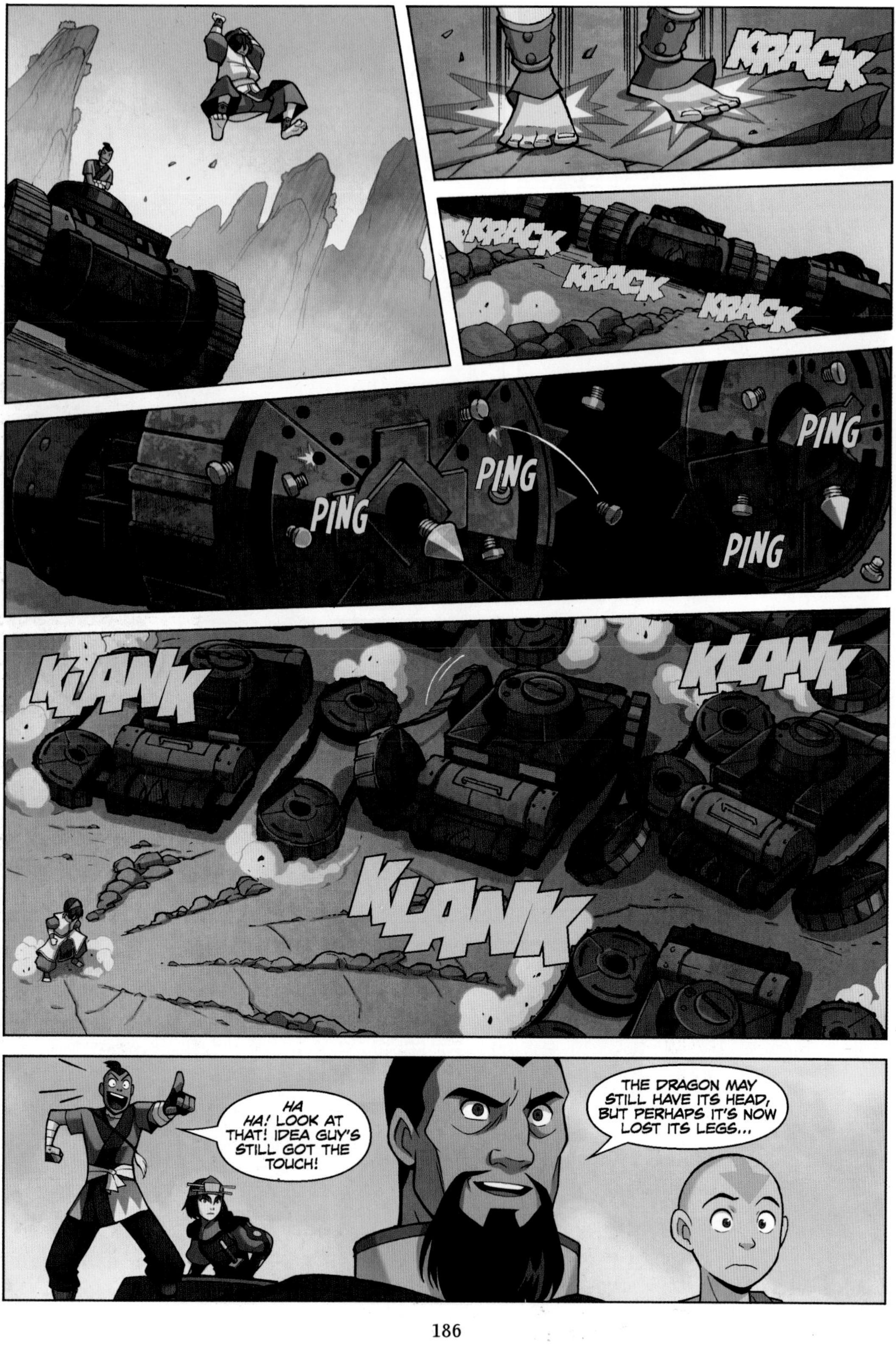
KRACK
KRACK
KRACK
KRACK
PING
PING
PING
PING
KLANK
KLANK
KLANK
HA HA! LOOK AT THAT! IDEA GUY'S STILL GOT THE TOUCH!
THE DRAGON MAY STILL HAVE ITS HEAD, BUT PERHAPS IT'S NOW LOST ITS LEGS...

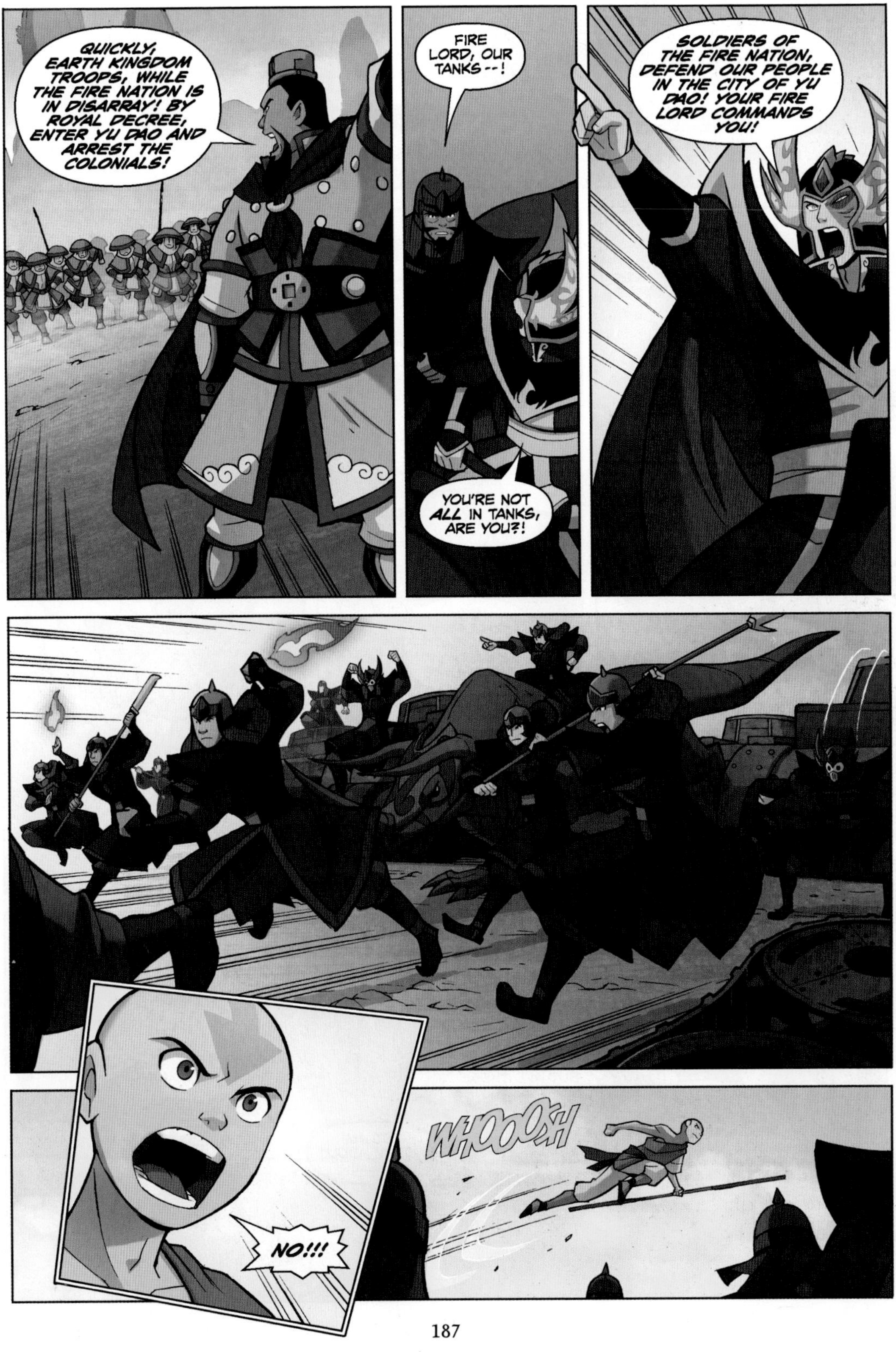
QUICKLY, EARTH KINGDOM TROOPS, WHILE THE FIRE NATION IS IN DISARRAY! BY ROYAL DECREE, ENTER YU DAO AND ARREST THE COLONIALS!
FIRE LORD, OUR TANKS --!
YOU'RE NOT ALL IN TANKS, ARE YOU?!
SOLDIERS OF THE FIRE NATION, DEFEND OUR PEOPLE IN THE CITY OF YU DAO! YOUR FIRE LORD COMMANDS YOU!
NO!!!
WHOOOSH

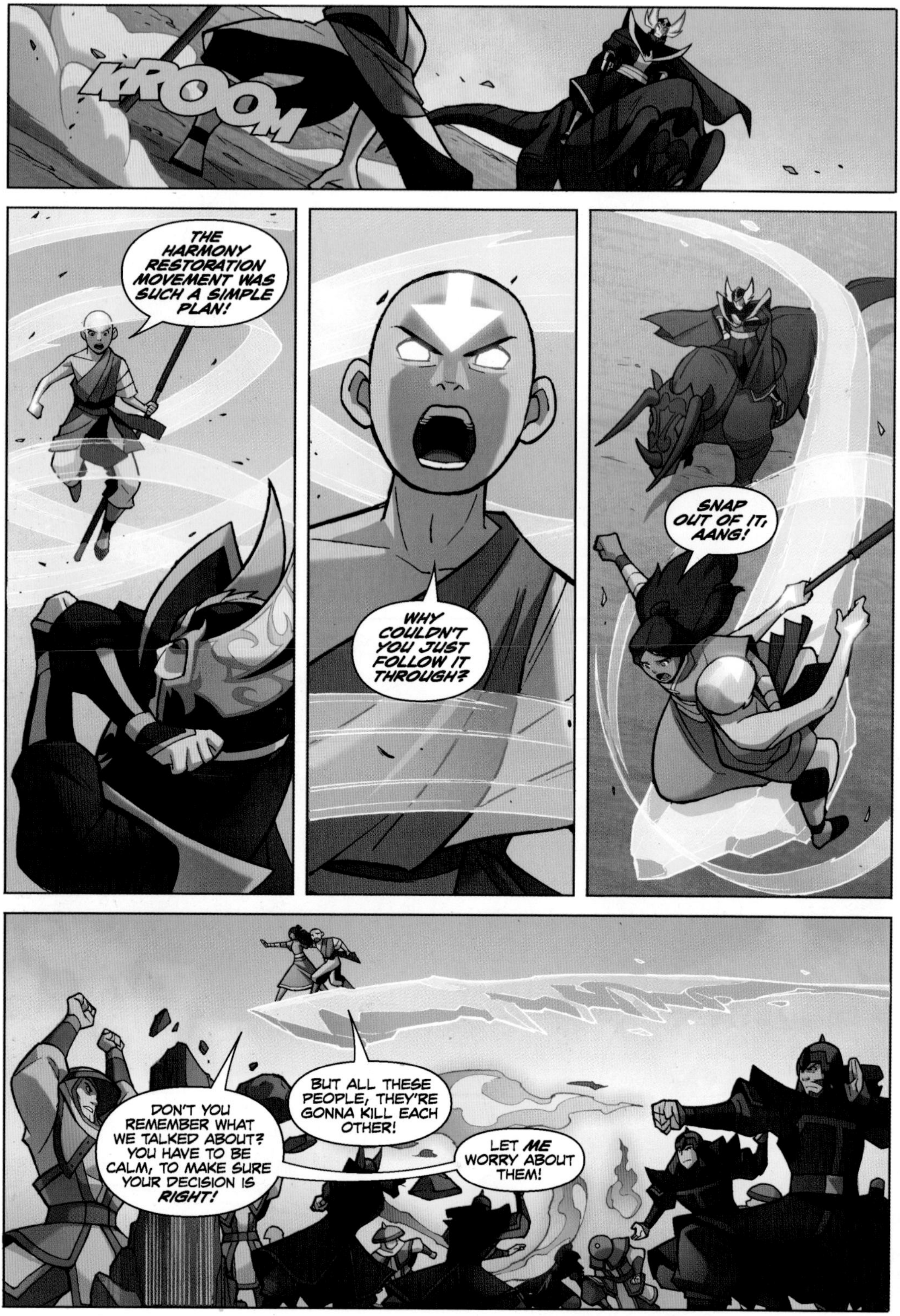
KROOM
THE HARMONY RESTORATION MOVEMENT WAS SUCH A SIMPLE PLAN!
WHY COULDN'T YOU JUST FOLLOW IT THROUGH?
SNAP OUT OF IT, AANG!
DON'T YOU REMEMBER WHAT WE TALKED ABOUT? YOU HAVE TO BE CALM, TO MAKE SURE YOUR DECISION IS *RIGHT!*
BUT ALL THESE PEOPLE; THEY'RE GONNA KILL EACH OTHER!
LET *ME* WORRY ABOUT THEM!

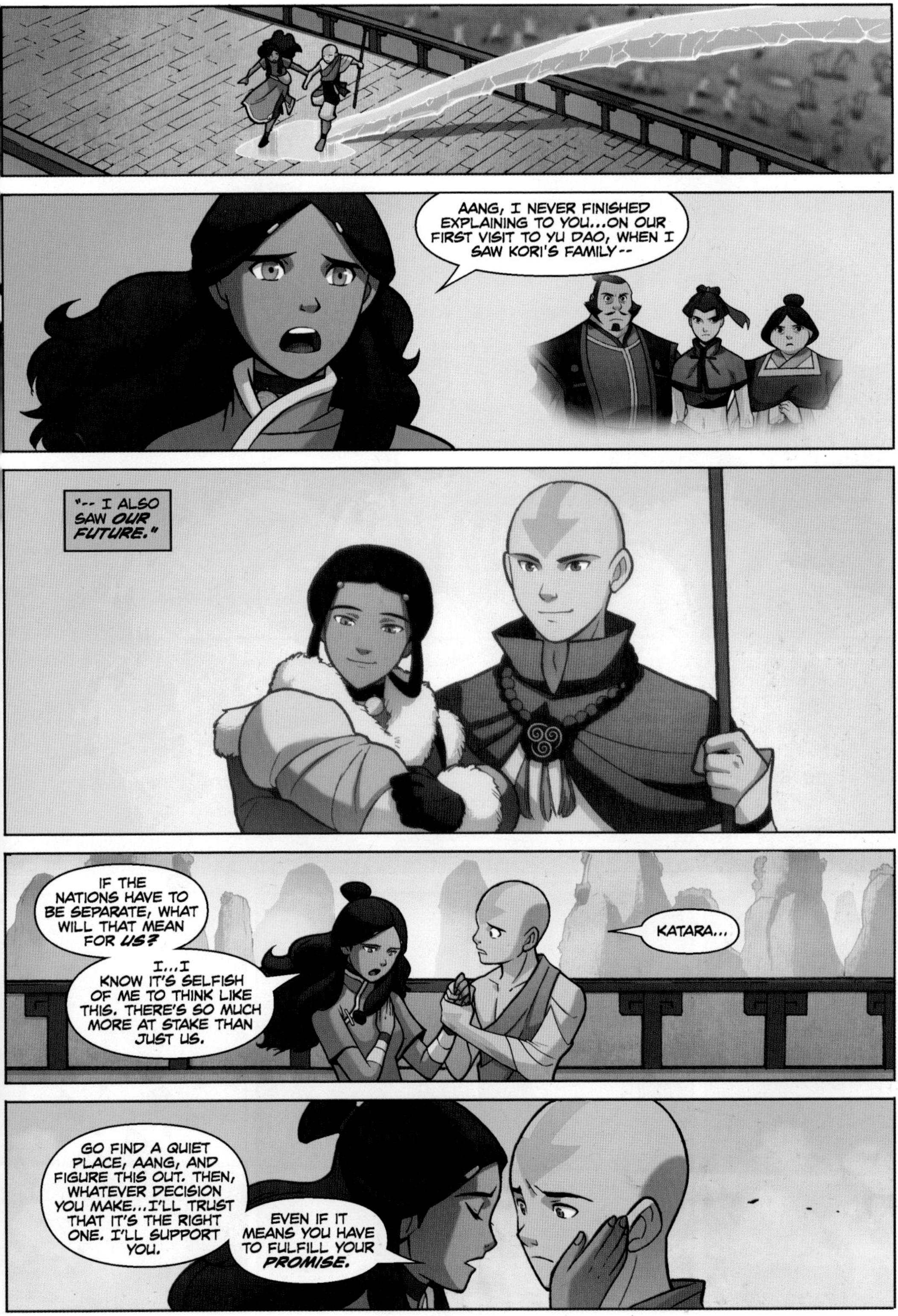
AANG, I NEVER FINISHED EXPLAINING TO YOU...ON OUR FIRST VISIT TO YU DAO, WHEN I SAW KORI'S FAMILY--
"--I ALSO SAW OUR FUTURE."
IF THE NATIONS HAVE TO BE SEPARATE, WHAT WILL THAT MEAN FOR US?
I...I KNOW IT'S SELFISH OF ME TO THINK LIKE THIS. THERE'S SO MUCH MORE AT STAKE THAN JUST US.
KATARA...
GO FIND A QUIET PLACE, AANG, AND FIGURE THIS OUT. THEN, WHATEVER DECISION YOU MAKE...I'LL TRUST THAT IT'S THE RIGHT ONE. I'LL SUPPORT YOU.
EVEN IF IT MEANS YOU HAVE TO FULFILL YOUR PROMISE.

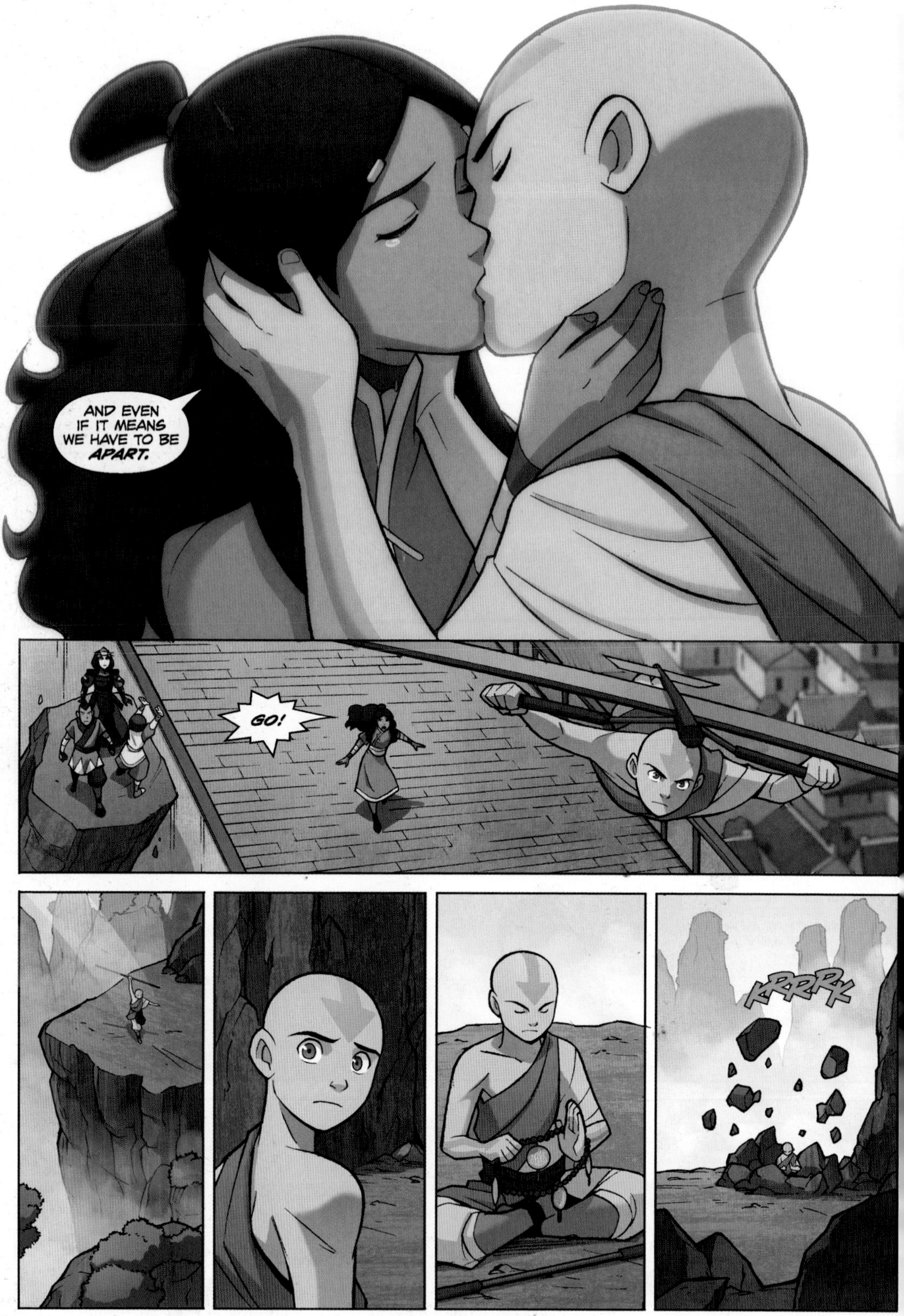
AND EVEN IF IT MEANS WE HAVE TO BE *APART.*
GO!
KRRRK

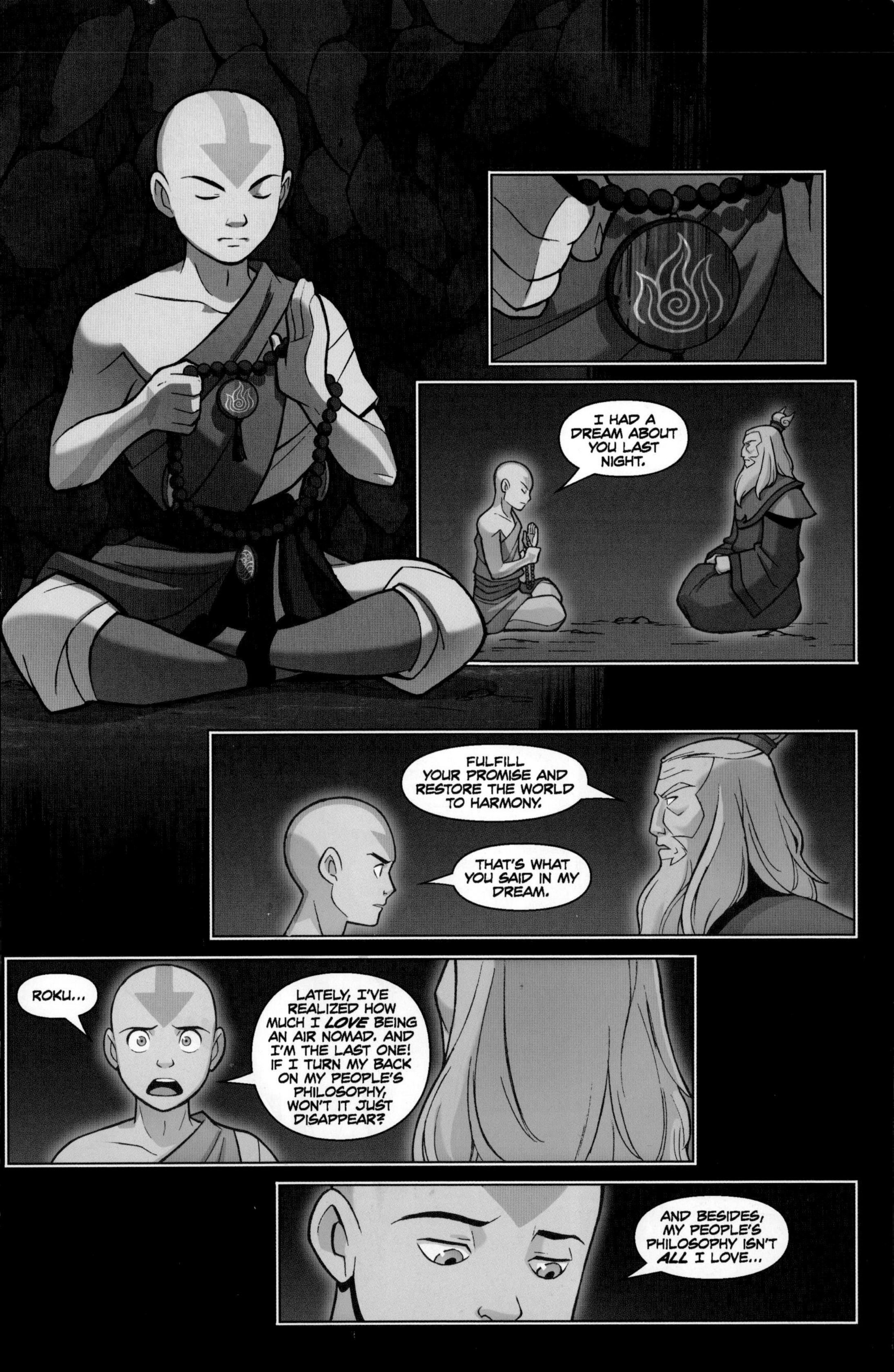
I HAD A DREAM ABOUT YOU LAST NIGHT.
FULFILL YOUR PROMISE AND RESTORE THE WORLD TO HARMONY.
THAT'S WHAT YOU SAID IN MY DREAM.
ROKU...
LATELY, I'VE REALIZED HOW MUCH I LOVE BEING AN AIR NOMAD. AND I'M THE LAST ONE! IF I TURN MY BACK ON MY PEOPLE'S PHILOSOPHY, WON'T IT JUST DISAPPEAR?
AND BESIDES, MY PEOPLE'S PHILOSOPHY ISN'T ALL I LOVE...

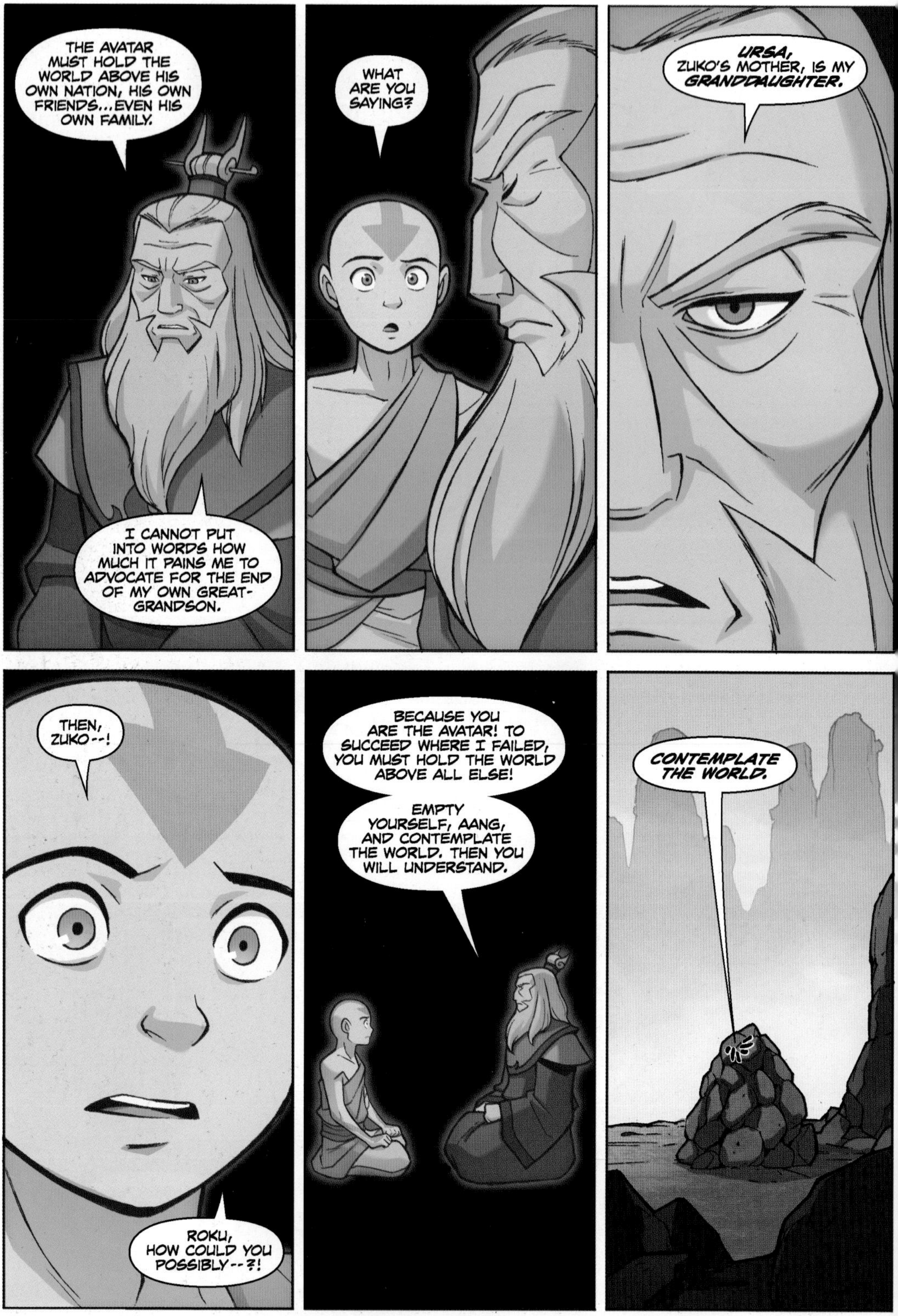
THE AVATAR MUST HOLD THE WORLD ABOVE HIS OWN NATION, HIS OWN FRIENDS...EVEN HIS OWN FAMILY.
I CANNOT PUT INTO WORDS HOW MUCH IT PAINS ME TO ADVOCATE FOR THE END OF MY OWN GREAT-GRANDSON.
WHAT ARE YOU SAYING?
URSA, ZUKO'S MOTHER, IS MY GRANDDAUGHTER.
THEN, ZUKO--!
ROKU, HOW COULD YOU POSSIBLY--?!
BECAUSE YOU ARE THE AVATAR! TO SUCCEED WHERE I FAILED, YOU MUST HOLD THE WORLD ABOVE ALL ELSE!
EMPTY YOURSELF, AANG, AND CONTEMPLATE THE WORLD. THEN YOU WILL UNDERSTAND.
CONTEMPLATE THE WORLD.

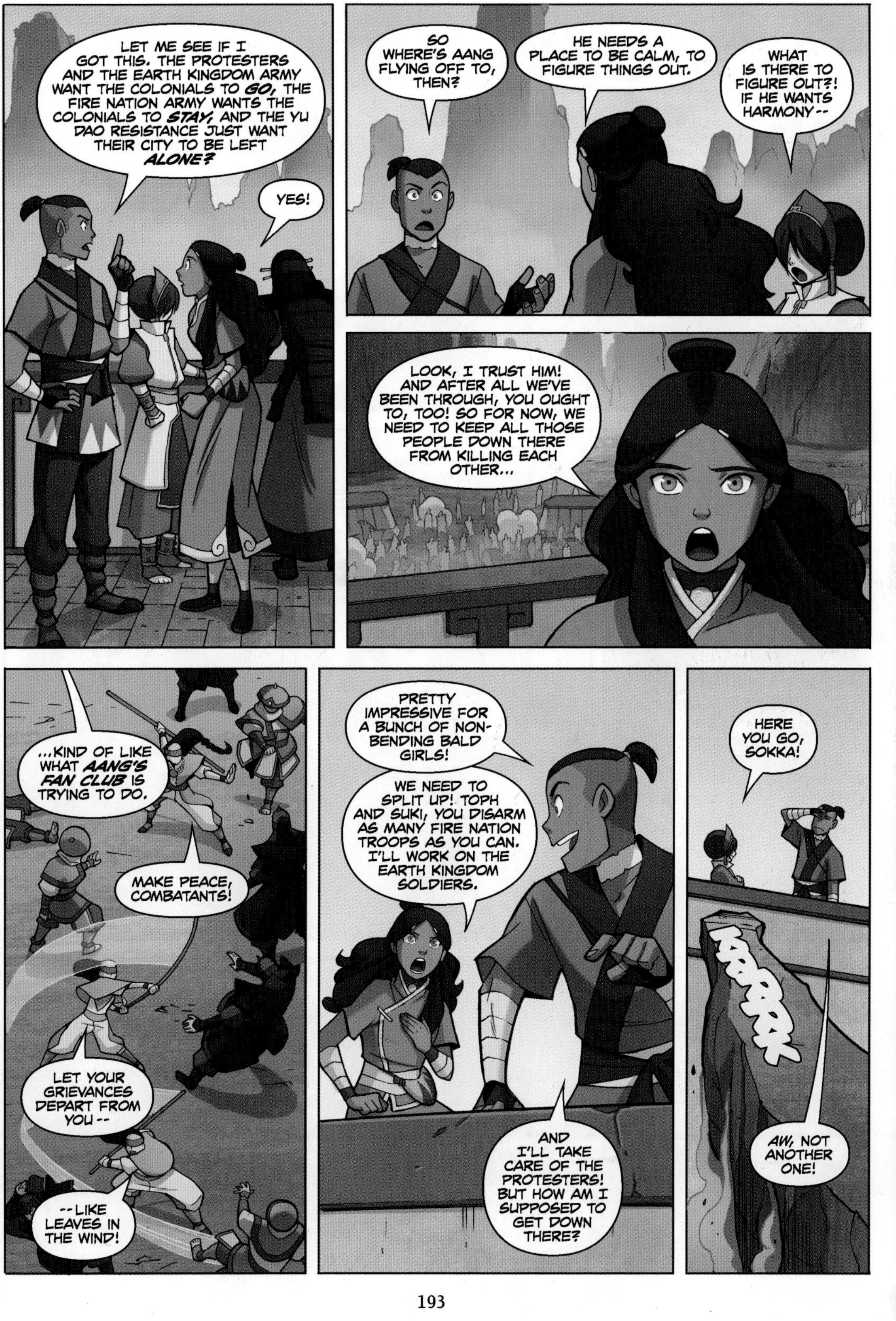
LET ME SEE IF I GOT THIS. THE PROTESTERS AND THE EARTH KINGDOM ARMY WANT THE COLONIALS TO *GO*, THE FIRE NATION ARMY WANTS THE COLONIALS TO *STAY*, AND THE YU DAO RESISTANCE JUST WANT THEIR CITY TO BE LEFT *ALONE*?
YES!
SO WHERE'S AANG FLYING OFF TO, THEN?
HE NEEDS A PLACE TO BE CALM, TO FIGURE THINGS OUT.
WHAT IS THERE TO FIGURE OUT?! IF HE WANTS HARMONY--
LOOK, I TRUST HIM! AND AFTER ALL WE'VE BEEN THROUGH, YOU OUGHT TO, TOO! SO FOR NOW, WE NEED TO KEEP ALL THOSE PEOPLE DOWN THERE FROM KILLING EACH OTHER...
...KIND OF LIKE WHAT *AANG'S FAN CLUB* IS TRYING TO DO.
MAKE PEACE, COMBATANTS!
LET YOUR GRIEVANCES DEPART FROM YOU--
--LIKE LEAVES IN THE WIND!
PRETTY IMPRESSIVE FOR A BUNCH OF NON-BENDING BALD GIRLS!
WE NEED TO SPLIT UP! TOPH AND SUKI, YOU DISARM AS MANY FIRE NATION TROOPS AS YOU CAN. I'LL WORK ON THE EARTH KINGDOM SOLDIERS.
AND I'LL TAKE CARE OF THE PROTESTERS! BUT HOW AM I SUPPOSED TO GET DOWN THERE?
HERE YOU GO, SOKKA!
KRRRAK
AW, NOT ANOTHER ONE!

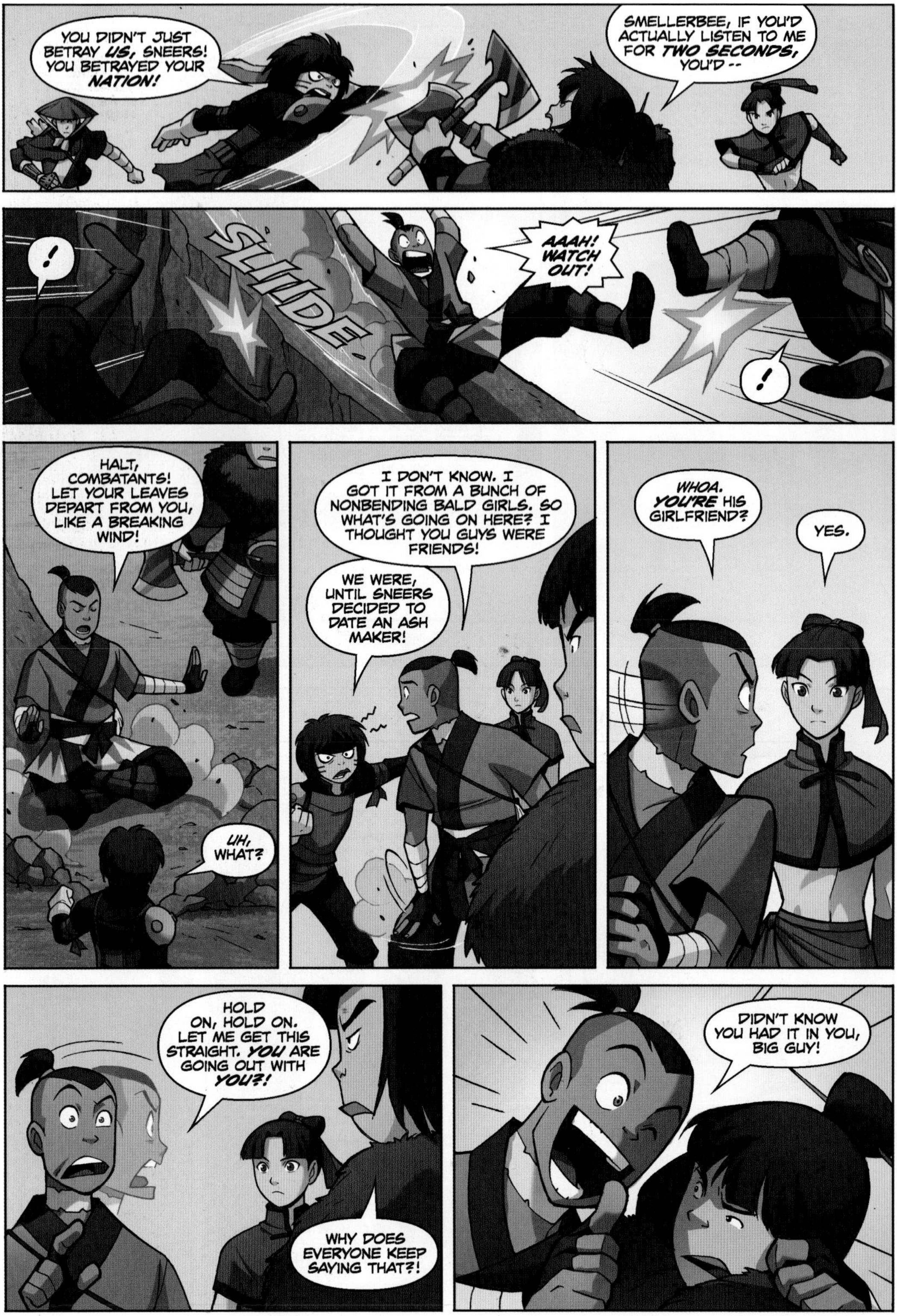
YOU DIDN'T JUST BETRAY US, SNEERS! YOU BETRAYED YOUR NATION!
SMELLERBEE, IF YOU'D ACTUALLY LISTEN TO ME FOR TWO SECONDS, YOU'D --
!
SLIIIDE
AAAH! WATCH OUT!
!
HALT, COMBATANTS! LET YOUR LEAVES DEPART FROM YOU, LIKE A BREAKING WIND!
UH, WHAT?
I DON'T KNOW. I GOT IT FROM A BUNCH OF NONBENDING BALD GIRLS. SO WHAT'S GOING ON HERE? I THOUGHT YOU GUYS WERE FRIENDS!
WE WERE, UNTIL SNEERS DECIDED TO DATE AN ASH MAKER!
WHOA. YOU'RE HIS GIRLFRIEND?
YES.
HOLD ON, HOLD ON. LET ME GET THIS STRAIGHT. YOU ARE GOING OUT WITH YOU?!
WHY DOES EVERYONE KEEP SAYING THAT?!
DIDN'T KNOW YOU HAD IT IN YOU, BIG GUY!

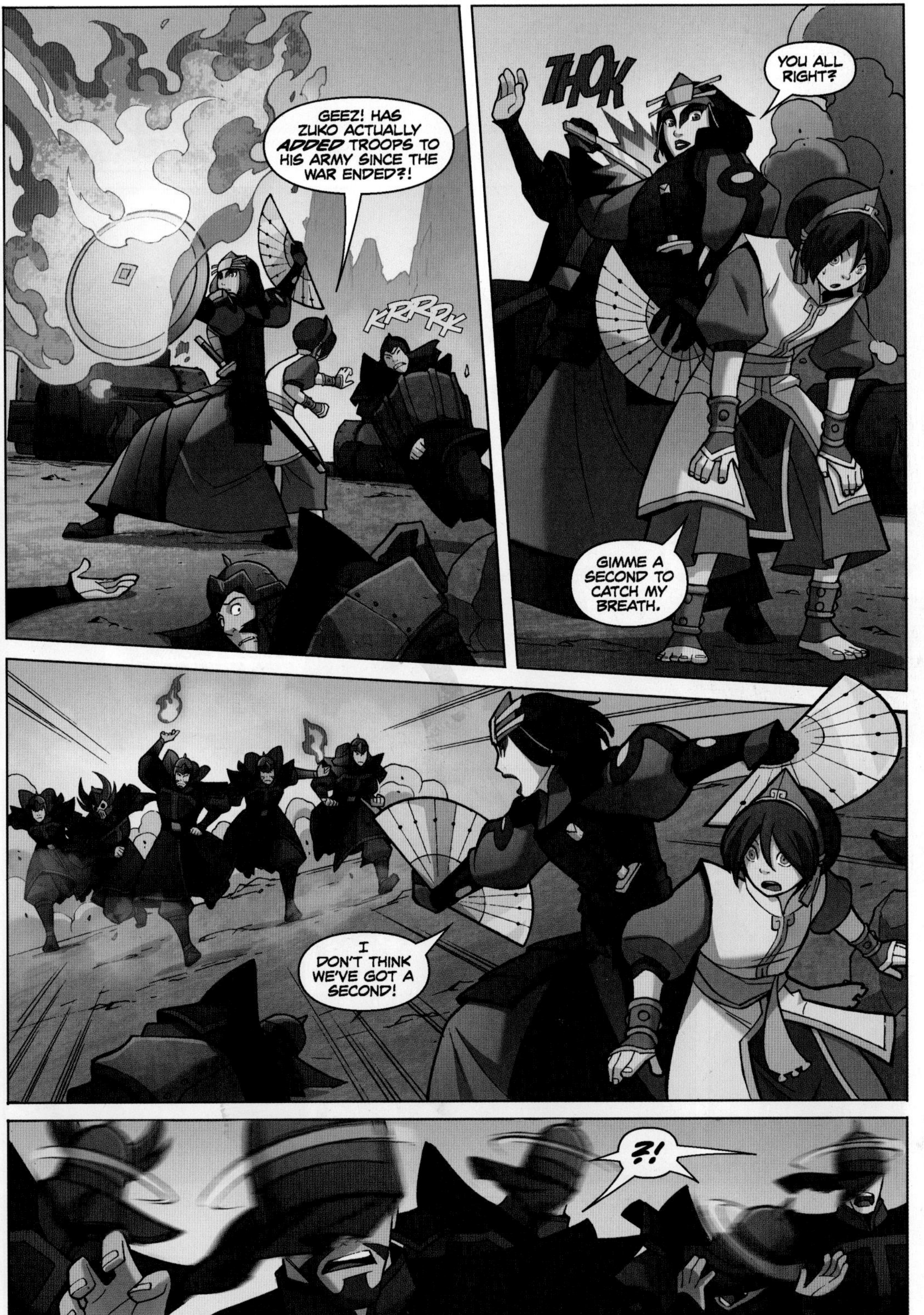
GEEZ! HAS ZUKO ACTUALLY ADDED TROOPS TO HIS ARMY SINCE THE WAR ENDED?!
KRRRK
THOK
YOU ALL RIGHT?
GIMME A SECOND TO CATCH MY BREATH.
I DON'T THINK WE'VE GOT A SECOND!
?!

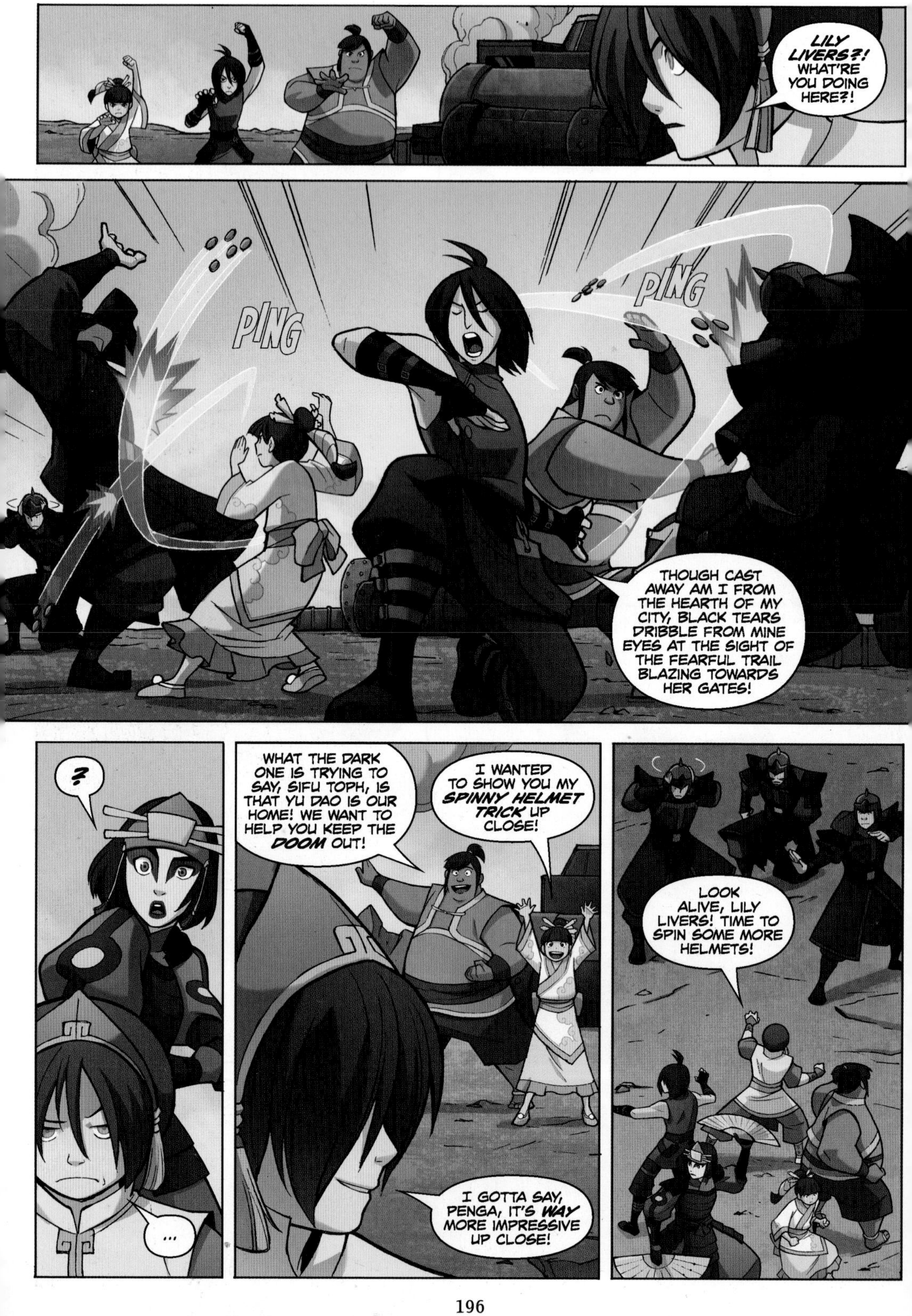

LILY LIVERS?! WHAT'RE YOU DOING HERE?!
PING
PING
THOUGH CAST AWAY AM I FROM THE HEARTH OF MY CITY, BLACK TEARS DRIBBLE FROM MINE EYES AT THE SIGHT OF THE FEARFUL TRAIL BLAZING TOWARDS HER GATES!
?
...
WHAT THE DARK ONE IS TRYING TO SAY, SIFU TOPH, IS THAT YU DAO IS OUR HOME! WE WANT TO HELP YOU KEEP THE DOOM OUT!
I WANTED TO SHOW YOU MY SPINNY HELMET TRICK UP CLOSE!
I GOTTA SAY, PENGA, IT'S WAY MORE IMPRESSIVE UP CLOSE!
LOOK ALIVE, LILY LIVERS! TIME TO SPIN SOME MORE HELMETS!

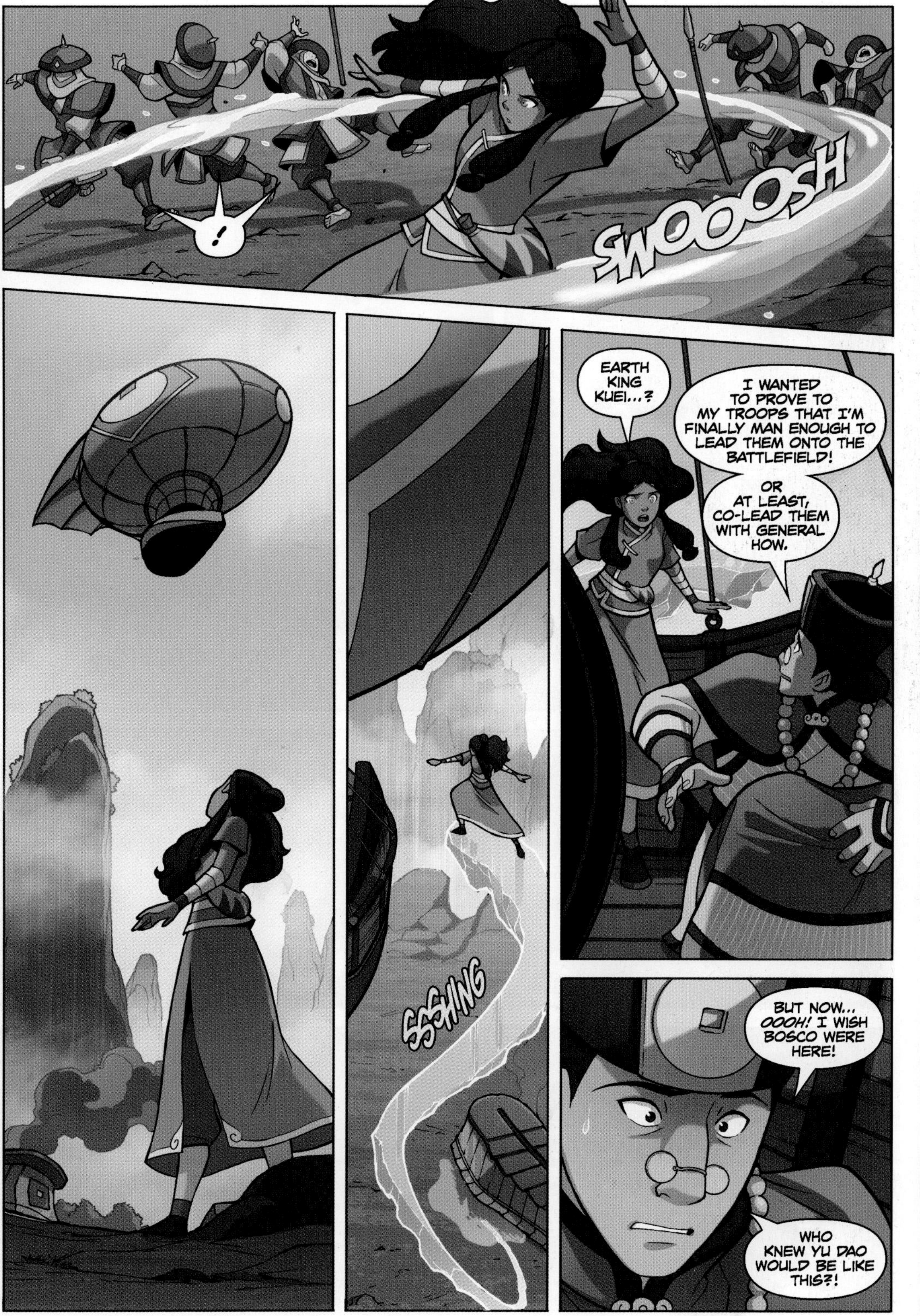
!
SWOOOSH
SSSHING
EARTH KING KUEI...?
I WANTED TO PROVE TO MY TROOPS THAT I'M FINALLY MAN ENOUGH TO LEAD THEM ONTO THE BATTLEFIELD!
OR AT LEAST, CO-LEAD THEM WITH GENERAL HOW.
BUT NOW... *OOOH!* I WISH BOSCO WERE HERE!
WHO KNEW YU DAO WOULD BE LIKE THIS?!

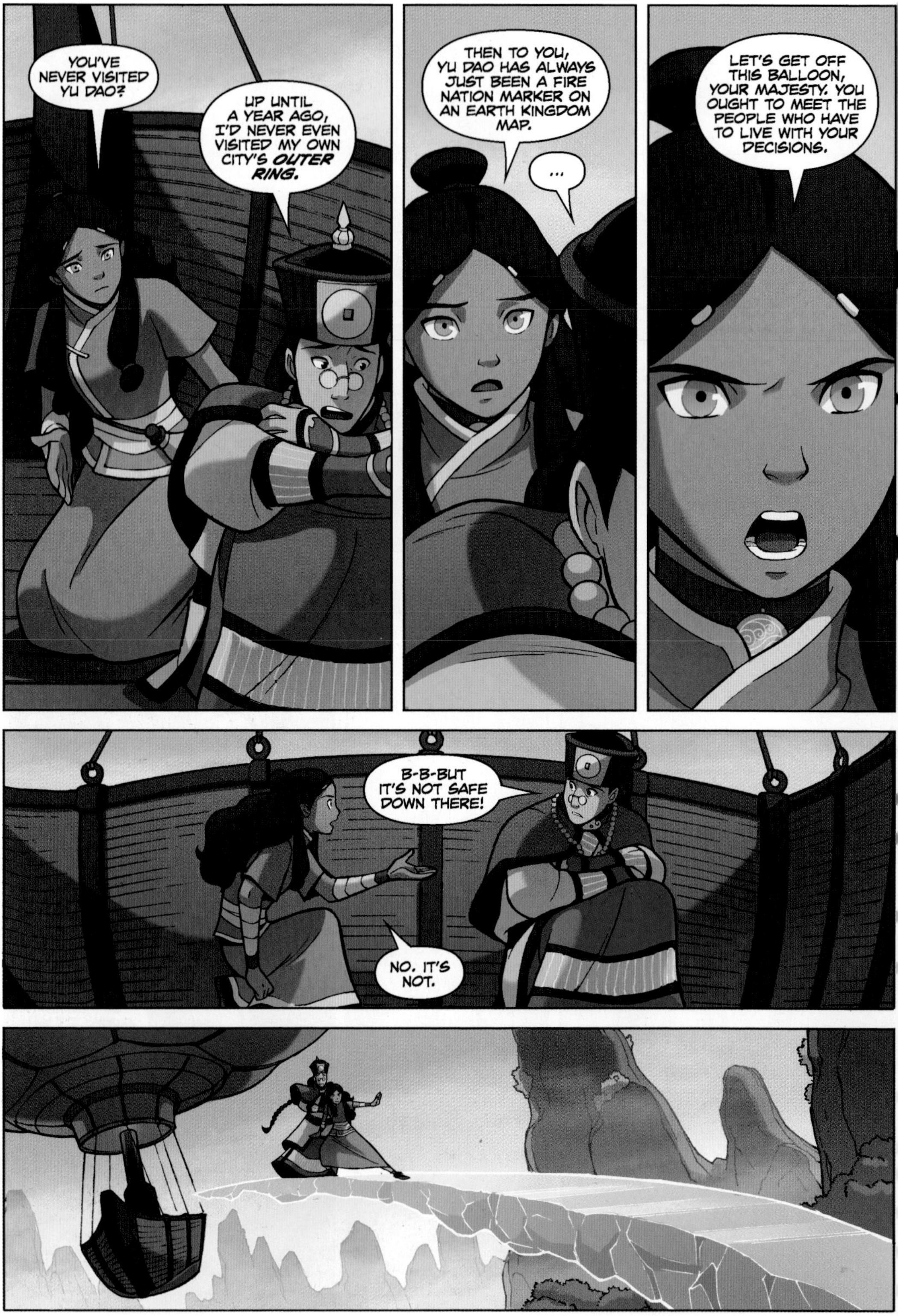
YOU'VE NEVER VISITED YU DAO?
UP UNTIL A YEAR AGO, I'D NEVER EVEN VISITED MY OWN CITY'S OUTER RING.
THEN TO YOU, YU DAO HAS ALWAYS JUST BEEN A FIRE NATION MARKER ON AN EARTH KINGDOM MAP.
...
LET'S GET OFF THIS BALLOON, YOUR MAJESTY. YOU OUGHT TO MEET THE PEOPLE WHO HAVE TO LIVE WITH YOUR DECISIONS.
B-B-BUT IT'S NOT SAFE DOWN THERE!
NO. IT'S NOT.

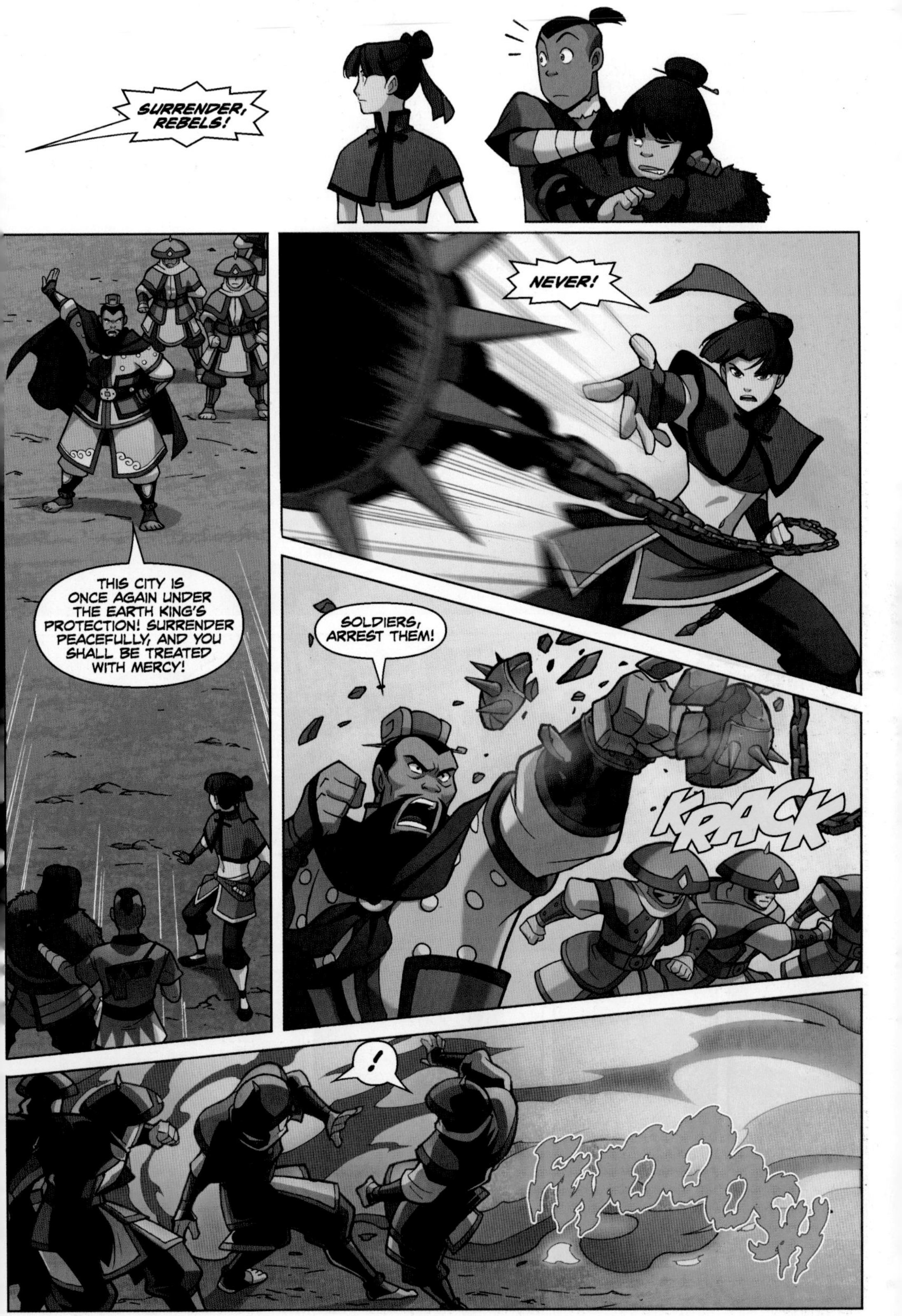
SURRENDER, REBELS!
NEVER!
THIS CITY IS ONCE AGAIN UNDER THE EARTH KING'S PROTECTION! SURRENDER PEACEFULLY, AND YOU SHALL BE TREATED WITH MERCY!
SOLDIERS, ARREST THEM!
KRACK
!
FWOOOSH

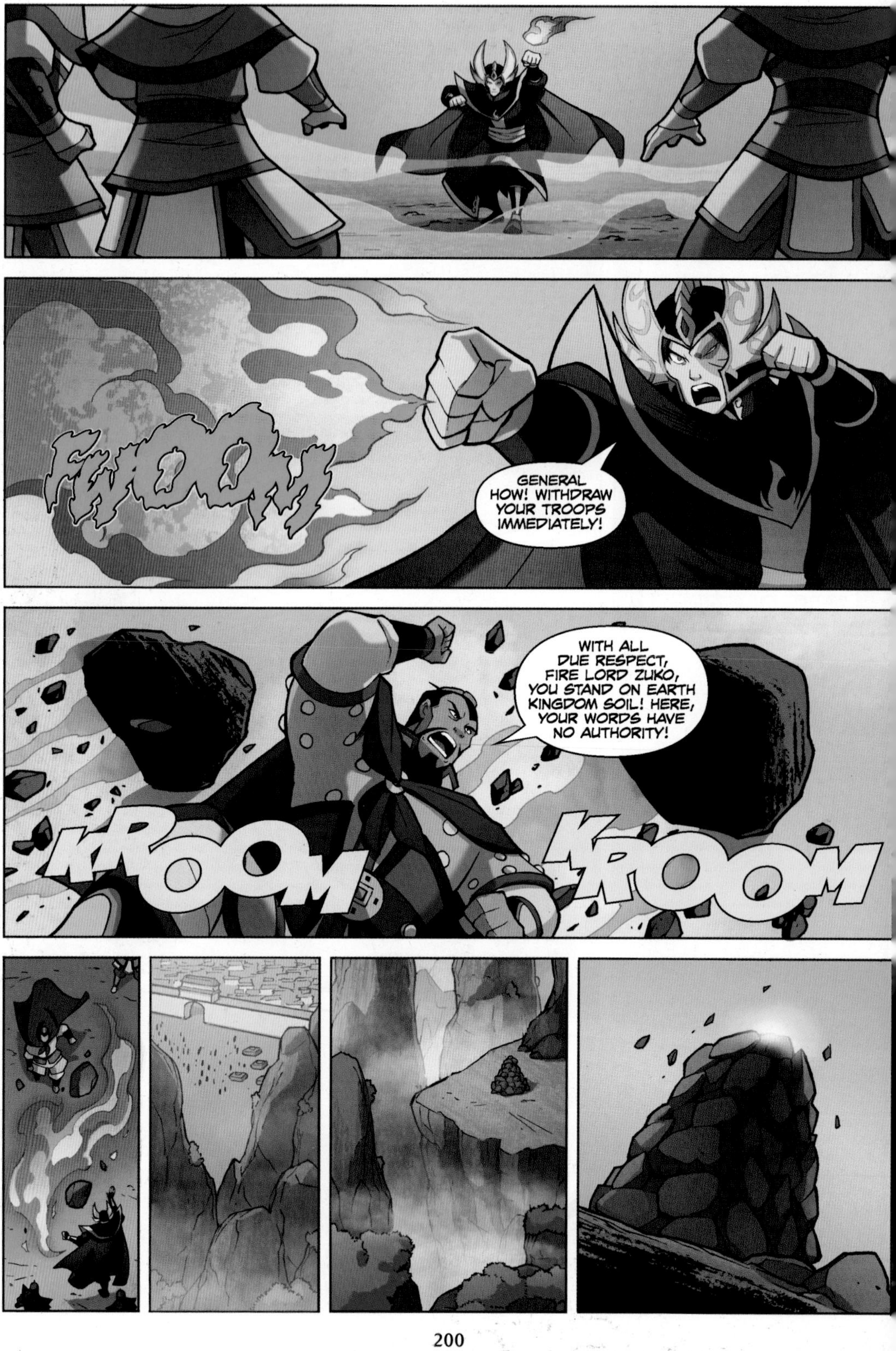
FWOOM
GENERAL HOW! WITHDRAW YOUR TROOPS IMMEDIATELY!
WITH ALL DUE RESPECT, FIRE LORD ZUKO, YOU STAND ON EARTH KINGDOM SOIL! HERE, YOUR WORDS HAVE NO AUTHORITY!
KROOM
KROOM

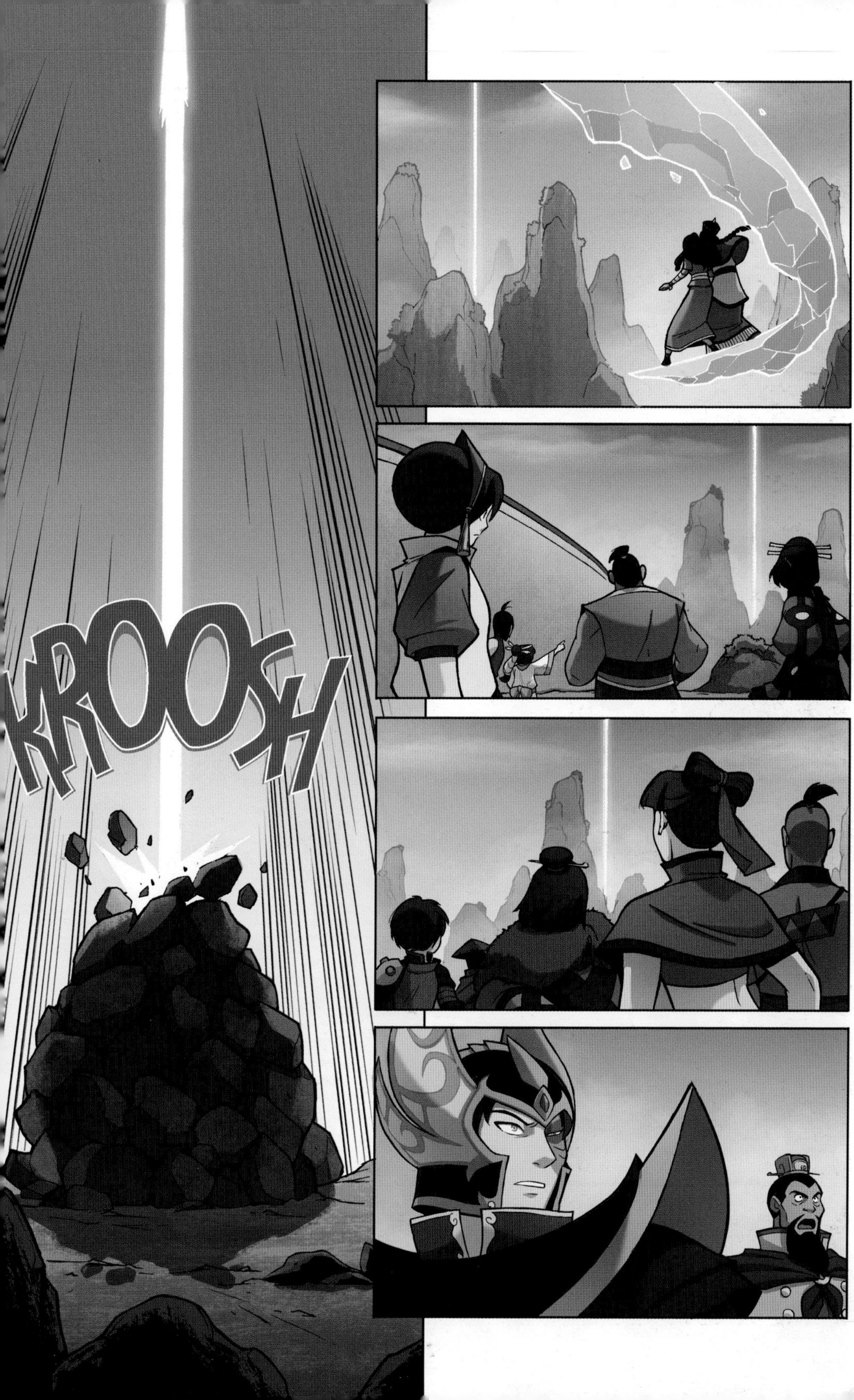
KROOSH

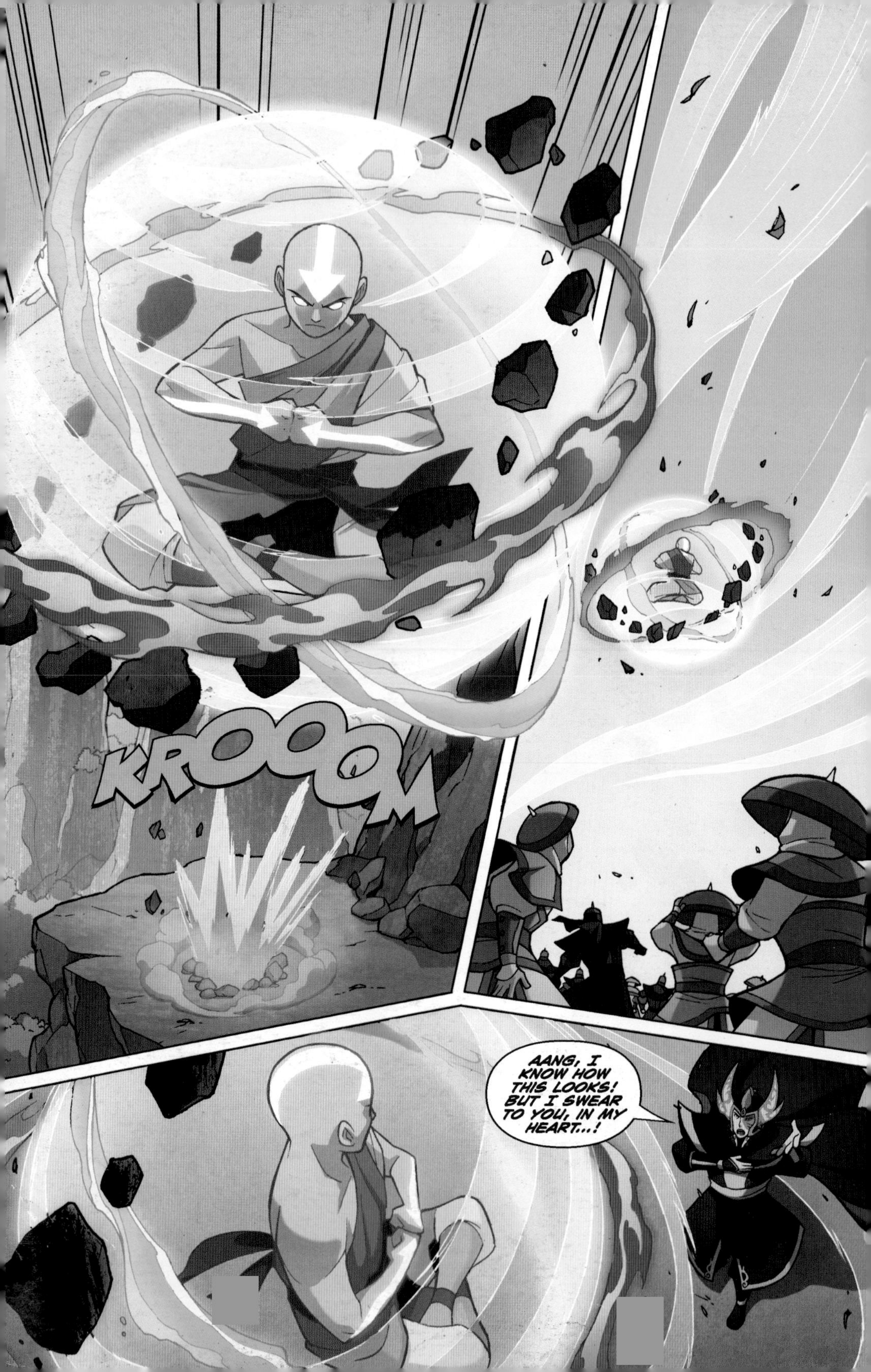
KROOOM
AANG, I KNOW HOW THIS LOOKS! BUT I SWEAR TO YOU, IN MY HEART...!

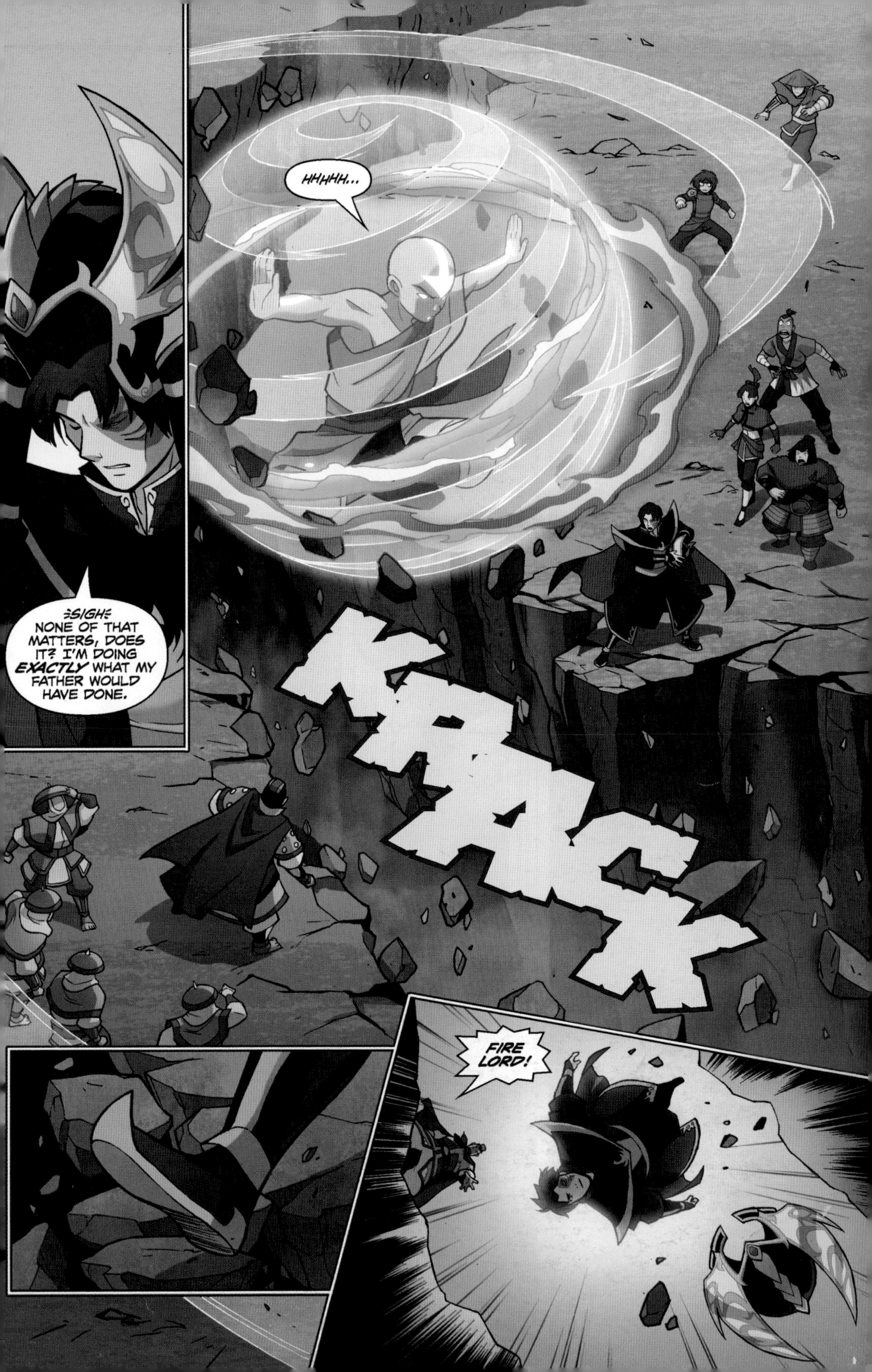

HHHHH...
:SIGH: NONE OF THAT MATTERS, DOES IT? I'M DOING *EXACTLY* WHAT MY FATHER WOULD HAVE DONE.
KRACK
FIRE LORD!

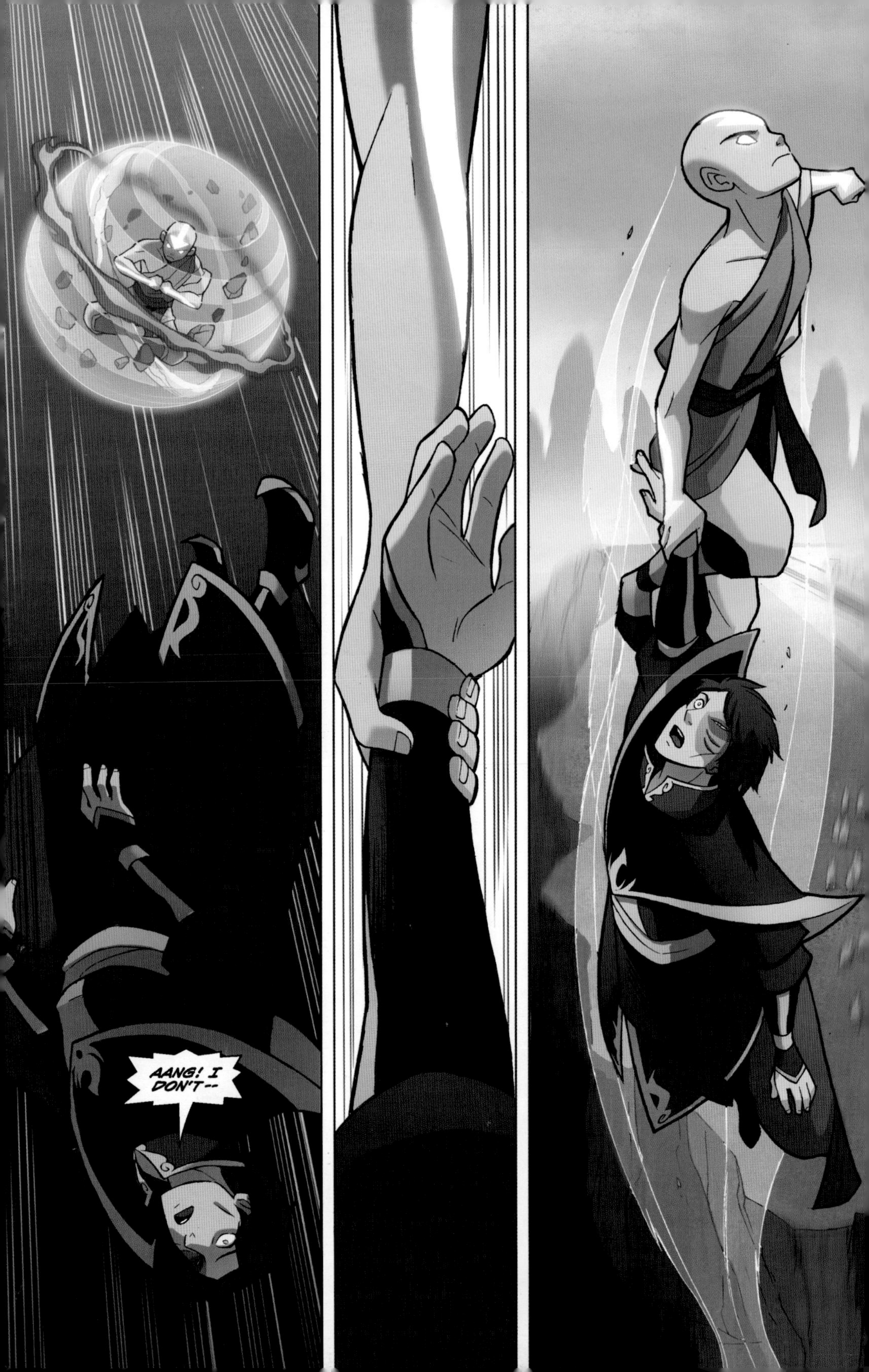
AANG! I DON'T--

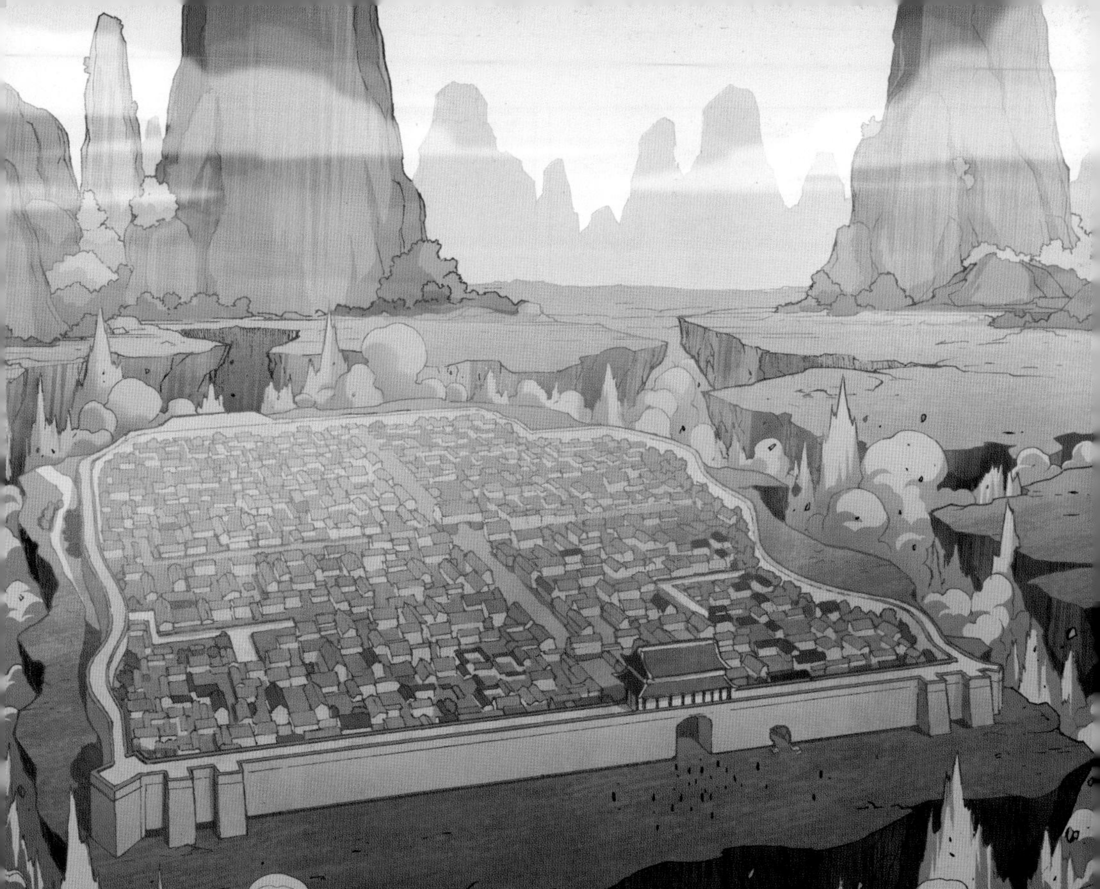

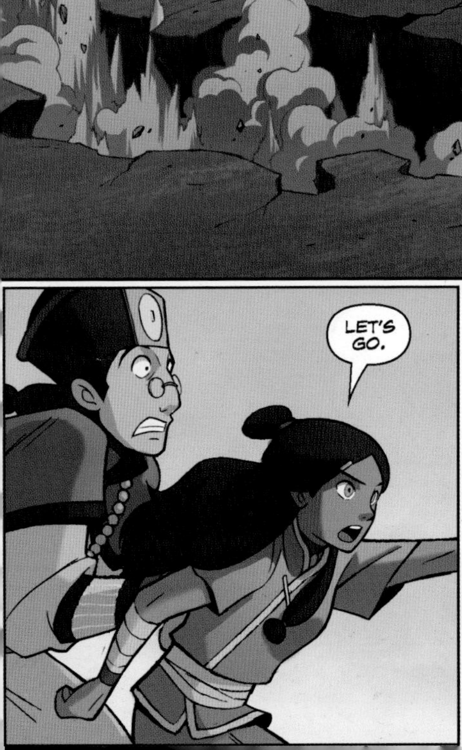
LET'S GO.

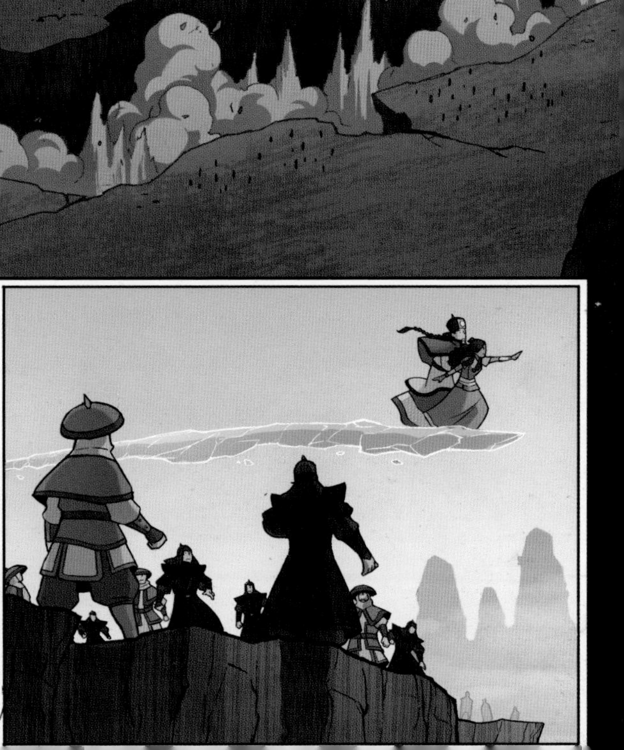

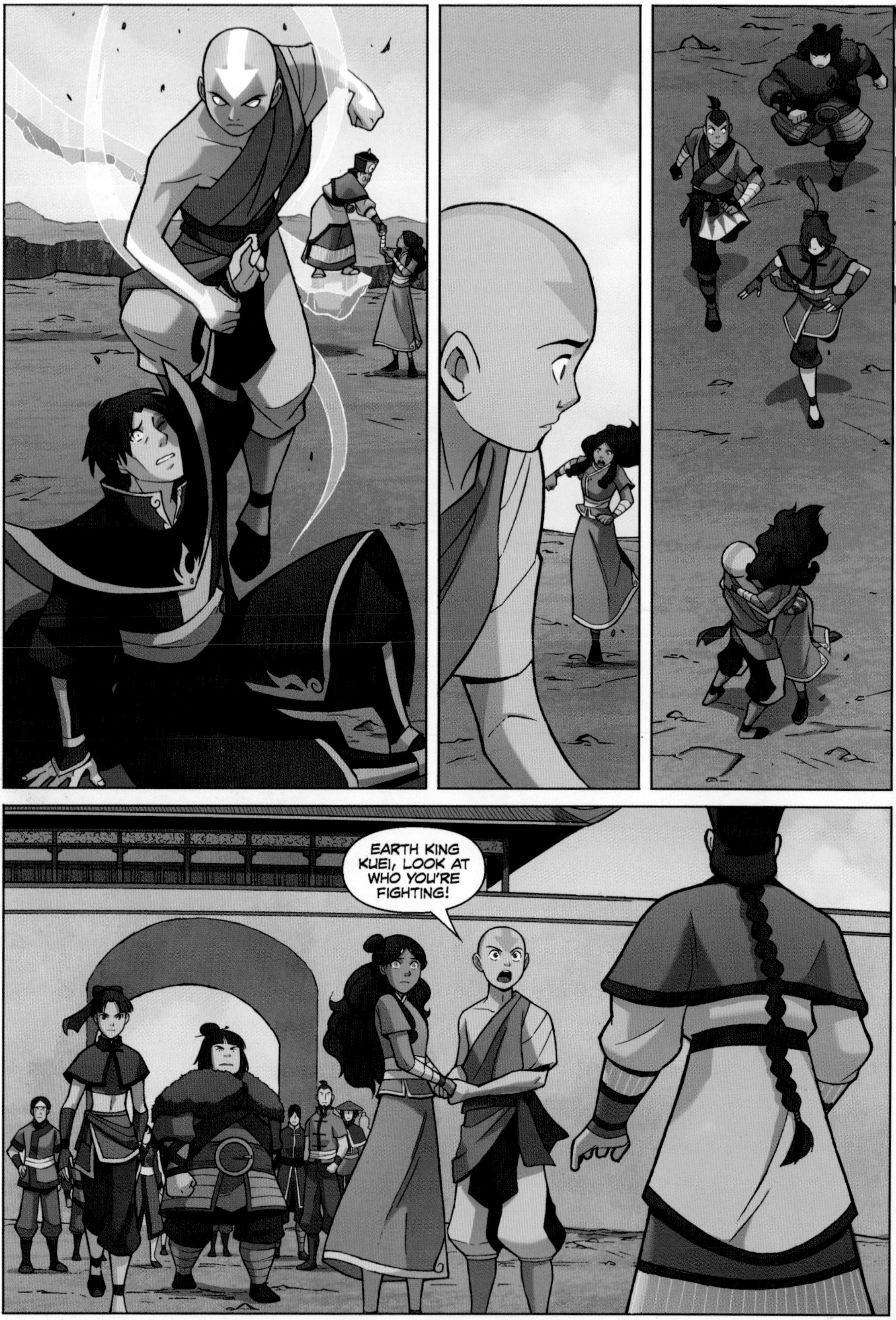
EARTH KING KUEI, LOOK AT WHO YOU'RE FIGHTING!

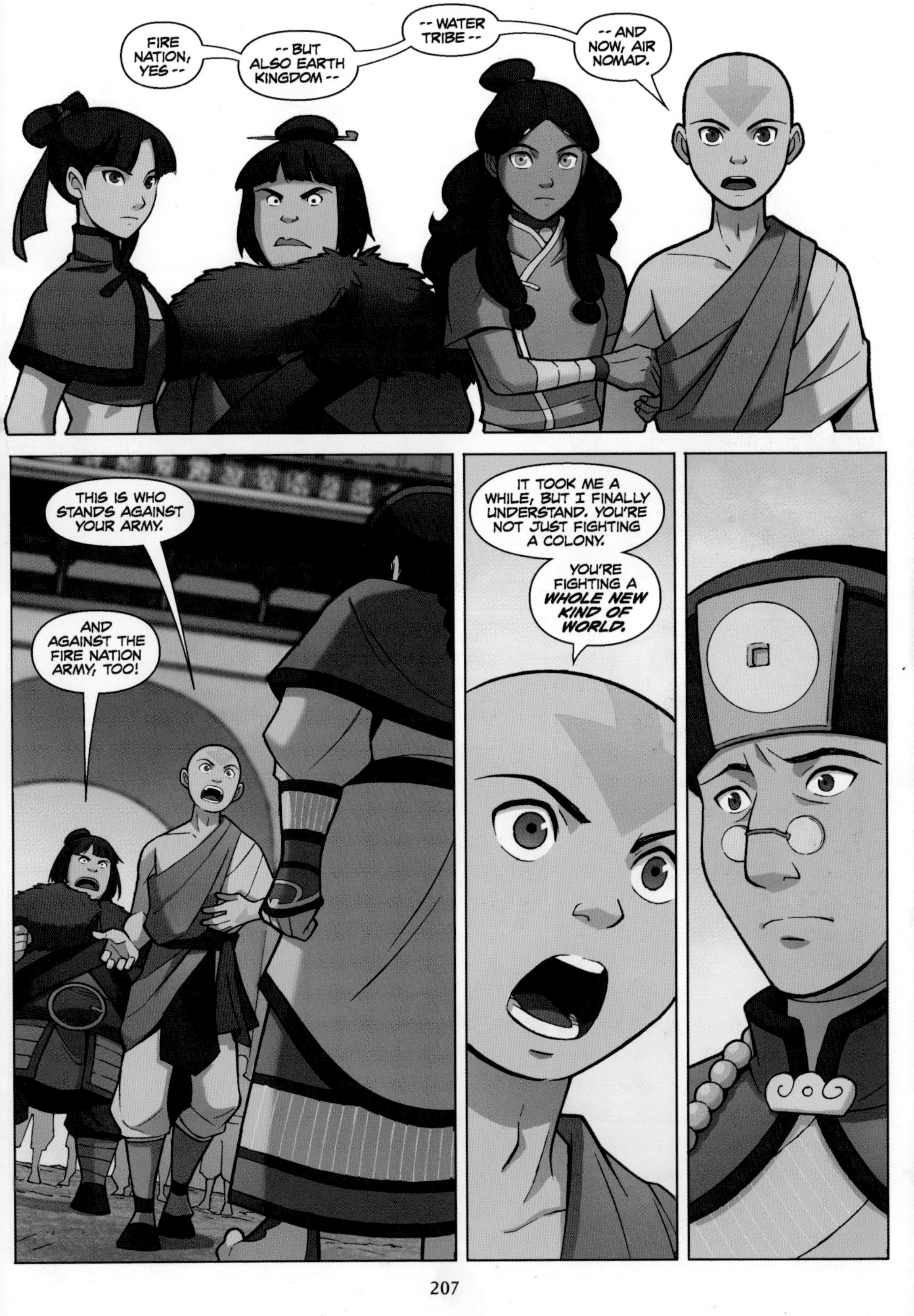
FIRE NATION, YES --
-- BUT ALSO EARTH KINGDOM --
-- WATER TRIBE --
-- AND NOW, AIR NOMAD.
THIS IS WHO STANDS AGAINST YOUR ARMY.
AND AGAINST THE FIRE NATION ARMY, TOO!
IT TOOK ME A WHILE, BUT I FINALLY UNDERSTAND. YOU'RE NOT JUST FIGHTING A COLONY.
YOU'RE FIGHTING A WHOLE NEW KIND OF WORLD.

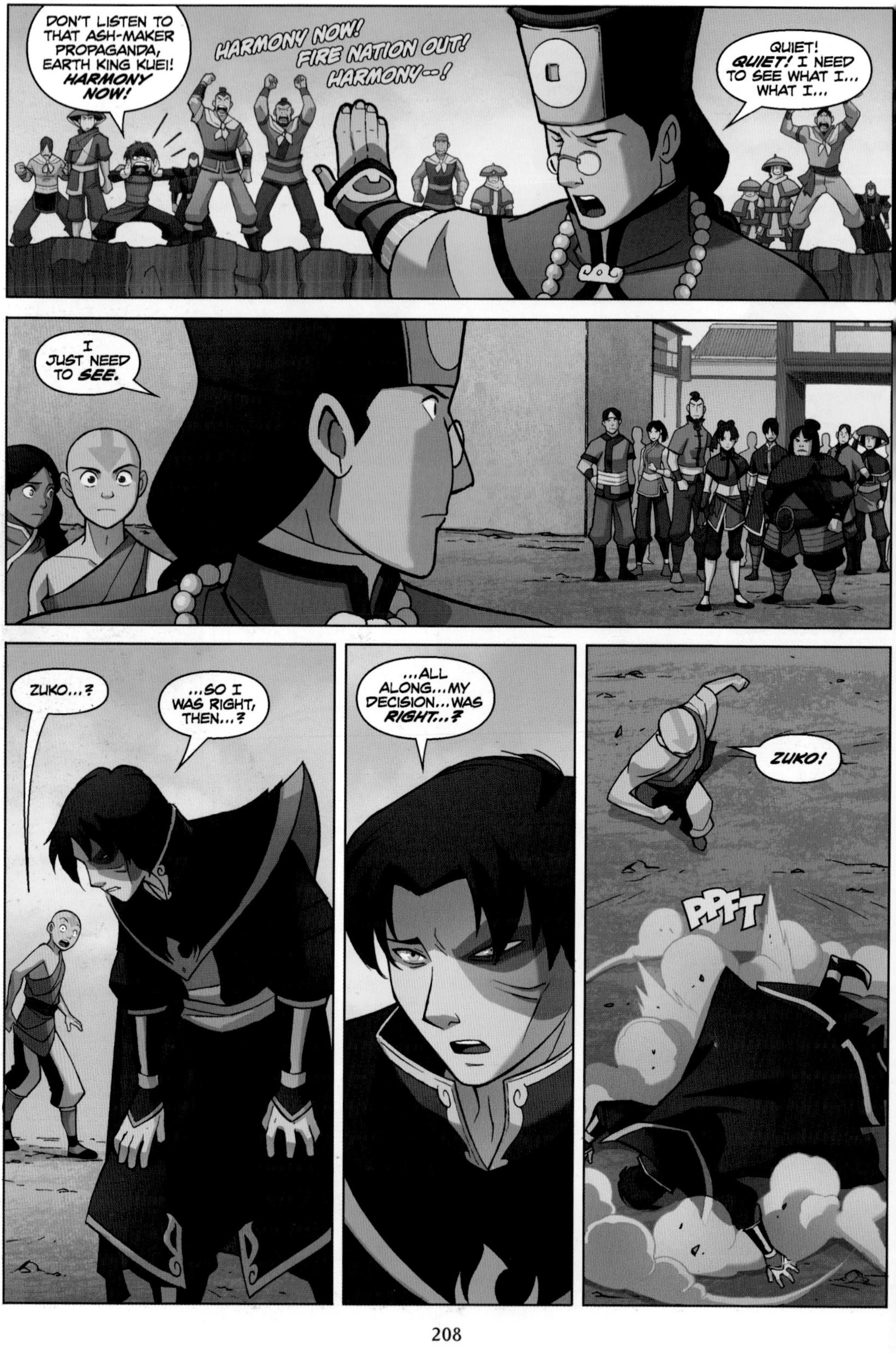
DON'T LISTEN TO THAT ASH-MAKER PROPAGANDA, EARTH KING KUEI! HARMONY NOW!
HARMONY NOW! FIRE NATION OUT! HARMONY--!
QUIET! QUIET! I NEED TO SEE WHAT I... WHAT I...
I JUST NEED TO SEE.
ZUKO...?
...SO I WAS RIGHT, THEN...?
...ALL ALONG...MY DECISION...WAS RIGHT...?
ZUKO!
PPFT

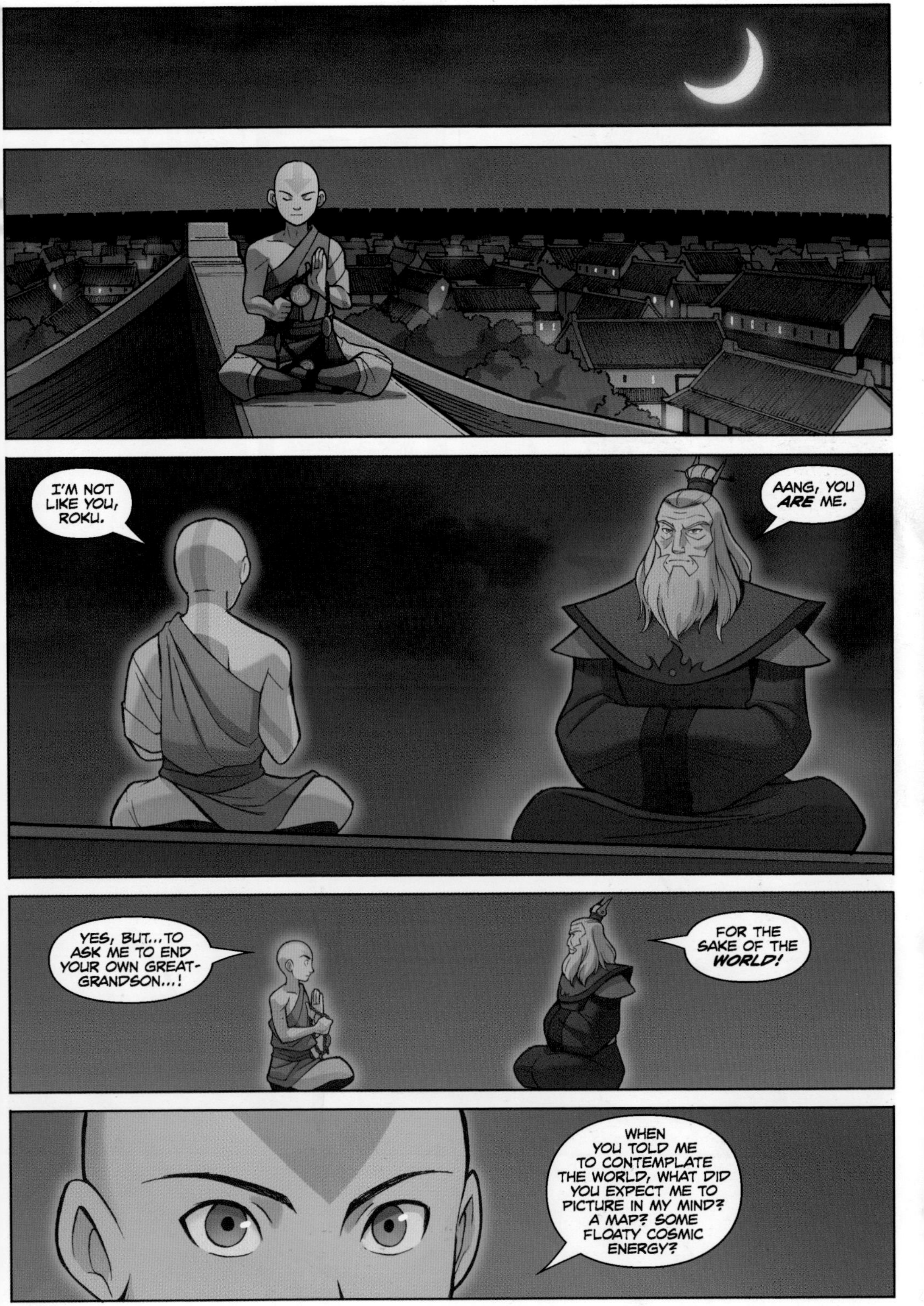

I'M NOT LIKE YOU, ROKU.
AANG, YOU *ARE* ME.
YES, BUT...TO ASK ME TO END YOUR OWN GREAT-GRANDSON...!
FOR THE SAKE OF THE *WORLD!*
WHEN YOU TOLD ME TO CONTEMPLATE THE WORLD, WHAT DID YOU EXPECT ME TO PICTURE IN MY MIND? A MAP? SOME FLOATY COSMIC ENERGY?

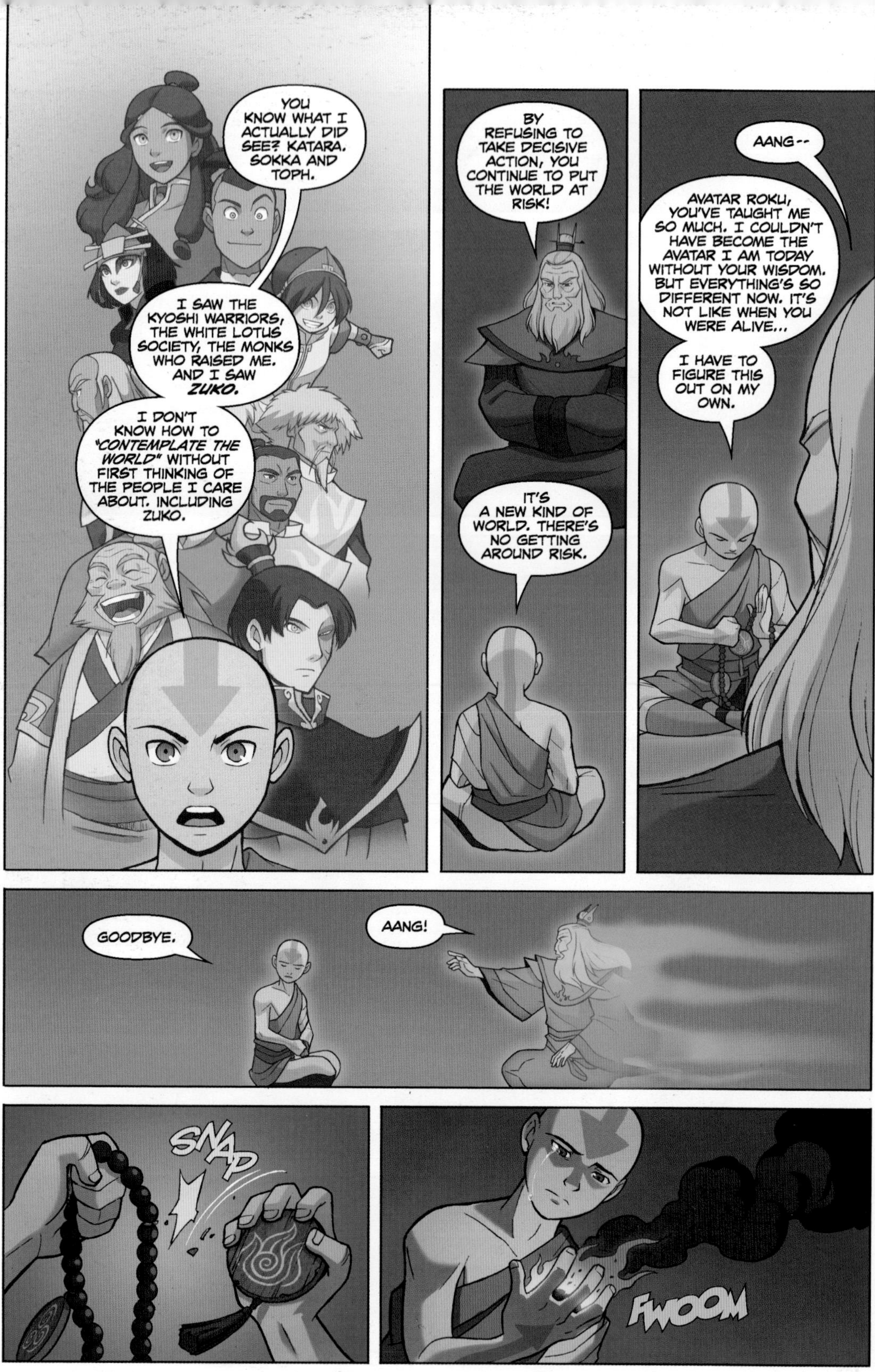
YOU KNOW WHAT I ACTUALLY DID SEE? KATARA. SOKKA AND TOPH.
I SAW THE KYOSHI WARRIORS, THE WHITE LOTUS SOCIETY, THE MONKS WHO RAISED ME. AND I SAW ZUKO.
I DON'T KNOW HOW TO "CONTEMPLATE THE WORLD" WITHOUT FIRST THINKING OF THE PEOPLE I CARE ABOUT. INCLUDING ZUKO.
BY REFUSING TO TAKE DECISIVE ACTION, YOU CONTINUE TO PUT THE WORLD AT RISK!
IT'S A NEW KIND OF WORLD. THERE'S NO GETTING AROUND RISK.
AANG--
AVATAR ROKU, YOU'VE TAUGHT ME SO MUCH. I COULDN'T HAVE BECOME THE AVATAR I AM TODAY WITHOUT YOUR WISDOM. BUT EVERYTHING'S SO DIFFERENT NOW. IT'S NOT LIKE WHEN YOU WERE ALIVE...
I HAVE TO FIGURE THIS OUT ON MY OWN.
GOODBYE.
AANG!
SNAP
FWOOM

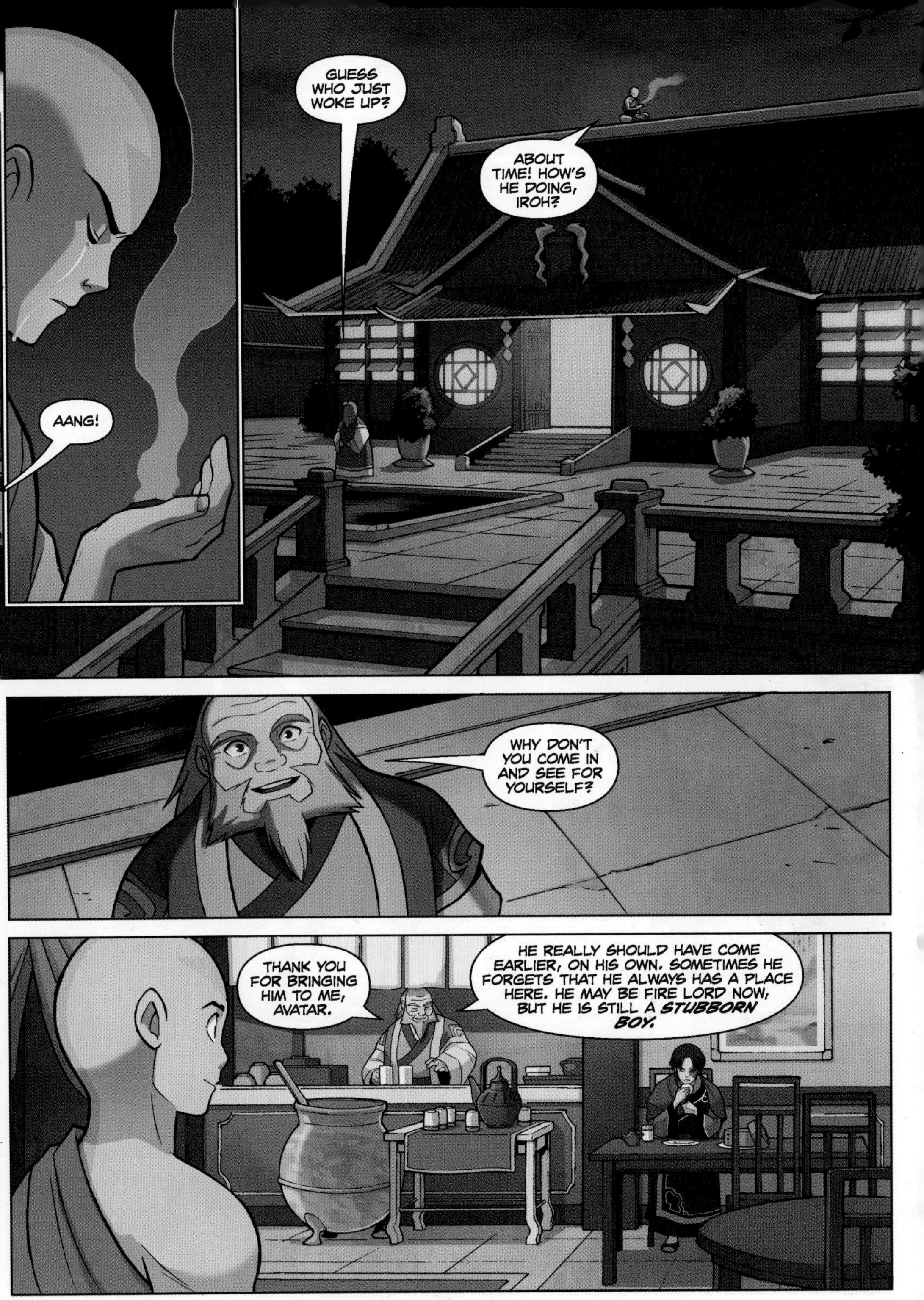
GUESS WHO JUST WOKE UP?
AANG!
ABOUT TIME! HOW'S HE DOING, IROH?
WHY DON'T YOU COME IN AND SEE FOR YOURSELF?
THANK YOU FOR BRINGING HIM TO ME, AVATAR.
HE REALLY SHOULD HAVE COME EARLIER, ON HIS OWN. SOMETIMES HE FORGETS THAT HE ALWAYS HAS A PLACE HERE. HE MAY BE FIRE LORD NOW, BUT HE IS STILL A *STUBBORN BOY.*

I FEEL LIKE I'VE BEEN ASLEEP FOR A WEEK.

NO. JUST FOUR DAYS.

HM.

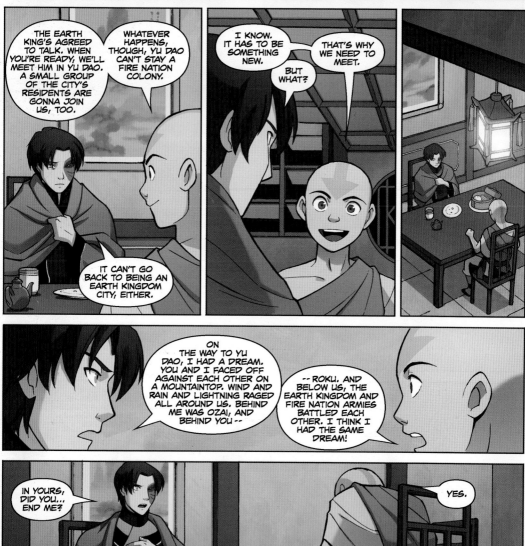

THE EARTH KING'S AGREED TO TALK. WHEN YOU'RE READY, WE'LL MEET HIM IN YU DAO. A SMALL GROUP OF THE CITY'S RESIDENTS ARE GONNA JOIN US, TOO.

WHATEVER HAPPENS, THOUGH, YU DAO CAN'T STAY A FIRE NATION COLONY.

IT CAN'T GO BACK TO BEING AN EARTH KINGDOM CITY, EITHER.

I KNOW. IT HAS TO BE SOMETHING NEW.

BUT WHAT?

THAT'S WHY WE NEED TO MEET.

ON THE WAY TO YU DAO, I HAD A DREAM. YOU AND I FACED OFF AGAINST EACH OTHER ON A MOUNTAINTOP. WIND AND RAIN AND LIGHTNING RAGED ALL AROUND US. BEHIND ME WAS OZAI, AND BEHIND YOU --

-- ROKU. AND BELOW US, THE EARTH KINGDOM AND FIRE NATION ARMIES BATTLED EACH OTHER. I THINK I HAD THE SAME DREAM!

IN YOURS, DID YOU... END ME?

YES.

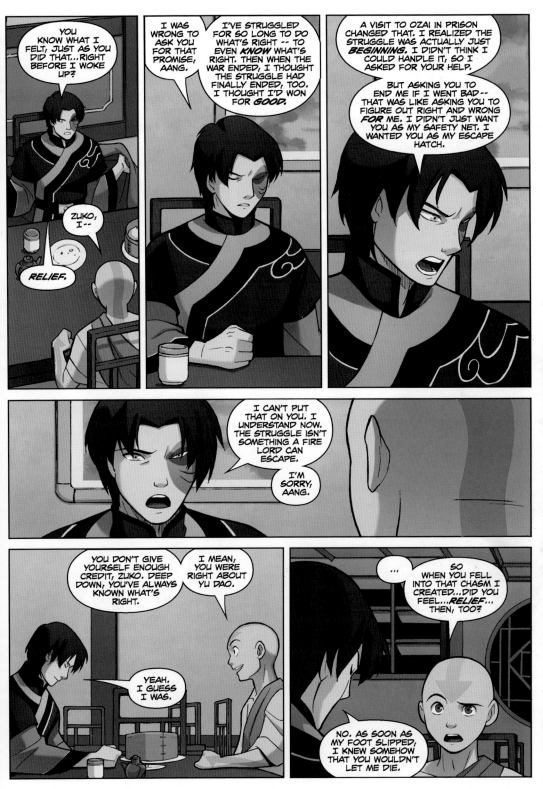

YOU KNOW WHAT I FELT, JUST AS YOU DID THAT...RIGHT BEFORE I WOKE UP?

ZUKO, I--

RELIEF.

I WAS WRONG TO ASK YOU FOR THAT PROMISE, AANG.

I'VE STRUGGLED FOR SO LONG TO DO WHAT'S RIGHT -- TO EVEN *KNOW* WHAT'S RIGHT. THEN WHEN THE WAR ENDED, I THOUGHT THE STRUGGLE HAD FINALLY ENDED, TOO. I THOUGHT I'D WON FOR *GOOD.*

A VISIT TO OZAI IN PRISON CHANGED THAT. I REALIZED THE STRUGGLE WAS ACTUALLY JUST *BEGINNING.* I DIDN'T THINK I COULD HANDLE IT, SO I ASKED FOR YOUR HELP.

BUT ASKING YOU TO END ME IF I WENT BAD -- THAT WAS LIKE ASKING YOU TO FIGURE OUT RIGHT AND WRONG *FOR* ME. I DIDN'T JUST WANT YOU AS MY SAFETY NET. I WANTED YOU AS MY ESCAPE HATCH.

I CAN'T PUT THAT ON YOU. I UNDERSTAND NOW. THE STRUGGLE ISN'T SOMETHING A FIRE LORD CAN ESCAPE.

I'M SORRY, AANG.

YOU DON'T GIVE YOURSELF ENOUGH CREDIT, ZUKO. DEEP DOWN, YOU'VE ALWAYS KNOWN WHAT'S RIGHT.

I MEAN, YOU WERE RIGHT ABOUT YU DAO.

YEAH. I GUESS I WAS.

...

SO WHEN YOU FELL INTO THAT CHASM I CREATED...DID YOU FEEL...*RELIEF*... THEN, TOO?

NO. AS SOON AS MY FOOT SLIPPED, I KNEW SOMEHOW THAT YOU WOULDN'T LET ME DIE.

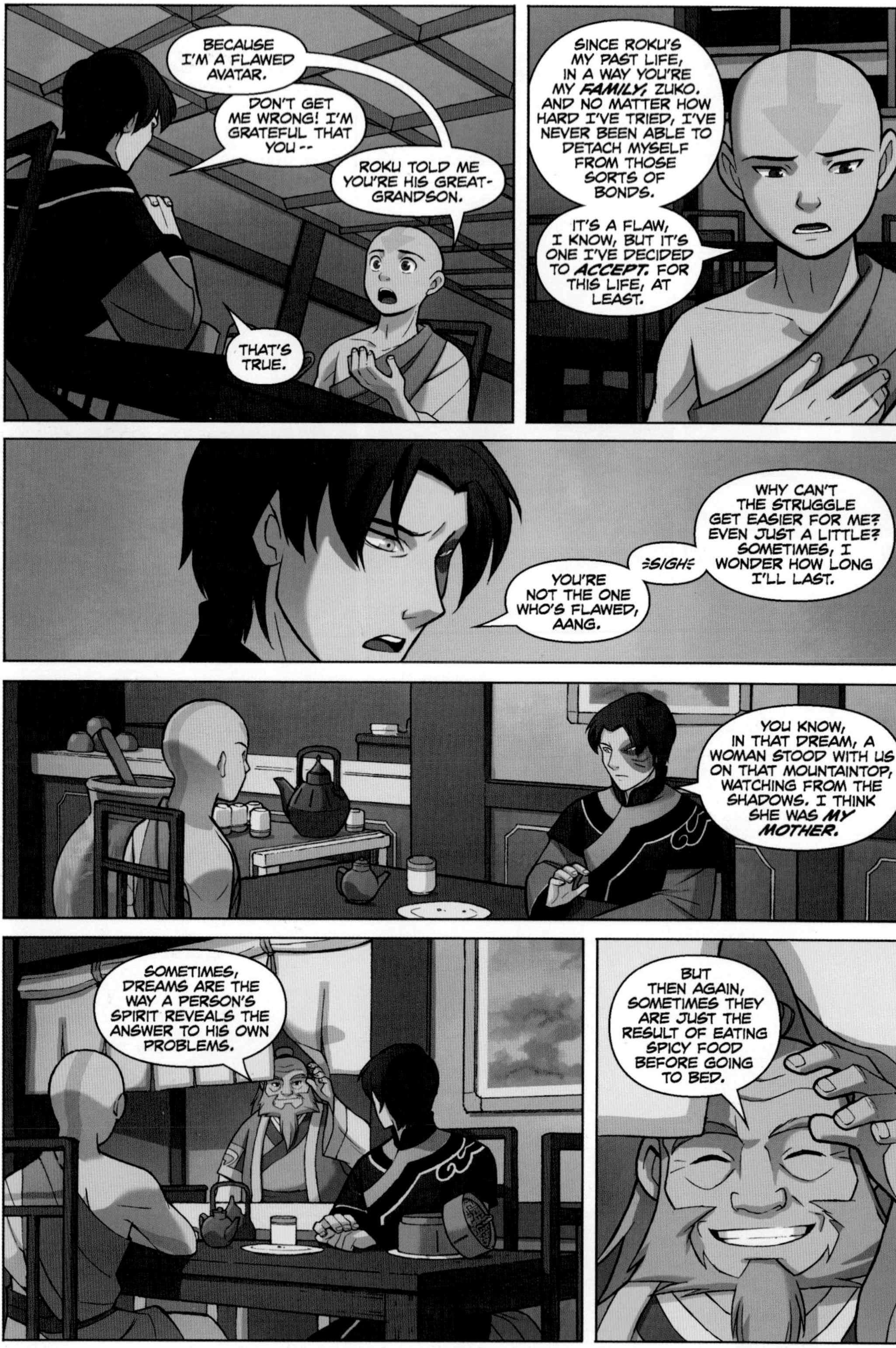
BECAUSE I'M A FLAWED AVATAR.
DON'T GET ME WRONG! I'M GRATEFUL THAT YOU --
ROKU TOLD ME YOU'RE HIS GREAT-GRANDSON.
THAT'S TRUE.
SINCE ROKU'S MY PAST LIFE, IN A WAY YOU'RE MY *FAMILY,* ZUKO. AND NO MATTER HOW HARD I'VE TRIED, I'VE NEVER BEEN ABLE TO DETACH MYSELF FROM THOSE SORTS OF BONDS.
IT'S A FLAW, I KNOW, BUT IT'S ONE I'VE DECIDED TO *ACCEPT.* FOR THIS LIFE, AT LEAST.
WHY CAN'T THE STRUGGLE GET EASIER FOR ME? EVEN JUST A LITTLE? SOMETIMES, I WONDER HOW LONG I'LL LAST.
SIGH
YOU'RE NOT THE ONE WHO'S FLAWED, AANG.
YOU KNOW, IN THAT DREAM, A WOMAN STOOD WITH US ON THAT MOUNTAINTOP, WATCHING FROM THE SHADOWS. I THINK SHE WAS *MY MOTHER.*
SOMETIMES, DREAMS ARE THE WAY A PERSON'S SPIRIT REVEALS THE ANSWER TO HIS OWN PROBLEMS.
BUT THEN AGAIN, SOMETIMES THEY ARE JUST THE RESULT OF EATING SPICY FOOD BEFORE GOING TO BED.

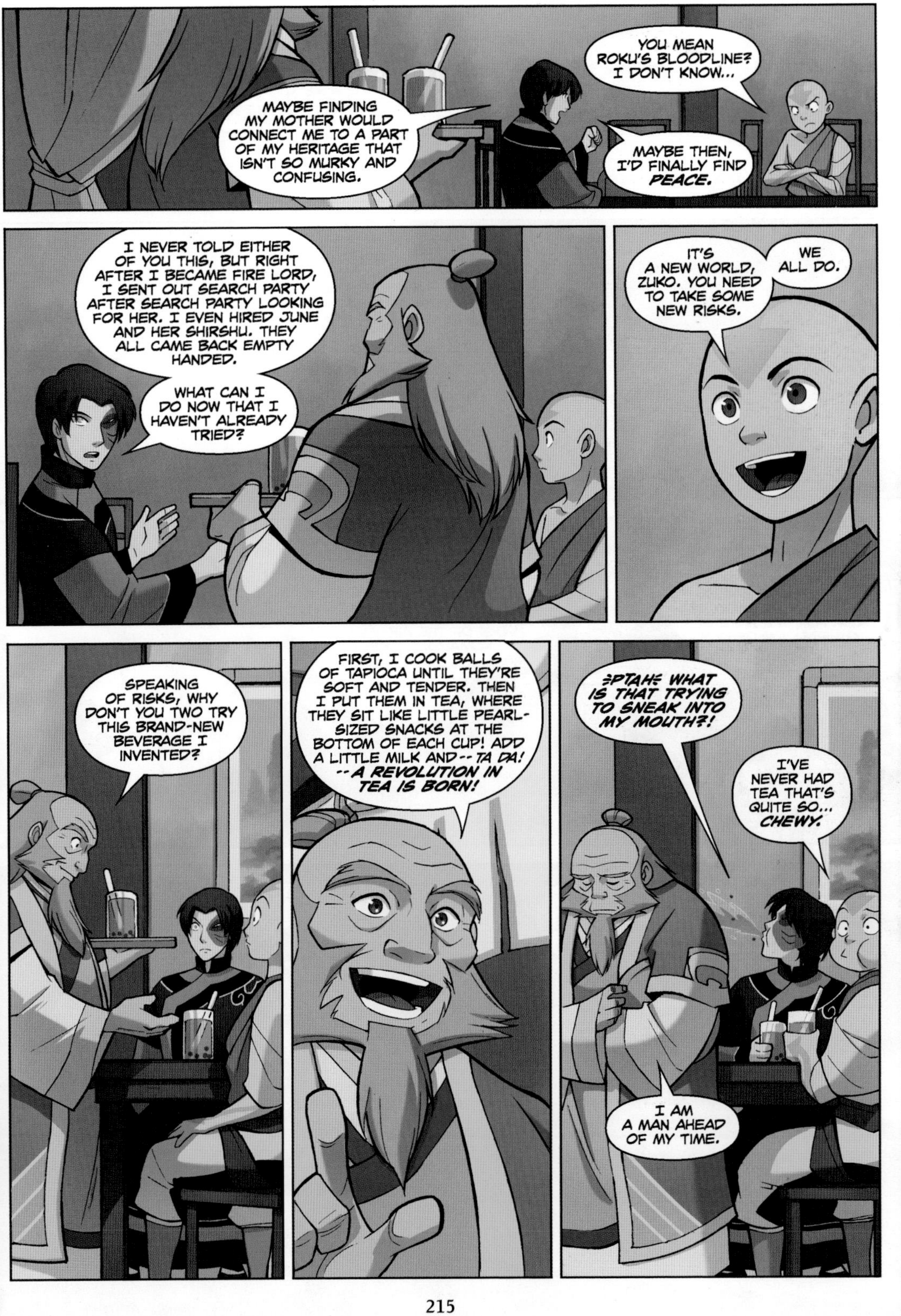
MAYBE FINDING MY MOTHER WOULD CONNECT ME TO A PART OF MY HERITAGE THAT ISN'T SO MURKY AND CONFUSING.
MAYBE THEN, I'D FINALLY FIND PEACE.
YOU MEAN ROKU'S BLOODLINE? I DON'T KNOW...
I NEVER TOLD EITHER OF YOU THIS, BUT RIGHT AFTER I BECAME FIRE LORD, I SENT OUT SEARCH PARTY AFTER SEARCH PARTY LOOKING FOR HER. I EVEN HIRED JUNE AND HER SHIRSHU. THEY ALL CAME BACK EMPTY HANDED.
WHAT CAN I DO NOW THAT I HAVEN'T ALREADY TRIED?
IT'S A NEW WORLD, ZUKO. YOU NEED TO TAKE SOME NEW RISKS.
WE ALL DO.
SPEAKING OF RISKS, WHY DON'T YOU TWO TRY THIS BRAND-NEW BEVERAGE I INVENTED?
FIRST, I COOK BALLS OF TAPIOCA UNTIL THEY'RE SOFT AND TENDER. THEN I PUT THEM IN TEA, WHERE THEY SIT LIKE LITTLE PEARL-SIZED SNACKS AT THE BOTTOM OF EACH CUP! ADD A LITTLE MILK AND-- TA DA! --A REVOLUTION IN TEA IS BORN!
PTAH! WHAT IS THAT TRYING TO SNEAK INTO MY MOUTH?!
I'VE NEVER HAD TEA THAT'S QUITE SO... CHEWY.
I AM A MAN AHEAD OF MY TIME.

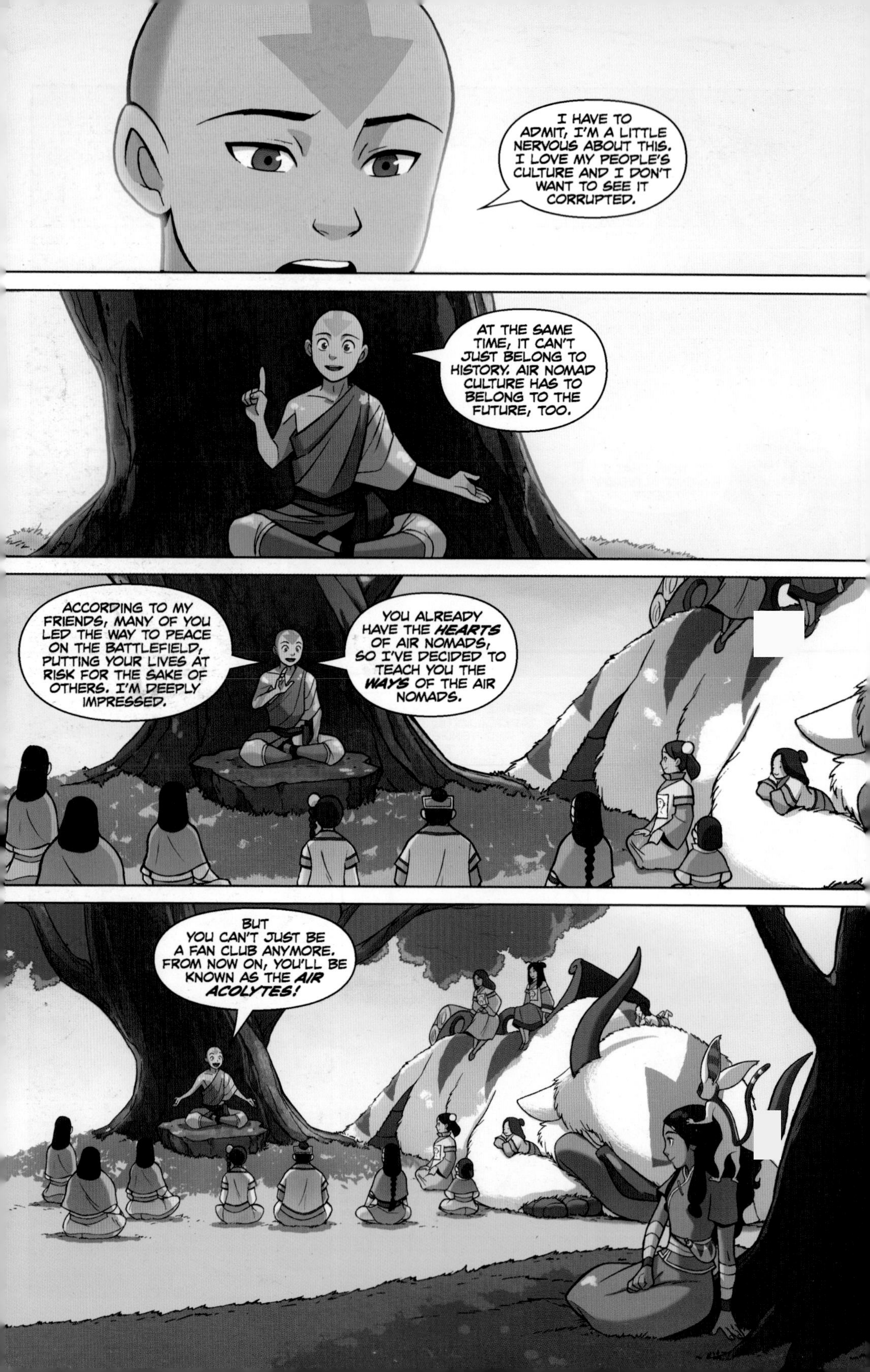
I HAVE TO ADMIT, I'M A LITTLE NERVOUS ABOUT THIS. I LOVE MY PEOPLE'S CULTURE AND I DON'T WANT TO SEE IT CORRUPTED.
AT THE SAME TIME, IT CAN'T JUST BELONG TO HISTORY. AIR NOMAD CULTURE HAS TO BELONG TO THE FUTURE, TOO.
ACCORDING TO MY FRIENDS, MANY OF YOU LED THE WAY TO PEACE ON THE BATTLEFIELD, PUTTING YOUR LIVES AT RISK FOR THE SAKE OF OTHERS. I'M DEEPLY IMPRESSED.
YOU ALREADY HAVE THE *HEARTS* OF AIR NOMADS, SO I'VE DECIDED TO TEACH YOU THE *WAYS* OF THE AIR NOMADS.
BUT YOU CAN'T JUST BE A FAN CLUB ANYMORE. FROM NOW ON, YOU'LL BE KNOWN AS THE *AIR ACOLYTES!*

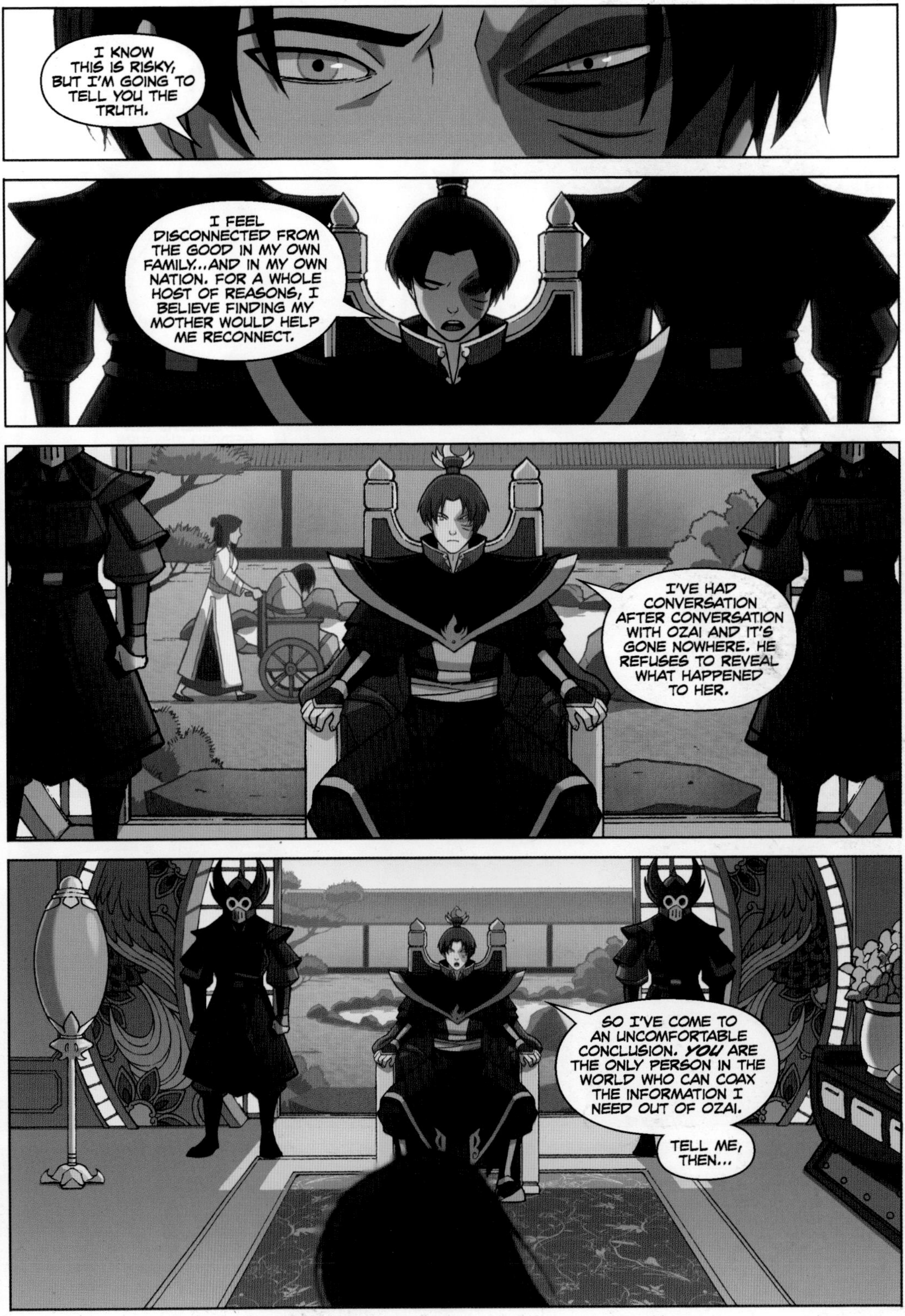
I KNOW THIS IS RISKY, BUT I'M GOING TO TELL YOU THE TRUTH.
I FEEL DISCONNECTED FROM THE GOOD IN MY OWN FAMILY...AND IN MY OWN NATION. FOR A WHOLE HOST OF REASONS, I BELIEVE FINDING MY MOTHER WOULD HELP ME RECONNECT.
I'VE HAD CONVERSATION AFTER CONVERSATION WITH OZAI AND IT'S GONE NOWHERE. HE REFUSES TO REVEAL WHAT HAPPENED TO HER.
SO I'VE COME TO AN UNCOMFORTABLE CONCLUSION. *YOU* ARE THE ONLY PERSON IN THE WORLD WHO CAN COAX THE INFORMATION I NEED OUT OF OZAI.
TELL ME, THEN...

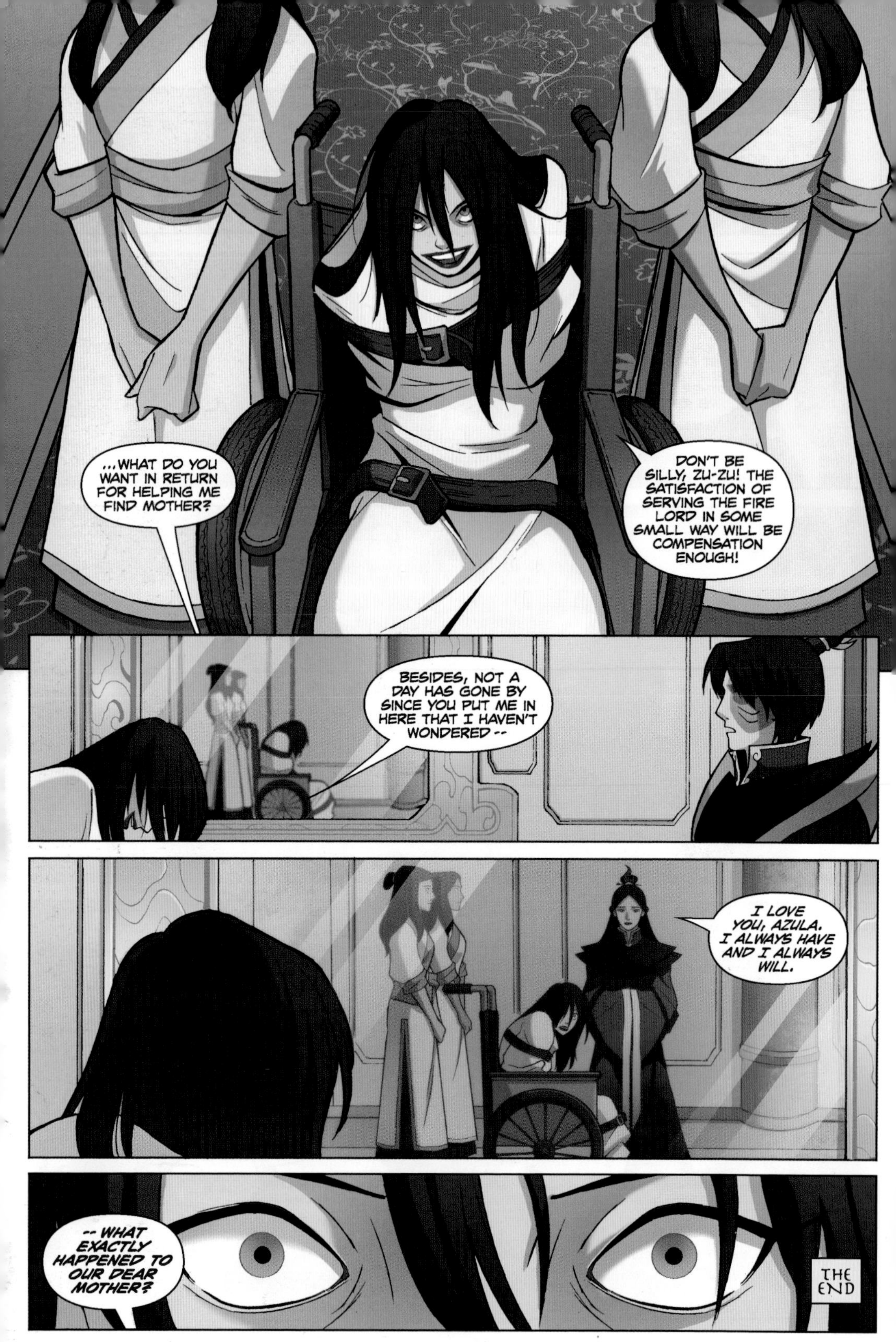
...WHAT DO YOU WANT IN RETURN FOR HELPING ME FIND MOTHER?
DON'T BE SILLY, ZU-ZU! THE SATISFACTION OF SERVING THE FIRE LORD IN SOME SMALL WAY WILL BE COMPENSATION ENOUGH!
BESIDES, NOT A DAY HAS GONE BY SINCE YOU PUT ME IN HERE THAT I HAVEN'T WONDERED --
I LOVE YOU, AZULA. I ALWAYS HAVE AND I ALWAYS WILL.
-- WHAT EXACTLY HAPPENED TO OUR DEAR MOTHER?
THE END

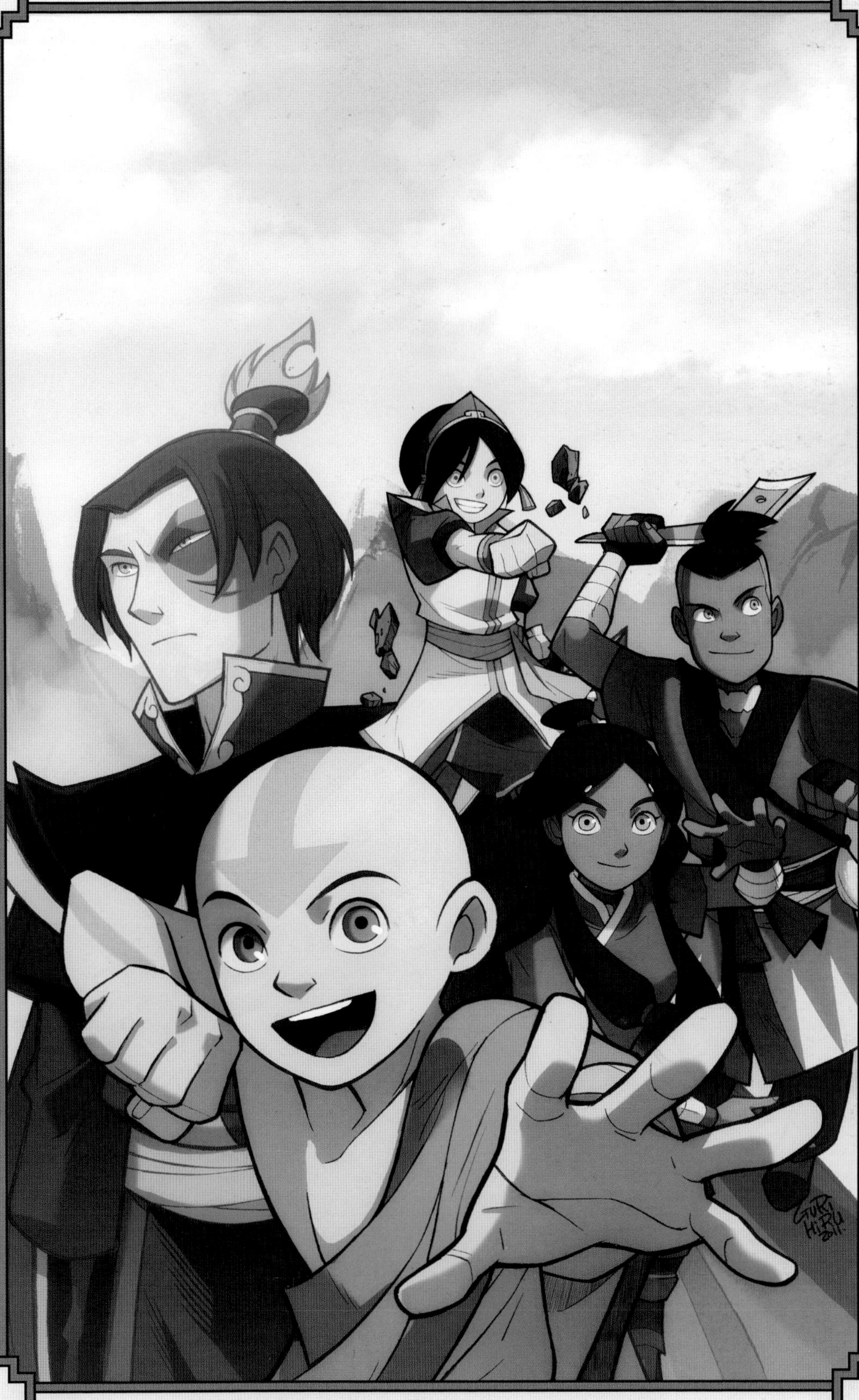
GURI HIRU 2011.

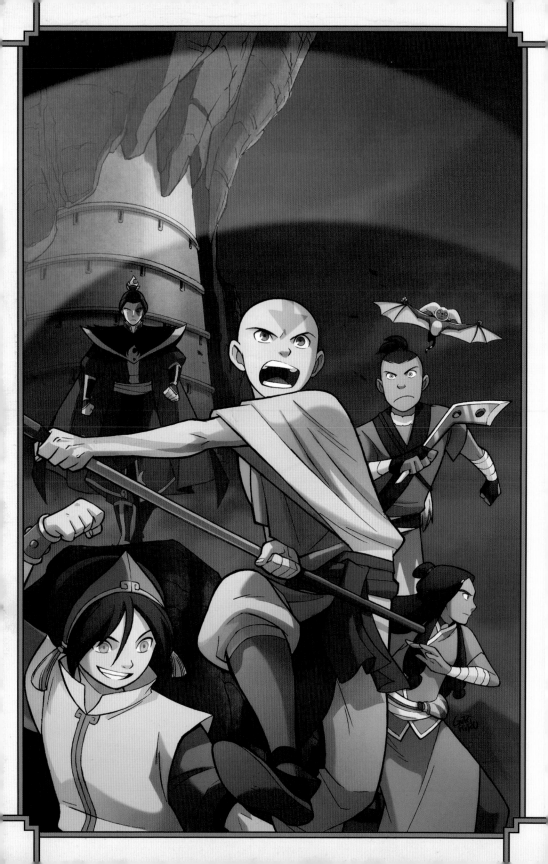

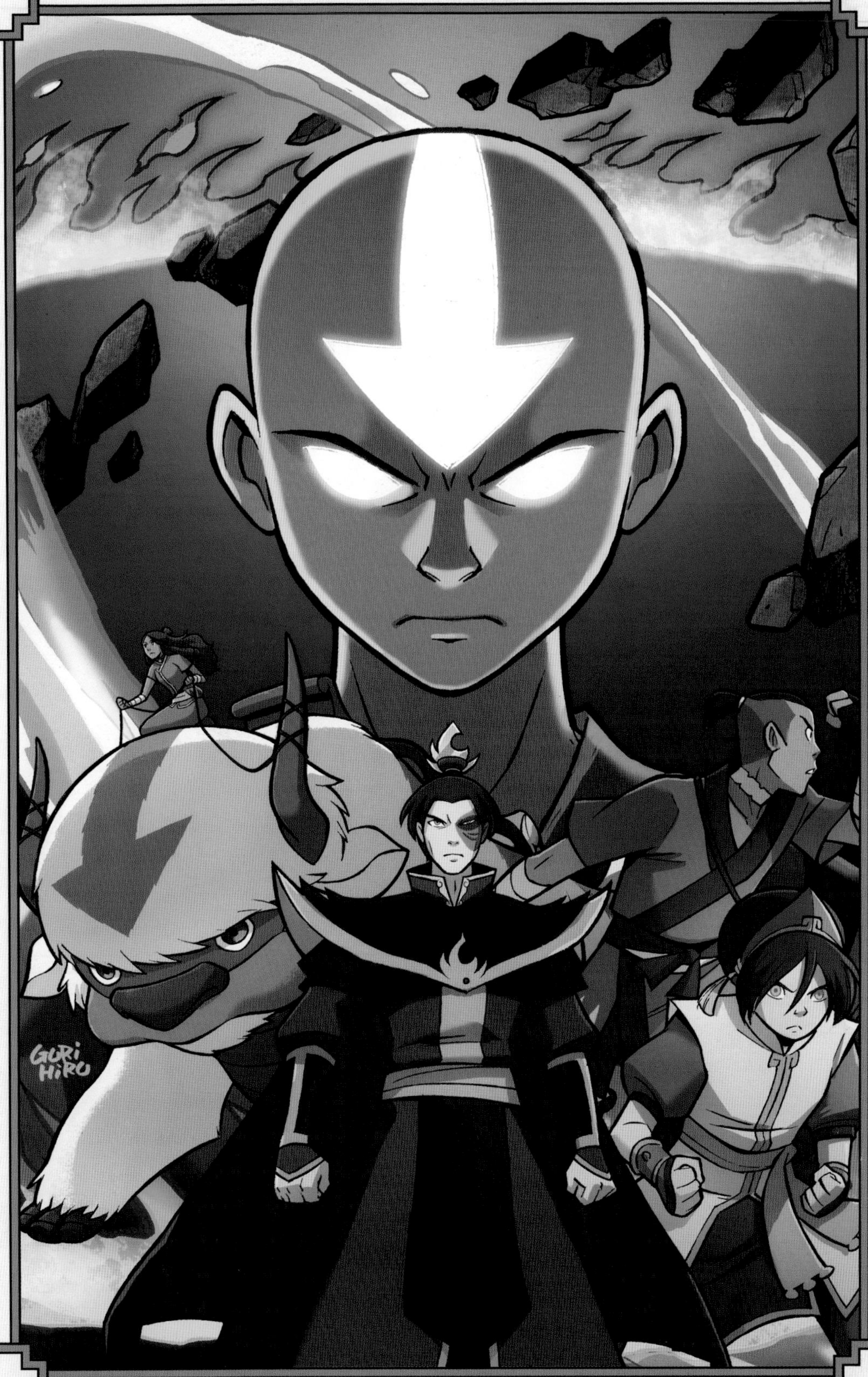
GURI HIRU

Artwork and captions by Gurihiru

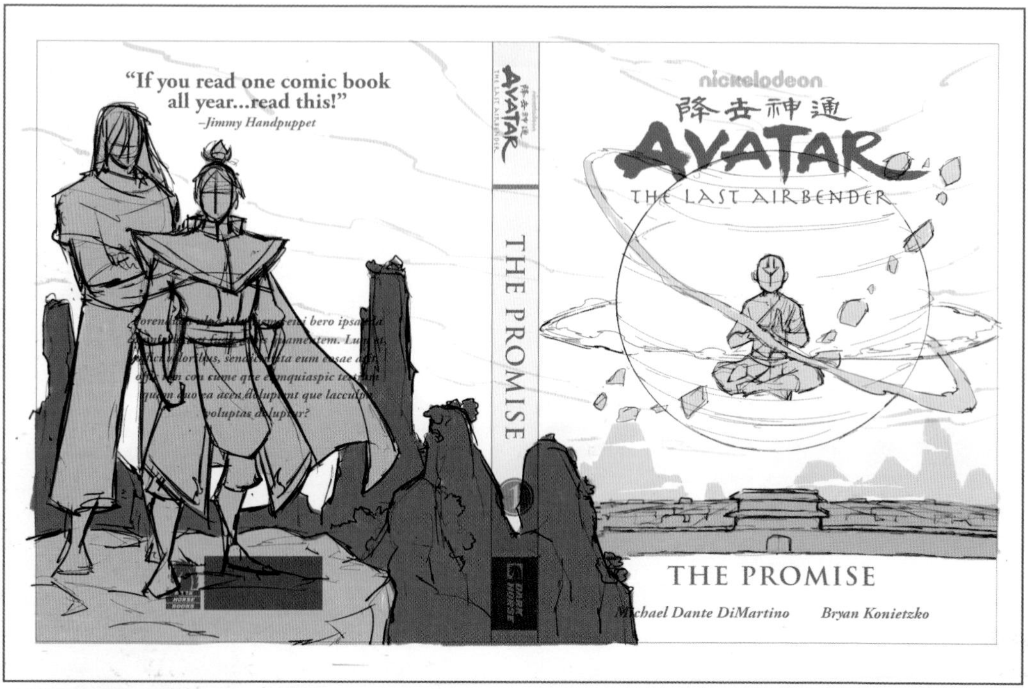
"If you read one comic book all year...read this!"
–Jimmy Handpuppet
nickelodeon
AVATAR
THE LAST AIRBENDER
THE PROMISE
THE PROMISE
Michael Dante DiMartino
Bryan Konietzko

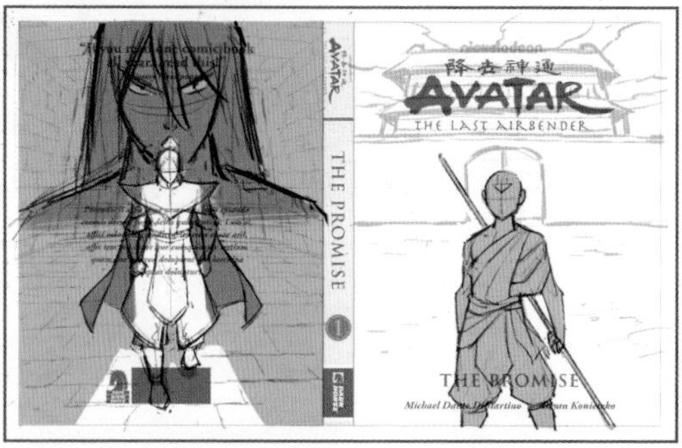
nickelodeon
AVATAR
THE LAST AIRBENDER
THE PROMISE

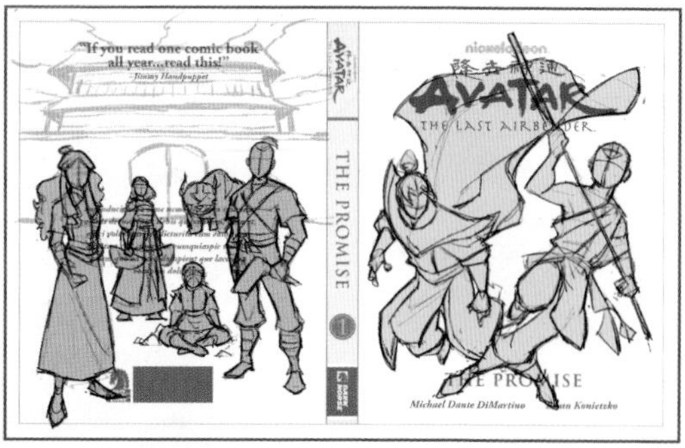
"If you read one comic book all year...read this!"
–Jimmy Handpuppet
nickelodeon
AVATAR
THE PROMISE
Michael Dante DiMartino

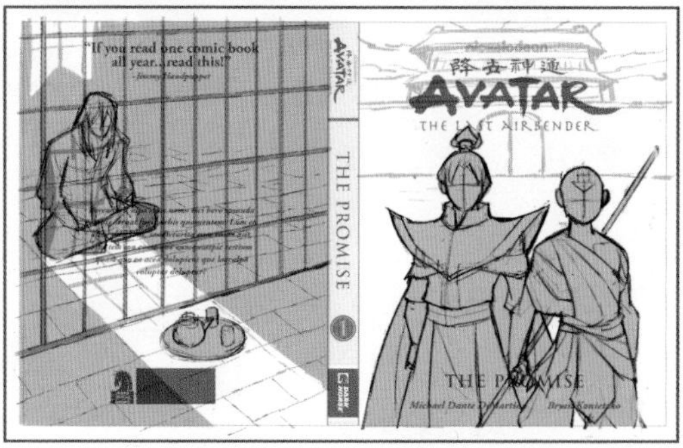
"If you read one comic book all year...read this!"
–Jimmy Handpuppet
AVATAR
THE LAST AIRBENDER
THE PROMISE

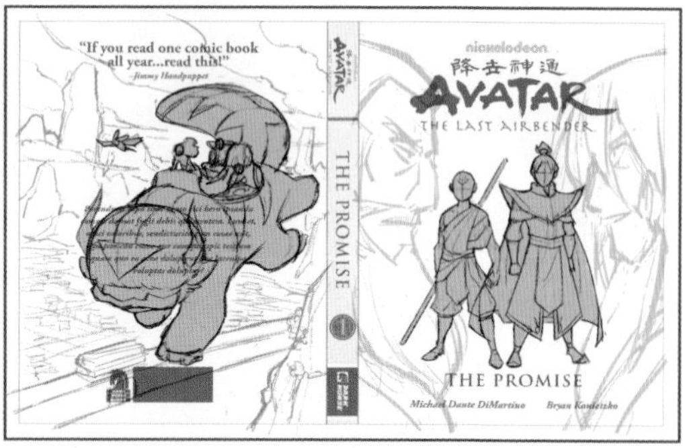
"If you read one comic book all year...read this!"
–Jimmy Handpuppet
nickelodeon
AVATAR
THE LAST AIRBENDER
THE PROMISE
THE PROMISE
Michael Dante DiMartino
Bryan Konietzko

We wanted to make a gorgeous cover for *The Promise* hardcover. We tried to express the bond between Aang and Roku, and the antagonism between Zuko and Ozai.

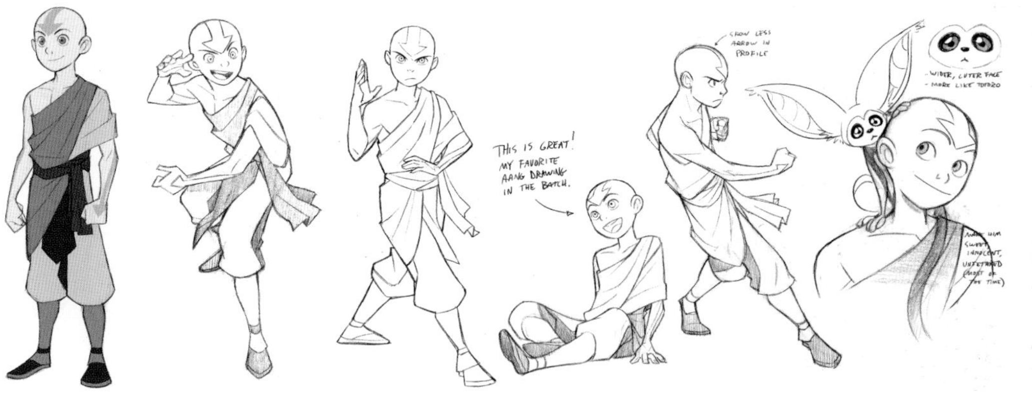
SHOW LESS ARROW IN PROFILE
- WIDER, CUTER FACE
- MORE LIKE TOTORO
THIS IS GREAT! MY FAVORITE AANG DRAWING IN THE BATCH.

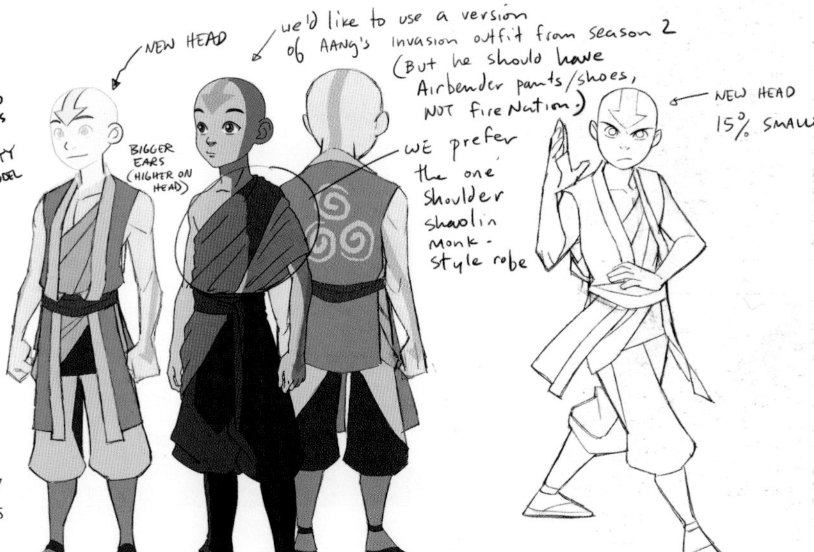
NEW HEAD
we'd like to use a version of Aang's invasion outfit from season 2 (But he should have Airbender pants/shoes, NOT fire Nation.)
TRY TO CAPTURE HIS DEFAULT PERSONALITY FOR THE MODEL SHEET.
BIGGER EARS (HIGHER ON HEAD)
WE prefer the one shoulder shaolin monk-style robe
NEW HEAD 15% SMALLER

AANG

Because of other projects we had been working on at the time, we drew everyone's heads too big at first, especially Aang's. The characters ended up looking too childish, so we went back and fixed this. We worked especially hard on Aang, since it was so important that we get him right.

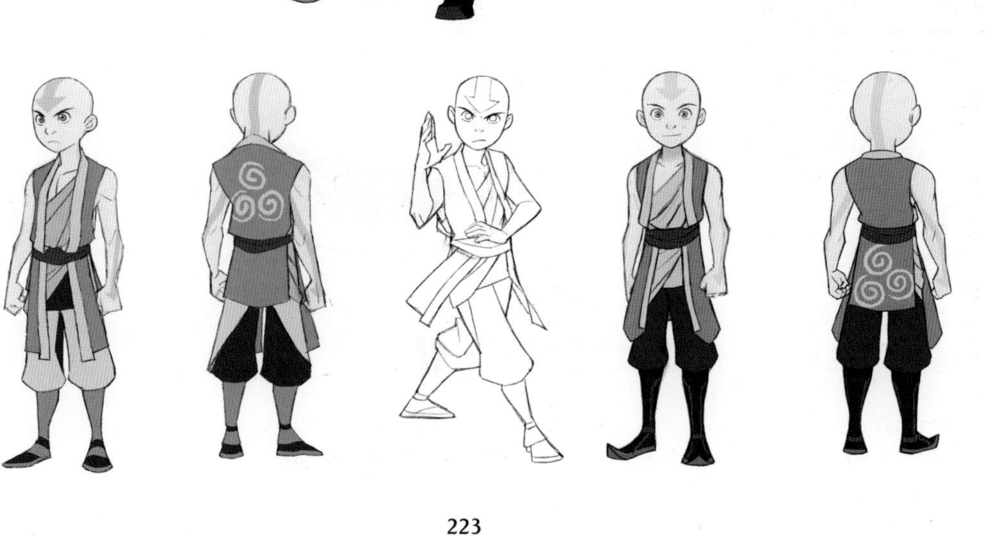

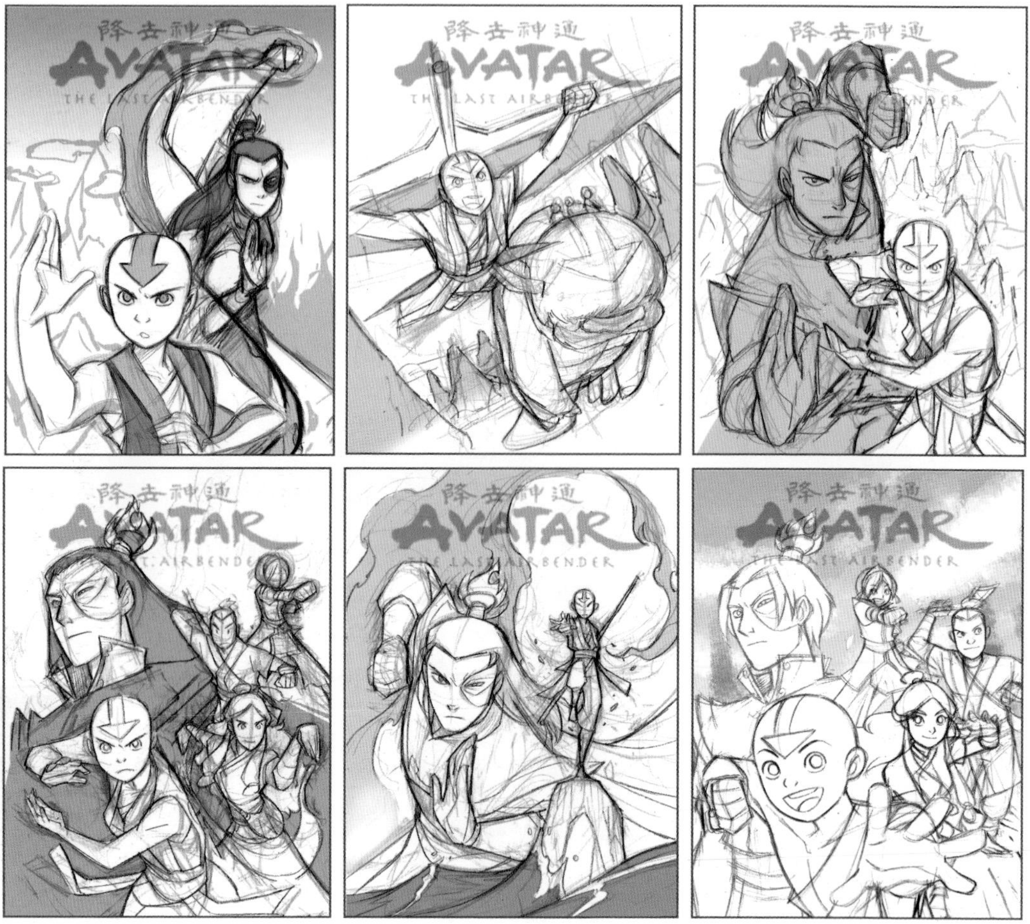
AVATAR
THE LAST AIRBENDER

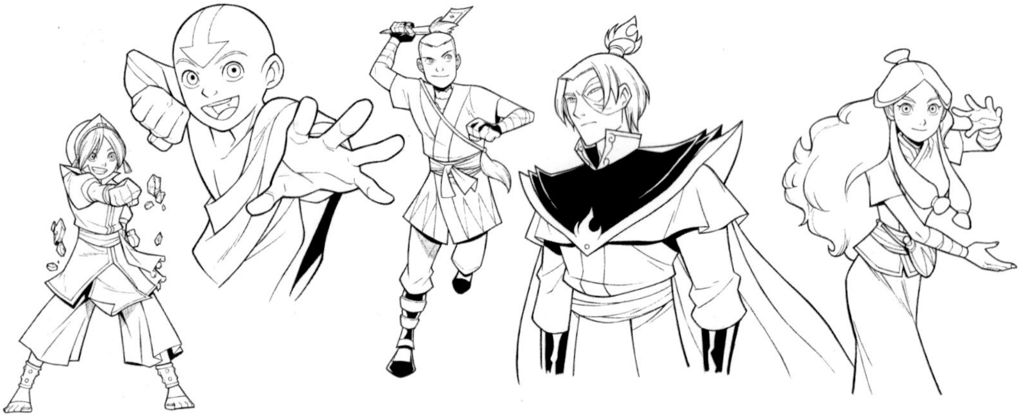

We sent several cover ideas for each part of *The Promise*. It was very challenging to fit all five characters on each cover.

SOKKA

We really enjoyed drawing Sokka. We based his costume on the design of his father's costume, so that you could feel the bond between them.

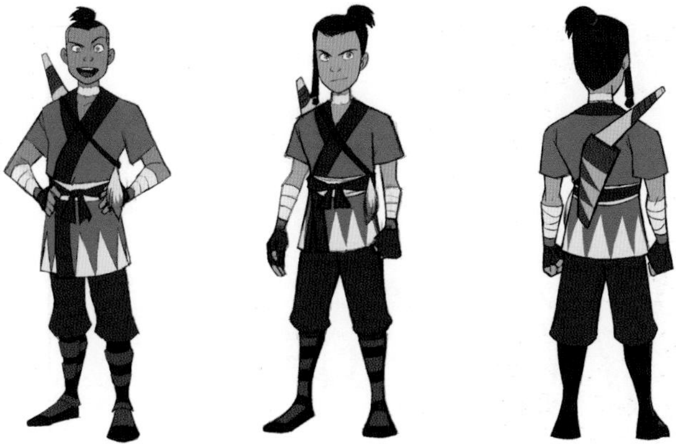

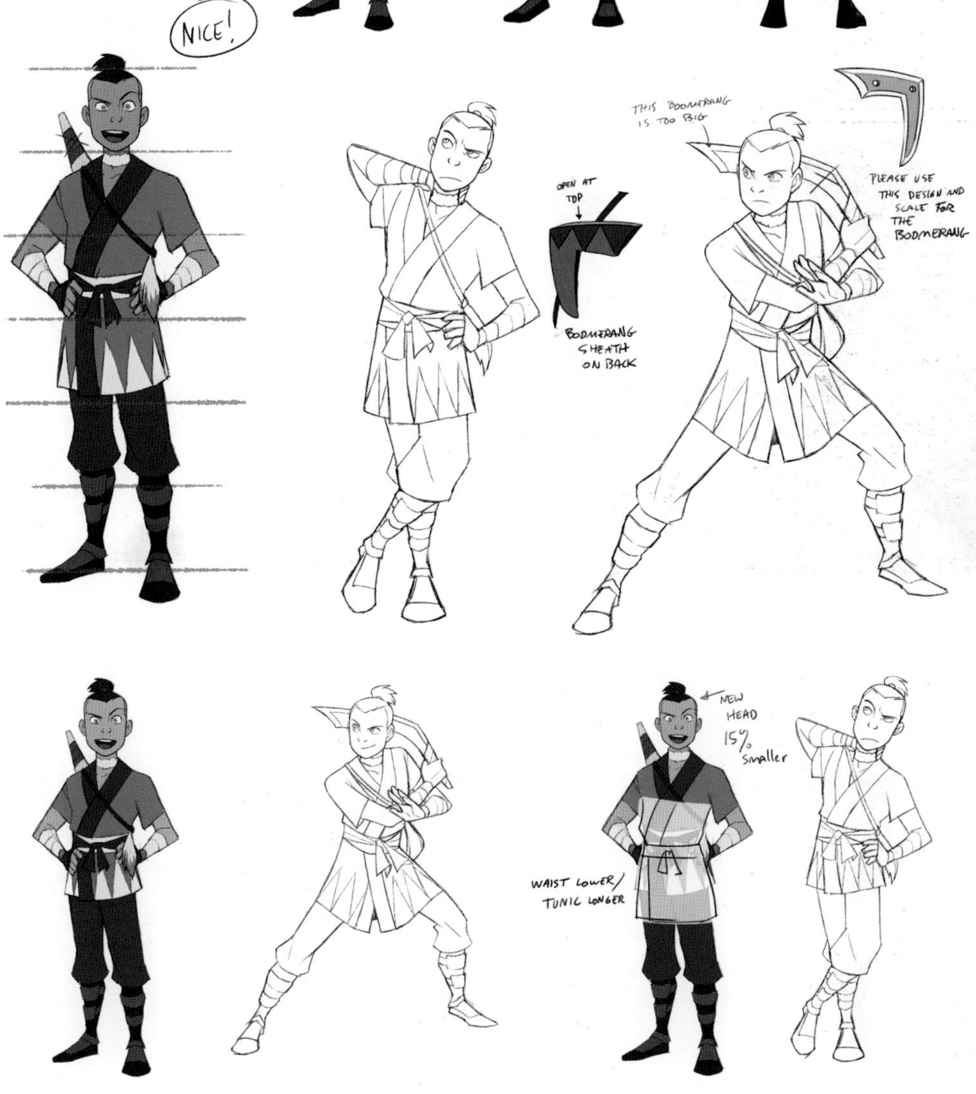
NICE!
THIS BOOMERANG IS TOO BIG
OPEN AT TOP
BOOMERANG SHEATH ON BACK
PLEASE USE THIS DESIGN AND SCALE FOR THE BOOMERANG
NEW HEAD 15% smaller
WAIST LOWER/ TUNIC LONGER

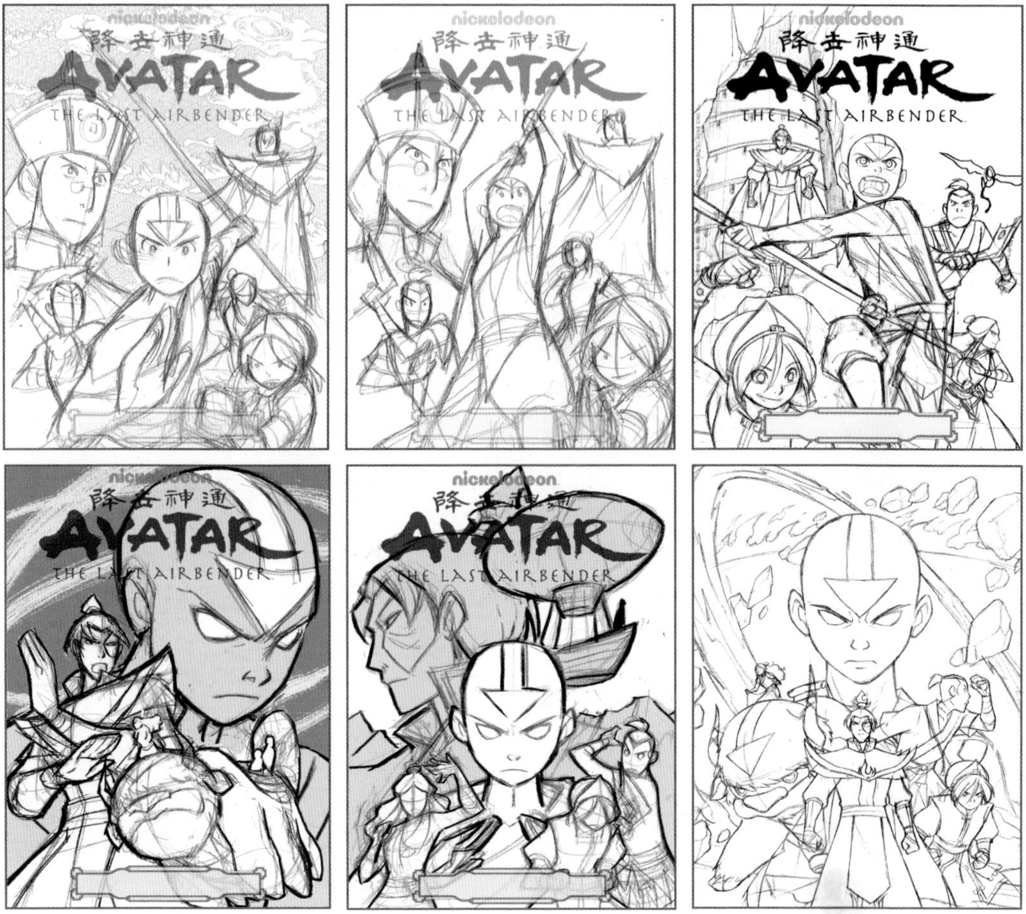
nickelodeon
降去神通
AVATAR
THE LAST AIRBENDER
nickelodeon
降去神通
AVATAR
THE LAST AIRBENDER
nickelodeon
降去神通
AVATAR
THE LAST AIRBENDER
nickelodeon
降去神通
AVATAR
THE LAST AIRBENDER
nickelodeon
降去神通
AVATAR
THE LAST AIRBENDER

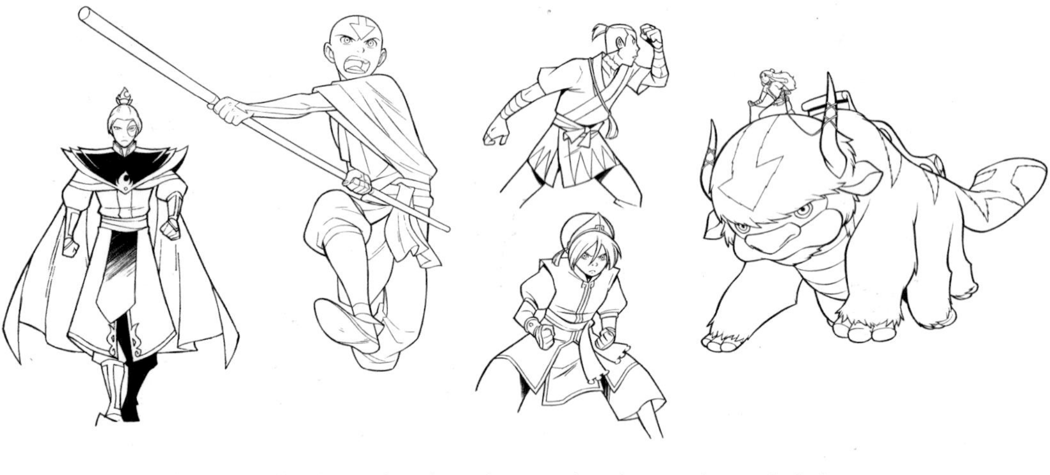

We always think about how to draw the readers' eyes along the page when we do the layouts.

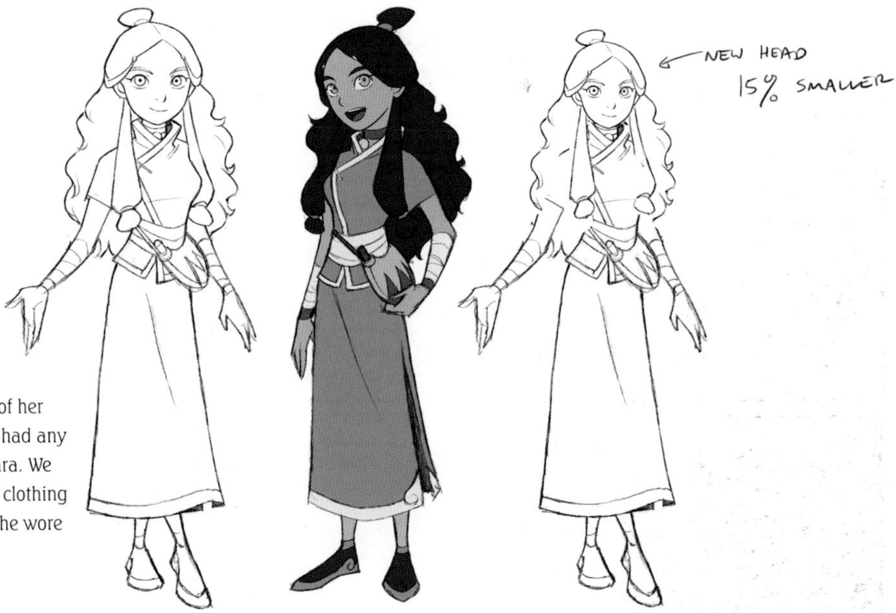
NEW HEAD
15% SMALLER

KATARA

Besides the size of her head, we hardly had any changes for Katara. We tried to keep her clothing similar to what she wore in the TV show.

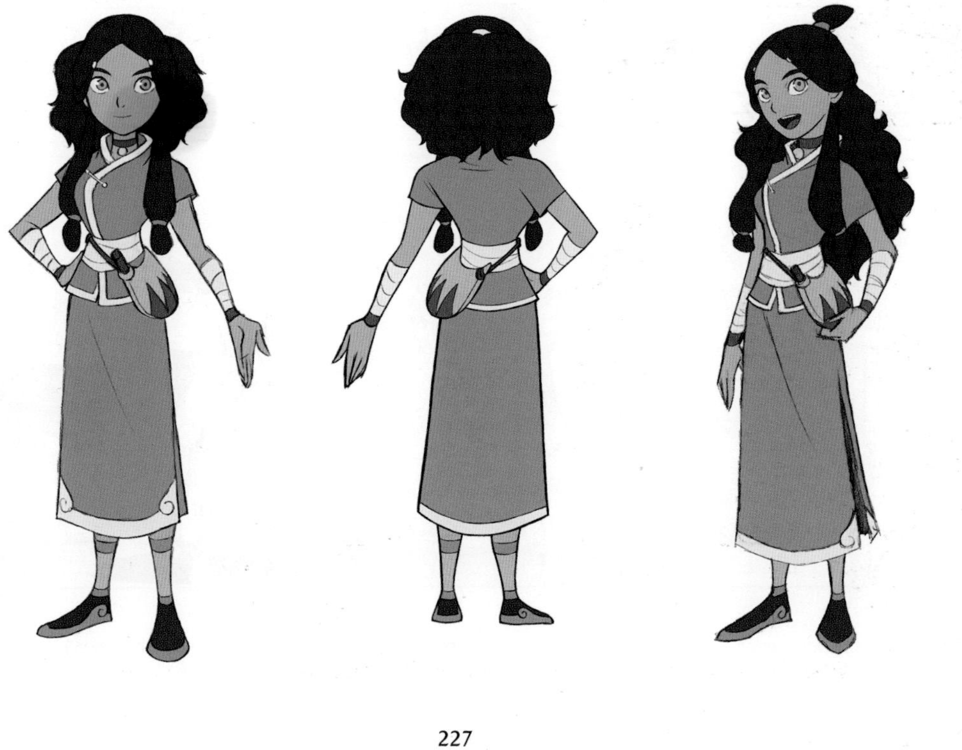

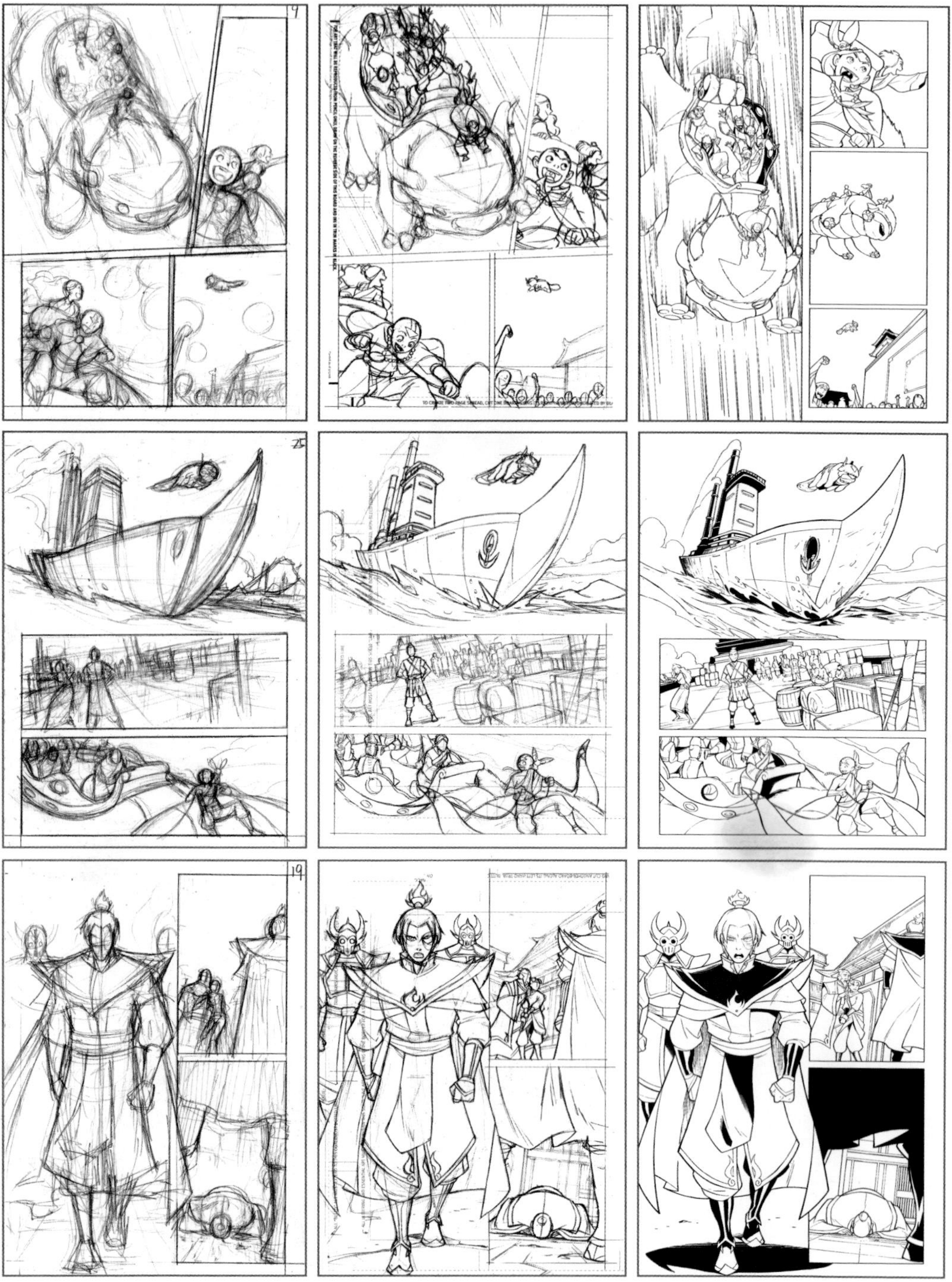

Here are the stages from rough layouts to pencils to inks. We worked on paper from layouts to inks and then digitally after that.

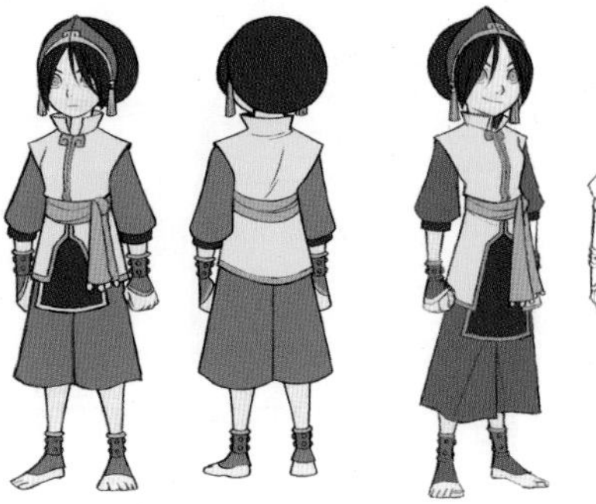

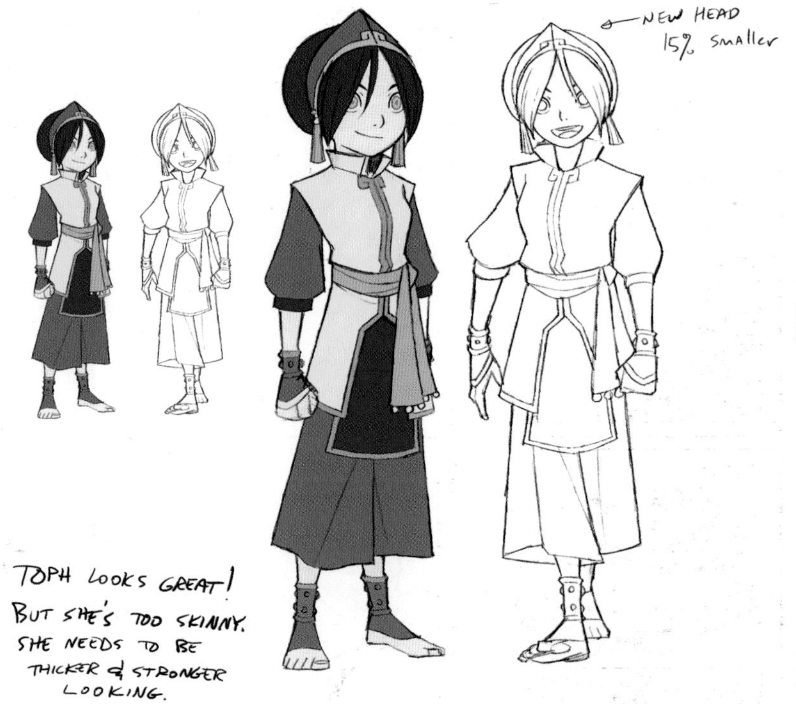

← NEW HEAD
15% smaller
TOPH LOOKS GREAT!
BUT SHE'S TOO SKINNY.
SHE NEEDS TO BE
THICKER & STRONGER
LOOKING.

TOPH

In our initial sketches, Toph was a little too skinny, so now we try to keep her more husky.

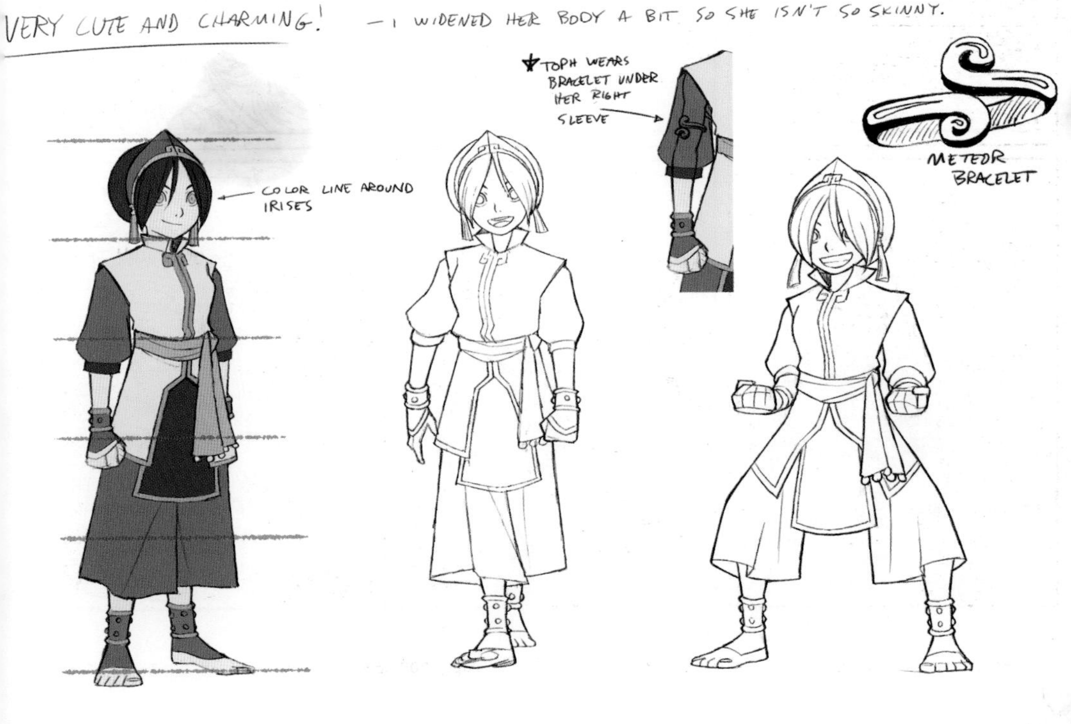

VERY CUTE AND CHARMING!
— I WIDENED HER BODY A BIT SO SHE ISN'T SO SKINNY.
★ TOPH WEARS BRACELET UNDER HER RIGHT SLEEVE
METEOR BRACELET
COLOR LINE AROUND IRISES

Firebending master Kunyo was inspired by actor James Hong.

ZUKO

At first, Zuko's costume was very formal and regal. However, that would not work for action scenes, so we changed to a costume that would allow for easier movement, and made Zuko's hairstyle short instead of long.

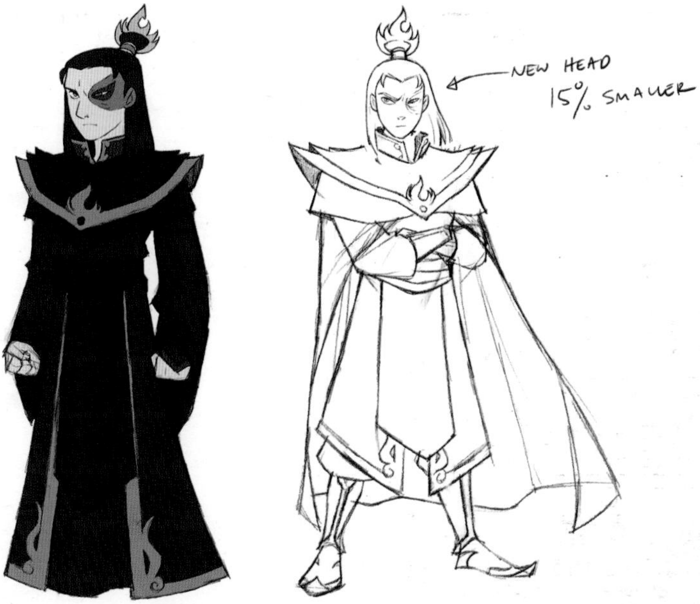
NEW HEAD
15% SMALLER

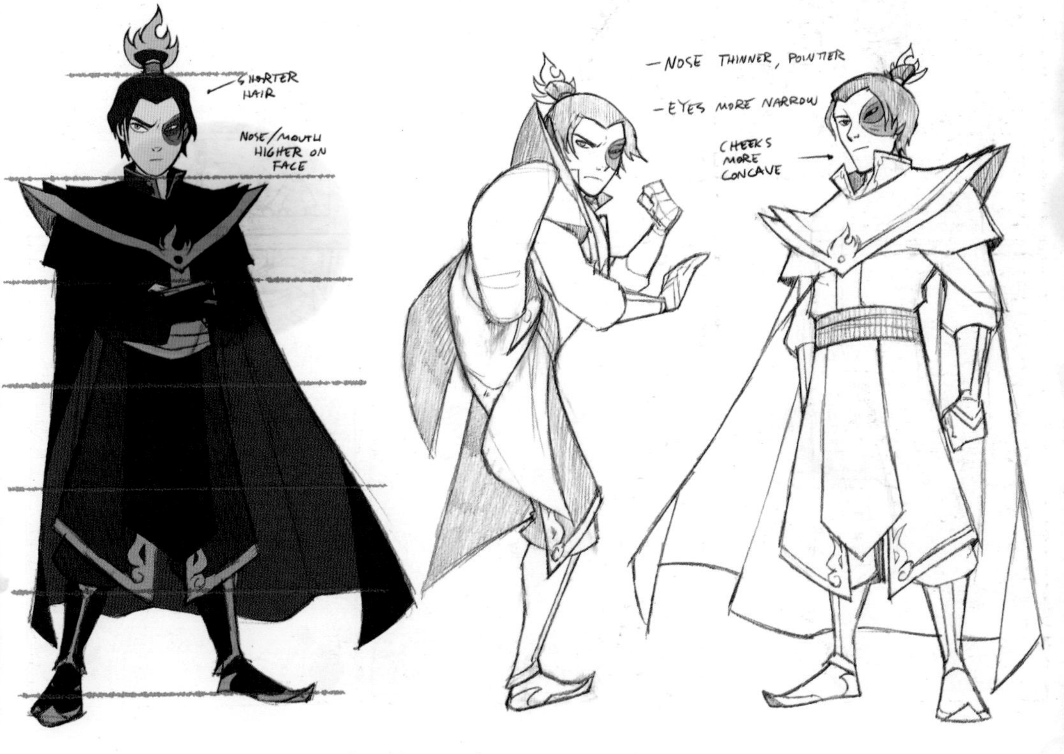
SHORTER HAIR
NOSE/MOUTH HIGHER ON FACE
–NOSE THINNER, POINTIER
–EYES MORE NARROW
CHEEKS MORE CONCAVE

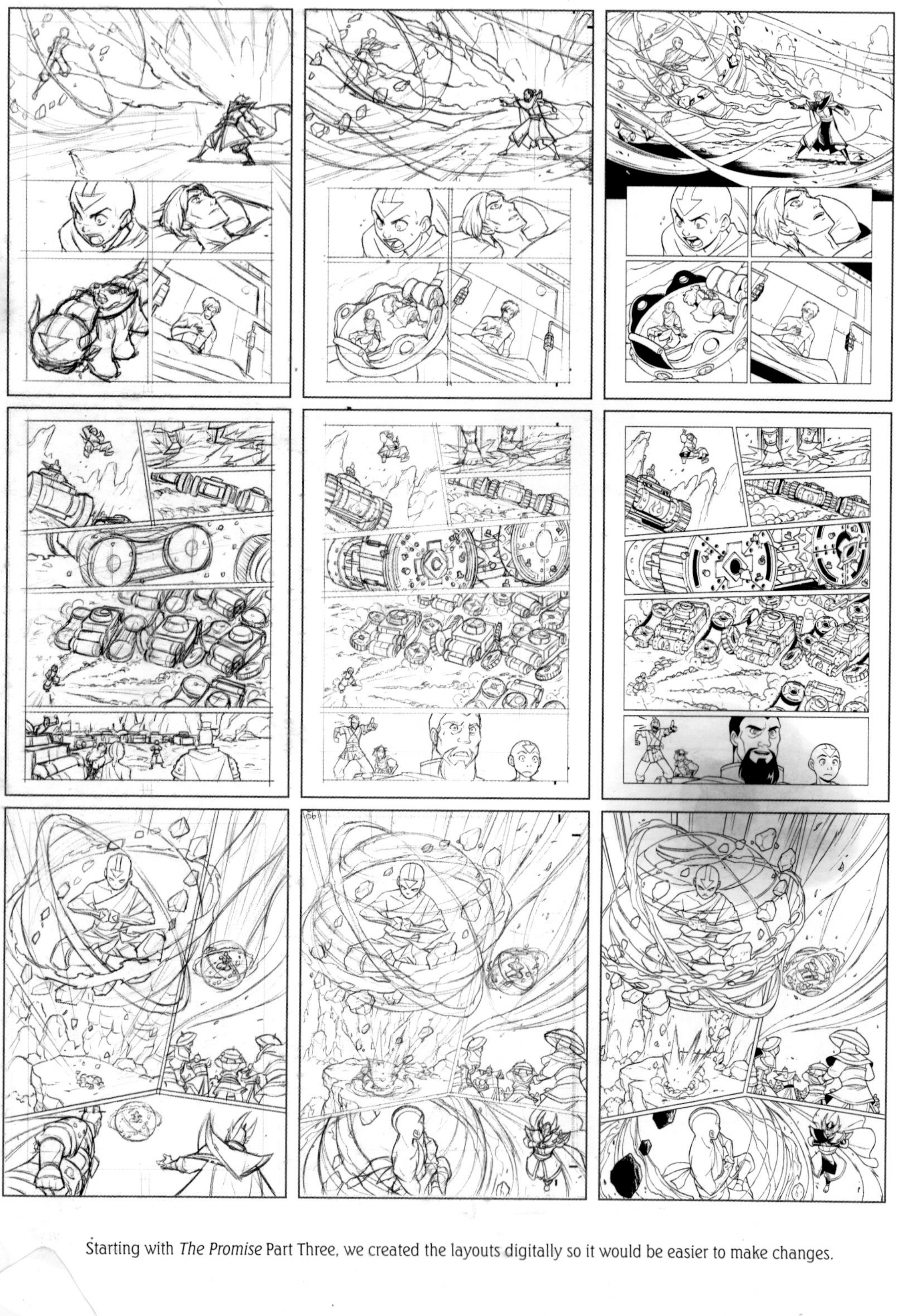

Starting with *The Promise* Part Three, we created the layouts digitally so it would be easier to make changes.